PROVENCE

Bonnieux

G. Magnin/ MICHELIN

Executive Editorial Director	David Brabis
Chief Editor	Cynthia Clayton Ochterbeck

THE GREEN GUIDE PROVENCE

Editor	Gwen Cannon
Principal Writer	Beebe Bahrami
Production Coordinator	Allison Michelle Simpson
Cartography	Alain Baldet, Michèle Cana, Peter Wrenn
Photo Editor	Brigitta L. House
Proofreader	Lydia Dishman
Layout	Allison Michelle Simpson, Nicole D. Jordan, Chris Robinson
Cover Design	Laurent Muller
Interior Design	Agence Rampazzo
Production	Pierre Ballochard, Renaud Leblanc

Contact Us :

The Green Guide
Michelin Travel Publications
One Parkway South
Greenville, SC 29615
USA
☎ 1-800-423-0485
www.michelintravel.com
michelin.guides@us.michelin.com
or
Hannay House, 39 Clarendon Road
Watford, Herts WD17 1JA, UK
☎ 01923 205 240 - Fax 01923 205 241
www.ViaMichelin.com
TheGreenGuide-uk@uk.michelin.com

Special Sales :

For information regarding bulk sales, customized editions and premium sales, please contact our Customer Service Departments:
USA   1-800-423-0485
UK   (01923) 205 240
Canada   1-800-361-8236

Note to the reader

One Team...
A Commitment to Quality

There's just one reason our team is dedicated to producing quality travel publications—you, our reader. We want you to get the maximum benefit from your trip—and from your money. In today's multiple-choice world of travel, the options are many, perhaps overwhelming.

In our guidebooks, we try to minimize the guesswork involved with travel. We scout out the attractions, prioritize them with star ratings, and describe what you'll discover when you visit them.

To help you orient yourself, we provide colorful and detailed, but easy-to-follow maps. Floor plans of some of the cathedrals and museums help you plan your tour.

Throughout the guides, we offer practical information, touring tips and suggestions for finding the best views, good places for a break and the most interesting shops.

Lodging and dining are always a big part of travel, so we compile a selection of hotels and restaurants that we think convey the feel of the place, and organize them by geographic area and price. We also highlight shopping, recreational and entertainment venues, especially the popular spots.

If you're short on time, driving tours are included so you can hit the highlights and quickly absorb the best of the destination.

For those who love to experience a destination on foot, we add walking tours, often with a map. And we list other companies who offer boat, bus or guided walking tours of the area, some with culinary, historical or other themes.

In short, we test and retest, check and recheck to make sure that our guidebooks are truly just that: a personalized guide to help you make the most of your visit. After all, we want you to enjoy traveling as much as we do.

The Michelin Green Guide Team
michelin.guides@us.michelin.com

PLANNING YOUR TRIP

WHEN AND WHERE TO GO

Driving Tours.................... 14
Themed Tours................... 16
When to go 19

KNOW BEFORE YOU GO

French Tourist Offices............ 20
International Visitors 21

GETTING THERE

By Air........................... 24
By Sea 24
By Rail 24
By Coach........................ 25

DRIVING IN FRANCE

Know Before You Go............. 26
Rules of the Road................ 26
Vehicles......................... 27

WHERE TO STAY AND EAT

Where to Stay 28
Finding a Restaurant............. 30
Menu reader 31

WHAT TO DO AND SEE

Outdoor Fun 32
Activities for Children............ 37
Calendar of Events............... 37
Shopping 39
Sightseeing 42
Books and Films................. 43

USEFUL WORDS & PHRASES   46

BASIC INFORMATION   49

INTRODUCTION TO PROVENCE

NATURE

Topography..................... 56
Flora............................ 59
Caves and Chasms............... 61

HISTORY

Time Line 62
Hallmarks of Diversity 64

ART AND CULTURE

Architecture 68
Architectural Terms.............. 74
Roman Culture 76
Roman Influence 80
Gothic Style..................... 82
Fine Arts 83
Decorative Arts.................. 86
Language and Literature......... 88
Legends and Tales............... 90

THE REGION TODAY

Economy........................ 92
Popular Games.................. 95
Festivals and Costumes 97
Food and Wine.................. 99

SYMBOLS

🖐	**Tips to help improve your experience**
👁	**Details to consider**
💰	**Entry fees**
👣	**Walking tours**
⚿	**Closed to the public**
🕐	**Hours of operation**
🕐	**Periods of closure**

CONTENTS

EXPLORING PROVENCE

Aigues-Mortes 106
Aix-en-Provence 110
Les Alpilles 122
Ansouis 126
Apt 128
Gorges de l'Ardèche 132
Arles 139
Aubagne 151
Avignon 153
Bagnols-sur-Cèze 171
Barbentane 174
Les Baux-de-Provence 175
Beaucaire 181
Étang de Berre 184
Bollène 188
Bonnieux 190
Massif des Calanques 192
La Camargue 196
Carpentras 203
Cassis 208
Cavaillon 210
Châteauneuf-du-Pape 214
La Ciotat 215
Grotte de la Cocalière 218
Chaîne de l'Estaque 218
Chaîne de l'Étoile 221
Fontaine-de-Vaucluse 223
Fos-sur-Mer 225
Gordes 226
Le Grau-du-Roi 229
Grignan 230
L'Isle-sur-la-Sorgue 232
La Beaume 234
Le Luberon 235
Marseille 243
Martigues 266
Ménerbes 268
Abbaye de Montmajour 269
Dentelles de Montmirail 270
Nîmes 273
Nyons 284
Orange 286
Aven d'Orgnac 290
Bois de Païolive 292
Pernes-les-Fontaines 293
Pont du Gard 295
Pont-St-Esprit 297
Rochefort-du-Gard 299
Roussillon 299
St-Blaise 301
St-Gilles 302
St-Maximin-la-Ste-Baume 307
Abbaye de St-Michel-de-Frigolet . 309
St-Rémy-de-Provence 310
La Ste-Victoire 317
Les Stes-Maries-de-la-Mer 319
Salon-de-Provence 321
Sault 326
Abbaye de Sénanque 328
Abbaye de Silvacane 331
Tarascon 332
La Tour-d'Aigues 337
Uzès 341
Vaison-la-Romaine 348
Vallon-Pont-d'Arc 354
Valréas 355
Venasque 357
Mont Ventoux 359
Villeneuve-lès-Avignon 362

How to Use this Guide

Orientation

To help you grasp the "lay of the land" quickly and easily, so you'll feel confident and comfortable finding your way around, we offer the following tools in this guide:

- Detailed table of contents for an overview of what'll you find in the guide, and how it is organized.
- Map of Principal Sights showing the starred places of interest at a glance.
- Detailed maps of city centers, regions and towns.
- Floor and site plans of museums and cathedrals.
- Principal Sights ordered alphabetically for easy reference.

Practicalities

At the front of the guide, you'll see a section called "Planning Your Trip" that contains information about the best time to go, getting to Provence and getting around, basic facts, tips for making the most of your visit, and more. It includes suggested itineraries, a calendar of annual events and festivals worth planning for, and tips about national and regional cuisines, and what to expect in the way of lodging. Then comes information on shopping, sightseeing, kids' activities, sports and recreational opportunities.

LODGING

We've made a selection of hotels and classified them according to room price in high season (without tax and breakfast, except where indicated) to fit all budgets *(see the Legend at the back of the guide for an explanation of the price categories)*. For the most part, we've selected accommodations for their uniquely Provençal or regional character, so unless the individual hotel embodies local ambience, it's rare that we include chain properties, which typically have their own imprint. If you want a more comprehensive selection of lodgings throughout the region, see the red-cover *Michelin Guide France*.

RESTAURANTS

We thought you'd like to make eating part of your experience of the region. So we selected restaurants that capture the essence of Provence—those that are well-frequented and popular, and conveniently located. As we did with the hotels, we categorized them by price to appeal to all wallets *(see the Legend at the back of the guide for an explanation of the price categories)*. If you want a more comprehensive selection of eating places, see the red-cover *Michelin Guide France,* which describes hundreds of restaurants throughout the region.

Attractions

Contact information, admission charges and hours of operation are given for the majority of attractions. Unless otherwise noted, admission prices shown are for a single adult only. Discounts for seniors, students, military personnel, etc. may be available; be sure to ask. If no admission charge is shown, entrance to the attraction is free.

Within each Principal Sight, attractions within a town or city are described first , sometimes in the form of a walking tour. Then come outlying sights and Excursions. If you're pressed for time, we recommend you visit the three- and two-star sights in a city or area first: the stars are your guide.

STAR RATINGS

Michelin has used stars as a rating tool for more than 100 years:

★★★	Highly recommended
★★	Recommended
★	Interesting

SYMBOLS IN THE TEXT

Besides the stars, other symbols in the text indicate tourist information 🖪; wheelchair access ♿; on-site eating facilities ✗; camping facilities △; on-site parking 🅿; entry fees ☜; hours of operation ◷; hours closed ◷; and sights of interest to children Kids.

See the box appearing on the Contents page for other symbols used in the text.

See Maps explanation below for symbols appearing on the maps.

Throughout the guide you will find peach-colored text boxes or sidebars containing anecdotal or background information. Green-colored boxes contain information to help you save time or money.

Maps

All maps in this guide are oriented north, unless otherwise indicated by a directional arrow.

See the map legend at the back of the guide for an explanation of other map symbols.

A complete list of the maps found in the guide appears at the back of this book.

Addresses, phone numbers, opening hours and prices published in this guide are accurate at press time. We welcome corrections and suggestions that may assist us in preparing the next edition. Please send your comments to:

Michelin Travel Publications
Editorial Department
P.O. Box 19001
Greenville, SC   29602-9001 USA
Email: michelin.guides@us.michelin.com
Web site: www.michelintravel.com

Aqueduc:	Aqueduct	Corniche:	Scenic road		
Bassin:	Dock	Défilé:	Narrow-gorge	Massif:	Massif (mountain mass)
Bois:	Wood	Étang:	Lake		
Chartreuse:	Charter house	Fontaine:	Fountain	Moulin:	Mill
Chaîne:	Mountain range	Forêt:	Forest	Plage:	Beach
Col:	Mountain pass	Gorges:	Gorge	Plaine:	Plain
				Rocher:	Rock

Principal sights

AVIGNON	★★★	Highly recommended
Orange	★★	Recommended
Carpentras	★	Interesting
Bollène		Other sight described in this guide

Seaside resorts ⛱ are classified according to the quality and range of facilities offered.

Itinerary described in this guide: look up one of the sites in the index at the back of the guide to find the page where the tour is described.

0   20 km

DRÔME

GRENOBLE

GAP
Sisteron

Valréas

Nyons

Vaison-la-Romaine

Séguret
Dentelles de Montmirail

MONT VENTOUX

le Barroux

ALPES-DE-

N.D. d'Aubune

Flassan

Sault

Plateau

Carpentras

Mormoiron

d'Albion

HAUTE-PROVENCE

COMTAT VENAISSIN

Nesque

Venasque

St-Hubert

Belvédère de Castellaras

Pernes-les-Fontaines

Gorges de la

Lagarde-d'Apt

VAUCLUSE

Fontaine de Vaucluse

Sénanque

PARC

Colorado de Rustrel

les Bories

Roussillon

NATUREL

Gordes

N 100

Apt

N 100

Ménerbes

Bonnieux

RÉGIONAL

DU

Oppède

LUBERON

MOURRE NÈGRE

Gorges du Régalon

Lourmarin

Cadenet

Glanum

Calès

Ansouis

la Tour-d'Aigues

Verdon

Silvacane

LUBERON

Salon-de-Provence

Château-Bas

D 572

Peyrolles-en-Provence

VAR

la Barben

LA STE-VICTOIRE

A 8

CROIX DE PROVENCE

Étang

Vallée de l'Arc

Aix-en-Provence

St-Maximin-la-Ste-Baume

de

Aqueduc de Roquefavour

Berre

Rocher de Vitrolles

Gardanne

Martigues

Cabriès

St-Jean-du-Puy

Massif et forêt de la Ste-Baume

Blaise

Canal souterrain du Rove

Chaîne de l'Étoile

Chaîne de l'Estaque

Niolon

Col de l'Espigoulier

SAINT-PILON

Mazaugues

Sausset-les-Pins

Carry-le-Rouet

Allauch

Parc de St-Pons

MARSEILLE

Parc OK Corral

Château d'If

Aubagne

Cassis

Corniche des Crêtes

Calanques

la Ciotat

CAP CANAILLE

Île verte

TOULON

MÉDITERRANÉE

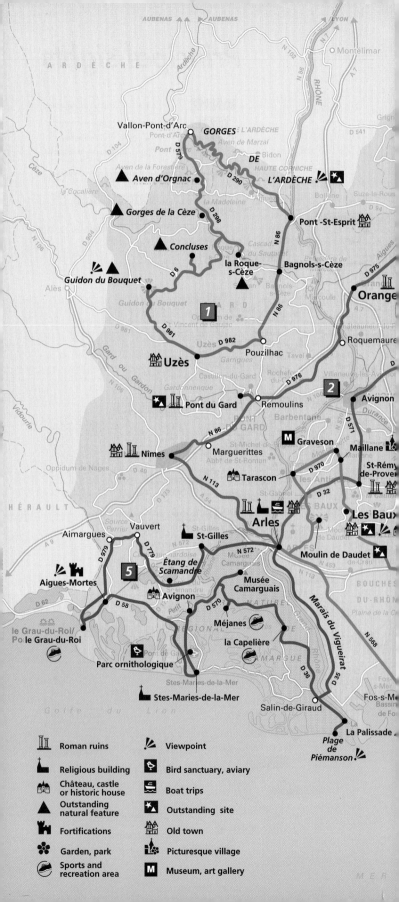

Driving tours

For descriptions of these tours,
turn to the *Planning Your Trip* section following.

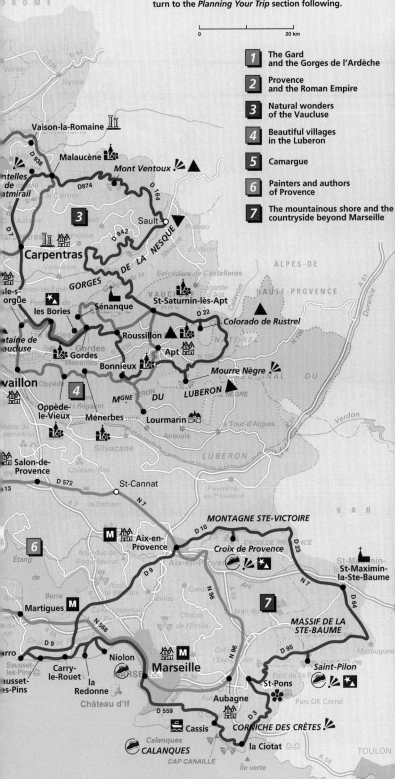

1 The Gard
and the Gorges de l'Ardèche

2 Provence
and the Roman Empire

3 Natural wonders
of the Vaucluse

4 Beautiful villages
in the Luberon

5 Camargue

6 Painters and authors
of Provence

7 The mountainous shore and the
countryside beyond Marseille

Fresh Vegetables

WHEN AND WHERE TO GO

Driving Tours

See the map of Driving Tours on page 10.

1 The Gard and the Gorges de l'Ardèche

▶*198km/123.8mi leaving from Uzès*

The old ducal seat of Uzès, with its elegant Tour Fenestrelle, its stately ducal palace, and the charming Place aux Herbes, is the starting point for this itinerary. Explore Bagnols-sur-Cèze and its museum of modern figurative art, the old city of Pont-St-Esprit, and have a first look at the Gorges de l'Ardèche, the profusion of caves, cliffs and spectacular viewpoints. The route climbs up the gorges to the astonishing natural arch at Pont d'Arc, near Orgnac cave and its fantastic rock formations. Explore the pleasant Gorges de la Cèze and remember to stop off at Goudargues before admiring the waterfalls at Sautadet in La Roque-sur-Cèze and at Les Concluses. If you're feeling energetic, climb the Guidon de Bouquet, for the view over the typical landcape of the garrigue – thyme, rosemary, and arbutus (also known as strawberry trees) scattered among holm oaks.

2 Provence and the Roman Empire

▶*233km/145.6mi leaving from Orange*

This itinerary starts at Orange, with a visit to the triumphal arch, the magnificent Roman theatre and the museum just opposite the theatre. From there continue on to the extraordinary archaeological site at Vaison. Other sites on the itinerary include a triumphal arch at Carpentras, remains of the Roman wall in Avignon, the Roman monuments of the Plateau des Antiques and the ancient city of Glanum, both situated just outside St-Rémy. Then it's on to Arles, the amphitheatre, the Roman theatre, the mysterious Cryptoporticus, Constantine's baths, the melancholy necropolis of Les Alyscamps, and the excellent Musée de l'Arles Antique. Then to Nîmes: the amphitheatre, the temple of Diana, the Maison Carrée and the vestiges of the city's fortifications, the most impressive example of which is the Tour Magne. The Castellum, a Roman water distribution tank, is an appropriate introduction to the majestic Pont du Gard, the most spectacular part of the ancient aqueduct that brought water from the Eure fountain near Uzès to Nîmes. This Roman aqueduct crosses 50km/31.2mi of hinterland.

3 Natural wonders of the Vaucluse

▶*258km/161.2mi leaving from Carpentras, after a visit of the old town*

Start your tour admiring the views and landscapes of the Dentelles de Montmirail, with a stop in the picturesque village of Malaucène. Choose a clear day to climb Mont Ventoux and enjoy the spectacular views. From the Nesque gorges, carry on to the remarkable ochre quarries of Colorado de Rustrel, gateway to the Luberon. Climb the Mourre Nègre summit and acquaint yourself with Mount Luberon, and the *villages perchés* (hilltop villages) of Bonnieux, Rousillon (where ochre reigns) and Gordes, with its stepped alleyways and the surprising *village des bories*. Make a stop in Fontaine-de-Vaucluse, where you can see the resurgent spring of the Sorgue river. It comes to the surface here after winding its way below the Vaucluse plateau – while you were winding your way above.

4 Beautiful villages in the Luberon

▶*128km/80mi leaving from Cavaillon*

Don't go anywhere without tasting the famous melons of Cavaillon. Then set out to visit the town: the synagogue and Jewish museum in the old town; and the antique shops on the shores of the River Sorgue at Isle-sur-la-Sorgue. If your memory is in high gear, you may wish to recite the poems of Petrarch in Fontaine-de-Vaucluse, his retirement home in the 14C. The curious group of drystone huts known as the *village des bories* may inspire you to write some poetry of your own, in praise of the beautiful Luberon region. In the village of Gordes, go up and down the *calades*, the steep staircases that serve as streets, and admire the view of the Calavon valley. The Abbey of Sénanque is nestled in a lavender field nearby, a heavenly place in more than one way. Explore Roussillon, with its ochre-coloured buildings and extraordinary quarries from which ochre is extracted, as well as the workshop where the pigment was processed with time-consuming and complex techniques. Visit Saturnin-lès-

Apt, with its mill and cherry orchards, before going to Apt, where you can enjoy the crystallized fruits and the large Saturday market. Climbers will appreciate the rock spur of Buoux, but you can by just resting in the charming hamlet at the base. To round off your tour, take a walk in the cedar forest of Bonnieux before visiting Lacoste and the lovely hillside villages of Ménerbes and Oppède-le-Vieux.

5 Camargue

▶228km/143mi leaving from Arles

Start in Arles with a visit to the Museon Arlaten, founded by the legendary local poet Frédéric Mistral. Next board a boat for a relaxing trip down the Rhône. Off starboard, you will have a glimpse at the unique and beautiful ecosystem of the Camargue. Discover the intricate network of marshes and streams, and the fabulous fauna and fora of the wetlands. Visit the salt marshes of Salin-de-Giraud and walk the footpaths of the Domaine de la Palissade (the only area of the delta not to have been enclosed by dikes) to Piémanson beach near the mouth of the Rhône. Learn more about the birds and flora on the footpaths around La Capelière or take a seat aboard the small train in Méjane and visit the shores of the Vaccarès lagoon. The Musée Camarguais is devoted to the customs of the inhabitants of the Camargue; the bird sanctuary of Pont-de-Gauoffers, a unique opportunity to become better acquainted with the unusual and rare birds that frequent the lagoons. Take a stroll through the streets of Stes-Maries, with its white houses nestled around the imposing fortified church, before going to the walled city of Aigues-Mortes, either via the Sylvereal bridge or by boat. Savour some fish soup and other local specialities in the port of Grau-du-Roi before starting the return journey to Arles. On the way back explore the profusion of reeds that conceals the Scamandre lagoon and then stop to contemplate the sculptures adorning the façade of the Abbey of St-Gilles, a masterpiece of Provençal Romanesque architecture.

6 Painters and authors of Provence

▶250km/156.2mi leaving from Baux-de-Provence

What better place to start this tour devoted to artists than the magnificent town of Baux, which has inspired many painters and writers? It is only fitting to make the pilgrimage to Maillane where the great master of the Félibrige movement, Frédéric Mistral, was born and lived, before going to admire the paintings of Auguste Chabaud in Graveson. A visit to the château of Tarascon will evoke the pageantry of the court of King René, and be sure to pay a visit to Tartarin's house before going to explore the landscape and the mill of Fontvieille, which inspried the author Alphonse Daudet. In Arles follow the footsteps of Vincent Van Gogh: visit the foundation that bears his name and the hospice where he was interned, which has been faithfully reconstructed exactly as it was.

The Picasso donation in the Musée Réattu is well worth a visit for the remarkable modern sculpture and fine photographic collection. To learn more about the late 19C Provençal school go to the Musée Ziem in Martigues, while the Musée des Beaux-Arts in Marseille will deepen your appreciation of the great Baroque master Pierre Puget. Others may prefer to see the installations in the MAC (Musée d'Art Contemporain) or to settle down on Prado beach with one of Jean-Claude Izzo's detective novels. The classical Aix is the place to go to trace Cézanne's footsteps (as well as finding out more about Vasarely) and to re-read Zola who described Aix (under the name of Plasson) as the birthplace of the Rougon family in his Rougon-Macquart series of novels. And if you're curious, why not visit Salon to find out what the future holds in Nostradamus' prophecies?

7 The mountainous shore and the countryside beyond Marseille

▶290km/175mi leaving from Baux-de-Provence

This itinerary is the ideal opportunity to use your walking shoes, or your flippers! Consider that after a pleasant stroll through the Panier and Notre-Dame-de-la-Garde quarters of old Marseille, the Chaîne de l'Estaque provides creeks and *calanques* with some superb seawater for swimmers and divers. Niolon in particular is ideal for divers while the tiny beaches of Redonne are good for catching sea urchins and spotting octopuses (*pourpres*). If you prefer to swim without the octopus, head for Carry-le-Rouet, Sausset-les-Pins or Carro. Aix is a good place for an evening stroll, when the light falls on the façades of the old *hôtels particuliers*. Trace Cézanne's footsteps by exploring Ste-Victoire, where the steep footpaths provide some superb views from the Croix de Provence. This is now a favourite spot for paragliders. A visit to the Royal Monastery at St-Maximin makes an ideal prelude to an excursion on the Ste-Baume massif, which attracts pilgrims, ramblers, and climbers who enjoy the challenge of its steep rock faces. The bucolic St-Pons park offers a pleasant rest in the shade before returning to the sea at La Ciotat and travelling up the Corniche des Crètes. Finally, at Cassis get on a boat for a voyage of discovery of the sumptuous *calanques*.

Themed Tours

HISTORICAL ITINERARIES

The historical itineraries, known as *Routes Historiques*, are intended to present France's architectural heritage in its historical context (*www.routes-historiques.com*). You can find out more about these many routes by contacting the various tourist offices, or, *La Demeure historique (Hôtel de Nesmond, 57 quai de la Tournelle, 75005 Paris,* ☎ *01 55 42 60 00. www.demeure-historique.org*).

Four important historical itineraries are covered in this the region:

♦ **Route historique du patrimoine juif du Midi de la France**
Comité départemental du tourisme de Vaucluse,
☎ *04 90 80 47 00*
www.provenceguide.com

♦ **Route historique des Vaudois en Luberon**; **Routes historiques en Languedoc-Roussillon**
Château de Flaugergues - 1744 av. Albert-Einstein - 34000 Montpellier -
☎ *04 99 52 66 37*

♦ **Via Domitia**
Delran - Association Régionale Via Domitia - CRT - 417 r. Samuel-Morse CS79507 - 34960 Montpellier Cedex 2 - ☎ *04 67 22 81 00 - www.viadomitia.org*).

You may also be interested in the Route Historique Musicale and part of the Route Historique du Gévaudan au Golfe du Lion.

Historical itineraries are signposted along country roads. All of them are detailed in handbooks available from local tourist offices.

PAINTERS' PATHS, WRITERS' FOOTSTEPS

The **Route des Peintres de la Lumière en Provence** offers an introduction to the region through the various sites painted by artists who created radiant works suffused with light (♨ *see Introduction to Provence; 19C and 20C art*). For details inquire at the *Comité Régional de Tourisme Provence-Alpes-Côte d'Azur.*

The tourist offices in Aix-en-Provence and St-Rémy de Provence (♨ *see AIX-EN-PROVENCE; see ST-RÉMY-DE-PROVENCE*) have information on two thematic itineraries – **"Cézanne"** and **"Visiting the Sites Painted by Van Gogh."**

In Aubagne, you can walk or take a bus tour to explore the life of writer/filmmaker **Marcel Pagnol** (*ask at the tourist office in Aubagne;* ♨ *see Aubagne*).

For a tour on **Alphonse Daudet** to visit the sites that inspired his famous, *Lettres de mon moulin,* inquire at the tourist office in Fontvieille (♨ *see Les ALPILLES*) .

NATURE PARKS

Parc Naturel Régional de Camargue (♨ *see La CAMARGUE*) – *Centre d'Information de Ginès, RD 570, Pont de Gau, 13460 Les Stes-Maries-de-la-Mer* ☎ *04 90 97 86 32 – info@parc-camargue.fr – www.parc-camargue. fr; Musée Camarguais, Mas du Pont de Rousty, 13200 Arles* ☎ *04 90 97 10 82 – musee@parc-camargue.fr. Information can also be obtained from Tourist Information Centres in Arles, Salin-de-Giraud, and Les Stes-Maries-de-la-Mer.*

Parc Naturel Régional du Luberon (♨ *see Le LUBERON*) – *Maison du Parc, 60 Place Jean-Jaurès, 84404 Apt* ☎ *04 90 04 42 00 – www.parcduluberon.fr.*

MARINE PARKS

Marine parks feature preserved areas where fishing and diving activities, as well as boat anchoring, are strictly regulated and where experiments with artificial reefs are being carried out. The aim of these parks is to fulfil a number of well-defined objectives: protecting the natural environment (controlling all activities concerned with the development and survival of plant and animal species); exploiting the available resources (immersion of artificial reefs to encourage the growth of fauna and flora); installing blocks to hinder illicit trawling; and providing information to increase public awareness of ecological issues.

Parc Régional Marin de la Côte Bleue – Lying west of Marseille harbour, it laps the Massif de la Nerthe, a rocky mountain range separating the Étang de Berre from the sea. *Information can be obtained from the Parc Régional Marin de la Côte Bleue - Observatoire du Parc Marin - Plage du Rouet - 31, avenue Jean Bart - B.P. 42 - 13620 Carry-le-Rouet – syndicatmixte@ parcmarincotebleue.fr – or from local Tourist Information Centres in Carry-le-Rouet, Ensuès-la-Redonne, Martigues, Le Rove and Sausset-les-Pins.*

Parc Régional Marin de la Baie de La Ciotat – The park is defined by La Ciotat bay. The underwater topography is remarkably varied: rocks, sand, sloping ledges, underwater slabs, and mossy beds of posidonia, home to a great many small molluscs. *Information available from the Parc Régional Marin de la Baie de La Ciotat, Hôtel de Ville, 13712 La Ciotat ☎ 04 42 83 90 09, or from the Ciotat tourist office.*

- **Never forget** that the marine environment is extremely fragile and needs to be respected by all those who venture near it. Make a point of observing the following rules:
- Dispose of plastic bags on shore in closed containers;
- Throw any fish you have caught back into the sea;
- Do not damage or remove the long, green posidonia leaves that cleanse seawater by renewing its oxygen.

OLIVES AND THE OIL INDUSTRY

There are several types of olives in Provence: the *tanche* or *olive de Nyons*, delicious when served pickled in brine; the *angladau*, pressed for its oil; the *grossane*, a big, black fleshy olive; the *salonenque* or *olive des Baux*, a green variety served crushed; the *picholine*, a long, narrow green olive, crushed and then pickled. *To learn more about olives and oils, contact l'Institut du Monde de l'Olivier, in Nyons ☎ 04 75 26 90 90.*

Provence offers thematic circuits that focus on the olive: those in the Bouches-du-Rhône (**Route de l'olivier des Alpilles et de la vallée des Baux**, and **Route de l'olivier du pays d'Aix-en-Provence**); and in the Drôme (**Route de l'olivier en Baronnies**, around Nyons and Buis-les-Baronnies). These tours include visits to olive groves, mills, presses, and museums. *Information can be obtained from the Association française interprofessionnelle de l'olive, 22 r. Henri-Pontier, 13626 Aix-en-Provence Cedex 1, ☎ 04 42 23 01 92.*

LAVENDER FIELDS

Created by the Regional Tourist Committee of the Provence-Alpes-Côte d'Azur area, the **Route de la Lavande** enables you to visit a great many places associated with the growing and processing of lavender around the Mont Ventoux, the Luberon, and the Provençal Drôme. This circuit is complemented

Olive trees in blossom

G. Magnin/ MICHELIN

by various festivities: Fête de la Lavande in Sault on 15 August, the **Corso Nocturne de la Lavande** in Valréas in the beginning of August. The *association Routes de la Lavande (2 Avenue de Venterol, 26111 Nyons Cedex* ☎ *04 75 26 65 91, www.routes-lavande.com)* publishes a handbook with general information as well as cards with practical data about each site which can be picked up from local tourist offices.

Pays de Sault et du Ventoux

Ferme St-Agricol in Savoillans: tour of the farmhouse and botanical gardens, practical demonstration of distillation techniques ☎ *04 75 28 86 57.*
Lavender garden in Sault: collection of lavender plants. *Hameau de Verdolier* ☎ *04 90 64 14 97.*
You can also visit a cooperative at the *Maison des Producteurs de Sault, rue de la République,* ☎ *04 90 64 08 98.*

Pays d'Apt and Luberon

There is a lavender distillery at Lagarde d'Apt. Guided tours available on request ☎ *04 90 75 01 42.*
Lavender farm at Lagarde d'Apt: tour of a lavender field and visit to the distillery. *Château du Bois* ☎ *04 90 76 91 23.*
Lavender Museum in Coustellet (*see Le LUBERON*).

Provençal Drôme

Bleu Provence Distillery in Nyons ☎ *04 75 26 10 42.*
Jardin des Arômes in Nyons: collection of aromatic plants, promenade along the pier ☎ *04 75 26 04 30.*

TRUFFLES

The Vaucluse is the main truffle-producing region. If you are here from mid-November to mid-March, you can delight in visiting the regional truffle markets that take place in the morning. Be sure to seal the deal with a good elixir!

- ◆ **Carpentras**
  The most important truffle market of the Vaucluse, runs from mid-Nov to mid-Mar: Fri, 9am.
- ◆ **Richerenches**
  A very reputable market: Sat, 10am.
- ◆ **Valréas** – Wed.

To visit a *truffière*, go to Uzès (*see Uzés*) and Grillon (*see Valréas*).

TOURS OF WINE COOPERATIVES

Tours of cooperative wine cellars *(caves)* are offered all over the wine-producing regions: the east and west banks of the Rhône, areas surrounding Aigues-Mortes, Aix, Les Baux-de-Provence, Cassis, etc. The addresses of wine cellars and domains can be obtained from the *Syndicats et Maisons des vins*. Details about events linked to vineyards and wine festivals are available at the tourist offices. Also consult Michelin's *The Wine Regions of France.*

⚜ Côtes-du-rhône wines
Maison des vins d'AOC côtes-du-rhône et Vallée du Rhône — 6 r. des Trois-Faucons - 84021 Avignon Cedex 1 - ☎ *04 90 27 24 00 - www.vins-rhone.com,* **Wine fesitvals**: of Vacqueyras, 14 July; of Véraison to Châteauneuf-du-Pape, first Sun in Aug; of Rasteau, the weekend of 15 Aug; in Avignon, third Thur in Nov. Ask for the pamphlet **Routes des vins**, which details nine itineraries.
See Dentelles de Montmirail, Orange, Vaison-la-Romaine.

⚜ Coteaux d'Aix-en-Provence wines
Syndicat des Coteaux d'Aix-en-Provence — Maison des Agriculteurs - 22 av. Henri-Pontier - 13626 Aix-en-Provence - ☎ *04 42 23 57 14 - www.coteauxaixenprovence.com.*

⚜ Baux-de-Provence wines
Syndicat des vignerons des Baux, Mme Marie-France Bigourdan, ☎ *04 32 61 90 67.*

⚜ wine festivals
Concour des vin du Baux, June; *Fête du vin et de l'artisanat* in St-Rémy-de-Provence, end of July; *fête du vignoble des Baux*, second weekend in Oct.

⚜ Cassis wines
Syndicat des vignerons de Cassis — Domaine du Bagnol - 12 avenue de Provence - 13260 Cassis - ☎ *04 42 01 78 05 -* A **wine feast** with a procession and tasting sessions takes place the first Sun in September.

⚜ Côtes-du-luberon wines
Syndicat général des vins des côtes-du-lubéron - BP 12 - La Tour-d'Aigues - 84125 Pertuis Cedex - ☎ *04 90 07 34 40 - www.vins-cotes-luberon.fr*

⚜ Côtes-de-provence wines –
See La Sainte-Victoire.

⚜ Costières de Nîmes wines
See Nîmes.

⚜ Vins de pays des sables du golfe du Lion –
See Aigues-Mortes.

When to Go

SEASONS

The region of Provence is blessed with mild weather throughout the year, especially along the coast. The rhythm of the seasons fluctuates somewhat, especially in the spring; even in winter the temperature can rise or fall dramatically in one day.

Summer – This is "the" season. in those three or four months, the heat and lack of rain attract sun-loving crowds to this popular region, which is most charming at this time. It rains no more than 70mm/2.5in and the temperature rarely drops below 30°C/86°F. The dry heat is not overpowering; its constancy is explained by the presence of a hot air mass from the Sahara, protected from the west's humid depressions by the Massif Central.

Autumn – The reflux of high pressure of tropical origin opens the way to Atlantic depressions. From mid-September to late November, rain appears; sometimes violent rainstorms provoke flash floods. The rainfall can amount to more than 100mm/3.75in in 1 hr (annually 600mm/23.5in).

Winter – The cold season—which is often sunny—is relatively mild and dry. The temperature can drop 10°C/50°F in a few hours because of the mistral (see Winds below). The Mediterranean's liquid mass reduces the cold front and prevents snow falls except on the peaks.

Spring – High pressure from Siberia abates from February on, allowing the Atlantic rains to fall. These rains are less violent than those in the autumn and bright and clear days are frequent. The mistral, especially in March, can provoke a surprising chill for those

who are not used to the whims of a Provençal spring.

Winds – The wind is an essential part of the Provençal climate. The most well known is the mistral (mistrau means master in Provençal, thus master-wind). This strong, dry, cold north-northwesterly wind sweeps down when the pressure is high over the mountains. It can rage like a storm, then disappear as suddenly as it arrives. Two other common winds in this region are the southeast marin, bringing rain and fog; and the southwest labech, bringing rainstorms.

CLIMATE

Writers have acclaimed Provence's temperate climate, low rainfall and exceptional light. Nonetheless, weather conditions are changeable from year to year. Provence's land relief and the sea play an important role. Maritime Provence enjoys a more agreeable climate (less rain and hotter) than the hinterland, where altitude modifies the temperature considerably. But the dominant factor remains the long periods of sunshine (more than 2 500hr per year) in the region.

WHAT TO PACK

As little as possible! Cleaning and laundry services are available everywhere. Most personal items can be replaced at reasonable cost. Try to pack everything in one suitcase and a carry-on bag. Take an umbrella—and an extra tote bag for packing new purchases, shopping at the open-air market, carrying a picnic, etc. Be sure luggage is clearly labelled and old travel tags removed. Do not pack medication in checked luggage, but keep it with you.

Temperature chart

°F/°C
Maximum temperatures in black.
Minimum temperatures in red.

Jan	Feb	Mar	Apr	May	Jun	Jul	Aug	Sep	Oct	Nov	Dec
33°/50°	35°/52°	38°/59°	44°/62°	52°/62°	57°/79°	62°/82°	62°/82°	57°/77°	50°/66°	42°/57°	37°/50°
1°/10°	2°/11°	3°/15°	7°/17°	11°/21°	14°/26°	17°/28°	17°/28°	14°/25°	10°/19°	6°/14°	3°/10°

Precipitation

Jan	Feb	Mar	Apr	May	Jun	Jul	Aug	Sep	Oct	Nov	Dec
43mm	32mm	43mm	42mm	46mm	24mm	11mm	34mm	60mm	76mm	69mm	66mm

KNOW BEFORE YOU GO

Useful Web Sites

www.ambafrance-us.org

The French Embassy in the USA has a web site providing basic information (geography, demographics, history), a news digest, and business-related information. It offers special pages for children, and pages devoted to culture, language study, and travel. Through it you can also reach other selected French sites (regions, cities, ministries) with a hypertext link.

www.franceguide.com

The French Government Tourist Office – *Maison de la France* – site is packed with practical information and tips for travelling to France. The home page has a number of links for more specific guidance, such as information tailored to your country of origin (such as for British, Irish, American, and Canadian travellers, or to the FGTO's London pages).

www.FranceKeys.com

This sight has plenty of practical information for visiting France. It covers all the regions, with links to tourist offices and related sites. Very useful for planning the details of your tour in France.

www.visiteurope.com

The European Travel Commission provides useful information on travelling to and around 27 European countries, and includes links to some commercial booking services (vehicle hire, for example), rail schedules, weather reports and calendar of events.

www.degrifprovence.com

This site offers last minute discounts on accommodations.

French Tourist Offices

For information, brochures, maps, and assistance in planning a trip to France travellers should apply to the official French Tourist Office or Maison de France in their own country.

AUSTRALIA – NEW ZEALAND

Sydney

Level 22, 25 Bligh Street,
NSW 2000 Sydney

☎ (02) 9231 5244
Fax: (02) 9221 8682.
info.au@franceguide.com.

CANADA

Montreal

1981 McGill College Avenue,
Suite 490,
Montreal Que H3A 2W9
☎ (514) 288 2026
Fax: (514) 845 4868.
canada@franceguide.com.

EIRE

Dublin

10 Suffolk Street, 2
☎ 01560 235 235.
info.ie@franceguide.com.

SOUTH AFRICA

P.O. Box 41022, 2024 Craighall,
☎ 00 27 11 880 80 62
Fax 00 27 11 770 16 66
mdfsa@frenchdoor.co.za.

UNITED KINGDOM

London

178 Piccadilly, London WIV 0AL
☎ 09068 244 123
Fax: 020 7493 6594. info.uk@franceguide.com.

UNITED STATES

East Coast

New York – 444 Madison Avenue,
NY 10022
☎ (514) 288 1904
Fax: (212) 838-7855.
info.us@franceguide.com.

Mid West

Chicago – 205 N.Michigan Ave,
Suite 3770, Chicago, IL 60601
☎ (514) 288 1904.
info.chicago@franceguide.com

West Coast

Los Angeles – 9454 Wilshire Boulevard, Suite 715, Beverly Hills, CA 90212-2967
☎ (514) 288 1904
Fax: (310) 276-2835.
info.losangeles@franceguide.com.

Information can also be requested from **France on Call**, ☎ (202) 659-7779.

Local and Regional Tourist Offices

Visitors may also contact local tourist offices for more precise information, and to receive brochures and maps. The addresses, telephone numbers, and web sites of local tourist offices are listed after the symbol 🖪 at the beginning of most of the Principal Sights described in this book. Below are addresses for the regional tourist offices and the *départements* tourist offices for Provence.

COMITÉ REGIONAUX DE TOURISME

Provence-Alpes-Côte d'Azur
Les Docks - Atrium 10.5 -
10 pl. de la Joliette -
BP 46214 - 13567 Marseille Cedex 02
☎ *04 91 56 47 00*
www.crt-paca.fr.

Languedoc-Roussillon
(For the *département* of Gard)
r. de la République - CS 79507,
34960 Montpellier Cedex 2
☎ *04 67 22 81 00*
www.sunfrance.com.

Rhône-Alpes
(for the gorges de l'Ardèche)
rte de Paris -
69260 Charbonnières-les-Bains -
☎ *04 72 59 21 59*
www.rhonealpes-tourisme.com.

COMITÉ DÉPARTEMENTAL DU TOURISME

Ardèche
cours du Palais - 07000 Privas
☎ *04 75 64 04 66*
www.ardeche-guide.com
www.ardeche-resa.com.

Bouches-du-Rhône
Le Montesquieu,
13 r. Roux-de-Brignoles,
13006 Marseille
☎ *04 91 13 84 40*
www.visitprovence.com.

Gard
rue Cité Foulc - BP 122 -
30010 Nîmes Cedex 04
☎ *04 66 36 96 30*
www.tourismegard.com.

Vaucluse
r. du Collège-de-la-Croix - BP 147
84008 Avignon Cedex 1
☎ *04 90 80 47 00*
www.provenceguide.com.

International Visitors

EMBASSIES AND CONSULATES IN FRANCE

Australia   Embassy
4 rue Jean-Rey, 75015 Paris.
☎ 01 40 59 33 00
Fax: 01 40 59 33 10.

Canada   Embassy
35-37 avenue Montaigne,
75008 Paris.
☎ 01 44 43 29 00
Fax: 01 44 43 29 99.

Eire   Embassy
4 rue Rude, 75116 Paris.
☎ 01 44 17 67 00
Fax: 01 44 17 67 60.

New Zealand   Embassy
7 rue Léonard-de-Vinci, 75116 Paris
☎ 01 45 01 43 43
Fax: 01 45 01 26 39.

South Africa   Embassy
59 quai d'Orsay, 75343 Paris. ☎ 01 53 59 23 23. Fax: 01 53 59 23 33.

UK   Embassy
35 rue du Faubourg St-Honoré,
75383 Paris.
☎ 01 44 51 31 00
Fax: 01 44 51 31 88.

UK   Paris Consulate
16/18 bis rue d'Anjou, 75008 Paris.
☎ 01 44 51 31 00
Fax 01 44 51 31 27.

UK   Marseille Consulate
4 rue du Prado, 13006 Marseille
☎ 04 91 15 72 10
Fax 04 91 37 47 06.

USA   Embassy
2 avenue Gabriel, 75008 Paris.
☎ 01 43 12 22 22.
Fax: 01 42 66 97 83.

USA   Paris Consulate
2 rue St-Florentin, 75382 Paris.
☎ 01 42 96 14 88.

USA   Marseille Consulate
Place Varian Fry 13006 Marseille.
☎ 04 91 54 92 00.
Fax 04 91 55 09 47.
www.amb-usa.fr.

DOCUMENTS

Passport
Nationals of countries within the European Union entering France need only a national identity card. Nationals of other countries must

be in possession of a valid national **passport**. In case of loss or theft, report to your embassy or consulate and the local police.

Visa

No **entry visa** is required for Canadian, US, or Australian citizens travelling as tourists and staying less than 90 days, except for students planning to study in France. If you think you may need a visa, apply to your local French Consulate.

US citizens should obtain the booklet *Safe Trip Abroad*, which provides useful information on visa requirements, customs regulations, medical care, etc, for international travellers. Published by the Government Printing Office, it can be ordered by phone (☎ *(202) 512-1800)* or consulted on-line (*www. access.gpo.gov*). General passport information is available by phone toll-free from the Federal Information Center (*item 5 on the automated menu)*, ☎ *800-688-9889*. US passport application forms can be downloaded from *http://travel.state.gov*.

CUSTOMS

Apply to the Customs Office (UK) for a leaflet on customs regulations and the full range of duty-free allowances; available from *HM Customs and Excise, Dorset House, Stamford Street, London SE1 9PS*, ☎ *0171 928 3344*. The US Customs Service offers a publication *Know Before You Go* for US citizens: for the office nearest you, consult the phone book, Federal Government, US Treasury (*www.customs.ustreas.gov*). There are no customs formalities for holidaymakers bringing their caravans into France for a stay of less than six months. No customs document

is necessary for pleasure boats and outboard motors for a stay of less than six months but the registration certificate should be kept on board. Americans can bring home, tax-free, up to US$ 400 worth of goods (limited quantities of alcohol and tobacco products); Canadians up to CND$ 300; Australians up to AUS$ 400; and New Zealanders up to NZ$ 700.

Persons living in a member state of the European Union are not restricted with regard to purchasing goods for private use, but the recommended allowances for alcoholic beverages and tobacco are as follows:

HEALTH

First aid, medical advice and chemists' night service are provided by chemists/drugstores *(pharmacie)* identified by the green cross sign. Since the recipient of medical treatment in French hospitals or clinics must pay the bill, it is advisable to take out comprehensive insurance coverage. Nationals of non-EU countries should check with their insurance companies about policy limitations. Reimbursement can then be negotiated with the insurance company according to the policy held. All prescription drugs should be clearly labelled; it is recommended that you carry a copy of the prescription.

British and Irish citizens should apply to the Department of Health and Social Security for **Form E 111**, which entitles the holder to urgent treatment for accident or unexpected illness in EU countries. A refund of part of the costs of treatment can be obtained on application in person or by post to the local Social Security Offices (*Caisse Primaire d'Assurance Maladie).* **Americans** concerned about travel and health can contact the International Association for Medical Assistance to Travelers, which can also provide details of English-speaking doctors in different parts of France: ☎ *(716) 754-4883. www.iamat.org*.

The American Hospital of Paris is open 24hr for emergencies as well as consultations, with English-speaking staff, at *63 boulevard Victor-Hugo, 92200 Neuilly sur Seine*, ☎ *01 46 41 25 25*. Accredited by major insurance companies.

The British Hospital is just outside *Paris in Levallois-Perret, 3 rue Barbès*, ☎ *01 46 39 22 22*.

Duty-Free Allowances	
Spirits (whisky, gin, vodka etc)	10 litres
Fortified wines (vermouth, port etc)	20 litres
Wine (not more than 60 sparkling)	90 litres
Beer	110 litres
Cigarettes	800
Cigarillos	400
Cigars	200
Smoking tobacco	1 kg

Accessibility

The sights described in this guide that are easily accessible to people of reduced mobility are indicated by the symbol ♿. Useful information on transportation, holidaymaking, and sports associations for the disabled is available from the *Comité National Français de Liaison pour la Réadaptation des Handicapés (CNRH), 236bis rue de Tolbiac, 75013 Paris.* Call their international information number ☎ *01 53 80 66 44*, or write to request a catalogue of publications. Web-surfers can find information for slow walkers, mature travellers, and others with special needs at *www. access-able.com* and *www.handitel. org.* For information on museum access for the disabled contact *La Direction, Les Musées de France, Service Accueil des Publics Spécifiques, 6 rue des Pyramides, 75041 Paris Cedex 1,* ☎ *01 40 15 35 88.* ♿ *Also see: http://museofile.culture.fr.*

The **Michelin Guide France** and the **Michelin Camping Caravaning France** indicate hotels and camp sites with facilities suitable for physically handicapped people.

GETTING THERE

By Air

The various national and other independent airlines operate services to Paris (Roissy-Charles-de-Gaulle and Orly airports). Major companies offering regularly scheduled flights from the UK and the US to Marseille and Nîmes include Air France, American Airlines, Delta and British Airways. For connecting flights from Paris, you can fly Air Littoral or Airlib. Discount flights from London to Nîmes or Marseille are offered by Ryanair and Buzz.

Air France (*www.airfrance.fr*) has daily flights from Marseille to Ajaccio, Brest, Bastia, Bordeaux, Clermont-Ferrand, Calvi, Figari, Lille, Lyon, Nantes, Paris, Rennes, Strasbourg, and Toulouse. Easyjet (*www.easyjet.com*) also flies Paris-Marseille.

Airports that serve the region:

Aéroport international de Marseille Provence
3727 Marignane
☎ 04 42 14 14 14
www.marseille.aeroport.fr

Aéroport d'Avignon-Caumont
☎ 04 90 81 51 51
www.avignon.aeroport.fr.

There are also package tour flights with a rail or coach link-up as well as Fly-Drive offers. Information, brochures and timetables are available from the airlines or travel agents.

By Sea

From the UK or Ireland

There are numerous **cross-Channel services** (passenger and car ferries, hovercraft) from the United Kingdom and Ireland, as well as the rail Shuttle through the Channel Tunnel (**Le Shuttle-Eurotunnel**, ☎ 0990 353-535). To choose the most suitable route between your port of arrival and your destination use the *Michelin Tourist and Motoring Atlas France, Michelin map 726* (which gives travel times and mileages) or Michelin maps from the Local series (with the yellow cover). For details apply to travel agencies or to:

P & O Stena Line Ferries
Channel House, Channel View Road,
    Dover CT17 9JT
☎ 0990 980 980
☎ 01304 863 000 (switchboard)
www.p-and-o.com.

Hoverspeed
International Hoverport, Marine Parade, Dover, Kent CT17 9TG
☎ 0990 240 241
Fax 01304 240088,
www.hoverspeed.co.uk.

Brittany Ferries
Millbay Docks;
Plymouth, Devon. PL1 3EW,
☎ 0990 360 360
www.brittany-ferries.com.

Portsmouth Commercial Port (and ferry information)
George Byng Way, Portsmouth, Hampshire PO2 8SP
☎ 01705 297391
Fax 01705 861165.

Irish Ferries
50 West Norland Street,
Dublin 2
☎ (353) 16 610 511
www.irishferries.com.

Seafrance
Eastern Docks, Dover,
Kent, CT16 1JA
☎ 01304 212696
Fax 01304 240033
www.seafrance.fr.

By Rail

British Rail and **French Railways** (SNCF) operate a 3hr daily service via the Channel Tunnel on **Eurostar** between **London** (Waterloo International Station) and **Paris** (Gare du Nord). Since June, 2001, the operation of high-speed TGV trains from **Paris** (Gare de Lyon) has greatly reduced the time it takes to reach **Marseille** (3hr 15min), **Avignon** (2hr 30min), and **Nîmes** (2hr 45min). You can also start your journey in Lille (add 1hr). The city centre to city centre service is nearly as fast as flying, and many find it more convenient.

Eurailpass, Flexipass, Eurailpass Youth, EurailDrive Pass, and **Saverpass** are travel passes that may be purchased by residents of countries outside the European Union. In the US, contact your travel agent or **Rail Europe** (*2100 Central Ave. Boulder, CO, 80301, ☎ 1-800-4-EURAIL, or Europrail International, ☎1 888 667 9731*). If you are a European resident, you can buy an individual country pass, if you are not a resident of the country where you plan to use it. In the UK, contact

Europrail at *179 Piccadilly London W1V OBA* ☎ *0990 848 848*. Information on schedules can be obtained on web sites for these agencies and the **SNCF**, respectively: *www.raileurop.com.us, www.eurail.on.ca, www.sncf.fr*. At the SNCF site, you can book ahead, pay with a credit card, and receive your ticket in the mail at home.

There are numerous discounts available when you purchase your tickets in France, from 25-50% below the regular rate. These include **discounts** for using senior cards and youth cards (the nominative cards with a photograph must be purchased – 44.21€ and 41.16€, respectively), and lower rates for 2-9 people travelling together (no card required, advance purchase necessary). There are a limited number of discount seats available during peak travel times, and the best discounts are available for travel during off-peak periods. Tickets bought in France must be validated *(composter)* by using the orange automatic date-stamping machines at the platform entrance (failure to do so may result in a fine). The French railway company SNCF operates a **telephone information, reservation** and **prepayment service in English** from 7am to 10pm (French time). In France call ☎ 08 36 35 35 39 (when calling from outside France, drop the initial 0).

By Coach

The Provence region can be reached by coach via Paris. **Eurolines** has daily services to the towns of Marseille, Avignon, and Nîmes. For further information, contact:

London: 52 Grosvenor Gardens, Victoria, London SW1 0AU ☎ 0171 730 8235.

Paris: 28, Avenue du Général-de-Gaulle, 93541 Bagnolet ☎ 01 49 72 51 51.

Internet: www.eurolines.com.

DRIVING IN FRANCE

Know Before You Go

ROUTE PLANNING

The area covered in this guide is easily reached by main motorways and national routes. **Michelin map 726** indicates the main itineraries as well as alternate routes for avoiding heavy traffic during busy holiday periods, and gives estimated travel times. **Michelin map 723** is a detailed atlas of French motorways, indicating tolls, rest areas and services along the route; it includes a table for calculating distances and times. The latest Michelin route-planning service is available at **www.ViaMichelin. com.** Travellers can calculate a precise route using such options as shortest route, route avoiding toll roads or the Michelin-recommended route. The site also provides tourist information (hotels, restaurants, attractions). The roads are very busy during the holiday period (particularly weekends in July and August) and, to avoid traffic congestion it is advisable to follow the recommended secondary routes *(signposted as Bison Futé – itinéraires bis)*. The motorway network includes rest areas *(aires)* and petrol stations, usually with restaurant and shopping complexes attached, about every 40km/25mi, so that long-distance drivers can stop for a rest every now and then.

DOCUMENTS

Travellers from other European Union countries and North America can drive in France with a valid national or home-state **driving licence**. An **international driving licence** is useful because the information on it appears in nine languages (keep in mind that traffic officers are empowered to fine motorists). A permit is available (US$ 10) from the **National Automobile Club**, *1151 East Hillsdale Blvd., Foster City, CA 94404 b 650-294-7000 or www. nationalautoclub.com*; or contact your local branch of the **American Automobile Association**. For the vehicle, it is necessary to have the registration papers (logbook) and a nationality plate of the approved size.

Certain motoring organisations (AAA, AA, RAC) offer accident **insurance** and breakdown service schemes for members. Check with your current insurance company in regard to coverage while abroad. If you plan to hire a car using your credit card, check with the company, which may provide liability insurance automatically (and thus save you having to pay the cost for optimum coverage).

Rules of the Road

REGULATIONS

The minimum driving age is 18. Traffic drives on the right. All passengers must wear **seat belts**. Children under the age of 10 must ride in the back seat. Headlights must be switched on in poor visibility and at night; use side-lights only when the vehicle is stationary.
In the case of a **breakdown**, a red warning triangle or hazard warning lights are obligatory. In the absence of stop signs at intersections, cars must **yield to the right**. Traffic on main roads outside built-up areas (priority indicated by a yellow diamond sign) and on roundabouts has right of way. Vehicles must stop when the lights turn red at road junctions and may filter to the right only when indicated by an amber arrow.
The regulations on **drinking and driving** (limited to 0.50g/l) and **speeding** are strictly enforced, usually by an on-the-spot fine and/or confiscation of the vehicle.

SPEED LIMITS

Although liable to modification, these are as follows:

- ◆ toll motorways *(autoroutes)* 130kph/80mph (110kph/68mph when raining);
- ◆ dual carriageways and motorways without tolls 110kph/68mph (100kph/62mph when raining);
- ◆ other roads 90kph/56mph (80kph/50mph when raining) and in towns 50kph/31mph;
- ◆ outside lane on motorways during daylight, on level ground and with good visibility – minimum speed limit of 80kph/50mph.

PARKING

In town there are zones where parking is either restricted or subject to a fee; tickets should be obtained from the ticket machines (*horodateurs* – small change necessary) and displayed inside the windscreen on the driver's side; failure to display may result in a fine, or towing and impoundment. Other parking areas in town may require you to take a ticket when passing through a barrier. To exit, you must pay the parking fee (usually there is a machine located by the exit – *sortie*) and insert the paid-up card in another machine which will lift the exit gate.

TOLLS

In France, most motorway sections are subject to a toll (*péage*). You can pay in cash or with a credit card (Visa, Mastercard).

Vehicles

CAR RENTAL

Car rental agencies are located at airports, at railway stations, and in all large towns throughout France. European cars have **manual transmission**; automatic cars are available in larger cities only if an advance reservation is made. Drivers must be over 21 years of age. Drivers between the ages of 21-25 years are required to pay an extra daily fee. Some companies rent to drivers under 23 years of age only if the reservation has been made through a travel agent. It is relatively expensive to hire a car in France; Americans in particular will notice the difference and should make arrangements before leaving. We recommen that you take advantage of fly-drive offers, or seek advice from a travel agent, specifying requirements. There are many on-line services that will

search internationally for the best prices on rental cars. Access **Nova** on-line at www.rentacar-worldwide.com, or by telephone ☎ 0800-018 6682 (free-of-charge in the UK); if calling from outside the UK, dial ☎ 44 28 4272 8189. All car-rental agencies appearing in the chart *(below)* have Internet sites for information and reservations, or call the phone numbers shown.

MOTORHOMES

 Worldwide Motorhome Rentals

Offers fully equipped camper vans for rent. You can view them on the company's web page.

☎ 888- 519-8969 *US toll-free*
☎ 530-389-8316 *outside the US*
Fax 530-389-5490.
www.mhrww.com

 Overseas Motorhome Tours Inc.

Organises escorted tours and individual rental of recreational vehicles.

☎ 800-322-2127 *US*
☎ 1-310-543-2590 *outside the US*
www.omtinc.com.

PETROL

French service stations dispense:

- *sans plomb 98* (super unleaded 98)
- *sans plomb 95* (super unleaded 95)
- *diesel/gazole* (diesel)
- *GPL* (LPG).

Petrol, or gasoline as Americans call it, is considerably more expensive in France than in the USA. Prices are listed on signboards on the motorways; it is usually cheaper to fill up after leaving the motorway; check the large hypermarkets on the outskirts of town.

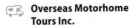

Rental Cars – Central Reservation in France (phone charge may apply)		
Avis:	☎ 08 20 05 05 05	www.avis.fr
Europcar:	☎ 08 25 35 23 52	www.europcar.com
Budget France:	☎ 08 00 10 00 01	www.budget.com
Hertz France:	☎ 01 39 38 38 38	www.hertz.com
SIXT-Eurorent:	☎ 01 43 33 27 47	www.e-sixt.com
National-CITER:	☎ 01 44 38 61 61 (Paris) ☎ 08 00 20 21 21 (outside Paris)	www.citer.fr
Baron's Limousine:	☎ 01 45 30 21 21 (chauffeur-driven)	

WHERE TO STAY AND EAT

Where to Stay

FINDING A HOTEL

The **MICHELIN GREEN GUIDE** is pleased to offer a selection of hotels and restaurants for Provence. Turn to the "Address Book" section within individual site listings for descriptions and prices of typical places to stay (**Where to Stay**) and eat (**Eating Out**) with local flair. The key at the back of the guide explains the symbols and abbreviations used in these sections. Use the map of **Places to stay** opposite to identify recommended places for overnight stops. For an even greater selection, use The **Michelin Guide France**, with its well known star-rating system and hundreds of establishments throughout France. The **Michelin Charming Places to Stay** guide contains a selection of 1 000 hotels and guest houses at reasonable prices. Be sure to book ahead, especially during the high season: Provence is a very popular holiday destination. For further assistance, **Fédération nationale des services de réservation Loisirs-Accueil** (*280 bd St-Germain - 75007 Paris -* ☎ *01 44 11 10 44 - www.resinfrance. com ou www.loisirsaccueilfrance.com*) is a booking service with a detailed brochure that has offices in some French *départements*. (You can also contact the tourist offices listed above for further information. Another resource, which publishes a catalog for each *département* for vacation villas, apartments, or chalets is the **Fédération nationale Clévacances France** (*54 bd de l'Embouchure - BP 52166 - 31022 Toulouse Cedex -* ☎ *05 61 13 55 66 - www.clevacances.com*). A guide to good-value, family-run hotels, **Logis et Auberges de France**, is available from the French Tourist Office, as are lists of other kinds of accommodation, such as hotel-châteaux, bed-and-breakfasts, etc. **Relais et châteaux** provides information on booking in luxury hotels with character: ☎ 0 823 32 32 32; within the UK ☎ 00 800 2000 00 02; within the US ☎ 1-800-735-2478; Internet, www.relaischateaux.com.

ECONOMY CHAIN HOTELS

If you need a place to stop en route, these can be useful, as they are inexpensive (around 42€ on average for a double room) and generally located near the main road. While breakfast is available, there may not be a restaurant; rooms are small, with a television and bathroom. Central reservation numbers:

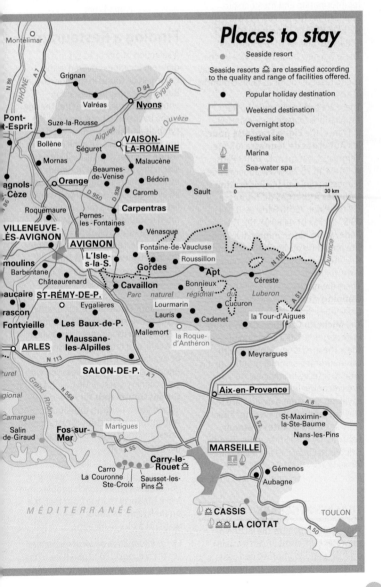📷 **Akena** ☎ 01 69 84 85 17.

📷 **B&B** ☎ 0892 78 29 29.

📷 **Etap Hotel** ☎ 0892 688 900.

📷 **Mister Bed** ☎ 01 46 14 38 00.

📷 **Villages Hôtel** ☎ 03 80 60 92 70.

The hotels listed below are slightly more expensive (from 58€), and offer a few more amenities and services. Central reservation numbers:

📷 **Campanile** ☎ 01 64 62 46 46.

📷 **Kyriad** – ☎ 0 825 003 003.

📷 **Ibis** – ☎ 0 825 88 22 22.

Many chains have on-line reservations:

📷 www.etaphotel.com

📷 www.ibishotel.com.

COTTAGES AND BED & BREAKFASTS

The **Maison des Gîtes de France et du Tourisme vert** is an information service for self-catering accommodation in Provence (and the rest of France). *Gîtes* usually take the form of a cottage or apartment decorated in the local style where visitors can make themselves at home, or bed and breakfast accommodation *(chambres d'hôtes)* that consists of a room and breakfast at a reasonable price. Contact the Gîtes de France office in Paris: 59 rue St-Lazare, 75439 Paris Cedex 09, ☎ 01 49 70 75 75, or contact their representative in the

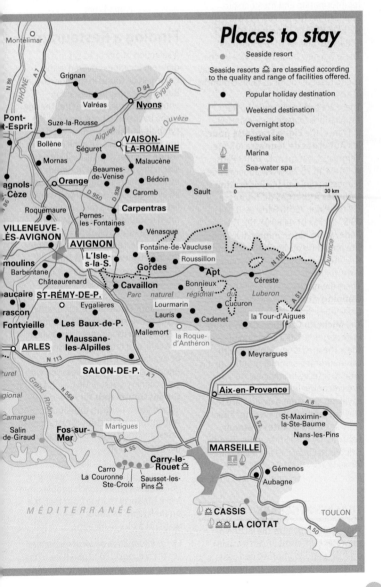

Places to stay

● Seaside resort

Seaside resorts ⚓ are classified according to the quality and range of facilities offered.

● Popular holiday destination

▢ Weekend destination

▭ Overnight stop

Festival site

⚓ Marina

♨ Sea-water spa

0   30 km

UK, **Brittany Ferries** (address above); www.gites-de-france.com (select English by clicking the flag on the home page), You can rder a catalogue on-line. **Fédération des Stations vertes de Vacances et Villages de Neige** (BP 71698 - 21016 Dijon Cedex - ☎ 03 80 54 10 50 - www.stationsvertes.com), offers similar options, in the mountains or the countryside, with access to local life and leisure activities.

HOSTELS, CAMPING

To obtain an International Youth Hostel Federation card (there is no age requirement, and there is a "senior card" available too), you should contact the IYHF in your own country for information and membership applications (US ☎ 202 783 6161; UK ☎ 1727 855215; Canada ☎ 613-273 7884; Australia ☎ 61-2-9565-1669). There is a new booking service on the internet (www.iyhf.org), which you may use to reserve rooms as far as 6 months in advance.

There are two main youth hostel associations (auberges de jeunesse) in France, the **Ligue Française pour les Auberges de Jeunesse** (67, rue Vergniaud, bâtiment K, 75013 Paris, ☎ 01 44 16 78 78, www.auberges-de-jeunesse.com) and the **Fédération Unie des Auberges de Jeunesse** (27 rue Pajol, 75018 Paris, ☎ 01 44 89 87 27, Fax 01 44 89 87 10). The **Féderation** has an informative web site providing on-line booking through the International Booking Network: www.fuaj.org.

There are numerous officially graded **camping sites** with varying standards of facilities throughout Provence. The **Michelin Camping Caravaning France** guide lists a selection of camp sites. The area is very popular with campers in the summer months, so it is wise to reserve in advance.

Are you going hiking, skiing, or kayaking and want a rustic place to stay overnight in the evening? Then consult the guide **Gîtes d'étapes, refuges**, by A. et S. Mouraret (Rando Éditions La Cadole, 74 r. A.-Perdreaux, 78140 Vélizy, ☎ 01 34 65 11 89, in French) and www.gites-refuges.com.

THALASSOTHERAPY

Thalassotherapy uses the virtues of seawater to prevent or cure certain disorders and to improve general fitness and well-being. The healing and relaxing properties of the marine climate (iodine, radiant light, etc), seawater, sea mud, algae and sand have given rise to a variety of therapeutic cures: fitness programmes, beauty treatments, therapy for relief from backache, stress, and addiction to smoking. The mild Mediterranean climate is a good place to rest and restore your energy.

There are various thalassotherapy centres in the region, at **Le Grau-du-Roi**, **Marseille**, and **Les Stes-Maries-de-la-Mer** (ⓒ See Le GRAU-DU-ROI; see MARSEILLE; see Les STES-MARIES-DE-LA-MER). Or, contact the national association for information: **Fédération Mer et Santé**, r. de l'Isly, 75008 Paris, ☎ 01 44 70 07 57, www.thalassofederation.com.

Finding a Restaurant

A selection of places to eat in the different locations covered in this guide can be found in the Address Books appearing in the section entitled Discovering Provence. The key at the back of the book explains the symbols and abbreviations used in the Address Books. Use the **Michelin Guide France**, with its well known star-rating system and hundreds of establishments throughout France, for an even greater choice. If you would like to experience a meal in a highly rated restaurant from The Michelin Guide, be sure to book ahead. In the countryside, restaurants usually serve lunch between noon and 2pm and dinner between 7.30-10pm. It is not always easy to find something in-between those two meal times, as the "non-stop" restaurant is still a rarity in the provinces. However, a hungry traveller can usually get a sandwich in a café, and ordinary hot dishes may be available in a brasserie.

Another guide series to help you with your culinary quest is Michelin's **Les Guides Gourmands** for Provence, Côte-d'Azure, Corse. In those guides you will find a fine selection of restaurants, cafes, and food shops catering to every gastronomic taste.

In French restaurants and cafés, a service charge is included. Tipping is not necessary, but French people often leave the small change from their bill on their table, or about 5% for the waiter in a nice restaurant.

ⓒ For information on local specialities, see the section on Food and Wine in the next chapter, Introduction to Provence.

MENU READER

La Carte...The Menu

ENTRÉES ....**STARTERS**

Crudités ....Raw vegetable salad

Terrine de lapin ....Rabbit terrine (pâté)

Frisée aux lardons ....Curly lettuce with bacon bits

Escargots ....Snails

Cuisses de grenouille .... Frog's legs

Salade au crottin ....Goat cheese on a bed of lettuce

PLATS (VIANDES) ....**MAIN COURSES (MEAT)**

Bavette à l'échalote..................................Sirloin with shallots

Faux filet au poivre ....Sirloin with pepper sauce

Côtes d'agneau...................................Lamb chops

Filet mignon de porc ....Pork filet

Blanquette de veau...................................Veal in cream sauce

Nos viandes sont garnies...... Our meat dishes are served with vegetables

PLATS (POISSONS, VOILAILLE) .... **MAIN COURSES (FISH, FOWL)**

Filets de sole ....Sole fillets

Dorade aux herbes .... Sea bream with herbs

Saumon grillé .... Grilled salmon

Coq au vin .... Chicken in red wine sauce

Poulet de Bresse rôti.............Free-range roast chicken from the Bresse

Omelette aux morilles .... Wild-mushroom omelette

PLATEAU DE FROMAGES.....................**SELECTION OF CHEESES**

DESSERTS ....**DESSERTS**

Tarte aux pommes.. Apple pie

Crème caramel .... Cooled baked custard with caramel sauce

Sorbet: trois parfums ....Sherbet: choose 3 flavours

BOISSONS..**BEVERAGES**

Bière... Beer

Eau minérale (gazeuse) .... (Sparkling) mineral water

Une carafe d'eau ....Tap water (no charge)

Vin rouge, vin blanc, rosé ....Red wine, white wine, rosé

Jus de fruit..Fruit juice

MENU ENFANT...................................**CHILDREN'S MENU**

Jambon..Ham

Steak haché.. Ground beef

Frites ....French fried potatoes

WHAT TO DO AND SEE

Outdoor Fun

MARINAS

Most of the seaside resorts lying between Le Grau-du-Roi and La Ciotat (♿ *see Places to Stay at the beginning of the guide)* have well-equipped marinas. The main ones, running from west to east, are: Aigues-Mortes, Le Grau-du-Roi, Port-Camargue, Les Stes-Maries/Port Gardian, Port-St-Gervais to Fos-sur-Mer, Martigues, Les Heures Claires at Istres, Carro, Sausset-les-Pins, Carry-le-Rouet, L'Estaque, Le Frioul, Marseille Pointe Rouge and Le Vieux Port, Cassis and La Ciotat.

Les Stes-Maries/Port Gardian and Port-Camargue have been awarded the label Pavillon Bleu d'Europe, granted on the basis of the following criteria: clean site and surroundings, special equipment and amenities, reception and information services, educational facilities.

Most seaside resorts have sailing schools where courses are organised. In season, you can hire boats with or without a crew. For further information, contact the local harbour-master's office or the Fédération **Française de Voile**, 55 Avenue Kléber, 75784 Paris Cedex 16 ☎ 01 44 05 81 00.

SCUBA DIVING

Marseille and its surroundings have always been a privileged setting for diving activities. It was here that Jacques-Yves Cousteau and Émile Gagnan achieved their record-breaking performances that paved the way for modern diving with the invention of the Aqualung.

The most popular spot for deep-sea diving are the calanques around Marseille, where the seabed is truly a feast for the eyes. Despite subsequent damage caused by pollutant waste, excessive harpoon fishing and the combing of wrecks for their valuable archaeological significance, the *calanques* still provide exceptional interest for divers with their abundance of multi-coloured fish, gorgonia, sponge, purple sea urchins, crayfish and mother-of-pearl.

Six exceptional sites can be explored: *Le Chauoen*, a Moroccan cargo ship which ran aground on the Île du Planier (off Marseille); *La Drôme*, a shipwreck lying at a depth of 51m/168ft; *Le Liban*, a liner that sunk in front of the Île Maïre in 1903; Les Impériaux, a site renowned for its huge gorgonian fish; La Cassidaigne, a seaway teeming with fish at the foot of the lighthouse (4 nautical miles from Cassis); Île Verte, an islet with luxuriant vegetation peopled with myriads of fish.

This sport requires a lengthy and challenging training which can only be provided by fully-trained instructors holding nationally-recognised diplomas. For a list of clubs offering scuba-diving courses, contact the local branch of the **Fédération Française d'Études et de Sports Sous-Marins**, 24 Quai de Rive-Neuve, 13007 Marseille ☎ 04 91 33 99 31. This federation publishes the magazine Subaqua every two months. There is also a local branch, the Comité regional des sports sous-marins, 46 boulevard Fenouil, 13016 Marseille. b 04 91 09 36 31. The Centre UCPA in Niolon is Europe's biggest training centre for deep-sea diving: Centre UCPA, Niolon, 13740 Le Rove ☎ 04 91 46 90 16. Books about diving can be found at the Librairie Maritime bookshop, 26 Quai de Rive-Neuve, 13007 Marseille ☎ 04 91 54 79 26. In La Ciotat the Atelier Bleu du Cap de

---

Safety Measures for Deep-Sea Divers

The growing popularity of scuba-diving along the Mediterranean coast, where one can admire superb underwater landscapes, must not detract from the potential hazards of this sport. To protect yourself against the risk of an accident, the consequences of which may be serious, you should bear in mind the following instructions. It is highly inadvisable to dive on your own, after a heavy meal, after a meal washed down with alcohol, after drinking fizzy beverages or when you are tired. Also, make sure to avoid the fairways used by boats and the areas frequented by windsurfers. When diving, it is essential that you respect the decompression stops.

In the event of an accident, give precise details of what happened to the emergency team on land so that they can provide appropriate care in a hyperbaric chamber (the only solution to decompression problems, however slight).

l'Aigle (Parc du Mugel – ☎ 04 42 08 07 67. Summer: every afternoon except Sun. 38.11€ - children: 28.97€) has courses for beginners and provides all equipment. At the end of the course, you receive a certificate.

SEA FISHING

Although the Mediterranean is not the busiest fishing spot in France, shoals of rock fish abound: scorpion fish (an essential ingredient in a *bouillabaisse*), red mullet, conger and moray eels as well as numerous octopuses, spider crabs, various squid and even the odd crayfish. In shallow, sandy waters there are skate, sole and dab. Offshore, shoals of sardines, anchovies and tuna fish intermingle with sea bream, bass and grey mullet. No permit is necessary for sea angling, provided that the day's catch is for personal consumption only.

BOAT TRIPS

By sea – Leaving from Marseille, you can visit the Château d'If, the Îles du Frioul and the Calanques; leaving from Cassis, you can visit the calanques at Port-Miou, Port-Pin and En-Vau. See the section on Admission times and charges under the heading Les CALANQUES.
Leaving from La Ciotat, you can visit the Île Verte (👁 *see La CIOTAT*). The excursions leaving from La Ciotat are on board a catamaran-type boat offering views of the sea depths cruising among the calanques of La Ciotat, between Cassis and Marseille. For details apply to Les Amis des Calanques, 6 Place de la Liberté, 13600 La Ciotat ☎ 04 42 83 54 50.
Leaving from the Tour de Constance in Aigues-Mortes, Le Pescalune will take you on a trip along the canals and the Vidourle, a coastal river. For details, apply to M. Griller, B.P. 76, 30220 Aigues-Mortes ☎ 04 66 53 79 47.
Along the River Rhône – Tiki III, 13460 Les Stes-Maries-de-la-Mer, b 04 90 97 81 68. From mid-March to mid-Nov: from 1 to 5 departures a day depending on the season. 9.15€ (children: 4.57€). Trips upstream the Petit Rhône as far as Bac du Sauvage offer insight into the Camargue of the gardian: herds of bulls and horses grazing on the plains and herons on the banks of the river dotted with tamarisk.

Back from fishing

In Le-Grau-du-Roi, you can hire a boat (licence required in some cases) to cruise the canals: Cap 2000 (ZA Port de Pêche, ☎ 04 66 51 41 54) or A2M at Port-Camargue (☎ 04 66 53 35 18). Sea lovers will enjoy the Nautiques de Port-Camargue (beginning of April), a nautical fair devoted to used boats.

WALKING/HIKING

Walking/Hiking

Exploring Provence on foot is an enchanting way of discovering the all-encompassing brightness of Provençal light as it sets off the beauty of the landscape to perfection, both in its natural, unspoiled state, and featuring the evidence of man's passage through village and countryside.
Leave the car behind and experience a different, more relaxed pace of life in a landscape that rings with the echoes of days gone by.
Many long-distance footpaths (*sentiers de Grande Randonnée – GR*) cover the area described in this guide. The GR 4 crosses the lower Vivarais country as far as Mont Ventoux; to climb up the mountain, you can start in the Bédoin Forest and follow GR 91 and 91B (information in the Bédoin Tourist office). GR 42 leads along the valley of

> 😊 A French bylaw rules that access to forests and other wooded massifs is strictly forbidden between 1 July and the second weekend in September, and when winds blow at over 40kph/25mph.

S. Sauvignier/MICHELIN

Stepping Smart

Choosing the right equipment for a hiking expedition is essential: flexible hiking shoes with non-slip soles, a rain jacket or poncho, an extra sweater, sun protection (hat, glasses, lotion), drinking water (1-2l per person), high energy snacks (chocolate, cereal bars, banana), and a first aid kit. Of course, you'll need a good map (and a compass if you plan to leave the main trails). Plan your itinerary well, keeping in mind that while the average walking speed for an adult is 4kph/2.5mph, you will need time to eat and rest, and children will not keep up the same pace. Leave your itinerary with someone before setting out (innkeeper or fellow camper).

Respect for nature is a cardinal rule and includes the following precautions: don't smoke or light fires in the forest, which are particularly susceptible in the dry summer months; always carry your rubbish out; leave wild flowers as they are; walk around, not through, farmers' fields; close gates behind you.

If you are caught in an electrical storm, avoid high ground, and do not move along a ridge top; do not seek shelter under overhanging rocks, isolated trees in otherwise open areas, at the entrance to caves or other openings in the rocks, or in the proximity of metal fences or gates. Do not use a metallic survival blanket. If possible, position yourself at least 15m/15yd from the highest point around you (rock or tree); crouch with your knees up and without touching the rock face or any exposed part of your body. An automobile is a good refuge as its rubber tires ground it and provide protection for those inside.

the Rhône; GR 6 follows the River Gard as far as Beaucaire and then plunges into the Alpilles and Luberon ranges; GR 9 takes the line of the north face of Mont Ventoux, then crosses the Vaucluse plateau, the Luberon range, Montagne Ste-Victoire and the massif of Ste-Baume. Further variations on the above are offered by the GRs 63, 92, 97 and 98. Besides the long-distance footpaths, there are short to medium-distance paths ranging from walks of a few hours to a couple of days.

The **Fédération française de la randonnée pédestre** publishes "topo-guides" available from its information centre, 14, rue Riquet, 75019 Paris. ☎ 01 44 89 93 90; www. ffrp.asso.fr. Some English-language editions are available. The regional guides describe long-distance trails (GR, for *Grande Randonnée* and GRP for *Grande Randonnée de Pays*) and shorter ones (PR – petite randonnée) in detail, distances and approximate times. Another source of maps and guides for excursions on foot is the Institut National Géographique (IGN), which has a boutique in Paris at 107, rue de La Boétie (off the Champs-Elysées), ☎ 01 43 98 85 12. Among their publications, France 903 is a map showing all of the GR and PR in France; the "Série Bleue" and "Top 25" maps, at a scale of 1:25 000 (1cm=250m), show all paths, whether blazed or not, as well as refuges, campsites, beaches, etc for a precise area. In the region, you can find many of the publications cited above in bookstores, at sports centres or equipment shops, and even in local newspaper shops, or from the town hall or a friendly innkeeper.

For information on walking the calanques, contact Les Excursionnistes Marseillais, 16 rue Rotonde, 13001 Marseille 01, ☎ 04 91 84 75 52, www. excurs.com.

HORSEBACK RIDING

The Fédération Française d'Équitation (9 boulevard MacDonald, 75019 Paris, ☎ 01 53 26 15 50; Fax: 01.53.26.15.88; www.ffe.com) and the **Comité National de Toursime Équestre** (59 bvd Mac Donald 75019 Paris ☎ 01 53 26 15 50; Fax 01 53 26 15 51; e-mail cntemagic.fr) are useful sources of information if you would like to plan a riding holiday. The latter publishes "Estafette" (12.20€ for a year – 4 issues + the catalogue), a review of local events and information on maps for riders, children's activities, etc, and the catalogue *"Cheval Nature"*(4.50€ + postage), where you will find further information including the addresses of riding centres (Centres de Tourisme Equestre) region-by-region, and practical tips on holidays for kids, insurance and more. Both can be ordered from the internet site. Riding is a favourite pastime in **Camargue**. Contact Promenades à cheval de la Fadaise, route d'Arles, 13460 Les Stes-Maries-de-la-Mer, ☎ 04 90 97 86 79 if you dream of riding one of the famous white horses of Camargue on the plain, in the marshes or along the beach.

In Le Grau-du- Roi: on the beach and on the dunes of Espiguette: rides of

1 or 2hr or a whole morning (4hr). On the Espiguette road there are several stables: Écurie des Dunes (☎ 04 66 53 09 28), Mas de l'Espiguette (☎ 04 66 51 51 89), Ranch du Phare (☎ 04 66 53 10 87), Lou Seden (☎ 04 66 51 74 75) and Abrivado Ranch (☎ 04 66 53 01 00).

CYCLING

For general information concerning France, write or call the **Fédération Française de Cyclotourisme** (12, rue Louis-Bertrand, 94200 Ivry-sur-Seine, ☎ 01 44 16 88 88, 12, rue Louis Bertrand Fax: 01 56 20 88 99). They have an attractive web site (in French): www.ffct.org. Off-road enthusiasts, contact the Fédération Française de Cyclisme (5 rue de Rome, 93561 Rosny-sous-Bois Cedex, ☎ 01 49 35 69 00; www.ffc.fr) and request the "Guide des centres VTT". The IGN (see address above, under Walking/hiking) offers Map 906, "Mountain Bike and Cycle Touring in France". Both web sites provide addresses of local clubs and a calendar of events. A favourite challenge is to tackle Mont Ventoux by bike. Contact the Tourist office in Bédoin for information on trails. Local tourist offices have a list of cycle hire firms, (including some SNCF train stations).
The firm Europbike offers bike rental facilities seven days a week to discover the Provençal countryside leaving from the city of Avignon: Europbike, Station Shell, Les Remparts, 16 Boulevard St-Michel, 84000 Avignon ☎ 04 90 86 54 47.

SKIING

You can practice both downhill and cross-country skiing at the Mont-Serein resort (the secondary peak of Mont Ventoux, 1 445m/4 741ft high). For details apply to the town hall (Mairie) in Beaumont-du-Ventoux (84340), Tuesdays, Thursdays and Fridays ☎ 04 90 65 21 13 or the Reception Chalet (Chalet d'Accueil) ☎ 04 90 63 42 02.

ROCK-CLIMBING

Rock-climbing is possible all year up the Dentelles de Montmirail or the cliffs in the *calanques* near Marseille. *Access to the calanques is forbidden from 1 July to the second Saturday in September*. The local branch of the **Club Alpin Français de Provence** (12 Rue Fort-Notre-Dame, 13007 Marseille ☎ 04 91 54 36 94, fax 04 91 54 36 94) organises accompanied climbing trips.
General information can be obtained from the **Fédération Française de la Montagne et de l'Escalade**, 10 Quai de la Marne, 75019 Paris ☎ 01 40 18 75 50. For the Dentelles de Montmirail, contact the Tourist Information Centre of Gigondas, ☎ 04 90 65 85 46.

CANOEING

This is a good way of exploring the less accessible stretches of the Ardèche, Cèze, Gardon, Durance and Sorgue rivers. As far as the **Gorges de l'Ardèche** are concerned, conditions for hiring boats are mentioned in the section on Admission times and

Vallon Pont d'Arc

charges under the heading Gorges de l'Ardèche; bear in mind that the stretch between Charmes and Sauze has been designated a natural reserve and special rules are enforced: no windsurfing; no boats with more than three people allowed, compulsory life jackets. Camping is possible only in Gaud and Gournier, for no longer than two nights. For further practical information, contact the **Maison de la Réserve** at Gournier ☎ 04 75 38 63 00. The Association de Protection des Gorges de l'Ardèche publishes a plastic-coated map showing difficult stretches of river and possible refuelling stops along the river. (It can be found at local Tourist Information Centres).

For a trip in the area around Bagnols-sur-Cèze, contact the association CAPCANOE, route de Barjac, 30500 St-Ambroix – www.canoe-France.com - ☎ 04 66 24 25 16. There is a choice of 3 routes along the River Cèze (4, 8 and 30km/2.5, 5 and 18.8mi) and a route of 15km/9.3mi through the Cèze gorges. Upstream from the Pont du Gard, you can safely practise canoeing on the Gardon (4 trips of 6, 11, 22 and 29km/3.5, 7, 14 and 19mi). KAYAK VERT, 30210 Collias ☎ 04 66 22 84 83. Between Fontaine-de-Vaucluse and Isle-sur-la-Sorgue, a 8km/5mi trip on the Sorgue will enable you to discover the beauty of the local landscape. KAYAK VERT, 84800 Fontaine-de-Vaucluse ☎ 04 90 20 35 44.

In conjunction with the **Fédération Française de Canoë-Kayak** (87 Quai de la Marne, 94344 Joinville-le-Pont ☎ 01 45 11 08 50), IGN publishes a map called France, Canoë-Kayak et Sports d'Eau Vive which lists all the different excursions, classifying them in terms of difficulty. Further information can be obtained from the Minitel on 3615 CANOË PLUS.

BULLFIGHTING EVENTS

The Camargue area, and especially the famous Camargue bull, have always been at the heart of French bullfighting tradition. *Cocarde* races (also called *courses camarguaises* or *courses libres*) involve going down into the arena in a bid to remove the ribbon that is pinned between the horns of the animal.

These events take place in Arles (April to early October) - *Cocarde d'Or* on the first Monday in July), Beaucaire (late July), Les Stes-Maries-de-la-Mer (April to August), St-Martin-de-Crau (May and October), Châteaurenard (May to October) and Le-Grau-du-Roi (April to October). Newspapers give the dates for these events, which are widely reported in the local press.

Originally, bullfighting was a Spanish tradition but it gradually spread to Provence. *Corridas* and *novilladas* are usually held during *ferias*, large celebrations that bring huge crowds to the arenas and create a lively atmosphere in the town centre: *abrivados* (bulls are let loose on the streets), *peñas* (brass bands) playing along pavements and in the *bodegas* (bars), dances, etc. The city of Nîmes hosts three *ferias* every year and Arles stages the famous Feria de Pentecôte at Easter. In Les Stes-Maries-de-la-Mer, the *corridas* are performed on horseback (Feria du Cheval). To attend a *corrida* or a *novillada*, it is best to book in advance by calling one of the following offices: Nîmes: Bureau de Location des Arènes, Rue Alexandre-Ducros, 30000 Nîmes ☎ 04 66 67 28 02; Arles: Location Arènes d'Arles, B.P. 216, 13635 Arles Cedex ☎ 04 90 96 03 70.; Les Stes-Maries-de-la-Mer: Arènes des Stes-Maries-de-la-Mer ☎ 04 90 97 85 86; Camargue: Arènes de Méjanes ☎ 04 90 97 10 60. The best seats are in the front row, on the side of the arena.

Small Bullfighting Lexicon

Aficionado: enthusiastic spectator; expert in tauromachy

Bravo: said of an aggressive bull

Chaquetilla: short embroidered jacket; an essential part of the matador's outfit

Coleta: small plait worn by the torero during bullfights

Faena: series of passes that the bullfighter performs with the muleta

Matador de toros: Master of Bulls who confronts the bull during a corrida

Montera: bullfighter's hat

Muleta: square of red material affixed to a wooden mast that the matador brandishes during the faena

Novillada: fight with a young bull under four years of age; the first stage in a bullfighter's career

Rejoneador: bullfighter who performs on horseback

Zapatilla: shoes traditionally worn by the matador

Activities for Children

Here are a few things that children will especially enjoy, and it makes a change from a day at the beach!
OK Corral, between Aubagne and La Ciotat is a theme park with fun rides in a super setting. **Amazonia** (near Roquemaure, Gard ☎ 04 66 82 53 92) is another, with an Aztec-Mayan theme.

The **Bonbon Museum** in Uzès is a treat for children. At Parc du Soleil et du Cosmos (Angles, near Villeneuvetlès-Avignon), the stars and planets are the featured performers.

Little animal lovers can go for a pony and cart ride at the **Monde merveilleux de Daudet** in Beaucaire, watch birds of prey in the flight at the château in the same town, or visit the zoo in the park of **Barben Château**. If you are in the area at the right time (last weekend in June), be sure to see the Fête de la Tarasque in Tarascon, an enchantment for all ages!

Calendar of Events

The list below is a selection of the many events that take place in the region. Contact local tourist offices for fuller details.

TRADITIONAL CELEBRATIONS

FIRST SUNDAY IN FEBRUARY

Nyons - Festival of New Oil.

2 FEBRUARY

Marseille - Candlemas Procession *(Fête de la Chandeleur)* in the Basilique St-Victor.

SUNDAY BEFORE LENT

Graveson - Carnival Procession of Floats *(Corso carnavalesque).*

LAST WEEKEND IN FEBRUARY

Nîmes - Spring Festival *(Feria de Primavera).* ☎ 04 66 67 28 02.

EASTER WEEKEND

Arles - Easter Festival *(Feria Pascale)* Spanish style bull fights.

1 MAY

Arles - Gardians' Festival.
☎ 04 90 18 41 20.

24 AND 25 MAY

Les Stes-Maries-de-la-Mer - Gypsy Pilgrimage on 24 May, procession and blessing of the sea on 25 May. ☎ 04 90 97 82 55.

WHITSUN

Nîmes - Whitsun Festival.
☎ 04 66 67 28 02.

St-Rémy-de-Provence - Festival of Transhumance Festival.

23 JUNE

Valréas - Feast of Little St John.
☎ 04 90 35 04 71.

THIRD WEEK IN JUNE

Martigues - Le Grau-du-Roi - Fishermen's Festival on St Peter's Day. ☎ 04 42 42 31 10.Music Festival

LAST WEEKEND IN JUNE

Tarascon - Tarasque Festival. Folklore procession with Daudet's character Tartarin. Bullfights.
☎ 04 90 91 03 52.

JULY

Marseille - International Folklore Festival at Château-Gombert: ☎ 04 90 94 23 2791 05 15 65.

FRIDAY BEFORE FIRST SUNDAY

Arles - Pegoulado. Night-time procession in traditional costume.
☎ 04 90 96 47 00.

FIRST SATURDAY

Martigues - Venitian Festival. Fireworks display and nocturnal flotilla of decorated boats.
☎ 04 42 42 31 10.

FIRST SUNDAY IN JULY

Châteaurenard - Celebration of Old Trades (Journée des Vieux Métiers). Blacksmith, sheep shearer, washerwoman.St Eligius' cart, decorated and drawn by 40 horses in Saracen harness; bullfights.

WEEKEND BEFORE 14 JULY

Nyon- International Olive Festival.

ABOUT 14 JULY

Les Stes-Maries-de-la-MerSalin-de-Giraud - Feria du Cheval. Competitive events for thoroughbreds, games in the arena.
☎ 04 90 97 82 55.Mediterranean Festival (classical music, jazz).

SECOND HALF OF JULY

Carpentra - Nocturnal procession of floats (Corso de Nuit).Provençal style bullfight (Course de la cocarde d'or).

LAST WEEKEND OF JULY

Graveson - Feast of St Eligius.
☎ 04 90 95 71 05.

JULY TO MID-SEPTEMBER

St-Rémy-de-ProvenceNyons - Feria. Provençal-style bull runs and bull-fightsInternational olive festival.

MID-JULY TO MID-AUGUST

Valréas - Nocturnal procession of floats.Bullfights: Spanish style (to the death) and Provençal style (courses à la cocarde).

TUESDAY AFTER 4TH SUNDAY IN AUGUST

MonteuxCarpentras - St John's Fireworks Display. Monteux is renowned for its fireworks.Nocturnal procession of floats; Festival of Our Lady of Good Health.

END OF AUGUST

Aigues-Mortes - Feast of St Louis.
☎ 04 66 53 73 00.

SEPTEMBER

NîmesValréas - Grape Harvest Festival.Evenings of the Papal Enclave (Nuits de l'Enclave des Papes – theatre): ☎ 04 66 67 28 02 90 35 04 71.

WEEKEND AROUND 22 OCTOBER

Les Stes-Maries-de-la-MerSalon-de-Provence - October Pilgrimage. ☎ 04 90 97 82 55.

EARLY DECEMBER

Istres - Shepherds' Festival. Migrant shepherds march through the streets with their herds.

24 DECEMBER

Allauch - Midnight Mass in Provençal. Shepherds come down from the hill of Notre-Dame du Château. ☎ 04 91 05 31 21.

Les Baux de Provence - Shepherds' Festival. Midnight Mass in Provençal.

Arles - Christmas Eve watch and Midnight Mass in Provençal. ☎ 04 90 18 41 20.

St-Michel-de-Frigolet - Midnight Mass in Provençal. ☎ 04. 90.95 70 07.

St-Rémy-de-Provence - Midnight Mass in Provençal with pastorale.

Les Stes-Maries-de-la-Mer - Midnight Mass with offerings from shepherds, fishermen and rice growers.
☎ 04 90 97 82 55.

Séguret - Enactment of the Li Bergié de Séguret Mystery.
☎ 04 90 46 91 08.

Tarascon - Midnight Mass in Provençal.

FESTIVALS

JUNE TO SEPTEMBER

Nîmes - L'Été de Nîmes. Summer festival of music, theatre, dance, art exhibitions. ☎ 04 66 67 28 02.

EARLY JULY

Îles du Frioul - Atout Frioul. Jazz, variety entertainment, folklore.
☎ 04 91 54 91 11

JULY

Fontaine-de-Vaucluse, L'Isle-sur-la-Sorgue, Lagnes, Le Thor - Festival de la Sorgue. Music, theatre, dance.

Aix-en-Provence - Dance Festival.
☎ 04 42 96 05 01.

Villeneuve-lès-Avignon - International Summer Events at the Charterhouse. Theatre.
☎ 04 90 15 24 24.

JULY-AUGUST

Valréas - Evenings of the Papal Enclave (Nuits de l'Enclave des Papes). Theatre.

EARLY JULY TO EARLY AUGUST

Avignon - Festival of Theatre, Dance and Music.
☎ 04 90 27 66 50.

EARLY JULY TO LATE AUGUST

La Tour-d'Aigues - Festival of South Luberon.

JULY TO SEPTEMBER

Cabrières d'Avignon, Fontaine-de-Vaucluse Goult, Roussillon, Abbaye de Silvacane - International String Quartet Festival in the Luberon. ☎ 04 90 75 89 60.

St-Rémy-de-Provence - Organa Festival. Organ concerts.
☎ 04 90 92 49 67.

FIRST FORTNIGHT IN JULY

Arles - International Photography Show.

Marseille - International Folklore Festival at Château-Gombert.
☎ 04 91 05 15 65.

MID-JULY TO EARLY AUGUST

Orange - Chorégies. Opera, symphonic concerts.
☎ 04 90 51 83 83.

SECOND FORTNIGHT IN JULY

Aix-en-Provence - International Festival of Opera and Music.

Carpentras - Les Estivales. International Festival of Theatre, Opera and Dance. ☎ 04 90 60 46 00.

Marseille - Boules Competition held in the Parc Borély.

Salon-de-Provence - Jazz Festival.
☎ 04 90 56 00 07.

Uzès - Nuits Musicales d'Uzès. Evening music concerts.
☎ 04 66 22 68 88.

MID-JULY TO MID-AUGUST

Vaison-la-Romaine - L'Été de Vaison. Theatre, dance, music concerts.
☎ 04 90 28 84 49.

MID-JULY TO LATE AUGUST

Bollène - Polymusicales de Bollène. Music Festival.
☎ 04 90 40 51 17.

Martigues - International Folk Festival. ☎ 04 42 42 12 01.

FIRST THREE WEEKS IN AUGUST

La Roque-d'Anthéron Abbaye de Silvacane - International Piano Festival. ☎ 04 42 50 51 15.

Orange - Nuits d'Été au Théâtre Antique. Opera, dance, variety entertainment.

SECOND FORTNIGHT IN AUGUST

Pont-St-Esprit - Rencontres Musicales. Classical concerts.
☎ 04 66 39 44 45.

THIRD WEEK IN SEPTEMBER

St-Maximin-la-Ste-Baume - Autumn Festival. Organ concerts.
☎ 04 94 78 00 09.

EARLY NOVEMBER

Vaison-la-Romaine - Gastronomic Festival. ☎ 04 90 36 02 11.

Shopping

Most of the larger shops are open Monday to Saturday from 9am to 6.30 or 7.30pm. Smaller, individual shops may close during the lunch hour. Food shops – grocers, wine merchants and bakeries – are generally open from 7am to 6.30 or 7.30pm; some open on Sunday mornings. Many food shops close between noon and 2pm and on Mondays. Bakery and pastry shops sometimes close on Wednesdays. Hypermarkets usually stay open non-stop until 9pm or later.

VALUE ADDED TAX

There is a **Value Added Tax** (VAT) in France of 19.6% on almost every purchase (books and some foods are subject to a lower rate). However, non-European visitors who spend more than 182.94€ in any one participating store can apply for a refund of the the VAT. Usually, you fill out a form at the store, showing your passport. Upon leaving the country, you submit all forms to customs for approval (they may want to see the goods, so if possible don't pack them in checked luggage). The refund is usually paid directly into your bank or credit card account, or it can be sent by mail. Big department stores that cater to tourists provide special services to help you; be sure to mention that you plan to seek a refund before you pay for goods (no refund is possible for tax on services). If you are visiting two or more countries within the European Union, submit the forms only on departure from the last EU country. The refund is worth while for those visitors who would like to buy fashions, furniture or other fairly expensive items, but remember, the minimum amount must be spent in a single shop (though not necessarily on the same day).

People travelling to the **USA** cannot import plant products or fresh food, including fruit, cheeses and nuts. It is acceptable to carry tinned products or preserves.

Among the souvenirs you might like to bring home are the famous santons, figurines from Aubagne, Arles or Marseille. Tarascon is famous for its Provençal cloth, although this can be bought throughout the entire region. Provence is famous for its candied fruit (Apt) or its olive oil (Alpilles region).

SPECIALITIES FROM PROVENCE

Crafts and Workshops – Numerous craft workshops can be found along the coast and inland, representing a wide variety of cottage industries. Most of them welcome visitors during the summer but it is always advisable to book in advance.

Provençal cloth – Annie Sotinel, Les Pourquiers, Route de Goult, 84220 Gordes ☎ 04 90 72 05 71 (hand weaving).

Shops – Souleiado, 39, Rue Proudhon, 13150 Tarascon ☎ 04 90 91 08 80. Les Olivades, Avenue Barberin, 13103 St-Étienne-du-Grès ☎ 04 90 49 19 19.

Soaps – Savonnerie Rampal-Patou, 71, Rue Félix-Pyat, 13300 Salon-de-Provence ☎ 04 90 56 07 28. Savonnerie Marius Fabre, 148, Avenue Paul-Bourret, 13300 Salon-de-Provence ☎ 04 90 53 24 77.

Santons and faience pottery – Ateliers Marcel Carbonel (santons), 47, Rue Neuve-Sainte-Catherine, 1 3007 Marseille ☎ 04 91 54 26 58. Maison Chave (santons), 37, Rue Frédéric-Mistral, 13400 Aubagne ☎ 04 42 70 12 86 or 14, Rond-Point des Arènes, 13200 Arles ☎ 04 90 96 15 22. Santons Fouque, 65, Cours Gambetta, 13100 Aix-en-Provence ☎ 04 42 26 33 38. Atelier d'Art-Maison Sicard (santons and faience), 2, Boulevard Émile-Combes, 13400 Aubagne ☎ 04 42 70 12 92. Poterie Ravel (faience), Avenue des Goums, 13400 Aubagne ☎ 04 42 03 05 59. Établissement Vernin Carreaux d'Apt (tiles in baked clay), Quartier du Pont St-Julien, RN 100, 84480 Bonnieux ☎ 04 90 04 63 04.

Provençal furniture – Meubles Provençaux Mélani et Fils, Route d'Eyguières, Pont de Crau, 13200 Arles ☎ 04 90 93 61 09 (tour of workshops for small groups by appointment). Meubles Bonjean, Route de l'Isle-sur-la-Sorgue, 84250 Le Thor ☎ 04 90 33 82 94 (tour of workshops during the week).

Antiques – Those with a passion for antique furniture will enjoy browsing at l'Isle-sur-la-Sorgue, where no less than 160 dealers have set up shops in five separate "villages." The largest one is the Village des Antiquaires de la Gare, 2 bis Avenue de l'Égalité, 84800 L'Isle-sur-la-Sorgue ☎ 04 90 38 04 57. Village des Antiquaires du Quartier de Lignane, RN 7, Lignane, 13540 Puyricard ☎ 04 42 92 50 03.

Sweets – Calissons du Roy-René, La Pioline, 13545 Aix-en-Provence ☎ 04 42 39 29 89.

Ciprial-Aptunion: Visit the crystallized fruit factory on the main road (RN 100), just outside the town. By appointment only. No charge. ☎ 04 90 76 31 43.

Miellerie des Butineuses (honey, nougat, gingerbread), 189, Rue de la Source, 84450 St-Saturnin-les-Avignon ☎ 04 90 22 47 52.

Production centre for berlingot sweets: apply to the Tourist Information Centre in Carpentras.

Liquor – Distillerie Liqueur Frigolet (Élixir du Révérend Père Gaucher), 26, Rue Voltaire, 13160 Châteaurenard ☎ 04 90 94 11 08.

PROVENÇAL MARKETS

The picturesque markets of Provence, which liven up both city streets and village squares, are much appreciated by foreign visitors, who are impressed by the variety and quality of the local produce and crafts (fruit and vegetables, flowers, spices, Provençal herbs, olives, honey, cheese, Provençal fabric etc) as well as by the loquacious stallholders and their broad southern accent.

Aigues-Mortes – Traditional market Wednesdays and Sundays.

Aix-en-Provence – Traditional market on Place Richelme every day. Flower market on Place des Prêcheurs Mondays, Wednesdays, Fridays and Sundays. Flea market on Place Verdun Tuesdays, Thursdays and Saturdays. Market offering produce on Place de la Croix-Verte at Jas-de-Bouffan on Thursdays.

Apt – Traditional market Saturdays. Farmers' market Tuesdays May to November.

Arles – Traditional market Wednesdays (Boulevard Émile-Combes) and Saturdays (Boulevard des Lices and Boulevard Clémenceau). Flea market on Boulevard des Lices the first Wednesday of each month.

Aubagne – Traditional market on Cours Voltaire Tuesdays, Thursdays, Saturdays and Sundays.
Flea market at La Tourtelle the last Sunday of each month.

Avignon – Traditional market daily except Mondays at les Halles.
Flower market on Place des Carmes Saturdays.
Flea market on Place Crillon Saturdays.

Beaucaire – Traditional market Thursdays and Sundays.

Bédoin – Provençal market Mondays.

Cadenet – Farmers' market Mondays and Saturdays.

Carpentras – Traditional market around the station every day.
Truffes market Fridays, November to March.

Cavaillon – Traditional market Mondays.

La Ciotat – Handicraft market every evening 8pm to midnight at the Vieux Port in July and August.

Fontvieille – Handicraft market once a week 4pm to 9pm in June, July and August.

Gardanne – Traditional market in the town centre Wednesdays, Fridays and Sundays.

Graveson – Farmers' market on Place du Marché 4pm to 8pm Fridays from 21 May to 31 October.

L'Isle-sur-la-Sorgue – Traditional market Thursdays and Sundays.
Flea market Sundays.

Marseille – ♿ *See MARSEILLE.*

Ménerbes – Truffes market on the last Sunday in December.
Honey market on the third Sunday in July.
Artists and artisans market on the second Sunday in August.

Nîmes – Traditional market Mondays.

Nyons – Traditional market Thursdays.

Orange – Traditional market Thursdays.

Pertuis – Traditional market Fridays.
Farmers' market Wednesdays and Saturdays.

Ruoms – Traditional market Fridays and Saturdays.

St-Rémy-de-Provence – Traditional market Wednesdays on Place de la République and Place Pélissier.

Les Stes-Maries-de-la-Mer – Traditional market on Place des Gitans, Mondays and Fridays.

Salon-de-Provence – Traditional market on Place Morgan and along the Cours, Wednesdays.
Flea market on Place Morgan the first Sunday of each month.

Tarascon – Traditional market in the town centre Tuesdays.

Uzès – Traditional market Saturdays.

Vaison-la-Romaine – Traditional market Tuesdays.
Provençal market in the upper town Sundays, June to September.

Vallon-Pont-d'Arc – Traditional market Thursdays.

Valréas – Traditional market Wednesdays and Saturdays.

Aperitives and liquors from Provence

S. Sauvignier/ MICHELIN

FAIRS AND EXHIBITIONS

Arles – Santonmakers' Fair (Salon International des Santonniers) late November to mid-January ☎ 04 90 18 41 22.

Aubagne – Santon and Ceramics Fair (Foire aux Santons et à la Céramique) July and August and early December to early January ☎ 04 42 03 49 98.

Barjac (Michelin map no 81 fold 12) – Antique Fair (Foire aux Antiquités) on Easter weekend and on 15 August ☎ 04 66 24 50 09.

L'Isle-sur-la-Sorgue – Antiques Fair (Foire aux Antiquités) Easter Sunday and the Sunday around 15 August ☎ 04 90 38 04 78.

Marseille – International Fair early September.

Santon Fair (Foire aux Santons) at La Canebière from the last Sunday in November to 31 December ☎ 04 91 13 89.

St-Quentin-la-Poterie – Biennial Pottery Fair (Terralha) around 14 July (upcoming fairs in 2006,etc).

Sightseeing

FROM ABOVE

One way of discovering the beautiful landscapes of Provence from above is gliding. There are several associations throughout the region that organise air trips:

Association Vélivole de Carpentras, BP 129, 84204 Carpentras Cedex ☎ 04 90 60 08 17.

Association Vélivole du Luberon, 26 Avenue de la Fontaine, 13370 Mallemort ☎ 04 90 57 43 86. Aerodrome.

Aéro-Club St-Rémy-les-Alpilles, Aérodrome du Romarin, 13210 St-Rémy-de-Provence ☎ 04 90 92 08 43; Fax 04 90 92 20 89. Gliding school, courses and flights for beginners.

Aéroclub de Romanin, on the former voie Aurélia, 13210 St-Rémy-de-Provence, ☎ 04 90 92 08 43 or ☎ 06 03 47 02 98, fax 04 90 92 46 35, offers beginners' lessons and gliding courses.

Centre de Vol à Voile de la Crau, Aérodrome Salon-Eyguières, BP 81, 13651 Salon Cedex ☎ 04 90 42 00 91.

Soleiado – Outside Tarascon on the route d'Arles – ☎ 04 90 43 51 67. Christine Garcia offers a choice of five circuits: Tartarin (around the Montagnette hills), Daudet (around the windmill), Van Gogh (St-Rémy, Glanum), Mireille (Camargue) or Altera Roma (Pont du Gard, Avignon).

General information can be obtained from the Fédération Française de Planeur Ultra-Léger Motorisé, 96 bis Rue Marc-Sangnier, B.P. 341, 94709 Maisons-Alfort Cedex ☎ 01 49 81 74 43.

FROM THE WATER

Along the River Rhône – Tiki III, 13460 Les Stes-Maries-de-la-Mer, ☎ 04 90 97 81 68. From mid-March to mid-Nov: from 1 to 5 departures a day depending on the season. 9.15€ (children:4.57€). Trips upstream the Petit Rhône as far as Bac du Sauvage offer insight into the Camargue: herds of bulls and horses grazing on the plains and herons on the banks of the river dotted with tamarisk. In Le-Grau-du-Roi, you can hire a boat (licence required in some cases) to cruise the canals: Cap 2000 (ZA Port de Pêche, ☎ 04 66 51 41 54) or A2M at Port-Camargue (☎ 04 66 53 35 18). Sea lovers will enjoy the Nautiques de Port-Camargue (beginning of April), a nautical fair devoted to used boats.

By Sea – Leaving from Marseille, you can visit the Château d'If, the Îles du Frioul and the calanques; leaving from Cassis, you can visit the calanques at Port-Miou, Port-Pin and En-Vau.
Leaving from La Ciotat, you can visit the Île Verte. The excursions leaving from La Ciotat are on board a catamaran-type boat with views of the sea depths cruising among the calanques of La Ciotat, between Cassis and Marseille. For details apply to Les Amis des Calanques, 6 Place de la Liberté, 13600 La Ciotat ☎ 04 42 83 54 50.

ARCHEOLOGICAL EXCAVATIONS

Provence is packed with archeological sites which welcome voluntary diggers during the summer. Every spring the journals Archeologia, L'Archéologue and Archéologie list sites which are looking for new recruits. Contact regional archeology departments (Services Régionaux de l'Archéologie) for details.

Ardèche and Drôme: DRAC Rhône-Alpes, 6 Quai St-Vincent, 69283 Lyon Cedex 01 ☎ 04 72 00 44 50. **Bouches-du-Rhône, Var and Vaucluse**: DRAC Provence-Alpes-Côte d'Azur, 21-23, Boulevard du Quai-Roy-René, 13167 Aix-en-Provence ☎ 04 42 16 19 40. **Gard**: 5, Rue de la Salle-l'Évêque, BP 2051, 34026 Montpellier Cedex ☎ 04 67 02 32 71.

Books and Films

Copies of titles mentioned below may be obtained through public libraries.

PERSONAL EXPERIENCE

Village in the Vaucluse by Laurence Wylie *(3rd edition Harvard University Press, 1976)*. This thoughtful book was written by Wylie, a sociologist, in the years following the Second World War. There is nothing glib about this sincere and in-depth look at rural France in the years of post-war recovery. The local inhabitants had to adjust their world view as the modern era encroached upon this once-isolated village. Never condescending, keenly observant, Wylie reveals much about how the villagers get along with each other and how the younger generation faces the challenges of the future.

Two Towns in Provence by M.F.K. Fisher *(Peter Smith, reprinted 1994)*. This is a reissue under one cover of *A Considerable Town* (Marseilles) and *Map of Another Town* (Aix-en-Provence). If you don't know Fisher's writing, you are in for a treat. Well-known for her cookbooks and treatises on culinary arts, she has here set down parts of her life story when she was living in southern France in the 1950s. Rich in detail and evocative of the beautiful places and eccentric people she met, this book will send you looking for Fisher's work on food and travel, or perhaps her excellent translation of Brillat-Savarin's masterful *Physiology of Taste*.

A Year in Provence, Toujours Provence, Provence Encore by Peter Mayle *(Vintage Paperbacks, all published or reprinted between 1990-2000; UK publisher Hamish Hamilton)*. Unless you've been living in a cave in recent years, you have certainly heard of these best-selling books, also available in video and audio formats. You either love them or you leave them, but in any event they have been credited for stirring up interest (and prices?) in Provence and things Provençal, including fixer-up houses and the game of *boules*.

The Magic of Provence: Pleasures of Southern France by Yvonne Lenard *(Broadway Books, 2001)*. Lenard is an American with French origins who, after a teaching stint in Aix, decided to stay on in the Luberon. She tells some entertaining stories about local characters and events, and closes most chapters with a recipe, thoughtfully suggesting substitute ingredients for those who are not living in southern France, but would like to eat as though they were.

FOOD AND WINE

The Provence of Alain Ducasse by Alain Ducasse *(Assouline, 2001)*. This book is by a Michelin-starred chef whose love for the region of Provence is apparent in every page. In addition to recipes, luscious photographs, information about regional products (flowers, olive oils, herbs, etc), there are tips on the finding the best markets, café terraces, wineries and gardens. The only drawback is that the hardcover format makes it a bit unwieldy to carry when travelling.

Patricia Wells at Home in Provence: Recipes Inspired by her Farmhouse in France, by Patricia Wells, photographs by Robert Freson *(Fireside paperback, 1999)*. Lovers of French fare, whether prepared at home in the kitchen or savoured in restaurants both grand and humble, are well acquainted with Wells' reviews and recipes. Not only is the style friendly and informative, the instructions are clear and the results are good!

Markets of Provence: A Culinary Tour of Southern France by Dixon Long, Ruthanne Long, Patricia Wells, photographs by David Wakely *(Collins 1996)*. This book offers those who use it the rare advantage of suggesting ways to really blend in to the local life, by discovering the daily markets (and asking vendors about their specialities), visiting vintners, finding the freshest goat cheese and bread. it even includes directions to the best picnic spots!

FICTION

Hotel Pastis: A Novel of Provence by Peter Mayle (*Vintage Books reprint 1994 – also available on tape from AudioFile*). More Mayle anyone? This one is a tale of fun, love and outlandish schemes in the sunny south.

The Sacred Pool by L. Warren Douglas (*Baen Books 2001*). Here is a book to offer to any fantasy and science fiction fans that you would like to convince to visit Provence. Set in the early Middle Ages, it is full of magic and mysticism but also offers an interesting perspective on history and is greatly inspired by folklore. If you like it, you're in luck, because it's the first of a trilogy.

Toujours Dead by Susan Kiernan-Lewis (*Abdale Books paperback 2001*). A whodunit that does it in the setting of a quaint village in Provence, and involves the handsome heir to an ancient vineyard, who also happens to be a great cook. Your adventures in Provence may be a bit tamer than the heroine's, but the characters she meets and the places she goes will certainly seem familiar – whether you bring this book along on vacation or save it for a rainy night after your return home.

Jean De Florette and **Manon of the Springs** by Marcel Pagnol, translated by W.E. van Hayningen (*North Point Press paperback reissue 1988*). These two books, which follow one another in sequence, are acclaimed works of French literature, and admirable in their faithfulness to the region's character. The story of the vengeful shepherdess is one that haunted the author for years before he committed it to paper. These books have everything a great novel needs, including strong characters, life struggles, crime, betrayal, judgement and forgiveness. Other works by Pagnol available in translation (*Picador*) include *My Father's Glory* and *My Mother's Castle*. In French, you can enjoy, among other works, the masterful trilogy *Marius, Fanny* and *César*.

REGIONAL INTEREST AND ART

The Most Beautiful Villages of Provence by Michael Jacobs, photographs by Hugh Palmer (*Thames and Hudson 1994*). If you love France, you have probably had a look at the books in this series, each one a gem. The villages of Provence are especially photogenic, drenched in colour, bright with flowers, fountains sparkling in the squares.

Colours of Provence by Michel Biehn, Rosanna M. Giammanco Frongua, photographs by Heinz Angermayr (*Stewart Tabori & Chang 1997*). This intriguing book is divided into chapters entitled "Red," "Orange," "Yellow," "Green," "Blue" and "White, Black & Gray". The text ventures from Van Gogh and Picasso to local fabric designs and other crafts, and delves into the realm of flower and herb gardens. The photographs of landscapes, villages, interiors and objects also illustrate personal reminiscences, historical anecdotes, and descriptions of local culture, poetry, folklore and cuisine.

Crafts of Provence: Projects and Inspiration from the South of France by Amelia Saint George (*Trafalgar Square 2000*). If you are not quite ready to realise your dream of retiring to southern France, here is a book that will advise you on transforming your home into a bright and sunny place that will make you feel like you're on holiday. Fabrics, ceramics, tiles and gardens are discussed at length and some DIY projects are outlined (but these will require skill and the right materials). Read it before you go to Provence, and look for the finished crafts or materials while you're there.

The Women Troubadours by Magda Bogin and Meg Bogin (*W.W.Norton paperback 1980*). This book casts a new light on the famous 12C poetry of Provence: finally we get a peek at courtly love from the feminine perspective. The translations are rather literal, and thus something is lost, but the story of the *trobaritz*, women troubadours, deserves telling and this book is well worth reading if you are interested in this literary tradition.

The Memoirs of Frédéric Mistral by Frédéric Mistral, translated by George Wickes (*New Directions 1986*). This book was first published in Provençal in 1906 under the title *Moun espelido: memori e raconte*. The region's best-loved bard, Mistral was awarded the Nobel Prize in literature in 1904 and founded the Félibrege association of poets to protect and revitalise the Provençal language. His memoirs are a charming collection of proverbs and stories, hyperbole and myth; the seasons change and with them the farm work and the festivities. Mistral gives us a look at the ordinary people of his time, singing and telling tales, and delights the reader with examples of medieval and modern Provençal poetry. The culture of the author's youth was a rich blend of Italian, Spanish and French influences, and his work stands as a testimony to the beauty, grace and vitality of this vanished time.

The Letters of Vincent Van Gogh edited by Ronald De Leeuw, translated by Arnold Pomerans *(Penguin Classics 1998).* These letters are a precious companion work to art book reproductions *(see below)* and will certainly move any reader who is interested in Van Gogh's paintings. In his letters, the artist reveals an unsuspected strength of character along side his famous instability, and he expresses himself quite clearly on matters pertaining to friendship and love, family, society, religion and, of course, art.

Van Gogh in Provence and Auvers by Bogmila Welsh-Ovcharov *(Hugh Lauter Levin Associates 1999).* This oversize book has 270 excellent reproduction of the artist's paintings, focused on his 15 months in Arles and the last feverish days of his life in Auvers, where he painted 70 pictures in as many days. The text provides insight and analysis of Van Gogh's achievements.

Cézanne in Provence by Evmarie Schmitt (Pegasgus Library Paperback; US publisher Prestel 2000). This series has become popular for the quality of the text and the reproductions as well as the price range. The artist's work was deeply rooted in his native region, and the 50 paintings reproduced

here emphasise the landscapes in particular, but his Bathers and still lifes are also included.

LITERATURE IN FRENCH

Jean de Florette, Manon des Sources, Marius, Fanny, Céésar, Topaze, La Gloire de mon Père, Le Château de ma Mère, Le Temps des Secrets, Le Temps de l'a'Aamour by M. Pagnol (Éditions de Fallois, collection *Fortunio*)

Lettres de mon Moulin, Tartarin de Tarascon by A. Daudet (Paris, Presses Pocket)

Regain, Le Grand Troupeau, Le Chant du Monde by J. Giono (Paris, Gallimard, collection *Folio* or *la Pléiade*)

GENERAL INTEREST

A Guide to Provence by M. Jacobs *(Viking Penguin)*

A Little Tour in France by H. James *(Sidgwick & Jackson)*

Aspects of Provence by J. Pope-Hennessy *(Penguin)*

A Spell in Wild France by B. and L. Cooper *(Methuen)*

A Year in Provence and Toujours Provence by P. Mayle *(Hamish Hamilton)*

Caesar's Vast Ghost (Aspects of Provence) by L. Durrell *(Faber & Faber)*

Food Lover's Guide to France by P. Wells *(Eyre and Spottiswoode)*

French Dirt by R. Goodman *(Pavilion)*

Gardens in Provence by L. Jones *(Flammarion)*

My Father's Glory and My Mother's Castle by M. Pagnol *(English-language edition from Picador)*

Next Time Round in Provence: The Vaucluse and the Bouches-du-Rhône by I. Norrie *(Aurum Press)*

Provence by F.M. Ford *(Ecco)*

Provence and the Côte-d'Azur by J. Bentley *(Aurum Press)*

O, for a draught of vintage! That hath been
Cooled a long age in the deep-delved earth,
Tasting of Flora and the country green,
Dance, and Provençal song, and sunburnt mirth!
O, for a beaker full of the warm South,
Full of the true, the blushful Hippocrene,
With beaded bubbles winking at the brim,
And purple-stained mouth.

John Keats
Ode to a Nightingale

When the Riviera was Ours by P. Howarth *(Century)*

South of France by A. Lyall *(Collins)*

The Camargue by C. Dix *(Victor Gollancz)*

The Roman Remains of Southern France by J. Bromwich *(Routledge)*

The Time of Secrets and The Time of Love by M. Pagnol *(English-language edition from Deutsch)*

The Water of the Hills by M. Pagnol *(English-language edition from Picador)*

Two Towns in Provence by M.F.K. Fisher *(Chatto and Windus)*

Van Gogh: Letters from Provence edited by M. Bailey *(Clarkson N Potter)*

Wild France: A Traveller's Guide edited by D. Botting *(Aurum Press)*

FILMS

Manon des Sources *(1952) by Marcel Pagnol*

Jean de Florette *(1985) by Claude Berri*

Manon des Sources *(1986) by Claude Berr*

La Gloire de mon père *(1990) by Yves Robert*

Le Château de ma mère *(1990) by Yves Robert*

Les Âmes Fortes (Savage Souls) *(2001) by Raoul Ruiz*

Borsalino *(1970) by Jacques Deray*

Jean de Florettee, Manon des Sources *(1985-1986) by Claude Berri*

Manon des Sources *(1986) by Claude Berri*

La Gloire de mon Père , Le Château de ma mère *(1990) by Yves Robert*

Le Château de ma Mère *(1990) by Yves Robert*

Marius et Jeannette *(1996) by Robert Guédiguian*

À l'Attaque! *(2000) by Robert Guédiguian*

La Ville est Tranquille *(2001) by Robert Guédiguian*

USEFUL WORDS & PHRASES

SIGHTS

abbaye	abbey
beffroi	belfry
chapelle	chapel
château	castle
cimetière	cemetery
cloître	cloisters
cour	courtyard
couvent	convent
écluse	lock (canal)
église	church
fontaine	fountain
halle	covered market
jardin	garden
mairie	town hall
maison	house
marché	market
monastère	monastery
moulin	windmill
musée	museum
parc	park
place	square
pont	bridge
port	port/harbour
porte	gateway
quai	quay
remparts	ramparts
rue	street
statue	statue
tour	tower

NATURAL SITES

abîme	chasm
aven	swallow-hole
barrage	dam
belvédère	viewpoint
cascade	waterfall
col	pass
corniche	ledge
côte	coast, hillside
forêt	forest
grotte	cave
lac	lake
plage	beach
rivière	river
ruisseau	stream
signal	beacon

source . . . . spring
vallée . . . . valley

ON THE ROAD

car park . . . . parking
driving licence . . permis de conduire
east . . . . Est
garage (for repairs) . . . . garage
left . . . . gauche
motorway/highway . . . . . . autoroute
north . . . . Nord
parking meter . . . . horodateur
petrol/gas . . . . essence
petrol/gas station . . . station essence
right . . . . droite
south . . . . Sud
toll . . . . péage
traffic lights . . . . feu tricolore
tyre . . . . pneu
west . . . . Ouest
wheel clamp . . . . sabot
zebra crossing . . . . . . passage clouté

TIME

today . . . . aujourd'hui
tomorrow . . . . demain
yesterday . . . . hier
winter . . . . hiver
spring . . . . printemps
summer . . . . été
autumn/fall . . . . automne
week . . . . semaine
Monday . . . . lundi
Tuesday . . . . mardi
Wednesday . . . . mercredi
Thursday . . . . jeudi
Friday . . . . vendredi
Saturday . . . . samedi
Sunday . . . . dimanche

NUMBERS

0 . . . . zéro
1 . . . . un
2 . . . . deux
3 . . . . trois
4 . . . . quatre
5 . . . . cinq
6 . . . . six
7 . . . . sept
8 . . . . huit
9 . . . . neuf
10 . . . . dix
11 . . . . onze
12 . . . . douze

13 . . . . treize
14 . . . . quatorze
15 . . . . quinze
16 . . . . seize
17 . . . . dix-sept
18 . . . . dix-huit
19 . . . . dix-neuf
20 . . . . vingt
30 . . . . trente
40 . . . . quarante
50 . . . . cinquante
60 . . . . soixante
70 . . . . soixante-dix
80 . . . . quatre-vingt
90 . . . . quatre-vingt-dix
100 . . . . cent
1000 . . . . mille

SHOPPING

bank . . . . banque
baker's . . . . boulangerie
big . . . . grand
butcher . . . . boucherie
chemist . . . . pharmacie
closed . . . . fermé
cough mixture . . . . sirop pour la toux
cough sweets . cachets pour la gorge
entrance . . . . entrée
exit . . . . sortie
fishmonger's . . . . poissonnerie
grocer's . . . . épicerie
newsagent, bookshop . . . . . . librairie
open . . . . ouvert
post office . . . . poste
push . . . . pousser
pull . . . . tirer
shop . . . . magasin
small . . . . petit
stamps . . . . timbres

FOOD AND DRINK

beef . . . . bœuf
beer . . . . bière
butter . . . . beurre
bread . . . . pain
breakfast . . . . petit-déjeuner
cheese . . . . fromage
chicken . . . . poulet
dessert . . . . dessert
dinner . . . . dîner
fish . . . . poisson
fork . . . . fourchette
fruit . . . . fruits
glass . . . . verre

ice cream	glace
ice cubes	glaçons
ham	jambon
knife	couteau
lamb	agneau
lunch	déjeuner
lettuce salad	salade
meat	viande
mineral water	eau minérale
mixed salad	salade composée
orange juice	jus d'orange
plate	assiette
pork	porc
restaurant	restaurant
red wine	vin rouge
salt	sel
spoon	cuillère
sugar	sucre
vegetables	légumes
water	de l'eau
white wine	vin blanc
yoghurt	yaourt

PERSONAL DOCUMENTS AND TRAVEL

airport	aéroport
credit card	carte de crédit
customs	douane
passport	passeport
platform	voie
railway station	gare
shuttle	navette
suitcase	valise
train/plane ticket	billet de train/d'avion
wallet	portefeuille

CLOTHING

coat	manteau
jumper	pull
raincoat	imperméable
shirt	chemise
shoes	chaussures
socks	chaussettes
stockings	bas
suit	costume
tights	collants
trousers	pantalon

COMMONLY USED WORDS

goodbye	au revoir
hello/good morning	bonjour
how	comment
excuse me	excusez-moi
thank you	merci
yes/no	oui/non
I am sorry	pardon
why	pourquoi
when	quand
please	s'il vous plaît

USEFUL PHRASES

Do you speak English?
Parlez-vous anglais?

I don't understand
Je ne comprends pas

Talk slowly
Parlez lentement

Where's...?
Où est...?

When does the ... leave?
À quelle heure part...?

When does the ... arrive?
À quelle heure arrive...?

When does the museum open?
À quelle heure ouvre le musée?

When is the show?
À quelle heure est la représentation?

When is breakfast served?
À quelle heure sert-on le petit-déjeuner?

What does it cost?
Combien cela coûte?

Where can I buy a newspaper in English?
Où puis-je acheter un journal en anglais?

Where is the nearest petrol/gas station?
Où se trouve la station essence la plus proche?

Where can I change traveller's cheques?
Où puis-je échanger des traveller's cheques?

Where are the toilets?
Où sont les toilettes?

Do you accept credit cards?
Acceptez-vous les cartes de crédit?

BASIC INFORMATION

Electricity

The electric current is 220 volts. Circular two-pin plugs are the rule. Adapters and converters (for hairdryers, for example) should be bought before you leave home; they are on sale in most airports. If you have a rechargable device (video camera, portable computer, battery recharger), read the instructions carefully or contact the manufacturer or shop. Sometimes these items only require a plug adapter, in other cases you must use a voltage converter as well or risk ruining your device.

Public Holidays

Museums and other monuments may be closed or may vary their hours of admission on the following public holidays:

Holidays	
1 January	New Year's Day (Jour de l'An)
(late March/late April)	Easter Day and Easter Monday (Pâques)
1 May	May Day
8 May	VE Day
Thurs 40 days after Easter	Ascension Day (Ascension)
7th Sun-Mon after Easter	Whit Sunday and Monday (Pentecôte)
14 July	France's National Day (Bastille Day)
15 August	Assumption (Assomption)
1 November	All Saint's Day (Toussaint)
11 November	Armistice Day
25 December	Christmas Day (Noël)

National museums and art galleries are closed on Tuesdays; municipal museums are generally closed on Mondays. In addition to the usual school holidays at Christmas and in the spring and summer, there are long mid-term breaks (10 days to a fortnight) in February and early November.

Post

Main post offices open Monday to Friday 8am to 7pm, Saturday 8am to noon. Smaller branch post offices generally close at lunchtime between noon and 2pm and at 4pm.

Postage via air mail:

- ✉ UK: letter (20g) 0.46€
- ✉ North America: letter (20g) 0.67€
- ✉ Australia and NZ: letter (20g) 0.79€

At press time, postage stamps in euros were not available.

Stamps are also available from newsagents and *bureaux de tabac*.

Stamp collectors should ask for *timbres de collection* in any post office.

Metric System

France operates on the metric system. Some equivalents *(see Conversion Tables at the the end of this section)*:

1 gram = 0.04 ounces
1 metre = 1.09 yards
1 kilogram = 2.20 pounds
1 kilometre = 0.62 miles
1 litre = 1.06 quarts

Money

CURRENCY

There are no restrictions on the amount of currency visitors can take into France. Visitors carrying a lot of cash are advised to complete a currency declaration form on arrival, because there are restrictions on currency export.

Notes and Coins

The European currency unit, the **euro**, went into circulation as of 1 January 2002 and, since **17 February 2002**, euros are the only currency accepted as a means of payment. Coins in francs will be accepted only by the Banque de France until 2005 and notes until 2012).

BANKS

Banks are open from 9am to noon and 2pm to 4pm and branches are closed either on Monday or Saturday. Banks close early on the day before a bank holiday. A passport is necessary as identification when cashing travellers cheques in banks. Commission charges

Notes and Coins

The euro banknotes were designed by Robert Kalinan, an Austrian artist. His designs were inspired by the theme "Ages and styles of European Architecture." Windows and gateways feature on the front of the banknotes, bridges feature on the reverse, symbolising the European spirit of openness and co-operation. The images are stylised representations of architecture typical of each period, rather than specific structures.

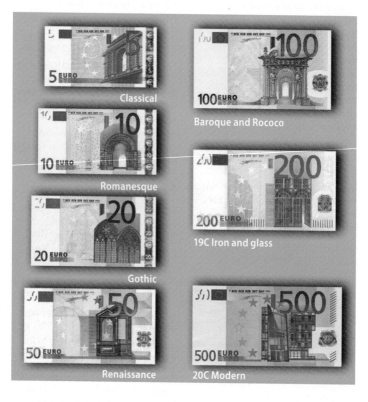

Euro coins have one face common to all 12 countries in the European single currency area or "Eurozone" (currently Austria, Belgium, Finland, France, Germany, Greece, Ireland, Italy, Luxembourg, The Netherlands, Portugal and Spain) and a reverse side specific to each country, created by their own national artists.

Euro banknotes look the same throughout the Eurozone. All Euro banknotes and coins can be used anywhere in this area.

vary and hotels usually charge more than banks for cashing cheques. One of the most economical ways to use your money in France is by using **ATM machines** to get cash directly from your bank account or to use your credit cards to get cash advances. Be sure to remember your PIN number, you will need it to use cash dispensers and to pay with your card in most shops, restaurants, etc. Code pads are numeric; use a telephone pad to translate a letter code into numbers. PIN numbers have 4 digits in France; inquire with the issuing company or bank if the code you usually use is longer. Visa is the most widely accepted credit card, followed by MasterCard; other cards, credit and debit (Diners Club, Plus, Cirrus, etc) are also accepted in some cash machines. American Express is more often accepted in premium establishments. Most places post signs indicating the cards they accept; if you don't see such a sign, and want to pay with a card, ask before ordering or making a selection. Cards are widely accepted in shops, hypermarkets, hotels and restaurants, at tollbooths and in petrol stations. If your card is lost or stolen, call one of the following 24-hour hotlines:

CC **American Express**
☎ 01 47 77 72 00

CC **Visa**
☎ 08 36 69 08 80

CC **Mastercard/ Eurocard**
☎ 01 45 67 84 84

CC **Diners Club**
☎ 01 49 06 17 50

You must report any loss or theft of credit cards or travellers' cheques to the local police who will issue you with a certificate (useful proof to show the issuing company).

TIPPING

Since a service charge is automatically included in the price of meals and accommodation in France, any additional tipping is up to the visitor, generally small change, and generally not more than 5%. Taxi drivers and hairdressers are usually tipped 10-15%. As a rule, prices for hotels and restaurants as well as for other goods and services are significantly less expensive in the French regions than in Paris.

Restaurants usually charge for meals in two ways: a *menu*, that is a fixed price menu with 2 or 3 courses, sometimes a small pitcher of wine, all for a stated price, or à la carte, the more expensive way, with each course ordered separately.

Cafés have very different prices, depending on where they are located. The price of a drink or a coffee is cheaper if you stand at the counter *(comptoir)* than if you sit down *(salle)* and sometimes it is even more expensive if you sit outdoors *(terrace)*.

DISCOUNTS

Tourist Pass: 100 sights for 42€. This pass gives unrestricted access to more than 100 historic buildings managed by the Centre des Monuments Nationaux. It is valid for one year throughout France as of the date of purchase and is for sale at the entrance to major historic buildings, monuments and museums. With the pass, you can save time by skipping the wait at the ticket window. For a list of all the monuments, plus details on their history, information on travel, and other entertaining features to help you plan your trip, visit the lively web site: www.monuments-france.fr. Significant discounts are available for senior citizens, students, youth under age 25, teachers, and groups for public transportation, museums and monuments and for some leisure activities such as movies (at certain times of day). Bring student or senior cards with you, and bring along some extra passport-size photos for discount travel cards.

The **International Student Travel Conference** (www.istc.org), global administrator of the International Student and Teacher Identity Cards, is an association of student travel organizations around the world. ISTC members collectively negotiate benefits with airlines, governments, and providers of other goods and services for the student and teacher community, both in their own country and around the world. The non-profit association sells international ID cards for students, youth under age 25 and teachers (who may get discounts on museum entrances, for example). The ISTC is also active in a network of international education and work exchange programmes. The headquarters address is Herengracht 479, 1017 BS Amsterdam, The Netherlands ☎ 31 20 421 28 00; Fax 31 20 421 28 10.

Telephones

Public Telephones

Most public phones in France use pre-paid phone cards (*télécartes*), rather than coins. Some telephone booths accept credit cards (Visa, Mastercard/Eurocard). *Télécartes* (50 or 120 units) can be bought in post offices, branches of France Télécom, *bureaux de tabac* (cafés that sell cigarettes) and newsagents and can be used to make calls in France and abroad. Calls can be received at phone boxes where the blue bell sign is shown; the phone will not ring, so keep your eye on the little message screen.

National calls

French telephone numbers have 10 digits. Paris and Paris region numbers begin with 01; 02 in northwest France; 03 in northeast France; 04 in southeast France and Corsica; 05 in southwest France.

International calls

To call France from abroad, dial the country code (33) + 9-digit number (omit the initial 0). When calling abroad from France dial 00, then dial the country code followed by the area code and number of your correspondent.

International dialling codes

(*00 + code*):

☎ Australia	☎ 61
☎ New Zealand	☎ 64
☎ Canada	☎ 1
☎ United Kingdom	☎ 44
☎ Eire	☎ 353
☎ United States	☎ 1

To use your **personal calling card** dial:

AT&T	☎ 0-800 99 00 11
Sprint	☎ 0-800 99 00 87
MCI	☎ 0-800 99 00 19
Canada Direct	☎ 0-800 99 00 16

International Information, US/Canada: 00 33 12 11

International operator: 00 33 12 + country code

Local directory assistance: 12

☺ **Emergency numbers** ☺

Police:	17
SAMU (Paramedics):	15
Fire (Pompiers):	18

Minitel

France Télécom operates a system offering directory enquiries (free of charge up to 3min), travel and entertainment reservations, and other services (cost per minute varies). These small computer-like terminals can be found in some post offices, hotels and France Télécom agencies and in many French homes. 3614 PAGES E is the code for **directory assistance in English** (turn on the unit, dial 3614, hit the *connexion* button when you get the tone, type in "PAGES E", and follow the instructions on the screen).

Cell Phones

Cellular phones in France have numbers which begin with 06. Two-watt (lighter, shorter reach) and eight-watt models are on the market, using the Itinéris (France Télécom) or SFR network. *Mobicartes* are pre-paid phone cards that fit into mobile units.

Cell phone rentals

(delivery or airport pick-up provided):

Rent a Cell Express
☎ 01 53 93 78 00
Fax 01 53 93 78 09

A.L.T. Rent A Phone
☎ 01 48 00 06 60
E-mail altlocjve.fr

Time Difference

France is 1hr ahead of Greenwich Mean Time (GMT).

When it is noon in France, it is. . .

⊘	3am	in Los Angeles
⊘	6am	in New York
⊘	11am	in Dublin
⊘	11am	in London
⊘	7pm	in Perth
⊘	9pm	in Sydney
⊘	11pm	in Auckland

In France "am" and "pm" are not used but the 24-hour clock is widely applied.

Conversion Tables

Weights and measures

| 1 kilogram (kg) | 2.2 pounds (lb) | 2.2 pounds |
| 1 metric ton (tn) | 1.1 tons | 1.1 tons |

to convert kilograms to pounds, multiply by 2.2

| 1 litre (l) | 2.1 pints (pt) | 1.8 pints |
| 1 litre | 0.3 gallon (gal) | 0.2 gallon |

to convert litres to gallons, multiply by 0.26 (US) or 0.22 (UK)

| 1 hectare (ha) | 2.5 acres | 2.5 acres |
| 1 square kilometre (km²) | 0.4 square miles (sq mi) | 0.4 square miles |

to convert hectares to acres, multiply by 2.4

1 centimetre (cm)	0.4 inches (in)	0.4 inches
1 metre (m)	3.3 feet (ft) - 39.4 inches - 1.1 yards (yd)	
1 kilometre (km)	0.6 miles (mi)	0.6 miles

to convert metres to feet, multiply by 3.28, kilometres to miles, multiply by 0.6

Clothing

Women							Men
	35	4	2½	40	7½	7	
	36	5	3½	41	8½	8	
	37	6	4½	42	9½	9	
Shoes	38	7	5½	43	10½	10	Shoes
	39	8	6½	44	11½	11	
	40	9	7½	45	12½	12	
	41	10	8½	46	13½	13	
	36	6	8	46	36	36	
	38	8	10	48	38	38	
Dresses &	40	10	12	50	40	40	Suits
suits	42	12	14	52	42	42	
	44	14	16	54	44	44	
	46	16	18	56	46	46	
	36	30	8	37	14½	14½	
	38	32	10	38	15	15	
Blouses &	40	34	12	39	15½	15½	Shirts
sweaters	42	36	14	40	15¾	15¾	
	44	38	16	41	16	16	
	46	40	18	42	16½	16½	

Sizes often vary depending on the designer. These equivalents are given for guidance only.

Speed

kph	10	30	50	70	80	90	100	110	120	130
mph	6	19	31	43	50	56	62	68	75	81

Temperature

Celsius (°C)	0°	5°	10°	15°	20°	25°	30°	40°	60°	80°	100°
Fahrenheit (°F)	32°	41°	50°	59°	68°	77°	86°	104°	140°	176°	212°

To convert Celsius into Fahrenheit, multiply °C by 9, divide by 5, and add 32.
To convert Fahrenheit into Celsius, subtract 32 from °F, multiply by 5, and divide by 9.

Gordes

NATURE

Topography

FORMATION OF THE LAND

Approximately 600-220 million years ago, during a period called the Primary Era, what is now Provence was covered by a sea that surrounded the continent of Tyrrhenia, contemporary with the Massif Central. Tyrrhenia was formed by crystalline rocks. Vestiges of this land mass included the Maures, Corsica, Sardinia and the Balearic Islands.

During the Secondary Era (220-60 million years ago), erosion gradually leveled Tyrrhenia; the Cretaceous Sea covered practically the whole region. Variations in sea level were caused by the materials from the Primary strata carried down by rivers and deposited at the bottom of the sea, forming sedimentary deposits composed either of limestone (e.g. from Orgon) or marl and transformed into regular, parallel layers of rock (strata) in a strip of land lying east to west; this was the Durancen Isthmus surrounded by the sea.

The Tertiary Era (60-2 million years ago) was marked by important tectonic upheavals that uplifted the sedimentary cover and created the young folded mountains of the Alps and Pyrenees. The strata were uplifted and folded in an east-west direction, giving rise to the Provençal secondary mountains north of Marseille, Toulon, and Draguignan (Ste-Baume, Ste-Victoire, Mont Ventoux, Baronnies, Alpilles, Luberon). The sea level rose to the present-day Rhône valley, and while the Alpilles chain was thrust upwards, the Crau plain sank.

During the Quaternary Era (beginning about 2 million years ago) land mass development continued: Tyrrhenia was submerged beneath the present-day Mediterranean Sea leaving such outliers as the Maures, Esterel, and Canaille mountains. The relief adopted the form it has now, the Rhône corridor emerged, widened, and became an important travel route.

The subsiding Crau plain modified the course of the River Durance so that it deviated to join the Rhône. Erosion during glaciation and interglacial periods put the final touches to the landscapes (calanques).

PLAINS

The plains, such as the Rhône delta, were formed by the constant deposits of alluvial sediments that reclaimed territory from the sea. These plains first spread over the Rhône's east bank, **Comtat Venaissin**, then spread over both banks. On the west side of the river the plains extended to the Lower Languedoc dominated by the garrigues near Nîmes. To the east they became the fertile **Petite Crau** and **Grande Crau**.

Romans, medieval monks, and small property holders throughout the centuries have improved the land with drainage and irrigation systems. Two regions, especially, have profited from such systems: Comtat Venaissin and Petite Crau. Market gardens now cover the land creating a fine pattern of tiny plots separated by windbreaks of tall cypress and lower screens of reeds.

The **Grande Crau**, separated from Camargue by the Grand Rhône, is an immense desert of pebbles and boulders between which grow tufts of grass known locally as coussous. It was used traditionally for the winter pasturing of large flocks of sheep. The expansion of Fos' industrial zone and the clearing of the land of stones as well as the irrigation systems have transformed the area; it has lost its pastoral image and with it much of its charm.

Olive groves, almond trees, vineyards, and undulating grassland make up the new wealth of these areas.

The **Camargue** is a delta of recent alluvium or silt formed by the Rhône. This man-made delta holds the sea back by means of dikes. The wetland thus created is one of France's most picturesque regions. The sansouires, vast salt-marshes, give the area the appearance of an untamed immensity.

PLATEAUS AND MOUNTAINS

The Provençal plains are flanked or penetrated by folded mountain chains lying east to west that rise quite abruptly, blocking the horizon. The relief often appears confused, presenting an undisciplined alternation of limestone heights and partitioned-off fertile basins: Apt country, Aigues country (south of Luberon), Aix country (irrigated by the Provence canal) where very varied crops (grain, vineyards, fruit, market gardening) are cultivated. East of the Rhône, from north to south, different landscapes follow one after the other.

The western fringe of the **Baronnies** form a complicated structure of hills and slopes of pure beauty wherein reign olive groves and the hybrid *lavandin*. Unique to Provence, the rocky summits of the **Dentelles de Montmirail** display a finely carved-out relief (*dentelle* means lace) of oak and pine forest with vineyards carpeting the slopes. Backed up against the Baronnies is **Mont Ventoux**, an imposing limestone massif that dominates the Comtadin plain at a height of 1 909m/6 263ft.

The **Vaucluse plateau**, also known as the Vaucluse hills, is a vast arid land of karstic relief devoted to raising sheep and to the cultivation of lavender. This limestone countryside is potted with chasms and carved out by gorges. An underground hydrographic network, still largely uncharted, penetrates the limestone and opens out at the Fontaine de Vaucluse.

The **Montagne du Luberon** stretches over some 60km/37mi. Cut in half north to south by the Lourmarin combe, it culminates in the Grand Luberon at Mourre Nègre (alt 1 125m/3 691ft). This region has some rugged but beautiful mountain sites to which villages cling precariously. There is a striking contrast between its wild, forest-clad north face and its more cultivated south face. In the middle of the Rhône plain stand two picturesque ranges: La **Montagnette** and Les **Alpilles**.

East of Aix, **Montagne Ste-Victoire**, a limestone mass pock-marked with caves and chasms, dominates the Aix basin, whereas to the southeast the Trévaresse and Vitrolles ranges bar it from the Étang de Berre. This lagoon is closed to the south by **Chaîne de l'Estaque** and is separated from the St-Mitre hills by the Caronte depression.

The **Chaîne de l'Étoile**, Chaîne St-Cyr, and Massif Marseilleveyre surround Marseille whereas on the horizon looms the long rocky barrier of the **Massif de la Ste-Baume,** which reaches an altitude of 1 447m/3 763ft at the Ste-Baume signal station.

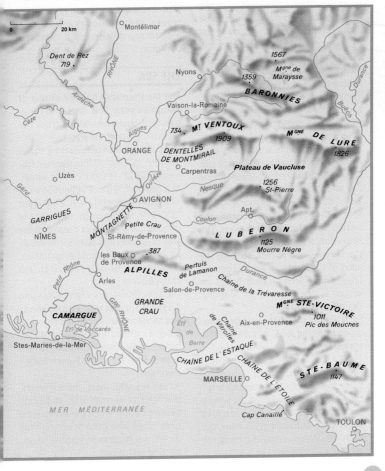

West of the River Rhône, the Cévennes foothills lie north to south receding in the river's direction and the vine-carpeted plain via the *garrigues* of Nîmes. A series of desolate limestone plateaux cut by canyons and gouged out by sometimes huge chasms succeed in tiers; it is an arid, rocky terrain only fit for grazing sheep. In the past, local people earned income by harvesting wild aromatic plants, olives, and almonds, and by making goats' cheese (*migou*). The countryside is criss-crossed by a multitude of dry-stone enclosures, in the middle of which once stood a modest hut (*mazet*), or *capitelle*, similar to the present-day dry-stone huts known as *bories*. There are, however, a few isolated fertile areas: the Uzès basin, the Vistre plain, and the Vaunage (southwest of Nîmes), which are devoted to growing crops, such as orchards and vineyards.

WATERWAYS

On its Provençal passage, the Rhône receives water to the west from the Ardèche and Gard rivers, which come down from the Cévennes, and to the east from the Aigues, Ouvèze, and Durance rivers, which come down from the Alps. They all have the same appearance: a trickle of water in an oversized stony bed during periods of drought, a torrent of foaming water during rain storms. The Cévennes receive rainfalls of unusual severity – a single downpour can exceed the annual rainfall of Paris. The rivers expand dramatically. The Ardèche has risen 21m/69ft in one day and its flow has increased from 2.5m³/88.3 cubic ft per second to 7 500m³/264 855 cubic ft; frequently the water rises 10m/33ft and more. The heavy flow of the Ardèche cuts through the Rhône like a rocket, striking the dikes of the left bank across the way. These 5m/16.5ft high flash-floods are known as "the blows of the Ardèche" (*les coups de l'Ardèche*).

For the tributaries of the east that come down from the Alps, it is the melting snows that multiply the volume of water. The Durance, for example, expands up to 180 times its usual volume. Fortunately these spates occur in the spring, when the Ardèche and Gard rivers are low. On the other hand, the Durance is almost dry in winter and autumn while the rains from the Cévennes expand the tributaries of the west bank.

COASTLINE

From the Languedoc coast to the Marseille *calanques,* the form of the coastline changes often. As far as the Golfe de Fos, the shoreline is marked by vast lagoons separated from the sea by narrow sand bars: the mass of alluvial deposits dropped by the Rhône and shaped by the coastal currents has formed offshore bars closing off the lagoons. The encroachment of sand has pushed old ports like Aigues-Mortes inland.

At the Chaîne de l'Estaque, limestone relief reappears and cuts the coastline. From Marseille to La Ciotat the littoral is cut into a great number of coves of which the deepest and most uneven are called **calanques** – they are in fact the submerged extremities of the valleys when the sea level rose after the Quaternary Era's glacial period. Steep cliffs, brown and reddish rocks plunge vertically into the deep, blue sea from which emerge a number of nearby islands. With small well-sheltered ports and lovely wild creeks, the *calanques* are at once a deep-sea diver's and a climber's paradise.

THE SEA

The Mediterranean is the bluest of European seas. This deep cobalt, in painters' parlance, arises from the great limpidity of the water.

The surface water temperature varies from 20°-25°C/68°-77°F in summer, falling to only 12°-13°C/53°-55°F in winter. At a depth of 200 to 4 000m/656 to 13 123ft, the temperature is a constant 13°C/55°F, an important factor in the climate: this great liquid mass cools the area in summer and warms it in winter. As a result of very rapid evaporation, the water is noticeably saltier than that of the Atlantic.

The sea's tide is very slight, averaging 0.25m/9.5in and yet, strong winds can cause variations in height of as much as 1m/3ft. This relative stability has singled out the Mediterranean as base level for all the French coast's altitudes.

A calm sea, with short, choppy waves, the Mediterranean can suddenly become violent. When the *mistral* wind rises, often with little or no warning, dangerous storms can surprise unsuspecting yachtsmen.

Flora

In addition to its beautiful country-side, backdropped by a luminous sky, Provence possesses a unique natural habitat.

CLIMATE AND ZONES

All vegetation is closely dependent on climatic conditions. In Provence, flowering occurs during the spring, although there is a second blossoming in the autumn that goes on well into winter. The dormant period is during the summer, when the climate's heat only permits plants that are especially adapted to resist drought to grow, such as those with long taproots, glazed leaves that reduce transpiration, bulbs that act as reservoirs of moisture and a protective perfumed vapour. The olive tree and holm oak mark out the distinctly Mediterranean zones, known as *garrigues*. In Haute-Provence the *garrigues* disappear to be replaced by forest cover (downy oak, Scots pine, beech) and moors (broom, lavender, boxwood).

In the Vivarais, chestnut trees add an unusual touch to the landscape.

OLIVE TREES

Olive tree

The Greeks brought olive trees to Provence 2 500 years ago because they grow equally well in limestone or sandy soils. The olive has been called the immortal tree since, grafted or wild, it will continually renew itself. Those grown from cuttings die relatively young, at 300 years of age. Along the coast the trees reach gigantic dimensions attaining 20m/65.5ft in height, their domes of silver foliage 20m/65.5ft in circumference and trunks 4m/13ft round the base. The olive tree—there are more than 60 varieties—will grow at altitudes of up to 600m/1 968ft, mainly on valley floors and hillsides, often mingling with almond and fig trees. Its presence marks the limit of the Mediterranean climate. It begins to bear fruit between 6 and 12 years of age and is in full yield at 20-25 years; it is harvested every two years.

Locals cultivate early vegetables in the shade of the light-coloured, evergreen foliage of the olive tree.

OAK TREES

There are several varieties of oaks.
The **holm oak** (*quercus ilex*) has a short thick-set trunk with a wide-spreading thick dome. It grows on arid, calcareous soil at less than 1 000m/3 281ft. It is an evergreen oak, the leaves of which remain a fine dark green. In stunted form it is a characteristic element of the *garrigues* in association with all sorts of shrubs and aromatic plants.

The **kermes,** or scrub oak, is a bushy evergreen shrub rarely exceeding 1m/3ft in height. It has a trunk of grey bark with a thick dome of shiny, tough, ragged, and prickly leaves. Its name, kermes, comes from the scale-insect that lives on its branches and from which a bright red dye is obtained. The tree can grow on stone-free dry soil but prefers fertile, cool soil.

The **downy oak** or **white oak** (*quercus pubescens*) is a deciduous tree; the undersides of the leaves are covered with dense short white hairs. It requires more water than the evergreens noted above. The downy oak can be found in the valleys and on the more humid mountain slopes. It is at times found with the maple, service tree, and rowan. In its undergrowth grow a variety of shrubs and flowers, most notably the orchid. Truffles develop around the roots of this tree.

PINE TREES

The three types of pine found in the Mediterranean can be easily distinguished by their shape.
The **maritime pine** (*pinus pinaster*) grows on limestone soil; its foliage is dark blue-green, the bark a purply red.
The **umbrella** or **stone pine** (*pinus pinea*) is one of the Mediterranean's most characteristic sights; it owes its name to its easily-recognisable shape. It is often found growing alone.

Umbrella pine

The **Aleppo pine** *(pinus halepensis)* is a Mediterranean species that grows well in the chalky soil along the coast. Its foliage is light and graceful. Its grey bark-covered trunk twists as it grows.

OTHER PROVENÇAL TREES

In towns and villages, the streets and squares are shaded by the smooth-barked **plane trees** or the dark green canopy of the branching **lotus tree** *(micocoulier)*, which yields a fruit mentioned by Homer in the *Odyssey* as inducing a state of dreamy forgetfulness and loss of desire to return home – hence lotus-eaters. Some have identified it as the jujube tree.

The outline of the dark **cypress**, a coniferous evergreen, marks the Mediterranean landscape with its tapered form pointed towards the sky. It is often planted in serried ranks to form a windbreak.

Cypress

The cypress variety with scattered branches is used for reforestation. The rosaceous species, the most common **almond tree** prevalent in Provence, bears lovely early-spring pink blossoms.

Almond tree

The noble elm tree has practically disappeared from the landscape.

FOREST COVER

There are not many forests in Provence and those that exist grow especially in the mountain ranges below 1 600m/5 249ft.

Fine forests of holm or downy oak grow in Grand Luberon, on Montagne Ste-Victoire, and on the Vaucluse plateau.

Petit Luberon is covered with a cedar forest. Beech tree forests grow on the north face of the Massif de la Ste-Baume. A moor of broom spreads along the limestone peaks.

The designation of the word forest beyond these areas indicates copses carpeting vast areas north of the Durance.

GARRIGUES

The word comes from the Provençal language – *garriga* – and defines an area of second-growth vegetation that appears on calcareous soils in the Mediterranean region following the destruction of the forest. Small *garrigues* can be found in most parts of Provence, but the vast stretch north of Nîmes, carved deeply by the River Gardon is what most people think of when they hear *"garrigue."* Here the low limestone hills are interspersed with minute parcels of land between the outcrops of white calcareous rock; sometimes the rain has washed the soil down into the valleys leaving vast rocky table-lands.

The sparse vegetation is mostly composed of holm oaks, stunted downy oaks, thistles, gorse, and cistus, as well as lavender, thyme, and rosemary. Short dry grass also provides pasture for flocks of sheep.

In addition to the wild aromatic plants that grow in the *garrigues*, herbs such as basil, marjoram, savory, sage, melissa, mint, laurel, and absinth are cultivated commercially.

ENVIRONMENTAL THREATS

Provence's, and the Mediterranean's, natural habitat is under constant attack due to the influx of tourists, and to industrial and urban development.

Forest fires

The Provençal forest is particularly vulnerable to fires (those of 1979, 1985, and 1986 were catastrophic), the majority of which are due to negligence or arson. Fire's two natural allies are drought and wind.

During the summer the dried-up plants of the underbrush, pine needles, resins exuded by leaves, and twigs are highly combustible and sometimes catch fire spontaneously. Once a fire has started, it spreads to the pines, and if the wind is strong, disaster may follow. Enormous walls of flame, sometimes more than 10km/6mi long and 30m/98ft high, spread at speeds of 5-6kph/2-3mph. When the fire has passed, nothing remains except the blackened skeletons of the trees and a thick layer of white ash covering the ground.

Often the fire wins, stopping only at the coast, unless the wind drops or changes direction. Over time, these fires gradually disrupt the ecological balance. The oak forests are receding and the soil remains barren for a long period of time. Fire prevention (systematic watch, periodically clearing the underbrush, creation of fire-breaks, etc.) and public awareness (especially that of tourists) will best help combat this devastating problem.

Dial 18 to reach the Fire Department (pompiers).

Pollution

The fast-developing urbanisation and industrialization programmes in Provence have dealt a heavy blow to the beauty of many natural sites.

The Fos-sur-Mer industrial complex spreads out over the Plaine de la Crau; the area around Étang de Berre, especially its eastern side, has become the bustling suburb (airport, refineries, etc.) of Marseille. In 1957, owing to the high level of polluted water, fishing was strictly forbidden in the lagoon. Discharge of used water from the surrounding towns, St-Martin-de-Crau's rubbish tip and Marseille's main sewer flow into the Calanque Cortiou all were harmful.

Increased traffic in the region has resulted in the construction of more and more road networks that are cutting up the countryside and diminishing natural land.

Caves and Chasms

In contrast to the deeply-dissected green valleys with their many settlements, the Bas Vivarais limestone plateaus roll away to the far horizon, grey and deserted. The calcareous nature of the rock absorbs rain like a sponge and makes the soil very dry.

At the end of the last century, the methodical, scientific exploration of the underground world, with which the name of **Édouard-Alfred Martel** is associated, led to the discovery of a number of caves, which have become a tourist attraction.

In 1935 **Robert de Joly** explored Aven d'Orgnac and encountered its wealth of cave formations. Later on, the discovery of a gaping hole in the chasm led in 1965 to the discovery of a vast network of upper galleries. Our knowledge of the underground system is at present very incomplete and a great many chasms remain unknown to speleologists.

WATER INFILTRATION

Rainwater, charged with carbonic acid, dissolves the carbonate of lime in the region's limestone. Depressions then form that are usually circular in shape and small in size and are known as **cloups** or **sotchs**. This dissolution of the limestone rocks, containing especially salt or gypsum, produces rich soil particularly suitable for growing crops. When the cloups increase in size they form large, closed depressions known as **dolines**. Where rainwater infiltrates deeply through the fissures in the plateau, the hollowing out and dissolution of the calcareous layer produces wells or natural chasms that are called **avens** or **igues**. Little by little the chasms lengthen and branch off, communicating with each other and widening out into caves.

UNDERGROUND RIVERS

The infiltrating waters finally produce underground galleries and collect to form a more or less swift flowing river. The river widens its course and often changes level, falling in cascades. Where the rivers run slowly they form lakes, above natural dams, known as **gours**, which are raised layer by layer by deposits of carbonate of lime. The dissolution of the limestone also continues above the water-level in these subterranean galleries: blocks of stone fall from the roof and domes form, the upper parts pointing towards the surface of the earth. Such is the case with the Upper Chamber at Orgnac, which lies only a few feet beneath the surface of the plateau. When the roof of the dome wears thin it may cave in, revealing the cavity from above and opening the chasm.

CAVE FORMATION

As water circulates below ground it deposits the lime it carries, thus building up concretions of fantastic shapes that seem to defy the laws of gravity and equilibrium.

In some caverns, the seeping waters produce calcite (carbonate of lime) deposits that form pendants, pyramids, and draperies. The best known calcite formations are stalactites, stalagmites, and eccentrics.

Stalactites are formed from the cave roof. Every droplet of water seeping through to the ceiling deposits on it some of the calcite with which it is charged, before dripping off. Gradually the concretion builds up layer by layer as the drops are attracted and run down its length, depositing particles before falling.

Stalagmites are formed in the same way but rise from the floor towards the roof. Drops of water, always dripping from the roof in the same place, deposit the calcite particles they carry and build up to form a candle-like shape. This rises towards a stalactite with which it ultimately joins to form a pillar linking the cave floor with the ceiling. Concretions form very slowly indeed; the rate of growth in a temperate climate is about 1cm/0.4in every 100 years.

The **eccentrics** are very fine protuberances which seldom exceed 20cm/8in in length. They emerge at any angle, either as slender spikes, or in the shape of small, translucent fans. They are formed by crystallization and seem to disregard gravity. Aven d'Orgnac, Aven de Marzal, and Grotte de la Madeleine contain remarkable examples.

HISTORY

Events in *italics* indicate milestones in history

Time Line

PREHISTORY TO THE ROMAN CONQUEST

BC

c 90 000-40 000 – Neanderthals occupy coastal Provence.

c 30 000 – Modern early humans (Cro-Magnon) settle in the region, leaving traces, such as the cave paintings in Grotte Cosquer (see *CASSIS*).

c 6000 – Neolithic impressed pottery: the first potters begin turning to agriculture and settle on the sites of Châteauneuf-les-Martigues and Courthézon.

c 3500 – hassey culture: the appearance of true stock-raising farmers living in villages.

1800-800 – Bronze Age. Ligurian occupation.

8-4C – Progressive installation of the Celts.

c 600 – Founding of Massalia (Marseille) by the Phocaeans (see *MARSEILLE*).

4C – Massalia is at its apex; travels of the Massaliote, Pythéas, into the northern seas.

218 – Hannibal passes through Provence and crosses the Alps.

125-122 – Conquest of southern Gaul by the Romans. Destruction of Entremont and founding of Aix.

102 – Marius defeats the Teutons at Aquae Sextiae (Aix).

58-51 – Conquest of long-haired Gaul by Julius Caesar.

55 – *Caesar lands in Britain.*

27 – Augustus establishes the Narbonensis.

AD

2C – Nîmes at its apex.

284 – Narbonensis is divided into two provinces: Narbonensis on the west bank of the River Rhône, and Viennoise on the east bank.

4C – Arles at its apex; establishment of the dioceses.

416 – Jean Cassien, from the Far East, founds the Abbaye de St-Victor in Marseille.

THE COUNTY OF PROVENCE

471 – Arles taken over by the Visigoths.

476 – F*all of the Roman Empire.*

536 – Provence ceded to the Franks.

843 – By the Treaty of Verdun Provence, Burgundy and Lorraine are restored to Lothair (one of Charlemagne's grandsons).

855 – Provence is made a kingdom by Lothair for his third son, Charles.

879 – Boson, Charles the Bald's brother-in-law, is king of Burgundy and Provence.

8C - 10C – Saracens, Vikings, and Magyars terrorise the land.

1032 – Provence is annexed by the Holy Roman Empire; the counts of Provence, however, retain their independence; the towns expand and assert their autonomy.

1066 – *William the Conqueror lands in England.*

1125 – Provence divided up between the counts of Barcelona and Toulouse.

c 1135 – First mention of a consulate in Arles.

1215 – *Magna Carta.*
St-Louis embarking in the port of Aigues-Mortes.

1229 – By the Treaty of Paris, Lower-Languedoc returns to France; founding of the royal seneschalship in Beaucaire.

1246 – Charles of Anjou, brother of St Louis (Louis IX), marries Beatrice of Provence, the count of Barcelona's daughter, and becomes count of Provence.

1248 – St Louis embarks from Aigues-Mortes on the Seventh Crusade.

1274 – Cession of the Comtat Venaissin to the papacy.

1316-1403 – The popes and schismatic popes at Avignon. Great Schism of the West (1378-1417).

1337-1453 – *Hundred Years War.*

1348 – Clement VI buys Avignon from Queen Joan I. Great Plague epidemic.

1409 – University of Aix founded.

1434-80 – Reign of Good King René, Louis XI's uncle. (see *AIX-EN-PROVENCE*)

1450 – Jacques Cœur sets up his trading-posts in Marseille.

1481 – Charles of Maine, nephew of René of Anjou, bequeaths Provence to Louis XI.

THE ESTATES OF PROVENCE

1486 – The Estates of Provence meet at Aix to ratify the union of Provence to the crown.

1492 – *Christopher Columbus discovers America.*

1501 – Inauguration of the Parliament of Aix as Supreme Court of Justice with limited political authority.

The Plague in Front of Marseille Townhall, by M. Serre

J. Barnard/Musée de Beaux-Arts de Marseille

1509-47 – *Henry VIII's reign.*

1524-36 – Provence is invaded by the Imperialists (soldiers of the Holy Roman Empire).

1539 – Edict of Villers-Cotterêts decrees French as the language for all administrative laws in Provence.

1545 – Suppression of Vaudois heretics from Luberon.

1555 – Nostradamus publishes his astrological predictions, *Centuries*.

1558-1603 – *Elizabeth I's reign.*

1558 – The engineer Adam de Craponne builds a canal.

1567 – Michelade tragedy occurs in Nîmes.

1588 – *Defeat of the Spanish Armada.*

1622 – Louis XIII visits Arles, Aix, and Marseille.

1660 – Solemn entry of Louis XIV into Marseille.

1685 – Revocation of the Edict of Nantes. Huguenots flee France.

1713 – Under the Treaty of Utrecht the Principality of Orange is transferred from the House of Orange-Nassau to France.

1714-27 – *George I's reign.*

1720 – The great plague, which originated in Marseille, decimates Provence.

1763 – Peace of Paris ends French and Indian War (1754-63); it marks the end of France's colonial empire in North America.

1771 – Suppression of Aix's *Parliament.*

FROM THE REVOLUTION TO THE PRESENT

1789 – *The French Revolution*; storming of the Bastille.

1790 – The constitutional Assembly divides southeast France into three *départements*: Basses-Alpes (capital: Digne), Bouches-du-Rhône (capital: Aix-en-Provence), Var (capital: Toulon).

1791 – Avignon and Comtat Venaissin are annexed to France.

1792 – 500 Marseille volunteers parade in Paris to the song of the Rhine Army, called *La Marseillaise*.

1805 – Battle of Trafalgar.

1815 – *Battle of Waterloo*; Napoleon's fall.

1837-1901 – *Victoria's reign*.

1854 – Founding of the Provençal literary school: Félibrige.

1859 – Frédéric Mistral publishes the Provençal poem *Mirèio*.

1861-65 – *American Civil War.*

1886 – *Statue of Liberty erected.*

1899 – *Second Boer War.*

1904 – Frédéric Mistral wins the Nobel Prize for Literature.

1933 – Founding of the Compagnie Nationale du Rhône for the harnessing of the river.

1942 – German forces invade Provence.

1944 – 15 August: Allied troops land on the Côte d'Azur.

22-28 August: General de Montsabert and his troops aided by the Resistance movement liberate Marseille from German occupation.

1962 – First hydroelectric power stations of the Durance begin operating.

1965 – Construction of Bassins de Fos complex begins.

1970 – A 6-A 7 motorways link Paris and Marseille.

Creation of the Parc Naturel Régional de Camargue.

1977 – Marseille's underground begins service.

Creation of the Parc Naturel Régional du Luberon.

1981 – The TGV, France's high-speed train, links Paris to Marseille.

1991 – Discovery in the Calanque de Sormiou, south of Marseille, of cave paintings and engravings dating from the Upper Paleolithic Era, now known as the Grotte Cosquer.

1993 – Olympique de Marseille become the first French football club to win the European Cup.

1994 – A painted cave, known as the Grotte Chauvet, is discovered in the Ardèche gorges.

1999 – Celebrations mark Marseille's 2 600th anniversary of its founding.

2000 – Avignon is one of nine towns designated a Cultural Capital of Europe.

2001 – The new TVG Méditerranée line south of Valence opens, making Paris a mere 3 hours away from Marseille.

2004 – The Millau Viaduct, the world's highest car bridge, opens west of Avignon, facilitating higher speed travel to southern France.

Hallmarks of Diversity

Provence is the product of one of the highly used crossroads of the Mediterranean world, ancient, medieval, and modern. Provence received migrations and invasions from diverse peoples: the Bronze-Age Ligurians, the Iron-Age Celts, the early Greeks, Romans, Visigoths, and Arabs, among others. No lesser diversity greets the visitor today as Provence has become a highly sought global travel destination.

PRE-ROMAN SOUTHERN GAUL

Origins: A Melting Pot

During the Bronze Age (1800-800 BC) Ligurians, the probable descendants of the native Neolithic population in northern Italy and southeastern France, inhabited the region. Celts began to infiltrate the area in the 7C, though their mass influx did not occur until about the 5C-4C. In the 7C, the first Greeks were also settling in the area. Phocaeans (Greeks from Phocaea in Asia Minor (Ionia, near Izmir in modern Turkey) founded Massalia (Marseille) in 600 or 620 BC in agreement with a Celtic tribe. This period represents a mixing of populations that established ancient Provence's roots in the Celtic-Ligurian civilization. These diverse populations settled progressively in *oppida*, fortified hill sites. Nages, near Nîmes, St-Blaise overlooking the Golfe de Fos, and Entremont, near Aix, were important settlements and fortified townships.

Greek presence

Greek settlement and influence is an essential part of the history of Provence's civilization. The Rhodian Greeks most likely gave their name to the great Provençal river (Rhodanos). However, the Phocaeans were the first to establish a permanent colony: **Massalia**. Massalia rapidly became a powerful commercial city, which founded in turn a number of trading posts: Glanum, Avignon, Cavaillon, and had commercial exchanges with the people of the north (wine and pottery for pewter from Armorica and agricultural products and livestock from Brittany). The colonists brought with them a number of improvements, such as a wine and olive oil industry, the introduction of coinage, and more intricate architecture. But by the 2C, relations between the natives and the Phocaeans from Massalia were deteriorating. The Salian Confederation, which had grouped together the Provençal population, rose against Massaliote imperialism.

Rome and Massalia

During the Second Punic War (218-201 BC), Massalia supported Rome whereas the Salian Franks helped Hannibal cross the region in 218. In 154 Massalia, worried about the threat of attack by the Gauls, obtained the protection of Rome. In 130 BC the powerful Arverni empire threatened southern Gaul's security, Gaul being the key trading centre between Italy and Spain. Rome came to Massalia's aid in 125 and the Roman legions easily conquered the Vocontii and Salian Franks, toppling their capital, Entremont. In 122, date of the founding of Aquae Sextiae (Aix-en-Provence), the Arverni and Allobroges suffered a bloody defeat. The consul Domitius Ahenobarbus relaxed the boundaries of a new province, **Gallia Transalpine**, which became **Narbonensis** (from the name of the first Roman colony of Narbonna) in 118. Massalia remained independent and was recognized as a territory. The Roman domination, which at one time was threatened by the Cimbrian and Teuton invasions in 105 (disaster at Orange) and halted by Marius near Aix in 102, spread irreversibly over the region, not without abuse and pillaging.

ROMAN COLONISATION

Pax Romana

Gaul Transalpine rapidly became integrated in the Roman world and actively supported the Proconsul Caesar during the Gallic Wars (58-51BC). Marseille, as

Apollo's head

Pratt – D. Fries/DIAF

a result of having supported Pompey against Caesar, was besieged in 49BC, fell, and lost its independence. The important Roman towns were Narbonne, Nîmes, Arles, and Fréjus. Romanisation accelerated under Augustus, and the Narbonensis *(see above)* was reorganized in 27BC. Antoninus Pius' (*see NÎMES*) reign (2C) marked the apogee of Gallo-Roman civilization. Agriculture remained Provence's principal activity and trade enriched the towns. Arles profited the most from Marseille's disgrace. Urban affluence was reflected in a way of life entirely focused on comfort, luxury, and leisure. Excavations have given us a glimpse of that life.

Arles, the Favoured City

After the troubled times of the 3C, the 4C and 5C brought considerable religious and political transformations. Christianity triumphed over the other religions after the conversion of Constantine. Arles became his favourite town in the west.

Marseille remained a commercial centre. Aix became an administrative capital. Nîmes declined, and Glanum was abandoned. Rural areas suffered from the general impoverishment of the Gallo-Roman world. Large landowners placed heavy demands, and insecurity led to the resettlement of fortified hill sites, such as St-Blaise.

FALL OF THE ROMAN EMPIRE TO PAPAL AVIGNON

Invasion after Invasion

Until 471 AD, the date Arles was taken by the Visigoths, Provence had been relatively free from invasions. The Burgundian and Visigoth domination (476 to 508) was followed by the Ostrogoth restoration, a period of some 30 years whereupon the Ostrogoths considered themselves the mandatories of the Far

Eastern emperor and revived Roman institutions: Arles thus recovered its praetorian prefects. Religious life continued to progress; several synods were held in Provence towns (Vaison-la-Romaine).

The bishop of Arles, Saint Caesarius, had a vast following in Gaul. In 536, Provence was ceded to the Franks and followed the same uncertain destiny as other provinces, tossed from hand to hand according to the Merovingian dynastic divisions. Decline was rapid.

The first half of the 8C was confusion and rife with tragedy: Arabs and Franks transformed the region into a battleground. In 855 Provence was made a kingdom, its limits corresponding more or less with the Rhône basin. It soon fell into the hands of the kingdom of Burgundy, whose possessions spread from the Jura to the Mediterranean and were under the protection of the Holy Roman Emperors, who inherited it in 1032. This was a major date in the history of Provence as it made Provence a part of the Holy Roman Empire, with the area west of the Rhône under the yoke of the counts of Toulouse.

Occitanian Provence

The 10C and 11C marked a major shift in the evolution of Provence's civilization, which until then was deeply defined by its Greco-Roman past. A new society developed out of the feudal anarchy. Rural life, henceforth, was concentrated in the hillside villages – Luberon, Ste-Baume and the Vaucluse mountains – which depended upon the seigneuries. Many towns sought to recover a degree of autonomy. The Oc language spread. Close links were established between Provence and Languedoc.

The failure of Occitania facilitated Capetian intervention. The Albigensian heresy resulted in the delayed union of the Catalan and Toulousain peoples, who until then had been fighting over Provence against the invaders from the north. The defeat at Muret in 1213 dashed all hope of a united Occitania.

Louis VIII's expedition (siege of Avignon in 1226) and the Treaty of Paris in 1229 brought about the founding of the royal seneschalship in Beaucaire: the west bank of the Rhône was part of France. In the east, the Catalan Count, Raimond Bérenger V, maintained his authority and endowed Provence with an administrative organizations. The towns became powerful locally: as early as the 12C they elected their own consuls, whose power increased to the detriment of the traditional lords (bishops, counts, and viscounts). In the 13C they sought their independence.

House of Anjou's Provence

The marriage of **Charles of Anjou**, St Louis' brother, to Beatrice of Provence, Raimond Bérenger V's heir, in 1246 linked Provence to the House of Anjou. Charles had large political ambitions: he interfered in Italy and conquered the kingdom of Naples in 1266 before turning towards the Far East.

In Provence, Charles of Anjou's government was very much appreciated. It re-established security. Honest administration managed public affairs, and prosperity returned. Concerning the territories, Comtat Venaissin was ceded to the papacy in 1274 by the king of France and evolved separately.

Charles I's successors, Charles II and Robert I, continued their father's and grandfather's political ideas and political order, and peace reigned during the first half of the 14C. Aix was raised to administrative capital with a seneschal and a court where the officers who presided were in charge of the finances of the county.

The key city was henceforth Avignon, where the Bishop Jacques Duèse, elected Pope in 1316 under the name John XXII, established himself. French-born Pope Clement V was already resident in Comtat Venaissin and benefited from the protection of the king of France. Thus John XXII's decision was confirmed by his successor Benedict XII, who began the construction of a new papal palace. The popes' stay in Avignon, which lasted almost a century, brought expansion and extraordinary brilliance to the city.

FROM ANNEXATION TO THE FRENCH CROWN

The End of Provence's independence

After the second half of the 14C, Provence entered a difficult period. Famine and the plague (which struck in 1348), pillaging road bandits, and political uncertainty brought about by the slackness of Queen Joan (granddaughter to King Robert; she was assassinated in 1382), badly damaged Provence's stability. The population was decimated, the country in ruins. After a violent dispute over succession, Louis II of Anjou (nephew to the king of France, Charles V) aided by his mother,

Marie of Blois, and the pope re-established the situation (1387).

Pacification was temporarily slowed by the activities of a turbulent lord, Viscount Raymond de Turenne who terrorized the country (1389-99), pillaging and kidnapping. His lairs were the fortresses of Les Baux and Roquemartine. Peace was not achieved until the early 15C.

Louis II of Anjou's (d 1417) youngest son, **King René**, inherited the county at the death of his brother in 1434. He was primarily concerned with the reconquest of the kingdom of Naples but every attempt of his failed, whereupon he turned all his attention to Provence (1447) and came to love it. His reign left happy memories; it coincided with a political and economic restoration that was felt through all of France. King René was a poet and had a cultivated mind fed by his love of the arts. He attracted a number of artists to Aix, who came to take up where the popes' Avignon had left off.

His nephew Charles of Maine briefly succeeded him. In 1481 Provence ceded to Louis XI of France. The history of Provence was henceforth interlaced with that of the kingdom of France, in spite of the Rhône boatmen who, for a long time, continued to distinguish between the Holy Roman Empire and the kingdom of France.

Vaudois and Huguenots

The Reformation spread in the south of France as early as 1530, thanks largely to the impetus from merchants and pedlars. Through the Rhône and Durance valleys and Vivarais, Protestantism was stimulated by the brilliance of the Vaudois church located in the Luberon village communities.

The Vaudois heresy went back to the 12C: a certain Vaudès or **Valdès**, a rich merchant from Lyon, had founded a sect in 1170 preaching poverty, Evangelism, refusal of the sacraments, and ecclesiastical hierarchy. Excommunicated in 1184, the Vaudois had since been pursued as heretics. In 1530 they were targeted by the Inquisition, and in 1540 the Aix *Parliament* decided to strike hard by issuing a warrant for the arrest of 19 Vaudois from Mérindol. François I temporized and prescribed a deferment. Instead of calming things down, the religious controversy came to a head. The heretics pillaged Abbaye de Sénanque in 1544. As a riposte, the *Parliament's* president obtained royal authorisation to enforce the Mérindol warrant and organized a punitive expedition. From 15 to 20 April 1545 blood ran through the Luberon village streets: 3 000 people were massacred, 600 were sent to the galleys, and many villages were razed.

Nevertheless, Protestantism continued to spread, especially west of the Rhône in Vivarais, Cévennes, Nîmes, and Uzès. East of the Rhône it was Orange (a Nassau Family principality since 1559) that became a Reformation stronghold. In 1560 the inevitable happened. Numerous churches and abbeys (St-Gilles, Valbonne charterhouse) were pillaged by the Huguenots; violence gave rise to more violence and with it the capture of Orange (1563) by the Catholic partisans. This in turn was answered by the fall of Mornas.

During these tumultuous times Provence and Languedoc-Cévennes split, taking different paths. Provence opted for Catholicism, and the Catholic League recruited fervent partisans in such cities as Aix and Marseille (both of which would have liked to become an independent republic). On the Rhône's opposite shore the situation was different. The people, influenced by the merchants and textile craftsmen who kept the Reformation alive, generally tended to believe in the Protestant movement and Nîmes was its capital.

The violent Wars of Religion in southern France brought about a conflict between two peoples of opposing mentalities who were to clash again during the Camisard Insurrection (1702-04) and who were never able to forget this crucial period of their history.

17C TO THE PRESENT DAY

Provence licked its wounds and revived, particularly in the 18C, which was the golden age for agriculture and commerce. The 19C was a less successful period: industrialization progressed but rural life suffered from the failure of the silkworm farms and phylloxera which spread through the vineyards.

In the face of these changes, Mistral sought to defend the Provençal identity and its traditions. When he died in 1914, Provence was nevertheless wholeheartedly engaged in modernisation.

In the 21C Provence is now a highly successful society, relying on heavy industry, speculative agriculture, and ever-increasing tourism. Its position as a major Mediterranean crossroad endures.

ART AND CULTURE

Architecture

Architectural terms

ORANGE – Roman Theatre (early 1C BC)

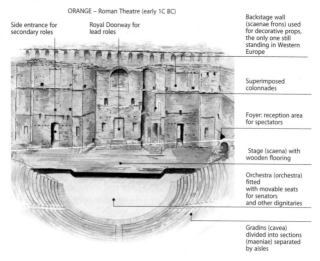

Side entrance for secondary roles

Royal Doorway for lead roles

Backstage wall (scaenae frons) used for decorative props, the only one still standing in Western Europe

Superimposed colonnades

Foyer: reception area for spectators

Stage (scaena) with wooden flooring

Orchestra (orchestra) fitted with movable seats for senators and other dignitaries

Gradins (cavea) divided into sections (maeniae) separated by aisles

NÎMES – Maison Carrée (late 1C BC)

The Maison Carrée in Nîmes is a temple consecrated to the Imperial cult: it consists of a vestibule lined by a colonnade and a room housing a statue of the divinity, the cella

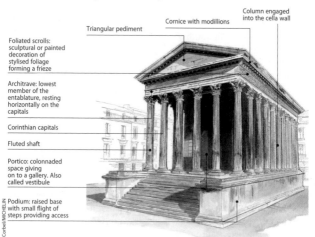

Triangular pediment

Cornice with modillions

Column engaged into the cella wall

Foliated scrolls: sculptural or painted decoration of stylised foliage forming a frieze

Architrave: lowest member of the entablature, resting horizontally on the capitals

Corinthian capitals

Fluted shaft

Portico: colonnaded space giving on to a gallery. Also called vestibule

Podium: raised base with small flight of steps providing access

R. Corbel/MICHELIN

Religious architecture

VAISON-LA-ROMAINE – Plan of the Ancienne Cathédrale
Notre-Dame-de-Nazareth (11C)

This cathedral is a typical example of Provençal church architecture, consisting of a nave without a
transept ending in a semicircular apse.

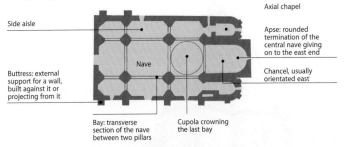

Side aisle

Axial chapel

Apse: rounded
termination of the
central nave giving
on to the east end

Nave

Chancel, usually
orientated east

Buttress: external
support for a wall,
built against or
projecting from it

Bay: transverse
section of the nave
between two pillars

Cupola crowning
the last bay

Vertical section of a Romanesque Provençal church

The two following drawings reflect the type of Romanesque church most frequently encountered in
Provence.

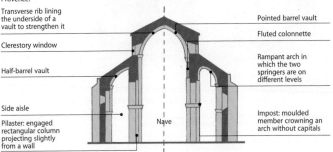

Transverse rib lining
the underside of a
vault to strengthen it

Pointed barrel vault

Fluted colonnette

Clerestory window

Half-barrel vault

Rampant arch in
which the two
springers are on
different levels

Side aisle

Pilaster: engaged
rectangular column
projecting slightly
from a wall

Nave

Impost: moulded
member crowning an
arch without capitals

Abbaye de SILVACANE – Vaulting in the Chapter-house (13C)

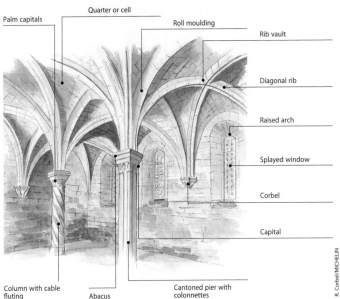

Palm capitals

Quarter or cell

Roll moulding

Rib vault

Diagonal rib

Raised arch

Splayed window

Corbel

Capital

Column with cable
fluting

Abacus

Cantoned pier with
colonnettes

R. Corbel/MICHELIN

Abbaye de MONTMAJOUR – Chapelle Ste-Croix (12C)

The quadrilobed plan of the Chapelle Ste-Croix, based on a Greek cross and representative of 12C Provençal architecture, can be seen in several other buildings of the area.

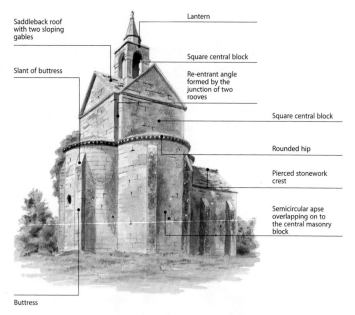

Saddleback roof with two sloping gables

Lantern

Slant of buttress

Square central block

Re-entrant angle formed by the junction of two rooves

Square central block

Rounded hip

Pierced stonework crest

Semicircular apse overlapping on to the central masonry block

Buttress

CARPENTRAS – South Door of the Ancienne Cathédrale St-Siffrein (late 15C)

The South Door, known as the Jewish Door, is Flamboyant or late Gothic: this is evidenced by the window tracery and its sinuous, tapering lines evoking tongues of flame.

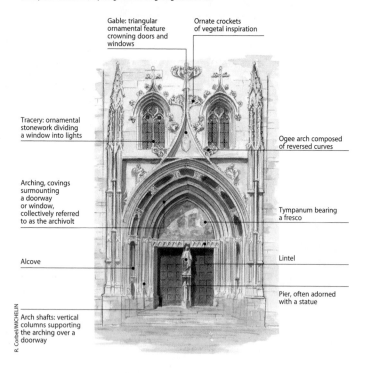

Gable: triangular ornamental feature crowning doors and windows

Ornate crockets of vegetal inspiration

Tracery: ornamental stonework dividing a window into lights

Ogee arch composed of reversed curves

Arching, covings surmounting a doorway or window, collectively referred to as the archivolt

Tympanum bearing a fresco

Alcove

Lintel

Pier, often adorned with a statue

Arch shafts: vertical columns supporting the arching over a doorway

R. Corbel/MICHELIN

Abbaye de ST-MICHEL-DE-FRIGOLET – Retable in the Chapelle
Notre-Dame-du-Bon-Remède (17C)

This 11C chapel is richly decorated with Baroque panelling dating from the 17C. At the far end stands an
imposing altarpiece.

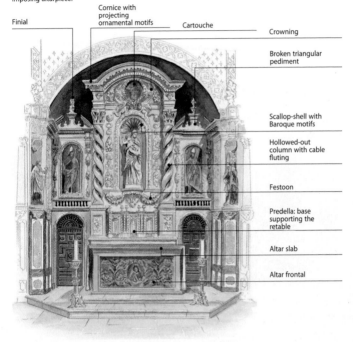

Finial

Cornice with
projecting
ornamental motifs

Cartouche

Crowning

Broken triangular
pediment

Scallop-shell with
Baroque motifs

Hollowed-out
column with cable
fluting

Festoon

Predella: base
supporting the
retable

Altar slab

Altar frontal

UZÈS – Organ in the Cathédrale St-Théodorit (18C)

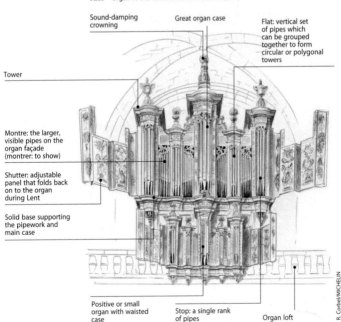

Sound-damping
crowning

Great organ case

Flat: vertical set
of pipes which
can be grouped
together to form
circular or polygonal
towers

Tower

Montre: the larger,
visible pipes on the
organ façade
(montrer: to show)

Shutter: adjustable
panel that folds back
on to the organ
during Lent

Solid base supporting
the pipework and
main case

Positive or small
organ with waisted
case

Stop: a single rank
of pipes

Organ loft

R. Corbel/MICHELIN

Military architecture

TARASCON – Fortified castle (14-15C)

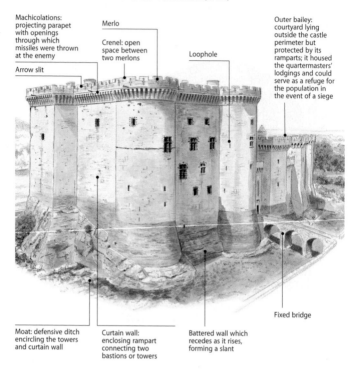

Machicolations: projecting parapet with openings through which missiles were thrown at the enemy

Arrow slit

Merlo

Crenel: open space between two merlons

Loophole

Outer bailey: courtyard lying outside the castle perimeter but protected by its ramparts; it housed the quartermasters' lodgings and could serve as a refuge for the population in the event of a siege

Moat: defensive ditch encircling the towers and curtain wall

Curtain wall: enclosing rampart connecting two bastions or towers

Battered wall which recedes as it rises, forming a slant

Fixed bridge

PORT-DE-BOUC – Fort (17C)

This fort was built by Vauban in 1664. Its defensive system allows for a great many salients and bastions in order to avoid both dead angles and areas lacking artillery.

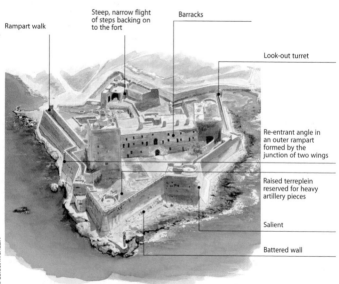

Rampart walk

Steep, narrow flight of steps backing on to the fort

Barracks

Look-out turret

Re-entrant angle in an outer rampart formed by the junction of two wings

Raised terreplein reserved for heavy artillery pieces

Salient

Battered wall

R. Corbel/MICHELIN

Civil architecture

AIX-EN-PROVENCE – Pavillon de Vendôme (17-18C)

The main façade features the "great order" advocated by Palladio as early back as the Renaissance, characterised by the display of three superimposed orders: Doric, Ionic and Corinthian.

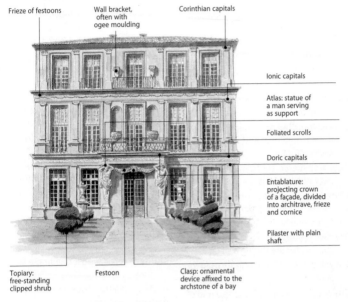

Frieze of festoons

Wall bracket, often with ogee moulding

Corinthian capitals

Ionic capitals

Atlas: statue of a man serving as support

Foliated scrolls

Doric capitals

Entablature: projecting crown of a façade, divided into architrave, frieze and cornice

Pilaster with plain shaft

Topiary: free-standing clipped shrub

Festoon

Clasp: ornamental device affixed to the archstone of a bay

MARSEILLE – Water tower of the Palais Longchamp (19C)

Seeking inspiration from Bernini's work in Rome, the architect Espérandieu built a monumental fountain whose decoration draws heavily upon the aquatic theme.

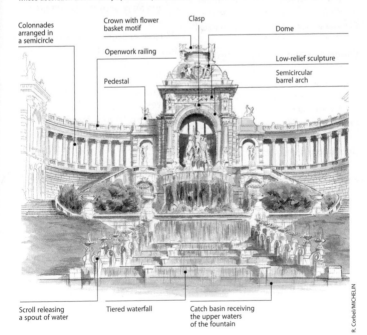

Colonnades arranged in a semicircle

Crown with flower basket motif

Clasp

Dome

Openwork railing

Low-relief sculpture

Semicircular barrel arch

Pedestal

Scroll releasing a spout of water

Tiered waterfall

Catch basin receiving the upper waters of the fountain

R. Corbel/MICHELIN

Architectural Terms

Acroterion: ornaments placed at the apex and ends of a pediment of a temple.

Aisle: lateral division in a church flanking a nave or chancel.

Ambulatory: aisle running around the east end of a church.

Apse: rounded termination of the central nave opening on to the east end.

Archivolt: arch moulding over an arcade or upper section of a doorway.

Barrel vault: vault in the form of a half-cylinder.

Basket-handled arch: depressed arch in late-medieval and Renaissance architecture.

Bay: transverse section of the nave between two pillars.

Blind arcading: sequences of arches, sometimes intersecting, applied to a blank wall for decorative effect.

Brattice: temporary wooden gallery or parapet for use during a siege.

Caryatid: carved female figure used for support.

Chevet: French term for the east end of a church.

Cippus: small pillar used to mark a burial place or serve as a sepulchral monument.

Claustra: stone railings with vertical bars.

Coffered ceiling: vault or ceiling decorated with sunken panels.

Crocket: carved ornament in the form of a curled leaf or cusp used in Gothic architecture.

Crypt: underground chamber or chapel.

Diaphragm arch: transversal arch used to relieve side walls.

Entablature: projecting crown of a façade, divided into architrave, frieze and cornice.

Exedra: niche, usually semicircular, with a bench around the wall.

Flamboyant: latest phase (15C) of French Gothic architecture; the name was taken from the tapering (flame-like) lines of the window tracery.

Fluting: vertical, shallow grooving decorating a column or pilaster.

Foliated scrolls: sculptural or painted ornamentation depicting foliage, often in a frieze.

Fresco: mural paintings executed on wet plaster.

Gable: triangular part of an end wall carrying a sloping roof; the term is also applied to steeply-pitched ornamental pediments in Gothic architecture.

Génoise: decorative frieze under the eaves, composed of a double or triple row of tiles embedded in the wall.

Historiated: decorated with figures of people or animals.

Hypocaust: an underground furnace to heat the water for the baths or rooms of a house.

Jambs: pillars flanking a doorway and supporting the arch above.

Keystone: middle and topmost stone in an arch or vault.

Lintel: horizontal beam or stone slab surmounting a door or window frame.

Mascaron: medallion carved in the shape of a human head.

Modillion: small console supporting a cornice.

Mullion: vertical post dividing a window.

Narthex: interior vestibule of a church.

Peristyle: range of columns surrounding or fronting a building.

Pietà: Italian term designating the Virgin Mary with the dead Christ on her knees.

Pilaster: engaged rectangular column.

Pinnacle: slender upright structure crowning a buttress, gable or tower.

Piscina: basin for washing the sacred vessels.

Portico: a colonnaded space in front of a façade or in an interior courtyard.

Predella: base of an altarpiece, divided into small panels.

Pulpitum: front section of the stage in an antique theatre.

Retable: ornamental structure set up above and behind an altar, often used as a setting for a religious picture or carving.

Rood screen: open screen, often richly painted or carved, separating areas reserved for clergy (chancel) and laity (nave).

Rosette: circular window with ornamental tracery radiating from the centre to form a symmetrical rose-like pattern.

Stucco: mixture of powdered marble, plaster and strong glue; used for decoration.

Transom light: upper section of a door or window.

Triptych: three panels hinged together, chiefly used as an altarpiece.

Voussoir: wedge-shaped stone forming part of an arch or vault.

TRADITIONAL RURAL STYLE

The Provençal country house, whether a *mas*, a *bastide* or an *oustau*, features the following characteristics:

– a shallow sloping roof of Roman style; curved terracotta tiles, with a decorative frieze under the eaves, composed of a double or triple row of tiles embedded in the wall and known as a **génoise**;

– stone walls, more or less smoothly rendered (pink or lavender), with no windows on the north side and those on the other three sides just large enough to let in light but keep out the summer heat;

– a north-south orientation, with sometimes a slight turn to the east to avoid the direct blast of the *mistral*; cypresses serve as a windbreak to the north, plane and lotus trees provide shade to the south;

– floors covered with red or brown terracotta tiles *(mallons)*;

– vaulting in dried stone or masonry that completely replaced floor boards.

The **Provençal mas** is a large, low farmhouse rectangular in plan with a sprawling low roof covering the living quarters and annexes. The walls are made of stone taken from the fields or from the Plaine de la Crau, ashlar-stone surrounding the openings. Traditionally, it is divided into two parts by a corridor, for in times past, one side was for the master and the other for the farmer *(bayle)*. This was repeated on the ground floor and on the upper storey.

The kitchen is level with the courtyard, and functions as the centre of the house in spite of its small size. Upstairs are bedrooms with tiled floors, and the attic. The outbuildings and other rooms are used for various purposes according to the importance of the *mas* and the agricultural vocation of the region. The ground floor sometimes has a vaulted cellar facing north. This could be used for stables, shed, storeroom, sheep's pen (at times separated from the *mas*), bread oven, and cistern. Above this, the attic space once served as the cocoonery for silkworms, and also as a barn (above the sheep's pen), and dovecote.

The **mas of the Bas Vivarais** are slightly different. They have an attractive pattern of stonework and an additional storey. In a traditional farm, the ground floor, covered by solid vaulting, contains the stables for the smaller animals and the storeroom for wine-making tools. In the cold-room, harvested products as well as hams and sausages are kept. A stone staircase opens on to a **couradou**, a terrace that is generally covered, and leads to the stone or terracotta-tiled kitchen. The cocoonery was often off the *couradou* and until c 1850 was an essential part of the Vivarais *mas* architectural conception. The sleeping quarters are off the kitchen, and a small wooden staircase leads to the attic. In the wealthier *mas* this may be a spiral staircase in a turret with the bedrooms on the upper floor. Annexes were often added to the living quarters, such as bread oven, barn, and in the chestnut region, a chestnut dryer, **clède** (or *clédo*).

Nowadays, it is hard to find a *mas* occupied by a traditional farming family. Many of these properties have been bought up for use as holiday homes and have been completely transformed to accommodate modern desires: a jacuzzi where sheep once rested; a TV room where the silkworms once spun; or a microwave where the bread oven stood.

An **oustau** is a typical Provençal farmhouse smaller in size than a *mas* but with the same layout. In the upper Comtat it is called a *grange*. In the past these barn-like buildings were progressively enlarged to house the family, which formed a clan, and the workers. It constituted an intermediary type of building between the *mas* of the plain and the village house. It was small but people compensated for the lack of surface area by adding on upper storeys.

A **bastide** is built of fine ashlar-stone and displays regular façades with symmetrical openings. Most often its layout is square in plan with a hipped roof.

Unlike the *mas*, the *bastide* was not necessarily a farmhouse. Thus, its conception was more luxurious, using decorative elements such as wrought iron balconies, exterior staircase, sculpture, etc.

The **gardian's cabin**, the typical Camargue dwelling of bygone days, is a small building (10m x 5m/33ft x 16.5ft) with a rounded apse at one end. The cob walls are low. Only the front façade, with its entrance door, is built in rubble to hold a long ridge beam supported by another piece of wood sloped at a 45° angle, and crossed by a piece of wood to form a cross. Thatched with marsh reeds, *sagnos*, these cabins usually had just two rooms divided by a wall of reeds: the dining room and bedroom.

CELTIC-LIGURIAN

Ligurians and Celts settled in fortified hill sites known as *oppida,* such as Nages, Entremont, and Roquepertuse, and created towns organized on a regular plan. Within the fortified walls stood a group of uniform dwellings, a type of hut in unfired stone and brick.

Celtic-Ligurian sculpture honoured, above anything else, the cult of the dead warrior, the town's hero, who they represented in the form of warriors' statues seated cross-legged with people either free-standing or in relief. An important ritual consisted of setting the severed heads of the conquered peoples, or at least the carved version, in the stone lintels. The sculpture exhibited at Roquepertuse perfectly demonstrates this Celtic form of expression.

Analysis of pottery shards confirms that Roquepertuse was densely occupied from the final Neolithic Era (3 000 BC) to around 200 BC, the date of the last destruction of the site. The most prosperous period was between the end of 4 BC to the end of 3 BC, characterized by the widespread use of delicate Mediterranean dishes (cups and pitchers of either painted or unpainted clay, and black glaze from 3C). From being confined to a single sanctuary, as was long believed, Roquepertuse, which is still the subject of detailed research, is in fact a vast complex stretching from the oppidum in the north to the sloping village in the south.

Hellenistic influence was also crucial for the region; it directly influenced the native peoples, accelerating the development of their economy and society. Greek construction techniques are evident in the building of St-Blaise (see p 301) and Glanum (see p 311). Numerous pottery fragments and Greek black figure vases were excavated at Arles, and the stelae found in Rue Négrel in Marseille are the oldest examples (second half of the 6C BC) of Greek sculpture in France.

Roman Culture

Throughout Provence, towns were built on the Roman urban plan. They all boasted remarkable public and private buildings, some of which are still well preserved, giving them a charm all their own. Without dropping Hellenistic influence entirely, the great Provençal towns took Rome as their model.

TOWNS

Most of the towns were built either on native Hellenistic or Gallic sites. And yet, very often, the desire to settle in a particular spot was that of a colony of veteran legionnaires, as was the case in Nîmes and Orange, who were soon after joined by the civilian population. The urban foundation was laid according to precise rules: having determined the future town centre, two major streets were traced – the *cardo maximus* (north-south orientation) and the *decumanus maximus* (east-west orientation). This created a regular grid pattern in which the grids were squared with sides some hundred square yards wide. This geometric exactitude could appear only on sites where the local topography was suitable, such as in Orange or Arles as opposed to Nîmes and Vaison-la-Romaine.

Where previous edifices had existed, they were razed, as at Glanum, to make room for the new buildings. These towns were not surrounded with walls except at Nîmes, Arles, and Orange, which were granted the honour of surrounding themselves with ramparts (permission obtained from Rome). Defensive walls did not appear until the end of the 3C. Such walls were built with towers and gates corresponding to the main streets.

Streets

The main streets were lined with pavements, at times 50cm/19.5in high and bordered by porticoes that protected the people from sun and rain. The roadway, paved with large flagstones laid diagonally, was crossed at intervals by stepping-stones laid at the same level as the pavements but between which horses and chariot-wheels could pass and pedestrians could cross over above the dust and mud. Gutters also ran alongside the road and were slightly rounded.

Forum

The forum, a large paved open space surrounded by an arcade, was the centre of public and commercial life in a Roman town. Government offices were located round the forum. These included a temple devoted to the imperial cult, a civil basilica (a type of town hall where judicial and commercial affairs were conducted), the *curia* or headquarters of local government, and at times, a prison.

At Arles the forum had the particularity of being lined with a vast underground gallery, *cryptoporticus*, the origin of which remains a mystery.

THE ART OF BUILDING

The art of building was very advanced with the Romans. The rapidity with which their buildings went up was not so much due to the number of people working on a site as to the special training of the workers, their organized working methods, and the use of lifting devices such as levers, hoisting winches, and tackles, that moved heavy material into place.

Building materials

For building material the Romans used the local limestone, which was not hard to dress; the stone was easily extracted and shaped into blocks. Romans originally adopted the method of using large blocks of stone without mortar: the stones were held together by their weight, and with dowels or cramps. But builders then revolutionized wall construction by introducing the use of concrete, a manufactured material not unique to any one country. Concrete could be used in the construction of buildings throughout the Empire, giving a uniformity and similarity to their edifices.

They also used concrete to fill in cracks or joints, or give to a public building a uniform surface, such as at the Maison Carrée and Amphitheatre in Nîmes, or to wedge the stones together allowing the expansion of a vault.

Orders

The Roman architectural orders derived from the Greek orders but with some variation. Roman Doric, still called the Tuscan Order, the simplest and most solid,

Doric Order   Iconic Order   Corinthian Order

was found on the monuments' lower storeys. Too severe, it was rarely used by the Romans. The Ionic Order was very elegant but not ornate enough for the Roman architects. It was the Corinthian Order that Romans used frequently because of the richness of its ornamentation. The Composite Order was a combination of the Ionic and Corinthian Orders.

Roofs

Public buildings sometimes had rectangular-shaped roofs held by colonnades inside the rooms. But more often the Romans used rounded vaulting in corridors and galleries where the walls were parallel, groined vaulting in square rooms, and the dome in circular rooms.

PUBLIC BUILDINGS

The inhabitants of Roman towns enjoyed bloody combats as much as more peaceful theatrical representations (*see NÎMES*).

Due to the influence of Christianity, gladiator fights were forbidden in 404. The games were abandoned at the same time.

B. Kaufman/MICHELIN

Roman theatre, Vaison-la-Romaine

Amphitheatres

The amphitheatre, also known as **arena**, had two tiers of arcades on the outside surmounted by a low storey called the attic. Posts were fixed on the attic to carry a huge adjustable awning, the *velarium*, to shelter the spectators from the sun and rain. The arcades were divided by rectangular pillars decorated with engaged half-columns on the first storey. Inside, enclosing the arena, a wall protected the spectators in the front rows from the wild animals released in the ring. The *cavea* – terraces for the spectators – was divided into *maenia* – tiers of seats generally in groups of four, individually separated by a passage. The seats were strictly allocated, those nearest the arena being for the men with a superior social station. The first *maenia* were reserved for consuls, senators, magistrates, and members of local guilds (such as the boatmen of Arles) who arrived in litters. In another section sat priests, knights, and Roman citizens, whereas freedmen and slaves sat in the attic. The arcades and three circular gallery-promenades, and the hundreds of staircases and passages allowed spectators to reach or leave their stepped seats directly. At Nîmes it took less than five minutes for the audience of 20 000 to leave.

Theatres

The Roman theatre, in the form of a half-circle lengthened by a deep stage, was divided into three sections: the *cavea* (auditorium) built in the hollow of a hillside, as in Orange, and crowned by a colonnade; the orchestra, the semicircular section in front of the stage with movable seats reserved for dignitaries; the stage flanked by side rooms, rectangular in shape, which were higher in level than the orchestra. At the back of the stage was a wall (which was as high as the cavea) with three doors through which the actors entered.

The stage wall was the finest part of the building. Its decoration included several tiers of columns, niches containing statues (the central niche contained the emperor's statue), marble facing and mosaics. Behind this were the actors' dressing-rooms and store rooms. Beyond these again was a portico open to the garden through which the actors entered the theatre. In it, spectators would stroll during the intermissions or take shelter from rain. As in the arenas, a huge adjustable awning, known as the *velum,* could be opened to shelter the spectators from the sun and rain.

Theatrical scenery and machinery were ingenious. Some scenes were fixed; some were superimposed and uncovered by sliding others sideways.

The curtain was only 3m/10ft high. It dropped into a slit at the beginning of the play and rose at the end. The basement contained the machinery and communicated with the stage through trapdoors on which the actors could rise from or sink into the ground. Other machines, mounted in the flies, lowered gods or heroes from the heavens, or raised them into the clouds.

The effects men knew how to create were smoke, lightning, thunder, ghosts, and the accompaniment of apotheoses.

All sorts of means were used to obtain perfect acoustics. The mouths of the actors' masks were little megaphones. The large sloping roof over the stage threw the sound downwards, and the upward curve of the seats received it smoothly. The colonnades broke up the echo, and carefully graduated sounding-boards under the seats acted as loud-speakers. One detail shows how far these refinements were carried: the doors on the stage were hollow and made like violins inside. When an actor wished to amplify his voice he would stand against one of these sound-boxes.

Circuses

These were huge rectangular arenas, one end of which was oval-shaped, where chariot and horse races were held. All that remains of the circus at Arles is the obelisk that stands in front of St-Trophime.

Temples

The temple stood on a podium surrounded by columns and consisted of two rooms: the *pronaos* (a vestibule) and the *cella* (a place for the statue of the divinity).The prime example of a temple is the Maison Carrée at Nîmes. In the countryside there were small local temples, *fana* (singular *fanum*).

TRIUMPHAL ARCHES

The arches in Orange, Glanum, Carpentras, and Cavaillon resemble the triumphal arches of Rome, raised in honour of victorious generals, but these were built to commemorate the founding of the cities in which they stand and the exploits of the veterans who settled there. They had either one or three openings. The columns decorating the four sides and flanking the central arch were all engaged; later on they became detached. The upper storey was decorated with statues, horse-drawn chariots, and their feats of arms, usually in gilt bronze.

BATHS

The Roman baths, which were public and free, were also centres of physical culture, casinos, clubs, recreation centres, libraries, lecture halls, and meeting places, which explains the amount of time people spent in them. Decoration in these great buildings (👍 see plan of La Trouille baths under ARLES) was lavish: columns and capitals picked out in bright colours, mosaic ornaments, coloured marble facings, richly coffered ceilings, mural paintings, and statues.

Central heating

The bath's functioning demonstrated the Romans' understanding of the canalisation of water and its subsequent heating. Water was brought from the mountains via aqueducts and placed into cisterns and then distributed by a lead-pipe and cement system of canals; evacuation was conducted through a network of drain pipes.

To heat air and water a number of underground furnaces (hypocausts) like bakers' ovens, in which roaring fires were kept going, were used. The hot gases circulated among the brick pillars supporting the stone floors of rooms and baths, and rose through flues in the walls to escape from chimneys. In this way the rooms were heated from below and from the sides as in modern buildings. The warmest room, facing south or west, had large glazed windows and was used as a solarium. Water at three different temperatures, cold, lukewarm and hot, circulated automatically by thermo-siphon.

Bather's route

The bather followed a medically-designed route. From the changing room, where he would have left his clothes and anointed his body with oil, he entered the palestra (a gymnasium of sorts), where he would warm up performing physical exercises. Then came the tepidarium (a lukewarm room), where he thoroughly cleaned himself by scraping his skin with small curved metal spatulas (strigiles) that prepared him for the caldarium (hot room), where he took a steam bath. He then proceeded into the hot swimming-pool. Having been massaged, he once again returned to the tepidarium before continuing on to the frigidarium (cold bath) to tone up the skin.

Thoroughly revived the bather dressed and proceeded to take advantage of the baths' other activities, such as lectures, sports, gossip, and the like. The private baths located in the wealthy urban dwellings and villae were not as spacious but did possess a comparable level of luxury.

THE ROMAN TOWNHOUSE

Numbers below correspond to the illustration that follows. Excavations at Vaison-la-Romaine, Glanum, or the Fountain quarter in Nîmes have uncovered Roman houses of various types: small bourgeois houses, dwellings (several storeys high) for rent, shops open to the street, and finally, large, luxurious patrician mansions.

Mansions had modest external appearances owing to their bare walls and few windows. But the interiors, adorned with mosaics, statues, paintings, and marbles, and sometimes hot baths and a fish pond, reflected the wealth of their owners.

A vestibule and a corridor in the mansion led to the atrium.

The **atrium** (1) which opened on to the street through a vestibule containing the porter's lodge was a large rectangular court, open in the middle, to the sky (compluvium). A basin called the impluvium, under the open section, caught rainwater. Rooms opened off the atrium: a reception room (2), a private oratory, a tablinum or study, and a library of the head of the family.

The **peristyle** (3) was a court surrounded by a portico (a gallery with a roof supported by columns) in the centre of the part of the house reserved for the family. They reached it from the atrium along a corridor called the fauces. Here the peristyle was generally made into a garden with basins lined with mosaics, fountains, and statues. The living quarters opened all around it: bedrooms, triclinium (dining room 4), and oecus (main drawing room).

The annexes included the kitchen with a sink and drain, baths, and a flush lavatory. Other buildings housed slaves' quarters, attics, cellars, stables, etc.

R. Corbel/MICHELIN

Roman townhouse

RURAL HOUSING

Experts are just beginning to examine this kind of dwelling. The towns must have been numerous and the settlement of these sites by Romans was done on pre-existing sites. The *cadastral* plan of Orange seems to show that the Romans tried to organise their territory into square-shaped lots called centuries.

The most common type of house was the *villa*, 40 of which have been discovered in Provence.

AQUEDUCTS

Grandiose like the Pont du Gard or more modest like Barbegal, aqueducts played an important role in daily life as they carried the water from their source to the town.

ROMAN ROADS

As soon as they settled in Provence, the Romans decided to design and build a reliable network of terrestrial means of communication that would ensure supremacy over the lands they had conquered, while at the same time encouraging the exchange of both goods and ideas. The layout of these roads usually coincided with that undertaken by the Gauls or with the paths (*drailles*) traditionally used by herds of cattle. They were cobbled only at the entrance to cities (country ways were surfaced with small, flat stones arranged tightly together) and dotted with stone or wooden bridges (Pont Julien at Bonnieux, Pont Flavien at St-Chamas), military milestones (1 Roman mile = 1 481m/0.92mi), and relay posts. Three great Roman roads cut across Provence: the Aurelian Way (*Via Aurelia*), the Domitian Way (*Via Domitia*), and the road to Agrippa. The first connected Rome to the River Rhône, running along the coast through the towns of Antibes (*Antipolis*), Fréjus (Forum Jilii), Aix-en-Provence (*Aquae Sextiae*), and Salon-de-Provence (*Salo*) before joining up with the Domitian Way in Tarascon (*Tarusco*). The Via Domitia, which headed towards Spain, helped link northern Italy to southern Gaul. It served the cities of Briançon (*Brigantium*), Gap (*Vapicum*), Sisteron (*Segustero*), Apt (*Aptia Julia*), Cavaillon (*Cabello*), Tarascon (*Tarusco*), Nîmes (*Nemausus*), Béziers (*Julia Baeterrae*), Narbonne (*Noarb*), and Perpignan (*Ruscino*). Finally, the road to Agrippa started at Arles (*Arelate*) and extended towards Lyon, following the left bank of the Rhône and crossing Avignon (*Avenio*) and Orange (*Arausio*).

Roman Influence

The brilliant Gallo-Roman civilization took a long time to disappear after the fall of the Western Empire. The ancient public buildings remained standing and the architects of the Middle Ages took inspiration from them to build churches and monasteries.

A dark age followed (5C-10C) when few buildings were erected, of which only isolated specimens now remain, such as the small baptistries at Aix and Venasque. Early Romanesque art, which developed from Catalonia to northern Italy in the 10C and 11C, did not leave significant examples, either.

The 12C was for Provence one of its most outstanding historic periods during which it underwent a brilliant architectural renaissance. Churches, remarkable for the bonding of their evenly-cut stones with fine mortar work, appeared everywhere. Their style was closely-linked to a School which had evolved in the area between the River Rhône, the Drôme, the Alps, and the Mediterranean. This school was more original than innovative and knew how to capture different influences: from Roman Antiquity came the use of vaults and especially decoration; from Languedoc came the carved portals; from Lombardy came the Lombard arcade or the lions adorning the base of doors; and from Auvergne came the dome on squinches over the nave and in front of the apse.

Below are the essential characteristics of the Romanesque style, the best examples of which were the great sanctuaries in the Rhône valley: Cathédrale de la Major in Marseille, St-Trophime in Arles, St-Gilles, Cathédrale Notre-Dame-des-Doms in Avignon, Cathédrale Notre-Dame in Orange, and the church in Le Thor.

CHURCHES AND CHAPELS

Plan

Provençal Romanesque churches have descended directly from the Roman basilica and Carolingian church. Their general appearance was of a solid mass. Transepts were rare and shallow. Often there was a single nave with side chapels hollowed out of the thickness of the walls. The east end took the form of an apse with two flanking apsidal chapels, where there were side aisles. Only the great pilgrimage churches of St-Gilles (in St-Guilles) and St-Trophime (in Arles) have ambulatories.

Minor buildings (Chapelle Ste-Croix in Montmajour – St-Sépulcre in Peyrolles) present a quadrilobed plan.

St-Trophime cloister, Arles

Bell towers

The bell tower is, an imposing, most often square, sometimes octagonal structure, that dominated the dome above the transept crossing.

It was sometimes placed above the bay preceding the apse or on the façade. It was decorated with blind arcading known as Lombard arcades or fluted pilasters in the Antique style, or sometimes both.

Side walls

The walls were usually bare except for the cornice and the plain side doors. Massive buttresses, between which were set the windows of the nave, relieved the austere monotony of the exterior.

West fronts and doors

The west front was generally plain, opened by a door surmounted by an oculus as the main door was often located on the south side sheltered from the *mistral*.

The doors were probably the architectural element most influenced by ancient Greek and Roman art; sometimes they were decorated with a fronton directly influenced by the ancient temples, such as the porch at Notre-Dame-des-Doms and the Chapelle St-Gabriel near Tarascon.

During the 12C, façades became more ornate preceded at times by a porch: a large carved tympanum over a horizontal lintel began to be featured. The doorways of St-Gilles and St-Trophime, superbly carved examples, rivalled in quality, size, and beauty the Gothic cathedral masterpieces of northern France.

Interior

Upon entering the Provençal Romanesque church the visitor is struck by the simplicity and austerity of the inside structure, enhanced only by some carved mouldings and cornices, barely visible in the dimly lit interior.

Chancel

This is the part of the church reserved for the clergy. It was usually oven vaulted and linked to the transept crossing with rounded barrel vaulting.

Nave and vault

The lofty – moderate though it was – structure of the building's interior was remarkable for the purity of its lines.

The nave was roofed with pointed barrel vaulting in which the downward thrust was more direct than that of the rounded arches, which tended to splay the wall outwards.

The barrel vaulting had already been used in the Roman era, having replaced the easily flammable wooden roofing, used from the 5C to the 11C, which had caused the destruction of many buildings. It was buttressed by pointed arches, also called transverse arches, which came down on thick engaged pilasters in the side walls or down onto slender pillars lining the nave.

The nave was sometimes lined with aisles with quarter-circle or pointed barrel vaulting, which acted as buttresses. Owing to the height of the side aisles there were no tribunes but a decorative band of blind arcading, made of rounded arches, with three arches to each bay, the central arch pierced by a lancet window, which let in very little light. Where the churches had but a single nave the side walls were quite thick in order to compensate for the missing side walls and balance the whole structure.

Transept and Dome

The construction of the transept was a difficult problem for the architects in the Romanesque period. The groined vaulting made by the crossing of the nave and aisle vaulting had to be of great height in order to support the heavy weight of the central bell tower; the problem was solved by placing a dome on squinches over the crossing in the style of the Auvergne School.

Decoration

Interior decoration was as austere as exterior decoration: decorated capitals usually ornamented with stylized leaves, friezes with interlacing and foliated scrolls, fluting and rope moulding.

The capital with leaves of the Romanesque style was an adaptation of the ancient Corinthian capital: it was formed by a group of leaves arranged according to the style of the Romanesque period (interlacing and stylized decoration). The most picturesque of these capitals were historiated, inspired by religious stories taken from the Old and New Testaments. The cloisters offer the best examples: St-Trophime with its magnificent corner pillars adorned with statues of saints is remarkable. Fine capitals can also be found in the cloisters of Montmajour and St-Paul-de-Mausole (fantastic animals) and the apse of the church at Stes-Maries-de-la-Mer. There are also fragments of carved decoration worth seeing: in Avignon's cathedral there is the bishop's throne; in Apt's cathedral there is the altar.

ABBEYS

Provence boasts several fine abbeys. The Benedictine Abbaye de Montmajour near Arles, founded in the 10C, forms a superb architectural ensemble illustrating the evolution of Romanesque forms from the 11C to 13C. It includes two churches (an upper church and crypt or lower church), two chapels, cloisters and its annexes in the characteristic Provençal style: simplicity in the monumental size, the volumes of which were inspired by the Antique style, carved decoration similar to St-Trophime, and perfection in the stone bonding. Cistercian art was represented by three sister abbeys: Sénanque, Silvacane and Le Thoronet (*see the Michelin Green Guide French Riviera*).

Sober elegance, austerity, and lack of ornamentation were the required rules of the Cistercians, a reformed monastic order founded by St Bernard of Clairvaux. St Bernard had denounced the fanciful nature of Romanesque sculpture, which could distract the monks at prayer. The Cistercians imposed an identical plan everywhere, and they themselves directed the construction.

Gothic Style

EVOLUTION

Romanesque art survived longer in Provence than it did in the rest of France. In spite of the relatively early appearance of Gothic, limited to two buildings (crypt of St-Gilles, porch of St-Victor in Marseille) and quadripartite vaulting as early as pre-1150, Gothic art was late in taking hold in Provence.

In the early 13C the new vaulting was used to cover buildings only in the Romanesque style. The only buildings entirely in the 13C Gothic style are to be found in Aix: the central nave of Cathédrale St-Sauveur and Église St-Jean-de-Malte, the former priory of the Knights of Malta. The Gothic style finally caught on under the influence of two historic factors: Capetian presence in the south, as a result of the Albigensian Crusade and the marriage of Charles of Anjou with Beatrice of Provence, and the settling of the mendicant orders in the towns.

In the mid 14C, there began a new step in Gothic evolution: a school of architecture called the Papal Gothic style began developing in Avignon. The popes attracted to their court artists from different regions of France, Germany, Flanders, and Italy.

During the 15C the cardinals embellished Villeneuve-lès-Avignon with palaces (*livrées*), churches, and cloisters; aisles and chapels were added to certain churches. St-Trophime was altered, the Romanesque apse was replaced by an ambulatory and radiating chapels.

The main Gothic churches include: Palais des Papes (Clementine, Grand or Clement VI Chapel), St-Didier, St-Pierre, St-Agricol, Couvent des Célestines, all in Avignon; St-Laurent in Salon-de-Provence; Cathédrale St-Siffrein in Carpentras; the basilica of St-Maximin-la-Ste-Baume; the church in Roquemaure; and especially the charter house and church in Villeneuve-lès-Avignon.

ARCHITECTURE

The Gothic style is marked by the systematic use of quadripartite vaulting and pointed arches. This innovative style, which originated in northern France, revolutionized construction by concentrating the weight of the structure on four pillars directed by stringers and transverse arches. Due to the absence of flying buttresses (characteristic of Northern Gothic) the thrust of the vaults was assured by the massive buttresses between which chapels were built.

Inside, the nave was relatively dark, almost as wide as it was high, and ended in a narrower polygonal apse. Its width better accommodated the primary function of the church: Dominican preaching. The wall surfaces required painted decoration.

Église St-Didier in Avignon is considered the best example of Southern Gothic in the region, whereas in a building like the basilica in St-Maximin-la-Ste-Baume, southern and northern influences appear. The church of the Couvent des Célestines in Avignon is entirely Northern Gothic in style.

Religious edifices were not the only examples of Gothic art in Provence. Civic and military buildings also held an important place. The Palais des Papes in Avignon was one of buildings in the 14C that accommodated the demands of luxury and comfort with those of defence and security.

DECORATION

The austere elegance of Provençal Gothic churches is underlined by the lack of decoration.

Fine Arts

PAINTING

The Avignon region was for over two centuries (14C-15C) the great centre of Provençal painting. Already in the 13C the frescoes of the Ferrande tower recalled the miniatures painted during St Louis' reign. In the 14C the popes decorating the palace sought out the great Italian masters: **Simone Martini** from Siena and **Matteo Giovanetti** from Viterbo (👈 see the Michelin Green Guide Italy). The charterhouse in Villeneuve-lès-Avignon also contains fine works by Giovanetti. Once the popes had left Avignon, Italian influence diminished, but artistic life underwent a renaissance in the mid 15C. Good King René was a patron of the arts and attracted master-craftsmen – artists and architects – to his court. Fresco painting lost ground to the Avignon School of panel painting. Artists from the north, Flanders and Burgundy, painted splendid masterpieces such as the Triptych of the Annunciation (1443-45) in Aix's Ste-Marie-Madeleine

Annunciation by Taddeo di Bartolo

Church and the Coronation of the Virgin (1453-54) by Enguerrand Quarton, which is exhibited in the Musée Pierre de Luxembourg in Villeneuve-lès-Avignon.

Nicolas Froment, King René's court painter from Languedoc, painted the famous *Triptych of the Burning Bush* (in Aix's Cathédrale St-Sauveur). Avignon's Petit Palais contains a remarkable collection of lovely 14C and 15C paintings (Avignon and Italian Schools).

SCULPTURE

In the 14C, sculpture consisted of recumbent figures (John XXII in Avignon's Notre-Dame-des-Doms, Innocent VI in Villeneuve-lès-Avignon's charterhouse, and Cardinal Lagrange in the Petit Palais in Avignon), corbels, keystones, and slender capitals. Archaic in style, they tended to draw on the Romanesque tradition. The reason for this diminished representation was that mural painting was occupying an increasingly important role in the interior decoration of churches.

RENAISSANCE

Although the Rhône valley was the principal route by which personalities of the Italian Renaissance entered France, Provence remained virtually untouched by the movement. Such buildings as were erected in the 16C were in the Gothic style, except for a few chapels and châteaux.

CLASSICAL PERIOD

The 17C and 18C, by contrast, produced a large number of buildings. They were

Pierre Puget (1620-1694)

This highly-skilled, multifaceted artist began his career as a young sculptor in Italy, where he trained under Pierre de Cortone. In 1645, Fouquet commissioned him to execute the doorway for the town hall in Toulon – it was to be one of his first great masterpieces. Between 1660 and 1668, the most brilliant period in Puget's career, he was living in Genoa. He was called back to Paris by Colbert, who entrusted him with the decoration of ships' prows belonging to the fleet in Toulon. Wary of the plots and intrigues of Versailles, he chose to live away from the French Court and devoted himself to the ornamentation of several Provençal cities, such as Aix and Marseille. His work is said to be forceful rather than elegant, and his statues, often of monumental proportions, artfully convey power, movement and pathos. His style is strongly reminiscent of Italian Baroque (Bernini, Cortone) and he succeeded in gracing Provence with a personal and highly original touch at a time when the country was largely dominated by Classicism.

His paintings (*Achilles' Education*) and sculptures (*The Faun, The Plague in Milan*–see right), are displayed at the Musée des Beaux-Arts in Marseille, as well as at the Louvre Museum in Paris (the famous *Milon de Crotone* sculpture). His architectural feats include the ovoid dome of the Vieille Charité chapel in Marseille.

dignified and austere in design without distinctive regional characteristics. The so-called Jesuit style developed in the Comtat Venaison churches, bringing with it Italian monumental features such as ornate retables or altarpieces, panelling and baldachins, often obscuring the church's architectural lines. Avignon became the major centre once more, with local artists such as the Mignards and Parrocels producing religious pictures and **Jacques Bernus** of Mazan carving for churches throughout the region.

In the Gard, there was a great drive to rebuild churches damaged during the Wars of Religion (Église St-Gilles). An entirely novel element was the building of town houses by the old and new moneyed nobility, the magistracy and others: a few remain in Avignon and Nîmes but the finest line the streets of Aix. These well-proportioned, dignified stone houses are distinguished by doorways coroneted with ironwork balconies often supported by robust caryatids or muscular atlantes. The artists of these works were sculptor-decorators **Jean-Claude Rambot** (1621-94) and **Bernard Toro** (1672-1731), both contemporaries of Pierre Puget. **Pierre Puget** (1620-94), an artist and architect from Marseille, became one of the great Baroque sculptors of 17C France.

The 18C saw the continuation of the towns' and cities' embellishment programme, which had begun the previous century: in Nîmes the engineer J-P Mareschal designed the splendid Jardin de la Fontaine.

Among the painters of that period, two stand out: **Carle Van Loo**, who was susceptible to Provençal charm, and **Joseph Vernet**, the painter of seascapes and ports.

19TH CENTURY

The art of architects and civil engineers was mostly practised in the Marseille region where **Espérandieu** erected the new Cathédrale La Major and Basilique de Notre-Dame-de-la-Garde, in the fashionable late-19C Romano-Byzantine style, and Palais Longchamp. Roquefavour Aqueduct is a superb civil engineering project that brings to mind the ancient Roman Pont du Gard. The Rove Underground Canal also represents an incredible feat.

Around this time painting benefited from an explosion of talented artists all fascinated by the luminous beauty of the Provençal countryside. The first to study the landscapes of Provence were **J-A Constantin** (1756-1844) and **François-Marius Granet** (1775-1849). The Landscape School inspired by **Émile Loubon** (1809-1863) also explored the notion of light with painters such as **Paul Guigou** (1834-1871), a forerunner of Impressionism, and the Marseille artist **Adolphe Monticelli** (1824-1886). This School ceased to exist around 1870 and was replaced by the painters known as «Naturalists»: **Achille Emperaire** (1829-1898) and **Joseph Ravaisou** (1865-1925) in Aix; **Clément Brun** (1868-1920) and **Paul Sain** (1853-1908) in Avignon; **Joseph Garibaldi** (1863-1941), **J-B Olive** (1848-1936) and **Alphonse Moutte** (1840-1913 - strong realistic scenes of local fishermen) in Marseille, the first artists to paint L'Estaque. Finally **Félix Ziem**, a resident of Martigues, one of the first to paint in the hills beyond the fishing village of L'Estaque, chose to use colour in its own right and not to create light effects. Ziem's concerns were echoed by the great painters of the late 19C and the early 20C.

VAN GOGH

Vincent Van Gogh (1853-90), son of a Dutch Calvinist pastor, admirer of Millet and Rubens and influenced by the art of Japanese prints, was attracted to Impressionism, and brought his turbulent, strong personality to his work.

In February 1888, he decided to settle in Arles, seeking a "different light." The two years he spent discovering Provence (Arles, Stes-Maries-de-la-Mer, Les Baux, St-Rémy) correspond to an intense period of creativity: he sought to express with colours and dramatic forms the "terrible human passions" that tormented him and caused him to suffer. He painted intensely, with genius, the light and forms of Provence: landscapes (*View of Arles with Irises, The Alyscamps, Starry Night, Crau Plain, Boats along the Beach*) and portraits (*Portrait of an Old Provençal Peasant, L'Arlésienne, Madame Ginoux*). His quarrel with **Paul Gauguin**, who had joined him in October 1888, plunged him into despair and madness; he was cared for at St-Paul-de-Mausole near St-Rémy-de-Provence and continued to paint (*Wheatfields, Cypresses, Olive Trees, Self-Portrait*). He returned to Paris in May 1890 and committed suicide two months later. Precursor of the Fauves and Expressionism, Van Gogh left an enormous legacy of work, of which his Provençal period is perhaps the most intense and fascinating.

CÉZANNE

Cézanne (1839-1904), unlike Van Gogh, was from Provence. Son of an Aix-en-Provence banker, he left his studies to take up painting. Introduced to the Parisian Impressionists by his friend, the writer Émile Zola, he began as a Romantic studying Delacroix, whose theory of colours he adopted. Having assimilated the Impressionist techniques, he rapidly went beyond them as early as 1879 and began his constructive period; he experimented with large dabs of luminous colour and simple geometric forms. "Everything in nature is modelled after the sphere, the cone and the cylinder," he wrote. He painted still lifes and portraits where colour and form determined the painting's organization.

After 1890, he hardly ever left his native Provence and devoted all his energy to capturing the Montagne Ste-Victoire on canvas, painting it some 60 times without ever being entirely satisfied with his work. His research continued until his death and opened the way to Cubism.

20TH CENTURY

Clearly, for Cézanne, it was impossible for a painting to convey the full brilliance and subtleties of light; only colour could presume to fulfil that role. These views gave rise to a movement that influenced many late 19C and early 20C painters. Provence was now attracting many artists who settled in L'Estaque, following in the footsteps of Cézanne. First **Paul Signac** (1863-1935), who applied his Pointillist technique to Provençal colour (instead of the fine brushwork used in the north of France, here he opted for square, oblong touches, more suitable for catching the vivid sunlight). The Fauves found inspiration in this radiant Provençal setting. Their works played with colours and lines ignoring perspective and chiaroscuro. Matisse, Dufy and Derain all spent time in Provence, together with native artists from the region like **Charles Camoin** (1879-1965), **Auguste Chabaud** (1882-1955), **Alfred Lombard** (1884-1973), and **L-M Verdihan** (1875-1928). Around 1906-08, **L'Estaque** (Cézanne had painted views of it) became the privileged meeting place of those artists who were later dubbed the Cubists. **Georges Braque** and **Pablo Picasso** worked together closely in Sorgues; the product of this joint venture was revolutionary, pictorial compositions touching on abstraction. After the Second World War, a new generation was experimenting with novel theories, such as Expressionism and Surrealism. **André Masson**, father of spontaneous drawing (a technique that enabled him to break from figurative conventions), settled in the Aix region until his death in 1987 and drew a series entitled *Provençal Landscapes*. Other prestigious names were also linked to Provence: **Max Ernst, Nicolas de Staël, Yves Brayer,** and **Vasarely**, who has opened a foundation at Gordes to continue his research into optics and kinetics.

CONTEMPORARY TIMES

Today, many of the region's young artists have studied at the École d'Art de Lumigny in Marseille. Two contemporary art museums showcase recent, and often audacious works: the MAC in Marseille and the Carré d'Art in Nîmes.

Decorative Arts

PROVENÇAL FURNITURE

It was during the 15C that Provençal furniture, until that time considered to be of unsophisticated design, began to follow the lead set by Italy, with the introduction of delicate sculptures, finished off with a Spanish-influenced style of heavily-chiselled wrought iron and copper key-holes. The 18C and beginning of the 19C heralded the *grande époque* of Provençal furniture, with the main production centres scattered between the lower valley of the Rhône and the mid-section of the Durance. The period from the Second Empire onwards was characterised among other things by excessive sculptured decoration.

In lower Provence, the Louis XV style reigned absolute from the middle of the 18C onward. Artisans preferred working with walnut, resorting if necessary to the use of box, olive, cherry, or pear wood. The pieces of furniture, with their irregular curves, pronounced bends, and curled legs and bases are generally of quite slender proportion, with an abundance of storage units. They include: the **paneiro** or openwork bread bin (see photograph); **manjadou** or meat safe decorated with ornamental spindles; **estagnié** or pewter cupboard; **verriau**, for glasses; and **saliero** or salt container. The following original items also stand out: the elegant **buffet à glissants,** or sliding sideboard; **radassié**, a large straw-seated sofa adorned with esparto leaves or sprigs of rye, such as those of the *à la capucine* armchairs, distinguishable by their trapezoid seat, setback arm rests, and concave-strutted back. Ornamentation is based on abundant and deep mouldings and sculpted motifs with overriding importance given to vegetation in different forms: acanthus leaves, flower baskets, branches of olive or oak; and the addition of small, curved candle-rings to the angles and to the crest tops. The best-known decorative style is from Arles, a production centre of particular character, where the *paneiro* or bread container, the first mobile cabinets, and *à la capucine* chairs originated.

In upper Provence, sombre lines and decor triumph over furniture of a more rustic style, remaining steadfast throughout the period of influence of the Renaissance and Louis XIII styles. Craftsmen in this part of the region preferred working with mulberry, pine or limewood. Furniture not seen in lower Provence, such as the *vaisselier* or dresser, and the *banc à dossier* or backed bench, are a testimony to the influence of the neighbouring Dauphiné. Simple wall cavities also tend to replace the use of small storage units in evidence in lower Provence.

THE SUPREMACY OF CLAY

The abundance of excellent quality clay in Provence has given rise to a number of large ceramic centres in the region: the mottle decoration of **Apt** and **Avignon** faience; Allemagne-en-Provence and Moustiers (see *The Green Guide French Alps); * La Tour-d'Aigues*;* and above all, **Marseille**, where clay has been worked into vessels both useful and decorative since ancient times. Under Louis XIV, the wars that emptied the kingdom's coffers resulted in the banning of the use of gold and silver dishes, thus providing an opportunity for the faience industry. In 1679, the Fabre pottery works at **St-Jean-du-Désert** between Aubagne and Marseille transformed its production to that of faience under the influences of **Joseph Clérissy**, who was from an Aubagne family that had moved to Moustiers. As in Nevers and Rouen, its blue "Chinese-style" cameos drew inspiration from the first pieces of porcelain imported into France from China. Although St-Jean-du-Désert saw its importance decline after the Great Plague, other earthenware works started to spring up, many of which employed the sharp fire technique. **Fauchier** created *fleurs jetées*, designs of flowers painted in a seemingly haphazard fashion, and used a distinctive yellow enamel background decoration. The works of **Leroy** are recognizable for their fantastic creatures and human figures set on a background of star-like flowers.

The second half of the 18C represented the zenith of Marseille earthenware, mainly as a result of the activities and talent of **Pierrette Candellot**, a colourful personality originally from Lyon, and the wife of the Marseille pottery manufacturer **Claude Perrin**. Following his death in 1748, his widow, known as **La Veuve Perrin**, guided the family business towards the mild firing technique, consequently obtaining pieces of exceptional quality. She perfected the ornamental Marseille style, introduced fish motifs and sea landscapes, and developed an unusual sea-green background. She also drew inspiration from contemporary trends in jewelry design.

After Veuve Perrin, the last great Marseille earthenware producers were **Joseph-Gaspard Robert** and **Antoine Bonnefoy**, both of whom were able to give to faience an ornamental refinement that until that time had been the prerogative of porcelain. Bonnefoy is famous for his trademark *bouillabaisse* motifs and pastoral scenes reminiscent of the paintings of Boucher. Robert created floral motifs set off by black butterflies and a gold border; his dishes bordered in red, white, and blue were the last great series to come out of Marseilles. Ultimately, a combination of the competition from porcelain makers, the Revolution, and the blockade by the English naval fleet sounded the death knell for Marseille's faience industry.

Faience ware from St-Jean-du-Désert (Musée Cantini, Marseille)

THE CHRISTMAS CRÈCHE

Christmas cribs (*crèche* means crib) have a long tradition in Provence although it was not until the late 18C that they became common and developed a typically local character. A few 18C groups, often highly original and beautifully modelled, may still be seen at a collector's or in a church, but most are now in museums (Musée du Vieil Aix, Musée du Vieux Marseille, Museon Arlaten in Arles, and the Musée National des Arts et Traditions Populaires in Paris).

Church cribs

Christmas was not an important festival in the early church. Nativity scenes did not form part of the medieval celebrations except for rare low reliefs of the Adoration of the Shepherds or the Kings as in the St-Maximin crypt.

In 1545 the Council of Trent sought to advance the Counter-Reformation through the encouragement of popular piety. The practice of setting up a crib in church arrived in Provence from Italy in the 17C. There is a particularly beautiful crèche from this period in the church of St-Maximin; the carved figures, about 50cm/20in high, are of gilded wood. In the 18C, bejewelled wax figures were introduced with glass eyes and wigs.

Only the head, arms, and legs were carved and attached to a richly-dressed articulated frame. In the 19C, new materials were introduced, including printed or painted cardboard cut-outs with gaily coloured clothing, figures made from spun glass, cork, clay, and even bread dough. By then, all the Provençal churches had adopted the Christmas crib of dressed figures. This kind of Christmas crib can still be seen in the present.

Live cribs

At midnight mass in many churches today – Séguret, Allauch, Isle-sur-la-Sorgue, and Marseille – a Nativity play is performed. In Gémenos, children in costume place an infant Jesus in a straw-filled manger. In Les Baux, a little cart, decorated with greenery and bearing a new-born lamb, is drawn into church by a ram and accompanied by shepherds. The procession is headed by angels and fife and tabor players, while the congregation sings old Provençal carols. The lamb is offered to the church and the cart stands on one side in the aisle throughout the year.

Talking cribs

The 18C passion for marionettes was adapted to produce talking cribs in which mechanical figures enacted the Nativity to a commentary and carols.

Provençal Christmas crib

People came from far and wide to see and hear the talking cribs of Marseille and Aix. Characters were added to the already numerous cast and, as imagination ran wild, historical accuracy and relevance vanished: reindeer, giraffes and hippopotamuses joined the other animals in the stable, and the pope was made to arrive in a carriage to bless the Holy Family. It must have been a fantastic sight to see a Napoleon puppet, accompanied by his soldiers and a man-of-war firing salvoes, arriving at the manger! Another new idea came to those presenting a crib close to Marseille station: the Three Kings travelled to the scene in a steam train! This endearing tradition has today been replaced by the displays in department store windows.

Santon cribs

The *santon* cribs are the most typical of Provence. They first appeared in 1789 at the time of the Revolution when the churches were closed and Nativity scenes had lost their stage. **Jean-Louis Lagnel**, a church statue-maker from Marseille, had the idea of making small figures that families could buy at little cost. Labelled *santouns* (little saints) in Provençal, and *santoni* in Italian, abbreviated from *santibelli* (beautiful saints), these figurines had an immediate and wide appeal. They were modelled in clay, fired, and naïvely painted in bright colours. Limited at first to biblical personages, they were soon joined by men and women from all walks of life, dressed, of course, in the local costume; the Holy Family, the Shepherds and their sheep, the Three Kings at times beside the knife grinder, the fife and tabor player, the smith, the blind man and his guide, the fishwife, the wetnurse, the milkmaid, the huntsman, fisherman, and even the mayor!

So great was the figurines' success, as virtually every family began to build up a collection, that a Santons Fair was inaugurated in Marseille, which is still held on the Canebière from the last Sunday in November to Epiphany. Aubagne was also famous for its *santons*. *Santon* makers established workshops in towns throughout Provence, whereas in the country men and women made figures in the long winter evenings. The craft reached its peak in the 1820-30s, which is why so many of the characters, now mass-produced, appear in the dress of that period.

The *santons* of Provence are now known the world over and many families like to add to their collection of characters each year and set up displays during the Christmas holidays.

Language and Literature

Provence is an ancient civilized land, Greco-Latin then Occitanian, which has never stopped influencing poets and writers alike, who expressed themselves in Provençal (a group of South Occitan dialects).

LANGUAGE OF THE TROUBADOURS

The Romance languages evolved out of Vulgar Latin spoken at the end of the Roman Empire. These were Italian, Romanian, Catalan, Spanish, Portuguese, and in France, the Oïl language (*langue d'oïl*) in the north and the Oc language (*langue d'oc*) in the south. "Oïl" and "Oc" were the words used for "yes" in the north and south, respectively. This distinction, which was formed as early as the Merovingian period, was advanced enough in the 10C and 11C for the two languages to enter into literature separately. Occitan, which appeared in Latin texts for the first time in the 11C, owed its place and influence to the success of 12C courtly literature. The art of the **troubadours**, which developed in the feudal courts of Périgord, Limousin and Gascony, was not confined purely to Provence but encompassed all of Occitania, from Bordeaux to Nice.

These troubadours (*trobar* means to find) were inventors of musical airs, both melodies and words in the Oc language, and they created a linguistic community independent of political divisions: Jaufré Rudel from Blaye, Bernard de Ventadour from Limousin, Peire Vidal from Toulouse, and from Provence, Raimbaut of Orange, the countess of Die, Raimbaut of Vaqueiras and Folquet of Marseille.

Bibliotheque Nationals de France, Paris

*Folquet of Marseille
(13C manuscript)*

Under the Provençal or Limousin name, Occitanian was appreciated by noble foreigners and most of the European courts. The essential inspirational force of the troubadours was love, not passionate love but courtly love where the patience and discretion of the poet-lover finally won over the lady who accepted the homage of her vassal. Using sound, word pattern, and stanza-structure these poems told of the troubadours' anxieties and hopes.

PROSE AND POETRY

The courtly poem declined in the 13C, its themes having been exhausted. It was replaced by satirical poems known as *sirventès*, and prose that told of the lives of the troubadours (the famous *vidas*). This period is marked by the European influence of French, by the setting up of the Inquisition, and by the expansion of the Capetian monarchy.

Occitan, nevertheless, retained its importance. It is said that **Dante** (1265-1321) almost used it to write his *Divina Commedia* and that it was the language spoken at the pontifical court of Avignon. With Latin, Occitan was in the Middle Ages the only written administrative language. And yet beginning in the 14C regional differences began appearing in written texts and French was gradually adopted in its place.

Occitanian literature became popular in Italy where it was revived thanks to Dante and returned in force into the Rhône valley in the form of a sonnet with **Petrarch** (1304-74). Exiled in Avignon, Petrarch fell passionately in love with the lovely Laura de Noves in 1327. His *Canzonière* (1348) were a group of sonnets where he expressed his unrequited love for her. The poet, who had retired to Fontaine-de-Vaucluse, also wrote descriptions of Provençal life in his letters; he spoke of shepherds, the Sorgue fishermen, and his climb to Mont Ventoux.

The fatal blow fell upon the Occitan language in 1539, with the adoption of the Edict of Villers-Cotterêts, which decreed that for all administrative purposes the French language – the dialect spoken in the Île de France, and thus Paris – should be used. In spite of that, Occitan survived until the 19C in the theatre, poetry, short stories and legends, chronicles, and didactic and erudite works (dictionaries and anthologies).

One of the regional popular writers of the 16C was **Bellaud de la Bellaudière**. Born in Grasse in 1534, he lived a very active life as a soldier; he was opposed to the Huguenots. When he was in prison, he wrote 160 sonnets, his *Œuvres et Rimes*. His poetry – inspired by Marot, Rabelais, and Petrarch – was essentially personal, owing to its familiar realism. His work renewed the Occitan language and he inspired and was joined by Claude Bruey, Raynier from Briançon and François de Bègue.

In the 17C, when the moralist Vauvenargues was born in Aix, and Madame de Sévigné resided at Grignan, **Nicolas Saboly** was composing Provençal **Noëls**, charming, simple works of popular poetry. These happy yet pious canticles, touching and devout, depicted the entire world running in the night towards the newly-born baby Jesus. In Saboly's lifetime, church services were still held in Occitan in rural villages as well as in the cities. When French dramatist **Jean Racine** resided in Uzès in 1661 he had a great deal of difficulty making himself understood. Until the Revolution, Occitan was the language spoken daily; only a small elite spoke French, and even then they were bilingual. And yet, the use of Occitan declined steadily, breaking up into different local dialects.

THE FÉLIBRIGE

In the late 18C, Occitan, weakened by the centralised state, was reborn through literature. In 1795, Abbot Favre made history with his *Siège de Caderousse* (Caderousse's Seat), a satirical poem written in dialect, amusing because of its Rabelais-like truculence. In the 1840s Occitan experienced an explosion: **Joseph Roumanille** (1818-91), a teacher in Avignon and the author of a work *Li Margarideto* (1847), awakened in the young **Frédéric Mistral** (1830-1914) a passion for Provence, its culture, history, and Oc language. As early as 1851, Mistral began writing *Mirèio*. In 1852 the first congress of future *Félibres* was held in Arles. On 21 May 1854, at the castle of Fort-Ségugne, seven young poets writing in Provençal (Roumanille, Mistral, Aubanel, Mathieu, Tavan, Giéra, and Brunet), founded the Félibrige. *Félibre* was a word taken from an old song meaning doctor. Félibrige was an association whose goals were to restore the Provençal language and to codify its spelling. It published a periodical *Armana Provençau*, which spread its ideas.

In 1859 Mistral published *Mirèio*, an epic poem of 12 cantos that brought him immense success. Lamartine praised his work and Charles Gounod made it into an opera in 1864. Mistral's literary works included: *Calendau* (1867), *Lis Isclo d'Or* (1875), *Nerto* (1884), *La Reino Jano* (1890),

The Song of the Rhône (1896), and *Lis Ouli-vado* (1912). In 1904 he was awarded the Nobel Prize for Literature. Mistral was also a fine philologist who patiently collected the scattered elements of the Oc language and recorded their spelling in a monumental dictionary *Lou Trésor du Félibrige*, published in 1878-86. It still serves as a reference book. The Félibrige brought together Occitanian poets and novelists as different as Alphonse Daudet, Paul Arène, Félix Gras, Baptiste Bonnet, Joseph d'Arbaud, Charles Rieu, Dom Xavier de Fourvière, Jean-Henri Fabre, Folco de Baroncelli-Javon, and Charles Maurras (political theorist). During the same period, renowned writers of French included: Jean Alcard (a member of the Academy, who wrote *Maurin of the Moors*); Émile Zola, who went to secondary school in Aix and who in his Rougon-Macquart series described the evolution of a family from the south; and Edmond Rostand, born in Marseille, who wrote the unforgettable *Aiglon*.

THE PRESENT

Although Provence is always present in their works, the contemporary writers have gone beyond the regional level and have attained the ranks of the top French writers: Jean Giono from Manosque *(see Le Guide Vert)*; Marcel Pagnol *(Jean de Florette, Manon des Sources)* from Aubagne; René Barjavel from Nyons; René Char (one of France's greatest poets) from Isle-sur-la-Sorgue; and Marie Mauron, to name but a few.

Among the English and American writers who settled in Provence are Lawrence Durrell, Graham Greene, F. Scott Fitzgerald, and H.G. Wells.

Provençal as a spoken language regressed while as a language of culture – successor to the troubadours and Félibres – it progressed. Admittedly the local dialects remain but they are most often ignored by the young and are more prevalent in rural than in urban areas. At the same time, the centralising and unifying role of the state has enhanced the language: The Oc language is recognised in official teaching programmes.

Continuing with the work of the Félibrige society, the goal of the *Institut des Études Occitanes* (Institute of Occitanian Studies), while still promoting the use of authentic everyday speech, is to seek the unity of a common language, and to restore to Occitania the status it enjoyed in Middle Ages when it extended beyond political limits from the Atlantic to the Mediterranean.

Legends and Tales

The legends and tales of Provence are a colourful account of its history and geography. These stories depict regional people, customs, institutions, lifestyles, beliefs, monuments, and sites. The Greco-Roman heritage shows in Provençal legends where the wondrous accompanies daily life in its humblest activities, where the gods are omnipresent and miracles occur at their behest.

ANCIENT MYTHS

For the ancient Greeks, the western Mediterranean was awe-inspiring, yet at the same time, frightening. Each evening the sun set with Apollo's chariot. **Heracles**, Zeus' son, had been to this land and had married Galathea from Gaul. Endowed with incredible strength, he had opened the passages through the Alps. To protect his son's passage through Provence, Zeus showered his enemies with stones and boulders, which became a desert, the Crau. The attraction of this western Mediterranean land inspired the Phocaeans later to found a colony here. The legend of **Protis** and **Gyptis** illustrates this episode (☙ *see MARSEILLE*). The Marseille navigator, **Pytheas**, is said to have sailed in the 4C BC, between the columns of Heracles (Straits of Gibraltar), across the waters to Cornwall and on to Iceland.

LEGENDS OF THE SAINTS

Christianity, too, brought its collection of stories. A thousand-year-old tradition ascribes the conversion of Provence in the 1C to the miraculous landing of a boat from Judaea bearing **Lazarus**, **Mary Magdalene**, **Martha**, and their saintly companions, disciples of Christ. With **St Victor** and **Cassien** they formed a sort of mystic Provençal state and are credited with many wondrous acts. Among the most dramatic is Martha's defeat of the monster of Tarasque (☙ *see TARASCON*).

Local saints were not in short supply either. **Eleazarius de Sabran** was so precocious that every Friday he refused milk from his wet nurse for mortification. **St Mitre**, the beheaded martyr, as the legend goes, picked up his head, kissed it, and bore it to the cathedral where he placed it on the altar. Then there is **St Caesarius**, who captured a puff of sea air in his glove and carried it back to Nyons country, locked in an amphitheatre of impenetrable mountains. From that moment, a light wind began to blow over the region; the local people took heart and started to cultivate the land. The prosperity of Nyons country dates from this period, and the advantages of the local climate have made it a perfect place for growing olives.

TROUBADOUR TRADITION

The legends of Provence were inspired by epic poetry (chansons de geste) and courtly prose.

Pierre of Provence, a valiant knight and talented troubadour, lived at his father's court in the Château de Cavaillon. Seeing her portrait, the knight fell in love with Princess Maguelone, daughter of the king of Naples, and set out to find her. Received at the Neapolitan court, he was victorious in a series of tournaments where he wore Maguelone's colours. But one day Pierre was kidnapped by Barbary pirates and taken to Tunis where he was imprisoned for seven years. Having served his term, he was finally able to set sail for Provence, but not far from Aigues-Mortes, his boat sank. Mortally wounded, he was brought to the Aigues-Mortes hospital, headed by Princess Maguelone herself, who had sought through charitable works a way to forget her unhappy love. The lovers met and recognised each other. Pierre was cured.

Not all endings were so happy. One day **Guillem de Cabestaing**, a son of a noble and well-known troubadour, came to sing at the court of the lord of Castel-Roussillon, an ugly, vulgar old man who had a lovely young wife named Sérémonde. Love kindled quickly between these two young people. The lord, having discovered this, killed the handsome Guillem in an ambush, ripped out his heart, and served it to his wife for dinner. Sérémonde responded with: "My lord, you have served me such delicious fare that nothing could ever equal it and so I swear before Christ, in order to keep the taste fresh for all time, I will never eat again." She then threw herself from the top of a cliff in Roussillon. As her blood spread it coloured the soil, bringing about the origin of ochre.

SORCERY

Rare were the villages that did not have at least one masc or masco. These people had the power to bewitch humans and animals. If a baby stopped suckling, if horses stopped for no apparent reason, if hunting dogs lost their scent, they had been emmasqués. Méthamis, in Vaucluse, is still – even today – a sanctuary of Provençal sorcery. To fight against evil spells a démascaire was called in. This person was often a shepherd, because the shepherd was a holder of supernatural powers but was said to be a sworn enemy of sorcerers, someone who held the secrets of nature. The demascaire was good and broke the evil spell. He was also a bone-setter and cured sickness with plants. Other ways of warding off evil spells were possible, such as wearing a piece of clothing inside out or back to front, throwing salt into the hearth, or reciting different invocations while crossing oneself at the same time. To protect houses from the evil eye the custom was to cement a vitrified pebble into the wall. On the sheep-pen door people nailed a magic thistle. Some places are totally magical and mysterious, such as Garagaï at Vauvenargues, a bottomless chasm where strange things happen. Between Arles and Montmajour is the fairies' hole, peopled with supernatural beings.

CHILD HEROES

A great number of Provençal legends recount the memorable exploits of children and adolescents gifted with a force and extraordinary ingenuity. They generally appeal to Almighty God, the intervention of the saints, or magic. This is the case of little **Bénézet** from Avignon, who built the bridge at Avignon. **Jean de l'Ours**, so-called because he had been brought up with a bear, was another. At the age of 12 he conceived the idea of journeying round France. He forged himself a stout iron staff and thus armed killed the horrible dragons that kept a young princess in an enchanted castle. **Guihen l'Orphelin** (the orphan), thanks to his mysterious white hen, which he would stroke while murmuring a special incantation, could become invisible. He was able to free a king and the king's daughter, both whom had been imprisoned by a wicked baron. To thank him the king promised his daughter to Guihen and they lived, of course, happily ever after.

THE REGION TODAY

Economy

Of all the regions of France, Provence is perhaps the place where the local economy has undergone the greatest changes in the past 50 years. These changes have come about due to the transformation of the agricultural sector, increased industrialization—especially along the coast—adaptation to large-scale tourism, and runaway urbanization.

FACETS OF AGRICULTURE

Rural life in the past depended on three crops – wheat, vineyards, and olives . These, with sheep raising and a variety of other products gathered locally (herbs, almonds), ensured the existence of a mass of small farmers very attached to their native soil. This traditional polyculture has almost disappeared and been replaced by modern speculative agriculture, making the most out of Provence's natural resources, thus turning it into the garden of France.

Early Produce

The alluvial soil of the Rhône plain, the high mean temperature, and irrigation schemes have favoured the development of early market gardening and fruit growing, producing several crops a year in the Comtat Venaissin and Petite Crau. The whole region is now divided up into little parcels of land protected from the mistral by screens of cypress and reeds.

Strawberries, tomatoes, and melons from Carpentras, asparagus, new potatoes and melons from Cavaillon, cabbage from Rognonas, asparagus from Lauris, cherries from Remoulins, and peaches, pears, and apricots from the Rhône valley are all sold in the markets of Paris, northern and eastern France, as well as abroad.

Early produce, picked in the morning, is either sold to a private packer or sent to a cooperative where it is sorted, graded, packed, and conditioned. Cooperatives have been established at St-Rémy, Châteaurenard, Barbentane, Cabannes, and St-Andiol, west of Cavaillon, among others.

From the main railway heads (Châteaurenard, Cavaillon, Carpentras, Barbentane, Avignon), high speed trains transport the early produce up the Rhône valley to Paris and other large cities.

Cereals and Vineyards

The area between Arles and Tarascon, once the main centre for growing wheat in Provence, is now producing maize, rape and rice as well. The windmills so dear to Alphonse Daudet have been replaced by modern milling machinery in the towns.

Vineyards occupy some 110 000ha/424sq mi and in the plains produce large quantities of table wine (*vin ordinaire*). On the hillside, where the vineyards are cultivated with more care, a more delicate wine is produced carrying the general name **Côtes du Rhône**. The Côtes du Rhône's most celebrated vintage is Châteauneuf-du-Pape). It has an estimated 15 000ha/37 050 acres of vineyards that produce high quality wine.

Lavender and Lavandin

The delicate scent of lavender is characteristic of Provence. This plant is well suited to the climate and calcareous soils of Provence and Haute-Provence (*see The Green Guide French Alps*). *Lavandin*, a more productive but less fragrant hybrid, is cultivated on the lower slopes (400-700m/1 312-2 297ft) and in the valleys.

Pastis in Provence

Inextricably linked to the game of *boules*, *pastis* is usually drunk around apéritif time, on the outdoor terraces of cafés. Pastis made its first appearance in Marseille in 1922, after aniseed beverages were rehabilitated (they had been banned since 1915 because they were likened to absinth). Proper *pastis* is produced by leaving various aromatic plants (anise, star anise, liquorice, etc) to macerate in alcohol. By the late 1930s, a host of brands had already made a name for themselves in France: Capon, Pernod, Cap Anis, Pasty-Anis, Bisanis, Stop-Anis, but especially Ricard. During the World War II, *pastis* was sold in small packets on the black market: mixing the concentrated powder with half a litre of 90° proof alcohol and the same quantity of water would produce a litre of pastis. Demand for bottled pastis soared once again in the 1960s with such brands as Casanis and Poncié, or Janot, which is still made in Aubagne today. There are some chic new brands on the market as well, made by small companies using special combinations of the finest fresh aromatic plants.

Lavendar fields

Jacass/MICHELIN

Today, about 8 400ha/20 748 acres of lavender are cultivated as well as 2 350ha/5 805 acres of *lavandin*. The harvest takes place from July to September according to the region. Most of the picking is now done by machinery but the inaccessible or closely-planted older fields are still picked by hand. After drying for two to three days, the picked lavender is sent to a distillery equipped with the classic still. One hundred kilos of lavender blossom are needed to produce one litre of essence (the same amount of *lavandin* flowers yields 10 litres).

Lavender essence is reserved for the perfume and cosmetic industries whereas the hybrid lavandin are for perfumed laundry soap and cleaning products. The lavender flower can also be dried and placed in scent bags.

Superb lavender fields can be spotted on the Vaucluse plateau and in the Drôme and Gard *départements*, north of Nîmes.

Almonds and Olives

Almond trees, which grow all round the shores of the Mediterranean, were first imported into France from Asia in 1548. The development of later-blossoming varieties has led to increased cultivation. The most famous of the local almond confectionery are *calissons* from Aix and Salon, lozenge-shaped sweetmeats coated in white sugar icing.

The silver-green of the olive groves is a common sight in the country round Salon, Nyons, and the mountains' southern slopes.

Sometimes, in the olive plantations, old trees have been cut low to the ground and four suckers can be seen growing in a crown-like shape; these are kept as they create handsome new trees. The black olives of Nyons, preserved in brine, are a delicacy.

At the Pont du Gard, a maginificent 1100 year old olive tree holds sentry as you apporach the Roman bridge. It still bears fruit.

Truffles

The truffle is an edible, subterranean fungus that develops from the mycelium, a network of filaments invisible to the naked eye. They live symbiotically with the root of the downy oak, known in Provence as the white oak. The truffle is harvested in the winter when it is ripe and fragrant.

These small, stunted downy oaks are planted in rows in fields called *truffières*. They are found mainly in south Tricastin, Comtat Venaissin, the Claparèdes plateau, and in the Luberon. A superficial breaking-up of the soil and a specified

Street sign in Aix-en-Provence

J. Malburet/MICHELIN

pruning favours the truffle crop, which is harvested from November to April and marketed mostly in Apt, Carpentras, Richerenches, Uzès, and Valréas, where several tons of this "black diamond" pass through annually.

Lime Trees and Herbs

Although found in most parts of France, the lime tree (*tilleul*) is cultivated mainly in Provence between Buis-les-Baronnies and Carpentras. At the end of the 19C, the lime tree grew alongside most French roads, whereas today it is planted in orchards and pruned. The flower is picked in June, depending on the blooming, dried in a shaded, airy dry room, then sold in bags or by the ounce for tea. Mixtures of aromatic plants called *herbes de Provence* have doubled in popularity in recent years. Certain varieties are cultivated traditionally: basil and marjoram are cultivated around St-Rémy-de-Provence, tarragon on the Vaucluse plateau, whereas other varieties such as thyme, rosemary, and savory are still gathered from the hillsides where they grow wild, and supply a large proportion of the herbs gathered.

Stock raising

Sheep raising is an essential resource of all Mediterranean rural economies. Wool, no longer profitable, was abandoned and the sheep are now reared for meat. The Merino variety from Arles is predominant in the Bouches-du-Rhône *département*, however, the area allocated to it diminishes daily. The sheep graze on the meagre *coussouls* from the Plaine de la Crau from 15 October to 15 June. They are then moved up to Alpine pastures. Once a picturesque procession through villages and rugged countryside, the transfer of the sheep is now done in trucks. In the *garrigues*, flocks of sheep graze on the sparse vegetation that they find when roaming these vast territories. They spend the summer in Larzac, or in the Lozère mountains.

The Camargue is famous for the black bulls and white horses raised there in free-range herds called *manades*.

FISHING

Fishing is a traditional activity in the ports of Languedoc (Le Grau-du-Roi) and Provence (Port-St-Louis, Martigues, Carry-le-Rouet, Marseille, Cassis). And yet, fishing has come to occupy a minimal position and frequently suffers from the effects of water pollution. Nevertheless, fishermen in these areas annually catch several thousand tons of sardines, anchovies, mackerel, and eel. The coming and going of these sailor-fishermen unloading their catch and drying their nets still remains one of the ports' most attractive scenes.

In Marseille, the recent port of Saumaty, located at the foot of the Estaque, can shelter as many as 180 trawlers (1 400m/4 593ft of quays) and offers all the necessary equipment for the preservation of fish.

Small fishing boats still supply the fishmongers of Marseille's Vieux Port. The hustle and bustle and the sing-song cries of the stall-holders create a lively, timeless atmosphere that seems to have come straight out of Marcel Pagnol's novels.

INDUSTRIALIZATION

Provence has benefited from a geographical location propitious to commercial exchange. In the 1930s it witnessed spectacular industrial development.

Around Étang de Berre a vast industrial complex was built: oil refineries; and chemical, aeronautic, and iron and steel (today threatened) works. Its centre was the Bassins de Fos complex, inaugurated in 1968. From Marseille to Aix, industrial zones have multiplied and offer a vast range of activities: from soap-making plants to the most modern electronics factories, including the Gardanne thermal power station.

The hydroelectric installations of the lower valleys of the Rhône and Durance have also contributed to the profound economic upheavals. Hydroelectric production combined with nuclear (Marcoule) production has allowed France to strengthen its energy potential. Moreover, the domestication of the two undisciplined rivers has resulted in the possibility of irrigating an immense agricultural area, until then hindered by drought. All these transformations have made Provence one of France's great industrial areas juggling between two types of industry:

- **traditional:** minerals (ochre, bauxite, lignite), shipbuilding, foodstuffs, soap-making (Marseille area), building materials, construction, and salt-works;

- **modern:** petroleum and its derivatives, aeronautics, electronics, nuclear (Cadarache Centre for Nuclear Studies), and chemicals.

Light industries have also developed: packaging in Valréas and Tarascon, confectionery in Aix, Apt and Nyons, fruit preserving, and garment and shoe making in Nîmes.

Ochre

The Apt-Roussillon area is one of the main mining and treatment regions in France for ochre (an earthy red or yellow and often impure iron ore essentially used as a pigment for paints or as a wash applied for its protective value). The mineral beds can at times be 15m/49ft thick. Ochre in its natural state is a mixture of argillaceous sand and iron oxide. To obtain a commercially-pure ochre product, the mineral is first washed and the impurities, which tend to be heavier, settle to the bottom. The lighter weight "flower," which is made of iron oxide and clay, is passed through the filter and into settling tanks. There, after drying, it assumes the look of ochre. It is then cut into blocks. After drying, the ochre is crushed, sifted, and at times baked in ovens to darken the pigmentation and obtain a reddish orange colour. This process is called ochre calcining. The ochre then becomes an unctuous, impalpable powder used commercially. The quality of the ochre from Vaucluse has made France one of its most important producers, with an annual production of about 3 000 metric tons.

Olive oil

Typically Provençal oil has always been olive oil. Olives are treated when they are ripe and are picked while still green if used for food preservation. The quality of the oil depends on the quality of the fruit and the treatment (number of pressings). Once picked, the olives are crushed whole with the pit, either by a millstone, hammer mill, or roller. The paste obtained is then distributed on a trolley's nylon discs. The trolley, now loaded, is placed on the sliding piston of a hydraulic press that exerts pressure on the paste, resulting in a mixture of oil and water that is collected in tanks and then pumped into centrifugal machines where the oil and water will be separated. The oil that comes out of the machine is a virgin oil obtained by a first cold water pressing. The residual pulp (*grignon*) can be pressed again, yielding more oil, though of a lesser grade and taste.

In the past the olive paste was spread by hand onto coconut mats (*scourtins*) which were stacked under the press. For a long time the presses were worked by hand and a horse turned the millstone. The residual pulp was remashed with lukewarm water: a mixture of refined and virgin oil was obtained, classed as second quality and called second pressing. Today, as in the past, the residual

pulp treated with chemical solvents in Italy produces oil used for cutting or soap-making. Before this last pressing the olive pit can be separated from the pulp: the pit is ground down into powder and is used by the baker and pastry cook; the pulp is used for compost.

Salt marshes

People in the Camargue work two large salt marshes: one is south of Aigues-Mortes and spreads over 10 000ha/24 700 acres; the other is south of Salin-de-Giraud and covers over 11 000ha/27 170 acres. Already improved by the monks in the 13C, the salt marshes (see p. 183) increased production in the mid-19C, progressed, and then decreased. The present-day global annual production is evaluated at 850 000 metric tons.

Popular Games

BOULES

This popular game is emblematic of Provence, long lazy evenings, and animated debates, and is played with balls weighted with iron. Contests are played between teams of three (*triplettes*) or four (*quadrettes*), amid attentive and enthusiastic spectators. The *pointeurs* have to throw their balls as near as possible to a smaller ball (*cochonnet*), which has been set at the end of the bowling ground; the *tireurs* have then to dislodge the balls of the opposing team by striking them with their own. The most skillful succeed in doing this and in taking the exact place of their adversary (*faire le carreau*). Over short distances play is *à la pétanque*, standing within a circle, feet together. Over longer distances, above 10m/30ft, the game is called *la longue*; the *tireurs* take a running start and throw their balls after having made three hopping steps from the throwing-point.

Among all these shirt-sleeved players the two Provençal types form a piquant contrast. The one, a native of the mountains, somewhat reserved and distant, shows his pleasure or his disappointment by a smile or a frown. The other, a descendant of the traditional Marius, enacts quite a little drama, which has been happily described: "Here, then, is the last ball; it rolls out before the player and you can watch its progress in his face; he broods over it, protects it with his gaze; gives it advice, strives to make it obedient to his voice, hurries or slows its course, encourages it with a gesture or urges it on with a heave of his shoulder, slackens it with his hand; perched on tiptoe, his arm

La pétanque

flung out, his face animated by a wealth of varying emotions, he wriggles his body in bizarre undulations; one could almost say that his soul had passed into the ball."

Play is frequently held up by noisy, heated arguments about the distances separating the various balls from the *cochonnet*. Play resumes once measurements have been taken, often with small branches or twigs broken off a nearby tree.

CARD GAMES

The unforgettable scene in the Bar de la Marine, where a group of locals take part in a game of *manille*, indulging in the colourful dialogue that typified Marcel Pagnol's work, is a telling example of the importance of card games in Provençal society. Indeed, Provence was the first place in France where playing cards appeared. Minutes drawn up by a Marseille notary public, dated 30 August 1381, prohibiting a merchant of the city from playing *nahipi* or *naïbi*, a sort of Happy Families card game, attest to the fact. In the last quarter of the 14C this card game became a favourite table recreation that, nowadays, is considered the ancestor of modern-day tarot. Following their likely origins in the imperial Chinese court, playing cards reached the Occident during the course of the 13C, either in the luggage of Venetian passengers, bankers or merchants, or via the hordes of Tartars from central Asia. Venetian artists, hitherto devoted to religious and secular canvases, eagerly succumbed to this growing trend of painting on card and parchment. Venice quickly became the main distribution centre in Europe. Marseille, with its access to both the Mediterranean and the Orient, was soon drawn to the charms of this new pastime, as was the Comtat Venaissin, with its close ties with Italy. The 15C gave rise to the game *cinq cents*, also known as the *Marseillais*. By the 17C, the popularity of card games in the city was considerable, paving the way for the appearance of the first "professional" card makers around 1631. Their numbers fluctuated according to the laws and taxes of the period. With the development of new

Marseille tarot card

xylographic and typographic processes, replacing wooden printing moulds with copper ones, card production continued to increase dramatically, reaching a rate of 180 000 packs a year by the end of the 17C. The 18C was for Marseille the epoch of **tarot**, which originated in Italy. Apart from the set manufactured by Jean Noblet in Paris during the 17C, the oldest tarot cards, said to have been made in Marseille, did in fact appear in Avignon in 1713, a city where card makers were exempt from tax. This privilege was removed in 1754, at which time Marseille established itself as the leading manufacturer. Marseille Tarot, the French version of Venetian Tarot, from which it copied 78 signs, provided the game with its definitive form, principally under the aegis of the master tarot maker **Nicolas Conver**, who produced a particularly attractive set of cards in 1760. The *Tarot de Marseille*, which was adopted by clairvoyants and soothsayers alike, was also to act as a support for another regional game in the 18C, the **Portrait de Marseille**. By this time, production in the city was relatively evenly divided between eight card manufacturers.

However, the following century, the Camoin company, with its exports world-wide, was to distance itself from its competitors by producing over a million sets a year, based on traditional expertise acquired over more than two centuries. The company finally closed its doors in 1974, though its sparkling creations can still be admired in the large collection housed in the Musée du Vieux-Marseille.

Festivals and Costumes

FESTIVALS

The people of Provence have always had a taste for celebration. In the past it was the men who were in charge of the festivities. The fairs, either secular or religious (remnants of solemn Christian celebrations mixed with pagan tendencies), were numerous. There are the classic feast days that occur throughout the year, and the larger festivals, more or less traditional, attracting thousands of people in a typically colourful Provençal atmosphere.

From April to September, Nîmes and Arles rival each other in the organisation of their famous *férias* attracting *aficionados* whether it be the *corrida*, bullfights, or simply making the bull run through the streets (the bulls wear a *cocarde*, a rosette between their horns: it must be removed by the *razeteurs*, handrake holders).

In Camargue the roundup (*ferrade*) is always an exciting time: the young calves are thrown to the ground and branded with the mark of their owner. There are also horse races between *gardians*.

The Venetian Water Festival is held at Martigues and includes a nocturnal procession of decorated boats.

And of course there are theatre, opera and dance festivals that take place in Provence. Be it Avignon, Aix-en-Provence, Orange, Vaison-la-Romaine, Carpentras, Salon-de-Provence, or Arles, each of these cities is the venue for an annual artistic festival of top quality. *See Calendar of Events.*

FARANDOLES

Most of the festivals are a wonderful opportunity to listen to the fife and *tambourin* so delightfully characteristic of the Provence region. The **farandole** is a Mediterranean dance that dates back to the Middle Ages if not to Antiquity, and was danced throughout Arles country. Young men and women, either holding each other's hands or a handkerchief, dance to a six-beat rhythm. The typically Provençal instruments played by the *tambourinaires* are the **galoubet**, a small 3-holed flute that produces a piercing sound, and the **tambourin**, a type of drum 75cm/29.5in high and 35cm/13.5in wide, beaten by a *massette* held in the right hand while the other hand holds the *galoubet*. On the drum itself, the head of which is made from calf-skin, is stretched the *chanterelle*, a thin strand of hemp or a violin string that produces a rasping sound, poetically called the song of the cicada.

CHRISTMAS IN PROVENCE

Celebrations surrounding the end of the year begin on 4 December, the feast day of St Barbe, and end at Candlemas on 2 February. The locals start by sowing their "Christmas wheat" (*lou blad de Calendo*) on 4 December. When it starts to sprout, they place it above the fireplace. Three weeks later, people use it as decoration beside the crib or as a centrepiece for the long banquet table. Preparations for the crib take place on the Sunday before Christmas, but it is only at midnight on 25 December that the infant Jesus is laid in the crib. That same night, the whole family ritually performs *Cacho-Fio*, a ceremony during which a Christmas log (*bûche de Noël*) is blessed with a fortified wine and taken round the house three times, before being burnt. The family may then be seated to begin their Christmas feast. The table, covered with three overlapping tablecloths, is laid with three chandeliers and three saucers containing the Christmas wheat, as well as 13 loaves of bread. The meal ends with the traditional 13 desserts (*mendiants:* walnuts and hazel nuts, figs, almonds and raisins; fresh fruit; black and white nougat; *pompe à huile,* a flat, brittle loaf made with olive oil*)*. Midnight Mass starts with *lou Pastrage*: the shepherd, the miller and the ancestors enter the church, where the priest lays the infant Jesus in the crib. Then the bells are rung, inviting the procession of shepherds to enter the church: they draw a small cart with a lamb, an offering made to the Infant Jesus. Mass continues with a series of Christmas songs and carols. 26 December heralds the start of the Pastorales, which retrace the steps of Joseph who was seeking refuge for the night. On 31 December, Provençal people always celebrate the New Year (*an nou*) together as a family. On the first Sunday in January, they pay tribute to the Magi and throughout the month of January, in honour of the Three Wise Men, they eat Twelfth Night cake (*galette des rois*), a crown-shaped bun decorated with crystallized fruit and containing a lucky charm (*fève*). These Christmas festivities end on 2 February with Candlemas (*Chandeleur*), the feast marking the Purification of the Virgin Mary and the presentation of Christ in the Temple 40 days after his birth. Celebrations involve a procession of green church candles. In Marseille, one also eats *navettes*, small boat-shaped biscuits that evoke the arrival of the Saintes Maries in Provence.

PROVENÇAL COSTUMES

Thanks to the commercial relationship between Marseille and the Mediterranean ports of the Levant, Provence discovered oriental fabrics. Since the end of the 17C, it has made these its own by adopting printed floral calicos and stitching and quilting techniques.

Traditional Arles costume

J.D. Sudres/Photononstop

The characteristic patterns of colourful motifs now known as "Provençal prints" are the result of a long evolution of methods and fashions.

Traditional costume in Arles is but one of the several different costumes worn all over Provence. It is one reminder of the diversity of the clothing worn by the various social milieux of days gone by: the fishwife of the Vieux Port of Marseille, with the flaps of her coif blowing about in the wind; the flowergirl; the country farmer's wife; the washerwoman; or the peasant woman with her striped underskirts, her huge apron of deep purple canvas and the *capuch* or *capelino* enveloping her head.

In their traditional festive costume (there is an excellent collection in the Museon Arlaten in Arles), women from Arles wear long colourful skirts and a black underblouse (*eso*) with tight sleeves; on top a pleated shirt is covered with a shawl either made of white lace or matching the skirt. There are different varieties of headdress, all worn on top of a high bun: *à la cravate* (white percale knotted like rabbits' ears); *à ruban* (with a lace-trimmed velvet ribbon); or *en ailes de papillon* ("butterfly wings" of lace).

The men's costume is less colourful. They wear a white shirt knotted at the collar by a thin tie or ribbon, sometimes covered by a dark-coloured vest upon which hangs a watch chain; canvas trousers are held at the waist by a wide red or black woollen belt. They wear black felt hats with a wide, tilted brim.

Food and Wine

A SUCCULENT CUISINE

Provençal cooking is characterised by garlic and food fried in oil. Garlic was praised by many poets as the "truffle of Provence," the "divine condiment," this "friend of man." Oil (preferably olive oil) replaced butter in all the Provençal dishes. An old Provençal saying goes, "A fish lives in water and dies in hot oil."

Bouillabaisse

This most famous of Provençal dishes traditionally comprises "the three fishes": the spiny red hog-fish, gurnet, and conger eel (*rascasse, grondin, congre*). To these cooks add as many others as are available: sea bass (*loup*), turbot, sole, red mullet (*rouget*), monkfish (*lotte*) and crustaceans such as crabs, spider crabs (*araignées de mer*), mussels (*moules*) and sometimes, spiny lobsters (*langoustes*) or crawfish.

These sea delights are cooked together very rapidly in a bouillon, emulsified with a small quantity of olive oil and seasoned with salt, pepper, onion, tomato, saffron, garlic, thyme, bay leaf, sage, fennel, orange peel, and maybe a glass of white wine or cognac – the magic of the results depends on the seasoning.

A *rouille* or paste of Spanish peppers, served at the same time, sharpens the sauce and gives it colour.

In a restaurant one is usually presented with a soup plate and toast with which to line it. Some people then spread some of the toast with the *rouille* paste, others mix it directly into the by now thickened bouillon soup that arrives in a tureen. To your plateful of toast, *rouille* and soup, you then add titbits of the assorted cooked fish and crustaceans. *Bouillabaisse* is a main dish. The fish must be fresh and the dish freshly prepared. It is not a stew: the actual cooking time is only some 10 minutes. This freshness doubtless adds to its reputed flavour.

Aïoli

The other great Provençal speciality is a mayonnaise made with freshly pounded, mild, Provençal garlic to which are added the usual egg yolks, olive oil, and condiments. It is served with hors-d'œuvre, asparagus and other vegetables, and also as a sauce with *bourride*, the fish soup made from angler fish (*baudroie*), sea bass (*loup*), whiting (*merlan*), etc. You may find this soup worth trying as a comparison to the more complex flavours of *bouillabaisse*.

Fish and crustaceans

Local fish dishes include red mullet (*rouget*) cooked whole, sea bass (*loup*) grilled with fennel or vine shoots, and *brandade de morue*, a thick and creamy mash of pounded cod, olive oil and milk, seasoned with crushed garlic (and truffles in its more refined version).

Fish specialities are associated with individual towns. For Marseille, in addition to *bouillabaisse*, there are clams (*clovisses*), ascidia or iodine-rich sea-squirts (*violets*), mussels (*moules*) and edible sea urchins (*oursins*), all of which you will find most easily in the small restaurants around the Vieux Port. In St-Rémy you will encounter the *catigau*, a dish of grilled or smoked Rhône eel in sauce. In the Camargue, look for *tellines* or sand crustaceans served with a pungent sauce.

A dish of bouillabaisse

C. Fleurent/TOP

Vegetables and fruit

Raw onion and tomatoes, common favourites among vegetables, are followed closely by *cardoons* (vegetable related to the artichoke, served in white sauce), fennel, peppers, courgettes, and aubergines. The art of Provençal cuisine resides in the wide variety of its cooking methods: gratin dishes baked in the oven (*tians*), soups, salads, stews, fritters, stuffed vegetables, and the like. The most popular fruit is the small green fig or Marseille fig, a juicy, sweet fruit. Peaches, apricots, strawberries, cherries, and grapes are all top quality, not to mention the deliciously fragrant melons from Cavaillon and also watermelons.

Olives

Local olives are both the small, meaty green and black varieties, which are left whole, pitted, or stuffed. There is the green olive, picked early then marinated, which comes from Nîmes, and the black olive of Nyons preserved in brine. Nyons and Carpentras are the main olive producing centres.

Cheeses

Provençal artisinal cheeses abound in the weekly markets throughout the region, as well as in specialty shops (*fromagerie*) and covered markets, such as Les Halles in Avignon. Provence is especially known for its sheep (*brebis*) and goat milk cheeses, which often come in the form of small, palm-size package: firm, semi-soft, and soft . These cheeses impart the flavours of the hillside aromatic plants upon which the sheep and goats grazed, enriching their milk. Pair one of these dairy delights with a local wine and the *terroir* of Provence's earth will be an experience in itself. A cheese-inspired salad to sample is *salade de Chèvre Chaud*: the well-dressed greens are topped with toasted slices of baguette covered in melting goat's cheese and herbs.

Specialities

Among the numerous Provençal specialities are the *pieds-paquets* (a kind of tripe) from Marseille; Arles' sausages or *saucissons,* often made from bull's meat; Gardian beef stew from the Camargue; Avignon's preserved melons; Aix's *calissons* (almond paste sweets with sugar icing); and *berlingots,* hard candies from Carpentras. Also try, in Nîmes, *brandade de morue, (*cod fish paste), small *caladon* almond cakes, and crisp Villaret biscuits; in Tarascon, tartarinades chocolates; Apt's crystallised fruits; Sault's nougat; Nyons' black olives; and Modane's special bread, which is split and stuffed with crystallised fruit.

THREE TRADITIONAL RECIPES

Tapenade

This olive, anchovy and caper-flavoured paste is eaten either as an *hors-d'œuvre* or as an accompaniment to an *aperitif* and is generally spread on slices of bread. In a mortar, place two good handfuls of stoned black olives, 2-4 anchovy fillets, 2 soup spoons of capers, 1 crushed garlic clove, a pinch of dried thyme, and ground black pepper to taste. Crush until you get a rough paste. Add a dessert

---

The Herbs of Provence

The famous *herbes de Provence*, an integral part of the Provençal countryside, form, along with garlic and olive oil, the basis of the region's cuisine. Coupled with the magic touch of the cook, these fresh ingredients will add their own personality to the frugal, yet fully flavoured and characteristic cooking of Provence. Among these note: **savory**, often used to flavour goats' or sheep's cheeses; a mix of **thyme** and **bay**, which combined with tomatoes, aubergines, courgettes, red and green peppers, and onions, is used to make the popular ratatouille, as well as being an ideal addition to grilled and roast meats; **basil**, which when crushed with garlic, olive oil, and occasionally bacon and parmesan cheese, is an important ingredient in the preparation of the famous *pistou*; **sage**, its clear, velvety leaves boiled with garlic to make the traditional *aigoboulido* broth to which nothing more than olive oil and slices of bread are added; **rosemary**, a perfect seasoning for vegetable gratins and baked fish, is also used in herbal teas to ease digestion; **wild thyme**, particularly suited to wild rabbit dishes, but which also brings out the best in vegetable soups and tomato-based recipes; **juniper**, an irreplaceable seasoning for pâtés and game; **marjoram**, ideal for stews; **tarragon**, used to spice up white sauces; **fennel**, with its aniseed taste, a superb accompaniment to fish dishes.

Thanks to each chef's personal culinary skills, these ingredients all lend character to Provençal cuisine, whose simplicity does not detract from its strongly aromatic nature, earning it a fine reputation among all dedicated gourmets.

spoon of mustard, juice from a quarter of a lemon, a dash of brandy (optional), and mix. Lastly, add enough olive oil to give the paste a nice spreading consistency.

Artichauts à la barigoule

Serves 4. The term *barigoule* is Provençal for mushroom; the name of the dish comes from the manner in which the artichokes are cut, giving them the appearance of mushrooms. Select a dozen small fresh artichokes and remove the largest leaves. Cut off the top two-thirds of the remainder and cook in an open casserole dish over a low heat with some sliced onions and carrots; add some olive oil. After 20-25min, add two glasses of dry white wine, two glasses of stock, two cloves of garlic and a few bacon cubes. Add salt and pepper, then cover once more and simmer for 50min. Serve the artichokes in the sauce.

Daube provençale

Allow two days for the preparation of this dish. Marinate half a pound of beef cut up into pieces in red wine together with an onion cut in four, a clove of garlic, a bunch of mixed herbs (*bouquet garni*), salt and pepper. The next day, fry some bacon (*lard*) in hot olive oil, using either a casserole dish (preferably made of clay with a shallow lid). Add a chopped onion and two sliced carrots as well as two crushed tomatoes. After browning these, mix in with the meat and continue to fry. Pour in a glass of red wine and bring to a boil. Add two more glasses of water and the garlic, the *bouquet garni* and the peel of an orange. Season with salt and pepper. After the boiling point is reached, turn the heat down and leave to simmer for five hours.

PROVENÇAL WINES

It was the Greeks who first cultivated vines in Provence on the hills around Massalia (present-day Marseille); the lower Rhône valley also received an early initiation in the art of viticulture.
During the Middle Ages, it was the honest, full-bodied red wines of Provence that enjoyed the greatest renown. Only when King René encouraged the production of rosé in the 15C did the red wines' domination of the area loosen. Following the spread of phylloxera, it was not until after 1918 that the vineyards of Provence regained prominence. Over the past 20 years, winemakers have made huge leaps in quality, largely due to strict selection processes and to an often highly complex blending of grapes. Provençal wines are characterised by the blending of several grape varieties in the same wine. This technique was devised in order to anticipate extreme climatic changes (such as drought, which can be aggravated by the mistral winds) since these, under certain circumstances, can have an unpredictable effect on the ripening of the grape. In the course of time, Mediterranean French stock has been mixed with Spanish and Italian transplants, with the following drawback: the wines occasionally lack consistency and there are doubts about their ability to age.

The delightful, fruity rosé wines of Provence, with their sparkling colour and recollections of sunshine and summer holidays, have become immensely popular in recent years (for more information on the wines of Provence, see the Michelin guide The Wine Regions of France). Having fully benefited from the introduction of the new vinification process, the wines are now developing greater balance, possess a delightful bouquet and are exceedingly fresh on the palate, especially when enjoyed young. Compared to rosé wines from other parts of the world, they are delightfully dry and vibrant.

The mainly dry whites, with a similarly delicate bouquet, are a perfect accompaniment for fish and seafood dishes.
The contrasting Provençal vineyards have led to a wide variety of rapidly improving reds, ranging from generous and full-bodied to supple, delicate wines.
In addition to unique wines, Provence also has its own wine-producing vocabulary: an *avis* is a wine shoot; a *tine* is a vat; and a *crotte* is a cellar.

Southern Côtes du Rhône wines

They feature many prestigious appellations such as Lirac, Tavel, Châteauneuf-du-Pape, Gigondas, Vacqueyras, Rasteau, Muscat de Beaumes-de-Venise, Côtes du Ventoux, and Côtes du Luberon, as well as the regional appellation Côtes du Rhône-Villages.
The right bank of the Rhône offers some fine wines such as **Tavel**, one of the most popular French wines sold abroad. This is a smooth, crystalline rosé, described as "sunlight trapped in a bottle" by the poet Ronsard. North of Tavel, the **coteaux de Lirac** yield delicate, full-bodied reds and rosés. Listel is a rosé wine (*vin gris du sable*) from the Aigues-Mortes region.
To the west, the well-balanced **Costières de Nîmes** reds are both elegant and powerful although they are not strictly speaking part of the Côtes-du-Rhône appellation.

On the left bank, the warm, structured **Châteauneuf-du-Pape** appellation is one of the most famous names in the Côtes-du-Rhône area. The reds, characterised by a dark robe (colour) as well as spicy, woody and peppery aromas, are definitely wines for laying down. The whites have a bouquet reminiscent of flowers.

Vacqueyras produces well-constructed reds and elegant whites. The Séguret vineyard yields heady, scented wines; those of **Cairanne,** tannic wines that will improve with age.

Gigondas is a red wine that needs to age in oak casks for a few years; in this respect it can be likened to Châteauneuf-du-Pape.

The **Côtes du Lubéron** reds are light and should be drunk young whereas the whites tend to be fresh and fine. Red wines from the **Côtes du Ventoux** are both structured and tannic, made with grapes that have ripened on the exposed slopes of Mont Ventoux; the lighter varieties should be drunk very young, barely a few months after the harvest (*vins de primeur*).

Dessert wines are represented by **Rasteau**, with its red or amber robe, and by **Muscat de Beaumes-de-Venise,** renowned for its golden robe and strong bouquet with notes of flower and fruit. They are made by adding alcohol to the must (the grape juice) during the fermentation process, which ensures that the wine is rich in sugar. The Rasteau and Beaumes-de-Venise vineyards are also used to produce red and rosé Côtes du Rhône.

Provence appellations

In the hills of southern Provence, the wines of **Cassis** have an excellent reputation, particularly the flower-scented dry whites; the velvety reds are equally exceptional.

The outskirts of Aix-en-Provence are home to the small **Palette** appellation, a smooth tannic red, often referred to as the "Claret of Provence." Only two landlords share this vineyard, which features the famous Château Simone.

The **Coteaux d'Aix-en-Provence** produce warm, robust reds and dry, lively whites.

The **Baux-de-Provence** appellation is used for red, white, and rosé wines that may be drunk young.

As for the **Côtes de Provence** appelation, on the boundary of this guide around the Massif de la Sainte-Baume, it is best represented by its many different rosés, offering a wide choice of flavours and textures.

Finally, you can also sample many pleasant country wines (*vins de pays*), including those made in La Petite Crau and the Principality of Orange.

M. Guillot/MICHELIN

Gigondas bottle

Cassis

AIGUES-MORTES★★

POPULATION 6 012

MICHELIN LOCAL MAP 339: K7 OR 528 FOLD 27

Aigues-Mortes, from *Aquae Mortuae* meaning dead water, with its large towers and defensive curtain wall, stands in a melancholy landscape of pools, sea marshes, and salt pans. This solitary fortified city is a glorious sight, especially during the long sunsets of the summer evenings.

🖫 *Place St-Louis, 30220 AIGUES-MORTES, ☎ 04 66 53 73 00. www.ot-aiguesmortes.fr*

▶ **Orient Yourself:** Take the tourist train (*🕭 see Address Book*) or a 2hr guided tour of the town to get an overview of what there is to see and do *(contact the Tourist Office)*. A traditional market can be found on ave. Frederic-Mistral *(🕭 see Address Book)*. .

🅿 **Parking**: Parking *(fee)* is available at the lot at the foot of the ramparts.

🆇 **Don't Miss**: The panorama from the Tour de Constance.

🕒 **Organising Your Time**: See the fortifications first, allowing at least 45min for your visit. Then visit the town site before taking the Excursions.

A Bit of History

St Louis' Creation – In the early 13C the king of France, Louis IX (St Louis), possessed no Mediterranean seaport as such. As he was preparing to set out on a crusade to Palestine, Louis IX did not want to embark from a "foreign" seaport like Marseille for example (foreign, because Marseille was ruled by the counts of Provence and thus separate from central government). Instead, he sought a site on the coast where he could set up a port of embarkation and a city that would serve to establish and reassert Capetian influence in the region.

In 1240 he obtained, from the monks of the Abbaye de Psalmody, a tract of virgin land frequented only by fishermen. There he rapidly built the powerful Tour de Constance. In order to encourage people to settle on this rather desolate site, the king granted a charter in 1246 that offered many advantages, such as tax exemption and other commercial privileges. Like the southern bastides *(see The Green Guide Dordogne, Berry-Limousin)*, the new town was built on a regular grid plan within a rectangle (550m x 300m/1 804ft x 984ft) cut across by five straight streets that were in turn cut by five cross streets. Clusters of settlements developed in the vicinity of three religious establishments (Notre-Dame-des-Sablons, the Franciscan monastery, and the Psalmody monks' residence), which offered protection from the local winds.

Aigues-Mortes, a fortified city

Setting off for the Crusades – In 1248 a huge armada chartered from Venice and Genoa gathered at Aigues-Mortes, which at that time was linked to the sea by the channel of Grau Louis. An estimated 1 500 ships, carrying 35 000 men plus horses and equipment – the Seventh Crusade - set sail for Cyprus on 28 August. The crusaders arrived in Cyprus 23 days later and met with some success before being defeated at al-Mansurah. The king was captured in 1250. In 1270, St Louis embarked with a fleet from Marseille that sailed to Tunis. It was there that he died of the plague, a disease he contracted while attending to his afflicted crusaders.

The Salted Burgundians – In 1418, during the Hundred Years War, the Burgundians captured Aigues-Mortes by surprise. The Armagnacs laid siege to the town and were desperate to possess it. In the dead of night, a handful of their partisans within the city walls succeeded in killing the garrison guarding one of the gates. They opened the city gates to the besieging army. The Burgundians were decimated. So numerous were the dead that the corpses awaiting burial were thrown into a tower, named ever since the Tour des Bourguignons. To prevent putrefaction, the Armagnacs covered the dead bodies with salt until they could bury them.

Decline – Aigues-Mortes stayed prosperous until the mid-14C, when it had a population of 15 000. However, the sea withdrew and the channels silted up in spite of dredging. Even the construction of a canal to the coast could not prevent the decline.

The town participated in the Wars of Religion and became a Protestant stronghold. In the 18C the founding of Sète dealt the port a final blow.

The town's activities now include wine growing, which extends over 75percent of the municipality, and salt extraction.

Visit *Allow 1hr*

Tall ramparts protect Aigues-Mortes from the salty wind and so it is remarkably unscathed by the ravages of time. The areas surrounding place St Louis and the main streets are teeming with cafés, craft boutiques, souvenir shops, and art galleries. In season, the Aigues-Mortes sightseeing train departs every half hour from Porte de la Gardette; you can also enjoy a boat tour on the canal (🕯 *see Address Book*).

Chapelle des Pénitents Blancs

Jul and Aug 🔊 *guided tours, ask at the Tourist Office.* A service is held in this Baroque chapel once a year on Palm Sunday. It houses a number of mementoes (liturgical vestments, penitents' attributes) belonging to this brotherhood established at Aigues-Mortes in 1622.

Chapelle des Pénitents Gris

Jul and Aug 🔊 *guided tours, ask at the Tourist Office.* This 17C chapel contains an imposing altarpiece (1687) carved by Sabatier.

Église Notre-Dame-des-Sablons★

This Gothic church has been frequently modified over the years, even serving as a salt warehouse at one time. Inside, its timber-framed nave adds to the simplicity of the decor: 14C Christ, altar table from the former Abbaye de Psalmody and Chapelle St-Louis. It is lit by contemporary stained-glass windows by local artist Claude Viallat.

Place St-Louis

On this lovely shaded square that marks the heart of the town stands the statue of St Louis (1849) by Pradier. The 17C **Chapelle des Capucins** served as a covered market before being converted into an exhibition space.

To get to the fortifications, take rue Victor-Hugo to the Organeau gate. From there turn right into boulevard Sud followed by boulevard Ouest ,which formerly allowed garrisons to move swiftly. You will then reach the Porte de la Gardette.

Fortifications *45min*

Access from place Anatole France - Les Fortifications – ♿ 🕐 *May to Aug: 10am-7pm; Sept to Apr: 10am-5.30pm.* 🕐*Closed 1 Jan. 1 May, 1 and 11 Nov, 25 Dec.* ✎*6.10€ (* 🔖 *under 18 free admission).* ☎ *04 66 53 61 55 - www.monum.fr.*

Address Book

Tours by Sightseeing Train – *SEPTAM, 30220 Aigues-Mortes,* ☎ *04 66 53 85 20.* 🚂 The Aigues-Mortes sightseeing train (tour 20min) departs every 45min from Porte de la Gardette. From Apr to Sept, daily. ⟜4€ (children 2.50€).

Boat Tours – **Pescalune Barge**, *46 r. de la Pinède , 30220 Aigues-Mortes,* ☎ *04 66 53 79 47.* Departure from the foot of the Tour de Constance. Trips last 2h 30min and follow the canal of Le Grau-du-Roi, the Vidourle, and the canal that links the Rhône to Sète, daily in season at 10.30am and 3pm.

Rive de France – *route du Grau-du-Roi, Péniche St-Louis,* ☎ *04 66 53 81 21; booking* ☎ *01 41 86 01 01, www.rivedefrance.com* Adventurous travellers can rent their own boats (no licence required), which accommodate 2-9 people, to cruise on the Rhône canal from Sète.

For coin ranges see Legend at the back of the guide.

EATING OUT

◛◛ **Le Café de Bouzigues** – *7 rue Pasteur -* ☎ *04 66 53 93 95 – www. cafebouzigues@club-internet.fr – closed mid-Jan to mid-Mar, Tue evenings and Wed from Oct-Easter .* No, you won't find mussels from Bouzigues here, in spite of the café's name. Still, what a pleasure to savour the fragrant local cuisine in the colourful dining room, or in the unique courtyard-terrace with its collection of pitchers and birdcages.

◛◛ **Salicorne** – *11 rue Alsace-Lorraine -* ☎*04 66 53 62 67 - Closed 3 Jan - 10 Feb.* On a peaceful little street away from the activity of the central square, here you will encounter cuisine inspired by traditional Provençal cooking while adding its own interpretation. An excellent choice of wines, attentive service, and among the best eating experiences in the region.

◛◛◛ **Les Arcades** – *23 bd Gambetta -* ☎ *04 66 53 81 13 – info@les-arcades.fr – closed 2-23 Mar, 5-20 Oct, Mon, and Tues and Thu lunchtime, except evenings in Jul-Aug.* This 16C house is full of character with its arcades overlooking the street. The dining room, with its pretty hexagonal floor tiles and exposed stonework, offers an appetising menu that uses fresh produce. A few spacious rooms are available decorated with Provençal furniture.

WHERE TO STAY

◛◛ **St-Louis** – *10 rue Amiral Courbet -* ☎ *04 66 53 72 68 - hotel.saint-louis@ wanadoo.fr– closed Nov to Mar -* 🅿 *- 22 rooms -* ⌑ *10€ - restaurant 20/35€.* Inside the city walls, near the Tour de Constance, this charming 17C building offers colourfully decorated contemporary bedrooms. In winter, eat in the dining room with its modern Provencal décor and fireplace; in summer, in the pretty shaded inner courtyard. Traditional cooking; limited selection of local wines.

ON THE TOWN

Le Tac Tac – *rue de la République - BP80 -* ☎ *04 66 53 60 29 – Jun-Sep: daily 1pm-2am, Oct-May: Thu-Tue 1pm-1am. Closed second half of Oct.* More than 130 varieties of beer and 65 whiskies are on offer in this cosy little pub. If you're famished, you can order a huge platter of all-you-can-eat charcuterie for a paltry sum!

Les Huîtres d'un Autre Monde – *9 r. Alsace-Lorraine -* ☎ *04 66 51 49 20.* Whether from Brittany, Normandy, Bouzigues or from Aigues-Mortes, the oysters here are superb. Enjoy them with a white wine from the region.

3-D Cinema – *place de Verdun (near the station),* ☎ *04 66 53 68 50.* 30min film on the Camargue, gypsies, and bulls.

SHOPPING

Traditional Market – *avenue Frédéric-Mistral. every Wed and Sun morning, 8.30 - 12.30.*

🍷**Domaines de Jarras-Listel** – *Quai de Jarras, on the road to Salins du Midi* ☎ *04 66 51 17 00 - www.listel.fr - Tasting and guided tours, 35-40 min, Apr-Oct, 10 am - 6 pm ; Nov.-Mar , Mon-Fri, 10 - 11.30 am and 2 - 4.30 pm. Closed on public holidays.* The cradle of famous local *vins des sables,* these wines are grown in the sand. Tour includes the historic, giant-sized oak casks in use in the 19C. Be sure to sample the *vin gris,* rosé. Wines are for sale in the gift shop.

La Bandido – *12 rue Pasteur -* ☎ *04 66 53 72 31 - summer, 9.30am-noon, and 3-8pm; the rest of the year, 9.30am -noon, and 3-7pm. Closed Nov-Feb, Christmas, and New Year.* Specialising in regional clothing and footwear.

SPECIAL EVENTS

Feast of St Louis – *last weekend in Aug, call for information -* ☎ *04 66 53 73 00 .* Medieval market, processions in historical costumes, tournaments and troubadours, as well as the embarkation of the king.

Votive Feast – *8-15 and 21-23 Oct.* This feast is notable for the typical Camargue races that take place at the foot of the bastions: each family owns their own "theatre," a 2m/6.6ft wide step decked out one next to the other forming an arena. Races are preceded by *abrivados* and followed by lively *bandidos.*

Tour de Constance★★

This tower is a massive circular keep 22m/72ft in diameter and 40m/13ft high (including the turret), with walls 6m/20ft thick.

Located northwest of the town, from which it was originally isolated, the tower was built between 1240 and 1249. The entrance fort and bridge, which connected the tower to the ramparts, date from the 16C. An elaborate defensive system protected the entrance. You can still see the portcullis and the embrasures through which missiles were hurled onto assailants.

The lower room with fine pointed arches still has its bread oven. The upper floors are approached by a spiral staircase. St Louis' oratory is a minute chapel built into the wall and the upper room, which served as quarters for well-known prisoners. A display case presents various documents covering a period of 500 years and concerning these famous detainees, many of whom were political opponents of the regime: Templars, rebel barons, and Huguenots. Two Protestants held in the tower were **Abraham Mazel**, a leading Calvinist who escaped down knotted bedclothes with 16 co-religionists in 1705, and **Marie Durand**, whose indomitable courage finally secured her release together with 10 of her companions from the cell in which she had been incarcerated for 38 years (1730-68). Note her graffito: *Register* (the verb to resist in Vivarais dialect).

Climb to the summit of the watchtower *(53 steps)* crowned by a wrought-iron cage. In the 13C-16C this protected a lantern that served as a beacon. An immense **panorama**★★ extends over the town and its grid-patterned streets to the surrounding plain punctuated right to left by the Cévennes, the Grande-Motte "pyramids," Montagne de Sète, the Midi salt-marshes, and the Camargue.

Remparts★★

The ramparts were built after 1272 with stone quarried from Beaucaire and Les Baux. Four-sided, and of remarkable unity, the fortifications are a typical example of 13C military architecture. The walls, topped by a watch path, are flanked by towers of different size and importance. The more massive towers defending the main gates contained two vaulted rooms with terraces.

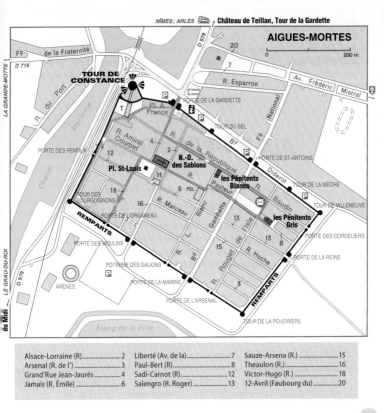

Alsace-Lorraine (R.) 2	Liberté (Av. de la) 7	Sauze-Arsena (R.) 15
Arsenal (R. de l') 3	Paul-Bert (R.) 8	Theaulon (R.) 16
Grand'Rue Jean-Jaurès 4	Sadi-Carnot (R.) 12	Victor-Hugo (R.) 18
Jamais (R. Émile) 6	Salengro (R. Roger) 13	12-Avril (Faubourg du) 20

The ramparts were punctuated by only two gates to the north, whereas, to the south, five gates or posterns offered access to the town from its loading docks. The towers in order of approach are: Tour des Bourguignons *(see above)*; Porte de l'Organeau, an *organeau* being the great iron ring to which the ships were moored; Porte des Moulins (Mill Gate) where grain was ground for the garrison; Porte des Galions (Galleons Postern), in front of which moored the galleys; Porte de la Marine (Maritime Gate), a ceremonial entrance; Tour de la Poudrière (the powder magazine); Tour de Villeneuve; Tour de la Mèche (Wick Tower), where a light was kept constantly burning to ignite firearms; and finally, Tour du Sel (Salt Tower).

Tour de Constance

Excursions

Salins du Midi

▶ *3km/2mi south of Aigues-Mortes on D 979 (access signposted by a small road on the left).* 🕐 *Mar to Oct;* 🚂 *guided tours (4hrs) by tourist train or by tour bus. Information and reservations:* ☎ *04 66 73 40 24 or 04 66 73 40 26; www.salins.fr.* This tour enables visitors to follow the various stages of salt production (both past and present procedures).

Tour Carbonnière

▶ *3km/2mi north for St-Laurent-d'Aigouze.* A 14C tower, complete with gates, portcullises and battlements, was the advanced barbican of Aigues-Mortes on the old salt road. A small garrison was quartered in the first-floor room, which was equipped with a big fireplace and a bread oven. The platform *(66 steps)* commands a panorama of Aigues-Mortes and the salt-marshes to the south, the Cévennes foothills to the northwest, and Petit Rhône to the east.

Château de Teillan

▶ *13km/8mi northeast on D 979, then, after St-Laurent d'Aigouze, left on D 288.* 🕐 *Mid-Jul to end of Aug;* 🚂 *guided tours of the interior (1hr) daily except Mon 3-5pm.* ⊜*4.50€.* ☎ *04 66 88 02 38.* Built on the site of a Gallo-Roman stronghold, this former priory of the Abbaye de Psalmody was sold in the 17C and subsequently enlarged.

A watchtower (15C) surmounts the main part of the building. You will encounter a fine view from the terrace, taking in the Cévennes, Languedoc plain, Aigues-Mortes, and the Camargue. In the park, landscaped with a fine variety of plants and trees, you will find a number of Roman altars and milestones. Note also the remarkable chain water pump in the small vaulted outbuildings.

AIX-EN-PROVENCE★★

POPULATION 134 222

MICHELIN LOCAL MAP 340: H-4 OR 114 FOLDS 15

AND 16 OR 528 FOLD 31 OR 524 FOLD J

This old capital of Provence has kept a great deal of its 17C and 18C character: the sober elegance of its mansions, the graceful charm of its squares, the majesty of its avenues, and the loveliness of its fountains. Aix is also a lively city whose large student population is abundantly evident on the busy café terraces.

Around old Aix a new town has developed that is both a spa and an industrial complex – it is the largest centre in France and Europe for processed almonds. Part of the production is used to make the cakes and confectionery of Aix, including the local speciality, sugar-coated *calissons*.

🛈 *2 pl. du Gén.-de-Gaulle, 13100 Aix-en-Provence,* ☎ *04 42 16 11 61, www. aixenprovencetourism.com.*

▶ **Orient Yourself** – Take a guided tour of the town *(2hrs)*; for information, contact the tourist office *(above)*. Buy a 2€ "visa" to Aix at the tourist office; use it to receive reduced admissions on guided tours, shows, museums, and the like.

A Bit of History

Good King René (1409-80) – Some traces of a prosperous civilization in Aix under the Roman emperor Augustus can still be seen in the sophisticated statuary in the Musée Granet. At the end of the 12C, the counts of Provence held a refined and literate court at Aix. The development of the town continued during the 13C, and yet in the 14C its surface area diminished. In 1409 Louis II of Anjou founded the university, but Aix's golden age occurred later, in the second half of the 15C under the reign of Good King René.

Address Book

Église St-Jean-de-Malte – *rue Cardinale* Open daily, 10am-noon and 3-7pm. Possibility of guided tours in Jul and Aug. ☎ 04 42 38 25 70.

Cézanne Tour – Mid-Mar to mid-Oct, Thur, 10am; ask at the tourist office - ☎ 04 42 16 11 61 - www.aixenprovencetourism.com.
For coin ranges see Legend at the back of the guide,

EATING OUT

Chez Charlotte – *32 r. des Bernardines* ☎ 04 42 26 77 56 - *Open for lunch and dinner. Closed Aug, Sun, and Mon.* Upon entering you are greeted with a nostalgic atmosphere. The main eating area's decor is dedicated to the cinema. Offering traditional and seasonal cuisine, the owner gives special attention to every dish.

Le Basilic Gourmand – *6 r. du Griffon (a small street NE of townhall from rue Paul-Bert) - ☎ 04 42 96 08 58 - Open for lunch and dinner, except Sun and Mon, open all evenings Jul - Aug. Terrace.* Light Mediterranean cuisine in a space with antique decor and warm, saffron-tones.

Chez Antoine "Côté Cour" – *19 cours Mirabeau - ☎ 04 42 93 12 51 - Closed Mon lunch and Sun.* This is a retreat with a luminous, verdant patio-veranda. All the flavours of Provence and Italy are at your fingertips. Try *aux aubergines à la parmesane* and *aux calamars farcis.* This is a place to be sure to visit.

La Vieille Auberge – *63 rue Espariat - ☎ 04 42 27 17 41 - closed 5-19 Jan and Mon lunchtime.* Set in a small square, which is lively in the evenings, this restaurant offers a rustic setting with exposed beams and columns and a huge fireplace in Rognes stone. Original cooking, with a good choice of dishes, and a seductive choice of regional wines.

WHERE TO STAY

La Manoir – *8 rue d'Entrecasteaux - ☎ 04 42 26 27 20 - msg@hotelmanoir.com – closed 7-30 Jan – ⊡ 40 rooms – ⊠ 11€.* A lovely old building, formerly a hat factory. Part of an adjoining 14C cloister has been converted into a summer terrace, creating a unique atmosphere.

Prieuré – *3km/1.9mi N of Aix-en-Provence, on the Sisteron road – ☎ 04 42 21 05 23 – ⊡ – 22 rooms – ⊠ 6.50€.* A former 17C priory which benefits from a peaceful setting. The romantically decorated bedrooms overlook an elegant park designed by Lenôtre.

Hôtel St-Christophe – *2 avenue Victor-Hugo – ☎ 04 42 26 01 24 – saintchristophe@francemarket.com – ⊡ – 51 rooms – ⊠ 8.50€.* This hotel is right in the centre of the city, near cours Mirabeau, and rooms are decorated in either a 1930s or Provençal style. The lively Brasserie Léopold is decorated in the Art Deco style and offers regional cuisine and typical brasserie dishes. Pavement terrace in fine weather.

Hôtel des Augustins – *3 rue Masse – ☎ 04 42 27 28 59 – hotel.augustins@wanadoo.fr –29 rooms – ⊠ 10€.* Stone vaulting and stained glass are reminders of the origins of this hotel, a stone's throw from cours Mirabeau, which was originally a 15C convent. The rooms, of which two have terraces with rooftop views, are decorated in a modern style.

ON THE TOWN

Café des Deux Garçons – *53 cours Mirabeau – ☎ 04 42 26 00 51 – www.les2garcons.com – daily 7am-2am.* Bordered by plane trees, cours Mirabeau is mainly frequented by Aix's bourgeoisie in search of a little fresh air on the terraces of one of its 13 cafés. The Deux Garçons café, more familiarly known as "le 2 G", is the oldest and most famous of these cafés and dates from 1792. Cézanne and Zola used to meet here every afternoon.

Château de la Pioline – *260 r. Guillaume-du-Vair, Les Milles – ☎ 04 42 52 27 27 – www.chateaudelapioline.fr – daily 24hr.* The bar of this hotel-restaurant (which dates from the 16C) is adorned with highly prestigious furnishings, such as those from the Medici hall (to commemorate the illustrious Catherine de' Medici) and the Louis XVI hall. Don't miss the large terrace overlooking the 4ha/10 acre French garden.

SHOPPING

Markets – ⊙Traditional market every morning in place Richelme and every Tuesday, Thursday, and Saturday in place des Prêcheurs and place de la Madeleine. Flower market every Tuesday, Thursday and Saturday in place de l'Hôtel de Ville, and in place des Prêcheurs on other days.

Antiques – Antique market every Tuesday, Thursday and Saturday in place Verdun. Antiques fairs take place in the center of town, throughout the year. Check with the tourist office. Village des **Antiquaires du Quartier de Lignane**, RN 7, Lignane, 13540 Puyricard. The place to hunt for antiques.

Crafts – Makers of vases, ceramics, fabrics, baskets and jewellery display their wares on cours Mirabeau at the end of Mar, in mid-May, mid-Jun, mid-October, and mid-Nov.

Calissons – The legend has it that these treats were invented to sweeten up Jeanne for her marriage to King René. It seems she felt much happier about her fate after savouring a *calisson* made of equal parts of almonds, sugar and candied melon. **Calissons du Roy René**, 10 rue Clemenceau – ☎ 04 42 26 67 86 – www.calisson.com; **Maison L. Béchard**, 12 cours Mirabeau – ☎ 04 42 26 06 78 – bechard-aix@wanadoo.fr (for *calissons* and biscuits, this is an Aix institution, having celebrated its 100th anniversary in 2001).

Aperitifs – The definitive shop for Provençal liquors and aperitifs is **Liquoisterie de Provence**, 36 av. de la Grand-Béude, 13770 Venelles – ☎ 04 42 54 94 65 – www.versinthe.net. Free tour and tasting.

Santons Fouque – 65 cours Gambetta, ☎ 04 42 26 33 38 – www.santonsfouque.fr. Visit the atelier where these figurines are made.

Books – Cité du Livre, 8-10 rue des Allumettes bookstore is a haven for book lovers - ☎ 04 42 91 98 88. (⭘ See Museums below.)

EVENTS

International Opera and Music Festival Founded in 1948 by Gabriel Dussurget, this prestigious festival takes place every summer in the courtyard of the archiepiscopal palace which is converted into a theatre for the event. Concerts and recitals are held in the cathedral, the cloisters of St-Saveur and the Hôtel Maynier d'Oppède. The festival focuses on important operas (in particular those by Mozart) as well as Baroque opera and contemporary music. Among the many illustrious artists who have contributed to the high standards of the festival are conductors Hans Rosbaud and Carlo Maria Giulini and the acclaimed singer Teresa Berganza. Working alongside the musicians, world-famous directors (Jorge Lavelli, Pier Luigi Pozzi) and set designers (Balthus, Derain, Masson) have also contributed to the creation of some unforgettable performances.

Santon Fair – These figurines can be purchased from the end of November until the end of December along cours Mirabeau.

Wine Festival – **Festivals des vins et Coteaux d'Aix** – cour Mirabeau – last Sunday in July.

Dance Festival – end of July - August. ☎ 04 42 96 05 01 – www.danse-a-aix.com.

A city of 4 000 to 5 000 people, a bishopric and county seat, Aix exerted a strong influence over the neighbouring countryside, occupied by wealthy townspeople and enhanced by Italian craftsmen. Within the walls lived the burghers, aristocrats and farmers; this category included the shepherds responsible for ensuring a return on livestock investments made by a handful of powerful merchants.

Second son to Louis II and Yolanda of Aragon, René became duke of Anjou, count of Provence, and titular king of Sicily and Naples at the death of his older brother, Louis III, in 1434. René spoke Latin, Greek, Italian, Hebrew, and Catalan. He played and composed music, painted illuminations with meticulous detail, wrote verses, understood mathematics, astrology, and geology. In short, René possessed one of the most universal minds of his time. He was an enlightened patron of the arts surrounded by artists, in particular Flemish painters. Dating from his rule are the famous triptychs of the *Annunciation* (said to be by the Master of King René) and the *Burning Bush* painted by Nicolas Froment (of Languedoc origin, he studied in Flanders and Burgundy). By the end of the 15C some 40 artists of quality lived and worked in Aix under contract to René and his nobles. They produced prestigious works of art and contributed to the decoration of mystery plays and popular festivals (such as Corpus Christi, which underwent a brilliant revival).

A man of arts and letters, René did not neglect his obligations as a ruler; he legislated, stimulated commerce, and encouraged agriculture. He introduced the Muscat grape into Provence and on occasion cultivated his own vineyards. He was concerned with the health standards of his people and instituted a public service of doctors and surgeons, promulgated a sanitation law and ordained the cleaning up of the different quarters of the city. He was, however, criticized for his heavy taxation as well as his weak currency; the coins he minted, called *parpaillottes*, were of rather base alloy. At the age of 12, René married Isabelle of Lorraine, who brought him as dowry the duchy of Lorraine. Their younger daughter, Margaret of Anjou (1429-82), married the English king, Henry VI (1421-71) in 1445. Two years after the death of Isabelle (at 44) to whom he had remained tenderly attached during the 33 years of their union, René married Jeanne of Laval, aged 21. This second marriage was as happy as the first. Queen Jeanne, who should not be confused with the 14C Queen Joan I of Sicily, was as popular as her elderly husband among the people of Provence.

Having lost both his son and two grandsons, King René sadly observed his nephew Louis XI annex Anjou to the kingdom of France. Thereafter, instead of dividing his time between Angers and Provence, René never set

King René

foot outside the land of sunshine and died at Aix in 1480, aged 72. His nephew Charles of Maine, who had been chosen as his heir, died one year later.

The New Faces of Aix – After the union of Provence to France in 1486, a governor appointed by the king lived in Aix. In 1501 the city became the seat of a newly-created parliament, and as a result in the 17C it experienced another period of growth as one of its social classes became prominent - the men of law. These well-to-do judges and lawyers led stimulating and active lives and consequently proceeded to build magnificent town houses (*hôtels*) worthy of their name and rank.

At the same time the urban landscape was transformed: new areas of the city sprang up and developed rapidly (notably the Quartier Mazarin, south of the city), the old ramparts were razed and replaced by an avenue for carriages, which later became cours Mirabeau. In the 18C, the city continued its transformation, with its wide avenues, squares, fountains, and new buildings. The old county palace was demolished and a new law court was built in its place.

Into the Modern Age – After the Revolution, Aix suffered a decline as a result of the newly prospering Marseille, although it retained its court and its university. It was not until the 1970s that it experienced a two-fold revival: economic, based the installation of high-tech industries; and cultural, with the growing influence of the university and the creation of the music festival. This growth in economic activity and population was accompanied by a major town-planning project, the extension of cours Sextius and cours Mirabeau, of which the Cité du Livre is the first stage, and which will help to redefine Aix in the 21C.

Cézanne Tour

A Bit of History

Born in Aix in 1839, **Paul Cézanne** studied at the Collège Bourbon, where he became friends with Émile Zola. He chose "humanities," then enrolled at the Faculty of Law in accordance with his father's wishes, while at the same time painting and writing poetry in the countryside around Jas de Bouffan. This residence in the midst of parkland, acquired by his father in 1859, was a propitious setting for the development of his artistic work.

Although Cézanne became friendly with Impressionist painters in Paris, he was not successful there. It was on his return to Aix that fame came to him, thanks to the good name he had made for himself among painters such as Monet, Manet, Sisley, and above all, Pissarro. However, it was not long before Cézanne shook off Impressionist techniques. Using large, luminous patches of colour and juxtaposing them in new ways, he created shapes with exaggerated outlines and relief but simple in form.

The countryside around Aix became the dominant subject of his painting. Fleeing Paris in 1870, Cézanne settled at Estaque in his mother's house. Finally, in 1904 he achieved recognition in the Paris Autumn Salon.

The **Cézanne Tour** (*see Address Book*) includes a visit to the parts of town habitually frequented by the artist and the areas of the surrounding countryside from which he drew inspiration, in particular **Montagne Ste-Victoire**.

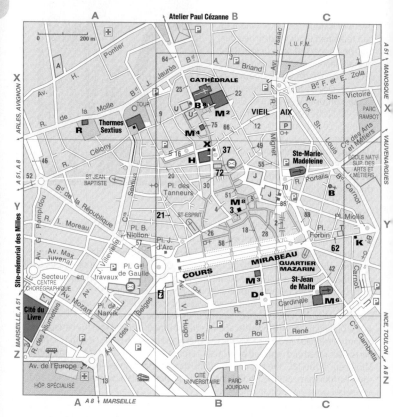

Agard Passage .... EY, CY
Albertas Pl. .... BY 3
Allumettes R.des .... AZ
Arts et Métiers
  Cours des .... CXY
Aude R. .... DY, BY 4
Bagniers R. des .... DY, BY 5
Bedarrides R. .... DY 6
Belges Av. des .... AYZ
Bellegarde Pl. .... EX, CX 7
Bon Pasteur R. .... DX, BX 9
Boulégon R. .... DX, BX 12
Briand Bd Aristide. .... DX
Brossolette Av. .... AZ 13
Cabassol R. Joseph .... DY 14
Cardeurs Pl. des. .... DY, BY 16
Cardinale R. .... DEY, BCY
Carnot Bd .... CY
Célony R. .... AY
Clemenceau R. .... DY, BY 18
Cordeliers R. des .... DY, BY 20
Couronne R. de la .... BY 21
Curie R.
  Pierre-et-Marie. .... BX, DX 22
David R. Émeric .... EY
Espariat R. .... DY, BY 26
Europe Av. de l' .... AZ
Fabrot R. .... DY, BY 28

Foch R. du Maréchal ...... BY, DY 30
Forbin Pl. .... EY
Forment Av. N. .... AY
Gambetta Cours .... CZ
Gaulle Pl. Gén.-de .... ABY
Goyrand R. .... DY
Hôtel de Ville Pl. .... DY, BY 37
Isaac Av. J. CX
Italie R. d' .... EY, CY 42
Jean-Jaurès Bd ...... DX, ABX
Jeanne-d'Arc Pl. .... ABY
De-la-Roque R. J. .... DX, BX 25
Laroque R. .... DY
Lattre-de-Tassigny
  Av. de .... AY 46
Martyrs de la
  Résistance Pl. des. .... DX 47
Matheron R. .... DY, BY 49
Mazarine R. .... DY
Méjanes R. .... DY, BY 51
Mignet R. .... EXY, CKY
Minimes Crs des .... AY 52
Miollis Pl. .... CY
Mirabeau Cours .... DY, BCY
Molle R. de la .... AX
Montigny R. de .... EY, BY 55
Moreau R. I. .... AY
Mozart Av. .... AY

Napoléon-
  Bonaparte Av. .... AY 57
Narvik Pl. de .... AY
Nazareth R. .... DY, BY 58
Niollon Pl. B. .... AY
Opéra R. de l' .... EY, CY 62
Pasteur Av. .... DX, BX 64
Paul-Bert R. .... DX, BX 66
Pompidou Av. G. .... AY
Pontier Av. H. .... AX
Portalis R. .... EY, CY 69
Prêcheurs Pl. des. .... EY, CY 70
René Bd du Roi .... BCZ
République Bd de la .... AY
Richelme Pl. .... DY, BY 72
St-Honoré Pl. .... DY 73
St-Louis Cours .... EXY, CXY
Ste-Victoire Av. .... EX, CX
Saporta R. G.-de .... DX, BX 75
Sextius Cours .... AY
Tanneurs Pl. des .... DY, BY
Thiers R. .... EY, CY 80
Vauvenargues R. .... DY
Verdun Pl. de .... EY, CY 85
Victor-Hugo Av. .... DY, BYZ
Zola Bd Émile .... EX, CX
4-Septembre R. .... DY, BZ 87

Ancienne chapelle des Jésuites .... CY, EY B	Musée du Vieil Aix .... BX, DX M⁴
Ancienne chapellerie .... DY B⁴	Muséum d'Histoire
Ancienne halle aux grains .... DY B⁶	naturelle (Hôtel Boyer
Atelier Paul-Cézanne .... BX	d'Eguilles) .... BY, DY M⁸
Cathédrale St-Sauveur .... BX, DX	Pavillon Vendôme .... AX R
Cité du Livre .... AYZ	
Cloître St-Sauveur .... BX, DX, B⁸	Quartier Mazarin .... CY, EY
Fontaine d'eau thermale .... DY D	Thermes Sextius .... AX
Fontaine des Neuf Canons ...... DY D²	Tour de l'Horloge .... BY, DY X
Fontaine des Prêcheurs .... EY D⁴	Église St-Jean-de-Malte ...... CY, EY
Fontaine des Quatre-Dauphins .... BY, DY D⁶	Église Ste-Marie-MadeleineCY, EY
Fontaine du roi René .... EY D⁸	
Hôtel Peyronetti .... DY L⁴	
Hôtel d'Agut .... EY E	
Hôtel d'Albertas .... DY E²	
Hôtel d'Arbaud .... DY E⁴	
Hôtel d'Arbaud-Jouques .... DY E⁵	
Hôtel d'Isoard de Vauvenargues .... DY E⁸	
Hôtel de Bonnecorse .... EY F	
Hôtel de Caumont .... DY F²	
Hôtel de Forbin .... DY F⁶	
Hôtel de Grimaldi .... EY F⁸	
Hôtel de Lestang-Parade .... EY G	
Hôtel de Marignane .... DY G²	
Hôtel de Maurel de Pontevès .... DY L²	
Hôtel de Panisse-Passis .... EY G⁶	
Hôtel de Roquesante .... EY G⁸	
Hôtel de Ville .... BY, DY H	
Hôtel du Poët .... EY L	
Maison natale de Cézanne .... CY K	
Musée Granet .... CY, EY M⁶	
Musée bibliographique et archéologique Paul-Arbaud .... BY, DY M³	
Musée des Tapisseries ...... BX, DX M²	

Atelier Paul-Cézanne (Cézanne's Studio)

9 av. Paul-Cézanne, in the north of Aix along av. Pasteur. ☎*04 42 21 06 53. - www.atelier-cezanne.com –* 🕐 *Jul and Aug: 10am-6pm; Apr to Sept: 10am-12pm, 2-6pm; Oct to Mar: 10am-12pm, 2-5pm.* 🕐 *Closed 1 Jan, 1 May, 25 Dec.* ▨ *5.50€.* When his mother died in 1897, Cézanne had a traditional Provençal-style house built about 500m (545yd) from the cathedral, outside the ramparts. It was surrounded by a garden with colourful leafy plants growing right up to the windows of the artist's studio.

The studio, called the "Lauves," where he painted *The Bathers*, among other works, has been left as it was at his death in 1906. A few items of memorabilia are on view.

Old Aix★★ *Allow half a day, including 1hr 30min for Quartier Mazarin.*

▷ *Start from place du Général-de-Gaulle, more commonly known as the "Rotonde," where there is a monumental fountain.*

The ring of boulevards and squares that encircles the old town marks the line of the ancient ramparts. North of cours Mirabeau, the town's focal point, lies old Aix, tucked between the cathedral and place d'Albertas. The many pedestrian streets criss-crossing this area make it the perfect setting for an exploratory stroll.

Cours Mirabeau★★

This wide avenue, shaded by fine plane trees, is the hub of Aix, where a verdant tunnel of foliage protects against the hot Provençal sun.

Built in the 17C on the site of the medieval ramparts, the avenue originally had no shops or boutiques, yet, now Aix's life revolves around this very area. Lining the north side of the street are cafés (namely the **Café des Deux Garçons**, once an important meeting place for artists and writers) and shops.

Atlantes, cours Mirabeau

G. Magnin/MICHELIN

A number of bookshops reveal Aix's intellectual and scholarly vocation. On the other side stand the aristocratic façades of the old hotels with their finely-carved doorways and wrought-iron balconies supported by caryatids or atlantes from the Puget School.

Hôtel d'Isoard de Vauvenargues

No 10. This mansion was built around 1710 with a wrought-iron balcony and fluted lintel. The Marchioness of Entrecasteaux, Angélique de Castellane, was murdered here by her husband, the president of Parliament.

Hôtel de Forbin

No 20. Ornamenting the 1656 façade is a balcony with lovely wrought-iron work.

Fontaine des Neuf Canons

This fountain marks the center of the avenue and dates to 1691.

Fontaine d'Eau Thermale

Farther up cours Mirabeau, at its junction with rue Clémenceau, is a natural hot water fountain covered with moss, dating from 1734, whose waters gush out at 34°C/93°F.

Hôtel Maurel de Pontevès

No 38. In 1660 the hôtel was the residence of Anne-Marie Montpensier, known as La Grande Mademoiselle. It now houses an annexe of the Aix-en-Provence Court of Appeal.

Fontaine du Roi René

This fountain marks the end of the avenue. Carved by David d'Angers (19C), the fountain portrays King René holding a bunch of muscat grapes, which he introduced into Provence.

Hôtel du Poët

This dates from 1730 and closes off the view down cours Mirabeau to the east. The three-tiered façade is decorated with *mascarons*, and some pretty ironwork adorns the first floor balcony.

▶ *Take the street to the right of the Hôtel du Poët.*

Rue de l'Opéra

There are a number of houses of interest on this street. *No 18* (**V**) Hôtel de Lestang-Parade was built around 1650 by Pavillon and Rambot and remodelled in 1830. *No 24* Hôtel de Bonnecorse (or Arlatan-Lauris) dates from the 18C. *No 26* Hôtel de Grimaldi was constructed in 1680 after drawings by Puget. And *no 28* was Cézanne's birthplace.

▶ *Return towards the Théâtre du Jeu de Paume, turning right and then left into rue Émeric-David.*

Hôtel de Panisse-Passis

No 16 rue Émeric-David. Built in 1739, the façade is enhanced by fine wrought-iron and corbelled balconies with fantastically carved heads.

Ancienne Chapelle des Jésuites

A detour to your right, on rue Portalis. Dating from the 17C, the former Jesuit chapel has an imposing façade pierced with five niches.

Église Ste-Marie-Madeleine

🕐*Open 8.30 to 11.30am.* The church's west front is modern although the church itself dates to the 17C. At the end of the south aisle, in the fourth chapel, an 18C marble **Virgin**★ by Chastel can be seen. The central panel of the 15C **Triptych of the Annunciation**★ hangs in the north aisle –near the altar to Our Gracious Lady (*the other two panels are elsewhere*)– and was ordered around 1443-45 and attributed to Barthélemy d'Eyck (a relative of the famous Van Eycks), an artist who used chiaroscuro effects subtly and inventively.

Fontaine des Prêcheurs

In the square of the same name you will find Chastel's 18C work.

Note the atlantes that decorate the doorway of the **Hôtel d'Agut** at No 2, before taking rue Thiers, where at No 2 you will find the 17C **Hôtel de Roquesante**.

Rue Thiers leads to the top of cours Mirabeau; take the right-hand pavement. At No 55 notice the sign of a hat shop founded by Cézanne's father in 1825.

▶ *Turn right into rue Fabrot.*

Properly speaking, this is the start of Old Aix. The pedestrian-only shopping street, rue Fabrot, leads to place St-Honoré.

▶ *Take rue Espariat.*

Hôtel Boyer d'Éguilles

No 6. This town house was built in 1675, most probably by Pierre Puget. Entrance is through a large porte cochère that opens into the main courtyard. The Musée d'Histoire Naturelle is housed here.

Place d'Albertas★

This square was opened in 1745 and was embellished with a fountain in 1912. It is arranged very much in the style of Parisian squares and has lovely mansions all around it. Concerts are held here every summer.

Hôtel d'Albertas

No 10. Built in 1707, this hôtel includes carvings by the sculptor Toro.

▶ *Bear right into rue Aude.*

Hôtel Peyronetti

No 13. Italian Renaissance in style, it dates from 1620.

▶ *Follow rue du Maréchal-Foch.*

Hôtel d'Arbaud

No 7. Fine atlantes frame the doorway.

Place Richelme

The south façade of the old grain market runs alongside this square, which is broken into sections by two corner statues. ⊕Every morning there is a fresh fruit and vegetable market here.

Place de l'Hôtel-de-Ville★

The northwest corner of this attractive square is overlooked by the **clock tower** (**F**), which in the 16 C used to be the town's belfry. A bell in a wrought-iron cage also dates from the 16C. Each season is represented by a different character. This is also the site of the weekly flower market.

Hôtel de Ville

Built between 1655 and 1670, the town hall was designed by the Parisian architect Pierre Pavillon. Both the lovely wrought-iron balcony and entrance gate are from the 17C. Around the splendid paved **courtyard**★, the buildings are divided by pilasters of the Classical order (⏾*see Introduction: Art*). There is a niche with scrolls on the inside façade.

Ancienne Halle aux Grains

This former grain market was built to the south of the square in the mid-18C. The central part of the building projects forward and is embellished with a pediment carved by Chastel, depicting the Rhône and the Durance. This sculptor spent his life in Aix, a fact evidenced by the many works of art left behind by him. The grain market now houses a post office and administrative centre.

▶ *Go along rue Gaston-de-Saporta.*

In place des Martyrs-de-la-Résistance is the 17C former archbishop's palace, the courtyard of which is used for the music festival, while the buildings house the **Musée des Tapisseries**★ *(⏾see "Museums").*

Cloître St-Sauveur★

🕐 *Open daily except during religious services: May-Oct, 9.30am-12pm and 2.30-5.30pm; Nov-Apr, 10am-12pm and 2.30-5.30pm. ⚑ Guided tours. Information ☎ 04 42 96 12 25.*

These Romanesque cloisters are a delight. Because the arcades are not buttressed, the cloisters seem delicate. The small, paired columns and the capitals are adorned with leaves or storiated and add a great deal of elegance to the construction. For the most part, the carvings on the capitals are badly damaged. However, on a fine corner pillar you will discover a remarkably carved St Peter.

▶ *A door northwest of the cloisters gives access to the adjoining cathedral.*

Cathédrale St-Sauveur

Cathédrale St-Sauveur★

St-Sauveur is a curious building where all styles from the 5C to the 17C can be seen side by side. In the vast Gothic central nave hang two 15C triptychs. Of the first triptych, depicting the Passion, only the central panel is from the 15C. The second series, the **Triptych of the Burning Bush**★★ *(currently being restored)*, is a masterpiece wrongly attributed to King René. In fact it was the work of his court painter Nicolas Froment. King René and Queen Jeanne are shown kneeling on either side of the Virgin. The Virgin holding the infant Jesus is in the Burning Bush, similar to that in which God appeared to Moses.

Behind the altar, in the Chapel of St-Mitre, hangs a painting on wood (*Martyrdom of St Mitre*) attributed to the School of Nicolas Froment. The great doorway is closed by **panels**★ *(masked by false doors)* in walnut; this masterpiece (1504) of sculpture in wood by Jean Guiramand of Toulon represents the four prophets of Israel and 12 pagan sibyls.

The cathedral's west front includes to the right a small door in the Romanesque Provençal style, in the middle a Flamboyant Gothic part (early 16C) and to the left a Gothic bell tower (14C-15C).

▶ *Return to cours Mirabeau via place de l'Hôtel-de-Ville and rue Vauvenargues, rue Méjanes, rue des Bagniers and rue Clemenceau.*

Hôtel d'Arbaud-Jouques

No 19 cours Mirabeau. Built in 1700, this *hôtel* displays a finely decorated façade with a carved frieze underlining the first floor, a medallion on the impost underneath the balcony and carved oak doors.

▶ *Turn left into rue Laroque and then left again into rue Mazarine.*

Quartier Mazarin★ *1hr 30min*

This district of orderly design was built between 1646 and 1651 by the Archbishop Michel Mazarin, brother of the famous cardinal of the same name, south of the old town.

Hôtel de Marignane

No 12 rue Mazarine. Late 17C. This *hôtel* was the scene of Mirabeau's scandalous behaviour towards Mlle. de Marignane.

Hôtel de Caumont

No 3 rue Joseph-Cabassol. An elegant mansion built in 1720, it presents a lovely façade adorned with balconies and pediments. It houses the Darius Milhaud Music and Dance Conservatory.

The Marriage of Mirabeau

Aix played an important role in the life of Mirabeau. He married here in 1772 and was divorced here in 1783. It was here, too, that he was elected to the Estates General in 1789.

The fiery Mirabeau was only 23 when he married Mlle. de Marignane. The bride was a rich heiress, and among her suitors featured the best of Provence nobility. Mirabeau, although a count, was ill-favoured. With a monstrous great head and a face disfigured by smallpox, he was penniless and moreover had a scandalous reputation. But he was aware of the mysterious attraction he held for women. He entered the competition and swept off with the prize. Cynically, he made a show of his good fortune and left his coach at the door of the Hôtel de Marignane (see "Quartier Mazarin") before spending the night there. After this scandal, a marriage had to take place. But Mirabeau's father-in-law showed resentment by cutting off the young couple's allowance. Mirabeau displayed no embarrassment at this blow and promptly ran up 200 000 *livres* of debts with Aix merchants. Their complaints were such that a warrant was issued sending him under house arrest to Château d'If and subsequently Fort Joux, where he published his *Essay on Despotism*.

No sooner was he freed than he seduced the lovely young Mme. Monnier and fled to Holland with her. Mirabeau returned to Aix in 1783 to answer a summons for separation instituted by his wife. The eminent orator presented his own defence. His prodigious eloquence secured him victory at a first hearing but he lost on appeal, although it is said that his pleading aroused such enthusiasm and the violence of his language was such that the opposing counsel fainted!

1789 dawned with the elections to the Estates General. The count of Mirabeau, who had encountered only contempt and rebuff among his peers, decided to represent not nobility but the Third Estate. His election was a triumph and his historic role as an orator began; however it was also the beginning of Aix's downfall.

Fontaine des Quatre-Dauphins★

At the center of a small square stands the charming fountain by J.C. Ribaut from 1667. It is one of the prettiest fountains in Aix!

Église St-Jean-de-Malte

🕐 *Open daily, 10am-12pm and 3-7pm -* ☎ *04 42 38 25 70*. The church, dating from the late 13C, was the chapel of the former priory of the Knights of Malta, and was Aix's first Gothic building. Although the façade is austere, the **nave**★ presents the elegant decorative detail of the High Gothic.

Museums and More

Musée Granet★

On rue d'Italie. 👁 *Closed for renovation; scheduled to re-open in July 2006.* A fine collection of paintings hang here that were acquired through various legacies, including those of the Aix painter, **François-Marius Granet** (1775-1849).

Works from among the great European Schools spanning the 16C-19C are exhibited beside the Flemish, Italian and Avignon (panels of a triptych by Matteo Giovanetti) Primitives.

The French School is represented by a series of paintings by Géricault, Philippe de Champagne, Le Nain, Rigaud, Largillière, Van Loo, Greuze, David and Ingres, among others. A number of works by the Provençal School are also on display. In particular note Granet, Constantin, Loubon, Parrocel, and Emperaire.

The Italian (Guercino), Flemish (Rubens, Master of Flémalle) and Dutch (Rembrandt's studio) Schools are also worth admiring.

A gallery devoted entirely to Cézanne presents eight of his paintings, including *Still Life* (1865), *Naked Woman Before a Mirror* (1872), *The Bathers* (1895), and *Portrait of Madame Cézanne* (1885).

Musée des Tapisseries★

🕐 *Open daily except for Tues: 10am-12.30pm and 1.30-5pm.* 🕐 *Closed 1-2 Jan, 1 May, and 25-26 Dec -* ☎ *04 42 21 05 78 –* 👁 *2.50€.* Housed in the former bishop's palace, the Tapestry Museum presents in particular the 19 magnificent tapestries made in Beauvais in the 17C and 18C, including nine famous panels illustrating the life of Don Quixote, after cartoons by Natoire.

Fondation Vasarely★

🕒 *Open daily except Sun and public holidays: 10am-6pm –* ☎ *04 42 20 01 09 – www. fondationvasarely.fr –2.5km/1.5mi west –* ♿*- 7€.* The foundation stands on a hill to the west of Aix, in an area known as the Jas d-e Bouffan, where Paul Cézanne used to live. This was the place selected for the foundation that was to bear his name by the Hungarian artist Victor Vasarely (1906-1997) who made no secret of his great admiration for the Aix painter.

The vast building, consisting of 16 hexagonal structures, has sober façades decorated with circles on alternately black and white squares. As early as 1930 Vasarely's research led him to geometric abstractions via lines and graphics. In 1955, the artist evolved into a more kinetic field where by various optical means he was able to produce visual illusion without the use of movement.

Cité du Livre

8-10 rue des Allumettes – ☎ *04 42 91 98 88 – www.citedulivre-aix.com.* The City of Books is a bibliophile's dream. Housed in a modern glass and metal structure, it is home to the prestigious Méjanes library – the 1786 legacy of the Marquis de Méjannes already included 80 000 volumes. The neigbourhood known as "Les Alumettes," beyond the end of cours Mirabeau and outside the town gates, had been a neglected, semi-industrial zone for many years when urban pressures required the establishment of new plan for the district. This ambitious and attractive project provides not only a new and more spacious home for the library's collection, but has also opened up new spaces for artistic creation in Aix, most notably a 1 300-seat auditorium, currently the home base of the Ballet Preljocaj. Numerous events and exhibits are organized in this premises. It should definitely be included on your tour of town if you are interested in urbanism and projects for the revival of run-down districts.

Musée d'Histoire Naturelle

🄺🄸🄳🅂 🕒 *Open daily, 10am-12pm and 1-5pm; Jul and Aug, 10am-6pm.* 🕒 *Closed 1 Jan, 1 May, and 25 Dec. –* ☎ *04 42 27 91 27 – www.museum-aix-en-provence.org.* *2€ (under 25 free).* This Natural History Museum houses interesting collections of mineralogy and paleontology. The paleontology section includes general as well as local exhibits, notably a collection of dinosaur eggs from the slope of Mont Sainte-Victoire. In addition, the *hôtel* is embellished with fine 17C doors, paintings, and interior paneling.

Musée du Vieil Aix

🕒 *Apr to Oct, daily except Mon: 10am-12pm and 2.30-6pm; Nov to Mar, daily except Mon: 10am-12pm and 2-5pm.* 🕒 *Closed public holidays.* *4€ –* ☎ *04 42 21 43 55.* *No 17.* Located in the Hôtel d'Estienne de St-Jean (17C), attributed to Laurent Vallon, the museum presents local memorabilia. On display is a collection of marionettes evoking the talking cribs and the local Corpus Christi procession, porcelain from Moustiers, and *santons*.

Musée Bibliographique et Archéologique Paul-Arbaud

🕒*Open daily 2-5pm.* 🕒 *Closed Sun, public holidays, and the second half of Aug –* ☎ *04 42 38 38 95.* *3€. No 2a rue du 4-Septembre.* This bibliographical and archeological museum is housed in a late-18C *hôtel.* Exhibited are books concerning Provence, a lovely collection of porcelain from the region and some fine paintings and sculptures.

Pavillon de Vendôme

🕒*Open daily except Tues, 10am-12.30pm and 1.30-5pm.* 🕒 *Closed 1-2 Jan, 1 May, 25-26 Dec –* ☎ *04 42 21 05 78.* *2.50€.* This mansion was built in 1667 from plans by A. Matisse and P. Pavillon, as Cardinal de Vendôme's country home. Displayed inside are Provençal furnishings and *objets d'art.*

Excursions

Montagne Ste-Victoire★★★ ⬜1

Round-trip of 74km/46mi. 👣 *See Mon SAINTE VICTOIRE.*

Vallée de l'Arc

Round-trip of 56km/35mi – about 3hr.

▷ *Leave Aix-en-Provence on N 8 towards Marseille as far as Bouc-Bel-Air.*

Jardins d'Albertas★ *At La Croix-d'Or.*

🕐 *Open May, and Sept-Oct: weekends and public holidays, 2-6pm; Jun to Aug: daily 3-7pm. – ☎ 04 42 22 29 77 – 🕭 www.jardins-albertas.com. 🕭 3.50 €.* These gardens were laid out in 1751 by the Marquis Jean-Baptiste d'Albertas. They blend together different styles: Italian (terraces, antique statues, artifical cave where visitors can enjoy the cool, Triton fountain); French (flower beds, canals, perspective); and Provençal (rows of plane trees).

▷ *At San Baquis, turn right onto D 60A.*

Cabriès

Cabriès is a picturesque hill village with a castle accessed through a clock gateway and a network of narrow streets inside what used to be its fortified town wall. The castle houses the **Musée Edgar-Mélik** (🕐*Open daily except Tues: 10-12pm and 2-5pm; Sundays, 2-6pm. 🕐 Closed 1 Jan, 1 May, and 25 Dec – ☎ 04 42 22 42 81. www. musee-melik.com. 🕭 4.60 €)* dedicated to this little-known painter (1904-76**)**, who kept company with the Montparnasse artists' group in Paris before traveling south and setting himself up in Cabriès in the 1940s. His work, some of which you will see on the walls, are executed in warm tones of yellow, orange, and red. His style heads toward Expressionism. There are also one or two archaeological exhibitions in the basement.

▷ *Take D 8 back to rejoin D 543 and at Calas, turn left onto 9B, then D 9. Drive alongside the **Réaltor Reservoir**, a fine 58 ha/143 acre stretch of water set amid lush vegetation, and take D 65D to the right, crossing over the Marseille canal. After Mérindolle, turn left.*

Aqueduc de Roquefavour★

This fine aqueduct was constructed to transport the Canal de Marseille across the Arc valley at a point 12km/7.5mi west of Aix-en-Provence. Built from 1842 to 1847 under the direction of Montricher, the aqueduct is a spectacular example of a 19C civil engineering project. Made up of three stages – three tiers of arches – supporting the water channel, it is 375m/1 230ft long and 83m/272ft high (Pont du Gard: 275m/902ft high and 49m/161ft high). Its lower level has 12 arches, the middle level 15 arches, and the top level with its 53 smaller arches carries the canal which transports the waters of the Durance to Marseille.

▷ *Follow D 65 towards Salon-de-Provence and 300m/328yd farther on bear right on D 64 uphill.*

Top level of Roquefavour Aqueduct (Sommet)

▷ *After 2.1km/1mi bear right on a path towards Petit Rigouès and right again to the keeper's house located on the aqueduct's topmost level.*

From the plateau's edge there is a lovely view of the Aix basin, Montagne Ste-Victoire, and the Étoile chain. From the car park walk to the top level of the aqueduct where the canal runs.

▷ *Return to D 64 and turn right.*

Ventabren

This tiny village is dominated by Queen Jeanne's castle, now in ruins. Take rue du Cimetière to the foot of the castle ruins to enjoy the splendid **view** of the Berre lagoon, Martigues, the Caronte gap and the Vitrolles chain.

▷ *From D 64A rejoin D 10 on the right, then, make a left onto D 543 for the village of Éguilles.*

Éguilles

The village, which has a wonderful view of the Arc valley, is situated on the old Aurelian Way, the present D 17. The town hall, an old castle bought by the Boyer d'Éguilles family in the 17C, has a beautiful façade interspersed with mullioned windows on four levels. From the esplanade, there is a magnificent **view** of the Étoile chain, Les Milles, and the Aix plain through which the TGV Med line passes. Stroll through the village to explore the old wash houses.

▷ *Leave Éguilles to the NE on D 63, and turn right onto D 14. Then, take the path to the left up to the plateau d'Entremont.*

Viaduc de Ventabren

Oppidum d'Entremont

🕐 *Open daily Feb-Oct, except Tues: 9am-12pm and 2-5.30pm; Nov-Jan, daily, except Tues: 9am-12pm and 2-5pm.* 🕐 *Closed 1 Jan, 1 and 8 May, 1 and 11 Nov and 25 Dec.* 🎫 *No charge.* ☎ *04 42 21 97 33.* This capital city of the Celtic-Ligurian Saluvii (*les Salyens*) was by 2C BC already looking like a fortified town, with a surface area of 3.5ha/9acres. It was naturally protected by steep slopes on one side and to the north by ramparts with a sturdy curtain wall reinforced with large round towers set at regular intervals. Between two of the towers on the ramparts is a gateway where archaeologists think the Saluvii may have displayed the skulls of their enemies.

Inside its walls a series of fortifications served to define a first town known as the "upper town" showing a remarkably even texture. Then there is a "lower town," which seems to have been the district of artisans and tradesmen (vestiges of ovens and oil presses have been found).

Excavations have uncovered a great many artefacts and works of art, proving that the *oppidum* possessed quite a high level of civilization and explaining how the town fell (stone balls, buried hoards) under the Romans. Entremont statuary is of significant interest for the history of art and may be seen at the Musée Granet (🕐 *see above*), a visit that makes a fitting complement to touring of the actual site.

The low-relief carvings and statues on display represent scenes of people making offerings, warriors on horseback or seated cross-legged, and full-length figures or women with long veils.

Les **ALPILLES**★★

MICHELIN LOCAL MAP 340: D3-E3 OR 528 FOLD 29

The limestone chain of the Alpilles, a geological extension of the Luberon range, rises in the heart of Provence between Avignon and Arles. From afar these jagged crests, rising 300-400m/984-1 312ft, appear to be really lofty mountains. The arid, white peaks of these summits standing out against the blue sky are reminiscent of some Greek landscapes. At the mouths of the dry valleys that cross the mountain chain, olive and almond trees spread their foliage over the lower slopes. Occasionally a dark line of cypress trees breaks the landscape. In the mountains, the gently sloping lower areas are planted with kermes oaks and pines, but often the rock is bare and peppered with a few scraggy bushes covered by *maquis* or poor pasture suitable only for sheep.

🚩 *Nature lovers can plan a guided tour of the Caume by contacting the Tourist Office in St-Rémy-de-Provence, ☎ 04 90 92 05 22.*

😵 Due to the high risk of fire, access to the forested areas of the Alpilles is forbidden from 1 Jul to 15 Sept.

Les Baux Alpilles★★ 1

🕐 *Round-trip starting from St-Rémy-de-Provence 40km/25mi – allow 4hr*

St-Rémy-de-Provence★

(♿ *See ST-RÉMY-DE-PROVENCE.*)

▶ *Leave St-Rémy-de-Provence going southwest on Chemin de la Combette; turn right into Vieux Chemin d'Arles. After 3.8 km/2mi, turn left at a T-junction onto D 27 (sign-posted: Les Baux).*

Les Baux Panorama (Table d'Orientation)★★★

Just before reaching the top of the hill, on your left, you will see a road tracing the ledge where you can stop and gaze at the magnificent **panorama**★★★ of les Baux.

♿ See *Les BAUX-DE-PROVENCE.*

▶ *Return to D 27; bear left on it.*

The road winds through Val d'Enfer (♿ *See Les BAUX-DE-PROVENCE*).

Les Baux-de-Provence★★★ – ♿ *See Les BAUX-DE-PROVENCE.*

▶ *Continue along D 27, then make a right before Massane-les-Alpilles to connect to Paradou on D 17.*

Paradou

This is the home to Provençal poet **Charloun Rieu** (1846-1924) who is buried in the village cemetery, beneath a very unusual tombstone. Rieu's works include *Chants du Terroir* and a translation of *The Odyssey* into Provençal.

La Petite Provence de Paradou

▶ *At the exit to the village, heading towards Fontveille (D 17), to the right of the road.*

🔳 In a decor redolent of rural Provence, *santons* are produced here by santon-makers from Aubagne. And so, they are dressed in the local costumes. Some are even mobile. They are arranged into evocative scenes of a Provence past, such as trades (fisherman, miller, shepherd), festivals, daily life (drinking holes, games of cards), and the like.

▶ *Return to the village, taking D 78 to the right through an olive grove.*

Aqueducs de Barbegal

▶ *15min round-trip on foot: follow the signposts for aqueduc romain.* Note the impressive ruins, on the left in particular, of a pair of Gallo-Roman aqueducts. The aqueduct branches off to the west, supplied Arles with water from Eygalières some 50km/31mi away. The other one cut through the rock and served a 4C hydraulic flour mill on the slope's south side, the ruins of which provide a rare example of Gallo-Roman mechanical engineering.

▶ *Go right on D 33.*

D. Pazery/MICHELIN

The Alpilles des Baux

Address Book

⚑ Hiking – Take the 15km/9mi footpath along the Alpilles ridge, from Glanum to Eygalières, via Val Saint-Clerg, following the GR 6 footpath. Other, shorter walks of 1-3hr are available.

EATING OUT

⚌ **La Pitchoune** – 21 place de l'Église – 13520 Maussane-les-Alpilles – ☎ 04 90 54 34 84 – closed mid-Nov to mid- Jan, Fri lunchtime, and Mon. Situated near the church this pretty, bourgeois house dating from the 19C has tastefully decorated rooms and tiles imitating mosaics on the floor. In the summertime there is a terrace shaded by pine trees. Home cooking.

⚌⚌ **Table du Meunier** – 42 cours Hyacinthe Bellon – 13990 Fontvieille – ☎ 04 90 54 61 05 – closed mid-Jan to mid-Mar, during holidays, 20-28 Dec, Tue evenings Sept-Jun and Wed except evenings in Jul-Aug. The tasty regional cooking in the rustic setting of this old mill attracts customers from far and wide. The terrace harbours a real treasure: a chicken house dating from 1765.

⚌⚌⚌ **Le Bistrot d'Eygalières (chez Bru)** – 28 r. de la République - 13810 Eygalières - ☎ 04 90 90 60 34 - sbru@club-internet.fr - closed mid-Jan to mid-Mar, and 6-11 Aug. An institution. Cuisine from the land with, it goes without saying, a lot of creativity and flavour.

WHERE TO STAY

⚌ **Hostellerie de la Tour** – Rte d'Arles - 13990 Fontvieille - 9 km toward les Baux then take D 78F, then D 17 – ☎ 04 90 54 72 21 - closed Nov to 14 Mars - ▣ - 10rooms : ⚏ 9 € - restaurant 11/18 €. A truly warm and attentive place awaits you here in this modest inn, which is consistent in its presentation. The rooms are small, pleasantly simple, and quite comfortable. The cuisine is good local fare.There is also a decent swimming pool.

⚌⚌ **Daudet** – 7 av. Montmajour - 13990 Fontvieille - ☎ 04 90 54 76 06 - closed the end of Oct to 26 Mar - ▣ - 14 rooms : ⚏ 7.50 €. Rooms partake of Daudet's joy – on the same level with the patio, the walls are white, the shutters lavender-blue, the furniture cast iron, the floor pétanque!

⚌⚌ **Chambre d'hôte le Mas du Petit Puits** – chemin Mario Prassinos – 13810 Eygalières – 0.5 km/0.3mi along the St-Rémy-de-Provence road via D 74A – ☎ 04 90 95 91 18 – 6 rooms : ⚏ 11.45€ – evening meal 23€. Before putting down your suitcases in one of the rooms decorated with antique furniture in this hundred-year-old mas, stop and admire the view of the Alpilles mountain range from the swimming pool. Provençal cuisine available on some evenings.

ON THE TOWN

La Maison Sucrée – R. de la République - 13810 Eygalières - ☎ 04 90 95 94 15 -open daily Jul-Aug; Mar-Oct, Mon-Thu, and Sun, 9.30am-9.30pm ; Nov.-May, Sat and Sun. Delicious ice cream and sorbets, such as mandarin and passion fruit. Also a lovely, restful crêperie and teahouse.

Fontvieille

⚑ 5 rue Marcel-Honorat, 13990 Fontvieille, ☎ 04 90 54 67 49 – www.fontvieille-provence.com.

For centuries the main industry in this small town, where Alphonse Daudet is remembered for his Lettres de mon Moulin, has been the quarrying of Arles limestone.

Moulin de Daudet (Daudet's Mill)

🕐 Jun to Sept: 9am-7pm; Apr-May: 9am-6pm; Feb-Mar and Oct-Dec: 10am-12pm, and 2-5pm. ⚌ 2€. ☎ 04 90 54 60 78.

Between Arles and Les Baux-de-Provence, the admirers of Alphonse Daudet's works can make a literary pilgrimage to his mill, the inspiration for his famous Lettres de mon moulin (Letters from My Mill), a charming and whimsical series of letters and tales from Provence. A lovely avenue of pines leads from Fontvieille to the mill.

Alphonse Daudet, the son of a silk manufacturer, was born in Nîmes on 13 May 1840 (d 1897). An outstanding author of tales of Provençal life and member of the Académie Goncourt, he was also a contemporary of such important 19C literary figures as Zola and Mistral. Long before 20C authors made it fashionable, Daudet left the fast-paced life of the big city to retire to Provence. He enjoyed strolling through the countryside, seeking inspiration, observing the farmers, meeting people, and listening to their stories. One of his characters is the garrulous miller, who rages against the modern steam-powered mills that are taking away all his customers. Other stories include the tale of the Pope's mule and old man Gaucher's elixir. The **view**★ from the mill is an inspiration to anyone, embracing the Alpilles, Beaucaire and Tarascon castles, the vast Rhône valley, and the Abbaye de Montmajour.

Le Moulin de Daudet's

Inside the mill, the first floor displays different kinds of millstones used in the grinding of grain. Note at roof level the names of the local winds, positioned according to their source.

The small **museum** contains memorabilia of the author remembered for the humour and sentiment with which he described the life and characters of Provence.

▸ *Continue along D 33. The road runs through a countryside of olive groves, pinewoods and fields of early vegetables.*

Chapelle St-Gabriel★

The chapel is closed but 🕐 *the key is available upon request at the Tourist Office in Tarascon – ☎ 04 90 91 03 52.*

This small 12C chapel has a richly carved façade. The plain interior, by contrast, is a fine example of Romanesque architecture.

▸ *Take D 32 to return to St-Rémy-de-Provence.*

Eygalières Alpilles★★ 2

Round-trip from St-Rémy-de-Provence. 42km/26mi – allow about 3hr

St-Rémy-de-Provence★

🕭 *See ST-RÉMY-DE-PROVENCE.*

▸ *Leave St-Rémy-de-Provence on D 5, in the direction of Maussane.*

The road passes the old monastery of St-Paul-de-Mausole and the Roman Monuments of Glanum, before continuing deep into the mountains where the landscape is dominated by pine trees.

▸ *After 4km/2.5mi leave the car by the side of D 5 and take the left footpath leading up to the Caume.*

Panorama de la Caume★★

🕐 *Access is forbidden from 1 July to 15 Sep. Alt 387m/1 270ft.*

A television relay mast is located at the top. Walk to the southern edge of the plateau to enjoy a vast panorama of the surrounding countryside, including the Alpilles in the foreground and the Crau and Camargue plains. From the northern edge, the view encompasses the Rhône plain, the Guidon du Bouquet with its characteristic beak-like outline, Mont Ventoux, and the Durance valley.

▸ *Return to D 5 and turn left.*

The road traverses a pinewood and several small gorges.

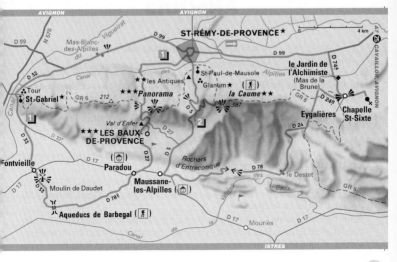

Rochers d'Entreconque

Lying to the left of the road, these rocks are, in fact, former bauxite quarries, as can be seen from their characteristic dark red colour. The road then runs through olive, apricot, almond and cherry orchard country.

Maussane-les-Alpilles

[Kids] ⚤ At the entrance to the town, to the left of the road stands a *santon* museum, **Musée des santons animés** (*Apr-Sept:10am-8pm; Oct-Mar: daily except Tues, 1.30-7pm.* ⏰*Closed Jan.* ∞*3€ (children 2€).* The displays show the evolution of these little figurines against a backdrop of Provençal scenery.

▶ *Turn round and by way of D 5, head toward Maussane-les-Alpilles. At the town entrance bear left and immediately left again onto D 78.*

The road runs through olive groves at the foot of the Alpilles before rising gently to a low pass from where there is a view of Les Opiès, a hillock crowned by a tower.

▶ *At Le Destet, turn left onto D 24, which, as it rises, reveals the crest of La Caume. After 7.5km/4.5mi bear right onto D 24B, which leads to Eygalières.*

Eygalières

This small town of narrow winding streets rises in tiers up the hill to an ancient castle keep. Once a Neolithic settlement, it was later occupied by a Roman legion sent to divert the local spring waters to Arles. From the top of the village a pleasant view opens out onto La Caume mountains, the Alpilles and then Durance valley.

▶ *Continue on D 24B, towards Orgon.*

Chapelle St-Sixte

This 12 C chapel, crowning a stony hill, stands on the site of a pagan temple erected in honor of the spirit of a local spring. The arch separating the nave from the fine oven-vaulted apse rests on consoles in the shape of a boar's head

▶ *Return to Eygalières and in the village turn left onto a small road signposted Mas de la Brune.*

Le Jardin de l'Alchimiste

The Mas de la Brune is a fine country residence built in 1572. It is now a charming hotel, set amid the alchemist's garden, where stones, water, and plants are landscaped. Their inspiration comes from the alchemist himself, and his quest for the philosopher's stone. The magical garden contains many plants local to the Mediterranean region, in particular, the Alpilles; these varieties have medicinal or symbolic properties. This delightful site has been laid out with skill and imagination. The result is a place that is different and that offers respite and relaxation.

▶ *Take D 74A, and turn left on D 99 for St-Rémy-de-Provence.*

ANSOUIS

POPULATION 1 033

MAP: SEE MONTAGNE DU LUBERON

MICHELIN LOCAL MAP 332: F-11 OR 114 FOLD 2 OR 528 FOLD 31

Located between the River Durance and the Grand Luberon foothills, the town was built on the southern slope of a rocky spur crowned by a castle.

🛈 *Pl. du Château, 84240 Ansouis,* ☏ *04 90 09 86 98.*

Visit

Château★

⏰*Open Feb to end of Dec: guided tours (1 hr) 2.30-6pm (July to Sept: 2.30-6pm); All Saints to Easter, June, and Oct: daily except Tues 2.30-6pm.* ⏰ *Closed in Jan.* ∞*6€ (children: 3€).* ☏ *04 90 09 82 70.*

At the beginning of the 12C the barons of Ansouis built a medieval castle on the foundations of an old fortress. The castle lost its defensive character, particularly in its southern section, during the 17C and 18C. The castle is of great interest as it has been in the

Sabran family for centuries and each generation has left its imprint. Stone steps and a ramp lead to a spacious chestnut walk, dominated by a monumental and harmonious façade in gold-coloured stone. The main door, lavishly decorated with pyramidal bosses and over which hangs the Sabran crest, is worthy of particular note. The coffer-vaulted grand staircase, dating from the Henri IV period, leads to the guardroom embellished with 17C-19C arms and armour. This room is connected, via a narrow corridor, to the well room, adjacent to the former guardroom, now a chapel. Cross the dining room, in which hang 17C Flemish tapestries depicting the story of Aeneas and

Château d'Ansouis

Dido, the **Charles X Room**, and the **St Eleazarius'** and **St Dauphine** de Sabran's rooms, which contain memorabilia of the two saints. The Provençal kitchen, the prison, and the chapel nicely round off the visit.

On the terrace you will find a beautiful view of the Durance gap and the Trévaresse range.

The gardens are a delightful surprise: hanging gardens planted with boxwood and dark-leafed trees fill every corner, giving it a romantic air.

Church

This former courtroom of the counts of Forcalquier and the counts of Sabran was constructed in the 13C on the original fortifications of the castle, as can be seen by its south wall pierced by thin arrow slits, giving it a military rather than a religious atmosphere.

Musée Extraordinaire

Guided tours (45min) daily except Tues 2-6pm (Apr to Sept: 2-7pm). ⓘ*Closed Jan and Feb and 25 Dec.* ⓘ*3.50€ (under 16, 1.5€).* ☎ *04 90 09 82 64.*

The 15C vaulted cellars of this ancient building house this small museum devoted to underwater life, which might come as a surprise here in the Luberon! Works displayed are by painter, ceramicist, and stained glass artist **G. Mazoyer** (first floor: artist's workshop). An underwater cave has been recreated. Provençal furniture is also exhibited.

Excursions

Le Luberon★★★ – (ⓘ*See Le LUBERON*)

Chateau Turcan: Musee de la Vigne et du Vin

▶ *Leave Ansous heading towards La Tour d-Aigues, then turn immediately right onto D 56 towards Pertuis. After 2km/1mi, turn left (signposted) onto a gravelled track lined with cypress trees.*

♿ ⓘ *Open mid-Jun to end of Sept: 9.30am-12.30pm and 2.30-7pm (Sun, by request); rest of the year: 9.30am-12pm and 2.30-6.30pm.* ⓘ *Closed Sun and public holidays, 1-10 Jan, and Mon in winter.* ⓘ *3 € (Under12, free) –* ☎ *04 90 09 83 33.*

APT

POPULATION 11 172

MICHELIN LOCAL MAP 332: F-10 OR 114 FOLD 2 OR 528 FOLD 31

The Roman colony of Julia Apt was a prosperous ancient city and a bishopric in the 3C. Today, Apt, a small bustling town in the Calavon valley known for its crystallized fruit and preserves, lavender essence, and truffles. It is also the main centre for ochre mining in France. Apt is a good excursion centre for trips to the Luberon range. A colourful, animated market is held here on Saturday mornings where you can find a rich variety of Provençal produce and products, including organic (*bio*) delights. Apt is also the scene of a traditional pilgrimage that takes place on the last Sunday in July.

🖿 *20 av. Philippe-de-Girard, 84400 Apt, ☎ 04 90 74 03 18 – www.ot-apt.fr.*

Walking Tour

🕐 *Allow 1hr and at least 2hr on market days.*

▶ *From place de la Bouquerie take rue de la République until you reach place du Septier, which is adorned with beautiful private residences. Go to place Carnot and turn right onto rue Ste-Anne.*

Cathédrale Sainte-Anne

🕐*Times vary according to the season and the availability of staff members. ☎ 04 90 04 61 71 – www.apt-cathedrale.com.*

This cathedral is the first sanctuary dedicated to Ste Anne in France. It holds the saint's reliquaries brought back from the Orient in the 3C, which, according to legend, were miraculously found by Charlemagne during a trip in 776. The actual building was constructed in the 11C or 12C and was remodelled many times. The south aisle is Romanesque, the north aisle is 14C Gothic and the nave was rebuilt in the 17C. Covering the transept crossing is a dome on squinches similar to the one at Notre-Dame-des-Doms Cathedral in Avignon. At the end of the apse, a 14C stained-glass window, given by Pope Urban V, depicts Ste Anne holding the Virgin and Child in her arms.

Chapelle Sainte-Anne

The first chapel off the north aisle was built in 1660, when Anne of Austria came on pilgrimage. The furnishings include: above the wooden gilt altarpiece, a large reliquary bust of Ste Anne; on the left, under the dome, a marble group of Ste Anne and the Virgin by the Italian Benzoni; and across the way the family tomb of the dukes of Sabran.

Treasury (Trésor)

♿ ▶ *Apr-Sept: guided tours (15min) daily, 11am-5pm; Sat, 11am; Oct-Mar: 11am. 🕐Closed Sun and public holidays. ⊛ No charge. ☎ 04 90 74 36 60 - www.apt-cathedrale.com.*

In the sacristy of Ste Anne's chapel are displayed 11C and 12C liturgical manuscripts, shrines decorated with 12C and 13C Limoges enamels, 14C Florentine gilded-wood caskets and Ste Anne's shroud, and an 11C caliph's coat brought back from the First Crusade (1096-99).

Crypt

Composed of two floors: the upper crypt is in the Romanesque style and contains an altar supported by a Romanesque capital and 13C sarcophagi; the lower crypt is Pre-Romanesque. At the back of the two crypts stand two tombstones.

▶ *Continue along rue des Marchands, which passes through the bell gate, to place du Postel.*

Porte de Saignon

Rue St-Pierre leads to this medieval gate, part of the town's remaining fortifications.

▶ *Go along cours Lauze-de-Perret to rue Louis-Rousset, which leads back into the old city.*

Note the 16C **Hôtel de Buoux** on the corner of rue Paul-Achard. The **Maison du Parc du Luberon** is housed in a former private hôtel in place Jean-Jaurès.

▶ *Turn right into rue Casin, which leads back to rue des Marchands; turn left and continue to place Gabriel-Péri.*

Note the lovely Classical façade of the *sous-prefecture*, flanked by two fountains with dolphins.

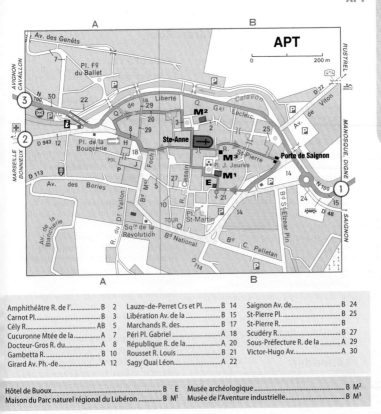

Amphithéâtre R. de l'......	B	2	Lauze-de-Perret Crs et Pl.	B	14	Saignon Av. de......	B 24
Carnot Pl.......	B	3	Libération Av. de la	B	15	St-Pierre Pl.....	B 25
Cély R.......	AB	5	Marchands R. des......	B	17	St-Pierre R.......	B
Cucuronne Mtée de la	A	7	Péri Pl. Gabriel	A	18	Scudéry R........	B 27
Docteur-Gros R. du	A	8	République R. de la	B	20	Sous-Préfecture R. de la	A 29
Gambetta R.......	B	10	Rousset R. Louis	B	21	Victor-Hugo Av.......	A 30
Girard Av. Ph.-de.....	A	12	Sagy Quai Léon......	A	22		

Hôtel de Buoux......	B	E	Musée archéologique	B	M²
Maison du Parc naturel régional du Lubéron	B	M¹	Musée de l'Aventure industrielle......	B	M³

▶ *Return to place de la Bouquerie via rue du Dr-Gros.*

Museums

Maison du Parc Naturel Régional du Luberon

60 pl. Jean-Jaurès, 84400 Apt. ⊙*Open Apr to end of Sept: daily except Sun 8.30am-12pm, 1.30-7pm; Oct to Mar: daily except Sat and Sun 8.30am-12pm, 1.30-6pm.* ⊙*Closed public holidays.* ☎ *04 90 04 42 00. www.parcduluberon.fr.*

Visitors to the centre learn about the natural environment and rural life in the Luberon Nature Park through various exhibitions, documents, local products and walking tours. In the cellars the emphasis is on the evolution of living specimens and geological phenomena. The displays include illuminated panels, animated tableaux of prehistoric landscapes and sculptures of primitive animals. The ground floor exhibition is devoted to the region's geological heritage, the different types of natural environment, habitat and hill villages.

Musée archéologique

⊙*June to Sept: daily 10am-12pm, 3-6.30pm, Sun 3-7pm; Oct-May: daily except Sun, 10am-12pm, 2-5.30.* ⊙*Closed Tues and public holidays.* ⊛4€ (under 12, free). ☎ *04 90 74 95 30.*

An 18C hotel houses this archaeological museum. The displays cover prehistory, proto-history, the Gallo-Roman period (mosaics, pottery, glassware, funerary furnishings, jewelry, coins), and items excavated from the *oppidum* of Chastellard-de-Lardiers, near Banon in the Alpes-de-Haute-Provence. The second floor displays 17C-19C ceramics from Apt, and works by local ceramicist **Léon Sagy** (1863-1939). A number of 17C-19C ex-votos are also exhibited.

Ochre Tour★★

49km/30mi – about 3hr 30min

▶ *Leave Apt on N 100 in the direction of Cavaillon. Turn right on D 149 in the direction of Bonnieux.*

Address Book

Access – ▶Getting to Apt requires some effort, but it is well worth it. *If you are approaching from the west on N 100, you will drive through endless suburbs before crossing the Cavalon river and on to place de la Bouquerie, which is Apt's town centre.* 🅿 There are car parks, no fee, on the river banks. Shuttle buses running every half hour are in service on Saturday market day, running from the car parks at Stade de Viton and the train station.

École Rustr'Aile Colorado – *Le Stade - 84400 Rustrel -* ☎ *04 90 04 96 53 - sud-parapente.com - 9am-7pm –closed Nov-Mar.* Hang-gliding school where you can take in an aerial view of the Colorado de Rustel.

ON THE TOWN

La Tour de l'Ho – *125 bd National -* ☎ *04 90 74 01 90 - closed Tues and Wed.* A highly recommended crêperie and ice cream parlor with a terrace in Luberon's capital.Open late, with music in the evenings.

EATING OUT

😊😊 **Auberge Le Rustréou** – *3 pl. de la Fête - 84400 Rustrel -* ☎ *04 90 04 90 90. For a long time this inn has had a very good reputation, which it retains.* Enjoy dining in a tranquil space decorated in cooling tones, situated in a serene village at the gate to the *colorado provençal.* All this enhances what is a deeply satisfying cuisine.

WHERE TO STAY

😊 **Le Ventoux** – *785 av. Victor-Hugo -* ☎ *04 90 04 74 60 - 15 rooms -* 🍽 *6 € - restaurant 12/21 €.* A nice little place with modest prices, the rooms are very comfortable. Away from the town centre, on the road to Cavaillon.

SHOPPING

Markets – There is a 😊**traditional** market every Sat morning and a **farmer's** market every Tues from May to Nov.

Boulangerie de Rustrel – *Brieugne - 84400 Rustrel -* ☎ *04 90 04 95 45 - Tues-Sat, 7am-12pm and 3-7pm; Sun, 7am-12pm.* This small bakery is so good it is well worth the extra mile. The bread made here is leavened on the premises, kneaded by hand, and best of all, cooked over a wood fire. Delicious!

Confiserie Aptunion – *N 100 - Salignan -* ☎ *04 90 76 31 43 - www.kerryaptunion. com – a guided tour is available upon prior arrangement.* In the heart of the Luberon, this superb factory shop offers a range of crystallized fruits. Clementines, oranges, pears, plums, apricots, and figs are presented in baskets or arrangements and can be sampled alone or as a part of a pastry or other confection. A film is included in the factory tour.

EVENTS

Festival Tréteaux de Nuit – *Second half of July – ask at the tourist office,* ☎ *04 90 74 03 18 – www.ot-apt.fr.* Comedy, variety shows, and world music festival.

Pont Julien

Spanning the River Coulon (or Calavon) in the 3C BC, this three-arched bridge was on the ancient Domitian Way linking Italy to Spain. It was mounted on two piers pierced to allow flood-waters to pass swiftly through them.

▶ *Take D 108, then D 149 in the direction of Roussillon.*

Roussillon★★ – 👓See ROUSSILLON.

▶ *Leave Roussillon on D 227.*

Watch for fine views, to the right, of the ochre cliffs and the Luberon range, and to the left, of the Vaucluse plateau.

▶ *Bear right on D 2 and right again on D 101.*

In a field to the right of the road you can see some 20 settling tanks used for the processing of ochre, extracted from neighbouring quarries.

▶ *On entering Gargas bear left on D 83 and left again on D 943.*

St-Saturnin-lès-Apt

This village, perched on the first foothills of the Vaucluse plateau, is overlooked by old castle ruins and a Romanesque chapel. 👓 Take the alley left of the village church and climb to the chapel for a view of the Apt countryside and Luberon range. The upper Porte Ayguier (15C gate) still preserves some of its defences. This village, with its narrow winding streets and drystone walled houses, is a cherry-growing centre, and makes a good base for walking 🚶: there are over 200km/125mi of signposted paths in the region, following the old droving routes (👓 *see SAULT*).

▶ *Follow D 179 and then D 30 to Rustel.*

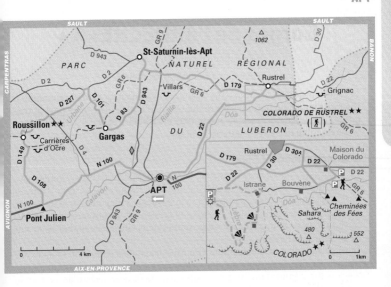

Colorado de Rustrel★★

🕐*Guides and maps available at the maison du Colorado, ☎ 04 90 04 96 07, and at Rustel's townhall, ☎ 04 90 04 97 43/98 49. Leave your car in one of the paying car parks, either by the banks of the Dôa, or on D 22. Footpaths are well-marked; walking time for each loop is indicated by a signpost at the start of the trail.*

🚶This gigantic colorado with its magnificent ochre quarries can be explored on many different walks. There is no better way to appreciate the ochre-coloured landscape of cliff faces, clay-capped earth pillars with jagged crowns (*Cheminées de Fées* – fairies' chimneys), the spot known locally as "the Sahara", the Cirque de Barries, waterfalls, and the "river of sand." All are the extraordinary combination of man's influence on the landscape and natural erosion.

🚶There is a 2hr loop *(recommended for experienced hikers)* that begins at the Colorado camp site, on D 22. Follow the yellow blaze marks. Leave the old workings of the Rustrel iron foundry to the right. The steep slope down into the little valley of the Lèbre contains vermilion rocks. Climb back up the valley to the foot of the old phosphate quarries, known as "Terres Vertes" (green earth). The countryside of pine forest and heathland leads to the rose-coloured cliffs of the Istrane quarry. Return to the car via the footpath from Rustrel to Caseneuve and a small country road.
Be sure to stop in the charming village of Rustel for well-deserved refreshment and to take in the skyline with its bell tower and manor house silhouette.

▷   *Return to Apt on D 22.*

Colorado de Rustrel

Gorges de l'ARDÈCHE★★★

MICHELIN LOCAL MAP 331: I7-J8 OR 528

FOLDS 1, 2, 14 AND 15 OR 524 FOLD 23

The Ardèche gorges, overlooked by an audaciously engineered road, rank among the most imposing natural sites in the south of France. The main part of the gorges is now a nature reserve and in 1993 the whole area was listed as a Major Site belonging to France's national heritage.

A Temperamental River

The Ardèche rises in the Mazan massif (alt 1 467m/4 813ft). After a 119km/74mi journey, it flows into the River Rhône, 1km/0.5mi upstream from Pont-St-Esprit. The river slope has a steep gradient, particularly so in the upper valley, but it is in the lower valley that the most surprising examples of erosion can be observed as the river carved a passage through the limestone strata of the plateau, already hollowed out by underground rivers.

The Ardèche's tributaries running down from the mountain accentuate its sporadic yet typically Mediterranean flow: autumn spates give way to a shallow rivulet in winter, then swell into spring torrents, before subsiding to a comparative trickle during the summer. During the peak flow there is a formidable convergence of flood-waters at Vallon-Pont-d'Arc. A powerful wall of water advances down the valley at 15-20kph/9-12mph! The strength of these erratic flood waters is such that the river pushes the flow of the Rhône eastwards and deposits a pile of rubble in its river bed. In 1890, the overflow of the Ardèche was so strong that it cut through the Rhône and broke the Lauzon breakwater on the opposite bank. Its drainage is just as erratic.

The nature reserve of the Gorges de l'Ardèche (situated between Charmes and Sauze) is a protected area and it is therefore essential to preserve its ecosystem by following a few simple rules:

It is strictly forbidden to light fires, leave litter, pick flowers or branches from trees and stray from designated footpaths. Camping is only allowed on official sites and windsurfing is forbidden.

Vallon-Pont-d'Arc to Pont-St-Esprit ⬚1⬚

▶ *38km/23mi – allow 1 day. Leave Vallons and drive south toward Pont d'Arc.*

A **panoramic road**, D 290, overlooks (in *corniche* style) the gorge, offering wonderful views along its way. It follows the left bank of the Ardèche, then after crossing the river at St-Martin-d'Ardèche, returns to Vallon via the *Plateau d'Orgnac*.

Cirque de la Madeleine

J. Damase/MICHELIN

Address Book

DESCENT BY BOAT

Ideal Time – This best time for the descent by boat or cano is from March to the end of November; May and June are ideal as days are longer and it is not too crowded (except on the weekends). September is also ideal.

Rental – The are about 60 rental firms at Vallon-Pont-d'Arc, Salavas, Ruoms, St-Martin, and St-Remèze, offering trips down the gorge independently or with a guide (1-2 days). To reduce the descent from 30km to 24km, start from Chaumes, the last of the rental spots. To fully enjoy the entire trip without concern for arrival time, allow two days. Rental rates vary from an average fee of 26-36€ (1 day) to 35€ (2 days, not including accommodation) per person. A list of rental firms is available from Tourist Offices (*syndicats d'initiative*) in Ruoms (*rue Alphonse-Daudet, 07120 Ruoms*, ☎ 04 75 93 91 90), Vallon-Pont d'Arc (*Cité administrative, 07150 Vallon Pont d'Arc*, ☎ 04 75 88 04 01) and St-Martin-d'Ardèche (*place de l'Eglise, 07700 St-Martin-d'Ardèche*, ☎ 04 75 98 70 91). If you are making the trip without a guide, make sure to reserve a pitch at a camp site through a central booking office at the Tourist Offices listed above.

Caution – Depending season and river water levels, allow 6-9 hours for the trip down the gorge (no departures allowed after 6pm). Ask about the trickier passages with rapids; these require expertise in the use of a canoe and are suitable for experts only. It is essential that you know how to swim. Life jackets are compulsory: failure to wear them can result in heavy fines. Navigation regulations can be consulted at all rental firms, town halls, tourist offices, and police stations (*gendarmeries*). It is advisable to obtain the map/guide of the area, the *Plan-guide des gorges de l'Ardeche,* published by Association Tourena. The safest way to descend the entire passage is with one of the trained boatmen of the Archèche.

Camping – The river flows through a nature reserve. It is possible to picnic anywhere along the river's banks as long as you respect the environment (leave no litter, etc.). Camping is only permitted at official sites at Gaud and Gournier (*5€ per person or to 7€ per tent per night:* ☎ 04 75 88 00 41). Longer stays are possible at the camp sites at Les Templiers (*nudist,* ☎ 04 75 04 28 58) and the St-Marcel caves (☎ 04 75 04 14 65).

DESCENT ON FOOT

Numerous passages require experience in assessing the terrain (slippery bends, passages through caves or fords). Proper hiking equipment is recommended. If you are walking along the left bank, check the water levels at local police stations or the local flood warning information service (*Service départemental d'alerte des crues*) before you leave. The "des Champs" and the "de Guitard" fords are unavoidable. ☎ 04 75 64 54 55.

For coin ranges, see Legend at the back of the guide.

EATING OUT

L'Esplanade – *place de l'Église - 30430 Barjac -* ☎ 04 66 24 58 42 *- closed Nov, Dec and Tue from 5 Jan-1 Jun.* A small 18C stone house whose flower-decked terrace offers a pretty view over the countryside. The interior has a vaulted ceiling and is decorated with old agricultural tools and other bric-a-brac objects.

L'Auberge Sarrasine – *rue de la Fontaine – 30760 Aiguèze –* ☎ 04 66 50 94 20. Exploring the little streets of the village you might well come across this little restaurant consisting of three vaulted rooms dating from the 11C. Originally from Burgundy, the chef incorporates Provençal flavours into his cooking.

WHERE TO STAY

Hôtel Le Clos des Bruyères – *route des Gorges - 07150 Vallon-Pont-d'Arc -* ☎ 04 75 37 18 85 *– closed Oct-Mar -* 🅿 *- 32 rooms -* ⬚ *6.60€ - restaurant 48€.* The Gorges de l'Ardèche road is magnificent, but its bends are exhausting. Take a break in this local-style house, with arcades opening onto the outdoor swimming pool. Rooms have balconies or overlook the garden. Country cooking in the restaurant with terrace.

Chambre d'hôte La Sérénité – *place de la Mairie – 30430 Barjac – 6km/3.7mi west of Aven d'Orgnac by D 317 and D 176 –* ☎ 04 66 24 54 63 *– closed Jan-Feb –* ⬚ *– 3 rooms.* Situated in the heart of the village, this 17C house with blue shutters is covered in Virginia creeper. Painted furniture, knick-knacks, the patina of the walls and hexagonal floor tiles adorn the individually decorated rooms. Delicious breakfast served in front of the fireplace or on the flower-decked terrace in fine weather.

The road passes the Château du Vieux Vallon and crosses the River Ibie before rejoining the Ardèche. On the left is the **Grotte des Tunnels**, a cave which once had an underground stream, and then the **Grotte des Huguenots**, which houses an exhibition on speleology and prehistory (mid-June to end of Aug: 10am-7pm. 3.50€ (children, 2.50€). 04 75 88 06 71).

Pont-d'Arc★★

▶ Park in the car par to the left of the road. To reach the foot of Pont-d'Arc, there is a path on the Vallon side 150m/164yd from the viewpoint. The river flows under the natural arch (34m/112ft high, 59m/194ft wide).

The scenic splendour begins immediately after Pont-d'Arc: the river flows in wide curves punctuated by rapids, all in the framework of a 30km/20mi gorge enclosed by rock walls 300m/984ft high in some places, dramatically coloured in tones of white, dark and light grey and overgrown with scrub oak and vegetation; the river is jade green.

Beyond Chames, on the floor of the **Tiourre valley**, the road curves to the left creating a grandiose rocky **cirque**★ before climbing to the plateau's edge.

Belvédère du Serre de Tourre★★

Poised almost vertically 200m/656ft above the Ardèche, this offers a superb **view** of the river winding round the **Pas du Mousse rock** on which stand the few remaining ruins of the 16C Château d'Ebbo. Also to be seen are the Falaises de Saleyron (Saleyron cliffs).

On the left bank, the tourist road follows the twisted outline of its cliffs and passes through forests of evergreen oaks, first the Bois Bouchas and then the Bois Malbosc.

Belvédères de Gaud★★

The **view** upstream takes in the Gaud meander and the turrets of its small 19C castle.

The discovery

The local word *marzal* identifies a wild grass. The name *marzal* was given in c 1810 to the forester Dechame, from St-Remèze, after he had fined his wife who had picked some for her rabbits. A little later Marzal was murdered and thrown into a well, the so-called Trou de la Barthe, with his dog. The crime was discovered and the local people began calling the well Marzal.

The chasm was actually discovered in 1892 when the speleologist **Édouard-Alfred Martel** (1859-1938) explored it for the first time, but its exact location was lost through incorrect signposting and it was not rediscovered until 1949.

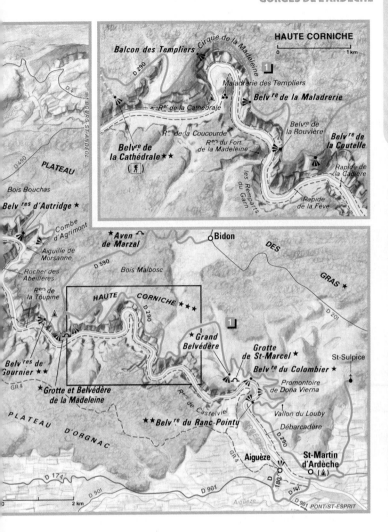

Belvédères d'Autridge★

To reach the two viewpoints take the panoramic curve. The Aiguille de Morsanne (Morsanne needle) soars above the gorges like the prow of a ship.

About 500m/0.3mi beyond the coomb, Combe d'Agrimont, new **vistas**★★ open up of the bend in the river with the Aiguille de Morsanne in the foreground.

Belvédères de Gournier★★

The viewpoints are well situated 200m/656ft above the river. Below, Le Gournier farm lies in ruins in a small field bordering the Ardèche, which carves its course through the Rochers de la Toupine (*toupine* means cooking pot).

▷ *Approach the Aven de Marzal by the road running along Gras plateau (D 590, opposite the road to the Belvédère de la Madeleine).*

Aven de Marzal (Marzal chasm)

Guided tours (1hr) – Apr - Sept: 10am-6pm; Mar and Oct-Nov: Sun and public holidays 2-5pm. ⊚7.80€ (children: 5.20€). ☎ 04 75 55 14 82 or ☎ 04 75 04 12 45.

Buried under the Gras plateau, this chasm is remarkable for the wealth of limestone formations which range in their oxide colouring from brown ochre to snow white. A metal staircase (743 steps) leads to the natural opening in the Gras plateau. The chasm opens into the Salle du Tombeau or Tomb Gallery. Nearby are bones of bear, stag, and bison that fell into the cave.

The **Salle du Chien** (Dog Gallery), whose entrance is surmounted by a flow of white draperies, contains a large variety of concretions, eccentrics, brightly-coloured organs, disc-like formations, and shapes resembling bunches of grapes. **Salle de la Pomme de Pin** (Pine Cone Gallery) is interesting for the wealth of its colours.

The **Salle des Diamants** (130m/426ft below ground) ends the visit; it presents a sparkling scene of fairy-like colours reflected in the glinting crystals which line the walls.

Musée du Monde souterrain

  Apr - Sept: 10am-6pm; Mar and Oct-Nov: Sun and public holidays 2-6pm. No charge. 04 75 55 14 82.

This museum recalls the great names and great moments of French speleology: Martel, Robert de Joly, Elisabeth and Norbert Casteret, and Guy de Lavaur.

Prehistoric Zoo

  Apr-Sept: 10am-6pm; Mar and Oct-Nov: Sunday and public holidays, 1-5.30pm. 7.80 € (children: 5.20 €) or with a combination ticket with Aven de Marzal, 13.40 € (children: 8.30 €). 04 75 55 14 82.

Displayed along a shaded path (800m/0.5mi) are life-size reproductions of animals from the Primary (Dimetrodon, Moschops) and Secondary Eras (Stegosaurus, Tyrannosaurus) through to the mammoth of the Quaternary Era.

▶*Follow the plateau des Gras via the picturesque D 201.*

Bidon

This tiny peaceful village with dry stone houses seems remarkably unaffected by the passage of time. The **Musée de la vie** traces the incredible evolution of the universe from the Big Bang to the present. *Daily from April to mid-Nov: 10am-6pm. 6€ (children, 3€).* 04 75 04 08 79.

▶ *Take D 590 back to the gorge as far as Madeleine crossroads.*

La Haute Corniche★★★

This, the most outstanding section of the drive. In close succession, there are unrivalled views of the gorges.

Belvédère de la Madeleine★

There is a fine view of the "Fort" de la Madeleine which bars the succession of gorges downstream.

Grotte de la Madeleine★

Guided tours (1hr)–July-Aug: 9am-7pm; Apr, June, and Sept: 10am-6pm; Oct: 10am-5pm (last admission 1hr before closing). 7€ (children: 4.50€). 04 75 04 22 20 – www.grottemadeleine.com.

This cave, discovered in 1887, was formed by an underground river which once drained part of Gras plateau. Enter through the Grotte Obscure, then follow a tunnel hewn out of the rock (*steep staircase*) to the Salle du Chaos or Chaos Cave.

Beyond this chamber, divided into two parts by a mass of columns detached from the vault, extends a vast gallery full of richly decorated concretions. The sides of the chamber are covered with small crystallisations resembling coral.

▶ *Approach Aven de Marzal by the road running along Gras plateau (D 590, opposite the road to the Grotte de la Madeleine).*

Belvédère de la Cathédrale★★

▶ *15min round-trip on foot.*

This affords a breathtaking view of one of the most curious sights of these gorges, the "Cathedral", a huge rock resembling a building in ruins whose stone spurs proudly overhang the river. Some of the path is quite rough, so be careful.

Balcon des Templiers

The viewpoint offers impressive views of a tight loop in the river flanked by the magnificent high rocky walls of the cirque. Down below, crowning a small spur, are the ruins of the Maladrerie des Templiers (Templars' Leper Hospital).

Belvédère de la Maladrerie

View of the Rocher de la Cathédrale.

Belvédère de la Rouvière

Facing the Garn "Ramparts."

Belvédère de la Coutelle

The viewpoint overlooks the river from a dizzying height of 180m/590ft. To the left the Castelviel rocks can be seen and the swift-flowing Fève and Cadière rapids.

Grand Belvédère★

View of the end of the gorges and the Ardèche's final bend.

▷ *Follow D 290 downstream from the Grand Belvédère; after 200m/656ft you will see the entrance building to the Grotte St-Marcel.*

Grotte de St-Marcel★

Guided tours (1 hr) – mid-Mar to end of Sept: 10am-6pm (July and Aug: 7pm); Oct to mid-Nov: 10am-5pm. ⊠ *7€.* ☎ *04 75 04 38 07.*

The opening to this cave, which was discovered in 1835 by a hunter from Aiguèze, is through a natural shelter cut into the side of the rock faces of the Gorges de l'Ardèche. The cave was formed by a subterranean river which has now dried up. It hollowed out a 32km/20mi network of chambers, a section of which is now open to the public.

A tunnel hollowed out of the rock leads through striking passages in which stalactites, stalagmites, draperies and other kinds of formations can be seen. There are various interesting stopping places along the route, where the nature of the concretions in evidence is reflected by the name given to that particular part of the cave: Chamber of the Virgin's Fountain; Painters' Gallery, with different coloured stripes in white (calcite), red (iron oxide) and black (manganese); Chamber of Kings; Cathedral etc. A footpath laid out on the site offers a good opportunity of discovering local flora (holm oak, boxwood, cistus, etc.) and two megalithic monuments *(information leaflet available at the ticket office).*

▷ *Return to D 290.*

Belvédère du Colombier★

There's a view down into the bend enclosed by rocky banks. The road follows a loop along a dry valley, skirts the Dona Vierna promontory and makes a wide detour around the Louby valley, the Ardèche's last enclosed bend.

Belvédère du Ranc-Pointu★★

Note the different types of erosion, striation, potholes, and caves.

Leaving the gorge, the countryside changes completely: the bare defile is replaced by a cultivated valley which opens out as it approaches the Rhône. On the right stands the village of **Aiguèze**, perched on a rocky outcrop overlooking the Ardèche, the first town since Vallon.

Saint-Martin-d'Ardeche

This friendly small town is situated at the exit to the gorge and is nowadays on more friendly terms with the river whose capricious floods used to be a bane to local residents. Surrealist painter Max Ernst stayed here in 1937-40. It is now a holiday centre for bathers, anglers, hikers, and canoeists.

Chapelle St-Sulpice

▷ *4km/2.5mi via Trignan from St-Martin-d'Ardèche.*

The dazzling white Romanesque chapel (12C-17C) stands on a slight hillock rising amid a sea of vines. The south wall is built of reused stones carved with interlacing designs.

▷ *Return to St-Martin-d'Ardèche and cross the Ardèche by the suspension bridge (pont suspendu St-Martin), then take D 901 on the right, and turn right again onto D 180.*

Aiguèze

This medieval village with its paved streets is set on top of the last cliffs of the gorges. After passing under an arch cut into the rock, one comes out into a 14C fortress. From the watch-path there is a pretty **view**★ of the end of the canyon, the ruined towers and the suspension bridge linking Aiguèze to St-Martin-d'Ardèche.

Orgnac Plateau 2

Aven d'Orgnac ★★★ – (See Aven d'ORGNAC.)

Plateau d'Orgnac

Round-trip of 45km/28mi leaving from the chasm.

▷ *Take D 317 and drive west as far as Barjac.*

Barjac

Barjac is famous for the antiquities fairs it organizes twice a year *(Easter weekend and the week of the Assumption of the Virgin Mary, 15 Aug, ☎ 04 66 24 50 09).* The upper part of town is a pleasant place to wander, through streets lined with 18C residences. The elegant château has been converted into a cultural centre, with a cinema and multimedia library. There is a good view of the Cévennes from the esplanade overlooking the plain.

▷ *Turn north onto D 979. At Vagnas, turn right onto D 355.*

Labastide-de-Virac

🕐*Easter to end of June and Sept: daily, except Wed, 2-6pm (July and Aug: daily 10am-7pm).* �. *Chateau, 5.5€, chateau and silkworm museum, 7.5€.* ☎ 04 75 38 61 13 – www.chateaudesroure.com.

North of this fortified village, an ideal departure point for outings to the Aveyron gorges or the Orgnac plateau, stands the 15C **château des Roure**. Since 1825 the castle has belonged to the family of the sculptor James Pradier (1795-1825), whose forebears were tenant farmers to the Counts of Roure. During the visit note the Florentine-style courtyard, spiral staircase and great hall (first floor) with its fine chimney. A fully operational silkworm farm enlightens visitors on the traditional breeding of silkworms. The visit ends with an exhibition of local handmade silks.

▷*After Labastides on D 217 turn left.*

Les Crottes

Just before Labastide, a small road on the right leads to this village, deserted since 3 March 1944, when all the villagers were shot by the Nazis. A marker commemorates this tragic event.

Belvédère du Méandre de Gaud★★

This commands an excellent view of the river at the foot of the Gaud cirque.

▷ *Retrace your steps and take D 217 to the left. Soon afterwards, a small road to the right leads to the Forestière chasm.*

Aven de la Forestière★

🕐*Apr to Sept: guided tours (1hr15min) 10am-6pm (July and Aug: 10am-7pm); Oct to Mar: school holidays, Sat-Sun and public holidays 10am-noon, 2-6pm.* 🕐*Closed 1 Jan and 25 Dec.* �. 6€. ☎ 04 75 38 63 08.

The dramatically lit chambers are rich in fine concretions such as the cauliflower-like shapes and macaroni-like strips, which hang from the roof, variegated stalactite curtains, phantasmagoric and eccentric formations, and floors bristling with stalagmites.
A small zoo presents a variety of crustaceans, fish, frogs, toads, and insects.

The Descent★★★

Vallon-Pont-d'Arc to St-Martin-d'Ardèche: By Boat

After a long calm stretch, the river bends and one enters the gorges. Almost immediately, the impressive Charlemagne rapid is passed, dominated on the right by the large rock of the same name. The river then passes under the natural porch of the famous Pont d'Arc. To the left extends the Estre cirque onto which opens a cave known as the Grotte Chauvet. Shortly after, to the right, are the Grotte d'Ebbo and Pas du Mousse rock, a narrow passage through the cliff to the plateau. The rock on the north bank is the Rocher de l'Aiguille. The first rapids, Rapide de la Dent Noire, are just below the immensely tall Saleyron cliffs and are followed by the wide Gaud meander and cirque with its small château.

Rapids and smooth flowing stretches, overlooked by canyon-high cliffs, alternate as landmarks such as the Aiguille de Morsanne, a needle-like rock on the north bank, and the jagged red and black spikes of the Rocher des Abeillères appear on the south bank.

After approximately 4hr you should have negotiated the Rochers de la Toupine, rocks strewn in the river's course, which in places is 18m/60ft deep, and be able to see Rocher de la Cathédrale in the distance. Before you actually reach Rocher de la Cathédrale, you pass one of the natural openings of the Grotte de la Madeleine, on the left. Shortly afterwards, the river flows below the enormous Rocher de la Cathédrale and

Down the Ardèche by canoe

past the Templars peninsula (12C remains), a popular spot with naturists.

The Cirque de la Madeleine is among the most spectacular on the trip, when seen from water level. Straits, rapids and smooth iridescent reaches follow one another as the river continues downwards between sheer cliff walls, bare of all but occasional evergreen oaks. Below the peculiar-looking Coucourde (Provençal for crane) rock and the Castelvieil cliff, the opening of the Grotte St-Marcel can be seen on the left, and, as you round the bend, the Dona Vierna promontory and the Belvédère de Ranc-Pointu. The cliffs melt away, the valley widens out, allowing a view of Aiguèze's tower on the edge of the rock escarpment to the right.

Vallon-Pont-d'Arc to St-Martin-d'Ardèche: On Foot

For a dry walk, leave from Chanes to Gué du Charmassonet (left bank), then cross the river twice, at Charmassonet to Gué de Guitard (right bank) and Gué de Guitard to Sauze (left bank). Otherwise, numerous loops are possible leaving from the plateau.

ARLES★★★

POPULATION 53 057

MICHELIN LOCAL MAP 340: C-3 OR 528 FOLD 28 OR 524 FOLD 26

Roman capital and a major religious centre in the Middle Ages, Arles preserves glorious Gallo-Roman antiquities and gems of Romanesque art. The development of the Camargue as a protected natural environment has made Arles the rice capital. It is a central market for agricultural produce (market gardening, raising of Crau sheep) and a city with diversified light industry and administrative and cultural functions. It is also the largest commune in France, encompassing 77 000ha/30sq mi.

Arles women inspired the praise in poetry or music of Mistral, Daudet, Gounod, and Bizet. Although their splendid costumes can be seen only during the festivals (🍷 see Address Book), the beauty of these women survives from one generation to the next.

🔖 Espl. Charles-de-Gaulle, Bd des Lices, 13200 Arles, ☎ 04 90 18 41 20. www.tourisme.ville-arles.fr

▶ **Orient Yourself:** Boulevard des Lices is a pleasant place for a stroll, particularly on a sunny day, with its huge plane trees and its busy cafe terraces; the atmosphere is especially lively during the market on Saturdays. The Old Town is reached by passing through pleasant Jardin d'Été and following rue Porte-de-Laure, with its many restaurants. Take a 90min guided tour of the town to get a quick overview (🍷 see Address Book).

🌀 **A Word of Caution:** Watch out for the plane trees on boulevard Georges-Clemenceau, and don't even try to venture by car through the maze of little streets within Old Arles.

🔅 **Don't Miss:** Alyscamps, a cemetery well known in Roman times, or the cloisters of St-Trophime, famous in Provence for their decoration.

🕐 **Organising Your Time:** Arles' public buildings and museums deserve a minimum two days. Allow at least 30min for Alyscamps alone. The tour of the Crau Plain requires about 3hr.

A Bit of History

Arles and Marseille – The excavations undertaken in 1975 under the Jardin d'Hiver have revealed the existence of a Celtic-Ligurian town (known as Theline) colonised by the Greeks from Marseille as early as the 6C BC.

The town, which soon took the name of Arelate, met with new prosperity when the Consul Marius, in 104 BC, built a canal that joined the Rhône to the Fos gulf, greatly facilitating navigation. In 49 BC when Julius Caesar defeated Marseille, Arles developed economically, becoming a prosperous Roman colony: it became a crossroads for seven important roads and a major sea and river port.

Address Book

TOURS AND DISCOUNTS

Tours of the town – (1hr30min) guided tours. Contact the tourist office for information and hours (☎ 04 90 18 41 20. www.tourisme.ville-arles.fr). 4€.

Monuments and Museums – At the tourist office, you can buy a single pass (☎13.50€) for all sights and museums, except the Museon Arlaten.

Les Alpilles train – 👣 see Les ALPILLES.

ENTERTAINMENT

The newspaper Le César, available free of charge for tourists at the Tourist Office and other cultural spots, gives listings of shows in the city.

Le Méjan – Pl. Nina-Berberova - ☎ 04 90 49 56 78. Evening and afternoon musicals, jazz concerts, lectures, conferences, and exhibitions in the chapel Saint-Martin-du-Méjan.

SHOPPING

Markets – **Traditional** market every Wed in boulevard Émile-Combes and every Sat in boulevard des Lices and boulevard Clemenceau. **Antique** market first Wed of the month in boulevard des Lices. **Christmas** market the end of November.

Provençal fabrics – Les Étoffes de Romane (maison Carcassonne), 10 boulevard des Lices - ☎ 04 90 93 53 70.

Patisserie – De Moro, 24 rue du Prés.-Wilson (near the Espace Van Gogh) – 🕐closed Sun and public holidays. ☎ 04 90 93 14 43. Specializes in delicious almond biscuits.

Provençal furniture – Melani Fréderic, route d'Eyguères, Pont-de-Crau, 13200 Arles, ☎ 04 90 49 72 83. The workshops can be visited in small groups by appointment only.

Fashion and jewelry – Christian Lacroix, rue de la République – ☎ 04 90 96 11 16.

Books – Librarie Actes Sud – Pl. Nina-Berberova, Le Méjan – ☎ 04 90 49 56 77. Find the latest publications of this local publishing house. La Boutique des

Passionnés – 14 r. Réattu (town center, walknig pedestrian zone) - b 04 90 96 59 93 - www.passion.toros.com - Mon, 2-7pm, Tues-Sat 9am-7pm, Sun in Dec. Closed public hoildays. At once a book and music shop, this is a gold mine for tauromachie and for music from the south.

Crafts – Maison Chave – 14 rd-pt des Arènes – ☎ 04 90 96 15 22 – May-Sept: Tue-Sat 9am-7pm; low season 9am-12.30pm, 2-7pm – Closed Jan. In this workshop, four craftsmen model and decorate santons, and a wide choice of figures is on sale. Exclusive hand-made santons, using two or three different types of clay, made here for three generations.

Olive Oil – Huiles Jamard – 46 rue des Arènes – ☎ 04 90 49 70 73 – pjamard@aol.com – Tue-Sat 11am-12.30pm, 4-6pm – closed 25 Dec to 2 Jan – prices for bottles of oil range from 6.10P to 18.29€, according to the variety. Provençal olive oil, but also varieties from Spain, Greece and Italy, each with its particular flavour. Pierre, the master oil producer and former engineer will allow you to taste the different types of oil, accompanied by anecdotes about the secrets of their manufacture.

EVENTS

Rencontres Internationales de la Photographie – Throughout this international photography festival (*from July to mid-Sept*) there are evenings at the Roman theatre, exhibitions, courses, talks, and activities in the field of photography in various locations throughout the town. *For more information: 10 rond-point des Arènes, ☎ 04 90 96 76 06 – www. rencontres-arles.com.*

Fête des Gardians – 1 May. A mass in the Provençal dialect is held in Collégiale Notre-Dame-de-la-Major. This includes the blessing of horses, typical Camargue games, dancing to the sounds of pipes and drums as well as beautiful girls competing for the title of "Queen" of Arles.

Tauromachia – The architectural beauty of the amphitheatre acquires even greater appeal when **bullfights** and Camargue races take place and one can almost breathe a sense of antiquity. As well as shows organized on specific occasions, bullfights also take place during the ferias at Easter (*Easter weekend*), and during the Rice Festival (*second weekend in September*) which sees the participation of tauromachy's most illustrious figures. With the arrival of spring come the **Camargue races**, although the most important of these races take place during the **fêtes d'Arles** with **Cocarde d'Or** (*early July*) and in the finals of the **Trophée des As**, which takes place every two years in October, alternating with Nîmes.

Booking: **Bureau des Arènes** (*to the right of the main entrance*), ☎ 04 90 96 03 70, www.label-camargue.com).

Festival Les Suds – *second half of July.* www.suds-arles.com. World music festival.

For coin ranges, see Legend at the back of the guide.

WHERE TO EAT

🍴 **La Charcuterie** – *51 rue des Arènes –* ☎ *04 90 96 56 96 – restaurant.la-charcuteriewanadoo.fr – Closed 1-15 Aug, 23 Dec-6 Jan, Sun and Mon except Jul and weekends in May.* A real reveller from Lyons, the jovial proprietor couldn't have chosen a better spot for this old charcuterie with its marble counters. Pork lovers can treat themselves to a range of carefully chosen products, from Arles sausages to pig's trotters from Lyons.

🍴 **Le Criquet** – *21 R. Porte-de-Laure –* ☎ *04 90 96 80 51 – Closed end of Dec to end of Feb and Wed.* Go for the charming dining room with its beams and exposed stonework rather than the terrace in this little restaurant near the amphitheatre. Once you're comfortably seated, savour the young chef's *bourride* (a kind of fish soup) and other specialities.

🍴 **Jardin de Manon** – *14 avenue des Alyscamps –* ☎ *04 90 93 38 68 – Closed 4-24 Feb, 21 Oct-10 Nov.* This restaurant, situated just outside the city centre, is aptly named. Its interior courtyard terrace, full of trees and flowers, will appeal to lovers of alfresco dining. There are two dining rooms with wood panelling and the local cooking, which uses seasonal market produce, offers good value for money.

🍴🍴 **Lou Calèu** – *27 r. Porte-de-Laure - montée Vauban -* ☎ *04 90 49 71 77 - contact@lou-caleu.com - Closed 5 Jan-15 Feb .* A real classic: fresh salads, *taureau* stew, lamb with rosemary... All Arle's delights are at your fingertips. An excellent wine list. The place for the ultimate gourmet.

WHERE TO STAY

🛏 **Le Relais de Poste** – *2 r. Molière -* ☎ *04 90 52 05 76 - le.relais.de.poste@* wanadoo.fr - Closed Jan - 15 rooms: - 🖵 6€ - restaurant 17/22 €. A couple steps from the boulevard des Lices and the espace Van-Gogh, this centrally-based hotel was once the 18C postal relay. The restaurant evokes its era, with beams and frescos. The rooms are simple and warmly decorated with Provençcal textiles.

🛏🛏 **Hôtel du Musée** – *11 r. du Grand-Prieuré -* ☎ *04 90 93 88 88 - contact@hoteldumusee.com.fr - Closed Jan - 28 rooms -* 🖵 *7€.* Facing the Musée Réattu, this is hotel was built in the 17C : a labyrinth of green pathways through intimate courtyards, the rooms are tranquille and warm. An absolutely charming place!

🛏🛏 **Muette** – *15 r. des Suisses -* ☎ *04 90 96 15 39 - Closed for Feb vacation - 18 rooms -* 🖵 *6€.* A beautiful building (originally from the 15C and 17C) at home in the heart of historic Arles. Visible stone in veritable Provençal rooms guarantee that the walls are soundproof.

🛏🛏🛏 **Hôtel Calendal** – *5 rue Porte-de-Laure -* ☎ *04 90 96 11 89 - contact@lecalendal.com - 38 rooms -* 🖵 *7€.* This hotel has all the stylishness of Provençal interiors with its colourful façade, pretty inner shaded garden and cosy sitting room. Blue and yellow make up the colour scheme of furniture, fabrics and ceramics. Small tearoom.

🛏🛏 **Mireille** – *2 place St-Pierre, Trinquetaille –* ☎ *04 90 93 70 74 – contact@hotel-mireille.com – Closed 4 Nov-14 Mar –* 🅿 *– 34 rooms –* 🖵 *11€ – restaurant 22/31€.* Dive into the swimming pool in total peace in this hotel situated outside the city centre. Good size rooms with vibrant colours and Provençal furniture. Airy dining room with red and yellow fabrics.

🛏🛏🛏 **Hôtel D'Arlatan** – *26 rue Sauvage, near place du Forum –* ☎ *04 90 93 56 66 – hotel-arlatan@wanadoo.fr – closed 5 Jan to 8 Feb –* 🅿 *– 41 rooms –* 🖵 *10.50€.* Fall under the spell of this old mansion dating from the 15C, a stone's throw from place du Forum. Admire the underground Roman fragments through the glass floor of the bar and the drawing room. Rooms furnished with antiques and pretty fabrics. Small courtyard planted with trees where breakfast is served in the summer.

ON THE TOWN

Far from being stuck in the past, Arles is a lively town that integrates its traditions with a sense of modernity. Between a bullfight and the International Photography Festival, the craft market and the music programme, set aside a few moments to sit at the sidewalk cafes that Van Gogh so skilfully depicted.

Bar de l'Hôtel Nord Pinus – *place du Forum –* ☎ *04 90 93 44 44 – www.nord-pinus.com – daily 10am-1am.* An essential stopping place in Arles, the small bar of the Hotel Nord Pinuas, dating from the 17C has indiscriminately entertained artists, writers, film stars, and bullfighters: Picasso, Jean Cocteau, Yves Montand, Nimeno 2, Ruiz Miguel, Jean Giono. The charm of this place is made of small details such as its boat-shaped lamps, the bullfighting bar, squat armchairs and, in the background, refined flamenco music.

Café Van Gogh – *11 place du Forum –* ☎ *04 90 96 44 56 – low season: daily 9am-midnight; July-Aug 9am-2am.* This café, with its large terrace in place du Forum owes its fame to Vincent Van Gogh who made it the subject of one of his paintings in 1888: "This is a nocturnal painting with no blackness, nothing but beautiful blue and violet and green and, in this setting, the lit square takes on the hue of sulphur yellow and lime. It amuses me enormously to paint in this square at night…" (extract from a letter from Van Gogh to his sister Wilhelmina, dated September 1888).

L'Entrevue – *23 Quai Marx-Dormoy –* ☎ *04 90 93 37 28 – Oct-May: 8.30am-midnight; June-Sept: 8.30-2am.* It is a well known fact that Arles is the birthplace of the flourishing Actes Sud publishing house: the publishers of Paul Auster and Nina Berberova are also responsible for the creation of this café-restaurant that is the cultural hub of the ancient Roman capital. On the other side of the square there is a space for concerts, readings, plays, and photography exhibitions.

Roman Arles – A colony of veterans of the Sixth Legion, Arles was granted the privilege of building a fortified wall around the 40ha/99 acres of the official city. A forum, several temples, a basilica, baths, and a theatre were built. An aqueduct brought pure water in abundance from the Alpilles. The town was spreading at the end of the 1C, with the construction of an amphitheatre. To the south lay the Roquette shipyards. To the east, the Jardin d'Hiver district and the Esplanade were residential, while on the right bank of the Rhône, at Trinquetaille, was the large bustling dockland frequented by sailors, boatmen, and merchants. A bridge of boats joined the two banks of the river northeast of the town, level with the Bourg-Neuf district.

A golden age – In the 5C Arles was an active industrial centre. Textiles and gold and silver work were manufactured, ships were built, sarcophagi and arms were made, and imperial money was minted. Wheat, pork butcher's meat (already famous), olive oil, dark and thick wine from the Rhône hills, were all exported. Moreover, stonecarvers, masons, and architects from Arles were famous for the quality of their work.

The town possessed five guilds of boatmen. Some sailed the Rhône, the Durance and the many lakes in the region, using rafts carried on inflated goatskins called *utriculaires*. Other Arlene watermen sailed the Mediterranean.

Prosperity brought political importance: Emperor Constantine established himself and the expansion of Arles reached its maximum. The emperor remodelled the northwest district where an imperial palace and the La Trouille baths were built. In 395 AD Arles became the political and administrative capital of the Gauls (made up of Spain, Gaul as such, and Brittany). It was also a great religious centre where 19 synods were held, and its bishops were constantly acquiring importance under the protection of imperial rule.

The decline – In the 8C, the Franks and Saracens fought over the country, causing a great deal of destruction. In the 9C Arles was but a shadow of its former self when it became the capital of the Kingdom of Arles, which included Burgundy and part of Provence. It was not until the 12C that the town experienced a political and economic revival and acquired the status of a district governed by elected consuls. Its prestige was considerable as the Germanic emperor Frederick Barbarossa came to the town in 1178 to be crowned King of Arles in the newly completed, superb Romanesque Cathedral of St-Trophime. In 1239 the burghers of Arles submitted to the Count of Provence. From that time onwards, the town followed the fortunes of the province: political status was transferred to Aix, and Marseille took its revenge and surpassed Arles in economic prosperity.

As long as the Rhône remained the main commercial route, Arles continued to be relatively prosperous. This was even more the case when the land was upgraded by the Crau irrigation project and the drainage of the marshland. However, the arrival of the railway made river traffic obsolete and dealt a severe blow to trade. Until recently it was only the agricultural market centre for the Camargue, Crau, and Alpilles.

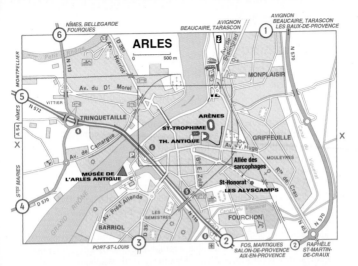

ARLES

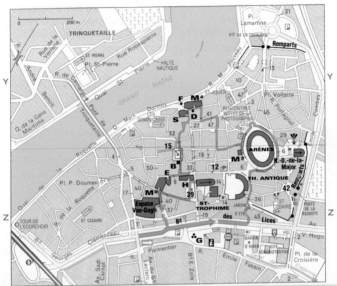

Allende Av. Président X	Doumer Pl. Paul .... Z	Président Wilson R. du .... Z	37
Alyscamps Av. des .... Z 2	Fassin R. Émile .... Z	Réattu R. .... Y	41
Amphithéâtre R. de l' .... Y	Forum Pl. du .... Z 3	Redoute Pl. de la .... Z	42
Anatole-France R. .... Z	Gambetta R. .... Z 4	République Pl. de la .... Z	39
Antonelle Pl. .... Z	Gare Maritime Q. de la .... Y 5	République R. de la .... Z	40
Arènes R. des .... YZ	Herriot Av. .... X 7	Robespierre R. .... Y	
Arènes Rd-Pt des .... YZ	Hôtel de Ville R. de l' .... Z 6	Roquette Q. de la .... YZ	
Balze R. .... Z	Jean-Jaurès R. .... Z 8	Roquette R. de la .... Z	
Benoît R. André .... Y	Jouveau R. Marius .... Y	Sadi-Carnot Av.	
Blum R. Léon .... Y 10	Lamartine Av. .... Y 10	St-Pierre Pl. .... Y	
Calade R. de la .... Z	Lamartine Pl. .... Y 12	St-Pierre Quai .... Y	
Camargue Av. de X	Leclerc Av. du Général .... Z	Sarcophages Allée des X	
Camargue R. de .... Z	Lices Bd des .... Z	Stalingrad Av. de .... Y	
Cavalerie R. de la .... Y	Maïsto R. Dominique .... Y 13	Trinquetaille Pont de .... Y	27
Clemenceau Bd Georges .... Z	Major Pl. de la .... Y	Vauban Montée .... Z	29
Cloître R. du .... Z	Mistral R. Frédéric .... Z 14	Verrerie R. de la .... Z	30
Combes Bd Émile .... YZ	Parmentier R. .... Z	Victor-Hugo Av. X	
Crau Rte de X	Place R. de la .... Y 32	Voltaire .... Pl. Y	
Croisière Pl. de la .... Z	Plan de la Cour R. du .... Z 33	Voltaire R. .... Y	45
Docteur-Morel Av. du X	Portagnel R. .... Z	Zola Bd Émile X	
Dormoy Q. Marx .... Y	Porte de Laure R. .... Z 36	4-Septembre R. du .... Y	47

Alyscamps (Les) X	Espace Van-Gogh .... Z	Musée de l'Arles antique X
Arènes .... Z	Fondation	Palais Constantin
Collégiale N.-D.-de-la-Major .. Z	Vincent-Van-Gogh-Arles .... Z M²	(thermes de la Trouille) .... Y S
Colonnes corinthiennes .... Z	B Fouilles de l'Esplanade .... Z	Remparts .... YZ
Commanderie Ste-Luce .... Y	D Hôtel de ville .... Z	H Théâtre antique .... Z
Cryptoportiques .... Z	E Museon Arlaten .... Z M⁶	Église St-Honorat X
Espace Méjean .... Y	F Musée Réattu .... Y M⁴	Église St-Trophime .... Z

Public Buildings *1 day*

Roman Theatre (Théâtre Antique)★★

🕐 *Open May-Sept: 9am-6.30pm; Mar-Apr and Oct : 9am-12pm and 2-6pm; Nov-Feb: 10am-12pm and 2-5pm -* 🕐*closed 1 Jan, 1 May, 1 Nov, and 25 Dec.* ⊜*3 €.* ☎ *04 90 49 36 74.*

Built during Augustus' reign c 27-5 BC, this theatre was much more badly damaged than the amphitheatre. As early as the 5C it was used as a quarry for the construction of churches, and in the 9C it was transformed into a redoubt before disappearing completely under houses and gardens. Rediscovered in the 17C, it was excavated from 1827 to 1855.

The theatre measured 102m/335ft in diameter and had a seating capacity of 12 000. Unlike the one in Orange, which was built on a natural height, this theatre was backed up by a 27-arched portico made up of three levels of arcades, of which only one bay remains.

All that is preserved of the stage wall are two columns in African breccia and Italian marble standing whole amid the ruins, a reminder of the theatre's great past. The stage, curtain slit, orchestra, and part of the tiers are still visible.

Turn right by the amphitheatre to the parvis of the **Collégiale Notre-Dame-de-la-Major**, an important place for the Confrérie des Gardiens. A terrace allows a fine view of the rooftops of Arles, the Rhône, the Alpilles, and the Abbaye de Montmajour.

▶*Bear right to reach the steps that lead to the amphitheatre.*

Amphitheatre (Arènes)★★

🕐*Open June -Sept: 9am-6.30pm (Wed, 2pm); May: 9am-6.30pm; Mar- Apr and Oct: 9am-6pm; Nov-Feb: 10am-5pm –* 🕐*closed Easter weekend (Fri-Mon), second weekend in Sept, 1 Jan, 1 May, 1 Nov, 25 Dec.* ⊜*5.50€.* ☎ *04 90 49 35 97.*

Roman Amphitheatre, Arles

G. Magnin/MICHELIN

This amphitheatre probably dates from the end of the 1C. Transformed into a fortress during the early Middle Ages, it constituted a system of defence. Later on, under the filled-in arcades, in the galleries, on the tiers and in the arena itself arose a small town of 200 houses and two chapels, built with materials taken from the building itself, which was mutilated but saved from complete destruction. The excavation and restoration began in 1825. Three out of the four medieval watchtowers remain.

The amphitheatre measured 136m x 107m/446ft x 351ft and could seat more than 20 000 spectators. The arena (69m x 40m/226ft x 131ft) as such, was separated from the tiers by a protective wall. The arena was floored and underneath it were machinery, animal cages, and the backstage area.

Wander through the upper level of arches of half the amphitheatre in order to under-stand the building's construction; finally go around the arena at the lower level of arches. The spectators would have enjoyed all kinds of games and gladiatorial fighting, which was finally forbidden in 404, under the influence of Christianity.

Continue around the amphitheatre to the 18C Palais de Luppé, which houses the Vincent Van Gogh foundation (*see MUSEUMS*).

▶ *Take rue des Arènes to the right of the palace, then the second street on the right.*

You will pass the former Grand Priory of the Order of the Hospital of St John of Jerusalem (15C), which today houses the Musée Réattu (*see MUSEUMS)*. Take a look opposite at the courtyard of the Commanderie de Sainte-Luce (Social Action Centre).

Palais Constantin - Thermes de la Trouille★

▶ *Access rue Maïsto.*

The same hours as those for visiting the Roman Theatre (see above). 3 €. 04 90 49 31 32

The baths of Arles are the largest (98 x 45m/322 x 148ft) remaining in Provence. They date from Constantine's era, the 4C.

Enter by the *tepidarium*, through to the *caldarium*, which still has its hypocaust.

▶ *Return to rue Maïsto, turn left and left again to reach place and rue de la Sauvage.*

Note the lovely old buildings, including the former palace of the counts of Arlatan de Beaumont(15C), today the Hotel Arlatan. *Continue to place du Forum.*

Place du Forum

The actual place du Forum is not on the site of the ancient forum, which lay more to the south. Left of the Hôtel Nord-Pinus, two Corinthian columns surmounted by a fragment of pediment are all that remain of a 2C temple.

A small street to the left leads to the Plan de la Cour, a small square lined with historical buildings, including the **Hôtel de Podestats** (12C-15C) and the **Hôtel de Ville**, town hall (*currently under restoration*).

Hôtel de Ville

The town hall was rebuilt from 1673 to 1675 to plans by Hardouin-Mansart and the architect Peytret from Arles. It includes the clock tower, a vestige of the original building, which was built from 1543 to 1553 and inspired by the Glanum mausoleum. The vestibule's flat **vaulting**★ is a masterpiece. At one time it was studied by the craftsmen touring France (as a part of their training to became master craftsmen).

▶ *Turn left into rue Balze, where the former Chapelle des Jésuites (17C) gives access to the Cryptoporticus.*

Cryptoporticus★

Closed for security reasons. 04 90 49 36 74.

This double, horseshoe-shaped, underground gallery dates from 1C BC. The two rounded-arched corridors were divided by a line of massive rectangular pillars. Ancient air shafts let the light in. The use of the Cryptoporticus is unclear, apart from the fact that the galleries enhanced and ensured the stability of the forum's monuments. One theory is that they were huge granaries, or more prosaically, just walkways.

Returning to the Plan de la Cour the vestibule of the Hôtel de Ville gives access to place de la République, in the middle of which stands a fine **obelisk** from Arles' Roman circus which was moved here in the 17C. The setting is completed by the town hall's Classical façade and the sumptuously decorated doorway of St-Trophime.

Église St-Trophime★

The same hours as for visiting the Ampitheatre. Closed 1 Jan, 1 May, 1 Nov, and 25 Dec. 3.50€.

This church, dedicated to St Trophimus, who was possibly the first bishop of Arles in the early 3C, was destroyed and then rebuilt during the Carolingian era (part of the façade built of rubble remains). It was again rebuilt at the end of the 11C (transept) and in the first half of the 12C (nave). In c 1190 the building was enhanced by a magnificent **carved doorway**★★, a perfect example of late Provençal Romanesque style. It displays an ancient classical arrangement, suggesting the form of a triumphal arch, often used in 12C Provence.

Doorway of St-Trophime

G. Magnin/MICHELIN

Inside, the main body of the building is surprisingly high and the aisles very narrow. The Romanesque severity contrasts with the rib and moulding work of the Gothic chancel. Among the works of art of particular interest are 4C Christian sarcophagi (one of which serves as an altar in the Chapel of Grignan and represents the crossing of the Red Sea), and an admirable *Annunciation* by Finsonius in the transept chapel.

Cloître St-Trophime★★

🕑 *The same hours as for visiting the amphitheatre.*

These cloisters, the most famous in Provence for the elegance and richness of their carved decoration, may have been carved with the collaboration of the craftsmen of St-Gilles. The best work is to be found in the north gallery *(on the left upon entering)*, particularly on the magnificent corner pillars decorated with large statues and low relief. The capitals are adorned with scenes from the Resurrection and the origins of Christian Arles, as well as foliage. Note especially, on the northeast pillar, the statue of St Paul, with the deeply-incised folds, very long under the elbows, the work of a craftsman who was familiar with St Gilles' central doorway. Of a later period, the east gallery's capitals and pillars recount the major episodes of Christ's life. The south gallery tells of the life of St Trophimus and the west gallery concentrates on typically Provençal subjects such as St Martha and the Tarasque(👤 *see TARASCON*). From the south gallery you can see the cloisters, and above, the former chapter premises, the church nave. Dominating the whole stands the stout plain bell tower. Along the east gallery the refectory and dormitory display temporary exhibitions, such as the famous annual santon fair *(end of Nov to mid-Jan)*.

▸ *Turn right into rue de la République, then rue Président Wilson, which leads to the former Hôtel-Dieu.*

Espace Van-Gogh

🕑 *Open 7.30am-7pm. No charge.* ☎ *04 90 49 38 05.*

This centre was originally a hospital where Van Gogh was treated in 1889; the courtyard is lined with arcades. Here you will see the recreated garden based both on Van Gogh's painting of this space, *Garden of Arles Hospital,* and from a letter to his sister containing details of the plants grown herein. The buildings house various organisations: a multimedia reference library, an academic centre, a school for literary translators, archives, etc. It is a sweet and serene courtyard where you can take in the garden while enjoying some refreshment.

A Pilot Restoration Project

Following important and delicate restoration work, the doorway of St-Trophime church, a masterpiece of Provençal Romanesque art on UNESCO's world heritage list, has regained its former splendour.

Threatened by wind, rain and pollution, the sculptures on the doorway have benefited from the work carried out by many specialists, whose joint expertise has managed to save them just in time.

Van Gogh in Arles

Vincent Van Gogh (1853-1890) came to Arles from Paris on 21 February 1888. He first lived at the Hôtel-Restaurant Carrel, on rue de la Cavalerie, and then rented a small house, the "Yellow House" on place Lamartine: both buildings were destroyed during the war. He adapted quickly to Arles. His health improved, and he made friends. In October, he received Gauguin.

Van Gogh's style changed as he moved away from Impressionism. He sought to find "another Japan," as Japanese wood prints fascinated him. The Provençal countryside and its luminosity provided the answer. He painted non-stop: nature, working in the fields, portraits, views of Arles and its surroundings, producing in all more than 200 paintings and 100 drawings. His Arles subjects, including *House of Vincent, The Alyscamps, L'Arlésienne, Crau Plain* and *Langlois Bridge,* were some of the most exciting works of his Arles period.

Plagued increasingly by fits of madness, made worse by his brutal break with Gauguin (24 December 1888, when he cut off part of his left ear, *Self-Portrait*), Van Gogh was hospitalised. His fortunes went from bad to worse: Gauguin abandoned him, his friend Roulin, the postman, was sent to Marseille, and in February 1889 a petition circulated in Arles demanding that he be confined. He finally decided to leave Arles for the asylum at St-Rémy-de-Provence, where he arrived on 3 May 1889.

Les Alyscamps★★★ 30min

🕐*The same hours as those for visiting the Roman Theatre (*🕐 *see above).* 🎫*3.50€.*

From Roman times to the late Middle Ages, the Alyscamps was one of the most famous necropolises (cemeteries) of the western world.

In ancient times, when a traveller arrived by the Aurelian Way to the gates of Arles, he made his way to the city's entrance passing along a line of inscribed tombs and mausoleums. And yet the Alyscamps' great expansion occurred during the Christianisation of the necropolis around the tomb of St Genesius, a Roman civil servant, beheaded in 250 for having refused to write down an

Les Alyscamps — Allée des sarcophages

imperial edict persecuting the Christians. Miracles began to happen on this site and the faithful, more and more numerous, asked to be buried here. Added to all this was the legend of St Trophimus, which confirmed that he too was buried here.

The transfer of St Trophimus' relics to the cathedral in 1152 removed part of the prestige of this immense cemetery. During the Renaissance the necropolis was desecrated. The city councillors took to offering their honoured guests one or several of the better carved sarcophagi as presents, and monks in charge took funerary stones to build churches and convents and to enclose monastery grounds.

Thanks to the Musée de l'Arles Antique some of the admirable sarcophagi, which enable us to get an idea of the splendour of the Alyscamps in the past, were saved and are exhibited.

Excavations (Fouilles de l'Esplanade)

The remains of a Gallo-Roman district, destroyed in the 3C, have been discovered, including baths, shops and houses (including a fine mosaic of Leda and the swan).

▷ *Continue along rue Émile-Fassin to the alley of sarcophagi.*

Allée des Sarcophages

A 12C porch, all that remains of the Abbaye St-Césaire, opens onto the avenue bordered with two rows of sarcophagi and also lined with chapels. A large number of the sarcophagi are Greek in style with double-pitched roof with four raised corners. The Roman-style ones are identified by their flat top. Some sarcophagi are carved with the three symbols: a plumb line, a mason's level, both signifying the equality of men before death, and a trowel, a type of axe, intended to protect the sarcophagi from robbers.

Église St-Honorat

Rebuilt in the 12C by the monks of St-Victor of Marseille who were keepers of the necropolis, this church is dominated by a powerful two-storey bell tower (13C), or lantern tower, opened by 8 round-arched bays. Besides the bell tower, the chancel, to which several chapels were added later, and a carved doorway, remain.

Museums

Musée de l'Arles et de la Provence antique★★

▷ *Follow boulevard Georges-Clemenceau to the edge of the Rhône, before passing left under the flyover.*

♿ 🕐*Apr-Oct: 9am-7pm; Nov-Mar: 10am-5pm.* 🕐*Closed 1 Jan, 1 May, 1 Nov, and 25 Dec.* 🎫*5.50 € (under 18, free), free admission the first Sun of every month.* ☎ *04 90 18 88 88 – www.arles-antique.org.*

Built on the edge of the Rhône, this bold triangular construction, designed by Henri Ciriani, houses behind its blue enamel walls the extensive Arles collection of ancient art. Greeting you is the 1C Arcoule Lion. A single room groups together large statues. Arranged around the **colossal statue of Augustus** (marble torso, limestone drape), which once decorated the theatre stage wall, are statues of dancers, altars dedicated to the god Apollo, and a cast of the famous **Venus of Arles**. The copy of a masterpiece of Hellenistic statuary, this statue is now displayed in the Louvre. The large **votive**

shield of Augustus (26 BC), a marble copy of the golden Roman shield, shows the extent and speed of Romanization in Arles.

Different models illustrate Roman civilisation in Imperial times. The museum presents town plans, marked with the important monuments of the Augustan (forum, theatre), Flavian (amphitheatre), Antonine (circus), and Constantine (baths) eras.

Also exhibited is the daily life of the people of Arles (household equipment, jewels, medical care), alongside their traditional activities (agriculture, breeding, craftwork, trade) either through objects –tools for weaving, bronze, glass and clay dishes –or through sarcophagus reliefs. The economic role of Arles is evoked through the depiction of its road network (military limits) and both its land and sea trade (set of amphorae and marine anchors, lead, tin and copper ingots). One area is given over to religions of the time, wherein you will find a small faun in bronze (1C BC), and the torso of Sarapis (2C) wrapped in a serpent's coil.

The splendour of the Imperial age is evident in the sumptuous nature of the **mosaics**, taken from the rich villas of Trinquetaille (late 2C). A footbridge allows visitors to explore the patterns and colours of the mosaics, which are either geometrical or illustrate a theme, such as the Abduction of Europa, Orpheus, or the Four Seasons. Take a look at the central medallion of the Aiön mosaic where you will see the god of time holding the wheel of the zodiac in his hand.

Next to the collection of funerary steles, typical of incineration rites, is the dazzling display of **sarcophagi**★★, both pagan and Christian, which constitutes one of the most important collections in the world after that of Rome. These magnificent marble works, carved predominantly in the 4C by craftsmen from Arles and some of which originate from the Alyscamps necropolis, exalted the new triumphant Christian faith. As well as the sarcophagus known as Phaedra and Hippolytus, note that of the Trinity or the spouses. The visit ends with late Antiquity and the presentation of the 6C ivory shield of St Caesarius, which depicts soldiers asleep in front of Christ's tomb.

Museon Arlaten★

▶ *On rue de la République.* ⏱ *Open June-Aug: 9.30am-1pm, 2-6.30pm ; Apr-May and Sept: 9.30am-12.30pm, 4-6pm; Oct-Mar: 9.30am-12.30pm, 2-5pm – last admission 1hr before closing –* ⏱*closed Mon (Oct-Jun), 1 Jan, 1 May, 1 Nov, and 25 Dec.* ⬤*4€, free admission first Sun and last Wed of each month.* ☎ *04 90 52 52 31.*

This fascinating Provençal Ethnographic Museum was created by Frédéric Mistral in 1896 and installed, from 1906 to 1909, in the 16C Hôtel de Castellane-Laval, bought by Mistral with the money he was given when awarded the Nobel Prize for Literature in 1904. Worried by the loss of Provençal identity in the face of the national centralisation policy, Mistral wanted to preserve the details of Provençal daily life for future generations. At the entrance to the courtyard you will encounter a small tiled forum with exedra that led to a small 2C basilica.

The Museon, with its attendant in traditional Arles costume as Mistral had wished, consists of some 30 rooms devoted in the main to the Arles country and organised according to theme or scene. This museum is the most comprehensive of its kind in Provence, with furnishings, costumes, ceramics evoking local customs, crafts and music, items of popular devotion, and documents on the Félibrige and the history of Arles and its surroundings.

⊛ Don't miss the reconstructed interiors (such as the delivery room, or Christmas Eve in the dining room of a *mas*) capturing the delightful atmosphere of a past way of life.

Musée Réattu★

⏱*Open May-Sept:10am-12.30pm, 2-7pm; Mar-Apr and Oct: 10am-12.30pm, 2-5.30pm; Nov-Feb: 1-5.30pm – last admission 30min before closing* ⏱*closed 1 Jan, 1 May, 1 Nov, 25 Dec.* ⬤*4€.* ☎ *04 90 49 38 34.*

The museum takes its name from the painter Jacques Réattu (1760-1833), who formerly lived here, and whose work is exhibited in five of the museum's galleries. There are also works from the 16C-18C Italian, French, Dutch, and Provençal Schools, as well as a large collection of modern and contemporary art. These include paintings by Dufy, Prassinos, Vlaminck, Sarthou, and Alechinsky; and sculpture by César, Richier, Bourdelle, and Zadkine.

The **Picasso Donation**★ is exhibited in three galleries and displays the variety of techniques mastered by Picasso through 57 of his drawings created in 1971.

Temporary exhibitions offer an imposing **collection of photographs**★.

Fondation Vincent Van Gogh-Arles

▸ *13 r. Aristide-Briand*

🕐*Open Apr to Oct: 10.30am-8pm; Nov-Mar: daily, except Mon, 11am-5pm -* 🕐*closed 1Jan, Easter, 1 Nov, and 25 Dec.* ✆*7 €.* ☎ *04 90 49 94 04.*

The permanent collection includes works of art executed in homage to Van Gogh by some of the greatest names in contemporary art, be they painters (Francis Bacon, David Hockney, Fernando Botero, Olivier Debré), sculptors (Karel Appel, César), photographers (Lucien Clergue, Robert Doisneau), writers (Viviane Forrester, Michel Tournier), musicians (Henri Dutilleux) or even fashion designers (Christian Lacroix).

Every year, while the permanent collection is on tour in France and abroad, there is an exhibition on the subject of one of these artists, all who have made a donation to the foundation.

Abbaye de Montmajour★ – 🖎 *See ABBAYE DE MONTMAJOUR.*

▸ *2km/1.2mi north of Arles, in the direction of Fontvieille.*

Plaine de la Crau

The Crau plain, which extends over 50 000ha/200sq mi between the Rhône, the Alpilles, St-Mitre hills, and the sea, is a grey-white desert of shingle (round rocks) and gravel that in places reaches a depth of 15m/50ft.

Cultivation – Since the development of a network of irrigation channels, two areas in the north of the Crau are now cultivated. One stretches from Arles to St-Martin-de-Crau, the other lies to the west of Salon. These two areas are gradually merging, so that a drive along N 113 from Arles to Salon gives little idea of the stony desert that defines the Grande Crau. Windbreaks of poplar and cypress shelter pastures and fields of fruit and vegetables. There are four crops a year of the famous Crau hay (annual crop approximately 100 000 metric tons) – the last of which is grazed in the fields by sheep wintering on the plain.

Sheep farming – The Grande Crau, resembling a huge steppe, is devoted to **sheep farming**. The traditional breed is the fine-wooled Merino, a cross between the Crau country breed and the Spanish Merino introduced into France around the early 19C. About 100 000 head graze on *coussouls* (tufts of fine grass growing between the stones) between mid-October and early June. The shepherds (belonging to the Union of Arles Breeders) own their personal flock. In the spring they settle on the grazing land, which they rent and which includes a sheepfold and a well. The well is crowned by a well-head made of Alpilles stone carved in one piece. All the sheepfolds, totaling in 40, were built

Sheep grazing in La Crau

from 1830 to 1880 on an identical plan: a rectangle (40m x 10m/131ft x 33ft) open on two sides and covered by stones placed like fish scales. Sometimes the shepherd lives nearby in a one-room hut.

The departure for summer pastures takes place in early June when the grazing disappears and water becomes scarce. In the past this droving to the Savoie or Briançon region followed established routes, along which the procession of sheep, goats, dogs, and heavily laden donkeys would be guided by the steward, followed by his shepherds. It took 12 days on foot to reach the Alps, after passing through many villages, whose inhabitants celebrated the passing of the flocks each year at the same date. The return journey, which took place as the first snows began, enjoyed the same festive atmosphere, and the shepherds were glad to regain the more temperate climate of the Crau.

Nowadays the flock is moved by truck from its summer pastures to its winter ones (and vice versa). The sheep, although well integrated into the local rural economy, pose a number of problems: the Merino is not sufficiently profitable, shepherds are hard to find, and the area of sheep-grazing land is diminishing.

Tour of the Crau Plain

🕐 *93km/58mi – allow 3hr, excluding the Vigueirat.*

▶ *Leave Arles on N 453.*

St-Martin-de-Crau

🕐 *Open 9am-12pm and 2-6pm.* 🕐 *Closed Sun, 1 May, and 25 Dec-1 Jan.* ✆ *1.50€.*
☎ *04 90 47 02 01.*

The village houses a museum, **l'Écomusée de la Crau**, containing an exhibition on this unique region, which can be explored through guided tours around the nature reserve at Peau de Meau.

▶ *Take D 24 south as far as the main road (N 568), where you will head in the direction of Martigues.*

La Grande Crau

Green countryside gives way to a progressively more barren landscape, devoid of villages, farms, and agriculture, apart from the very occasional sheepfold and cabin near a well, reflecting the decline of such pastoral activities as sheep farming. In addition to the encroachment of agriculture from the north, and the installation of several aerodromes, the continued expansion of the Bassins de Fos in the south has changed the appearance of the landscape so dear to Mistral. The Provençal desert is gradually disappearing.

▶ *At La Fossette turn right and take N 268 to Port-St-Louis-du-Rhône, then turn right onto D 35, and take D 24 to Mas-Thibert.*

Coustière de Crau

This is the marshy part of the Crau plain, situated near the so-called "great Rhône," where a Spanish race of bulls used for the *novilladas* of this region are bred.

Marais du Vigueirat★

🕐 *For thematic tours:* ☎ *04 90 98 70 91, www.marais-vigueirat.reserves-naturelles.fr, or contact the Tourist Office in Arles. Allow 6hr and take a picnic.* The presence of this land, situated between the Arles canal at Bouc (dug in 1827) and the Vigueirat canal (1642), is the work of a Dutch engineer and depicts a moving testimony to man's perpetual struggle with water and salt. Thanks to complex drainage and irrigation systems, the level of the water and its salinity are kept under control, thereby maintaining the Camargue's ecosystems.

▶ *Return towards Arles via D 35; take the small signposted street to the right.*

Pont de Langlois

The original bridge, the subject of a famous painting by Van Gogh, was destroyed in 1926. The current bridge, identical to the one in the painting, was taken down and rebuilt on the canal that links Arles to Fos, not far from its original site.

Étang de Vaccarés – 🕭 *See the CAMARGUE.*

AUBAGNE

POPULATION 42 638

MICHELIN LOCAL MAP 340: I-6 OR 114 FOLDS 29 AND 30 OR 528 FOLD 45 OR 524 FOLD L

In the Huveaune valley, Aubagne lies in a verdant basin, dominated to the north-west by the Chaîne de l'Étoile. Its location is favourable to industrial expansion and local food production (important agricultural market centre). The once-fortified town has preserved some of its old ramparts and a 12C church remodelled in the 17C. The beloved Marcel Pagnol (1895-1974), author, playwright and film-maker was born here, and lived at 16 cours Barthélemy.

🄸 *Av. Antide-Boyer, 13400 Aubagne, ☎ 04 42 03 49 98. www.aubagne.com.*

A Bit of History

Aubagne's pottery tradition, which developed as a result of its clay quarries, dates back to Antiquity. This tradition became established during the Gallo-Roman period with the manufacture of amphora and ceramics and turned to tile production in the Middle Ages.

In the 19C, the production of santons was started, carried on today in a score of cottage industries dotted throughout the old town. The ceramic coating of ships such as the Normandie, the France or the De Grasse originates from Aubagne's workshops.

Walking Tour

The historic centre lies within the ancient fortified ramparts of which a few vestiges remain, namely the 14C Gachiou doorway, one of the seven original gates that gave access to the medieval city. The small, narrow streets reveal a number of architectural curiosities - the quaint triangular belfry of the late 17C Chapelle de l'Observance (place de l'Observance), the Tour de l'Horloge and its superb wrought-iron bell tower, the fine, white Baroque front of the Chapelle des Pénitents Blancs and the more Classical façade (1551) of the Chapelle des Pénitents Noirs (chemin de St-Michel).

Address Book

Parking – 🄿 Parking can be tough to find in the town's center, but there is a car park (fee charged) about 300m/330yd from the town hall.

Train – The TER train connects Marseille to Aubagne in 15 min.

SHOPPING

Santon and ceramic worshops – The historic centre of Aubagne contains about 20 *santon* workshops where the tradition is kept alive. Open daily except Sunday. Contact the Tourist Information Centre for addresses. Every two years in August (odd-numbered years) there is a large market of terracotta ware (Argilla), while in Dec (even numbered years) the Art of Santon-making Biennale take place. In the summer and in December there are several santon fairs along cours Mar.-Foch.

Marius Chave – *8 cours Mar-Foch – ☎ 04 42 03 86 33 – www.santons-chave. com – Mon-Sat 8am-12.30pm, 2-7pm; Sun 9am-noon.* A friend of the playwright Marcel Pagnol, Marius Chave depicted the celebrated card game played by the actor Raimi and his friends in the cinematic version of novel *Marius* using santons. Today his grandson upholds the family expertise and carries on producing the colours of traditional Provençal santons.

Atelier d'Art-Maison Sicard – *2 bd Émile-Combes, ☎ 04 42 70 12 92 – – www. santons-sylvette-amy.com. – open Mon-Fri, 9am-12pm, 2-6:30 pm; Sat, 2.30-6pm – closed one week in Aug, one week at Chrsitmas, and public holidays.* Santon and ceramic ware, including the typical cicadas which are very common in the region.

Poterie Ravel – *avenue des Goumes, ☎ 04 42 82 42 00 – 8am-noon, 2-6pm (Mon-Sat).* Terracotta objects and pottery for the garden.

Markets – Traditional market Tue, Thu, Sat and Sun along cours Voltaire. Antique market on the last Sunday of the month at the Tourtelle.

ON THE TOWN

La Belle Époque – *4 cours Mar.-Foch - ☎ 04 42 03 13 66 – daily 7am-2am.* There are countless reasons for frequenting this spot which is both trendy and cultural and offers a rich programme of events: Wednesday is chess day; rock concerts on Friday or Saturday; one Monday a month a philosophy debate. And on occasion the Belle Époque is transformed into a café-theatre.

Ateliers Thérèse-Neveu

&. ⏱*Daily except Mon 10am-noon, 2-6pm.* 🕐*Closed 1 Jan and 25 Dec. No charge.*
☎ *04 42 03 43 10.*

This huge exhibition hall occupies the former workshop of Thérèse Neveu, who
was a famous santon maker from Aubagne. It is devoted to the art of clay and other
related industries. It features a standing retrospective on the history of ceramics in
Aubagne and hosts temporary exhibitions on a variety of themes associated with
santons and pottery.

Le Petit Monde de Marcel Pagnol

🕐*9am-12.30pm, 2.30-6pm.* 🕐*Closed 1 May, first fortnight of Feb, and second fortnight
of Nov. No charge.*

This display on Esplanade Charles-de-Gaulle consists of a crib with santons illustrating
the popular characters that feature in Pagnol's films and literary works.

EXCURSIONS

Musée de la Légion★

▶ *Access via D 2 towards Marseille, turn right on D 44A.* 🕐 *June to Sept: daily except
Mon 10am-noon, 3-7pm, Fri 10am-noon; Oct to May: Wed and Sat-Sun 10am-noon,
2-6pm. No charge.* ☎ *04 42 18 82 41*

On the ground floor, the great hall opens onto the Salle d'Honneur which exhibits
memorabilia belonging to the legion's great leaders. The museum, on the first floor,
presents numerous historical documents, photographs, arms, and uniforms.

Chapelle St-Jean-de-Garguier

▶ *5.5km/10mi northeast on D 2, turn left on D 43C and right on D 43D.*

Rebuilt in the 17C, this chapel, consecrated to St John the Baptist, is the object of an
annual pilgrimage on 24 June. More than 300 ex-votos (painted on wood, canvas or
zinc), mainly dating from the 18C and 19C, although some go back to the 15C, hang on
the chapel walls. A small museum giving off the chapel displays documents relating
to this small priory's history (17C missals, 18C religious art, two carved low reliefs).

Parc d'Attractions OK Corral – ♿ *See La CIOTAT.*

▶ *16km/10mi east on N 8.*

AVIGNON ★★★

POPULATION 88 312

MICHELIN LOCAL MAP 332: B-10 OR 528 FOLD 16 OR 524 FOLD 25

Designated city of art and culture, on the borders of three *départements* (Bouches-du-Rhône, Gard, and Vaucluse), Avignon stretches in all its beauty along the banks of the River Rhône. Bell towers emerge from a mass of pink roofs and the city is surrounded by ramparts, dominated by the Rocher des Doms, the majestic cathedral, and the Palais des Papes.

The city is known for its **Festival d'Art dramatique** (Festival of Theatre, Dance, and Music) founded in 1947 by actor/ director **Jean Vilar** (1912-71). Theatrical events, perhaps not so different from the pageants of the Middle Ages, illustrate various art forms (dance, music, cinema, etc) and use the city's enchanting historical monuments.

▸ **Orient Yourself:** Take the sightseeing train (*see Address Book*) or a guided tour of the city, for an overview *(contact the tourist office)* 📄*41 cours Jean-Jaurès, 84000 Avignon, ☎ 04 32 74 32 74. www.ot-avignon.fr; also www.vpah.culture.fr and www. avignon-tourisme.com.*

◉ **Don't Miss:** The best view of the skyline is from across the river, in Villeneuve-lès-Avignon, especially beautiful at sunset.

A Bit of History

Before the Popes – Only a few ruins remain of the monuments which embellished the flourishing Gallo-Roman settlement of Avenio. Following the barbaric invasions of the 5C, Avignon fell into oblivion through the early Middle Ages. Its rebirth occurred in the 11C and 12C, when Avignon took advantage of the feudal rivalries between the Houses of Toulouse and Barcelona to protect and reinforce its independence: like its Italian counterparts, Avignon formed a small city state. But its commitment in favour of the Albigensians brought about royal reprisals: in 1226, Louis VIII seized the town, ordering its defences razed. Nevertheless, Avignon rose again quite quickly, and, in spite of losing its independence, regained its former prosperity under the rule of the House of Anjou.

The Popes at Avignon – Avignon's destiny changed in the early 14C with the exile of the pontifical court to France, bringing with it a century of brilliance.

The court in Rome had become more or less impossible for the popes, who were incessantly the object of political differences. The Frenchman Bertrand de Got, elected pope under the name of **Clement V** (1305), decided to establish the court in France, where since 1274 the Holy See possessed the Comtat Venaissin. Clement V solemnly entered Avignon on 9 March 1309, though, he did not reside here permanently as he preferred the calm of Groseau priory, near Malaucène, or Monteux castle, not far from Carpentras. He died in 1314. In 1316, the former bishop of Avignon, Jacques Duèse was elected. As **Pope John XXII** he established the papacy here; from 1309-77, seven French popes succeeded each other at Avignon, among them **Benedict XII**, who built the papal palace, and **Clement VI** who purchased Avignon from Queen Joan I of Sicily, countess of Provence, in 1348.

The Constructive Popes – The city was transformed, and took on the appearance of a vast building site: convents, churches and chapels, not to mention the splendid cardinals' palaces, livrées (◉ *see VILLENEUVE-LÈS-AVIGNON*), sprouted everywhere, while the pontifical palace was constantly being enlarged and embellished. The university, founded in 1303, numbered thousands of students. The pope wanted to be considered the most powerful ruler in the world. His wealth and munificence shone brilliantly, attracting the notice of the envious, which was why he lived in a fortress and established a line of fortifications to protect the town from mercenary soldiers who pillaged the countryside.

Life in Avignon was pleasant: liberty and prosperity existed and the population jumped from 5 000 to 40 000. A place of asylum for political refugees like Petrarch, the pontifical city also housed a Jewish community. But this tolerance extended, unfortunately, to adventurers, escaped criminals, smugglers, counterfeiters and all kinds of rogues. In these circumstances, the popes thought of returning to Rome; **Urban V** left for the Eternal City in 1367, but hostility in Italy forced him to return to Avignon after three years. **Gregory XI** finally left Avignon in 1376 and died in 1378.

Address Book

TOURS AND DISCOUNTS

Pass – The city offers a tourist pass, valid for two weeks and offering significant price reductions for visitors to Avignon and Villeneuve-les-Avignon (museums and monuments, guided tours of the town, boat and tourist train trips, coach excursions). To obtain it, simply pay full price at one of the sites mentioned on the pass. Therafter, you will qualify for Pass reductions. Show it each time you purchase a a ticket. Ask about the Pass at the tourist office.

Avignon by boat – *(45mn) audioguide tour, from pont Saint-Bénezet and along the Rhône. July-Aug: 1-6pm (each hour); May-June, and Sept: 1pm, 2pm, 3pm, 3.30pm, and 4.45pm.* 8€. 04 32 74 32 74 *(tourist office).*

Sightseeing train –*Guided visit through Avignon (45mn). Mid-Mar to mid-Sept: 10am-8pm; mid-Sept to mid-Oct: 10am-7pm - 7* € *(under 9 years, 4€). Departs from the place du palais des Papes.* 04 50 60 05 55 - www.petittrainavignon.fr.

Trips on the Rhône – "Grands Bateaux de Provence," organizes several full day roundtrip boat outings from Avignon along the Rhône, to such destinations as Arles, Châteauneuf-du-Pape, the Camargue, etc. 04 90 85 62 25 - www.avignon-et-provence.com/mireio .

Coach excursion – Provence Vision (Cars Lieutaud) – *36, bd Saint-Roch (near the central train station),* 04 90 86 36 75, contact@cars-lieutard.fr, or, inquire and make reservations at the tourist office – Offers half and full-day excursions from Avignon to the Camrague, Pont du Gard, Fontaine de Vaucluse, the Alpilles, a Lavender tour (Coustellet, Gordes, Abbaye de Sénanque), a wine tour (Orange and Châteauneuf du Pape). A tour of Avignon proper is also offered.

SHOPPING

Markets – Les Halles Centrales, *Place Pie,* traditional covered market, *open daily except Mon, 6am-1.30pm.* **Flower** market every Saturday in *place des Carmes.* **Fair** Sat and Sun, *rempart St-Michel.* **Flea** market every Sunday in *place des Carmes.*

Honey – Miellerie des Butineuses, *189 rue de la Source, 84450 St-Saturnin-lès-Avignon,* 04 90 22 47 52 – www.miellerie.fr. Honey, pollen, and royal jelly, as well as honey-based products.

Chocolate – Puyricard, *33 rue Joseph-Vernet,* 04 90 85 96 33. *Open Mon, 2-7pm; Tues-Sat, 9am-12pm and 4-7pm. Closed Mon and July-Aug.* Chocolate lovers go no further: herein find some 92 varieties of chocolate in all its possible forms.

Pastries and Confections – Nicole Poutet – *15 rue des Trois-Faucons -* 04 90 82 08 31 – *Mon-Sat, 7.30am-8pm;* *Sun, 7.30am-6pm. Closed 15-28 Feb and 15-31 Aug.* Are you familiar with *papalines*? This speciality of Avignon was created in 1960 by the current owner's father: pink delicacies filled with an exquisite liqueur made from oregano, a plant of the Comtat Venaissin.

Home decor – Terre è Provence – *26 r. de la République -* 04 90 85 56 45 - terre-provence@waandoo.fr - *Mon-Sat, 10am-1.30pm, 2-7pm (June-Aug: 10am-7pm).* In the same family for several generations, this shop is dedicated to all that is Provence : table settings, textiles with Provençal prints, pottery, and porcelain and many lovely idea for your home.

EVENTS

The festival : mainstream and fringe events – Theatre, dance, lectures, exhibitions, meetings, and concerts given in the main courtyard of the Palais des Papes, in the municipal theatre, in the many cloisters and churches of the town, as well as at Villeneuve-lès-Avignon and other outlying areas, such as the Boulbon quarry (Carrière de Boulbon), Montfavet or Châteaublanc. **Fringe events are** dotted around the town.

Booking – Programmes and tickets are available at the Bureau du Festival d'Avignon, Cloître Saint-Louis - *20 r. du Portail-Boquier - 84000 Avignon,* 04 90 27 66 50 - réservations 04 90 14 14 14. From the first two weeks of June onwards it is also possible to make reservations by internet (www.festival-avignon.com), by minitel 3615 FNAC, at FNAC booking counters, and at the main office located at St-Louis d'Avignon (20 *rue Portail-Bocquier). Festival programmes are available by mail: send a check for 5€ to: Avignon Public Off, BP 5, 75521 Paris Cedex 11 (* 01 48 05 01 19, contact@avignon-off.org, www.avignon-off.org).

Hivernales d'Avignon – This choreography festival takes place in February but it never attains the atmosphere of the summer festival as the shows (luckily) take place indoors. 04 90 82 33 12. www.hivernales-avignon.com.

Horse festival – In January this event includes dressage, show jumping, competitions, and shows at the sports stadium. 04 90 84 02 04. www.cheval-passion.com.

For coin ranges, see Legend at the back of the guide.

EATING OUT

Le Mesclun - Le Petit Bistrot de Brunel – *46 r. de la Balance -* 04 90 86 14 60 - closed evenings Sun, and Mon. There's no better place for lunch, be it on the shaded terrace or inside. The daily dishes and menu mingle market freshness,

Provence, and gastronomy with the zest of good cheer. The choice spot to take a pause between excursions.

Le Grand Café – *cours Maria-Casares, La Manutention* – ☎ *04 90 86 86 77* – *closed Jan, Sun and Mon except July-Aug* – *booking recommended*. Backing onto the buttresses of the Palais des Papes, these old barracks have become an essential part of local life. Locals and tourists all flock here to savour inventive cooking with Provençal accents. Pleasant décor that combines the styles of a Parisian bistro and a Viennese café. There is also an attractive terrace.

Au Coin des Halles – *4 r. Grivolas* - ☎ *04 90 82 93 49* - *closed Sun and public holidays*. Enjoy this central spot among the Avignonnais, with its reading space and two little dining areas, all infused with jazzy music. And check out the menu: simple dishes, like a delicious *reblochon* cheese tart, a *salade landaise*, a winter squash soup

Entrée des Artistes – *1 place des Carmes* – ☎ *04 90 82 46 90* – *closed 23 Dec-3 Jan, 17 Aug-8 Sept, Sat and Sun*. The dining room of this restaurant is decorated in the style of a Parisian bistro, with its old posters and movie memorabilia. Tables are placed close together and the cooking is traditional. Service is friendly and there is a real scent of the Mediterranean in the air.

Le Moutardier – *15 place du Palais-des-Papes* – ☎ *04 90 85 34 76* – *moutardier @wanadoo.fr* – *closed 6-25 Jan, 24 Nov-19 Dec, and Wed from Oct-Mar*. This 18C building, listed in France's National Heritage, makes an exceptional setting for a simple, fresh meal. There is a pleasant atmosphere, both in the bistro room, where frescoes depict the story of "The Pope's mustard maker," and on the terrace facing the Palais des Papes.

Compagnie des Comptoirs – *83 r. Joseph-Vernet, Le Cloître des Arts* - ☎ *04 90 85 99 04* - *jc.toussaint@ lacompagniedescomptoirs.com* - *closed Sun and Mon*. Inspired by the colonial trading posts of the French East Indies Company, this restaurant, situated in the 14C cloisters, is the "in" place to eat. The bar decor is glass and bamboo, there are colonial etchings in the dining rooms, and the terrace is decked out with a palm tree and straw huts. The menu combines the flavours of East Asia with those of southern France.

WHERE TO STAY

Hôtel Le Provençal – *13 r. Joseph-Vernet* - ☎ *04 90 85 25 24* - *hotel. leprovencal@wanadoo.fr* - *11 rooms* – 5€. Le Provençal offers the advantage of being in the very heart of Avignon without being too pricey, a rare mix for this town. Moreover, the rooms are comfortable and decent.

Hôtel Médiéval – *15 rue de la Petite-Saunerie* – ☎ *04 90 86 11 06* – *hotel. medieval@wanadoo.fr* – *closed 3 Jan-7 Feb* – *34 rooms* – 7€. A simple hotel in the city centre, the Médiéval also offers special reduced rates for stays of a week or longer. Some rooms (studios) have kitchenettes. A stone's throw from the Palais des Papes, this is a wonderful base for exploring the heart of Avignon (and for picking up market delights at Les Halles!). The owner and staff are very welcoming and helpful.

Chambre d'hôte La Prévoté – *354 chemin d'Exploitation* – *84210 Althen-les-Paluds* – *17km/10.5mi northeast of Avignon towards Carpentras* – ☎ *04 90 62 17 06* – *prevote@aol.com* – *closed Nov-1 Mar* – *5 rooms* – 5€. After a peaceful night spent in one of the spacious, colourful rooms of this *mas*, you will certainly enjoy breakfast, which is served in the shade of the vine arbour or under the chestnut tree. Let your gaze roam over the apple trees or have a dip in the swimming pool.

Hôtel Garlande – *20 rue Galante* – ☎ *04 90 80 08 85* – *hotel-de-garlande@ wanadoo.fr* –*closed Jan* – *11 rooms* - 6.10€. Situated in two renovated old houses in a peaceful street, this small, family-run hotel is close to the church of St Didier. Colourful rooms with Provençal floral fabrics.

Hôtel Cloître St-Louis – *20 rue Portail Boquier* – ☎ *04 90 27 55 55* – *hotel@ cloitre-saint-louis.com* – *77 rooms* – 16€ - *restaurant 38/55€*. Situated in 16C cloisters, part of this hotel was designed by the architect Jean Nouvel. The building uses a variety of materials including glass, steel, and stone. Rooms are stylishly minimalist. Pool and solarium on the roof. Sunday mass in the chapel at the heart of the hotel.

ON THE TOWN

La Cave Breysse – *41 r. des Teinturiers* - ☎ *04 90 86 00 44* - Open 6-10.30pm. A very popular wine bar, this is a nice place to enjoy a well-priced glass of wine or an aperitif, and to take in the night, the ambiance, and the festivities.

Café In&Off – *place du Palais-des-Papes* – ☎ *04 90 85 48 95* – *www.cafeinoff.com* – *Summer: daily 7.30am-10pm and until 3am during the festival; rest of year: 7.30am-8pm* – *closed from mid-Nov to the end of Feb*. Don't miss the only café that enjoys unbeatable views of the Palais des Papes. The interior is not lacking in appeal but the terrace is definitely the highpoint of this café.

Cloître des Arts – *83 rue Joseph-Vernet* - ☎ *0490861232* - *www.avignon-et-provence.com/gambrinus/* - *Daily 7am-1.30pm except Sun. During the festival 7am-3am. Closed the first fortnight of Jan*. Sixty varieties of beers from all over the world and a relaxed atmosphere attract beer enthusiasts of all ages, whether among friends or with the family.

Woolloomooloo – *16 bis rue des Teinturiers* - ☎ *04 90 85 28 44* - *www. wooll.com* - *Daily noon-1am*. Bearing a long, wild cry for a name, this bar-restaurant nevertheless occupies the very civilised site of a former printing works inthe oldest street of the city. The myriad objects brought back by the owner from his worldwide travels adorn this place Everything from musical evenings in the bar to exotic dishes (always using fresh produce from the market) evokes travel.

SHOWTIME

Le Rouge Gorge – *10 bis rue Peyrolerie* - ☎ *04 90 14 02 54* - *www.le.rougegorge.fr* - *Tues-Sun 8.30pm-3am. Closed July-Aug.* The only cabret in Avignon, the Rouge-Gorge, modestly sheltered by thePalais des Papes, unveils the sensual charms of its show every Friday and Saturday from 8.30pm, while two Sundays a month there is an operetta lunch. During the week the atmosphere remains lively with numerous themed evenings (Corsican, Latino, Oriental).

Popes and Schismatic Popes – Hostile to the reforms of the Italian pope **Urban VI**, successor to Gregory XI, the mainly French cardinals of the Sacred College, elected another pope, **Clement VII** (1378-94), who returned to Avignon. The Great Schism divided the Christian world; the Avignon pope was recognised mainly in France, Naples, and Spain. Popes and schismatic popes mutually excommunicated each other and attempted by any means possible to bring the other down, vying with each other for the papacy's great wealth. **Benedict XIII** (1394-1409) succeeded Clement VII; however, he no longer had the support of the king of France. He fled Avignon in 1403, yet his followers resisted in the palace until 1411. The Great Schism finally ended in 1417 with the election of **Martin V**. Meanwhile life continued in Avignon as is suggested by the presentation of the *Mystères* (mystery plays enacting an episode of the Scriptures) during Whitsun in 1400, with huge living tableaux and processions that went on for three days and dramatised the Passion of Christ.

Until the Revolution, Avignon was governed by a papal legate and a vice-legate. Intolerance toward the Jews increased: confined to a ghetto, which was locked every night, the Jews had to wear a yellow cap, pay dues, and listen to sermons preached to convert them. Moreover, they were not allowed to mix with Christians, they could only occupy certain positions, and they were under constant surveillance.

Avignon was a society of contrast, with a gulf between the wealthy and poor, as evidenced by the confrontation between them from 1652 to 1659. At the Revolution, Avignon was split between the partisans wanting to belong to France and those who wanted the pontifical state maintained. The former won, and on 14 September 1791 the constitutional assembly voted the union of the Comtat Venaissin to France.

Palais des Papes★★★ *Allow 1-2hr.*

🕐*Jul: 9am-9pm; Aug-Sept: 9am-8pm; 15 Mar-June and Oct: 9am-7pm; Nov-14 Mar: 9.30am-5.45pm (last admission allowed 1hr before closing) – Audioguided tour.* 👓 *High season, 9.50€ (11.50€ combined admission with pont St-Bénezet) - low season, 7.50€ (9.50€ combined admission with pont St-Bénezet).* ☎ *04 90 27 50 83 - www. palais-des-papes.com.*

The palace is a maze of galleries, chambers, chapels and passages, now empty and deserted. Yet, try to imagine what it was like at the time of the popes.

Picture its luxurious furnishings; sumptuously-painted decoration; discreet comings and goings of prelates and servants; changing of the guards in dress uniform; cardinals, princes and ambassadors arriving and departing; the pilgrims gathered in the courtyard waiting to receive the pope's blessing; or to see him leave on his white mule; the litigants and magistrates creating commotion around the pontifical court; and many other activities.

Construction – This princely residence counts among the largest of its time with an area of 15 000m2/2.6 acres. It is both a fortress and a palace and is made up of two buildings joined together: the **Palais Vieux** to the north and the **Palais Neuf** to the south; its construction lasted 30 years. The Cistercian, Benedict XII, brought up in contempt of luxury, had the old episcopal palace razed and entrusted to his compatriot Pierre Poisson, from Mirepoix, the task of building a vast residence that would lend itself to prayer and be well defended. The Palais Vieux thus acquired the appearance of an austere fortress.

Palais des Papes

Planned around cloisters, its four wings are flanked by towers, the strongest of which, the north tower, Tour de Trouillas was used as a keep and prison. Clement VI, a great prince of the church, artist, and prodigy, ordered the architect Jean de Louvres from the Ile de France to carry out the expansion of the palace. The Tour de la Garde-Robe and two new buildings closed off the main courtyard that preceded Benedict XII's palace. The exterior was not modified. However, inside, artists directed by Simone Martini and then Matteo Giovanetti sumptuously decorated the different rooms and notably the pope's private apartments. The works continued under Clement VI's successors: Innocent VI had Tour St-Laurent built to the south and Tour de la Gache to the west and the decoration completed (fresco on the vault in the Grande Audience); Urban V had the main courtyard laid out with its well and had buildings constructed linking the palace to the gardens, behind the Tour des Anges.

In 1398 and again from 1410 to 1411, the palace was under siege resulting in the dilapidation of the buildings. Allocated to the legates in 1433, it was restored in 1516 but continued to deteriorate. In a bad state when the Revolution broke out,

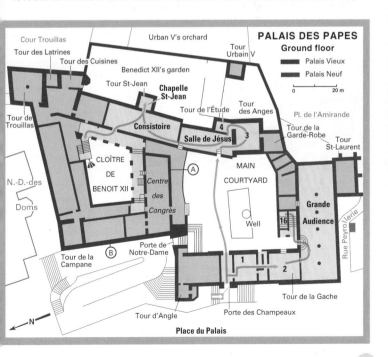

it was pillaged, with furniture dispersed and statues and sculptures broken. After a particularly bloody episode in 1791, the palace was transformed into a prison and barracks (1810). Occupied by military engineers, it was again mistreated: at least the statutory wash on the walls protected some of the mural paintings. Unfortunately, in many places, this safeguard came too late: the soldiers had had time to cut the protective coating off the frescoes and sell the pieces to collectors or antique dealers from Avignon.

Visit

Exterior

The palace from the outside has the appearance of a citadel built straight out of the rock. Its walls, flanked by 10 large square towers, some more than 50m/164ft high, are buttressed by huge depressed arches holding up the machicolations: this is one of the first known examples of such military architecture.

Ground Floor

▶ *Go through the Porte des Champeaux and enter the former guard room (reception and ticket office).*

The walls here are decorated with 17C paintings (1).

Petite Audience (2)

In the 17C, when this room was in use as an arsenal, the vaulting was decorated with *grisaille* paintings representing military trophies.

▶ *Turn round and go back through the Porte des Champeaux.*

Main Courtyard (Cour d'Honneur)

Running along the main courtyard to the north is the machicolated Conclave Wing (A), which houses the Conference Centre. The Gothic south wing has a number of irregular openings in its façade and the Indulgence window (15) on the first floor. It is used during the summer as a backdrop for the theatrical performances of the Avignon festival.

Treasury

The **Lower Treasure House** (Trésor Bas) is a beautiful vaulted room hollowed out beneath the Tour des Anges. Underneath the flagging were the hiding places where bags of silver and gold, silverware and valuable ornaments were kept. The cupboards on the walls contained the accounts ledgers and archives.

The wealth of the popes was considerable. Ample proof of this is provided by a building such as the Palace at Avignon, which was built in less than 20 years. John XXII, born in Cahors, bequeathed 24 million ducats to his heirs after 19 years as pope. The

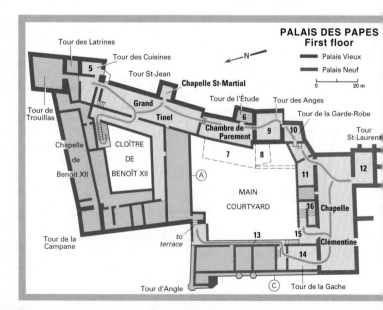

PALAIS DES PAPES
First floor

Palais Vieux
Palais Neuf

0   20 m

Tour des Latrines
Tour des Cuisines
5
Tour St-Jean
Chapelle St-Martial
Tour de l'Étude
Tour des Anges
Tour de la Garde-Robe
Grand
Tour de
Trouillas
Tinel
6
9 **10**
Tour
St-Laurent
**Chambre de
Parement**
Chapelle
de
Benoît XII
CLOÎTRE
DE
BENOÎT XII
7   **8**
(A)
11
12
MAIN
COURTYARD
16 **Chapelle**
Tour de la
Campane
to
terrace
13
15
Clémentine
14
Tour d'Angle
(C) Tour de la Gache

size of the Papal revenue explains why the most important court dignitary was the chamberlain, that is, the Minister of Finance. He was closely followed by the Treasurer, another very important figure.

Grande Trésorerie

This small room has an enormous fireplace decorating the north wall. Take the staircase to the **Salle de Jésus**, which used to serve as antechamber to the Consistoire.

Chamberlain's Bedchamber (3)

Situated on the third floor of the Tour des Anges, just below the Papal Bedchamber, this room is magnificently embellished with a 14C painted beam ceiling and with foliated scrollwork covering parts of the walls. Here, too, there are hiding places concealed in the flags on the floor.

Papal Vestiary (4)

This small room in the Tour de l'Étude was converted into a chapel in the 17C by the vice-legates. The original timberwork was reinforced by a stone vault. The walls feature 18C wood paneling.

Consistoire

To debate the great theories of Christianity, the pope and his cardinals met in council in this vast rectangular hall. It was here that the pope announced the name of the newly-appointed cardinals and received the sovereigns and their ambassadors in great pomp. It was here also that cases proposed for canonisation were examined. Exhibited in this hall are **frescoes** executed by the great artist **Simone Martini**, which were brought from the porch of Notre-Dame-des-Doms cathedral.

Chapelle St-Jean or Chapelle du Consistoire

This oratory is adorned with lovely frescoes painted from 1346 to 1348 by **Matteo Giovanetti**, Clement VI's official court painter.

On leaving the Consistoire, follow the lower gallery of Benedict XII's cloisters and take the staircase to the banqueting hall. There is a fine view of the **Staff Wing (B)**. This was where the staff – persons holding various functions – and the main servants lodged. Here you will also discover a fine view of the Tour de la Campane and of Benedict XII's chapel.

First Floor

Grand Tinel or Banqueting Hall

Exhibited in this hall, one of the largest in the palace (48m/157ft long and 10.25m/33ft wide), is a superb series of 18C Gobelins **tapestries**. The immense panelled keel-vaulted roof that takes the form of a ship's hull has been beautifully restored.

Continue into the **upper kitchen (5)** with its huge chimney in the form of an octagonal pyramid, located on the topmost floor of the Tour des Cuisines. This tower was also used as the pantry and provisions storeroom. Next to it, the Tour des Latrines (or Tour de la *Glacière – not open to the public*) offered common latrines on each floor for the soldiers and staff.

Chapelle du Tinel or Chapelle St-Martial

(*Slated for restoration.*) This oratory is named after the **frescoes** painted in 1344-45 by Matteo Giovanetti of St Martial (apostle from the Limousin, Clement VI's native region). They recount the life of the saint using a harmony of blues, greys, and browns.

Chambre de Parement

Next to the pope's bedroom, this antechamber, also known as the Robing Room, was used as a small waiting-room by those who had been accorded a private interview with the pope. Two 18C Gobelins tapestries hang on the walls.

Next to the Robing Room on the first floor of the Tour de l'Étude you will find Benedict XII's study (**Studium**) (6) with its magnificent tiles.

Situated along the west wall of the Robing Room is the pope's private dining room (7) called the Petit Tinel. Alongside it was the kitchen (or secret kitchen) (8). The rooms in this section of the palace were entirely destroyed in 1810.

Papal Bedchamber (9)

The walls of this room were richly painted against a blue background: birds entwined in vines and squirrels climbing oak trees. Exotic birdcages were painted in the window embrasures.

AVIGNON

Amirande Pl. de l'.EY 2
Annabelle R. .... DZ
Arroussaire Av. de l'FZ 3
Aubanel R.
  Théodore ......EZ
Balance R. de la....EY 7
Banasterie R. ......EFY
Bancasse R. ....EY 9
Bec Av. FerdinandGZ
Bertrand R. ....FY 10
Bon Martinet R. duFZ 13
Bonneterie R. ....EY
Bouquerie R.........EYZ
Buffon R. ....GYZ
Campane R. ....FY 14
Capdevila Bd .....GYZ
Carmes Pl. des......EY
Carnot Pl. ....EY
Carnot R. ....FY

Carretene R. ....FGY
Cloître St-Pierre Pl.EY
Collège d'Annecy R.EZ18
Collège du
  Roure R. du......EY 19
Corps Saints Pl. desEZ 20
Crillon Pl. ....EY
Croix R. de la........FY
Daladier Pont
  Édouard.............DY
David R. Félicien...EY 22
Dorée R. ....EY 23
Dr.-Pons Rte
  Touristique du...GY
Eisenhower Av. .... DZ
Fabre R. Henri ......EZ
Folco-de-
  Baroncelli R........EY 28
Folie R. de la ....GY
Four R. du ....EY 33
Four de la
  Terre R. du......FZ 35

Fourbisseurs R. desEY 34
Galante R..............EY 37
Grande Fusterie
  R. de la ....EY 39
Grottes R. des........EY 41
Horloge Pl. de l'....EY
Infirmières R. des.FY
Italiens Av. des ....GY 44
Jean-Jaurès Cours EZ
Jérusalem Pl..........FY 45
Ledru-Rollin R........FY 47
Lices R. des............FZ
Ligne Pte de la ....FY
Limas R. du............EY
Limbert Porte.......GZ
Lyon Rte de ....GY
Magnanen Porte...FZ
Manivet R. P.......EFZ 48
Marchands R. des.EY 49
Masse R. de la ......FZ 52
Molière R. ....EZ 54
Monclar Av. ....EZ 55

Mons R. de ....EY 59
Montfavet Rte de GZ
Muguet R..............GY 62
N.-D.-des-Sept-
  Douleurs R. ......FGY
Ortolans R. des ....EZ 63
Oulle Bd de l'........DY
Oulle Pte de l'.....DEY
Oulles Allées des. DY
Palais Pl. du..........EY 64
Palapharnerie R....FY 66
Pasteur R. Louis.FGY
Petite Calade
  R. de la ....EY 67
Petite Fusterie
  R. de la ....EY 68
Petite Saunerie
  R. de la ....FY 70
Pétramale R. ....EZ 72
Peyrollerie R..........EY 73
Philonarde R..........FZ
Pie XII Pl................FY

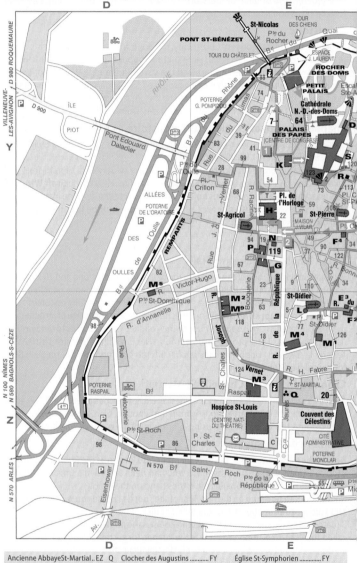

Ancienne AbbayeSt-Martial..EZ Q
Ancienne Aumône générale .
  (École des Beaux-Arts) ....FZ B
Cathédrale N.-D.-des-Doms..EY
Chapelle St-Nicolas.................EY
Chapelle des Pénitents Gris..FZ
Chapelle des Pénitents Noirs FY

Clocher des Augustins ....FY
Cloître.....................................FY E
Collection Lambert...................EZ M³
Couvent des Célestins.............EZ
Église St-Agricol......................EY
Église St-Didier........................EZ
Église St-Pierre ....EY

Église St-Symphorien ....FY
Église de la Visitation ....FY
Hospice St-Louis ....EZ
Hôtel Berton de Crillon, Hôtel de
  Jonquerettes, Hôtel d'Honorati,
  Hôtel de Fonseca ....EZ E³
Hôtel Fortia de Montréal ....EZ F²

Pignotte............... Pl. FY
 Pont R. du ....EY 74
Portail
 Magnanen R. du FZ
Président-Kennedy
 Cours.....................EZ 76
Prévot R. ....EZ 77
Puy R. Guillaume FYZ
Quai de la Ligne
 Bd du..................EFY
Racine R. ....EY
Rascas R. de ... GY 79
Raspail Bd...........DEZ
Rempart de
 l'Oulle R. du .... DY 82
Rempart du
 Rhône R. du...... EY 83
Rempart St-Lazare
 R. du .... FGY
Rempart St-Michel
 R. du ....EY 84

Rempart St-Roch
 R. du ....DEZ 86
République Pte de la EZ
République R. de la EYZ
Rhône Bd du......DEY
Rhône Pte du...... EY 88
Rocher Pte du ....EY
Roi-René R. du ....EFZ
Rouge R. ....EY 90
Saïn R. Paul ....FY
St-Agricol R. .... EY 94
St-Bénézet Pont ...EY
St-Bernard R. ...... GY
St-Charles Pte ....EZ
St-Charles R. ....EZ
St-Christophe R... FZ 97
St-Didier Pl. ....EZ
St-Dominique Bd DZ 98
St-Dominique Porte DZ
St-Étienne R.........EY 99

St-Jean Chemin de GZ
St-Jean le Vieux Pl. FY 101
St-Jean le Vieux R. FY 102
St-Joseph Pl. .... FY
St-Joseph Pte ......FY
St-Joseph R.........FY 104
St-Lazare Bd ...... FGY
St-Lazare Pte .... GY
St-Michel Bd ....FZ
St-Michel Pte ......EZ
St-Michel R.........EZ 105
St-Pierre Pl. ......EY 106
St-Roch Bd ....DEZ
St-Roch Porte ...... DZ
St-Ruf Av. ....FZ 108
Ste-Anne Escaliers EY
Ste-Catherine R. .. FY 109
Saraillerie R. de la EYZ 110
Semard Av. Pierre GZ
Soulier Bd Denis.. GZ
Sources Av. des.....FZ

Synagogue Av. de la GY
Taulignan R. de ... EY 113
Teinturiers R. des .FZ
Thiers Pte .... GZ
Thiers R. ....FYZ
Tour R. de la .... GY 116
Trillade Av. de la FGZ
Vallin R. Ninon .....FZ
Velouterie R. ....DZ
Vernet R. Horace ..EZ 118
Vernet R. Joseph EYZ
Viala R. Jean.......EY 119
Vice-Légat R. ....EY 120
Victor-Hugo R....DEY
Vieux Sextier R. du EFY 122
Vilar R. Jean ....EY 123
Violette R. ....EZ 124
3 Colombes R. des FY
3 Faucons R. des... EZ 126
3 Pilats R. des .... FY 127
58e R. I. R. du ......FGZ

Hôtel Gasqui de la Bastide..... FY K²
Hôtel Salvador...........................FZ K⁴
Hôtel d'Adhémar de Cransac EY R
Hôtel de Rascas ....EY F⁴
Hôtel de Sade............................EY G
Hôtel de Salvan Isoard ....FZ G²
Hôtel de ville............................EY H
Hôtel des Monnaies ....EY K
Livrée Ceccano ....EZ L
Maison du roi René ....FZ
Manutention (la) ....EY D
Musée Angladon.......................EZ M¹
Musée Calvet.............................EZ M²
Musée Lapidaire ....EZ M⁴
Musée Louis-Vouland...............DYZM⁵
Muséum Requien......................EZ M⁹
Palais des Papes ....EY
Palais du Roure ....EY N
Verger Urbain V........................EY S

Chambre du Cerf (10)

This room, known as the Stag Room, was Clement VI's study and is decorated with elegant **frescoes** painted by various Italian artists. The subjects are profane, illustrated against a verdant background: hunting, fishing, fruit and flower picking, and bathing scenes. The ceiling in larch wood is wonderfully ornate. This intimate and cheerful room had two windows. One offered a fine view of Avignon, and the other overlooked the gardens.

To get to the Chapelle Clémentine, cross the **north sacristy** (11) comprising two vaulted bays on diagonal ribs and containing plaster casts of characters who figured significantly in the history of the Avignon Papacy. The bridge was built by Innocent VI to link the pope's private dining room with the chapel and led into the east bay.

Grande Chapelle or Chapelle Clémentine

To the right of the pontifical altar, an opening leads into the **Cardinals' vestry** (12) in Tour St-Laurent, where the pope changed vestments when officiating at high mass. It contains casts of recumbent figures of the popes: Clement V, Clement VI, Innocent VI and Urban V.

In this chapel, the Conclave of cardinals came to hear the Mass of the Holy Spirit before returning to the Conclave Wing (A) via a narrow passageway called the **Conclave gallery** (13), which has marvellously elegant vaulting.

The **Conclave** was made up of the college of cardinals, who met 10 days after the death of the pope, to elect a successor. The first floor of the Palais Vieux was used to receive the cardinals. In order to isolate them from the rest of the world, they blocked up all the doors and windows and did not open them again until they had elected a pope with a two-thirds majority vote. The word *conclave* is derived from Latin, meaning "under lock and key."

A. Guerrand/Musée du Petit Palais, Avignon

The Virgin and Child by Botticelli

Chamberlain's New Bedchamber (14)

This occupies the far south end of the **High Dignitaries' Wing** (C), which also houses the bedchamber of the Treasury notaries and the Treasurer's apartment.

Terrasse des Grands Dignitaires

Located on the second floor of the High Dignitaries' Wing, this terrace offers an extensive **view**★★ over the upper storeys of the Palais des Papes, the Tour de l'Horloge, the dome of the cathedral, the Petit Palais and, further in the distance, Pont St-Bénézet, and the monuments at Villeneuve-lès-Avignon.

Turn back in the other direction to come across the loggia opposite the doorway of the Chapelle Clémentine. From the window of this loggia the pope would bless the gathered faithful in the courtyard below. This is how the window came to be known as the Indulgence window (15).

Ground Floor (Palais Neuf)

Go down the **Grand Escalier** (16). The right-hand flight of stairs is covered with pointed vaulting, a strong example of the bold architectural design for that time.

Grande Audience

This is a magnificent room with two aisles divided by a line of columns supporting the pointed arches of the vaulting. This is also called the Palais des Grandes Causes (Palace of the Great Causes), as it was here that the 13 ecclesiastical judges formed the Tribunal de la Rota – *rota* (wheel) comes from the circular bench on which they were seated and which is located in the room's last east bay. Around the judges sat the lawyers and the papal court's public servants. The rest of the room was for the public; seating ran along the whole of the room's wall. On the vaulting against a dark blue background sprinkled with stars is the **fresco of the Prophets** painted in 1352 by Matteo Giovanetti.

▷ *Cross the Petite Audience (2) and the guard room to leave the palace by the Porte des Champeaux.*

Walking Tours

Place Du Palais And The Quartier De La Balance ①

🕐 ⌖ *Allow 4hr for the round-trip circuit of the place du Palais.*

"Promenade des Papes"

This walk gives a striking impression of the height of the building. Follow the pretty little rue Peyrollerie that leads off from the southwest corner and goes under the enormous buttress supporting the Chapelle Clémentine to emerge on to a square in which there is an attractive 17C town house. Go along rue du Vice-Légat leading to Urban V's orchard, then go through a covered passageway which opens onto cour Trouillas. The Escaliers Ste-Anne lead up to the Rocher des Doms, giving a different view of the palace.

Rocher des Doms★★

There is a well-laid out garden planted with different species on this bluff. From the terraces you will behold superb **views**★★ of the Rhône and Pont St-Bénézet, Villeneuve-lès-Avignon with Tour Phillipe-le-Bel and Fort St-André, the Dentelles de Montmirail, Mont Ventoux, Vaucluse plateau, the Luberon hills, and the Alpilles.

▷ *Go back down to the garden, in the direction of the Petit Palais.*

Petit Palais

This was formerly Cardinal Arnaud de Via's residence (*livrée*) before being bought by the pope in 1335 to house the bishopric. The building deteriorated during the different sieges imposed upon the Palais des Papes, and had to be repaired and transformed in the late 15C, especially by Cardinal della Rovere, who subsequently became Pope Julius II.

Famous guests resided here: Cesare Borgia in 1498, François I in 1533, and Anne of Austria and the Duke of Orléans in 1660 during Louis XIV's visit to Avignon. Today it houses the paintings of the Musée du Petit Palais (⚫*see MUSEUMS*).

Cathédrale Notre-Dame-des-Doms

Built in the mid-12C, the cathedral was damaged many times and each time rebuilt and altered. In the 15C, the large bell tower was rebuilt from the first floor, crowned since 1859 by an imposing golden statue of the Virgin. A plain lantern tower crowns the bay preceding the chancel.

The porch was added in the late 12C and shelters two tympana (a semicircular one surmounted by a triangular one) once magnificently decorated with frescoes by Simone Martini and now located in the Palais des Papes.

Inside, the single nave with five bays is roofed with pointed-barrel vaulting. The Romanesque appearance of the building was tempered by the addition of side chapels (14C-17C), and with the reconstruction of the apse and the construction of Baroque galleries in the 17C. The Romanesque **dome**★ that covers the transept crossing is remarkable: to reduce the area, the master craftsman created a series of projections that supported the dome and its elegant columned lantern.

At the entrance to the chancel, on the left, stands a fine 12C white marble episcopal throne. Carved on its sides are animals symbolising St Mark (lion), and St Luke (ox). The chapel adjoining the sacristy contains the Flamboyant Gothic tomb of Pope John XXII. Its recumbent figure was lost during the Revolution and replaced by that of a bishop.

Hôtel des Monnaies (Mint)

This 17C town house (now the Conservatory of Music) is crowned with a balustrade and has an ornately carved **façade**★ of dragons, eagles, Borghese coat of arms, cherubs, and festoons of fruit.

▷ *Take the street to the right of the Hôtel des Monnaies to get to the Quartier de la Balance.*

Gypsies lived in the **Quartier de la Balance** in the 19C. In the 1970s it was renovated. This Quartier descends as far as the ramparts and the famous bridge of the French song, Pont d'Avignon.

Rue de la Balance

This is the Balance district's main street. On one side are old restored town houses with elegant façades, decorated with mullioned windows. By contrast, on the other side you will witness modern, Mediterranean style buildings with small flower-decked patios and ground level shopping arcades.

Pont St-Bénézet★★

Audioguided tour.   *Jul: 9am-9pm; Aug-Sept: 9am-8pm;15 Mar-Jun, and Oct: 9am-7pm; Nov-14 Mar: 9.30am-5.45pm (last admission 30 mins before closing) - 4 € or 11.50 €. ☎ 04 90 27 51 16 - www.palais-des-papes.com.*

In reality Pont St-Bénézet was originally a narrow bridge for people on foot or on horseback. It was never such that one could dance in a ring as in the song, *Sur le pont d'Avignon l'on y danse tous en rond*! Indeed, the people of Avignon did their dancing on the island beneath the arches of the bridge, in other words *sous le pont*.

Spanning two arms of the Rhône to Villeneuve-lès-Avignon at the base of the Tour Phillipe-le-Bel, the bridge was 900m/2 953ft long and composed of 22 arches. On one of the bridge's piers stands the Chapelle St-Nicolas consisting of two superimposed sanctuaries, one Romanesque and the other Gothic.

Legend has it that in 1177, a young shepherd boy, Bénézet, was commanded by voices from heaven to build a bridge across the river at a spot indicated by an angel. Everyone thought he was crazy until he proved his divine guidance by miraculously lifting a huge block of stone. Volunteers appeared and formed themselves as the **Bridge Brotherhood** *(Frères Pontifes)*, and funds flowed in. Within eight years they completed the bridge's construction.

Rebuilt from 1234 to 1237, the bridge was restored in the 15C and then broken by the flooded Rhône in the mid-17C.

On one of the bridge's piers stands the **Chapelle St-Nicolas**, consisting of two super-imposed sanctuaries, one dedicated to St Nicolas, patron saint of boatsmen, and the other to St Bénézet *(access via the steps)*. There is a small display on the history and iconography of this famous bridge to round off your visit.

Pont St-Bénézet

Remparts★

The actual fortifications (4.3km/2.75mi long) were built in the 14C by the popes. From a military standpoint this is not first-class work: the towers were open to the town, and part of the walls had no machicolations. In fact, the popes had simply wanted to build a preliminary obstacle against attack on the palace.

The most interesting part is along rue du Rempart-du-Rhône to the pleasant **place Crillon**, where Maréchal Brune was assassinated on 2 August 1815.

▸ *Return to place de l'Horloge via rue St-Etienne bordered by old town houses, rue Racine to the right, and rue Molière to the left.*

Old Avignon 2

▶ *Start in place de l'Horloge – allow half a day.*

This route explores the churches, museums, and the particularly notable town houses in the part of Old Avignon to the south and to the east of the Palais des Papes. It also offers you the opportunity to appreciate the past and present contrasts in this lively city.

Place de l'Horloge

The theatre and town hall overlook this vast square shaded by plane trees and partly occupied by open-air cafés.

In the little streets around place de l'Horloge there are windows painted with effigies of famous actors that call to mind the city's theatrical vocation.

Avignon — place de l'Horloge

Hôtel de Ville

Built in the 19C, the town hall includes the 14C and 15C **clock tower**.

▶ *Take rue Félicien-David and go around St-Agricol's east end.*

Note the Gallo-Roman rampart ruins.

Église St-Agricol

A large staircase leads to the church's parvis overlooked by a finely carved 15C façade. Inside there are a number of works of art: a mid-15C white marble stoup, paintings by Nicolas Mignard and Pierre Parrocel, and in the south aisle near the sacristy door, the Doni altarpiece, a work in stone by Boachon (1525) representing the *Annunciation*.

▶ *Take a left on rue Agricol, then a right on rue Bouquerie.*

Rue Jean-Viala

The street runs between two 18C mansions housing the *Préfecture* (**P**) offices and the general council of the *département* (Conseil Général). To the north is the **Hôtel de Forbin de Ste-Croix**, once a school (Collège du Roure), and to the south is the **Hôtel Desmarez de Montdevergues**.

Palais du Roure

No 3, rue du Collège-du-Roure. ⟵⟶*Guided tours (1hr) at 3pm or by appointment 2 weeks in advance.* ⊙*Closed in Aug. 4.60€.* ☎ *04 90 80 80 88.*

This former residence of the Baroncelli-Javon houses the Flandreysy-Espérandieu Foundation, a centre of Provençal studies.

Hôtel de Sade

▶ *No 5 rue Dorée.* Elegant mullioned windows overlook the street. In the courtyard there is a fine pentagonal turreted staircase.

▶ *Head to rue Bouquerie, take a left, then a right on rue Horace-Vernet, which will take you to rue Joseph-Vernet.*

Rue Joseph-Vernet

You will see two fine hotels on the right, which house the Musée Calvet and the Requien museum (👆*see MUSEUMS).*

▶ *Go to the left on rue Joseph-Vernet.*

Rue de la République

This lively and commercial street, which runs into cours Jean-Jaurès (which heads straight into the train station), forms the main axis of the city.

▶ *Go back towards the Tourist Office.*

From cours Jean-Jaurès turn right (the arcades standing in the neighbouring square are all that remain of the **Abbaye St-Martial**), then left into rue Agricol-Perdiguier to reach the 15C **Couvent des Célestins**, built in the Northern Gothic style. Its church with its fine east end and the cloisters have been restored.

The Penitent Brotherhoods of Avignon

Appearing as early as the 13C, the penitent brotherhoods were at their peak in the 16C and 17C. The brothers were expected to help each other, do public penance, and perform good deeds. The brotherhood they belonged to was identified by the colour of their sackcloth and by the hood that covered their heads during processions. Avignon was a city where many different brotherhoods – grey, white, blue, black, purple, and red – coexisted. The White Penitents were the most aristocratic and included among their members Charles IX and Henri III. Each brotherhood had assets and a chapel: a number of these chapels are still standing (the most interesting are those of the Grey Penitents and Black Penitents). During the Revolution they were disbanded and yet several brotherhoods managed to survive.

▶ *Turn back north onto rue des Lices (on the right).*

Rue des Lices

This street traces the 13C curtain wall. On the left are the 18C buildings of the former almshouse with its façade divided into galleried storeys. It now houses the École des Beaux-Arts (School of Fine Arts).

▶ *At the end of the street bear right on rue des Teinturiers.*

Rue des Teinturiers

The picturesque cobbled street shaded with plane trees follows the course of the River Sorgue, the waters of which were used by the cloth-dyers (after whom the street is named). You can still see several of the large paddle-wheels once used by the printed calico manufacturers to make fine shawls until the end of the 19C. On the right is the Franciscans' bell tower, all that remains of a convent where Petrarch's Laura is believed to be buried.

Chapelle des Pénitents Gris

No 8. ○*Open 10am-12pm and 2-6pm.* ☎ *04 90 86 58 80.*

A bridge leads to this 16C chapel, which contains paintings by Nicolas Mignard and Pierre Parrocel. Above the altar is a 17C gold glory by Péru.

▶ *Turn around and walk back as far as rue de la Masse, on the left.*

Rue de la Masse

At no 36 is the **Hôtel de Salvan Isoard**, a 17C mansion with ornately carved window surrounds; and at no 19 **Hôtel Salvador** is an impressive 18C square mansion.

Rue du Roi-René

At the corner of rue Grivolas stands the **Maison du Roi René**, where the king lived during his visits to Avignon.

Farther on four 17C and 18C town houses form a remarkable **group**★.

The Hôtel d'Honorati de Jonquerettes (*nos 10* and *12*) is bare of decoration except for its pediments which are triangular, like basket-handles.

The **Hôtel Berton de Crillon** (*no 7*) is emblazoned with portrait medallions, masks, flowers, garlands, and adorned with a wrought-iron balcony. In the inner courtyard is a grand staircase with a stone balustrade.

Across from it at no 8 is the **Hôtel de Fortia de Montréal**, less ornate, with pediments and grotesques.

Église St-Didier

This 14C church is in the purest Provençal style with a pentagonal apse and single nave lined with chapels. Located in the first chapel on the south side is the dramatic 15C **altarpiece**★ of the *Carrying of the Cross* by a Dalmatian artist, Francesco Laurana.

The baptismal font chapel at the north end is adorned with a group of frescoes belonging to the second half of the 14C and attributed to Italian artists belonging to the School of Siena.

Livrée Ceccano

Across from St-Didier's south side rises the powerful tower of the mansion (livrée) built by the cardinal of Ceccano in the 14C and later incorporated into the Jesuit College. The building now houses the Avignon media centre.

▶ *Take rue des Fourbisseurs until you reach place Carnot.*

Hôtel de Rascas

▷ *At the corner of rue des Marchands and rue des Fourbisseurs.*

A fine 15C corbelled mansion.

▷ *From place Carnot turn right and head for place Jérusalem*

On the small place Jérusalem is the synagogue, which until the 19C was the heart of the Jewish District, also known as the Carrière.

Place St-Jean-le-Vieux

Set at one corner of the square is a tall square tower (14C), all that remains of the Commandery of the Knights of St John of Jerusalem destroyed in the 19C.

▷*From rue St-Jean-le-Vieux, go to place Pignotte.*

Église de la Visitation

This former convent chapel (17C) has a finely carved façade adorned with a pediment.

▷ *Take rue P.-Saïn to the left, then right on rue Carreterie, which leads to place des Carmes.*

Place des Carmes

On the south side of the square is the Clocher des Augustins, the only remnant of the convent founded here in 1261. The wrought-iron bell tower dates from the 16C.

Église St-Symphorien (or Église des Carmes)

15C façade – The first north chapel contains three fine 16C statues in painted wood: Christ, Virgin, and St John. In the succeeding chapels hang paintings by Pierre Parrocel (*Holy Family*), Nicolas Mignard (*St Eligius*), and Guillaume Grève (*Adoration of the Magi*). A wrought-iron gate to the left of the church marks the entrance to the 14C cloisters.

▷ *Turn left into rue des Infirmières, on the north side of the square, then take the second right onto rue des Colombes.*

Chapelle des Pénitents Noirs

🕐*Apr-Sept: Fri and Sat, 2-5pm; Oct-Mar: Sat, 2-5pm.* ☎ *06 08 06 36 73.*

On the chapel's façade, remodelled in the 18C, two angels carry St John the Baptist's head in a dish (the brotherhood's emblem is the beheading). The Baroque interior boasts a handsome group of woodwork and marble, paintings by Levieux, Nicolas Mignard, and Pierre Parrocel.

Rue Banasterie

This street is named for the basket-makers' guild (*banastiers* in Provençal). At no 13 the 17C **Hôtel de Madon de Châteaublanc** has a façade adorned with garlands of fruit, eagles, and masks.

▷ *From place Manguin take the narrow rue Taulignan to the right.*

Hôtel d'Adhémar de Cransec

No 11. 🕐*Guided visit (1hr); reservation required: 2-6pm. 8€.* ☎ *04 90 86 13 28 or 01 30 59 42 71.*

This small private mansion dating from the 17C, was redecorated in 18C: its drawing rooms were hung with silk hangings, fireplaces with overmantels and painted decorations. Only two rooms retain their original French style ceilings. The mansion used to be a part of the St-Martial cardinal's mansion. It was the residence of one Amélie Palun. Countess René d'Adhémar de Cransac (1873-1955), who along with her poet and Camargue *guardian* friends, dedicated her life to promoting Provençal folklore. There is a collection of items and documents on the subject of Frédéric Mistral, Joseph Roumanille, and the Marquis de Baroncelli-Javon.

▷ *Continue straight to place St-Pierre.*

Église St-Pierre

14C-16C – On the church's west façade are two doors adorned with fine richly-decorated Renaissance **panels**★. Carved in perspective in 1551 by Antoine Valard, the subjects illustrate, on the right, the Virgin and the angel of the Annunciation, and on the left St Michael and St Jerome. Inside, in the chancel, there are elegant 17C woodwork framed painted panels. You will also see a fine late-15C pulpit.

▷ *Take rue des Marchands, to the left, off place Carnot, to get back to the place de l'Horloge.*

Museums

Petit Palais★★

Pl. du Palais-des-Papes. ○ *June-Sept: 10am-1pm, 2-6pm; Oct-May: 9.30am-1pm, 2-5.30pm.* ○*Closed Tues, 1 Jan, 1 May, 14 July, 1 Nov, and 25 Dec.* ⊜ *6 €.* ☎ *04 90 86 44 58.*

The first two rooms of this museum contain **Romanesque and Gothic sculpture**. Note especially the carved figure (at the back of the room), which comes from the late-14C monumental **tomb of Cardinal de Lagrange**. The realism of the emaciated corpse, which formed the tomb's base, anticipates the macabre representations of the 15C and 16C.

The **Campana collection**, bringing together an exceptional group of Italian paintings from the 13C-16C, constitutes the major treasure of this museum. The presentation of the works by the different schools over consecutive periods allow a good appreciation of the evolution of the Italian style. Note particularly the strong Byzantine influence that still prevailed in the works of the 13C, the Siennese School, represented by Simone Martini and Taddeo di Bartolo, the international Gothic style (Lorenzo Monaco and Gherardo Starnina), the Florentine School, which concentrated on the form of the drawing in balanced compositions where perspective plays an important role, especially with Bartolomeo della Gatta (*Annunciation*), and the rediscovery of Antiquity, c 1500.

The remaining galleries are devoted to the **painting and sculpture of the Avignon School**. The Avignon School, which can be placed midway between the realism of the Flemish School and the stylisation of the Italian Schools. **Enguerrand Quarton** is represented here by the significant *Requin Altarpiece* (1450-55). On either side of a remarkable *Virgin of Pity* (1457) stand the works of Jean de la Huerta (*St Lazarus and St Martha*) and Antoine le Moiturier (*Angels*), both of whom worked for the dukes of Burgundy.

Musée Calvet★

65 r. Joseph-Vernet. ○ *Daily, except Tues, 10am-1pm and 2-6pm.* ○*Closed 1 Jan, 1 May, 25 Dec.* ⊜*6€ (children, free).* ☎ *04 90 86 33 84.*

This celebrated, recently restored museum is named after the physician Esprit Calvet who created the foundation that contains a great many works of art. Highlights include a wide range of sculptures, a fine collection of silverware and faience (Puech bequest), and French, Italian, and Flemish painting from the 16C to the 19C. Note in particular the moving *Death of Joseph Bara* by David, *The Four Seasons* by Nicolas Mignard, works by Elisabeth Vigée-Lebrun, Victor Leydet, and Corot, and especially, the large maritime canvases by the Avignon painter **Joseph Vernet** (1714-1780).

Musée Calvet, Avignon

Morning by the Sea by Joseph Vernet

Musée Angladon★

5 r. des Laboureurs. ○ *Apr-Oct, daily, except Mon, 1-6pm; Nov-Mar, daily except Mon and Tues, 1-6pm.* ⊜*6 € (7-14 years of age, 1.50 €).* ☎ *04 90 82 29 03 - www.angladon.com.*

This lovely 18C mansion was acquired in 1977 by the Avignon painters Jean Angladon-Dubrujeaud (1906-1979) and Paulette Martin (1905-1988) in order to display their art collections. The particularly wanted to display the prestigious collection of modern art belonging to famous Parisian couturier Jacques Doucet, which they inherited. It contains several remarkable paintings by Cézanne (*Still Life with Stoneware Pot*), Sisley, Manet, Derain, Picasso, Modigliani, and Foujita. Van Gogh's *Train Carriages*, painted during the artist's stay in Arles, is his only work to be found in Provence today.

Curators have furnished and decorated the first floor according to the former proprietors' wishes, giving the impression that "the owners have just gone out." You will witness here is a collection of furniture and paintings from medieval to modern times: a Renaissance dining room, an 18C library with painting by Joseph Vernet, a Chinese salon, famous for its collection of porcelain (dating from the reign of Emperor Kangxi, 1662-1722), and the studio where the couple's own work is exhibited.

Musée Lapidaire★

27 r. de la République. ⏰ *Daily, except Tues, 10am-1pm and 2-6pm.* ⏰*Closed 1 Jan, 1 May, and 25 Dec.* ♿ ᯤ *2€ (under 12, free).* ☎ *04 90 85 75 38 or 04 90 86 33 84.*

Located in the former chapel of the 17C Jesuit College, this building has a unique nave and is flanked by side galleries where you will find wonderfully intimate displays of sculpture and stone carvings that together represent the different civilisations that left their mark on the region. You will encounter the "Tarasque" of Noves, a man-eating monster that is a part of the Celtic bestiary collection. There are a number of statues: Greek, Greco-Roman (a remarkable copy of Praxiteles' *Apollo the Python killer*), and local (Gallic warriors from Vachères and Mondragon). Also, take in several sculpted portraits of emperors (Marcus Aurelius, Tiberius) and anonymous people, low reliefs (relief of Cabrières d'Aigues representing a towing scene), sarcophagi, and a remarkable series of masks from Vaison.

Musée Louis-Vouland★

17 r. Victor-Hugo. ⏰ *May to Oct: daily, except Mon, 10am-noon, 2-6pm, Sun and public holidays 2-6pm; Nov to Apr: daily, except Mon, 2-6pm.* ⏰*Closed 1 Jan, 1 May, 25 Dec.* ᯤ*4€.* ☎ *04 90 86 03 79 - www.vouland.com.*

The museum contains a decorative arts collection that concentrates on 18C French **furnishings**: a commode signed by Migeon, an inlaid backgammon table, a money-changer's desk, and an amusing travelling table service stamped with the Countess Du Barry's coat of arms.

A fine collection of porcelain and **faience**★ is displayed in two rooms; there are many examples of Moustiers and Marseille wares. A number of Flemish and Gobelins (*Diana the Huntress,* pastoral scenes) **tapestries** hang on the walls. The Far Eastern Art collection consists of a number of Chinese vases and plates and ivory polychrome statues. Two galleries are dedicated to the works of Provençal painters.

Muséum Requien

67 r. Joseph-Vernet, next to Musée Calvet. ⏰ *Daily, except Sun and Mon, 9am-12pm, and 2-6pm.* ⏰*Closed public holidays. No charge.* ☎ *04 90 82 43 51.*

Named after the Avignon naturalist Esprit Requien (1788-1851), this museum contains a very important natural history library, a herbarium with more than 200 000 specimens from all over the world, and a local geological, zoological, and botanical collection.

Collection Lambert

5 r. Violette. ⏰ *July: 11am-7pm; Aug-June: daily, except Mon, 11am-6pm.* ⏰*Closed 1 Jan, 1 May, and 25 Dec.* ᯤ*5.50 €. For information:* ☎ *04 90 16 56 20 - www.collection-lambert.com.*

This fine 18C mansion was once a secondary school and has been renovated, now housing the contemporary art collection belonging to Yvon Lambert, who intends to eventually donate it. Most of the avant-garde artistic trends championed by Lambert (Conceptual Art, Land Art, Minimal Art, New Figurative Art or Nouvelle Figuration) are represented by a collection of works, some of which were created for this exhibition space, by names such sa Cy Twombly, Christian Boltanski, Nan Goldin, Sol LeWitt, Anselm Kiefer, Daniel Buren, Robert Combas, and Bernard Lavier, The works are diplayed in rotation, by chronology ot theme.

Excursions

Villeneuve-lès-Avignon★

▶ *On the Rhône's south (right) bank. Leave Avignon via the bridge, pont Édouard-Daladier, on N 100, towards Nîmes. ☝See VILLENEUVE-LÈS-AVIGNON.*

Château de Barbentane★★

9.5 km/6mi SW on N 570, then right on D 35. ☝See Château de BARBENTANE.

Montfavet

6km/3.5mi to the east on D 100 and N 7F to the right.

This small town possesses an imposing **church**, the only vestige of a monastery built in the 14C by Cardinal Bertrand de Montfavet. Interesting carvings adorn the doorway's lintel. The vast and austere nave is covered by elegant Gothic vaulting and flanked by side chapels.

Les Alpilles to the Durance

▶ *Approximately 2hr. Leave Avignon via D 571.*

Châteaurenard

Of the feudal castle, once belonging to a nobleman named Reynard, only two towers remain on the hill. At its foot, the town, has become a important market handling the produce harvested from the market gardens and fruit farms in the neighbouring plain. *Access the castle on foot by taking the staircase to the right of the church, or by car, 1km/0.5mi via avenue Marx-Dormoy and a signposted road on the right.* The two towers house a **Regional History Museum** (*Musée d'histoire locale*) ⊙ *May-Sept: daily, except Sun and Mon, 10am-12om and 2.30-6.30pm.* ⊛2€. ☎ *04 90 24 25 50* . From the top of one, the Tour du Griffon, is a fine **panorama**★.

▶ *Head east along D 28.*

Noves

Noves is an old town with a network of narrow winding streets, two medieval gateways (Porte d'Agel and Porte Aurose) and a 12C stone-roofed church.

▶ *Exit Noves on N 7 for Avignon; after passing the motorway turn right towards Cavaillon. The signpost to the charter-house of Bonpas is on the left-hand side of the road.*

Chartreuse de Bonpas

⊙*Apr-Oct: 9am-12.30pm and 1.30-7pm; Nov-Mar: 9am-12.30pm and 2.30-5pm.* ⊛4€. ☎ *04 90 23 09 59.*

Next to a small chapel, the Templars built a church and monastery in the 13C, which took the name of Bonpas. It enjoyed a period of prosperity in the 17C when the chapter-house was constructed. The charterhouse has recently been restored, and today houses a wine-growing business: an excellent Côtes-du-Rhône, which can be sampled before visiting the well-kept formal French gardens. From the terrace there is a clear view of the Alpilles, which stand out in the distance, and the Durance spanned by a 500m/0.3mi-long bridge.

▶ *Return to Avignon via N 7.*

BAGNOLS-SUR-CÈZE

POPULATION 18 103

MICHELIN LOCAL MAP 339: M-4

To the old town of Bagnols, ringed by boulevards, on the site of the former ramparts, has been added the new city built for the workers of the Marcoule atomic works. The River Cèze is popular with kayakers.

🛈 *Espace St-Gilles, av. Léon-Blum, 30200 Bagnols-sur-Cèze, ☎ 04 66 89 54 61. www.ot-bagnolssurceze.com.*

Musée d'Art Moderne Albert-André★

Pl. Mallet, 2nd floor in the townhall. 🕐 *Daily, except Mon, 10am-12pm, 2-6pm -* 🚫*Closed Feb and public holidays.* ⏣*4.30 €, free the first Sun of the month (Oct-Jun).* ☎ *04 66 50 50 56.*

The Modern Art Museum shares the same building as the town hall, a fine 17C mansion. It exhibits contemporary works collected by the painter Albert André, curator from 1918 to 1954. The museum has also been endowed with the private collection of George and Adèle Besson. It is made up of artists' signed works – oils, watercolours, drawings, sculptures (Renoir, Valadon, Bonnard, Matisse, Marquet, Van Dongen).

Musée d'Archéologie Léon-Alègre

♿ *Mon, Tues, Wed 10am-12pm, 2-6pm (mid-June to mid-Sept: Mon, Tues, Wed 10am-12.30pm, 2-6.30pm).* 🚫*Closed Feb and public holidays.* ⏣*4.30 €, free the first Sun of the month (Oct-Jun).* ☎ *04 66 89 74 00.*

The Archeological Museum's collections originate from the Rhône valley and illustrate the different periods of Antiquity. Two rooms illustrate the Celtic-Ligurian civilisation and Greek influence from the 6C to the 1C BC: pottery, bronze wares, cult objects and sculpture. Along one gallery are assembled various Gallo-Roman remains: ceramics, amphorae, glassware, everyday objects and cinerary urns. Note the fine shop sign of a stone-carver with its mason's level, hammer and two scissors. One room is devoted to the site of the St-Vincent de Gaujac oppidum (see below): reconstructed hypocaust, small pool originally from the baths, pottery and documents (photographs and plans).

Excursions

Le Bas-Vivarais

▷ *Round-trip of 130km/81mi – allow 1 day.*

▷ *Leave Bagnols-sur-Ceze going west on D 6, then turn left on D 166.*

Sabran

This old town is perched on a rocky outcrop. In the castle ruins, from the foot of the giant statue of the Virgin a vast **panorama**★ unfolds over the surrounding countryside.

▷ *Return to D 6, which you will cross and take D 166.*

La Roque-sur-Cèze

The village appears grouped around its Romanesque chapel on a hilltop darkly plumed by cypresses, creating a peaceful **site**★. An old arched bridge with pointed cutwaters spans the River Cèze.

▷ *Follow the path on the left without crossing the bridge.*

Cascade du Sautadet★

☺ *This site is accessible but dangerous. pay attention to all the safety markings along the path.*

This waterfall is unique in the way it cuts deeply into the river bed and for the complicated network of crevasses in which the Cèze runs. Blocking the river's route, the limestone rock was attacked by the water, which carved rifts and potholes into it. Continue beyond the abandoned mill-race to the deeper ravines plumbed by the River Cèze. From the southern end there is a lovely view.

▷ *Return to D 166 and continue to D 980 where you will turn left. After 3km/1.86mi turn right.*

Cornillon

This ancient fortified site offers an enjoyable walk along its ramparts. From the center of the chateau, take in the **panorama**★ of the Cèze valley.

▷ *Proceed on D 298. After St-André-de-Roquepertuis, turn left on D 167, which runs across an solitary, wild plateau. Take D 16 in the direction of Rochegude, then take D 7 to Brouzet-les-Alès.*

Guidon du Bouquet★★

The highest point of the Bouquet range is a beak-shaped rock that dominates the vast horizon extending between the Gard and Ardèche rivers. From the steep approach road the ruins of the Château du Bouquet are visible through the clumps of holm oaks. The **panorama**★★ from the summit extends across the Cévennes *causses* to the west. The irregular crests of the Bas Vivarais range to the north, Mont Ventoux and the Alpilles to the east. From the statue of the Virgin there is a vertiginous view of the immense garrigue surrounding Uzès and to the rear of the television mast a view of the Bouquet range itself.

▷ *Returning to Brouzet-les-Alès, take D 7 . Turn right onto D 37.*

The road rises offering a good view of the **ruins**★ of Château d'Allègre. It continues through the garrigue to the hill village of **Lussan**.

▷ *At Lussan take D 143, then go left on D 643 which, lined with clipped boxwood, crosses a garrigue of holm oak to the Gorges de l'Aiguillon, also known as Les Concluses. Leave the car at the end of the road, preferably in the second of the two car parks, in a lay-by halfway down.*

From here there is a **view**★ upstream of the giant holes in the river bed.

Les Concluses★★

▷ 🚶 *1hr round-trip on foot.*

The Aiguillon torrent, dry in summer, has hollowed out of the calcareous grey-white rock a rocky defile some 1km/0.5mi long and opened upstream by a fine natural phenomenon: the **Portail** (Gateway).

▷ *Take the path on the right signposted: Portail.*

As you descend you see the caves on the opposite bank, most notably the Baume de Biou or Bulls' Cave, and come to the promontory and Beauquier pool, a widening of the stream fringed by trees at the feet of majestic rock escarpments. Note on the cliff face three abandoned eagles' eyries. The path ends at the gateway where the rock overhang finally meets above the river's course; the bottom forms a narrow gorge through which the Aiguillon flows when in flood. Pass under the gateway, then walk through the rocky straits following the river bed for about 200m/219yd. (🚶 *This walk is possible only in summer.*) The atmosphere in the bottom of the gorge is one of profound solitude.

On the way back, experienced walkers may enjoy climbing back to the car park by way of the riverbed upstream as far as Baume de Biou and from there a very rough path *(allow an extra 15min).*

▶ *Once on D 143, head for Goudargues.*

Goudargues

The village, ringed by massive plane trees, is dominated by its church. This former abbey church, partly rebuilt in the 17C and 19C, is interesting for its tall Romanesque apse, decorated inside by two storeys of arcading.

▶ *Turn right onto D 298 and return to Bagnols.*

The Garrigue and Côtes Du Rhône Vineyards

Round-trip of 50km/31mi – allow 3hr

▶ *Leave Bagnols-sur-Cèze on N 86 southwards (direction of Remoulins) to Gaujac, turn right onto D 310 which passes below the village. Take a dirt road (signposted) uphill (unsuitable for cars).*

Oppidum de St-Vincent-de-Gaujac

Perched on a height in the middle of a forest, this site was occupied intermittently between the 5C BC and the 6C AD and then again from the 10C to the 14C. During the Gallo-Roman era it was a rural sanctuary with temples and baths. Go through a fortified gate (the vestiges of a curtain wall) to discover the ruins of the medieval fortified stronghold with its cistern and the Gallo-Roman excavations. The latter dates from the Early Empire (1C-3C).

Above are the remains of a fanum, a small Roman temple; below are the baths, the arrangement of which can be seen with the remains of the hypocaust and drains. The sanctuary was abandoned in the 3C for an unknown reason.

▶ *Return to N 86 and 4km/2.5mi south, after Pouzilhac, turn left onto D 101.*

The narrow and winding road crosses a landscape of garrigues and forest; shortly before St-Victor-la-Coste, there is a good view of the ruins of an imposing feudal castle dismantled during the Albigensian Wars.

St-Victor-la-Coste

On the border of the garrigues and vineyards, this picturesque old village huddles at the foot of its castle.

▶ *Continue along D 101.*

On the left a narrow road leads to an isolated chapel. The countryside is now covered by the Côtes du Rhône vineyards. These wines are made from selected grapes and there are several different appellations; the best known are **Lirac** and **Tavel**.

St-Laurent-des-Arbres

In the past this village belonged to the bishops of Avignon. It has preserved some interesting medieval ruins. The Romanesque church was fortified in the 14C: the walls were raised and a crenellated parapet was added. Inside, the domes on squinches are adorned with symbols of the Evangelists. Near the church stands a rectangular keep from the Lords of the Sabran's castle. The base dates from the late 12C; it was raised in the 14C by a storey set back with crenellated arcades. Not far from the keep, above the village is located another 12C square tower.

▶ *Take D 26 to Lirac and Tavel.*

These two wine-growing villages have given their names to excellent wines.

▶ *Return to St-Laurent-des-Arbres. At the crossroads with N 580 turn left. At l'Ardoise, take D 9 to the left.*

Laudun

This village is dominated by its imposing 14C Gothic church. A long distance footpath, the GR 42 towards Orsan leads from the church up the Camp de César plateau, from where there is a good view of the Rhône. Julius Caesar almost certainly never came to Laudun. The "Camp de César" was a large encampment occupied from the 5C BC to the

6C AD. The ruins of the forum and a basilica have been uncovered. Artefacts discovered on the site are exhibited in Laudun in a gallery on Rue de la République.

▷ *From Laudun, drive to Orsan on D 121 (north) and then turn right to cross N 580.*

Belvédère de Marcoule★

Impossible to miss from afar, the nuclear power station with its tall towers is surrounded by vineyards and garrigue. From the raised terrace that seprates the two exhibit sapces in the *Centre d'informacion de Marcoule* there is an extensive **scenic view** of the Rhône, Orange and its Roman theatre, Mont Ventoux, the Comtat plain, the Alpilles, the Ardoise iron and metalworks, and the Lower Gard valley.

Centre d'information de Marcoule

🕐 *Closed temporarily.* ☎ *04 66 79 52 97.*

Two galleries exhibit information pertaining to nuclear energy: the activities of the plant, the nuclear fuel cycle, and different types of energy, and the various ways of protecting the environment.

▷ *Return to Bagnols via Chusclan, then to N 580 to the right.*

BARBENTANE

POPULATION 3 645

MICHELIN LOCAL MAP 340: D-2

Château de Barbentane — Main façade

Built against the north slope of the Montagnette, Barbentane overlooks the plain near the confluence of the Rhône and the Durance and is devoted to market gardening. Lying at the foot of the Tour Angelica (1365), the village has retained part of its 14C fortifications and is worth visiting for its elegant castle.

🛈 *Le Cours, 13570 Barbentane, ☎ 04 90 90 85 86. www.barbentane.fr.*

Visit

Château★★

♿ 🕐*Easter to Oct: guided tours (45min) daily except Wed. 10am-noon, 2-6pm (July to Sept: daily); Mar and Nov: Sun, 2-6pm. 6€. ☎ 04 90 95 51 07.*

A classical 17C façade and terraces lined with stone railings decorated with lions and flower-filled urns overlook the formal Italian-style gardens. The interior, which is enhanced by the mementoes belonging to the marquis of Barbentane, features rich 18C decoration of Italian influence. The vaulting, which used a particular stone-carving technique, plasterwork, painted medallions, coloured marble, Louis XV and XVI furnishings, Chinese porcelain and Moustiers faience all add to the charm of this delightful château.

Old Village

All that remains from the fortifications are the two entrance gates, Porte Calendale, which opens onto the Cours, and Porte Séquier above the village.

Maison des Chevaliers (House of the Knights)

This 12C residence has a lovely Renaissance façade composed of a turret and two basket arches topped by a columned gallery. Across the street is a 12C church, much remodelled, with its 15C bell tower (badly damaged).

Tour Anglica

Overlooking the village, the tower is the keep of the former castle, built in the 14C by the brother of Pope Urban V, Cardinal Anglic de Grimoard. From the terrace there is a good view of Avignon, Châteaurenard and in the distance Mont Ventoux.

A short walk through the pines leads to the well-preserved 18C **Moulin de Bretoul** (Bretoul mill), from where there is a lovely view of the Rhône plain. This is the only remaining example of the many windmills formerly present in the region.

Les BAUX-DE-PROVENCE★★★

POPULATION 434

MICHELIN LOCAL MAP 340: D-3

Detached from the Alpilles, this bare rock spur – 900m/2 953ft long and 200m/656ft wide – with vertical ravines on either side, a fortified castle lying in ruins, and old desolate houses, compose the spectacular site★★★ of the village of Les Baux, which boasts a proud history. The village gave its name to the mineral bauxite, discovered here in 1822.

🄸 *R. Porte-Mage, 13520 Les Baux-de-Provence,* ☎ *04 90 54 34 39, www.lesbauxdeprovence.com.*

Les Baux de Provence

B. Kaufmann/MICHELIN

Address Book

For coin ranges, see Legend at the back of the guide.

Wine tours – Les Baux is surrounded by vineyards in a region classified "Les Buax de Provence" for wines produced here. The area is blessed with a well-suited microclimate; reds and rosés dominate, though whites are also produced.

To explore the wine country, contact either the tourist offices at Les Baux or St-Rémy or the *Syndicat des Vignerons des Baux ed Provence, Château Romanin, 13210, St-Rémy-de-Provence.* ☎ 04 90 92 45 87.

Golf – **Domaine Manville**, ☎ 04 90 54 40 20, www.golf-provence.com. *Summer 7am-8pm; winter 9am-5pm.* This beautiful 9 hole course offers a splendid view of the castle ruins at Les Baux and of the Alpilles mountains.

EATING OUT

◎◎ **Café Cinarca** – *26 rue du Trencat* – ☎ 04 90 54 33 94 – *closed 6 Jan-6 Feb, 1 2 Nov-20 Dec, evenings from 15 Sept-30 Apr and Tues.* If the road to the castle seems never-ending, a pit stop in this café will refuel your energy. Invigorating, "traditional" food served in an original setting crammed with objects, posters, photographs and old work tools. Tables outside under mulberry trees.

◎◎◎ **Margaux** – *1 rue P.-Revoil – 13520 Maussane-les-Alpilles* – ☎ 04 90 54 35 04 – *closed 7 Jan-15 Feb, 15 Nov-7 Dec, Tue and Wed lunchtime.* Tucked away behind the church is this tastefully decorated little Provençal house with blue shutters. The shady inner courtyard is much appreciated in the summer. Southern-style cooking.

WHERE TO STAY

◎◎ **Hostellerie de la Tour** – *route d'Arles – 13990 Fontvieille – 9km/5.6mi west of Les Baux on D 78F and D 17 –* ☎ 04 90 54 72 21 – *open 15 Mar-31 Oct –* 🅿 *– 10 rooms* ⌂ *8€ – restaurant 14/18€.* A warm and friendly welcome is assured in this popular, well-kept auberge. Recently renovated rooms and small restaurant decorated in Provençal colours. Family-style cooking and local wines.

◎◎◎◎ **Auberge de la Benvengudo** – *2km/1.2mi southwest of Baux via D 27 –* ☎ 04 90 54 32 54 – *closed 15 Nov-20 Dec –* 🅿 *– 21 rooms –* ⌂ *12€ – restaurant 43€.* Nestled in a cluster of olive groves at the foot of the citadel is this charming Virginia creeper-covered inn. Rooms are plush and open onto a flower-filled garden. The dining room and veranda are decorated in Provençal style. Poolside terrace. Dishes are composed around fresh market produce.

◎◎◎◎ **Hôtel Mas de l'Oulivié** – *2.5km/1.5mi southwest of Baux via the D 27 -* ☎ 04 90 54 35 78 - *closed mid Nov-mid Mar -* 🅿 *- 25 rooms -* ⌂ *10€.* This pretty mas surrounded by olive trees is bound to appeal to people who want to relax. At sunset, when the crickets come to life, you can lounge about in the landscaped pool area. Friendly welcome, Provençal style rooms decorated in shades of almond green, magnificent garden.

EVENTS

Christmas at Les Baux – Midnight mass is held on Christmas Eve in the church of St-Vincent with a living nativity scene. The congregation flocks to watch musicians escorting shepherds swathed in cloaks, bringing a newborn lamb in a little chariot pulled by an ox.

A Bit of History

A warrior line – The lords of Baux were renowned in the Middle Ages, described by Mistral as "warriors all – vassals never." They were proud to trace their genealogy back to the Magi king, Balthazar, and, so that no one should ignore the fact, boldly placed the star of Bethlehem on their coat of arms.

From the 11C the lords were among the strongest in the south of France, having in their control 79 towns and villages. From 1145 to 1162 they warred against the House of Barcelona, whose rights to Provence they contested. Supported for a while by the German emperor, they finally submitted after having succumbed to a siege at Les Baux itself.

They won titles: members of different branches became variously princes of Orange, viscounts of Marseille, counts of Avellino, and dukes of Andria (having followed the Capetian Princes of Anjou who were campaigning in southern Italy). One of them married Marie of Anjou, sister of Joan I, queen of Sicily and countess of Provence, a beautiful woman much loved by the people of Provence. She was destined to tragedy: three times a widow, she died in 1382, smothered by an ambitious cousin.

Turenne, the brigand – The house of Turenne, from the Limousin, was a great family: two of its members were popes at Avignon, one of whom was the famous Clement VI. Another of its members was the Viscount Raymond de Turenne, nephew of Gregory

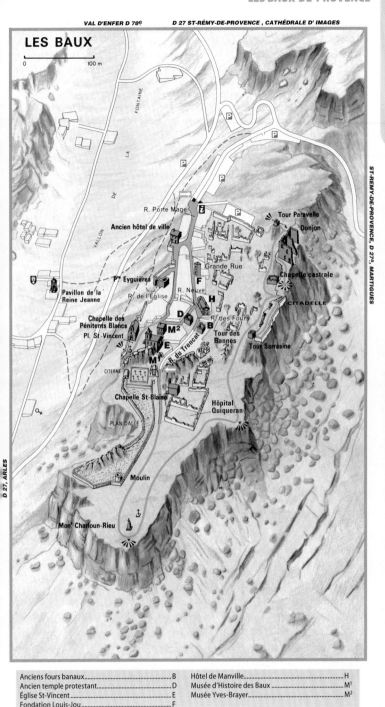

LES BAUX

VAL D'ENFER D 78ᴳ D 27 ST-RÉMY-DE-PROVENCE , CATHÉDRALE D' IMAGES

0   100 m

R. Porte Mage
Ancien hôtel de ville
Pᵗᵉ Eyguières
Pavillon de la Reine Jeanne
Rᵉ de l'Église
R. Neuve
Chapelle des Pénitents Blancs
Pl. St-Vincent
M²
E
M¹
Grande Rue
R. des Fours
R. du Trencat
Tour des Bannes
Tour Sarrasine
CITERNE
PLAN DALLE
Chapelle St-Blaise
Hôpital Quiqueran
Moulin
Monᵗ Charloun-Rieu

Tour Paravelle
Donjon
Chapelle castrale
CITADELLE

ST-RÉMY-DE-PROVENCE, D 27ᴬ, MARTIGUES

D 27, ARLES

Anciens fours banaux...B	Hôtel de Manville...H
Ancien temple protestant...D	Musée d'Histoire des Baux ....M¹
Église St-Vincent...E	Musée Yves-Brayer....................................M²
Fondation Louis-Jou...F	

XI, who became the guardian of his niece, Alix of Baux, in 1372. His ambitions caused civil war in the region. His pillaging and cruelty terrorised the countryside and he was appropriately named the "Scourge of Provence." His chief delight was to force his unransomed prisoners to jump off the castle walls.

The pope and the lord of Provence hired mercenaries to get rid of the brigands, but the mercenaries themselves ravaged the enemy territories as well as the territories to be protected; as a result their contract was broken and they were paid to leave the area. Pillaging and fighting broke out again quite soon. The king of France joined Turenne's enemies and in 1399 the "scourge" was surrounded at Les Baux; however, he escaped and fled into France.

The End – Alix was Baux's last princess, and on her death in 1426 the domain, incorporated into Provence, became simply a barony. King René granted it to his second wife Jeanne of Laval. Joined with Provence to the French crown, the barony revolted against Louis XI, in 1483, who subsequently had the fortress dismantled. As of 1528 the Constable Anne de Montmorency, who was titular lord of Les Baux, undertook a large restoration project on the town, which once again enjoyed a prosperous period. Les Baux then became a centre of Protestantism under the Manville family who administered it for the crown. In 1632, however, Richelieu, tired of this troublesome fief, had the castle and ramparts demolished and the inhabitants were fined 100 000 livres plus the cost of the demolition! What was once a proud town of 4 000 gradually disintegrated to become a shadow of its former self.

The Village★★★ 1hr

A walk through the streets of Les Baux is a magical experience, as long as they are not too crowded or full of souvenir sellers.

▶ *Enter through the Porte Mage and turn left towards place Louis-Jou.*

Ancien Hôtel de Ville

This deconsecrated 16C chapel, formerly the town hall, still has three rooms with pointed vaulting, which house a **Santon Museum** *(free admission)*.

Porte Eyguières

This used to be the town's only entrance gate.

▶ *Return to the street and walk to the end of rue de la Caldes, go towards the right on rue de l'Église.*

Place St-Vincent★

This is a charming, shaded little square. There is a lovely view of the Fontaine valley and the Val d'Enfer from the terrace. In the corner of the square, the hôtel Porcelet houses the Musée Yves Brayer (splendid 17C frescoes near the reception).
Chapelle des Pénitents Blancs – The 17C chapel was restored in 1936. Inside, the wall frescoes are by Yves Brayer and depict pastoral Provençal scenes set against the backdrop of the Alpilles or the Val d'Enfer.

Église St-Vincent★

This 12C church is flanked on its north side by a graceful campanile, the so-called lantern of the dead. Partly carved out of the bedrock, the simple interior is surprisingly light, with stained-glass windows by Max Ingrand.

Ancien Temple protestant

This former Protestant chapel was once a house dated 1571, part of the Hôtel de Manville. On the lintel of one of its fine windows is the Calvinist motto: *"Post tenebras lux"* (after the shadows comes light).

Hôtel de Manville

This 16C mansion, donated to the town by the prince of Manville, boasts a beautiful façade decorated with mullioned windows. It houses the town hall.

▶ *Go back up the Grande Rue.*

Anciens fours banaux

The townspeople came to bake their bread in these manorial ovens.

Rue du Trencat

This street, carved out of the bedrock, leads to the castle.
While descending Grande Rue, note the **Renaissance house** of Jean de Brion, home of the engraver, publisher, and printer **Louis Jou** (1881-1968), who devoted his whole life to the art of books.

▶ *Go to the Porte Mage.*

Château★ *45min*

▶ *Access to the citadel through the Musée d'Histoire des Baux, at the end of rue du Trencat.*

Since 1991 the citadel has been the subject of an important restoration and development project. The excavation work carried out in 1992 allowed three main periods of occupation of the rocky spur prior to the modern era to be determined: the 2C and 1C BC (second Iron Age), the 5C and 6C (construction of a rampart and scattered dwellings), and the medieval period (construction of a keep).

Musée d'Histoire des Baux

🕐 *- June-Aug: 9am-7.30pm; Mar-May and Sept-Nov: 9am-6.30pm; Dec-Feb: 9am-5pm. ☞7.30 € (7-17 years, 3.50 €). ☎ 04 90 54 55 56 - www.chateau-baux-provence.com.* Housed in the old residence of the powerful Tour du Brau family, this History Museum exhibits in a beautiful rib-vaulted room information concerning the most important moments in the history of Les Baux from Antiquity to the present day. Two models of the fortress in the 13C and the 16C illustrate the architectural evolution of the site.

Chapelle St-Blaise

This chapel was the seat of the woollen carders and weavers brotherhood from the 12C. Nowadays it houses a small museum devoted to the olive. Visitors can watch a video entitled "Van Gogh, Gauguin and Cézanne in the Country of the Olive."

Hôpital Quinqueran

This hospital was built in the 16C by Jehanne de Quinqueran, wife of the governor of Les Baux and was in operation until 1787. Nowadays in ruins, there are plans to rebuild it.

Moulin

The old communal mill, the use of which incurred a tax paid to the lord of Les Baux, stands alongside a paved area used to collect rainwater which then drains into a cistern carved into the rock.

Monument Charloun Riéu

From this monument erected in honour of the poet Charloun Riéu (1846-1924), there is a magnificent view a over the plain as far as the Berre lagoon.

Citadelle

Towering over the eastern side of the rocky spur are the impressive citadel ruins. The **Tour Sarrasine** (Saracen Tower) –from the top, a good **view** of the village and castle– and the **Tour des Bannes** remain to the south, dominating a group of houses built in the 16C. A beautiful bay of rib vaulting can still be seen in the **Chapelle Castrale** (12C-16C), dedicated to St Catherine.

Château and Chapelle Ste-Blaise

The **castle** and the **donjon** (keep) *(fairly difficult steps, not recommended for those who suffer from vertigo)*, are the remains of a 13C building constructed on the site of the 10C fortress. There is a magnificent **panorama**★★ embracing the Aix countryside, the Luberon, Mont Ventoux and the Cévennes; closer by, the tormented shapes of the Val d'Enfer to the north contrast with the gentle countryside of the Vallon de la Fontaine to the west.

Leaning against the northern rampart, the **Tour Paravelle** affords a pretty **view**★ of the village of Les Baux and the Val d'Enfer.

Musée Yves-Brayer★

◷*Apr–Sept: 10am–12.30pm, 2–6.30pm; Oct–Dec and mid-Feb–end Mar: daily, except Tues, 10am–12.30pm, 2–5.30pm.* ⊷ *4 €.* ☎ *04 90 54 36 99 - www.yvesbrayer.com.*

The museum houses a retrospective collection of the works of Yves Brayer (1907-1990), a figurative painter deeply attached to Les Baux (he is buried in the village cemetery). The canvases of his early travels in Spain, Morocco and Italy are characterised by contrasting shades of black, red and ochre, including bull-fighting scenes; there are also watercolours he executed on more recent journeys. But it is the glowing landscapes of Provence which inspired some of his best paintings; his palette lightened in works such as *Les Baux, Herds of Horses in the Marshlands*, or *Field of Almond Trees*.

Excursions

Cathédrale d'Images★

▷ *By D 27, 300m/330yd north of the village in Les Baux stone quarries.*
Kids ◷ *Apr–Sept: 10am–7pm; Oct–Dec: 10am–6pm -* ◷*closed 8 Jan–mid-Feb.* ⊷ *7.30€ (children, 3.50 €).* ☎ *04 90 54 38 65 - www.cathedrale-images.com.*

The potential of this colossal backdrop, which lay forgotten for more than a century, was realized by Albert Piécy (1914-77), who saw in it a place where he could carry out his research on the "total image." In the half-light, the immaculate limestone cliffs of the great galleries and pillars act as three-dimensional screens for a magical audiovisual projection show on a giant scale, immersing the viewer into a farytale world. The *30min* show changes theme every year.

Panorama★★★

▷ *Continue along D 27 for about 1km/0.5mi and bear right on a steep road (look for parking signs).*

This rocky promontory offers the best view of Les Baux and a far-reaching panorama (*signposted, car park, viewing table*): Arles and Camargue, Rhône valley, Cévennes mountains, Aix-en-Provence, the Luberon and Mont Ventoux.

Val d'Enfer

▷*Access from D 27 and D 78G.*

A path (15min return on foot) crosses this jagged and irregular gorge aptly named Hell Valley. The caves used to be lived in and are still the source of many legends as the place where witches, fairies, and sprites reign.

Queen Jeanne's Pavilion (Pavillon de la reine Jeanne)

On D 78G.

A path leads down to the pavilion from Porte Eyguières. The small Renaissance building, built by Jeanne of Les Baux c 1581, was beloved by the Provençal poets of the Félibrige. Mistral had a copy made for his tomb at Maillane.

BEAUCAIRE ★

POPULATION 13 748

MICHELIN LOCAL MAP 339: M-6

Formerly a stronghold of the Counts of Toulouse, Beaucaire kept watch over Tarascon, across the river, which was part of the Holy Roman Empire. It became famous for its fair, attracting huge crowds for many centuries. The town's facilities include a river marina, since the Rhône to Sète canal flows through the town, and the Rhône borders it to the east.

🛈 24 cours Gambetta, 30300 Beaucaire, ☎ 04 66 59 26 57. www.ot-beaucaire.fr.

Beaucaire Fair

The fair, launched in 1217 by **Raymond VI of Toulouse**, originally lasted one week. It became a great medieval fair and at its peak, in the 18C, it lasted a month when as many as 300 000 people gathered to do business, roister and celebrate every July. Streets were decorated, and houses beflagged and crammed with visitors and their merchandise. So prestigious was the fair that the prices negotiated there served as a reference throughout the kingdom. Streets specialised in single commodities after which many were named: Beaujolais was a wine street; Bijoutiers was a jewellers' row; rue des Marseillais was where oil and soap were sold; and elsewhere there were wool, silk, linen, cotton, lace, coloured woven cloth, clothing, weapons, hardware, rope and saddlery shops and harness makers. On the quayside and on board, traders proffered dried fish, sugar, cocoa, coffee, cinnamon, vanilla, lemons, oranges, and dates.

The fairground, on the large flat expanse between the castle cliff and the river, was set with stalls offering everything from games to perfume, pipes to pottery. It was, of course, also a horse fair. Tumblers and jugglers, acrobats and clowns entertained the crowds; bearded women, giants and dwarfs, monkeys, performing dogs, lions, bears and elephants amazed onlookers. There were even dioramas of Paris, Constantinople and Versailles to be viewed through magnifying lenses.

This huge success was almost certainly due to the town's position at a crossroads of land and river routes, aided by Louis XI's decree which made it a free port. The advent of industrialisation and rail transport brought about considerable changes in commerce and international exchanges, and, as a result, the Beaucaire Fair ceased to exist, except in the form of the "Estivales" festival, which still attracts a crowd.

Old Beaucaire ★

▸ Take rue Hôtel-de-Ville (to the right of cours Gambetta), which leads to place Georges Clemenceau.

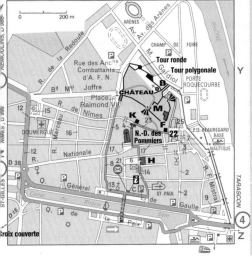

BEAUCAIRE

Barbès R.	Z	2
Bijoutiers R. des	YZ	3
Charlier R.	Y	4
Château R. du	Y	5
Clemenceau Pl. Georges	Z	6
Danton R.	Y	7
Denfert R.	Z	8
Écluse R. de l'	Z	9
Foch Bd Maréchal	YZ	12
Gambetta Cours	Z	13
Hôtel de Ville R. de l'	Z	14
Jean-Jacques-Rousseau R.	Y	16
Jean-Jaurès Pl.	Y	15
Ledru-Rollin R.	Z	17
Nationale R.	Z	
Pascal R. Roger	Z	21
République Pl. de la	Y	22
République R. de la	Y	23
Victor-Hugo R.	Y	25

Chapelle romane	Y	B
Hôtel de Roys de St-Michel	Y	F
Hôtel de ville	Z	H
Hôtel des Margailliers - Maison des cariatides	Y	K
Musée Auguste-Jacquet	Y	M²

Address Book

Guided tours of the town – *(1hr 30min to 2hr).* – One of the designated "towns of art and history," Beaucaire offers a Ministry of Culture and Communication approved tour. For information and reservations, inquire at the tourist office, or, at www.vpah.culture.fr.

Birds of prey in flight – *Château de Beaucaire,* ☎ 04 66 59 26 72 – www.aigles-de-beaucaire.com. *Apr-June: daily except Thurs and public holidays: 2pm, 3pm, 4.30pm; Mar and Sept-Nov: daily except Wed, 2.30pm, 3.30pm, 4.30pm.* ☎ *7€ (children, 5€).* Kites, eagles, buzzards, and other birds, are handled by falconers (in medieval attire!) in an evocative and entertaining presentation.

EATING OUT

Auberge l'Amandin – *Quartier St-Joseph – 3km/1.8mi south of the town centre of Beaucaire via D 15 for Fourques then south industrial zone –* ☎ *04 66 59 55 07 – lamandin@tiscali.fr –closed11-26 Aug, Sun evenings, and Mon .* Laid out in the stables of an old mas, this dining room has a charming Provençal atmosphere with its

rustic furniture and paintings. The traditional cuisine is livened up with specialities cooked over a wood fire. There are also tables on the terrace facing the garden.

WHERE TO STAY

Hôtel les Vignes Blanches – *67 rte de Nîmes -* ☎ *04 66 59 13 12 - 58 rooms - 7.50 €.* A recent total renovation here has resulted in beautiful colors and an overall fresh, bright feeling. The culinary offering is traditional cuisine; seasonal and market-fresh.

FESTIVALES

Les Estivale de Beaucaire –For 10 days in July, this summer festival recreates the glorious past of the Beaucaire fair. Entertainments include abrivados along the streets, Camargue races in the amphitheatre (where the "palme d'or" trophy is contested) *novilladas* and *corridas* in the last weekend of July, amusement parks, dance evenings, fireworks and "casetas" (tents) where Xères wine flows liberally to the rhythm of Seville dancing.

Hôtel de Ville

The town hall is a late-17C mansion by Mansart with a central block flanked by wings outlined by a high, balustraded wall; carved flower garlands surround the windows, and the grand staircase (courtyard) rises behind a double portico of Ionic columns.

Église Notre-Dame-des-Pommiers

Rebuilt (1734-44) in the Jesuit style by the architect Jean-Baptiste Franque, this church presents an elegant façade. The church's interior is majestic; above the transept crossing is a fine dome on pendentives. All that remains of the early-Romanesque church is the frieze imbedded in the upper part of the eastern wall which can be seen from rue Charlier. It depicts the Last Supper, Kiss in the Garden, Flagellation, Carrying of the Cross and Resurrection.

▸ *A small arched passageway leads to rue de la République.*

Hôtel des Clausonnettes

Note the Classical façade of this 18C building which backs onto the castle (▸*try to enter the courtyard).*

Hôtel del Margailliers

N° 23 rue de la République. This magnificent dwelling with its carved façade is known as the "house of caryatids" because of the caryatids flanking its porch.

▸ *Go back along rue de la République, then take the street on the right which leads up to the castle.*

Hôtel de Roys de Saint-Michel

▸ *A few yards farther along, opposite.* Another fine 16C mansion.

The street emerges onto **place de la République**, a pleasant square with arcades housing numerous craft workshops. In the center of the square is a statue of the *"drac,"* a local mythological monster who looks rather the worse from the ravages of time.

▸ *Go back along rue de la République, then take the street on the right side that leads up to the castle.*

Château★

🕐 *Apr-Aug, visits of the château every 1st and 3rd Wed in the month starting at 10.15am, by appointment with the tourist office.*

Built in the 11C on the site of a Roman camp and remodelled in the 13C, the castle was dismantled in the 17C on the orders of Cardinal Richelieu. It stood on the crown of the hill surrounded by ramparts (imposing ruins).
Romanesque Chapel – This small chapel (restored in the 19C) has a twin-bayed bell tower and carved tympanum.

Tour polygonale
This extremely unusually shaped tower is also called the triangular tower.

Tour ronde
A fine corner tower.

Curtain wall
A short walk enables the visitor to admire the sheer curtain wall, the barbican defending a castle entrance, and the rocky spur on which the Tour Polygonale stands.
Shows of birds of prey in flight are held on the esplanade of Beaucaire castle. Kites, buzzards, eagles and other birds of prey glide to a background of evocative music, handled by three falconers clad in medieval costume. After the demonstration, the birds can be seen in their aviary at the bottom of the polygonal tower.

Romanesque Chapel
This small chapel (restored in the 19C) has a twin-bayed bell tower and carved tympanum.

Additional Sights

Musée Auguste-Jacquet

🕐 *Apr to Oct: daily except Tues 10am-noon, 2-6pm: Nov to Mar: daily except Tues 10am-12pm, 2-5pm.* 🕐 *Closed public holidays. 4.35€ (children, 1.25€).* ☎ *04 66 59 47 61.*
Located within the castle walls, this museum has an archaeological section containing exhibits which date from prehistoric to Gallo-Roman times. On the first floor are documents on the famous Beaucaire Fair, the reconstruction of a typical Beaucaire hall and bedroom, costumes, head-dresses, Provençal utensils and ceramics from St-Quentin-la-Poterie.

Excursions

Abbaye de St-Roman★

▶ *5km/3mi NW by D 999 and the road to the right, then 15 min return on foot.*

🅿 🚶 *Park the car in the free car park and take the pleasant path to the abbey.*

🕐 *Jul and Aug: 6.30pm; Apr -Jun and Sept: 10am-6pm; Oct to Mar: Sat-Sun, public and school holidays, 2-5pm. 5€.* ☎ *04 66 59 19 72 - www.abbaye-saint-roman.com.*

This remarkable abbey, dependent in the 12C on the Abbaye de Psalmody near Aigues-Mortes, is located on a limestone peak. It was abandoned by the monks in the 16C, gradually transformed into a fortress and then enlarged by the construction of a castle on the upper terrace, using stone taken from the abbey without seriously affecting its original appearance. In 1850 the castle was demolished, and only vestiges of the fortifications can still be seen. A signposted circuit leads to the chapel, built into the rock, containing the tomb of Romanus. The **view**★ from the terrace extends to the Rhône and the Vallabrègues dam, Avignon, Mont Ventoux, the Luberon, the Alpilles and, in the foreground, Tarascon and its castle. Note the graves hollowed out of the rock, the basin from which rainwater was channelled to a collecting tank, the monks' cells and a vast hall three storeys high.

G. Magnin/MICHELIN

Abbaye St-Roman, tombs cut in the rock

Mas Gallo-Romain des Tourelles

▶ *4km/2.5mi- to the west. Leave Beaucaire by the road to Bellegarde. After 4km/2.5mi, turn right for the Mas des Tourelles.*

&♿ ⏰ *Jul and Aug: 10am-noon, 2-7pm, Sun and holidays, 2-7pm; Apr -Jun and Sept-Oct: 2-6pm; Nov - Mar: Sat 2-6pm. 4.80€. ☎ 04 66 59 19 72, www.tourelles.com.*

Between the 1C and 3C AD a Gallo-Roman villa covered this area, comprised of a dwelling, a farm and a pottery workshop. Its 17C buildings (sheep barn, present wine-cellar, farm house), containing archeological material found in pottery ovens and information on wine production during the Gallo-Roman period, are grouped around an attractive, flowered courtyard.

In the Cella vinaria, a life-size, working reconstruction of a Roman wine-cellar, a wine-press (*calcatarium*), vat (*lacus*), press (*torcula*) and large earthenware jars (*dolia*) are worthy of note. Nowadays the mas produces "archeological" wines such as Muslum, with its honey taste, enhanced with spices, Turriculae, developed according to the Columelle texts, Defrutum (grape juice), as well as the AOC Costières de Nîmes wines. The visit ends with a wine tasting session.

Croix Couverte

▶ *1.5 km/1mi at the junction of D 15 (to Fourques) and a small by-road to the right.*

Small, early-15C oratory surmounted by a delicate openwork balustrade.

Lae Vieux Mas

▶ *6.5 km/4mi S on D 15 (to Fourques), then a small road to the right towards Mas Taraud, which you follow for about 2 km/1mi as far as Mas Végère.*

♿ 🧒 ⏰ *Jul-Aug: 10am-7pm; Apr-Jun and Sept: 10am-6pm; Oct-Mar: Wed, weekends and holidays, 1.30-6pm. ⏰Closed 25 Dec and Jan. ☜5.50 € (children, 4 €). ☎ 04 66 59 60 13 - www.vieux-mas.com.*

Turkeys, geese, ducks, and cattle are raised here in this traditional *mas* where life seems to have stopped around 80 years ago. Staff are dressed in period costume and use traditional tools to revive trades and skills of long ago. A gentle air of nostalgia reigns, the atmosphere of a country life governed by the rhythm of the seasons.

Étang de **BERRE**★

MICHELIN LOCAL MAP 340: F5

The Étang de Berre (Berre Lagoon), 15 530ha/60sq mi in extent and nowhere more than 9m/30ft deep, has been France's principal petroleum port for the last 80-odd years. The Canal de Caronte, dredged out where there was once a lagoon of the same name, provides a passage to the Mediterranean, as does the underground Rove section of the Marseille-Rhône canal. The lagoon is fed fresh water by the Arc and Touloubre rivers and the EDF canal (Électricité de France) and is ringed by limestone hills: the Lançon chain to the north, the Vitrolles to the east, the Estaque to the south, and the St-Mitre to the west.

A Bit of History

The region was largely uninhabited when, in 1920, under the San Remo Agreement, France obtained the right to purchase the major part of Iraq's annual crude oil production. The lagoon was transformed into an ideal port for shallow-draught oil tankers; at the same time harbours also began to be developed on the Golfe de Fos: the French BP company set up at Lavéra in 1922-24, Shell-Berre at the Pointe de Berre in 1928 and the Compagnie Française de Raffinage at La Mède in 1934. Esso has had installations in Fos since 1965.

At the turn of the 19C, the peaceful lagoons and deserted Crau plain were an ideal testing ground for pioneer aviators. The very first military aerodrome was established in Istres before the First World War and it still operates today. Since then it has expanded considerably and now occupies 2 031ha/5 017 acres. Until 1940, Berre was the most important hydroplane base of the National Marines. When a civil airport was required for Marseille, the Marseille-Provence airport was sited at the east end of the Étang de Berre at Marignane.

The growth in demand for oil, apparent even in 1938, brought about the transformation of Lavéra soon after the war, to enable 90 000-ton tankers to dock and pump their cargoes directly into onshore installations. In the 1960s a completely new port was constructed at Martigues. The lagoon complex is also the terminal of the South European Oil Pipeline. This line, inaugurated in 1962, supplies a dozen European refineries.

However, the petrol crisis of 1973 led to a slight reduction in the capacity of the refineries, which were obliged to adapt

to the fall in demand. The petrochemicals industry has continued to develop in more recent years, contributing to a transformation of the landscape.

The modern installations are but the latest of man's constructions in the area; buildings still above ground and excavations reveal the presence of earlier inhabitants at St-Blaise, Pont Flavian, built by the Romans, the medieval hamlet of Miramas-le-Vieux and the 17C walls of Port-de-Bouc.

Driving Tour
113km/70mi round-trip– allow 1 day. ▶ *Start from Martigues.*

Martigues
⚓ *See MARTIGUES.*
▶ *Leave Martigues by D 5.*

St-Mitre-les-Remparts
The old town, encircled by 15C ramparts still pierced by only two gateways, stands just off the road. A network of small streets and alleys leads to the church where there is a view of the Étang d'Engrenier.
▶*Leave St-Mitre-les-Remparts by D 51.*
Good view on the right of the Étang de Berre; the road skirts the Étang de Citis in a cultivated site before passing the foot of the hill on which stands Chapelle St-Blaise, the east end of which is just visible among the pine trees.

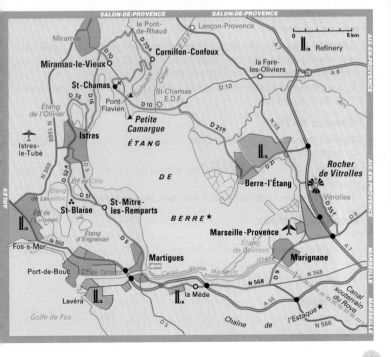

Pont Flavien (triumphal arch)

G. Magnin/MICHELIN

St-Blaise Archaeological Site

♿*See Site archéologique de ST-BLAISE.*

Istres

🛈 *30 allée Jean-Jaurès, 13800 Istres.* ☎*04 42 55 51 15.*

Despite the town's rapid development, the old village of Istres still retains its Provençal appearance. **Musée archéologique d'Istres** presents local history: paleontology, zoology, prehistory, underwater archeology, and the economic life of Istres, Fos and Miramas (🕔*open daily, 2-6pm –* 🕔*closed 1-2 Jan, 1 May, and 24-26 and 31 Dec –* 🚾 *1.50€/children, .75€*).

Parc aquatique de la Pyramide – 🄺🄸🄳🅂 The water park at Istres has splash pools, slides, and a swimming pool with waves (*place Champollion, 13800 Istres,* ☎*04 42 56 99 99*).

To the north of Istres lies the Greco-Ligurian town of **Castellan** also on the banks of the Étang d'Olivier; a surfaced path leads to the edge of the rocky spur from where there is a fine view.

🎭**Festival in Istres –** The *Feria de la Saint-Étienne* falls on the third weekend in June offering up five days of delirium in the town, with events in the brand new amphitheatre, such as corridas, bandas, and bodegas.

▶ *Circle the Étang d'Olivier by way of D 53 and then turn left onto D 16, which returns to the Étang de Berre.*

Miramas-le-Vieux

The small town on a flat ledge of rock has preserved its medieval ramparts and the ruins of the 13C castle.

▶ *Return to D 10 and take D 16 across the way and then D 70D. At Le Pont-de-Rhaud bear right onto D 70A.*

The road ascends a height overlooking the **Touloubre** on the right.

Cornillon-Confoux

At the centre of the hill village stands a small Romanesque church with a bell gable and modern stained-glass windows by Frédérique Duran. There are good local **views**★ from the walk which starts at the church and circles the village.

▶ *Take D 70 and a tourist road on the right to St-Chamas.*

St-Chamas

The town is dominated by a small, triple-arched aqueduct. The church is 17C with a Baroque west front.

Pont Flavien

This bridge, to the south of St-Chamas, crosses the Touloubre in a single span.

▶ *Continue along D 10 which passes the St-Chamas Power Station (Centrale de St-Chamas), the EDF canal's final project. Turn left onto D 21 and left again after 1.7km/1mi onto an unsurfaced road. Park the car.*

Lançon Viewing Table★★(Table d'orientation de Lançon)

▶ *15min return on foot.*

Steps (48) lead to the top of a rock from where there is a view over the lagoon to the surrounding hills.

▶ *Turn round and once on D 21 continue to Berre-L'Étang.*

Berre-l'Étang

The town lives off fishing and its chemical factories. The chapel, Notre-Dame-de-Caderot, displays at the altar a 16C polychrome wood retable and, in a recess opposite the door, a Roman crystal vessel known as the Caderot vase, said to have contained a lock of the Virgin's hair.

▶ *Continue first along D 21, then N 113 on the right. Finally, turn left for Vitrolles.*

Rocher de Vitrolles

▶ *Leave your car outside the main entrance of the cemetery and then go up the 75-step staircase.* The town of Vitrolles, now hidden by an ample industrial and residential area, is famous for the unusual ruiniform rock that dominates it. At the top of the rock, on the southernmost tip, there is a Saracen tower (11C), and on the opposite side a chapel dedicated to Notre-Dame-de-Vie, the aviators' guardian. The immense **panorama**★ embraces to the southwest the lagoons of Berre, the oil installations of Lavéra, the port of Fos-sur-Mer and the refinery of La Mède.

▶ *Leave Vitrolles by D 55F. At the N 113 crossroads, cross onto D 9 which runs alongside the Marseille-Provence airport.*

Marignane

In the 17C Marignane acceded to the status of marquisate. The castle, the **Château des Covet**, remains from this period and currently houses the town hall (*guided visit-visite guidée (1.5 hr), July-15 Aug: 8.30am-12pm, 1.30-5pm; rest of the year: 8.30am-12pm, 1.30-5.30pm - closed Sat-Sun, holidays - 1 €. ☎ 04 42 77 04 90).* Originally built in the 13C by Guillaume des Baux, the château was taken over in the 17C by the Covet, a wealthy family of tradesmen, who applied themselves to extending and embellishing the premises. It is to them that the château owes its fine Classical façade. Some of the rooms are open to the public: the boudoir, the Louis XV bathroom, the Grand Salon (Salon d'Honneur) and especially the former bedchamber of Jean-Baptiste Covet (Registry Office - Salle des Mariages), presenting a superb painted ceiling. The small **Musée d'Arts et Traditions populaires** evokes the traditions, history and activities of the area (*for information,* ☎ *04 42 31 12 40).*

Église St-Nicolas

The late-11C church nave has pointed-barrel vaulting with transverse arches set close together and no windows at all. Follow N 568 back to Martigues, which crosses the Marseille-Rhône canal. Fine views of the lagoon and the site of **La Mède** marked by two peculiar rocks at the harbour entrance.

BOLLÈNE

POPULATION 14 130

MICHELIN LOCAL MAP 332: B-8

The town, which stands on a hillside, has been an agricultural marketing centre since the days of the Avignon popes, when it was one of the popes' richest possessions. A few houses and fine doorways remain as mementoes of the past in what is now a typical Provençal town, with wide shaded boulevards marking the line of the ancient ramparts and a web of narrow streets at the centre.

From the terraces overlooking the Rhône you can see the Canal du Donzère-Mondragon, the Bollène hydroelectric power station and the vast Tricastin Nuclear Power Station. Beyond in the distance are the mountains of the Ardèche and the Bas-Vivarais.

🄸 *Pl. Henry-Reynaud-de-la-Gardette, 84500 Bollène, ☎ 04 90 40 51 45.*

Visit

Belvédère
Pasteur

From this small public garden, set around the former Romanesque Chapelle des Trois-Croix, there is a pleasant view of the town and its surrounding countryside.

EATING OUT

🥘🥘🥘 **Lou Bergamoutié** – *rue de l'Abbé-Prompsault* – ☎ *04 90 40 10 33 – closed Sun evening and Mon.* You will find this large restaurant in a little street near the former gates of the old fortified city. You can choose between the classical dining room with its tapestry armchairs or the airy patio embellished with plants. A friendly welcome with dishes based on fresh market produce.

Collégiale St-Martin

The former parish church (12C-16C) is now used for exhibitions. Its robust bell tower stands atop the hill overlooking the town's rooftops from the east. Go through the lovely Renaissance doorway to admire the size of the nave covered with a vast timberwork saddleback roof.

Belvédère Pasteur

From this small public garden, set around the former Romanesque **Chapelle des Trois-Croix**, there is a pleasant view of the town and its surrounding countryside.

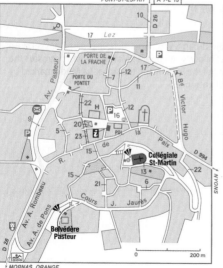

BOLLENE

Chabrières R. des	5
Cimetière R. Gd	6
Fabre R. Henri	7
Gambetta Bd	9
Giono Av. Jean	10
Louis R. Auguste	11
Mistral R. Frédéric	12
Paroisse Montée de la	13
Puy R. du	15
Récollets Pl. des	16
République Cours de la	17
Reynaud-de-la-Gardette Pl	20
Tour R. de la	21
Vietto Montée René	22
Zola R. Émile	23

Excursion

Mornas

▶ *11km/7mi south via D 26, which cuts through Mondragon and is dominated by the castle ruins. Then take N 7.*

The old village of Mornas clings to the foot of a sheer cliff (137m/449ft) on which lie the ruins of a powerful fortress. The fortified gates and old houses enhance the medieval atmosphere.

▶ P *Access by a steep alleyway (car park) and path.*

Fortress

Guided tours (1hr15min) July-Aug: 11am-5pm; Apr-Jun and Sept: Sun and festivals, 11am-5pm. 7€ (children, 5€). ☎ 04 90 37 01 26.

It features a vast curtain wall, 2km/1mi long, flanked by either semicircular or square towers. At the top are ruins of the keep and chapel. The castle was also the scene of a terrible episode during the Wars of Religion: it was held by the Catholics and fell into the hands of the sinister Baron des Adrets, who in reprisal forced all the inhabitants to jump off the top of the cliff.

Suze-la Rousse

▶ *7km/4.3mi east via D 994.*

Guided tours (45min) Sept-June: 9.30-11.30am, 2-5.30pm; Jul and Aug: 9.30-11.30am, 2-6pm; Nov to Mar: daily except Tues. ◑Closed 1 Jan and 25 Dec. 3.20€. ☎ 04 75 04 81 44.

Suze, picturesquely terraced on the south bank of the Lez, was the most important town of Tricastin during the Middle Ages. The former town hall displays a lovely 15C and 16C façade. The hill is dominated by an imposing castle (**château**) which is reached via an entrance drive through a plantation of truffle oaks (some 30ha/74 acres). It dates for the most part from the 14C, and its towers are a good example of military architecture of this period. It was remodelled inside during the Renaissance. The main courtyard features fine Renaissance façades.

The ground floor houses the staff and service quarters, the stables and 12C kitchen. The apartments are reached by a monumental grand staircase. Note the Four Seasons Room, and the armoury with its painted ceiling and great chimney flanked by two frescoes (restored) representing the siege of Montélimar.

In one of the corner towers there is an octagonal room, offering a fine view of Mont Ventoux, Lance mountain and the Dauphiné pre-Alps.

The castle houses the **University of Wine**, which is equipped with a laboratory and a tasting room and which offers courses in oenology (☎ 04 75 97 21 30).

BONNIEUX★

POPULATION 1 422

MICHELIN LOCAL MAP 332: E-11

This large, attractively-terraced village situated on a Luberon promontory still has vestiges of its ramparts.

🛈 Pl. Carnot, 84480 Bonnieux, ☎ 04 90 75 91 90.

Bonnieux, a typical hillside village

Visit

Upper Bonnieux

▶ *Start from place de la Liberté by the steep vaulted passageway, rue de la Mairie, to reach the terrace situated below the old church. By car take the road to Cadenet and a steep surfaced path on the left.*

Terrasse

From the terrace there is a lovely **view**★ of the Calavon valley, away to the left, of the hilltop village of Lacoste, and further to the right, of the edge of the Vaucluse plateau to which cling the hilltop villages of Gordes and Roussillon, blending into its red cliffs. In the background Mont Ventoux stands out.

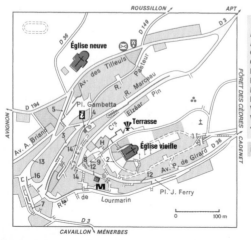

BONNIEUX

Ancien Presbytère R. de l'	2
Aurard R. J.-B.	3
Carnot Pl.	4
Gare Av. de la	5
Hugues Av. Clovis	7
Liberté Pl. de la	8
Mairie R. de la	9
République R. de la	12
Victor-Hugo R.	13
Voltaire R.	14
4-Septembre Pl. du	16
Musée de la Boulangerie	M

Address Book

BOAT TRIPS

From Marseille – *Groupement des Armateurs Côtiers Marseillais – 1 quai des Belges, Vieux Port de Marseille –* ☎ *04 91 55 50 09. Jul-Aug: guided tours (4hr) daily, 2pm; rest of year, Wed, Sat and Sun, 2pm.* ☞*25€.* Most of the calanques are visited though no stops are made for swimming.

From Cassis – ☎ *04 42 01 71 17 (Tourist Office). Departure from the port of Cassis (3-4hr) visiting Port-Miou, Port-Pin and En-Vau, without landing.* ☞*11€.* Direct number for Cassis boat companies: ☎ *04 42 01 90 83.*

From La Ciotat: *Les Amis des Calanques, chemin de la Louisiane, 13600 Ceyreste,* ☎ *06 09 35 25 68.* Trips in catamarans with glass bottoms. ☞ *13/22€.*

CLOSE-UP ON THE CALANQUES

Access – ⚠Caution! No access either on foot or by car to the *calanques* is allowed between 1 July to the second Sunday in September, or on days when the mistral is blowing fiercely. Even when access to the calanques is permitted, restrictions may apply in bad weather conditions, particularly on weekends. The spring is probably the best time for a visit.

Boat trips – An excursion by boat is a practical way of discovering the *calanques* in summer when access to them by land is strictly controlled.

Walking – There are no direct approach roads by car to the *calanques* with the exception of the less attractive coves of Les Goudes, Callelongue and Port-Miou. The only way to reach the others is on foot. Footpaths that are often steep and rocky: it is advisable to get yourself the IGN map *Les Calanques de Marseille á Cassis.* It is strictly forbidden to pick any form of vegetation, stray from marked paths, smoke or light a fire at any time of the year. Make sure you are equipped with walking boots and detailed maps; carry water with you as there is none available on the paths; take necessary precautions against the harmful effects of the sun.

Experienced hikers will be tempted to walk the GR 98-51 footpath from Callelongue to Cassis (see local map), an incomparable 28km/17mi hike (allow 11-12hr) along towering cliffs, with spectacular views of the most secret *calanques.*

A LOCAL FAVOURITE

⬭⬭⬭**Le Lunch** – *13009 Calanque de Sormiou –* ☎ *04 91 25 05 37 – closed Nov-mid Mar –* ✉ *– booking essential – 35€.* If you want to lunch by the water in a wild setting, this is the place to come. Seafood is very much in evidence here and is scrupulously fresh. Access to the calanque is strictly controlled and only those who have reserved at the restaurant may bring their cars.

Église Vieille

From the terrace, take the stairs to the former parish church (12C), remodelled in the 15C and surrounded by fine cedars.

▷ *Return to D 36.*

Musée de la Boulangerie

☉*Apr-Jun and Sept-Oct: daily except Tues 10am-12.30pm, 2.30-6pm (Jul and Aug: 10am-1pm, 3-6.30pm).* ☉*Closed Nov-Mar, 1 May, and 25 Dec. 3.50€ (under 12, free).* ☎ *04 90 75 88 34.*
The museum illustrates the work of a baker, with utensils, and literature on the bakery trade.

EXCURSION

Cedar forest

2km/1.25 mi along the Cadenet road. Allow 2hr. Imported from the Moroccan Atlas, these cedars were planted in upper Bonnieux in 1862. There is now a botanical foot-path with eight stopping points giving information on plants of the Luberon area.

Massif des **CALANQUES**★★

MICHELIN LOCAL MAP 340: H-6 TO I6

The Massif des Calanques, with Mont Puget (565m/1 850ft) its highest peak, stretches almost 20km/12.5mi between Marseille and Cassis. With its solid lime-stone, dazzling whiteness, and weather-worn pinnacles, it has long attracted nature lovers for its wild beauty. However, its unique character and exceptional charm stem above all from its deep and narrow indentations, the famous *calan-ques*, which have been chiselled out along its coastline, creating a majestic union of sea, sky, and rocks.

What is a Calanque?

The word *calanque* (from the Provençal *cala* meaning steep slope) describes a nar-row and steep-sided coastal valley that has been bored into the solid rock by a river, whose course was usually guided by a fault, during the periods of the sea's retreat, and which has subsequently been submerged by the waves during cycles of flooding. Such fluctuations in sea level result from the alternation of glaciation and deglaciation on the earth's surface over the course of the past two million years. The most recent rise in the water level, an average of 100m/330ft, occurred 10 000 years ago, flooding caves inhabited by prehistoric man. The *calanques*, none of which are longer than 1.5km/1mi, extend towards the open sea via large underwater valleys, and though they can be compared to the *abers* of Brittany, should not be confused with fjords, which are shaped by glaciers.

A fragile, remarkable site

The absence of any form of sur-face water and the area's dry-ness can be explained by the permeability of the limestone, the proliferation of faults, and low levels of rainfall. The tem-perature regulation of the sea, the sun's glare on the high, bare rocks, and the area's sheltered position away from the *mistral* all combine to create an excep-tionally hot microclimate on the southern slopes of this massif, conditions that occasionally result in winter temperatures 10°C higher than those on its northern side. Some typically tropical and extremely rare species of vegetation have been able to survive the periods of climatic cooling that occurred during the Quaternary period, creating today a botanical reserve of valuable scientific interest. This in a paradoxical context in which vegetation continues to suffer, the main culprits of which are the area's dryness, the felling of trees for the local lime kilns, excessive grazing and the repeated forest fires that decimate the range. From the time of the first fire ordered by Julius Caesar in 49BC to the catastrophic blaze on 21

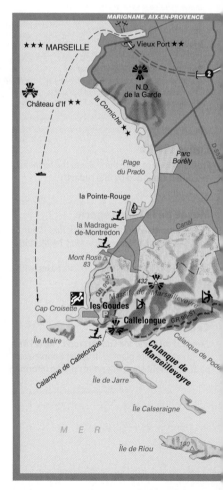

August 1990, the forests of the Massif des Calanques have suffered indescribable damage over the centuries. Increasing protective measures have been introduced in recent years: since 1975 the area has benefited from the protection granted natural monuments and sites. Following the 1990 disaster, measures restricting public access during the summer months were stepped up. A large reforestation project through the recycling of purified sludge is also being studied. For some ecosystems, however, the harm already done is irreversible and the threat ever present for those areas still spared.

Flora and fauna

In this semi-arid environment, the best adapted flora include copses or thickets of green oaks, viburnum, wild olive trees, myrtle, and mastic. In addition to woods of Aleppo pine, stony scrub oak, rosemary, and heather-carpeted *garrigue* also predominate. Ground where vegetation damage is widespread is also home to areas of brachiopods. Samphire (sea-fennel) and sea lavender also grow along the coast, replaced higher up the slopes by a thin cushion of plants including the rare Marseille astralagus or "mother-in-law's cushion" with its fearsome thorns.

Europe's largest lizard and longest snake can also be found in the *calanques*: the ocellar lizard can grow to 60cm/2 ft and the Montpellier grass snake can reach 2m/over 6ft in length.

Birds nest mainly on the coastal cliffs and outlying islands. The most common, the herring gull or *gabian*, which feasts on the rubbish left behind by careless visitors, is increasing rapidly in number. The most rare, Bonelli's eagle (about 15 pairs), is a beautiful diurnal bird of prey with white, grey, and dark brown plumage.

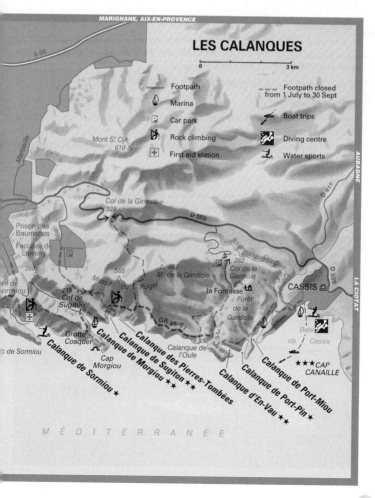

Address Book

For coin ranges, see Legend at the back of the guide.

EATING OUT

⊜⊜ **La Flambée** – *Pl. du 4-Septembre -* ☎ *04 90 75 82 20 - fermé Jan.* Grilled foods and wood fire pizzas among other specialties *(daube provençale, pain de chèvre, truffes, gibier)* in a familial, jovial restaurant lacking a snooty atmosphere. The decor is rustic and the terrace overlooks the *Calavon* valley. Reasonable prices.

⊜⊜⊜ **Le Fournil** – *place Carnot* – ☎ *04 90 75 83 62 – closed 28 Nov-3 Feb, Saturday midday, Tue except evenings from Apr-Sept, and Mon – booking essential.* The cave-like dining room of this house, which is built on the rock, assures a pleasant coolness during your meal. For sun worshippers there is a terrace in the square in the summer. Regional dishes on the menu.

WHERE TO STAY

⊜⊜⊜ **Chambre d'hôte Le Clos du Buis** – *rue Victor-Hugo -* ☎ *04 90 75 88 48 - www.luberon-news.com/le-clos-du-buis - closed 15 Jan-mid Feb and from 15 Nov-15 Dec - 6 rooms: – evening meal 22€.* Situated near the church, this old house used to be a grocery and bakery and there is still a bread oven in the sitting room. The attractive bedrooms are bright and airy and have terracotta flooring. Behind the house there is a pleasant garden and swimming pool.

CRAFTS

Établissement Vernin – *quartier du Pont-St-Julien, RN 100,* ☎ *04 90 04 63 04. www. carreaux-d-apt.com. Open Mon-Sat, 9am-12pm, 2-6pm.* Hand-painted ceramic tiles typical of Apt.

Tour

Les Goudes

▷ *Leave Marseille by the promenade de la Plage.* An old fishing village, nestled amid grandiose rocky scenery. There is no beach, but there are a number of small local restaurants frequented by the local Marseillais.

▷ *Continue as far as Callelongue where the tarmac road ends.*

Callelongue

This tiny cove, with its attractive **site**, has several cabanons or Provençal cabins and provides shelter for a small flotilla of boats.

🚶*(45min) From there you can get to the calanque of Marseilleveyre and its little beach of pebbles.*

Sormiou★

🚶 *(45min) Leave Marseille on either avenue de Hambourg or chemin de Sormiou.* 🅿 *Park in the car park at the entrance to the tarmac road blocked off to vehicles. Walk*

G. Magnin/MICHELIN

Calanque de Port Miou

A Peaceful Retreat

Faithful to a tradition that dates back to the 16C, no effort is spared on the part of the town dweller to purchase his *cabanon*, which was, until recently, a modest building "no bigger than a pocket handkerchief," a fisherman's hut, a cabin in the hills, or a small village house, where Sundays and summer holidays were spent. Although nowadays the hut is more likely to be a comfortable villa and the stay lengthened to weekends and school holidays, a typical day in the *cabanon* is not so far removed from the picture painted in the operettas of Vincent Scotto. The morning is reserved for fishing, hunting, or a trip to market. Afternoons, the household gathers in the shade of the terrace to sip an iced *pastis*, before a hearty lunch accompanied by *aïoli*. Cicadas chirp you to sleep during the siesta hour. Evenings are whiled away at the *pétanque* court, and the after-dinner hours devoted to *belote* card games, a last chance for amicable dispute before turning in for a sound sleep, with all the cares in the world having been left in the noise and pollution of the city.

The local fisherman, *pescadou*, still use old Provençal words for some of the fish they catch:

Arrapède: limpet (a shellfish in the shape of a Chinese hat)
Esquinade: spider crab
Favoiulle: small crab
Fielas: conger eel
Galinette: gurnard
Pourpre: octopus
Supion: squid
Totène: cuttlefish
Violet: sea-squirt (a delicious potato-shaped type of seafood)

down to the *calanque*. Considered by the local Marseillais population to be the best of all the *calanques*, there are numerous cabanons, a small port, a beach, and several fish restaurants.

Sormiou is separated from Morgiou by the **Cap Morgiou**, a viewpoint affording magnificent views of both *calanques* and the eastern side of the Massif. The opening to the **Grotte Cosquer** can be found on the north-east side of Sormiou at 37m/121ft below sea-level. The Grotte Cosquer is closed to the public.

Morgiou★★

(2hr) From Marseille take the same route initially as for Sormiou; turn left at the and follow the "calanque Morgiou" signs (you will pass the famous prison, Baumettes). Park near the "sens interdit" (no entry) sign; continue on foot along the paved road. A wild setting with an unobtrusive human presence; tiny creeks for swimming, crystal-clear water, cabanons clustered at the far end of the valley, restaurant, small port. Not to be missed!

Sugiton★★

(1hr30min) From Marseille take boulevard Michelet as far as Luminy; park in the car park near the Ecole d'Art et d'Architecture, and continue on foot along the forest track. A small calanque with turquoise water, it is well sheltered by its surrounding high cliffs. It is also popular with naturists.

En-Vau★★

(2hr30min) Access via Col de la Gardiole (Route Gaston-Rebuffat beginning opposite the Carpiagne military camp); leave your car in the Gardiole car park. (2hr) Or, from Cassis, walk past Port-Miou and Port-Pin calanques. The best known and most attractive of all the *calanques* with its high white cliffs, emerald water, and small stony beach. It is encircled by a forest of rock pinnacles overlooked by the "Doigt de Dieu" or Finger of God.

Port-Pin★

Access via Col de la Gardiole (same directions as En-Vau – 3hrs) or Cassis (skirting Port-Miou calanque – 1hr30min). A more spacious *calanque* with less steep rock walls and a sandy beach surrounded by pine trees.

Port-Miou

(30min) 1.5km/1mi to the west of Cassis. Access by car; car park always full in summer. The longest of the *calanques*; invaded by pleasure bo ats and slightly disfigured by an old "Cassis stone" quarry.

La **CAMARGUE**★★

MICHELIN LOCAL MAPS 339 AND 340: B-4 TO D-5

The Camargue, the most original and romantic region of Provence and possibly of France, has been largely preserved in its natural state through its designation in 1927 and 1970 as a botanical and zoological nature reserve. Late spring and early autumn are the best times for a visit: wildlife abounds, the sun shines (but not overpoweringly), and there are the famous pilgrimages to Stes-Maries-de-la-Mer.

Parc Naturel Régional de Camargue

This nature park occupies an area of 85 000ha/328sq mi in the Rhône delta, including the municipalities of Arles and Stes-Maries-de-la-Mer. The main objective of the park, besides its basic policy of protecting nature, is to allow its occupants to live in their natural habitat, while preserving agricultural activity and strictly monitoring both the hydraulic balance of the region and the growing influx of tourists.

Geographical Notes

The Rhône Delta

The Camargue is an immense alluvial plain, the product of the interaction of the Rhône, the Mediterranean, and the winds. During the end of the Tertiary Era and the beginning of the Quaternary Period while the sea was receding, waterways transported huge quantities of shingle that piled up along the shore creating a shingle bar some dozens of metres wide. On top of this rocky base, marine sediment was deposited after the last glacial period: then, the sea extended to the north shore of the Étang de Vaccarès. However, the landscape changed constantly owing to the conflicting forces of the freshwater Rhône and the sea. The powerful Rhône has shifted its course over the centuries – it has occupied the two present arms of its bed only since the 15C – transporting enormous amounts of alluvial deposits: barriers were formed which isolated the marshes; sandbanks created by the coastal currents closed off lagoons. Every year the Grand Rhône, which accounts for 90% of the flow, hollows out 20 million m³/2 6157cu yd of gravel, sand, and mud from its banks and sweeps them to the sea.

The construction of the **seawall** and the Rhône dikes in the 19C has partially helped to curb these phenomena. And yet the encroachment of the shore line – 10-50m/33-164ft a year – continues in several places (l'Espiguette and Sablon Points). Elsewhere however, owing to continental subsidence, the sea is invading the shore: the Vieux **Rhône and Petit Rhône** promontories have been swept away by southeasterly storms; Phare de Faraman, a lighthouse 700m/0.5mi inland in 1840 was swallowed up by the sea in 1917 so that a new one had to be built; and Stes-Maries-de-la-Mer, once an inland town, is now protected by breakwaters.

Different faces of the Camargue

Although Camargue is one vast plain, it is divided into three distinct regions: cultivated, salt marshes, and natural.

The cultivated region

North of the delta and along the two arms of its river bed, the Rhône has created banks of fine alluvium (*lônes*) that make up the best soil. This area, the upper Camargue, is well-drained and tillable and started being improved during the Middle Ages. People have battled against water and salt: the level of salt in the soil was increased by intense heat in summer causing evaporation.

Since World War II, great drainage and irrigation projects have been undertaken and have brought satisfactory results. The extent of arable land has considerably increased and large farming units are predominant. Wheat, vineyards, orchards, market gardens, maize, rape, and forage are grown in rotation on this productive soil. But the area is known above all for its **rice** production, even if cultivation has dropped drastically in recent times.

Growing here and there are small clumps of white oak, ash, elm, poplar, robinia and willow trees.

Boat in a roubine lined with reeds

G. Magnin/MICHELIN

The salt marshes

These lie near Salin-de-Giraud (11 000ha/27 181 acres) and Aigues-Mortes (10 000ha/24 710 acres), and appear as a checkerboard of evaporation pans and huge glistening mounds of salt. The production of salt goes back to Antiquity and made, during the Middle Ages, the wealth of the salt abbeys like Ulmet and Psalmody. Industrial salt production started in the 19C.

Between March and September a shallow flow of seawater (not more than a foot deep) is pumped across large "tables" for about 50km/30mi until a saturated solution of sodium chloride has been formed. This is then passed into 9ha/22 acre crystallising pans, 12cm/5in deep, divided by dikes (*cairels*). Between late August and early October, when evaporation is complete, the salt crystals are raked to the edge, washed and piled into huge white glistening mounds (*camelles*), some 21m/70ft high. After further washing, drying and crushing, the salt crystals are ready for use in industry and for animal and human consumption. La Compagnie des Salins du Midi is currently the most powerful company involved in salt harvesting.

The natural region

The wild southern delta comprises a sterile plain dotted with lagoons and smaller pools linked to the sea by a number of channels (*graus*). A desert of sand and marsh with small dunes lining the coast forms a fascinating nature reserve. Roads cross the Camargue, but for a better idea of this nature reserve, walk along the paths laid out by the Regional Nature Park or Nature Reserve. These flat expanses, cracked by drought and whitened by the efflorescence of salt, are covered with sparse vegetation known as **sansouire**. Halophilous plants (liking salt), sea lavender, and glasswort, green in the spring, grey in the summer, and red in the winter, proliferate and are used to feed the herds of wild bulls. The only shrubs are tamarisks. The reeds serve to make sagno, a screen that protects cultivated land and provides roofing material for the cabins of *gardians*. The **Îlots des Rièges**, islands that lie at the south end of the Étang de Vaccarès have a lush vegetation, creating a kaleidoscope of colour in the spring: of blue thistles, tamarisks, wild daisies and zinerar-ias, junipers, yellow irises and narcissi.

Fauna

The fauna is of exceptional variety and quantity. Besides racoons, otters, and beavers, which are difficult to find, birds reign supreme in this vast marshy land (see Address Book Birdwatching). There

Gray heron

R. Corbel/MICHELIN

Address Book

For coin ranges see Legend at the back of the guide.

EVENTS AND ACTIVITIES

Birdwatching – Leave early in the morning, before 10am, or at dusk, from Mar-Oct. Be sure to be quiet and still as the birds are wary of people. Don't forget your binoculars, and also, insect repellent and protective clothing (the mosquitos are voracious). The best places for watching are the footpaths around La Capelière and the Domaine de la Palissade, the seawall, and the Pont de Grau bird sanctuary. Avoid high season.

Walking – The ideal way to see the local flora and fauna is on foot. The best paths are: the GR 653 footpath; the seawall; and the footpaths around Domaine de la Palissade, La Capelière, and Salin-de-Badon.

Biking – Five routes: the salt landscape and flamingo route (29km/18mi); the Vaccarès route (46km/29mi); the seawall route (16km/10mi); the salt route (salt marshes); the horse and rice route (29km/18mi); and the bull and wine route(31km/19mi).

Swimming – The best spots are at Saintes-Maries and Piémanson, south of Salin-de-Giraud.

Horses – the *Association camarguaise de tourisme équestre* –☎ 04 90 97 10 40–will guide you in finding a good horseback riding outfit where the horses are properly cared for and well-rested. *Also see listing in Le GRAU-DU-ROI.*

Méjanes: Domaines Paul Ricard – *Horse rides:13€/hr; pony rides 4€/15mins; tourist train ride: 4€ (children, 3€).*

Bullfighting – Corridas and novilladas, corridas de rejoneo (on horseback), Portuguese corridas (on horseback, with no final killing and the intervention of forcados who seize the animals with their hands) *at Les Stes-maries-de-la-Mer, Arles, Dalin-de-Giraud* and *Méjanes*. Many typical Camargue races. Gardian in the arena of Méjanes on Sunday mornings.

July-Aug, Camarguises races in Arles' arena, Wed, 1 pm.

EATING OUT

Specialties – Look for *tellines*, little shellfish that live in the sand, and bull's meat sausages. Many establishments offer lovely preparations of these, as well as a lean, tender *taureau* steak with *frites* (fries) and salad. As of 1996, bull's meat from the Camargue has been classified AOC. Be sure to enjoy it with Camargue-grown rice and a nice red wine from the region!

😋😋😋 **Domaine de la Tour de Cazeau** – *13200 Le Sambuc – 24km/15mi southeast of Arles via D 570 and then D 36 – ☎ 04 90 97 21 69 – closed 1-15 Feb and Wed – ✄ – booking essential.* This 18C Camargue farm is surrounded by rice fields, bulls, and horses. Once upon a time boats on the Rhône used to be watched over from the tower, which is worth having a look at before sitting down to eat in what used to be the stables. Cooking is typical of this region. Two eating areas.

WHERE TO STAY

😋 **La Camargue** – *58 bd de Camargue - 13129 Salin-de-Giraud - ☎ 04 42 86 88 52 - hotel-restaurant-la-camargue@wanadoo.fr - closed Nov-Mar – ✄ – 20 rooms 🛏 4,60 € - restaurant 13/26 €.* The splendor of this hotel, such as its monumental staircase, harkens back to its heydey in the time of *Pechiney*. The reception is very friendly. The restaurant's specialty is *bouillabaisse*.

😋😋😋 **Hôtel Le Mas de Peint** – *13200 Le Sambuc – 24km/15mi southeast of Arles via D 570 then D 36 – ☎ 04 90 97 20 62 – hotel@ masdepeint.net –closed 9 Jan-17 Mar and 15 Nov-23 Dec – 🛏 – 11 rooms 🛏 19€ – restaurant 34/43€.* Bulls, white horses, and *gardiens* abound in this property of 500ha/1 235 acres, with its exceptional 17C house. In the combined kitchen and dining room, the chef concocts his unique dishes in front of you, using produce from the vegetable garden. Snacks are available around the swimming pool.

are some 400 different species, 160 of which are migratory. The bird population changes according to the season due to the migratory birds which come from northern Europe (Finland and Siberia) to spend the winter, such as the teal, or to stop over in spring or autumn, such as the purple heron. Other kinds of birds you might spot are: the cattle egret, which follows the *manades* so as to feed off the insects that the cattle (and bulls) put to flight; the egret; grey heron; black-headed gull; herring gull; cormorant; lark; tit; harrier; and finally, the incontestable star of the show, the pink flamingo, instantly recognizable by its pink plumage and long neck. Flamingoes live in colonies numbering several thousand and feed on shellfish.

The waters also teem with fish: pike, perch, carp, bream, and especially eel found in the *roubines,* which are fished with long nets (*trabacs*) composed of three pockets sectioned by passages that get narrower. In the past the people lived off their catch. The cistudo, a small aquatic tortoise, and the common snake are also happy in this watery zone.

The **bulls**, black, lithe and agile, with horns aloft, are the stars of the Provençal bull-fights or *cocardes*, where the bull survives the fight (as opposed to the Spanish-style bullfight). They formerly lived wild, but are now kept in **manades**, the local word for herds of livestock. The *manades*, which contribute to the ecological balance of the Camargue, are tending to decline in favour of agriculture and salt production.

The *mas*, the large farm of several hundred acres, is managed by a steward (*bayle-gardian*) and numbers an average of 200 horned cattle plus the horses. In the spring the roundup (*ferrade*) is a colourful event: the young calves (one-year-old) are separated from the herd for branding by the *gardians*. They are roped, thrown on to their side, and branded on their left thigh with the mark of their owner.

Camargue **horses** are descended from prehistoric animals, the skeletons of which were discovered in a vast horse cemetery at Solutré (north-northwest of Lyon). Small (not more than 10 hands), they possess stamina, sureness of foot, and lively intelligence. The foals are born brown and turn white only in their fourth or fifth year.

Gardians

The *gardian* is the soul of the *manades*, the cowboy of Camargue, in a large felt hat, carrying a long, three-pronged stick, and watching over his herd (checking the sick animals, caring for them, selecting the bulls for the bullfight – *cocarde*). Although the hat and three-pronged stick are kept more and more for traditional fairs, the horse remains the faithful companion of the gardian – an excellent horseman. The *gardian's* saddle, made especially by a saddle-maker of the region, must offer maximum comfort and security: padding, fenders which fall along the horse's flanks, cage-like stirrups, pommel in front, and cantle behind. The **Confrérie de Saint-Georges**, a brotherhood founded in 1512, laid down the first statutes regarding the profession of *gardian*.

Visit

It is advisable to avoid this remarkable region in the summer when only the mosquitos outnumber the tourists. Spring and early autumn are the ideal periods to appreciate the flora and fauna of the area, as well as the numerous herds of bulls on their way back from the Bas-Languedoc. There are some spendid days in winter as well, although the weather is hard to predict.

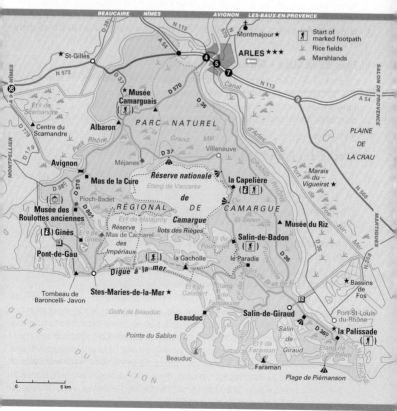

⊛Be sure to pack drinking water as there is none available outside the villages (Le Sambuc, Gageron, and Sain-de-Giraud). Insect lotion is important during mosquito season (summer and early autumn), and binoculars are also a good idea!

Excursion

▷ *Round-trip starting from Arles – 160km/99mi – allow one day.*
▷ *Leave Arles by the southwest (D 570), in the direction of Saintes-Maries-de-la-Mer.*

Musée Camarguais★

RD 570, Mas du Pont de Rousty, 13200 Arles, &. ⊙*July and Aug: (last admission 1hr before closing) 10am-6; Apr-June and Sept: 9am-6pm; Oct-Mar: daily except Tues 10am-5pm.* ⊙*Closed 1 Jan, 1 May, and 25 Dec.* ⊛ *5€.* ☎ *04 90 97 10 82, 3615 Camargue, musee@parc-camargue.fr.*

This museum has been set up in the old sheep-fold of the *mas* at Pont de Rousty and retraces the history of the Camargue region since the formation of the Rhône delta. The periods studied – including Antiquity, the Middle Ages and above all the 19C – will familiarize you with the traditional activities linked to the Camargue's natural environment. A model of a *mas* illustrates its social organisation around 1850, which includes an animated reconstruction of part of the sheep-fold. ⊛ A footpath of 3.5km/2.2mi through the estate reveals the crops, pasture, and marshlands in between the irrigation canals, all of which form a natural part of the grounds of a Camargue *mas*.

Albaron

Albaron, once a stronghold, as can be seen from its fine 13C-16C tower, is now an important pumping and desalination station.

Château d'Avignon

⊙*Guided visit (1hr) Apr-Oct: daily except Tues, 10am-5pm -* ⊙*closed 1 May - 3 €. Call for information* ☎ *04 90 97 58 60.*

This vast residence with its classical appearance was modified at the end of the 19C by the industrialist from Marseille, Louis Prat, and is a fine illustration of bourgeois tastes from that period. A tour of the interior reveals beautifully-panelled and furnished rooms on the ground floor that are decorated with 18C Aubusson or Gobelins tapestries. A botanical footpath (500m/just over 500yd) leads visitors past the variety of trees in the gardens.

Mas de la Cure – Maison du Cheval

⊙*Temporarily close for work.* The old farm estate at the Mas de la Cure now houses this centre aimed at promoting the Camargue horse. There are training courses in horsemanship, exhibitions, a footpath tracing different kinds of local natural environments, and of course, the horses themselves, along with bulls and merino sheep from Arles.

Musée des Roulottes anciennes

▷*À Pioch-Badet.* ⊙ *Summer: 10am-8pm; winter: 10am-5pm (call in advance:* ☎ *04 90 97 52 85).* ⊛*3.50 €.*

In homage to the Gypsies (Roma) who are an important part of this region's culture, this museum displays seven conserved caravans along with their furnishing.

Centre d'Information de Ginès/François-Hüe

▷ *RD 570, Pont de Gau, 13460 Les Stes-Maries-de-la-Mer,* ☎ *04 90 97 86 32 – info@ parc-camargue.fr – www.parc-camargue.fr.* ⊙*Apr to Sept: 9am-6pm; Oct to Mar: daily except Fri. 9.30am-5pm.* ⊙*Closed 1 Jan, 1 May, 25 Dec.*

The Information Centre of the Parc naturel régional de Camargue is located at Pont de Gau, on the edge of the Étang de Ginès. Its aim is to make visitors more aware of the fragility of the environment under the park's protection. A permanent exhibition describes the flora and fauna of the Camargue and the working methods and traditions of those who make a living from its natural resources. Large windows overlook the lagoon and marshlands, also giving visitors a good view of many examples of Camargue birdlife as they fly past. Upstairs, there are audiovisual presentations and video films on the subjects of the saltmarshes and related activities, pink flamingoes, and the various projects within the park.

Parc Ornithologique du Pont de Gau

 Apr-Sept: from 9am until the sun sets; Oct-Mar: from 10am until the sun sets- closed 25 Dec. 6.50 € (children, 4 €). ☎ 04 90 97 82 62. This bird sanctuary is next to the information centre. By following a trail marked with explanatory panels and observation posts, you can see firsthand most of the bird species that live in or pass through the Camargue in their natural habitat: nocturnal and diurnal birds of prey, such as the marsh-harrier; waders, such as the avocet or the oyster-catcher; grey herons; ducks of all sorts; pink flamingoes, and many more.

Les Stes-Maries-de-la-Mer★ – See Les STES-MARIES-DE-LA-MER.

▶ *Take D 38 west and after 1km/0.5mi, turn left onto a surfaced road.*

On the left is the tomb of **Folco de Baroncelli-Javon**, built in 1955 on the site of his property, the Mas du Simbeu, which was destroyed in 1944.

▶ *Return to Les Stes-Maries-de-la-Mer and take D 85A, north.*

The road crosses Couvin marsh, a saltwater landscape of stunted plants and swamp. Mas de Cacherel stands to the right; Stes-Maries can be seen to the rear.

▶ *At Pioch-Badet, turn right onto D 570, toward Arles; at the entrance to Albaron, turn right again, onto D 37. This winds through rice fields. You can make a 4.5km/2.5mi detour (bear right) to Méjanes.*

Méjanes

Horse-rides are organised at the Mas de Méjanes.Horse rides: 13€/hr; *pony rides* 4€/15mins; *tourist train ride:* 4€ (children, 3€). The amusement centre includes a bull ring, pony trekking and horse-drawn carriages; an electric railway runs 3.5km/2mi along Vaccarès lagoon.

▶ *Continue along D 37.*

The road crosses an expanse relieved by the occasional clump of trees, reeds, and isolated *mas*. On the right there is a small viewpoint that looks out over Vaccarès lagoon towards the Rièges islands.

▶ *In Villeneuve turn right towards Vaccarès lagoon.*

After a little wood the road runs alongside the lagoon, giving a lovely view★ over the Camargue, in all its wild splendour.

La Capelière

 Apr to Sept: 9am-1pm, 2-6pm; Oct to Mar: daily except Tues 9-1pm, 2-5pm. Closed 1 Jan and 25 Dec. 3€.(under 12, free). ☎ 04 90 97 00 97 – www.reserve-camargue.org. This is the information centre of the Réserve nationale de Camargue, founded by the national society for the protection of nature. The reserve covers more than 13 000ha/32 000 acres at the heart of the Rhône delta in the area of the Étang de Vaccarès. Protected here are the species of animal (in particular migratory birds) and plant life that feature in this complex natural environment. The centre offers a permanent exhibition, footpaths (1.5km/1mi), and two observatories to help you get better acquainted with the Camargue landscape. To the left, on St-Seren marsh, there is a typical *gardian's* cabin. The road skirts the Étang de Fournelet.

Salin-de-Badon

 observatories open from sunrise to sunset. Permits can be obtained from La Capelière (Camargue National Reserve information centre). 3€ (children, 1.5€). ☎ 04 90 97 00 97 or ☎ 04 90 97 20 74.

All year round birds flock to this old royal saltmarsh in their thousands. The Réserve Nationale de Camargue has laid out footpaths, put up explanatory panels, and built observatories for the visitors' use.

From Le Paradis two excursions (open to traffic at driver's own risk) can be undertaken in dry weather, enabling the tourist to discover the birds of the Camargue and particularly the pink flamingoes:

– one goes, via part of the seawall, to Phare de la Gacholle (La Gacholle lighthouse) where there is a telescope in a cabin (traffic prohibited from Perthuis de la Comtesse; do the last 1km/0.5mi on foot).

– the other is along the causeway running between two lakes, the Étang Fangassier and the Étang Galabert (access to cars is forbidden; leave the car at the pumping station); Galabert island is the only nesting site in France for pink flamingoes. An information center has been created at the end of the causeway, which can also be reached by car from Salin-de-Giraud, by following the road to Beauduc from La Belugue. It is extremely bumpy, however, and is better explored by mountain bike.

Beauduc

This "village" by the edge of the sand is actually more like an ecclectic collection of caravans and an old bus, ringed with a reed fence. There are certainly more sophisticated spots along the Mediterranean coast, but Beauduc is no less friendly for it. The small local restaurant prepares fish dishes that draw gourmets from miles around.

▶ *Retrace your steps to Faraman and carry on to Salin-de-Giraud.*

Salin-de-Giraud

In salt country, this small town on the south bank of the Rhône, with its grid pattern of streets shaded by plane trees, acacias, and catalpas, is a chemical manufacturing centre. Every district is named after a firm (Péchiney, Solvay). The surrounding countryside lives from cattle-rearing and mixed farming.

▶ *Follow the road that skirts the Grand Rhône in the direction marked "Plages d'Arles".*

Viewpoint over the saltmarsh

The viewpoint beside a salt heap looks out over the Giraud pans and workings.

Domaine de la Palissade★

From mid-June to mid-Sept: 9am-6pm; from mid-Sept to mid-June: 9am-5pm (last admission 45min before closing) - ⊙closed Mon and Tues from mid-Nov to end of Feb, 1 Jan, 1 May, 11 Nov, and 25 Dec. ◎ 3 € (under 12, free) . ☎ 04 42 86 81 28.
This estate, the property of the Conservatoire du Littoral (Society for the Preservation of Coastlines and River Banks), covers 702ha/1 735 acres and is the only area of the delta not to have been enclosed by dikes. The result is that the scenery here reflects the original character of the lower Camargue: alluvial deposits from the old course of the Rhône; riparial shrubs on the present banks; dunes or hummocks; a type of marsh samphire (*sansouires* in Provençal); fields of sea lavender used for grazing; and beds of reeds and rushes. Three footpaths lead visitors round the estate: one of 1.5km/1mi, intended for the general public, with explanatory panels, and two others of 3km/1.8mi and 7.5km/4.6mi, offering less explanations but allowing walkers to penetrate the Camargue and discover, according to the season and to chance, flora and fauna, as well as the traditional activity of the *paludiers*, the people who live in the area.

▶ *Continue towards Plage de Piémanson.*

The road goes along a dike, through a region of lagoons glistening white with salt. Take the chance to have a dip in the Mediterranean at the vast beach of Piémanson (25km/15.5mi) of fine sand.

▶ *Head towards Arles through Salin-de-Giraud.*

Musée du Riz

🚹 ⊙10am-5.30pm. 3.50€. ☎ 04 90 97 29 44.
The Petit Manusclat estate is given over to the cultivation of rice. Its museum describes methods used in the Camargue. Upstairs, there is a pretty santon scene displayed in a model of the Roman Theatre at Arles.

▶ *Take D 36 and then D 570, on the right, and head back to Arles.*

Walk

Along the Seawall

🔼 *From the eastern exit to Stes-Maries-de-la-Mer, the seawall is reserved only for those on foot or cross-country bike.*
The path leads to the **Phare de la Gacgolle**, a lighthouse with an information centre that houses a long-distance observatory and an exhibition on the coastline.
This walk gives ample opportunity to discover the Camargue's rich birdlife and landscapes, providing the weather is dry.
From Pertuis to la Comtesse, continue south: the causeway runs between the two lagoons, the **Étang Fangassier** and the **Étang Galabert**. Galabert island is the only nesting site in France for pink flamingoes. About 8 000 young birds are born here every year. It takes 3-4 years for their plumage to turn from black to pink.

CARPENTRAS ★

POPULATION 26 090

MICHELIN LOCAL MAP 332: D-9

This town continues to thrive as an active agricultural centre. You can witness this firsthand with a visit to the weekly market every Friday morning.

A Bit of History

Market centre for a Celtic-Ligurian tribe, then a Gallo-Roman city, and a bishopric, which was temporarily moved to Venasque, Carpentras blossomed when the popes came to Provence. Pope Clement V stayed here frequently from 1309 to 1314, as did the cardinals. A conclave met here in 1314, although it moved to Lyon where it elected John XXII. Capital of the Comtat Venaissin in 1320, the town profited from papal munificence. It expanded and protected itself, under Innocent VI, with powerful ramparts consisting of 32 towers and four gates, demolished in the 19C. With Avignon, Cavaillon and Isle-sur-la-Sorgue, it had a Jewish ghetto up until the Revolution.

The most famous local figure was the 18C Bishop Malachie d'Inguimbert, benefactor and founder of the hospital (Hôtel-Dieu), who also founded, in 1745, the famous library named after him, the Bibliothèque Inguimbertine. Carpentras grew prosperous from the production of madder, a dye-plant introduced in 1768, and the surrounding plain became a fertile garden when a canal, a branch of the Durance, was built in the 19C, enabling the area to be irrigated. At the same time the railway arrived.

🏛 *Hôtel-Dieu, pl. A.-Brand, 84200 Carpentras, ☎ 04 90 63 00 78. www.ville-carpentras.fr.*

The Old Town *Allow 3hr.*

▶ *Start south of town in place A.-Briand.*

Hôtel-Dieu

🕐*Visits by appointment, at the tourist office.* This majestic building housing the former hospital dates from the 18C. To the left of the chancel, the Baroque chapel houses the tomb of Monseigneur d'Inguimbert, the hospital's founder. The Hôtel-Dieu was built outside the city wall, to the south, so that the sick inmates were not subject to the foul air of the city.

Note the triangular fronton surmounted by Baroque flaming urns and the statue of the patron in the square. An elegant wrought-iron ramp runs along the main staircase. Note the numerous little votive paintings on the walls of the corridor. The tour includes a visit to the **pharmacy**★, largely in its original state, that contains cabinets painted with landscapes and amusing figures (monkey apothecaries) in which there is a large collection of Moustiers faïence (glazed earthenware) jars.

▶ *Cross place du 25-Août-1944 and enter the city along rue de la République, a pedestrian street.*

In the place Ste-Marthe note the fine 17C and 18C **Classical façade** to the right along rue Moricelly, the to the left the **Chapelle du collège**, built in the Jesuit style. It houses contemporary art exhibits.

▶ *Continue along rue de la République, into place du Gén.-de-Gaulle.*

Ancienne Cathédrale St-Siffrein★

The cathedral was started in 1404, on the orders of Pope Benedict XIII of Avignon, and is a good example of the southern Gothic style. It was finished in the early 16C, and its façade was completed in the 17C with the Classical doorway. Inside, the balcony on the nave's end wall connects with the bishop's apartments, and from the small room above the first bay he could follow services. There are paintings in the north chapels by Mignard and Parrocel and sculptures, including a gilded wooden glory, by the Provençal sculptor, Bernus, in the chancel. To the left is a late-15C altarpiece depicting the *Coronation of the Virgin*.

Palais de Justice

🔸*2 guided tours (1hr30min) per month (Apr-early Sept): make an appointment at the tourist office (☎ 04 90 63 00 78). ⌾ 4 €.*
Adjoining the cathedral is the old bishop's palace from the 17C, which now houses the law courts.

Address Book

Guided tours of the town – Carpentras and it surrounding area have been classified "Pays d'art et d'histoire." Tour guides acredited by the Ministry of Culture and Communication conduct *90min* tours: *Apr-Sep: daily, 10.30am, 3.30pm, and 5pm. ∞4€. www.vpah.culture.fr. Inquire at the tourist office.*

The Tourist office also provides a map for a self-guided tour which is marked out in town by distinctive signs made of enamelled lava stone.

EATING OUT

◯◯**Chez Serge** – *90 r. Cottier - ☎ 04 90 63 21 24 - closed Sun - 13 € lunch .* The decor is ecclectic and so is the food, varying from delicious traditional Provençal to the new and surprising. The shaded terrace fills up shortly after noon.

◯◯**L'Atelier de Pierre** – *30 place de l'Horloge, top of rue des Halles – ☎ 04 90 60 75 00 – closed Jan, Sun and Mon.* A smart restaurant with a painted wooden front in the centre of Carpentras. Inside, the Provençal style dining room with its exposed beams has pretty round tables, while there is a peaceful terrace at the back. Classic cuisine with hints of the Mediterranean.

WHERE TO STAY

◯◯◯ **Chambre d'hôte Bastide de Ste-Agnès** – *1043 chemin de la Fourtrouse – 3km/1.8mi northeast via D 974 for Bédoin and D 13 for Caromb – ☎ 04 90 60 03 01 – 5 rooms.* This old country house is constructed in dry stone. It is hard not to be won over by the ochre bedrooms, antique floor tiles, the charm of the Provençal scented garden and the tranquil atmosphere. Pretty swimming pool in what used to be the water cistern.

ON THE TOWN

Café du Siècle – *13 place Gén.-de-Gaulle – ☎ 04 90 63 58 52 – Mon-Sat 7.15am-10pm. Summertime: 7am-10.30pm, closed for a week for the All Saints' Day holiday and for a week during the Feb school holidays.* It is extremely pleasant having a drink in this café whose terrace faces St Siffrein's Cathedral. The décor inside is reminiscent of old-fashioned train carriages like the Orient Express.

SHOPPING

Market – *rue de Carpentras – Fri 8am-12.30pm.* The Carpentras market has produce of such fine quality that it was elected "marché exceptionnel" in 1996. There is a very colourful atmosphere, conducive to finding good bargains.

Truffle Market – *place Aristide Briand – Fridays, 8am-12pm, from mid-Nov to mid-March.* The region around Carpentras furnishes over half of France's truffles. This market is quite authentic.

Chocolaterie Clavel – *30 rue Porte-d'Orange – ☎ 04 90 63 07 59 – Summertime daily 9.30am-7pm. Low season: daily 9.30am-7pm (Sun, 9.30am-12pm). Closed Jan and 1 week in Mar.* A major personality in Carpentras, René Clavel never ceases in his search for perfection in the creation of new chocolates, the most celebrated of which are the rocailles de Provence. Other specialities worth trying are the plaques de chocolats fins, the lavender truffles, and amusing figures made of marzipan.

Berlingots: a Carpentras speciality

S. Sauvignier/MICHELIN

Confiserie Bono – *280 allée Jean-Jaurès - ☎ 04 90 63 04 99 - confiseriebono.fr - Mon-Sat, 9am-12pm, 2.15-6.30pm - closed June.* Established in 1925, Bono is a master of the Provençal confectioners' tradition and carries it on. Using ancient techniques, they make handmade candied fruits, a wide range of jams and conserves, including of lemon. All these delights are also packaged in earthy and elegant ways, such as beautiful boxes, baskets, and pots.

Nougats Silvain – *Rte de Vemasque - 84210 St-Didier - ☎ 04 90 66 09 57 - silvain.freres@free.fr - daily, 9am-12pm, 3-7pm – closed Jan.* The Silvain brothers invite you to share their passion, with a show and tasting. They call themselves "nougat farmers" because they grow their own almonds and collect their own honey. The result, you can imagine, is delicious.

Confiserie du Mont-Ventoux – *288 av. N.-D.-de-Santé – ☎ 04 90 63 05 25 - berlingots. net - Tues-Sat, 8am-12pm, 2-6.50pm - closed public holidays, except Christmas.* You will find the famous *berlingot* everywhere in town, but in this shop a rainbow of flavours awaits you. Moreover, stop by in the morning to watch these treats being made.

EVENTS

Estivales – *Information: 4 pl. du Marché-aux-Oiseaux - ☎ 04 90 60 46 01.* This festival of music, dance, theatre and fine arts, takes place the second half of July.

Truffle and Wine Festival – Come tempt yourself with everything having to do with truffles, fine food, and wine. Tastings, cooking demonstrations, and more. *First Sunday in February.*

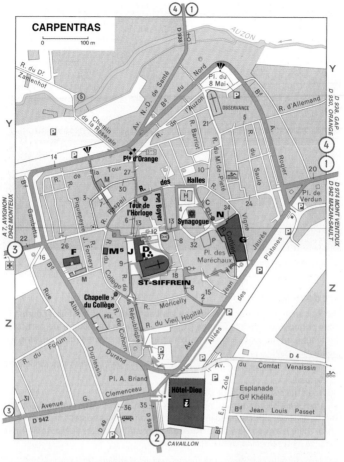

CARPENTRAS

Barjavel R.	Z	2	
Briand Pl. A.	Z		
Carmel R. du	Y		
Charretier Pl. M.	Y	3	
Clapiès R. de	Y	4	
Évêché R. de l'	Y	5	
Frères-Laurens R. des	Y	6	
Gaudibert-Barret R.	Z	7	
Gaulle Pl. du Gén.-de	Z	8	
Guillabert R. D.	Y	9	

Halles R. des	Y		
Inguimbert Pl. d'	Z	12	
Inguimbert R. d'	YZ	13	
Khélifa Espl. Gén.	Z		
Leclerc Bd Mar.	Y	14	
Marins R. des	Z	15	
Marotte Pl. de la	Y	16	
Mercière R.	Z		
Mont Ventoux Av. du	Y	18	
Observance R. de l'	Y	20	
Pétrarque Av.	Z	21	

Pte de Mazan R.	Y	24	
Pte de Monteux R.	Z	26	
Pte Orange R.	Y	27	
République R. de la	Y		
St-Jean R.	Y	34	
Stes-Maries R. des	Y	30	
Sémard Av. Pierre	Z	31	
Sous-Préfecture R.	Z	32	
Victor-Hugo Av.	Z	35	
Wilson Av.	Z	36	
25-Août-1944 Pl. du	Z	37	

Arc de triomphe	Z	D	Charité (La)	YZ	G
Bibliothèque Inguimbertine	Z	F	Musée Sobirats	Z	M⁵
Chapelle des Pénitents Blancs	Y	N	Palais de justice	Z	J

The old ceremonial hall of the bishops of Carpentras and the old meeting hall of the states of Comtat Venaissin are decorated with French style painted ceilings and a frieze of canvases painted in the 17C.

▷ *Take a right a go along the south side of the cathedral.*

Note the cathedral's Flamboyant Gothic south door (late 15C), known as the **Porte Juive** ★ or Jewish door, after the Jewish converts who passed through it to be baptised.

▷ *Continue around the cathedral's east end via rue de la Poste to reach place d'Inguimbert.*

Near the east end of the present church are the remains of the original Romanesque cathedral surmounted by an ornate dome (from the railing, look up to see the twisted column topped by a historiated capital).

Medicine cabinet in the Hôtel-Dieu

Arc de triomphe

The Roman municipal arch behind the law courts was built most likely during the same period as the arch in Orange (1C). Its decorations (mutilated) are particularly interesting on the east face, where two prisoners are chained to a tree hung with military trophies.

▶ *Take rue d'Inguimbert to the left, past place du Col.-Mouret, then turn right into rue Raspail.*

This road traces the line of the old city walls.

▶ *After 50m/55yards turn left onto rue des Frères Laurens.* After running alongside the chapelle des Visitandines (16C), the street comes to some steps, from the top of which there is a good view of the **Auzon valley** with Dentelles de Montmirail in the distance (*see Dentelles de MONTMIRAIL*).

▶ *At the bottom of the steps, take boulevard Leclerc to the right.*

Port d'Orange

North of the old town centre, this gateway was one of four fortified gateways leading into Carpentras. It is 26m/85ft high, and is all that remains of the fortified wall punctuated by 32 towers built at the end of the 14C.

▶ *Take rue de la Porte-Orange again and turn left into rue des Halles.*

Rue des Halles

This street is lined with arcades sheltering numerous shops, making it an ideal place to take refuge from the heat of summer. Note the **tour de l'Hortilage** (clock tower) at the entrance to the street, a remnant of the first town hall (15C). For a better view of the clock tower, go into the pleasant courtyard terrace of the Atelier de Pierre restaurant (*access via rue du Château*). Further on, **passage Boyer** opens off to the right. This glass-covered passage was built in 1848 by a group of unemployed members of the national workshops, *Ateliers Nationaux*.

▶ *At the far end of passage Boyer turn left onto rue d'Imguimbert. This leads into place Maurice Charretier, standing in the place of the old Jewish ghetto. Note the* **façade** *of the synagogue on the right.*

Synagogue★

Daily except Sat-Sun 10am-noon, 3-5pm. (Fri 4pm). Closed public holidays and Jewish feast days. 3.81€. ☎ 04 90 63 39 97.

The synagogue, dating from 1367, was rebuilt in the 18C. On the first floor is the panelled sanctuary, simple yet richly decorated. On the ground floor are the oven for baking unleavened bread and some annexes. In the basement is the pool for women's purification rites (**mikwe**, 14C).

▶ *Rejoin rue des Halles and walk around the town hall into rue Bidauld.*

Rue Bidauld leads down to the **Chapelle des Penitents Blanc**, a 17C chapel with a door featuring a triangular fronton.

▷ *Take rue Cottier.*

La Charité

Built in 1669 to shelter the poor, today the building houses various exhibitions in its cellars (*access via rue Vigne*).

▷ *Head to place des Maréchaux, turn right, and rejoin rue des Marin.* This street is lined with fine mansions, such as the Hôtel de Bassompierre with its caryatids.

▷ *Take rue Gaudibert-Barret to the left, an extension of rue Barjavel. Cross avenue Jean-Jaurès to rejoin allée des Platanes and return to the Hôtel-Dieu.*

SIGHTS

Musée Sobirats

🕙*Daily except Tues, 10am-12pm, 2-6pm (Oct-Mar, 4pm) -* 🕙*closed public holidays.* 👝 *2 €, free first Sunday of each month.* ☎ *04 90 63 04 92*
Lovely reconstruction of an 18C mansion: furniture , faïences, and tapistries.

Musée Comtadin-Duplessis

🕙*Daily except Tues, 10am-12pm, 2-6pm (Oct-Mar, 4pm) -* 🕙*closed public holidays.* 👝 *2 €, free first Sunday of each month.* ☎ *04 90 63 04 92*

One level displays regional mementoes that evoke the popular traditions of the area, such as coins and seals, local headdresses, and bells for the cattle and sheep traditionally driven through town to summer and winter pastures. Another level exhibits a collection of 16C-20C paintings, such as Parrocel, Rigaud, and the Carpentras artists Duplessis and Laurens.

Excursions

Monteux

▷*4.5km/2.5mi to the west via D 942.* This small market-garden centre had a moment of glory in the early 14C when Pope Clement V came here to rest. A tower remains from the castle where he stayed. Also standing are two gates from the 14C ramparts. The town is also the birthplace of St Gentius, patron saint of Provençal farmers, who reputedly had the ability to bring on rain.

Mazan

▷ *7km/4mi to the north on D 942, in the direction of Sault.*

🕙 *Mid-Jun to mid-Sept, except Tues, 2-7pm; the rest of the year, upon request. No charge.* ☎ *04 90 69 74 27.*
The small town in the Auzon valley is close to Mormoiron, Europe's largest gypsum deposit and quarry. The village was the birthplace of the Comtat Venaissin's most reputed sculptor, **Jacques Bernus** (1650-1728).
Sixty-six Gallo-Roman sarcophagi, which once lined the Roman road from Carpentras to Sault, now surround the **churchyard** of the 12C Notre-Dame-de-Pareloup, which has an underground chapel. From here there is a fine **view**⋆ of the Dentelles de Montmirail, Mont Ventoux, and Lure mountain.
Near the church, the 17C Chapelle des Pénitents Blancs houses a **local museum** (parchments, costumes, furnishings, and agricultural implements). Note the vestiges from the Stone Age found during the excavations on the south face of Mont Ventoux, and a carving by Jacques Bernus. In the courtyard is a 14C bread oven.
The Château de Mazan, today an old people's home (not open to the public), once witnessed the extravagant sexual antics of the notorious Marquis de Sade.

CASSIS ☼

POPULATION 8 001

MICHELIN LOCAL MAP 340: I6

Cassis, a small, bustling fishing port, lies in an attractive settinga at the end of a bay between the arid Puget heights to the west and the wooded escarpments of Cap Canaille to the east. It is a popular summer resort which has three small beaches, two of sand, one of shingle, each sheltered by rocks with a fairly steep slope. Boat trips to the calanques are a popular excursion.

The quarries not far from the village, notably by the Calanque de Port-Miou, produce a hard white stone which has been used for quaysides and gateways, such as for the Rove Tunnel, the Suez Canal and the Campo Santo in Genoa.

🛈 *Quai des Moulins, 13260 Cassis, ☎ 04 42 01 71 17. www.cassis.fr.*

Visitors arriving by yacht should reserve a mooring well in advance. The Cassis marina has 30 berths (☎ 04 42 01 24 95); Port-Miou has 40 (☎ 04 42 01 04 10).

Musée des d'Arts et Traditions populaires

🕐*Apr-Sept: 10.30am-12.30pm, 3.30-6.30pm; Oct-Mar: 10.30am-12.30pm, 2.30-5.30pm - 🕐closed Mon, Tues, Sun, and public holidays. No charge. ☎ 04 42 01 88 66.*

Address Book

Train tour – *40 min – mid-Apr to mid-Nov: 4-7pm; mid-Mar to mid-Apr: Sat&Sun, 2-7pm.* 🚶 *5€ (children 2.50P).* Promenade along the port to the *calanque* of Port-Miou.

Excursions to the calanques – Boat trips of 3-4hr, visiting the calanques of Port-Miou, Port-Pin and En-Vau, without landing. *Information and reservations at the Tourist office.*

EATING OUT

😋 **Romano** – *Port de Cassis* – ☎ *04 42 01 08 16.* A seafood bistro where the cooking has a Provençal flavour. Plain, contemporary decor, lit by picture windows which overlook the port.

😋 **La Vieille Auberge** – *14 quai Jean-Jacques-Barthélemy* - ☎ *04 42 01 73 54 - fermé fév. et mer. - réserv. conseillée.* Passed from father to son, the cuisine of this lovely inn is traditional and Provençal On the edge of the sea; terrace in summer.

😋 **La Presqu'île** – *2km/1.2mi southwest of Cassis on the Port-Miou road-* ☎ *04 42 01 03 77 – restaurantlapresquile@wanadoo.fr – closed 11 Nov-28 Feb, Sun evenings from Sept-May and Mon.* Perched on the Calanques road, just opposite Cap Canaille, admire the stunning sight of the steep cliffs plunging down to the turquoise-blue waters. If the chill of the evening makes you shiver, take shelter in the dining room decorated with Provençal colours.

WHERE TO STAY

😋 **Hôtel Le Clos des Aromes** – *10 rue Paul-Mouton* – ☎ *04 42 01 71 84 – closed 4 Jan-end of Feb, Tue lunchtime, Wed lunchtime and Mon – 14 rooms:* 🛏 *7€ – restaurant 21/29€.* Located in the centre of the village, this old building has all the charm of a mansion. Enjoy the Provençal cooking, served on a flower-decked terrace in the summertime. Its rather small bedrooms are colourful and cosy. Mediterranean atmosphere.

ON THE TOWN

Casino de Cassis – *avenue du Prof.-Leriche* – ☎ *04 42 01 78 32 – casino-cassislibertysurf.fr – July-Aug: daily 10am-4am.* Low season: daily 10am-3am, until 4am weekends and on the eve of public holidays. This place vibrates with the excitement of gambling. Slot machines and traditional table games are available but this casino also knows how to vary its entertainments by organising themed evenings. Sports also play an important part here with OM (the Marseille soccerl team) matches shown on a giant screen.

Bar de la Marine – *5 quai des Baux* – ☎ *04 42 01 76 09 – daily 7am-2am – closed mid-Jan to mid-Feb.* A simple, friendly place, this bar takes pride in attracting artists and actors passing through this popular summer resort. For those who wish to remain incognito behind a pair of Ray-Bans, it is worth ordering a pastis on the terrace while silently admiring the view of the port. At 10pm the K6 disco, also owned by the Bar de la Marine, opens.

The Cassis wine festival and the feast of St-Éloi (*first Sunday in September*) offers a good opportunity to sample some excellent wines, in particular white wine, of a region that is divided among 12 wine producers.

The port of Cassis

Located in an 18C restored town house, Maison de Cassis, this small museum contains archaeological finds from the area, including a 1C cippus, Roman and Greek coins, pottery, amphorae, various manuscripts relating to the town, and paintings and sculpture by local artists.

Corniche des Crêtes★★

▶ *From Cassis to La Ciotat 19km/11.5mi – allow 45min by car.*

The stretch of coast road between Cassis and La Ciotat skirts the crests of the Canaille, a short limestone range that rises from the sea in towering white cliffs, some of the tallest in France – 362m/1 188ft at Cap Canaille, and 399m/1 310ft at the Grande Tête. The tourist road and its viewpoints offer superb and dizzying views.

▶ *Leave Cassis in an easterly direction, on the road to Toulon (D 559), and during the ascent take a signposted road to the right. At Pas de la Colle turn left.*

Mont de la Saoupe

The **panorama**★★ from the television mast at the top of this mountain includes Cassis, the Île de Riou, Massif de Marseilleveyre and Chaîne St-Cyr to the west, the Chaîne de l'Étoile, Mont Garlaban and Massif de la Ste-Baume to the north, La Ciotat, Cap de l'Aigle and Cap de Sicié to the southeast.

▶ *Return to Pas de la Colle and continue uphill.*

Bends and viewpoints reveal an ever-wider view of Cassis and La Ciotat.

Panorama from the Mont de la Saoupe

The Grotte Cosquer

From 1985 onwards this underwater cave, located near the Cap Morgiou headland, was explored by the Cassis diver, Henri Cosquer. On 3 September 1991 the sensational public disclosure of its Paleolithic paintings and engraving shot it to the rank of the buried cathedral of cave art. Initially, it was feared that this was a huge "Marseille tall story" until scientists quickly proved the authenticity of the representations; the new neutronic activation dating method, able to analyse minuscule quantities of organic matter, has dated the "negative hands" to 27 000 BC and the animal drawings to approximately 17 000 BC, one or two millennia prior to those found at Lascaux which are similar in both style and technique. The unusual depiction of marine fauna such as seals, penguins and fish adds further originality to this ornate cave.

Cap Canaille★★★

From the guard rail on the cape there is an outstanding **view**★★★ of the cliff face, Massif de Puget and the calanques and Massif de Marseilleveyre.

▶ *Beyond Grande Tête, turn right towards the coastguard station.*

From the **Coastguard station (semaphore)** the **view**★★★ embraces La Ciotat and its shipyards, Aigle point, the Embiez islands, Cap Sicié, and Cap Canaille (telescope).

▶ *Return to the crest road; bear right for La Ciotat.*

The descent into town passes quarries, recently planted pinewoods, and the "pont naturel," a natural limestone arch standing on a pudding-stone base.

CAVAILLON

POPULATION 24 563

MICHELIN MAP 332: D-10

The name Cavaillon, to the French, conjures up fragrant melons and the early vegetables of spring. The melons are sweet and rose pink inside and their harvest begins in May. The melons are grown, along with other produce, in the extensive market gardens that surround the town and make it France's largest designated "national market," with an annual turnover of nearly 800 000 metric tons.

Ancient Cabellio was an oppidum of the Cavares, a Celtic-Ligurian people, and was located on the hill of St-Jacques. It was under Marseille's jurisdiction until the arrival of Roman conquerors. The town then left its hilltop site and became a prosperous Roman colony.

🛈 *79 pl. François-Tourel, 84300 Cavaillon, ☎ 04 90 71 32 01. www.cavaillon-luberon. com.*

Lower Cavaillon

▶ *From place Tourel walk toward the adjacent place du Clos which used to be the site of a melon market.*

Arc romain

On the square lie the ruins of a small, delicately-carved Roman arch dating from the 1C BC which stood near the cathedral at the intersection of the main streets of the Roman town and was re-erected here in 1880.

▶ *Take cours Sadi-Carnot and turn right into rue Diderot.*

Cathédrale St-Véran

The cathedral is dedicated to the patron saint of shepherds, who was bishop of Cavaillon in the 6C. The original Romanesque structure was enlarged by side chapels, which were added from the 14C to the 18C. The façade was almost entirely rebuilt in the 18C and the east end holds a fine pentagonal apse. Enter on the south side by crossing the small Romanesque **cloisters**. Inside, despite the darkness, one can admire paintings by Nicolas Mignard.

▶ *Take Grand Rue, which crosses the old part of Cavaillon.*

Pass the façade of the Grand Couvent before going through the Porte d'Avignon, part of the town's remaining fortifications.

▶ *Turn right along cours Gambetta to reach the square of the same name, then turn right again into the pedestrian-only shopping street, rue de la République.*

This area was known as the "carrière," formerly the Jewish ghetto. On the right is rue Hébraïque, which leads to the **synagogue**.

Synagogue and Musée juif comtadin

🕐*Apr to Sept: daily except Tues 9.30am-12.30pm, 2.30-6.30pm; Oct to Mar: daily except Tues and Sat-Sun 9am-noon, 2-5pm.* ▶*Closed 1 Jan, 1 May, 25 Dec.* ⊚*3€ (ticket includes admission to Hôtel-Dieu).* ☎ *04 90 76 00 34.*

The original synagogue was built on this site in the 14C, making it the oldest in France. Rebuilt in 1772-1774, this synagogue, together with that of Carpentras, is one of the last examples of Baroque Provençal architecture. The interior is ornamented with delightful wood panelling painted grey and decorated with blue and yellow touches. A superb wrought-iron balustrade encircles the gallery. The museum contains a miscellaneous collection of objects and documents: manuscripts, prayer books and sacred articles. In the basement are the baths reserved for the women's purification rites.

▶ *Return to place Tourel by rue Raspail and, on the right, cours Bournissac.*

Colline St-Jacques

🚶 *The hill can be reached on foot taking a signposted footpath which starts at the Roman arch (allow 45min).*

▶ *It is accessible also by car (5.5km/3mi) by way of D 938 towards Carpentras; then to a road to the left uphill, just beyond a crossroads.*

From the viewing table the **view**★ embraces the Cavaillon plain, Mont Ventoux, the Coulon valley, the Vaucluse plateau, the Luberon (quite near), the Durance valley, and the Alpilles. Continue to the **Chapelle St-Jacques**, a 12C chapel, which stands in an attractive garden among cypresses, pines and almond trees.

Napoleon's woes

Fleeing Avignon in April 1814, **Napoleon Bonaparte**, on his way to exile on the island of Elba, stopped at an inn in Orgon. A hostile crowd, alerted by the Royalist drummers, gathered. The excited mob wanted to lynch him but he was saved by the mayor of Orgon and fled. He was able to reach the Auberge de La Calade near Aix.
Leave Orgon via N 538 to the south, in the direction of Salon-de-Provence. After 3km/1.8mi turn right onto D 569.

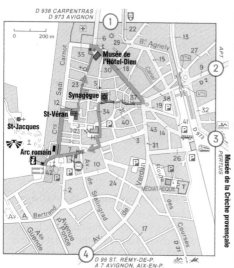

CAVAILLON

Berthelot Av.	2
Bournissac Cours	3
Castil-Blaze Pl.	5
Clemenceau Av. G.	6
Clos Pl. du	7
Coty Av. R.	9
Crillon Bd.	10
Diderot R.	12
Donné Chemin	13
Doumer Bd P.	14
Dublé Av. Véran	15
Durance R. de la	17
Gambetta Cours L.	18
Gambetta Pl. L.	19
Gaulle Av. Gén.-de	22
Grand-Rue	23
Jean-Jaurès Av.	24
Joffre Av. Mar.	26
Kennedy Av. J.-F.	27
Lattre-de-Tassigny R. P.-J. de	29
Pasteur R.	30
Péri Av. Gabriel	31
Pertuis Rte de	32
Raspail R.	34
Renan Cours E.	35
République R. de la	37
Sarnette Av. Abel	38
Saunerie R.	40
Sémard Av. P.	41
Tourel Pl. F.	42
Victor-Hugo Cours	43

Address Book

Guided tours of the town – Contact the tourist office which also offers theme trips through the Luberon leaving from the town.

Synagogue and Jewish Comtat Venaissin Museum – Apr to Sept: daily except Tues 9.30am-12.30pm, 2.30-6.30pm; Oct to Mar: daily except Tues and Sat-Sun 9am-noon, 2-5pm. Closed 1 Jan, 1 May, 25 Dec. 3€. ☎ 04 90 76 00 34.

EVENTS

Market – Traditional market *every Monday morning.*

The Melon Festival – This festival takes place in the weekend before 14 July. There are exhibitions, tastings, book sales, processions of flowered carts, reconstructions of an old market and fireworks all centred around the theme of the melon, symbol of Cavaillon. This is a welcoming town so confréries from other cities are invited to join the festivities, including candied-fruit makers from Apt and vintners from Beaumes-de-Venise. Délice de Melon is the name of an aperitif made from the pulp of melon steeped in alcohol with the addition of sugar, served with crushed ice.

EATING OUT

☒ **Côté Jardin** – 49 rue Lamartine – ☎ 04 90 71 33 58 – cotejardclub-internet.fr – Closed Tues evening in winter, Mon evening and Sun year round. Slightly out of the town centre, the discovery of this spruce, ochre-painted restaurant

with its wall friezes will come as a pleasant surprise. In the summertime tables are laid out around a small fountain in a pretty courtyard situated in the garden. Mediterranean cuisine.

☒ **Fin de Siècle** – 46 pl. du Clos (1er étage) - ☎ 04 90 71 12 27 - closed 8 Aug-8 Sept, Tues and Wed. ☒ 13 € lunch . THe decor is decidedly Empire style, with velvet shairs, crytal chandeliers, not to mention the framed effigy of Napoléon III. Traditional cuisine and very good service.

WHERE TO STAY

☒☒ **Chambre d'hôte Le Mas du Souleou** – 5 chemin St-Pierre-des-Essieux – 84300 Les Vignières – 3km/2mi north of Cavaillon via D 938 for Carpentras, then D 16, thenVC 25 for Châteaux – ☎ 04 90 71 43 22 – www.souleou.com – closed Feb – ☒ – 4 rooms – evening meal 19.82P. Situated in the heart of the countryside, this pretty, well-restored 19C mas welcomes its guests in spacious, well-furnished rooms. Attractive drawing room-cum-library with fireplace. In the summertime you will enjoy the sumptuous food under the pergola. Swimming pool.

SHOPPING

Patissier-chocolatier Étoile du Délice – 57 pl. Castel-Blaze - ☎ 04 90 78 07 51. Melons of course, this time enrobed in chocolate and baptized *melonettes.* The melon sorbet (seasonal) is very fragrant *(call ahead to order).*

Additional sights

Musée de l'Hôtel-Dieu

June to Oct: daily except Tues 9.30am-12.30pm, 2.30-6.30pm; Oct to May: by appointment. ⊙*Closed 1 Jan, 1 May, 25 Dec. 3€.* ☎ 04 90 76 00 34.

The museum is housed in the main building of an old hospital, as well as the chapel, which contains a lapidary section. There is an exhibition on the former hospital: note the ointment jars made of glass and earthenware. The first floor displays an important **archeological collection**★ of objects discovered for the most part on the hill of St-Jacques: ceramic pieces, coins, and funerary urns.

Excursions

Orgon

▷ *Leave Cavaillon via D 99 in the direction of St-Rémy and Tarascon. After the Durance river and the motorway, take D 26 on the left.*

The city, crossed by N 7, lies in the Durance plain. It overlooks the ridge which separates the Alpilles to the west and the Montagne du Luberon to the east. It is home to an interesting **church** (Église) from the 14C. The choir and nave are slightly out of alignment. On the nave's north side hang fine 14C painted panels.

Crowning the hill overlooking the town to the south (road subject to restrictions), the **Chapelle Notre-Dame-de-Beauregard**'s terrace presents a fine view of the Durance valley and the Luberon mountains.

Saint-Andiol

▷ *10km/6mi west, leave Cavaillon on D99 towards St-Rémy, then turn right in Pland'Orgon onto N 7 towards Avignon.*

This large farming town was founded by pioneering monks from Montmajour and is the birthplace of French Resistance hero Jean Moulin (1899-1943). The town, while lacking charm itself, is worth a visit for its church, **église Saint-Vincent**. The fortifications were added in the 14C crowning the church with imposing battlements that give it the air of a fortress. The church itself is Romanesque, and has a single nave with three vaults and a trefoil apse. Inside, there is a Flamboyant Gothic ciborium (15C).

Les Taillades

▷ *5km/3mi east via D 143. At the roundabout, follow signposts to "Vieux Village." Park the car on the square in the front of the town hall.*

At the far end of the Petit Luberon range, this delightful little village comes as a surprise with its houses perched on what look like enormous stone stalagmites, creating a striking yet serene **site**★. This effect is in fact man-made: quarrymen literally hacked away at the foundations of their homes to obtain molasses, a soft sandstone highly prized by the construction industry.

Follow the road to the church that climbs in a spiral and go past the tower, probably a remnant of an earlier keep. To your left you will see a strange statue, the "Morvellous," supposedly of St Veranus. Opposite the church of St-Luce, a small enclosed area, once a graveyard, overlooks the village: ancient dwellings, roofs of mossy tiles, troglodyte constructions and, wherever you look, vertical partitions carved into rock by those tireless stone-cutters.

▷ *Retrace your steps and turn right after Auberge des Carrières into rue des Carrières.*

A vaulted archway leads into this quarry hollowed out of the very heart of the village itself. Its sheer rock walls form a roughly circular space, the **théâtre des carrières**. This forms a striking setting for concerts of classical and jazz music every summer, beneath the starry Luberon sky.

▷ *Continue on D 143 to the Cavaillon crossroads.*

The road comes to **moulin St-Pierre**, a watermill on the canal de Carpentras that still featuers its great paddle-wheel. It was used for grinding madder before becoming a flour mill, a role it played until 1870.

Combe de Vidauque

▷ *5km/3mi southeast. Leave Cavaillon on D 973 and fork left towards Vidauque.*

The road is very steep and takes a hairpin course (*one-way traffic, speed limit of 30kph/18mph*), skirting the wild Vidauque combe and offering magnificent plunging **views**★★ of the surrounding countryside: the tip of the Vaucluse plateau and Cavalon valely (north), the Alpilles and Durance valley (south and west), and below, the Cavaillon plain.

▷ *Take the Trou-du-Rat road down to D 973 into which you turn right towards ChevalBlanc to return to Cavaillon.*

Le Luberon★★★

⌖ *See Le LUBERON.*

CHÂTEAUNEUF-DU-PAPE

POPULATION 2 062

MICHELIN MAP 332: B-9

The town has given its name to the most prestigious of all the Rhône wines. The original vineyard was planted in the 14C on land belonging to the Avignon popes, who summered here, and the wine was consumed locally until the mid-18C when its renown began to spread. For a long time it was sent in barrels to Burgundy for improvement. In c 1880 phylloxera ravaged the vineyard, resulting in its ruin. It was subsequently replanted. In 1923 the wine-growers' association laid down strict rules defining the area, the management of the vineyards, harvest dates, the selection of grapes (13 approved varieties), vinification, and vintage labelling. These strict controls have resulted in a highly refined and often superb product: Châteauneuf-du-Pape. Today, 300 vineyards grow 3 300ha of vines.

The emblem of the Holy Sea on a bottle of Chateauneuf-du-Pape

🛈 *place du Portail, 84230 Châteauneuf-du-Pape,* ☎ *04 90 83 71 08.*

Visit

Château des Papes

The ruined fortress commands a splendid **view**★★: the valley of the Rhône, Roquemaure and the ruins of Château de l'Hers, Avignon with Notre-Dame-des-Doms and the Palais des Papes clearly outlined against the more distant Alpilles, the Luberon and the Vaucluse plateau, the Dentelles de Montmirail and, further off, Mont Ventoux, the Baronnies, and Lance mountain.

Musée des Outils de Vigneron

🕘*Apr to beginning of Oct: 9am-12.30pm, 2-7pm, Sat-Sun and public holidays 10am-12.30pm, 2-7pm; beginning of Oct to end of Dec: 9am-noon, 2-6pm.* 🕘*Closed 1 Jan, 1 Nov, 25 Dec. No charge.* ☎ *04 90 83 70 07.*

Address Book

EATING OUT

🍽🍽 **Le Pistou** – *15 rue Joseph-Ducos –* ☎ *04 90 83 71 75 – closed 31 Dec-15 Jan, Sun evenings, Mon, and evenings from Nov to Easter except Sat.* A small restaurant located right in the middle of the village in a little street that leads to the castle. Simple, country-style dining room. Dishes from southwest France, and the day's specialities are presented on a blackboard. Very reasonable prices.

🍽🍽 **La Garbure** – *3 rue Joseph-Ducos –* ☎ *04 90 83 75 08 – garburewanadoo.fr – closed Jan, 1-12 Nov and Sun.* Once you're ensconced in the well-furnished, brightly coloured dining room, let your appetite guide you; you should find the regional menus concocted by the owner tempting. There are a few Provençal-coloured rooms if you wish to prolong your stay. Air conditioning.

Hostellerie Château des Fines Roches – *on the route to Sorgues –* ☎ *04 90 83 70 23 – reservation@chateaufinesroches.com – 8 rooms – restaurant 45/75€.* A remarkable, crenellated château with views of the vineyards and surrounding countryside. Offers fine regional cuisine and pleasant, spacious rooms.

This museum is devoted to the world of wine and the tools used to produce it. The tour is conducted in the order that wine is produced: from work in the vineyard (plough, hoes, pruning clippers), its treatment (copper sulphate spraying-machines), harvesting (baskets, wine press), work in the cellar (funnel, 16C press, huge 14C barrel) and related subjects such as cooperage, grafting, weights and measures, phylloxera, bottling and corking. In one room an exhibition describes the vineyard, which extends nowadays over 3 300ha/8 154 acres and involves 300 wine-growers. In the courtyard is a display of old ploughs.

Excursion

Roquemaure

Drive for around 10km/6mi along D 17, then take D 976.
The road runs through beautifully-kept vineyards. On the left, some 2km/1mi further on, appear the ruins of Château de l'Hers. Its machicolated tower seems to hover protectively over its precious vineyard. Opposite it, on the far bank of the Rhône, is Château de Roquemaure where Pope Clement V died on 20 April 1314. Cross the Rhône, which the road borders for a couple of miles, and continue to Roquemaure where you will find several preserved old houses (notably the one belonging to Cardinal Bertrand, near the church). The 13C church has a fine 17C organ.

La CIOTAT ☆☆

POPULATION 31 630

MICHELIN LOCAL MAP 340: I-6

La Ciotat, where the houses rise in tiers above the bay of the same name, has been a port since ancient times. when, as Citharista, it was an outpost of Marseille. Roman occupation, barbarian invasion, and devastation were followed by a revival in the Middle Ages, and from the 16C the provision of a merchant fleet in the eastern Mediterranean. The city continues to fulfill its maritime vocation, particularly by running large shipbuilding yards specializing in oil and methane tankers. However, the worldwide crisis in the shipbuilding industry has scored a direct hit here, and the city is having to adapt to different technologies and to seek new areas of commercial activity, such as tourism. Its beach and fishing port, its cliffs, calanques, and sea bed attract numerous visitors all year round.

🛈 *Bd Anatole-France, 13600 La Ciotat, ☎ 04 42 08 61 32. www.laciotatourisme.com.*

Shipbuilding yard at La Ciotat

Address Book

In the Lumière brothers' footsteps – *Ask at the tourist office.* Tour themed on the these inventor brothers' Ciotat.

Parc du Mugel – *Apr to Sept: 8am-8pm; Oct to Mar: 9am-6pm. No charge.*

Musée ciotaden – *Daily except Tues 3-6pm (July and Aug: 4-7pm). Closed Easter, 1 May, 25 Dec. 3.05P.* ☎ *04 42 71 40 99.*

EATING OUT

◖◖ **La Fresque** – *18 rue des Combattants* – ☎ *04 42 08 00 60 – closed 15 Dec-10 Feb, Sun evening and Mon.* The pretty, shady terrace of this old pharmacy overlooks the old port. Inside there are still a few remnants of its original decor, such as the fine fresco decorating the dining-room ceiling, and a few 19C pieces of pharmacy furniture.

WHERE TO STAY

◖◖ **Hôtel R.I.F.** – *Calanque de Figuerolles* – ☎ *04 42 08 41 71 – www.figuerolles.com – closed Nov – 9 rooms –* ⊐ *7€ – restaurant 39€.* A few steps lead down to this house tucked away in an isolated calanque. A terrace affords an excellent view. Provençal coloured rooms are in bungalows in the pretty garden. The beach is a stone's throw away and canoes are available. Best to reserve in advance

◖◖ **Résidence Motel Camping St-Jean** – *30 avenue de St-Jean* – ☎ *04 42 83 13 01* – *www.asther.com/stjean – closed 1 Oct-23 Mars –* ▣ *– 32 rooms –* ⊐ *5€ – meals 17/25€.* This is a useful address if you want to stay by the sea. You can either choose to stay in the hotel or rent a studio with kitchenette for weekly stays (sheets and towels provided). Alternatively you can pitch your tent on the shady camping site which has 80 places and offers direct access to the beach.

◖◖ **La Closeraie** – *8 av. Bellon* – ☎ *04 42 71 32 80 - 17 rooms* ⊐ *7 €.* A great location: only 6 min walking to the beach and only 2 min to port St-Jean. The rooms might be small but you will sleep soundly in this peaceful neighborhood.

LEISURE ACTIVITIES

Markets – The **traditional** market is held every Tuesday in place Évariste-Gras and on Sundays at the Vieux Port.

In July and August there is a **craft** market every evening from 8pm-midnight at the Vieux Port.

Parc Régional Marin de la Baie de la Ciotat – Information at the town hall. Famous for the rich diversity of its seabed life, La Ciotat bay is now a protected regional park, thanks to strict measures enforced for its preservation, whereby fishing, deep-sea diving and mooring are strictly regulated. These measures have assured the survival of animal and plant species (thanks to the immersion of artificial reefs which favour reproduction).

Marina – The new tourist marina has 13 berths for visitors. Call well ahead of time to reserve (☎ 04 42 08 62 90).

Sights

Clos des Plages

The district has been developed as a resort just north of the new harbour (*Nouveau Port*, with 850 berths), with hotels and seaside villas lining the beach, making it ideal for family outings. Marking one of the squares open to the sea is a monument to the Lumière brothers, who brought fame to the town with the first showing of a motion picture in 1895.

Vieux Port

This old harbour has all the charm of a small fishing port, with its quaysides overlooked by warm façades and lively restaurants.

Parc du Mugel

▸ *Access by quai de Roumanie.* ⏱ *Apr-Sept: 8am-8pm ; Oct-Mar: 9am-6pm. No charge.* ☎ *06 23 79 55 92.* Located at the tip of Cap de l'Aigle, this natural protected area favours abundant and varied vegetation (cork trees, mimosa, and arbutus). At the top (steep path), some 155m/509ft, there is a lovely view of La Ciotat and its surroundings.

The Ciotat calanques

▸ *1.5km/1mi. Leave La Ciotat along quai de Roumanie, avenue des Calanques and turn left into avenue du Mugel.* These rocky inlets known as calanques can also be visited on board a catamaran-type boat with a glass bottom, affording underwater views.

Calanque du Mugel

The inlet is dominated by the rock of Cap de l'Aigle. There is a good view of Île Verte from here.

▷ *Take avenue des Calanques and bear left into avenue de Figuerolles.*

Calanque de Figuerolles★

15min return on foot.

A short green valley leads to the small clear-water inlet. This curious site is characterised by strangely eroded rocks, including the "Capucin", an isolated crag projecting forward on the right, and cliffs featuring cavities with sharp edges and a smooth, polished interior.

Île Verte★

30min return by boat

By boat (from Vieux Port: ☎ 06 63 59 16 35 or 06 16 40 83 50): May to Sept: daily; Apr: Sat-Sun depending on the weather. Contact the companies at the landing stage. Return fare: 7€ (children, 4€). The rock at Cap de l'Aigle, so clearly a bird of prey (*aigle* means eagle) when seen from the small fort on Île Verte, is what gave the point its name.

Additional Sights

Église Notre-Dame-du-Port

This 17C church's lovely pink Baroque façade overlooks the harbour. Inside, the modern-looking interior is notable for a *Descent from the Cross* by André Gaudion, painted in 1616 (south aisle), and a modern frieze (22m/72ft long) by Gilbert Ganteaume of scenes from the *Gospels*. At the end of the nave are paintings by Tony Roux representing *Man* and *Woman*.

Musée ciotaden

Jul-Aug: 4-7pm; Sept-Jun: 3-6pm - closed Mar and certain public holidays. 3.20 €. ☎ *04 42 71 40 99.* Inside are mementoes and documents about this seafaring town and its past.

Chapelle Notre-Dame-de-la-Garde

▷ *Follow chemin de la Garde for 2.5km/1.5mi by car, until you reach a brilliant white housing estate, then 15min return on foot.*

At the chapel, bear right onto a path which leads to a terrace above the chapel (85 steps cut out of the rock). The **view**★★ embraces the full extent of La Ciotat bay.

Excursion

Parc OK Corral

▷ *19km/12mi NW on D 3 then N 8 to the left.*

10 am: mid-June to beginning of Sept: daily; May to mid-June: Wed, Sat-Sun, public holidays; Apr: Wed, Sat-Sun and zone B school vacations; Sept: Wed, Sat-Sun; Mar: Sat -Sun; Oct: Sat-Sun and public holidays. Closed Nov-Feb. 16.50€ (children, 14.10€). ☎ *04 42 73 80 05 – www.okcorral.fr.*

Downhill from the main road, N 8, in the centre of a pine forest clearing with the Ste-Baume massif serving as a backdrop, lies this exceptional amusement park (loop-the-loops roller coaster, Titanic, Tokaido Express, scenic railways, looping star). However there are also more restful activities and games for visitors of all ages. A chair-lift and a small train provide a quick, comfortable tour of the park. Snack bars, crêperies and picnic areas have been set up.

Grotte de la COCALIÈRE★

MICHELIN LOCAL MAP 339: J-3

This cave, northwest of St-Ambroix on the Gard plateau, contains a network of explored galleries running 46km/29mi underground. In addition the site of La Cocalière has revealed a very populated prehistoric settlement that was occupied from the Mousterian period (45 000 BC) to the Iron Age (400 BC).

▶ *From Les Vans bear left on a road which branches off D 904 on the left; not far after, the road to the right goes off to Courry.*

Tour *1hr 15min, temperature: 14°C/57 °F*

Kids ⏲ *Jul-Aug: 10am-6pm; mid-Mar through June and Sept-Oct: 10am-12pm, 2-5pm. 7€ (children, 5€). ☎ 04 66 24 34 74. www.grotte-cocaliere.com.*

At the bottom of the tunnel, a path follows along (about 1 200m/1 312yd) the bottom of a horizontal gallery that adjoins the other galleries. The cave is rich in its variety of concretions, reflected in the pools of water fed by small waterfalls. As you travel underground you will see discs – huge concretions with a wide diameter that specialists have not yet been able to explain; delicate stalactites that are white (if charged with calcite) or multi-coloured (if charged with metallic oxide); and gours (natural dams). After the speleologists' camp site, walk through the Chaos chamber, where the roof is covered with stalactites and other forms of erosion, to the gallery of frozen falls and eccentrics that overlooks an imposing sparkling waterfall and wells linked to the lower stages where underground rivers flow. Pass through a prehistoric deposit before returning to the entrance area on a small train.

🚶 *(20min)* Outside, the cave's immediate surroundings are a dolmen, tumuli, small constructions of dried stones, prehistoric shelters, and varied karstic phenomena (caves, sinkholes, and faults).

WHERE TO EAT AND STAY

🍴🍴🍴 **La Bastide des Senteurs** – 30500 St-Victor-de-Malcap – 8km/5mi from Grotte de la Cocalière via D 904 and D 51C – ☎ 04 66 60 24 45 – subileau@bastide-senteurs.com – www.bastide-senteurs.com – closed Nov-Mar, midday in July, Aug except Sun and public holidays. The young owners have made a charming spot out of this abandoned country house. You will enjoy the food, the restrained elegance of the decor and the warm welcome. Everything here sings with the flavours and colours of the south! Pretty rooms, swimming pool and an attractive terrace.

Chaîne de l'ESTAQUE★

MICHELIN LOCAL MAP 340: F-5 TO G-5

The Chaîne de l'Estaque, which divides the Étang de Berre from the Mediterranean, is an unusual limestone formation, arid in appearance and almost uninhabited except for a few small fishing villages sheltered by deep inlets (*calanques*) in the steep coastline. The area is much appreciated by the locals from Marseille and is known as the "Côte Bleue," from the intense cobalt or sapphire blue of its sparkling waters. The Parc Marin de la Côte Bleue, a natural marine reserve, extends along the coast between the ports of Niolon and Carro, at the foot of the Massif de la Nerthe. Fishing, scuba diving, and mooring are prohibited. There is one marina Carry-le-Rouet (☎ 04 42 45 25 13), with a few berths for visiting yachts.

By train – A fun way to explore the coastline and its beaches. 🔊*See the Address Book.*

Driving Tour

Marseille to Port-de-bouc 74km/46mi – about 4hr.

▶ *From Marseille take the motorway on the coast and exit at St-Henri-L'Estaque.*

Address Book

ACCESS

By car – A transverse road cuts across the mountian chain, running along the hinterland (except between Carry and Sausset-les-Pins). Most of the harbours can only be reached down a dead-end road. In the summe, especially during weekends, access to the *calanques* of Niolon and Redonne is sometimes prohibited to reduce the risk of fire in an area with a particularly fragile ecosystem.

By train – Between Port-de-Bouc and Marseille there is a train which makes several stops at the beaches of the Côte Bleue. The train is fun to ride, as it chugs along through tunnels and past gorgeous views of the sea, blowing its whistle to warn daydreamers who enjoy rambling along the tracks!

EATING OUT

Les Girelles – *3 avenue Adolphe-Fouque – 13960 Sausset-les-Pins – ☎ 04 42 45 26 16 – closed 2-24 Jan, Sun evening low season, Mon and Tues lunch from June-Aug, and Wed, except evenings in season.* The terrace bordering the beach is very popular with locals. Inside, there is a pretty model ship and plenty of picture windows that make the most of the view.

Appetizing and well-presented cooking.

WHERE TO STAY

Auberge du Mérou – *Calanque de Niolon - 13740 Niolon - 5 km from Rove, on the road to Niolon - ☎ 04 91 46 98 69 - aubergedumerou@wanadoo.fr - closed Sun and Mon evenings during low season- 5 rooms - �>< 5,50 € - restaurant 26/32 €.* Decorated as cabins in a boat, the rooms look out over the port of Niolon. The restaurant is known for its seafood specialties.

ACTIVITIES

Markets – Sausset-les-Pins – Traditional markets Thurs mornings, at the quai du Port, and Sun mornings along bd Armand-Audibert, especially the corniche. **Fish** market daily, from 9am, at quai du Port.

Centre UPCA de Niolon – *18 chemin de la Batterie - Le Rove - 13740 Niolon - ☎ 04 91 46 90 16 - niolon@ucpa.asso.fr - open 9am-12pm, 2-5pm – closed mid-Nov to end of Feb.* This is one of Europe's largest diving centres (all levels from beginner to instructor).

Marina-Port de Carry-le-Rouet – *☎ 04 42 45 25 13.*

L'Estaque

In July 1876 Paul Cézanne described the charms of this fishing village, dotted with workshops, to Camille Pisarro, saying it was "just like a playing card – red roofs on a blue sea." A number of avant-garde painters made the village famous between 1870 and World War I. It was partly here that the foundations of modern art were laid– especially Cubism from 1908-1910– by Cézanne, Renoir, Braque, Dufy, Derain, Marquet, and Othon Freisz.

Inhabitants from Marseille are now attracted here by the fish shops, the restaurants, as well as the odd stall that continues to make *chichi frégi*, delicious, long fried donuts. You can enjoy a panoramic view from the place de l'Église in the old village. From here take in the ports and islands, and the picturesque rooftops of the old village, to see what Cézanne was talking about.

▶*Turn right onto N 568 going west towards the Rove. Before the railway bridge, turn right along the Carrière Chagnaud road. Pass under the railway before turning down the slope to the entrance.*

Canal Souterrain du Rove

The tunnel was cut in the 1920s beneath the Chaîne de l'Estaque to link the Marseille docks and the Étang de Berre, and was used regularly by 1 200 metric ton barges until it was obstructed by a rockfall in 1963. It is more than 7km/4mi long and dead straight – one can still see daylight at the far end. Height, width and water depth respectively are 15.4, 22 and 4.5m (50, 72 and 14ft).

"Oursinades"

The glorious days that usually characterise the winter months are the setting for the "Oursinades", a sea urchin festival which takes place in January in Sausset and February in Carry. The streets around the port are literally invaded with long tables where people sit down to tuck into sea urchins and other seafood accompanied by white wine. A lively time is guaranteed!

Calanque de Niolon

▶ *After passing the village of Rove, which is famous for its fromage frais, made from goats' milk, turn left onto D 5 and left again onto D 48. On approaching Niolon, the winding road descends steeply towards the port.*

Niolon★

The lovely little village retains a traditional atmosphere where it clings to the hillside above a *calanque* of the same name. It is a good spot for deep-sea diving. (⚓ *See Address Book: Centre UPCA de Niolon*).

▶ *Return to D 5, which will be on your left. An arid landscape leads to Ensuès. On entering the village turn left and take D 48D.*

La Madrague-de-Gignac

The village, set in a lovely site, lines a *calanque*, which faces Marseille across the water. A narrow road (alternate traffic circulation) leads from the port to the Anse de la Redonne.

▶ *Returning to Ensuès make a left turn onto D 5, which goes down the Vallon de l'Aigle, bordered by pines and holm oaks.*

Le Rouet-Plage

An attractive creek with a beach and small harbour, and, half-hidden among the pine trees, some elegant houses.

Carry-le-Rouet⚓

🛈 *Espace Fernandel, av. A.-Briand, 13620 Carry-le-Rouet, ☎ 04 42 13 20 36.* This one-time fishing village is now a seaside resort. Summer residences can be seen in the woods that line the bay. There are plenty of seafood restaurants on the port where you can eat sea urchins, among other specialties.

Sausset-les-Pins⚓

This fishing village and seaside resort has a fine promenade from where one can look across the sea to Marseille.

▶ *D 49 leaves the coast and winds its way up the massif. Drive toward La Couronne by way of D 49B. Turn right before the church and head for Cap Couronne.*

Cap Couronne

From the lighthouse on the point there is a view right round to Marseille, with the Chaîne de l'Estaque in the foreground, the Chaîne de l'Étoile and the Marseilleveyre in the background. The huge beach of La Couronne is very popular and is a favourite spot among Marseille's young set.

Carro

The attractive small fishing village and resort lies well protected at the back of a rock-strewn bay. There is a fish market held every morning at the port.

▶ *Leave Carro via D 49 and continue to Les Ventrons.*

The road climbs through an arid landscape of dark pines against the white limestone and, at 120m/394ft, looks back (*observation tower*) over the industrial harbour complex of Lavéra, Port-de-Bouc, and Fos.

▶ *At Les Ventrons turn right onto D 5.*

St-Julien

A path (on the left) from the village leads to a chapel where embedded in the north wall there is a Gallo-Roman relief (1C) of a group of eight people in a funeral scene.
▶*On returning to Les Ventrons turn right onto D 5 for Martigues.*

Martigues

See MARTIGUES.

▶ *Turn left onto N 568.*

Port-de-Bouc

The port is protected by a fort erected by Vauban in 1664 on the southern bank of the passage. The 12C tower, part of these fortifications, is now a lighthouse. Situated at the western exit of the town, along N 568, the **Musée Moralès** offers an unusual walk through a veritable forest of gigantic creatures in the form of metal sculptures by **Raymond Moralès**, following themes that are in turn amusing, puzzling, and even occasionally disturbing (*Musée Moralès – Call for information and time.* ☎ *04 42 06 49 01*).

Chaîne de l'ÉTOILE★

MICHELIN LOCAL MAP 340: H-5

This chain of mountains, which belongs to the small Alps of Provence and is a result of the Pyrenean fold, separates the Arc basin to the north from that of the Huveaune to the east. It extends the Chaîne de l'Estaque beyond the shelf of St-Antoine. In spite of the low altitude of its mountain tops, the chain rises spectacularly above the Marseille plain. Its central crest, which spreads out like a fan, ends at 781m/2 562ft at the Tête du Grand Puech.

Driving Tour

Gardanne to Aubagne 61km/38mi – about 3hr 30min (not including the climb to Étoile peak).

Gardanne

bd Carnot - 13120 Gardanne - ☎ 04 42 51 02 73 - www.ville-gardanne.fr - daily except Sun and Mon: 9.30am-12pm, 2-6pm. This important industrial town with its coal mining, bauxite and cement works was painted by Cézanne. It is a lively place on market days (*ask at the tourist office*).

Écomusée de la Forêt méditerranéene

▶ *NW of Gardanne, on D 7 towards Aix and Valabre.*

Jul-Aug: 10am-1pm, 1.30-6.45pm; Sept-Jun: 9am-12.30pm, 1-5.45pm – closed Sat, 15Aug-5 Sept, 1 Jan, and 25 Dec. 5.30 €. ☎ 04 42 65 42 10.

G. Magnin/MICHELIN

One of the five mills in Allauch

Address Book

Feast of Saint-Jean – *Around 24 Aug, in Allauch*: folkloric groups, parades, and more.

EATING OUT

🍽 **La Grignote** – *22 r. Mignet - 13120 Gardanne* - ☎ *04 42 58 30 25 - lagrignote2@wanadoo.fr - fermé 1er-15 août – 12 €.* A restaurant with good, traditional cuisine.

WHERE TO STAY

🛏 **Les Cigales** – *Rte Enco-de-Botte - 13190 Allauch* - ☎ *04 91 68 17 07 - lescigales@9online.fr* - 🖵 *10 rooms: 55/85 - : 7- restaurant (evenings only) 15/17 €.* Between Marseille and Allauch, this new establishment offers tranquil and cozy rooms, a garden and swimmnig pool.

Dedicated to the Mediterranean ecology of this region, there are interactive displays, footpaths, and instructive panels, as well as a botanical trail that helps you explore and learn about the flora and fauna in its natural setting and from those who work in and around the forest everyday.

▶ *Return to Gardanne and take D 58 going south which becomes D 8. After 7km/4mi turn right to Mimet.*

Mimet

This small hill-top village is undergoing considerable expansion. From its terrace there is a fine **view**★ of the Luynes valley, Gardanne, and its furnaces.

▶ *Return to D 8 and bear right. The picturesque D 7 and D 908 skirt the Étoile chain. At Le Logis-Neuf turn left to Allauch.*

Allauch

A large suburb of Marseille, Allauch (pronounced Allau) rises in tiers up the foothills of the Étoile chain. 🚶From Allauch you can follow a series of footpaths leading up to the Garlaban hills, much loved by the great Provençal writer Marcel Pagnol.

Esplanade des Moulins

Appropriately named (*moulin* means mill), this esplanade, with its five windmills, one of which has been restored, offers a good **view**★ of Marseille.

Musée du Vieil Allauch

♿ ⏱*Daily except Mon: 9am-12pm, 2-6pm -*⏱*closed public holidays except weekends.* 💰 *3€.* ☎ *04 91 10 49 00 - http://musee.allauch.com.* Near the church. This museum contains objects and documents pertaining to local history.

Chapelle Notre-Dame-du-Château

🚶*30min return on foot.* This chapel belonged to an 11C and 12C castle of which only some ramparts remain. The terrace affords a fine view of Marseille.

▶ *Take D 44F northwest of Allauch.* After passing Plan-de-Cuques, you will reach Château-Gombert, a neighbourhood of Marseille that has retained the atmosphere of a village.

Musée du Terroir marseillais

▶ *At Château-Gombert.* ⏱*Daily except Mon 9am-12pm, 2-6.30pm, Sat-Sun 2.30-6.30pm.* ⏱*Closed public holidays. 3.80€.* ☎ *04 91 68 14 38.*

The museum is situated in the main square shaded by plane trees. Dedicated to local arts and traditions, it is set out as a traditional interior of an old provençal dwelling. The kitchen, with its fireplace hood and typical *pile* (sink), is full of ceramics from Marseille, pewter, terralhas (culinary pottery), the big clay tian (bowl) and mortars for aïoli (garlic mayonnaise).The middle-class living room and bedroom are arrayed with beautiful furniture from the region. Note the *radassié*, a long couch commonly found in country farmhouses.

▶ *Leave Château-Gombert towards Marseille and turn right into Traverse de la Baume-Loubière. Park the car at the Grottes Loubière. A footpath leads to the summit of the Étoile (4hr return on foot).*

Étoile peak

🚶 After a winding trail through a rocky passage you reach the **Grande Étoile** (alt 590m/1 936ft), where a telecommunications tower stands, and then **Étoile peak** (alt 651m/2 136ft). From the shelf separating these last two summits there is a splendid **panorama**★★ over the Gardanne basin to the north and the thresholds that cut the chain's southern slopes.

▶ *Return to Allauch by car by the same way you came. Continue south on D 4A. At Les Quatres-Saisons bear left and soon after, left again.*

Camoins-les-Bains

This pleasant little spa is surrounded by green countryside. **Marcel Pagnol** (1895-1974), the writer and film director who was born in Aubagne, is buried in **La Treille cemetery** at the town's entrance.

> **Nougats F et V Brémond** – *Parc d'activités Fontvieille – 13190 Allauch -* ☎ *04 91 68 19 06*. The inhabitants of Allauch claim that their town is the birthplace of nougat, which can be sampled at the manufacturers.

▶ *Return to Camoins-les-Bains and take D 44A to Aubagne.*

FONTAINE-DE-VAUCLUSE

POPULATION 610

MICHELIN LOCAL MAP 332: D-10

Vallis Clausa (the "enclosed valley") from which this département gets its name, is best known for its fountain, the famous resurgent spring that rises in a picturesque site dear to Petrarch and is the source of the River Sorgue. It is in winter or spring, during the floods, that the stream is at its most dramatic, when the water level rises 150m3/32 985 gallons per second. By dramatic contrast, in the summer or autumn the flow is reduced to a mere 4.5m3/159 cubic ft per second.

🗓 *Chemin de la Fontaine, 84800 Fontaine-de-Vaucluse,* ☎ *04 90 20 32 22.*

Petrarch

On 6 April 1327 in an Avignon church, this great poet and humanist – a familiar member of the pontifical court in Avignon – met the lovely **Laura de Noves**, with whom he fell passionately in love. However this love remained platonic: Laura was married and virtuous, but she inspired many of the poet's works throughout his life, and indeed his best works. Ten years after his first meeting with her, Petrarch, who was only 33 years old, retired to Vaucluse. He remained here for 16 years seeking peace in the tranquil Sorgue valley. During his stay Laura died of the plague in Avignon in 1348. The poet died 20 years later in Arquà Petrarca near Padua. He never forgot her in those long years.

Fontaine de Vaucluse

S. Sauvignier/MICHELIN

FONTAINE DE VAUCLUSE★★ *30min return on foot*

▶ *From place de la Colonne, where a commemorative column of the fifth centenary (1304-1804) of Petrarch's birth stands, take chemin de la Fontaine, which climbs gently, following the river Sorgue.*

The Fontaine de Vaucluse is one of the most powerful resurgent springs in the world. It is the outlet of an important underwater river fed by rainwater draining through the Vaucluse plateau pitted with numerous chasms (avens), through which the speleologists have searched in vain for the underground Sorgue. The exploration of the fountain's chasm began as early as the 19C and continues to this day. The last record was 315m/1 033ft deep and was achieved in August 1985 with the help of a small remote-controlled submarine equipped with cameras.

The cave from which the River Sorgue emerges is at the foot of a rocky cirque formed by high cliffs. In front of it stands a pile of rocks through which the waters usually filter. During heavy flooding the water reaches the level of the fig trees growing in the rock above the cave mouth, before racing away over the rocks in a vivid green fury of tumbling foaming water.

Sights

Église St-Véran★

This small Romanesque church has rounded vaulting over its nave and an oven-vaulted apse flanked by antique fluted columns. To the right of the chancel opens the crypt containing the sarcophagus of St Veranus, 6C bishop of Cavaillon, credited with having dispatched Coulobre, a monster that terrorised the region.

Opposite is a Provençal house, built in pinky-orange stone and decorated with bunches of grapes.

Musée-Bibliothèque Pétrarque

🕐 *Jun to Sept: 10am-12.30pm, 1.30-6pm; Apr-May and the first half of Oct: 10am-12pm, 2-6pm: 16 Oct - 1 Nov: 10am-12pm, 2-5pm (mid to end of Oct: 5pm).* 🕐*Closed Tues and 2 Nov-31 Mar and 1 May.* ⊜*3.50€ (12-16 years, 1.50 €).* ☎ 04 90 20 37 20.

This library-museum is located at the heart of the village in a house said to be built on the site of the house where Petrarch once lived. Upstairs, there is an exhibition of drawings and prints (16C-19C) on the subjects of Petrarch, Laura, Avignon, and the Fontaine-de-Vaucluse, as well as a collection of old editions of the writings of the poet and his followers. On the ground floor there is a rotating display of works by artists linked with the site of the Fontaine-de-Vaucluse, and of writings by René Char illustrated by Zao Wou Ki, Braque or Vieira da Silva.

Musée de Spéléogie

▶*On chemin de la Fontaine.* 🚶 ⌇*Guided tours (45min). Feb to 15 Nov: 9.30am-12.30pm, 2-6.30pm; Jul to Sept: 9.30am-7.30pm.* ⊜*4.50€ (children: 4€).* ☎ 04 90 20 34 13.

The underground museum presents the **Casteret collection**★ of limestone concretions (calcite, gypsum, aragonite) assembled over 30 years of underground exploration by the speleologist. Different sites have been reconstructed: stalactite and stalagmite caves, chasm and rubble, rivers, waterfalls, natural dams, and caves with human imprints. A detailed documentation introduces the visitor to Vaucluse speleology; a permanent display (documents, photos, models) explains the discoveries made on Fontaine-de-Vaucluse through the years.

Musée d'Histoire (1939-1945)

▶*On the left, near the Vallis Claus artisinal centre.* 🚶🕐*Jun-Sept: 10am-6pm; Apr-May and first half of Oct: 10am-12pm, 4-6pm; 16-31 Oct and All Saints Day: 10am-12pm, 2-5pm; Nov-Dec: Sat-Sun, 10am-12pm, 2-5pm; Mar: Sat-Sun, 10am-12pm, 2-6pm -* 🕐*closed Tues, 1 May, and 25 Dec.* ⊜ 3.50 € *(children, 1.50€).* ☎ 04 90 20 24 00.

This history museum, sited in a plain and functional building, offers a historical, literary, and artistic view of the years 1939-1945 within a modern framework. The first section of the museum describes daily life in occupied France; the second, the activity of the Resistance in the Vaucluse département, through the testimonies of those involved in or observing events during the "dark years." An audiovisual support helps to situate local history within the national context.

Santon Museum

♿ *Jul-Sep: 10am-8pm ; the rest of the year: 10am-6pm.* ⎈ *4€ (children 2€).* ☎ *04 90 20 20 83*

This houses a pretty collection of cribs and santons made by local artisans both recently and in the past.

Excursion

Saumane-de-Vaucluse

▷ *4km/2.5mi northwest. Leave Fontaine-de-Vaucluse on D 25, then turn right onto D 57.* The road follows the hillside across the limestone slopes of the Vaucluse mountains, before arriving at this attractive village perched above the Sorgue valley. Here stands the 15C castle belonging to the family of the **Marquis de Sade**. St-Trophime church, dating from the 12C but modified several times since, is crowned by an arcaded belfry. From the square, which contains a 16C stone cross, there is a broad **view** across the Sorgue valley, the Luberon and the Alpilles.

Cabrières-d'Avignon

▷ *5km/3mi south on D 100A. Leave the car in the car park by the town hall.*

The Château des Adhémar *(not open to the public)* was built in the 11C and partially rebuilt in the 17C in a slightly more approachable Renaissance style. It was the backdrop to the tragic events of 20 and 21 April 1545, when Vaudois Lutheran "heretics," who had taken refuge there under the leadership of local Eustache Marron, were massacred by Meynier d'Oppède's Roman Catholic forces. Walk around the château (*go along rue du Vieux-Four then go left up chemin Eustache-Marron at the edge of open countryside*) to see the ramparts linking the five towers, vestiges of the original fortifications.

Mur de la peste

▣ *1 hr return on foot.*

▷ *Take the chemin des Muscadelles to the left of the château, then a loose stone track uphill, waymarked in red.*

Once you reach the ridge (small commemorative monument) go back downhill straight ahead (*milestone*) then turn right. The dry stone wall, well-restored, was built to protect the Comtat from the plague that arrived in Marseille in 1720. It hugs the contours of the land, cutting through dense vegetation and wild olive trees and pines and inpenetrable thickets of prickly juniper.

▷ *Those with stamina can follow the fairly rocky track, GR 6, for good views of Gordes, then, take the chemin de Vaucluse back to Cabrières. Otherwise, retrace your footsteps back down to the village.*

FOS-SUR-MER ★

POPULATION 13 922

MICHELIN LOCAL MAP 340: E-5

Perched on a rocky outcrop, dominated by the ruins of its château, Fos evokes the typical idea of a Provençal village. It is named after the Fosses Mariennes, a canal dug at the mouth of the Rhône by Marius' legions in 102 BC (fosse: hole, pit, canal). The development of the new complex, the largest in southern Europe and which complements the port of Marseille, was begun in 1965 on the Golfe de Fos. The advantages of the site, some 10 000ha/24 700 acres, are a deep water channel, a low tidal range, and the extensive stony surface of the Plaine de la Crau that makes an ideal foundation on which to build an industrial estate.

Pl. de-l'hôtel-de-Ville, 13270 Fos-sur-Mer, ☎ 04 42 47 71 96. www.fos-tourisme.com.

Visit

The Village★

The village retains the ruins of its 14C castle, which once belonged to the Viscounts of Marseille, as well as the église St-Saveur, with its Romanesque nave. The chief attraction, however, lies in the views from the terrace and rampart garden.

The Port

With over 90 million metric tons of traffic per year, of which Fos handles two-thirds, the combined Marseille-Fos complex is the largest port in France and third in Europe.

*For a **boat tour**, contact the tourist office 10-15 days in advance.*

Excursions

Port-St-Louis-du-Rhône

▶*15km/10mi southwest.* A town and port have developed around the St-Louis tower, built to defend the mouth of the Grand Rhône in the 18C. The dock, constructed in 1863 and now part of the Marseille complex, is used both by seagoing ships and Rhône barges. Its lock and the large Fos-Rhône canal make it the key point for river and maritime-river traffic between Europe and the Mediterranean. It handles products as diverse as hydrocarbons, liquid chemicals, timber, and wine.

Port-de-Bouc
See Chaîne de l'ESTAQUE.

GORDES ★★

POPULATION 2 092

MICHELIN LOCAL MAP 332: E-10

The houses of Gordes rise in picturesque tiers above the Imergue valley on the edge of the Vaucluse plateau, facing the Luberon. The site was already occupied by humans as early back as the Neolithic era. The first inhabitants, the Vordeuses, a tribe of Celtic-Ligurian descent, named the city Vorda. Over the centuries this appellation underwent a number of phonetic changes to finally become Gordes. The site★ can best be seen from a rock platform (no barrier) about 1km/0.5mi from the village on the Cavaillon road, D 15.

Pl. du Château, 84220 Gordes, ☎ 04 90 72 02 75. www.gordes-village.com.

Visit

The Village★

It is pleasant to walk through this charming town along the *calades* – small paved, sometimes stepped alleyways lined with gutters defined by two rows of stone – with vaulted passageways, arcades of old, tall houses and rampart ruins. The shops, craft-shops and lively market add to the atmosphere.

For coin ranges see the Legend at the back of the guide.

EATING OUT

☺☺ **La Farigoule** – *Les Imberts (D 2, between Gordes and Cabrières-d'Avignon) - 84220 Gordes - 4 km from Gordes - ☎ 04 90 76 92 76 - lafarigoule@wanadoo.fr - closed Wed evening and Thu. Best to make reservations.* A beautiful covered terrace, this restaurant offers Provençal dishes that are really bursting with flavour, and at good prices.

WHERE TO STAY

☺☺☺ **Chambre d'hôte La Badelle** – *7km/4.3mi south of Gordes via D 104 for Goult – ☎ 04 90 72 33 19 - www.guideweb. com/provence/bb/badelle – closed Jan – 🍴 – reservation essential in winter – 5 rooms.* The outbuildings of this ancestral farm have been converted into bedrooms. They are pleasantly simple with antique furniture and terracotta floor tiles. There is a kitchen available for guests' use in the summertime.

☺☺☺ **Chambre d'hôte Le Mas de la Beaume** – *☎ 04 90 72 02 96 – www. guideweb.com/provence/bb/beaume – closed Jan and Feb – 🍴 – 5 rooms.* Peace, a view of the village of Go[...] song of cicadas will all se[...] dwellers! This Provençal [...] a garden with olive and almond trees, lavender and nice spacious rooms full of local colours. Swimming pool and Jacuzzi.

ON THE TOWN

Le Renaissance – *place du Château - ☎ 04 90 72 02 02 – daily 8am–midnight. Closed mid-Nov to mid-Feb.* This bar-restaurant-hotel has the benefit of a sunny terrace overlooking the streets of the historic centre of Gordes and the Renaissance castle in the square.

CRAFTS

Easter market – Easter weekend, the town turns into a big street market featuring arts and crafts.

Annie Sotinel – *Les Porquiers – route de Goult – ☎ 04 90 72 05 71.* Open in the afternoons and by appointment. Closed Jan. Textile designer and hand woven items.

EVENTS

Summer Festival – *Soirées – the first half of Aug: theatre, music, and dance.*

Château

🕐*10am-noon, 2-6pm.* 🚫*Closed 1 Jan and 25 Dec.* 💶*4€.* ☎ *04 90 72 02 75.*

The Renaissance château stands on the village's highest point. It was rebuilt by Bertrand de Simiane on the site of a 12C fortress. The north face flanked by round machicolated towers is austere, the south monumental, relieved by mullioned windows and small turrets. In the courtyard note the fine Renaissance door (the soft limestone has been worn away by erosion). Inside, in the great hall (first floor) two flanking doorways show off a splendid **chimney-piece**★ (1541) with ornate pediments and pilasters, shells and flowers. The three top floors of the château present a standing **exhibition** of works by the contemporary Flemish artist **Pol Mara**.

In the summer evenings in July and August plays and concerts are held in the courtyard of the castle.

Gordes

D. Pazery/MICHELIN

ve du palais Saint-Firmin

▶ *Access via place Genty-Pantaly, via the little rue de l'Élglise, then du Belvédère towards "point de vue."*

A visit to the cellars of this "mansion" reveals a little-known aspect of Gordes. Vast and vaulted and excuding a rather unreal atmosphere, the cellars contain cisterns, stairways, and the remains of an ancient oil mill, probably dating to the 15C and bearing witness to a trade practiced in Gordes centuries ago.

Les Bories to Sanctuaire de Répit

Round-trip of 12km/7.5mi – allow 2hr.

▶ *Leave Gordes on D 15 towards Cavaillon; just beyond the fork with D 2 turn right onto a tarred road which leads to a car park in the village.*

Abbaye de Senánque★★

⚓*See Abbaye de SENÁNQUE.*

Village des Bories★★

🕘*9am to dusk.* ⊘*Closed 1 Jan and 25 Dec.* 5.50P. ☎ *04 90 72 03 48.*

This village is now a Museum of Rural Life with 20 restored bories (⚓*see Montagne du LUBERON*) between 200 and 500 years old, grouped around a communal bread oven. The larger bories served as dwellings, the others were either sheep-folds or various outbuildings. They were inhabited until the early 19C but their origin and use remains something of a mystery: were they permanent or seasonal dwelling, or, were they used as refuges during troubled times?

Village des Bories

▶ *Return to D 2 and bear right; turn left on D 103 towards Beaumettes and left again onto D 148 towards St-Pantaléon; continue along this road about 100m/110yd to the place called Moulin des Bouillons.*

Moulin des Bouillons

♿ *Apr to Oct: daily except Tues 10am-noon, 2-6pm. 4.50€. ☎ 04 90 72 22 11.*

This bastide (16C-18C) has been transformed into a museum dedicated to the history of olive oil, and contains a remarkably large **olive press**★ made from a whole oak tree trunk weighing seven tonnes It is Gallo-Roman in appearance, and it is the oldest and the only one preserved with its tools. The history of lighting over the past 5 000 years is traced with the help of oil lamps, tools for the cultivation of olives, vessels, and weights and measures. The use of olive oil through the ages is also explained.

▶ *Continue along D 148 in the direction of St-Pantaléon.*

St-Pantaléon

The small village occupies a dominant position in the countryside. Its small Romanesque church is built out of the living rock and consists of three naves; the central part dates back to the 5C. Surrounding the church is a rock necropolis, or cemetery, most of the tombs of which are child-size. This necropolis was most likely a sanctuary of grace; there are other examples like it in Provence. Children who died before they were baptised were brought here by their parents; they revived – according to the beliefs of the period – for the duration of a mass during which they were baptised, they then died again and were buried here.

▶ *Leave St-Pantaléon from the north and join D 104A, then D 2 which returns to Gordes.*

Le GRAU-DU-ROI≗≗

POPULATION 5 253

MICHELIN MAP 339: J-7

This seaside resort was part of the town of Aigues-Mortes until 1879; it grew up around a pretty little port. This extends in part from an inland estuary or "grau" formed by a spate in the Rhône during the 16C (in Languedoc, grau designates an open breach in the offshore bar separating the lagoon from the sea). From the far end of the pier there is a view of the Grande-Motte pyramids, Boucanet beach and Port-Camargue. An 18km/11mi stretch of fine sandy beach runs past the resorts of Le Grau-du-Roi and Port-Camargue, which are equipped with a variety of sports facilities and attract many holiday-makers in the summer. For a break from driving, you may arrive from Nîmes on board an old-fashioned railcar travelling at a pleasant pace through the countryside dotted with lakes and ponds.

The Village

The grid-plan of low houses becomes a hive of activity in the summer months, with craft shops and restaurant, but the nerve-centre remains the canal, with its pontoons and old lighthouse, symbol of the town.

The Seaside

The Beaches

Between the Passe des Abymes and Les Baronnets stretch 18km/11mi of fine sand. A word of advice for bathers: swimming is better from the right bank of the canal (Le Boucanet) than the left.

Seaquarium et musée de la Mer

⚅ ⏱ *May to Sept: 9.30am-7pm (July and Aug: 10am-11pm); Oct to Apr: 10am-6pm. 8.38€ (children: 5.64€). ☎ 04 66 51 57 57.*
Access from boulevard du Front-de-Mer. Sharks and Mediterranean fish will entertain adults and children alike. The small museum is also worth a visit. It contains model boats, abandoned fishing nets as well as recounting the resort's history.

Port-Camargue

Via D 62B. Located between the fishing harbour and Point de l'Espiguette, the resort of Port-Camargue was created in 1969; it represents the farthermost eastern resort created in the development of the Languedoc-Roussillon coast, and has all the necessary facilities to house 4 300 boats. It is a good departure point for cruising along this coastline.

Looking for a pick-me-up? Try the special beauty and fitness treatments offered for men and women at **Thalassa Port-Camargue** in Port-Camargue *(Route des Marines, Plage Sud, ☎ 04 66 73 60 60).*

Grau-du-Roi, port

G. Magnin/MICHELIN

Address Book

EATING OUT

Le Chalut – *2 rue du Cdt Marceau* – ☎ *04 66 53 11 61 – closed 12 Nov-10 Dec, Sun evenings and Mon from Oct-Apr.* This restaurant is situated opposite a swing bridge and you will see trawlers and yachts pass before your eyes. Two attractive blue and yellow dining rooms on two levels. Needles to say seafood is very much in evidence here. Reasonable prices and a busy, small terrace.

L'Amarette – *Centre commercial Camargue 2000 – 30240 Port-Camargue – 3km/1.8mi south of Grau-du-Roi via D 62B –* ☎ *04 66 51 47 63 – closed Jan, Dec and Wed in low season.* This restaurant is situated on the first floor of a 1970s house. Seafood dishes can be enjoyed on the terrace which affords a good view of the coast.

WHERE TO STAY

Camping Le Boucanet – *route de la Grande-Motte – 1km/0.6mi northwest of Grau-du-Roi –* ☎ *04 66 51 41 48 – campingboucanetwanadoo.fr – open 29 Apr to Sept – booking recommended – 458 places.* For those who like to get their feet wet, some sites are 5m/16 feet from the sea! But the swimming pool also has a certain charm. Guaranteed relaxation for adults and children alike, tennis, windsurfing and entertainment for children. Mobile homes and bungalows can be rented.

Relais de l'Oustau Camarguen – *3 route des Marines – 30240 Port-Camargue – 3km/.8mi south of Grau-du-Roi via D 62B –* ☎ *04 66 51 51 65 – closed 15 Oct-29 Mars –* 🅿 *– 37 rooms –* ⌸ *8.38€ – restaurant 25.46€.* This Camargue style house is situated on the road to the southern beach. The spacious rooms are decorated in local style; some open out onto a small, private garden. There is a terrace for alfresco dining next to the swimming pool. Classic cooking, with grills at lunchtime. Turkish bath and spa.

ON THE TOWN

Maison Méditerranéenne des Vins et Produits Régionaux – *Domaine-de-l'Espiguette* – ☎ *04 66 51 52 16 – www.mdv30.com – mid-June to mid-Sept: 9am-1pm, 2.30-8pm. Low season: 9am-12.30pm, 2.30pm-6pm – closed 25 Dec and 1 Jan.* This spacious store is packed to the rafters with regional products to buy or taste: wines from Provence and Languedoc-Roussillon, olive oils, cooked dishes, honey and soaps.

Casino du Grau-du-Roi – *3 avenue du Ceinturion – Port Camargue –* ☎ *04 66 53 40 95 – www.groupetranchant.com – daily 10am-4am.* Two black-jacks, two English roulettes and many other machines are available for your entertainment, together with a disco and DJ and a bar-restaurant (cabaret dinner on Fri and musical spectacle Sat evenings and Sun afternoons).

Phare de l'Espiguette

6km/3.5mi south by a road from the roundabout at the entrance to Port-Camargue. Paying car park in summer.

The road, which passes between beaches and lakes, is a good place to discover a typical Camargue landscape, as well as to observe several species of bird *(observatory next to the Étang des Baronnets, opposite the Maison des vins du Domaine de l'Espiguette)*. The lighthouse which overlooks Point de l'Espiguette stands amid windswept dunes, where tamarisk, thistles, sea rockets and cakiles grow. The immense beaches are a haven for *naturistes* – that is people who prefer to bare it all.

GRIGNAN ★

POPULATION 1 300

MICHELIN MAP 332: C-7

Located on an isolated rocky hillock, the imposing château belonging to Adhémar de Monteil overlooks the old town of Tricastin and owes its fame to the delightful letters written in the late 17C by Mme de Sévigné to her daughter, Mme de Grignan.

Madame de Sévigné and Grignan

When Mme de Sévigné's daughter married the count of Grignan, Lieutenant-General of Provence in 1669, the girl's mother commented: "the prettiest girl in France is marrying not the most handsome of young men (the count was very ugly!) but one of the most honest in the kingdom". From that time onwards, she entered into a correspondence with her daughter which lasted 20 years, wherein she recounts with a keen eye and nice turn of phrase, life at the court of Louis XIV, Paris society, visits to the country and day-to-day domestic matters. Mme de Sévigné spent several long stays at the château. She enjoyed her visits and described the château as "very fine and magnificent", adding characteristically "one eats well and there are masses of visitors". She gives a mouthwatering description of how the partridges were fed on thyme, marjoram and other herbs to give them flavour, how the quail had fat and tender legs, the doves were succulent and the melons, figs and muscat grapes perfect. Although she admired the view from the terrace, she preferred the cool fragrance of the nearby grotto to write in; her only complaint was the mistral, which she viewed as a personal enemy, describing it as "'that bitter, freezing and cutting wind".

Mme de Sévigné died at the château in 1696 aged 69 from over-fatigue after nursing her sick daughter. She was buried in the château's chapel, but during the Revolution her head was dispatched to Paris for examination by avid phrenologists. It has since disappeared.

🏠 *Pl. Sévigné, 26230 Grignan,* ☎ *04 75 46 56 75.*

Grignan's Festival

Lovers and publishers of epistolary literature have elected Grignan as a place to hold the festival de la correspondance. The festival is held in July. *For information contact the Tourist office or www.festivalcorrespondance-grignan.com.*

Visit

Château★★

🕐 *Apr to Oct: guided tours (1hr) 9.30am-11.30am, 2-5.30pm (Jul and Aug: 6pm); Nov to Mar: daily except Tues 9.30-11.30am, 2-5.30pm.* 🕐*Closed 1 Jan and 25 Dec. 4.57€.* ☎ *04 75 46 51 56.*

The medieval castle was remodelled in the 16C by Louis Adhémar, governor of the Galleys of Provence, and from 1668 to 1690 by François de Castellane-Adhémar, Mme de Sévigné's son-in-law.

The Renaissance south façade (restored in 1913) overlooks the garden in the lower courtyard. The Well Court opens onto a terrace enclosed by a transitional Gothic gallery on the left and by Renaissance wings on the right and at the far end.

The great staircase, the drawing-rooms, the audience chamber, the Count of Grignan's apartments, Mme de Sévigné's bedroom and dressing room, the chapel, the Gothic staircase and the panelled Adhémar gallery are also open.

The **furnishings**★ recreate past settings: Louis XIII furniture, Italian writing desk in the audience chamber; Régence style and Louis XV period furnishings in the Grignans' apartments where the parquet flooring is lovely. The walls are hung with Aubusson tapestries (17C mythological scene).

Église St-Sauveur

Jan, Easter Monday and during the summer: organ concerts; Christmas: "Grignan" animated Provençal crib. Contact the tourist office

16C. Inside, the features of interest are the small gallery beneath the roof which connected directly to the castle; 17C **organ loft**, 17C altarpiece and fine chancel panelling. On the north side is the marble funerary stone to Mme de Sévigné.

From the terrace of the church, there is a vast **panorama**★ including the long ridge of the Lance, Mont Ventoux and the Dentelles de Montmirail, the Comtat Venaissin plain, the Alpilles, Grignan woods and the Vivarais mountains.

Beffroi

The belfry, the 12C town gateway, was transformed in the 17C into a clock tower.

Grotte de Rochecourbière

1km/0.5mi. Take D 541 south out of Grignan, at a Calvary take the road that branches off; after about 1km/0.5mi from D 541 park the car and walk back to the stone steps on the right.

WHERE TO EAT

🍽🍽 **Le Relais de Grignan** – *1km/0.6mi west of Grignan on D 541* – ☎ *04 75 46 57 22 – closed Wed evening from Sept-June, Sun evening and Mon.* This is a large, low house built alongside an olive grove with an attractive terrace under the trees. If you come here in the winter you will almost certainly eat truffles.

Le château de Grignan

This grotto was one of Mme de Sévigné's favourite places, where she loved to sit and write.

Excursion

Taulignan

7km/4mi northwest on D 14 and D 24. On the boundary between Dauphiné and Provence, this old agricultural town remains ensconced within its medieval fortifications. An almost uninterrupted circle, it has preserved 11 towers (nine round and two square) joined by a curtain wall (machicolations remain in several places), into which dwellings are integrated.

Walk along the old streets and admire the ancient façades with their ogee-arched doorways and mullioned windows (rue des Fontaines) and go through (to the northeast) Porte d'Anguille, the only fortified gate flanked by two towers still standing.

L'ISLE-SUR-LA-SORGUE

POPULATION 15 564

MICHELIN MAP 332: D-10

L'Isle-sur-la-Sorgue is set at the foot of the Plateau de Vaucluse. The branches of the River Sorgue and the avenues lined with plane trees add freshness to this charming site, which is particularly popular among antique dealers. For a long time the town was a very active industrial centre: weaving, dyeing, tanning as well as paper, grain and oil mills flourished; some 10 wheels set the beat of this bustling town. The town is also the birthplace of the poet René Char (1907-1988).

Sights

Roues à eau

Near place Gambetta at the corner of the Caisse d'Épargne's garden is a wheel, similar to those which worked the silk factories and oil mills. Seven other old water wheels still exist: one in place Émile-Char, two others in boulevard Victor-Hugo, three in rue Jean-Théophile and one in quai des Lices.

Collégiale Notre-Dame-des-Anges

Unaccompanied visits on weekdays only. 10am-noon, 3-5pm (6pm in summer). Contact the presbytery. ☎ 04 90 38 03 26.

The fascinating interior catches the attention on account of the ornate 17C decorationa, recalling Italian church interiors. The single nave is adorned on the back of the west face with an immense gilded wooden glory attributed to Jean Péru, as are the figures of the Virtues placed in the spandrels underneath the balustrades. The side chapels are decorated with fine woodwork and paintings by Mignard, Sauvan, Simon Vouet and Parrocel. In the chancel a large altarpiece frames a work by Reynaud Levieux representing the Assumption.

Hôtel Donadeï de Campredon (Centre Xavier-Battini)

&. ⏱ *Jul to mid-Oct: daily except Mon 10am-1pm, 3-6.30pm; mid-Oct to mid-Jun: 9.30am-noon, 2-6pm. Open for exhibitions only (enquire), 1 Jan and 25 Dec. 5.34€ (children: no charge).* ☎ *04 90 38 17 41.*
This lovely 18C mansion is a good example of the French classical style. Its renovated rooms are used for cultural events and are well-suited for housing interesting temporary exhibitions.

Hôpital

⏱ *Closed for renovation work.*
The hospital's entrance is on rue Jean-Théophile parallel to a branch of the River Sorgue. Admire in the hall the gilded wooden Virgin, the grand staircase,

---

Address Book

SHOPPING

Meubles Bonjean – *route de l'Isle-sur-la-Sorgue, 84250 Le Thor* - ☎ *04 90 33 89 54. Visit the workshop during the week:* ☎ *04 90 33 82 94. Daily except Mon and Sun, 2-7pm.* Manufacture of furniture of different styles, specialising in Provençal walnut pieces.

Le Village des Antiquaires – *2 bis avenue de l'Égalité* - ☎ *04 90 38 04 57 - www.villagegare.com - weekends and public holidays 10am-7pm.* This is one of the most important antique centres: 80 dealers grouped together in an old weaving factory.

Antique fairs – There is an antiques fair on Easter weekend, and one in mid-August.

EATING OUT

👄👄 **Le Carré d'Herbes** – *13 avenue des Quatre-Otages* – ☎ *04 90 38 62 95 – www.carredherbes.com – closed Jan, Tues and Wed except July-Aug.* This small restaurant is located in a courtyard surrounded by antique shops. It is unusually decorated with red walls, an oxidized metal ceiling, wooden seats and a terrace in the aviary. Provençal specialities on the menu.

👄👄 **L'Oustau de l'Isle** – *21 avenue des Quatre-Otages* – ☎ *04 90 38 54 84 – closed Jan-end Feb, 7-14 June, 14-21 Oct, Thu except evenings in Jul-Aug.* A stone's throw from the old town, this restaurant reflects the colours and flavours of Provence: painted furniture, brightly coloured tablecloths and southern-influenced dishes.

WHERE TO STAY

👄👄 **Chambre d'hôte Le Mas de la Coudoulière** – *1854 route de Carpentras –* 2km/1.2mi north of Isle-sur-la-Sorgue via D 938 for Carpentras – ☎ *04 90 38 16 35 – avignon-et-provence.com/mas-coudouliere/ – closed Nov – 6 rooms – evening meal 29€.* This hotel is situated in what was originally a 17C monastery that used to grow hemp and madder. Rooms have been decorated in the spirit of bygone times. The evening meal is served in the vaulted dining room or under the hundred-year-old chestnut tree in the summertime. Self-contained accommodation is also available.

ON THE TOWN

Au Rendez-vous des Marchands – *91 avenue de la Libération* – ☎ *04 90 20 84 60 – daily 10am-1.30am except Tues.* Is this an antique shop in a café or a café in an antique shop? It is hard to say where one ends and the other begins: what is certain is that this place is full of originality and charm. Terrace bordering the Sorgue.

Le Caveau de la Tour de l'Isle – *12 rue de la République* - ☎ *04 90 20 70 25 – Tues-Sat 9am-1pm, 3-8.30pm except Sun 9am-1pm. July-Aug: same hours, Mon-Sat.* This wine cellar has a pleasant aroma of Spanish bodegas. Behind the counter there is a tasting room where one can sample and buy over 120 wines, many of which are local.

Café de France – *14 place de la Liberté* - ☎ *04 90 38 01 45 – daily 7am-1.30am.* Don't miss the opportunity of enjoying this terrace, beautifully situated opposite the fine façade of the collegiate church of Notre-Dame-des-Anges (17C). This delightful café is also keen on philosophy (philosophy café on the first Sunday of the month) and music (concerts on Wednesday in the summer and in winter one Friday a month).

embellished by an 18C wrought-iron banister, a chapel with 18C woodwork, and pharmacy with Moustiers faience pottery jars and a huge 17C mortar. An additional attraction is the peaceful garden, ornamented by an 18C fountain.

Excursion

Le Thor

5km/3.1mi west along N 100 for Avignon. Once the capital of the white dessert grape, Chasselas, Le Thor has diversified its agricultural activities to include market gardening and tree and shrub growing. The bridge over the Sorgue, the church and its precinct create a picturesque scene. Remaining from the Middle Ages are the ruins of the ramparts and the belfry.

Water wheel

Church (Église)★

🕐*Daily 9.30am-noon. Guided tours possible, ask at the Tourist Office.*

Completed in the early 13C, the church as a whole is Romanesque in style, yet its single nave is covered with Gothic vaulting which counts among the most ancient in Provence. The exterior is imposing with its massive buttresses supporting the tall nave, its apse adorned with Lombard arcades and its heavy unfinished central bell tower. The doors were directly inspired by Antique art, particularly the south door.

Grotte de Thouzon

🕐*Apr to All Saints: guided tours (45min) 10am-noon, 2-6pm (Jul and Aug: 10am-7pm); Mar: Sun and public holidays 2-6pm. 6.10€ (children: 3.96€). ☎ 04 90 33 93 65.*

3km/2mi to the north; the trail to the cave branches left off D 16. The cave opens at the foot of the hill crowned by the ruins of Thouzon castle and a monastery. It was discovered in 1902 by chance after a blast on the site of a former quarry. The visitor walks 230m/755ft along the bed of the old underground river, which carved this gallery, to a not very deep chasm. On the cave roof, which rises to 22m/72ft, are delicate stalactites of rare quality. In addition the cave presents oddly-shaped, beautifully-coloured concretions.

LABEAUME★

POPULATION 455

MICHELIN MAP 331: H-7

When seen from afar, the old village situated on the bank of the gorges of the Beaume, a tributary of the Ardèche, merges almost totally into the rock face.

Visit

The Village

Leave the car on the large square at the village's entrance and enjoy a pleasant stroll along the steep streets, admiring the covered passageways and balconied houses, some of which have been restored by artists. To the left of the church, with its very high belfry-porch (19C) resting on two large round columns, take an alleyway which ends at the river bank and a shaded esplanade. For a better overall view of the village cross the low level bridge, with no parapet walls, and follow the uphill path for a couple of hundred yards.

Gorges de la Beaume★

The walk upstream along the river's north bank, beside the clear waters, across from the fascinating eroded limestone cliff, is worthwhile.

Excursions *11km/7mi – allow 1 hr.*

▶ *Leave Labeaume on D 245, then turn left onto D 4.*

Défilé de Ruoms★

The road goes through picturesque rock tunnels and affords plunging views of the river with its clear green waters. Following the Ruoms defile are the Ligne gorges; from the confluence of the two rivers (Ardèche and Ligne), framed by 100m/329ft high cliffs striped by the rock strata, there is a good view upstream. On the return trip, at the end of the tunnels, the silhouette of Rocher de Sampzon appears at the end of the valley.

▶ *Cross the Ardèche towards Ruoms.*

Ruoms

The old walled centre of the small commercial town lies within a quadrilateral of ramparts flanked by seven round towers. At the heart of the old town is a small Romanesque church with an unusual arcaded belfry faced with motifs worked in volcanic rock. The view is best from Ruelle St-Roch opening onto the parvis.
Leave Ruoms on D 579 towards Vallon, then turn right along the narrow D 161, which winds upwards towards Sampzon after crossing the Ardèche. Park below the old village church.

Rocher de Sampzon★

(45min return), first by the tarred path and then by the path level with the turning place.

From the summit (television relay mast) there is a panorama including the Vallon basin, the Orgnac plateau and the meanders of the Ardèche.

Le LUBERON★★★

MICHELIN MAP 332: E-11 TO G 11

Midway between the Alps and the Mediterranean lies the mountainous Luberon range. This region is full of charm: striking solitary woods and rocky countryside and picturesque, old hill-top villages and dry-stone huts.

Geological Notes

Natural Habitat

The Montagne du Luberon is a gigantic anticlinal fold of calcareous rock of the Tertiary Era running east-west. The range is divided from north to south by the Lourmarin coomb into two unequal parts: to the west the Petit Luberon forms a plateau carved by gorges and ravines where the altitude rarely exceeds 700m/2 297ft; whereas to the east, the massive summits of the Grand Luberon rise up to 1 125m/3 691ft at Mourre Nègre.
The contrast between the north and south slopes is no less great. The northern face, steep and ravined, is cooler, more humid and wears a fine forest of downy oaks. The southern face, turned towards Aix, is more Mediterranean in its vegetation (oak groves, rosemary-filled garrigues), and with its sunny slopes, crops and cypresses, announces the delightful countryside along the River Durance.
The diversity of the vegetation is a delight to nature lovers: oak forests, Atlas cedar (planted in 1862) on the heights of the Petit Luberon, beech, Scots pine, moors of broom and boxwood, *garrigues*, an extraordinary variety of aromatic plants (herbs of Provence) clinging here and there to the rocky slopes. The *mistral* contributes, provoking unusual local changes: holm oaks are blown onto the northern exposed slopes and downy oaks onto the southern exposed slopes. In winter the contrast between the evergreens and deciduous trees is striking. The fauna is equally rich: snakes (seven different varieties), lizards, warblers, blue rock thrushes, owls and eagles.

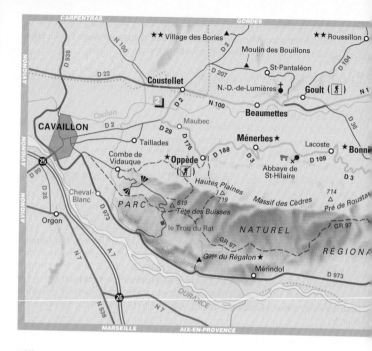

Hilltop Villages

The Luberon has been inhabited by man since prehistoric times. Villages appeared during the Middle Ages, clinging to the rock face near a water hole. The tall houses with their imposing walls huddled close together at the foot of a castle or church; most of them had rooms cut out of the rock. The men left their homes to work in the surrounding countryside and when necessary they lived in dry-stone huts called *bories (see below)*. Their livelihood was obtained mostly from sheep, olives, grain and vineyards as well as lavender and silkworms. Each parcel of cultivated land was carefully cleared of stones – the stones were grouped into piles called *clapiers* – and bordered by low walls which served to protect the land from soil erosion. The flocks were also contained within a close of dry stone. Traces of these arrangements are still visible in the rural landscape. This traditional economy was swept away by the agricultural improvements of the 19C and 20C: villages lost their inhabitants and fell into ruins. Nowadays, the trend is reversing itself; village populations are increasing at an almost constant rate, and the villages themselves have been well restored.

Bories

On the slopes of the Luberon and the Vaucluse plateau stand these curious dry stone huts, one or two floors high, called *bories*. They are either alone or in groups forming

Parc naturel régional du Luberon

Founded in 1977, the regional nature park includes 60 communes covering 165 000ha/396 000 acres including the *départements* of Vaucluse and Alpes-de-Haute-Provence (that is, from Manosque to Cavaillon and the Coulon – or Calavon – valley to the Durance). Its goal is to preserve the natural balance of the region with the aim of improving the living conditions of the village folk, the promotion of agricultural activity through irrigation, mechanisation and the reorganisation of the holdings. The main developments in the tourist industry are the opening of Tourist Information Offices and museums at Apt, Buoux and La Tour-d'Aigues, and the creation of nature trails (through the cedar forest at Bonnieux,
the ochre cliffs of Roussillon, the Viens *bories* and the cultivation terraces at Goult, as well as thematic tourist routes such as the "Route de Vaudois." It also produces attractive publications.

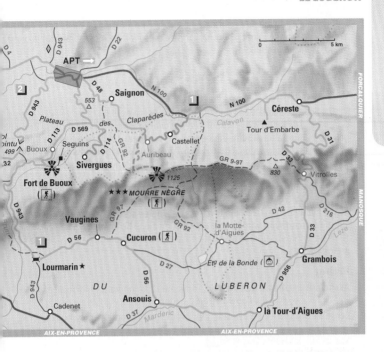

a very picturesque unit; there are about 3 000 of them. They were sometimes just tool sheds or sheep pens but many were inhabited over the different periods from the Iron Age until the 18C for the most recent, which in fact are better constructed. The *bories* were built with materials found on the spot: thin slabs of limestone which have become detached from the rock, or slabs picked when clearing the fields. These stones called *lauzes* are on average 10cm/3.75in thick. Specialised *masons* knew how to select the *lauzes* and assemble them without either mortar or water. The thickness of the walls obtained by the juxtaposition of several rows of slabs varied from 0.80m/31.5in to 1.60m/4.5ft; it was always reinforced at the base. The bonding whether from the outside or inside was remarkably regular. The technique used for the roofing of the *borie* consisted of a type of false corbelled vaulting. As the walls were raised, each stone course was carefully made to overhang the preceding one, so that at a height of 3 or 4m/10 to 13ft – the diameter diminished to the point of being reduced to a small opening which could be closed simply by placing one slab. To avoid the infiltration of water the different layers of stone were slightly inclined towards the exterior.

Inside, the vaulting appeared as a hemispheric dome on pendentives which allowed the plan to pass from a square or a circle or a cone. The *bories* offered a variety of forms. The simplest, round, ovoid or square, consisted of one room and one open-ing set east or southeast. The interior arrangement was rudimentary, lim-ited to hollow niches used for stor-age. The temperature of the *borie* remained constant whatever the season. Larger dwellings exist, espe-cially at Gordes. They are rectangular, with a few narrow openings, and the roof had double or quadruple pitch using the technique of false vaulting either rounded, pointed barrel or an inverted ship's hull (Gordes). Their organisation was similar to that of

Bories

a traditional farm: disposed around a courtyard encircled by a high wall were the living quarters (tiled floors, benches, and chimney for the most comfortable ones), bread oven and outbuildings.

Activities in the Park

Walking/Hiking

🚶 The French National Rambling Federation issues two guides called *Tour du Luberon, GR 9*, and *20 Ballades dans le Parc naturel régional du Luberon*. The Maison du Parc will give you information about guided walks 👣 *(free of charge)* as well as bed and breakfast accommodation. There is also a guidebook for footpaths in the region.

Cycling

The Maison du Parc has created a route especially for cyclists, stretching from Cavaillon to Forcalquier (around 100km/62mi): signposts have been set up at all main crossroads (white heading from Cavaillon towards Forcalquier, ochre in the opposite direction); additional road signs with further information are to be found in 25 nearby villages. The Vélo-loisirs en Luberon association has indicated accommodation where cyclists are welcomed.

Flying

Association vélivole du Luberon, *26 avenue de la Fontaine, 13370 Mallemort, ☎ 04 90 57 43 86*. Admire the Luberon from a glider.

École de Rustrel – *84400 Rustrel – ☎ 04 90 04 42 00*. Paragliding school.

Grand Luberon ★★ 1

Round-trip from Apt – 119km/74mi – allow half a day (not including climb to Mourre Nègre)

▶ *Leave Apt on D 48 going southeast on Avenue de Saignon.*

As the road climbs, the hill-top site of Saignon, Apt basin, Vaucluse plateau and Mont Ventoux come into view.

Saignon

The village, close to a tall rock, contains a Romanesque church with a west front rebuilt in the 16C to include beautiful, trilobed blind arcading.

▶ *Continue along D 48.*

The road skirts Claparèdes plateau with its scattered bories.

▶ *Leave the car at Auribeau; exit from town northwards and bear left on the unsurfaced road towards Mourre Nègre. The GR 92 leads to the summit.*

Mourre Nègre ★★★

🚶 *Half a day return on foot*. Mourre Nègre at 1 125m/3 691ft is the highest point of the Montagne du Luberon. The **panorama** ★★★ embraces four points of the compass: the Montagne de Lure and Digne pre-Alps (northeast), the Durance valley with Montagne Ste-Victoire in the background (southeast), Étang de Berre and the Alpilles (southwest), Apt basin, Vaucluse plateau and Mont Ventoux (northwest).

▶ *Return to D 48 and continue through Auribeau.*

Castellet

The tiny terraced hamlet is now a lavender distillery centre. The road crosses a garrigues landscape before reaching the Calavon valley.

▶ *Turn right on N 100. After crossing the River Calavon follow a small road on the right for 2km/1mi.*

Tour d'Embarbe

This tower dates from the 12C and presents a practically blind façade with only a few arrow slits along its spiral staircase.

Céreste

This old Roman village was on the Domitian Way, which linked Italy to the Rhône delta at the time of the Romans. The village still has some of its fortifications and constitutes a lovely architectural unit. The surrounding earth is rich in remarkable fossils (fish, plants) which have formed in the calcareous strata.

LE LUBERON

▷ *Leave Céreste in the direction of Forcalquier and turn left into avenue du Pont-Romain.*

The so-called Roman bridge, which is in fact medieval, can be seen on the right, spanning the River Encrème. The Nid d'amour or Love Nest (below the village near to the Encrème) is a curious fountain-tank beneath a stone vault, fed by two streams gushing from the rock and extended by a pool corbelled into the rock.

Follow the small road, keeping closely to the right, as it crosses the first foothills of the Vaucluse plateau. After 3.5km/2.2 mi, turn left into a road downhill.

Prieuré de Carluc

🕑*Visits by appointment only, all year round (Jul: 3-7.30pm). 1.52€. ☎ 04 42 54 22 70.*

The remains of the 12C priory of Carluc, dependent on the Abbaye de Montmajour, are tucked at the bottom of a peaceful little valley. A gallery cut into the rock opens from the north side of the church. Tombs in the shape of human figures and benches are visible on the ground. This gallery once led to a second church; the part hollowed out of the rock is all that now remains of this.

▷ *Return to Céreste and take D 31 to the left.*

The road winds up the north slope of the Grand Luberon offering lovely views over the Calavon valley to the Vaucluse plateau. The road then descends the southern slope passing through Vitrolles down onto the plain; via D 42; just before St-Martin-de-la-Brasque, continue along D 27, which skirts the Étang de la Bonde.

Cucuron

Museum – 10am-noon (by appointment), 2-7pm. No charge. ☎ 04 90 77 25 02.

Inside the church are a multicoloured marble pulpit and a 16C painted wood Christ Seated and Chained in the baptismal chapel. Opposite the church, on the first floor of the 17C Hôtel de Bouliers is a small museum: the **musée archéologique Marc Deydier** which is dedicated to prehistory, Gallo-Roman period, and later local traditions. From the terrace below the keep, there is a fine view over the Cucuron basin to Montagne Ste-Victoire on the horizon.

▷ *Leave Cucuron on D 56 going southeast.*

Ansouis

♿ *See ANSOUIS.*

▷ *Leave Ansouis on D 135 and turn right onto D 45 and then immediately left onto D 27.*

Lourmarin★

17 avenue Philippe-de-Girard – 84160 – ☎ 04 90 68 10 77

This village at the foot of the Montagne du Luberon is dominated by its château built high on a rock bluff. **Albert Camus** (1913-60), the author of L'Étranger (The Stranger) and La Peste (The Plague), is buried in the cemetery, together with the author **Henri Bosco** (1888-1976).

Château

Address Book

EATING OUT

L'Auberge du Cheval Blanc – *La Canebière – 84460 Cheval-Blanc – 5km/3.1mi from Cavaillon –* ☎ *04 32 50 18 55 –* . This unassuming roadside inn is a pleasant place to stop and eat. The sunny-coloured dining room is completely new. The cooking is classic, with some Provençal flavours.

La Table des Mamées – *1 rue du Mûrier – 84360 Lauris – 4.5km/2.8mi southwest of Lourmarin on D 27 –* ☎ *04 90 08 34 66 – closed 15 Nov-15 Dec and Mon – booking recommended.* In this village restaurant culinary traditions handed down by generations of women are cultivated with true passion. Grandmother's recipes can be enjoyed by guests eating in the 14C and 15C vaulted dining rooms. Musical evenings at weekends have a wonderful atmosphere.

Maison Gouin – *84660 Coustellet – 7km/4.4mi northwest of Ménerbes via D 103 and N 100 –* ☎ *04 90 76 90 18 – closed 15 Feb-10 Mar, 15 Nov-10 Dec, Tue evening from Oct to Mar and Wed.* Tables are laid out in the back room of a butcher's shop here! Run by the same family since 1928, the shop extends into a dining room and a terrace. Cooking based on fresh market produce, with wines that you select yourself from the cellar. An unusual place.

WHERE TO STAY

Hôtel L'Aiguebelle – *place de la République – 04280 Céreste –* ☎ *04 92 79 00 91 – closed 16 Nov-14 Feb and Mon except July-Aug – 17 rooms –* 5.79€ – *restaurant 13.57/33.54€.* Before or after visiting the medieval ruins, take a break in this unpretentious hotel in the heart of the village. Rooms are simple and bright. Simple local cooking which is both tasty and very reasonably priced.

Chambre d'hôte La Maison des Sources – *Chemin des Fraisses – 84360 Lauris – 4.5km/2.8mi southwest of Lourmarin via D 27 –* ☎ *04 90 08 22 19 –* – *4 rooms – evening meal 21.34€.* Standing against a cliff which shows traces of a cave dwellers' settlement, this renovated farmhouse has limewashed rooms. One very original room has four four-poster beds. Downstairs two vaulted rooms serve as a drawing room and dining room.

Hôtel L'Oustau dï Vins – *La Font du Pin – 84460 Cheval-Blanc – 7km/4.4mi west of Mérindol, Cavaillon road –* ☎ *04 90 72 90 90 –* – *6 rooms –* 7.50€. Situated in 20ha/49 acres of wooded land at the foot of the Luberon mountain, this well-restored old farm has pretty, ochre-coloured Provençal style rooms, all with a personalised decor. Attractive stove and wrought-iron furniture in the breakfast room. The wine-producing owner will help you discover the wines of the region. Swimming pool.

Chambre d'hôte Les Grandes Garrigues – *84160 Vaugines – 3km/1.8mi west of Cucuron via D 56 and D 45 (Cadenet road) –* ☎ *04 90 77 10 71 –* – *5 rooms – evening meal 20€.* Situated in 11ha/27 acres of land at the foot of the Luberon, this is a fine ochre-coloured building with comfortable rooms. From Easter to September guests can also have meals which are eaten outside facing the Alpilles and the St Victoire mountain.

Chambre d'hôte Domaine de Layaude Basse – *Chemin de St-Jean – 84480 Lacoste – 1.5km/0.9mi north of Lacoste towards Roussillon and a secondary road –* ☎ *04 90 75 90 06 – www.luberon-news.com/domaine-layaude – closed 1 Dec-1 Mar –* – *6 rooms – evening meal 22.90€.* Situated in the heart of a wine-producing property facing Mount Ventoux, your hosts will put you up in the pretty rooms of this cosy 18C mas. Meals are accompanied by wines produced on the estate while homemade honey and jams are available with your morning toast.

Château★

July and Aug: (every 30min) 10-11.30am, 3-6pm; May, June and Sept: at 10am, 11am, 2.30pm, 3.30pm, 4.30pm and 5.30pm; Oct to Dec and Feb to Apr: at 11am, 2.30pm, 3.30pm and 4.30pm. ◯*Closed Jan except Sat-Sun and 25 Dec. 4.57€.* ☎ *04 90 68 15 23.*

The château is partly 15C and partly Renaissance. The Renaissance wing has remarkable stylistic unity and contains large chimney-pieces ornamented with caryatids or Corinthian columns. The grand staircase ends dramatically with a slender pillar supporting a stone cupola. The château offers a lovely view of the Durance valley and the olive grove lying within the grounds. The 15C wing, which now houses the library and students' quarters, overlooks pretty stone or wood arcades.

▶ *D 943 travels northwest up the Lourmarin coomb.*

The River Aigue Brun has cut narrow gorges through the rock. The road goes through a children's holiday camp (16C-18C château) before crossing a bridge and reaching a group of houses.

▶ *Just before these houses turn right onto the narrow path (car park).*

Fort de Buoux

🕐 *From dawn to dusk. 2.29€.* ☎ *04 90 74 25 75.*
30min return on foot, plus 45min tour. Go through the gate and follow the path beneath a vertical rock wall to the porter's lodge.

The rock spur on which the fort stands is a natural defence which has, in succession, been occupied by Ligurians, Romans, Catholics and Protestants. Louis XIV ordered its demolition in 1660; there nevertheless remain three defensive walls, a Romanesque chapel, houses, silos hewn out of the rock, a keep, a Ligurian sacrificial altar and a concealed staircase. From the rock spur, where a medieval keep once stood, there is a fine view of the Upper Aigue Brun valley.

▶ *Return to the holiday camp and turn right onto D 113.*

Beyond Buoux village the road returns to Apt along a picturesque route.

Petit Luberon ★ 2
Round-trip from Apt – 101km/62.5mi – about 6hr

▶ *Leave Apt by D 943 and turn right immediately onto D 3, which winds through vineyards.*

Bonnieux★

👣*See BONNIEUX.*

▶ *Leave Bonnieux south on D 3 then bear left on D 109.*

The road winds along the slope of the Petit Luberon; pause and look back for a pretty view of Bonnieux.

Lacoste

Abbaye de St-Hilaire – ¤10144089am-7pm (winter: 10am-6pm). No charge.

This hill-top village has a small, elegant 17C belfry and is dominated by the imposing ruins (partially rebuilt) of a château which belonged to the Sade family and included 42 rooms. The **Marquis de Sade** (1740-1814), author of erotic works, was the lord of Lacoste for some 30 years. He was extremely fond of the stage and gave orders to build an extravagant, luxurious theatre that could accommodate over 100 people. Condemned several times, he escaped and hid here; but in 1778 he was caught and imprisoned. His château was wrecked during the Revolution.

▶ *Continue to Ménerbes via D 109; note the quarries which extract a well-known freestone in the area near Lacoste.*

Abbaye de St-Hilaire

Located on a pretty site facing the Luberon, this former monastery (now private property) was occupied by the Carmelites from the 13C to the 18C. It retains three chapels, from the 12C, 13C (broken barrel vault) and 14C respectively, in addition to the monastic buildings from the 17C.

Ménerbes★

👣*See MÉNERBES.*

▶ *Go south along D 3 and then take D 188.*

Oppède-le-Vieux★

Leave the car in the car park just after the village, to explore it on foot. The terraced **site**★ of the village on its picturesque rocky spur, once partially abandoned, has come to life again through its careful restoration by numerous artists and writers. An old gateway in the walls leads from the old village square to the upper village, crowned by its 13C collegiate church and ruined castle (founded by the counts of Toulouse and rebuilt in the 15C and 16C). The fine **view**★ from the church terrace is of the Coulon valley and Vaucluse plateau, Ménerbes and, from the rear of the castle, of the ravined north face of the Luberon.

▶ *Cross the Maubec wine region (D 176, D 29) and bear right on D 2.*

▶ *Turn left instead of right onto D 2 and, on leaving Robion, bear left on D 31 to the intersection with the Vidauque road, which you take to the left.*

This very steep winding road (one-way road; speed limit 30kph/20mph), skirts the wild Vidauque coomb and offers magnificent plunging **views**★★ of the surrounding countryside: tip of Vaucluse plateau and Coulon valley (north), Alpilles and Durance valley (south and west), and below, Cavaillon plain with its market-gardens hemmed in by cypresses and reeds.

▷ *The road branches off to the right on the so-called Trou-du-Rat road leading to D 973 which you take to the right in the direction of Cavaillon. Here, turn right to rejoin the D2.*

Coustellet

The **Musée de la Lavande** (on the right on the Gordes road) has a collection of old copper stills (♿☉ *open 10am-noon, 2-6pm, Jun to Sept until 7pm).* ☉*Closed Jan and Feb. 2.29€. ☎ 04 90 76 91 23).* Products on sale are made from lavender grown at the Château du Bois in the commune of Lagarde d'Apt.

▷ *3km/2mi after Coustellet bear right on D 207 towards Moulin des Bouillons.*

Musée du Moulin des Bouillons

♨*See GORDES Excursions.*

St-Pantaléon

♨*See GORDES: Excursions.*

▷ *D 104 and D 60 to the right lead to Goult.*

Goult

This hilltop village, dominated by a castle and a windmill, houses the "**conservatoire des terrasses**" which aims to preserve and enhance a building method which uses dry stone, which made construction on irregular land possible.

Notre-Dame-de-Lumières

A large ex-voto collection is on display in these convent buildings which stand in a fine park.

▷ *N 100 returns to Apt, climbing the Coulon valley. On the left is ochre country.*

MARSEILLE★★★

POP 800 550

MICHELIN MAP 340: H-6

Twenty-six centuries of history have contributed to making Marseille the oldest of the great French cities. Jealous of its independence, the city has always struck out on its own, resulting in its isolation from the regional and national community until the 19C. Even nowadays, although proud of being the second most populated city in France, it has retained its own distinct character: a combination of authenticity and hardworn clichés. The distinctive local dialect, the cries of the fishmongers on the Vieux Port or of the boule players, but also shady judicial proceedings combine to create the soul of Marseille. And yet it does not survive on its folklore, it is a city which has progressed with the times: modernising constantly and developing ambitious projects, especially cultural ones (a dozen museums to which have been added the Vieille Charité cultural centre, the Opera, the Criée theatre, the dynamic Luminy School of Art, a group of young artists, etc). 🚹 4 La-Canebière, 13001 Marseille, ☎ 04 91 13 89 00. www.marseille-tourisme.com.

▶ **Orient Yourself:** For an overview of the city, take the histobus or the tourist train (see Address Book). Use the map in this chapter to orient yourself to the various partss of Marseille.

All streets lead to the old port where visitors tend to congregate. Here the many cafés and restaurants offer bouillabaisse and other fish specialities. The water of the port almost disappears under the forest of masts belonging to the pleasure boats; occasionally warships tower above the **quai des Belges**, the liveliest of the quays, where a small **fish market** is held every morning, a scene enhanced by the thick Marseille accent of the locals. Excursion boats leave from here and the picturesque **ferry-boat** described by Pagnol in his novel *César* still plies the harbour waters between quai du Port and quai de Rive-Neuve.

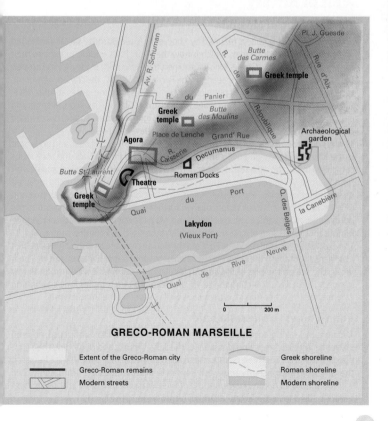

GRECO-ROMAN MARSEILLE

Extent of the Greco-Roman city	Greek shoreline
Greco-Roman remains	Roman shoreline
Modern streets	Modern shoreline

Marseille, Fort St-Jean and Cathédrale de la Major

Shopping: The rue St-Ferréol is the main pedestrian-only shopping street of the city; here you'll find the fashion boutiques, shoe shops, record stores and fast-food outlets are concentrated, as well as major stores such as Galleries Lafayette.

Parking: Like in any big city, finding a parking space is usually a problem. Consider taking the metro, the most convenient method of transport *(see Address Book)*.

Don't Miss: Admire the unique **site**★★★ on which the city was built. Notre-Dame-de-la-Garde is the best viewpoint and from the parvis and the area near the basilica, a splendid **panorama**★★★ extends over the roofs of the city, the harbour and the surrounding mountains. On the left rise Pomègues and Ratonneau islands, Château d'If and in the distance the Massif de Marseilleveyre; opposite is the port overlooked by Fort St-Jean (14C-17C) with Parc du Pharo in the foreground, farther to the right the city, and in the background, the Chaîne de l'Estaque with the Chaîne de l'Étoile in the distance.

A Bit of History

The founding of Massalia

Around 600 BC a few galleys manned by Phocaeans (Greeks from Asia Minor) landed on the coast in Lacydon creek, which is now the Vieux Port, hoping to expand their commercial activity. The Greeks, who were expert traders, quickly made the city prosperous. After the defeat of the Phocaeans by the Persians in 540 BC, the city became home to several different colonies of people. They set up busy trading-posts at Arles, Nice, Antibes, Agde, Le Brusc, the Hyères islands, and inland at Glanon, Cavaillon, Avignon and perhaps St-Blaise on Étang de Berre. With the Celtic-Ligurians, intense trade concentrated on arms, bronze objects, oil, wine, salt, most likely slaves and ceramics.

Masters of the sea between the straits of Messina and the Iberian coast, and dominant in the Rhone valley having overcome their Etruscan and Punic rivals, the Massalians controlled international trade in amber and raw metals in particular: silver and pewter from Spain or Brittany, copper from Etruria. After a period of eclipse, the city regained its splendour in the 4C. The coastal region was developed and planted with fruit and olive trees and vines. Greek sailors pushed further south as far as Senegal and to the north explored the Baltic coast as far as Iceland. Massalia was administered as a republic, famous for the wisdom of its laws, and widely recognised as a cultural centre.

The excavations around the Vieux Port and the Bourse commercial district have enabled historians to establish the layout of the town: it covered 50ha/124 acres and was built facing the sea on the hills of St-Laurent, Moulins and Carmes. It was surrounded by ramparts, aimed at protecting the town, and featured two temples (one celebrating Artemis and the other Apollo), a theatre as well as several other monuments.

Rome comes to Massalia's aid

The Romans, taking advantage of the occasion to acquire more influence, entered Provence in 125 BC, rescuing Massalia for the Salian Franks and beginning their conquest of the area. For three years battles raged as the Salian Frankish tribe harassed the land from entrenched camps, but Roman tenacity triumphed. Transalpine Gaul was founded with Aix and Narbonne as colonies. Massalia remained an independent republic allied to Rome; it kept a strip of territory along the coast.

Address Book

GUIDED TOURS:

Lecture tours – Contact the tourist office.

Histobus – A guided tour of the city by bus (3hr). Sun 2.30pm (daily Jul-Oct). 11.43€ (children: 4.57€). ☎ 04 91 91 92 10.

Taxis Tourisme – Guided tour with an audio guide (from 1hr to 1 day). From 30.49€ to 86.90€. To book, contact the Tourist Information Centre.

Tourist train – There are two itineraries: to N.-D.-de-la-Garde going past the Basilica of St-Victor and in the old town (the Panier and Vieille Charité quarters). Departures: quai des Belges. Not available mid-Oct to Easter. 4.57€ for 1 circuit (children: 2.29€), 7.62€ for both.

Cathédrale de la Major – Mid-June to end of Aug: Daily except Mon and Sun. 9am-6.30pm. Low season Mon to Thur 9am-noon, 2-5.30pm, Fri and Sat-Sun 9am-noon, 2.30-6pm.

Basilique de N.-D.-de-la-Garde – Guided tours possible by appointment. ☎ 04 91 13 40 80.

GETTING AROUND TOWN

Metro – This is the most convenient mode of transport; the two lines operate from 5am to 9pm. From 9pm to 1am the metro is substituted by the "fluobus". Tickets are sold in the form of magnetic cards and are valid for a single trip (carte solo), 1 day (carte journée) or for several journeys (carte liberté: 7.62€ or 15.24€). *Free network maps are given out at ticket offices. Information:* ☎ *04 91 91 92 10.*

Ferry Boat – Trips from place aux Huiles to the town hall. *8am to 6.30pm, weekends in the summer from 8am to 8.30pm. 0.76€ for a trip across and back, 0.46€ one-way.*

Guided tours are available for all ages and tastes: lecture tours on the history and architecture of Marseille, coach tours, taxi tours and a tourist train.

ENTERTAINMENT

Programmes are listed in local newspapers (*La Provence, La Marseillaise*), in a free weekly paper, Taktik, distributed by the Tourist Information Centre, cultural centres and at the paper's head office, 55 cours Julien. The Tourist Information Centre also distributes a small magazine, In Situ, which is published every three months.

Pastorals – In December and January pastorals are performed at the Mazenod theatre (88 rue d'Aubagne) and the Nau theatre (9 rue Nau).

Theatres – Marseilles boasts over 20 active theatres: classical and contemporary plays at the Théâtre National de Marseille-la-Criée, directed by Gildas Bourdet (30 quai de Rive-Neuve), at the Gymnase (4 rue du Théâtre-Français), at the Toursky (poetry and Mediterranean theatre, 16 passage Léo-Ferré) and at the Lenche (4 place de Lenche). "Art et Essai" at the Merlan-Scène nationale (avenue Raimu), at the Bernardines (17 bd Garibaldi) and at the Chocolat-Théâtre (59 cours Julien).

Classical music and dance – Classical music and opera at the Opéra municipal (2 rue Molière). Dance at the Ballet National now directed by Marie-Claude Pietragalla (20 bd de Gabès). A varied musical programme at the Cité de la Musique (4 rue Bernard-du-Bois) and at the Pharo auditorium.

Modern music – Rock concerts, jazz, reggae, etc. at the Espace Julien (39 cours Julien). Large concerts at the Marseille Dôme, with its huge cement arch: a vast room holding 8 000 where world-famous singers perform.

Cinema – Art house cinema: Le César (place Castellane), Breteuil (rue Breteuil), Paris (rue Pavillon) and Les Nouvelles Variétés (on the Canebière). Several multiplex cinemas on the Canebière and along avenue du Prado, near the Rond-Point.

Art galleries – All art events take place in the old warehouses of the Friche de la Belle-de-Mai, rue Jobin. There are also several galleries in rue Sainte, rue Neuve-Ste-Catherine, in the Arcenaulx quarter and on cours Julien.

SHOPPING

Markets – Fish market every morning on quai des Belges, food markets are open every morning (except Sunday) in cours Pierre Puget, place Jean-Jaurès (la Plaine), place du Marché-des-Capucins and avenue du Prado. La Canebière has a flower market every Tuesday and Saturday morning; this market is also set up on avenue Prado every Friday morning.

Every second Saturday of the month cours Julien has a book market and second-hand books and records can be bought daily outside the Palais des Arts. Finally, there is a fleamarket on Sunday mornings in avenue du Cap- Pinède.

Books – Librairie-galerie-restaurant des Arcenaulx, place d'Estienne-d'Orves, head office of the Jeanne Laffitte "regional" publications. Librarie maritime – 26 quai de Rive-Neuve – ☎ 04 91 54 79 26. Mon-Sat, 9am-noon and 2-7pm.

Le Cabanon des Accoules – 24 montée des Accoules – ☎ 04 91 90 49 66). Specialised in the manufacture of santons, in the picturesque Quartier du Panier.

Santons Marcel Carbonel – *47 rue Neuve-Ste-Catherine* – ☎ *04 9154 26 58* – *www. santonsmarcelcarbonel.com* – *shop: Tue-Sat 10am-noon, 2-7pm; workshop: guided visits Mon-Fri 8am-1pm, 2-5.30pm.* Visit the workshop where the famous santons are made, as well as the shop.

The "Four des Navettes" bakery

Marseille soap – *Au Père Blaize, 4-6 rue Méolan* – ☎ *04 9154 04 01*. Herbalist. This shop has remained unchanged since 1780 and sells a wide range of herbs: star anise, thyme, marjoram, pesto, rosemary as well as medicinal plants.

La Compagnie de Provence – *1 rue Caisserie* – ☎ *04 91 56 20 94 – lcdp@free.fr – Mon-Sat 10am-1pm, 2-7pm, closed public holidays.* Marseille soap and natural products: bath products, body care, decorations for the home.

Four des Navettes – *136 rue Sainte* – ☎ *04 91 33 32 12 – navettes@aol.com – Daily from 7am.* It is impossible to celebrate Candlemas without *"navette"* which protect houses from sickness and catastrophe! In the oldest bakery of the city people buy these biscuits **flavoured** with orange blossom; their recipe has been jealousy guarded for two centuries. There is also lavender flavoured chocolate, replete with the scent of Provence.

Provençal fabrics – Souleïado, 101 rue Paradis and in the shops on rue Vacon.

Pétanque – La Boule bleue, Z.I. La Valentine, montée de St-Menet, 13396 Marseille cedex 11, ☎ 04 91 43 27 20. The place to buy the balls used for the traditional game of pétanque, which is always followed by the traditional aperitif of pastis.

Fish auction, quai des Belges

LEISURE ACTIVITIES

Thalassa-Form Le Grand Large – *42 avenue du Grand-Large* – ☎ *04 96 14 05 40*. This sea-water spa has a range of health and beauty treatments for all the family.

EVENTS

Fiesta des Suds – In October and over some weekends throughout the year, this "southern fiesta" brings together the melting pot of races present in Marseille and vibrates with the music, traditions and atmosphere of the Mediterranean. It takes place in the J4 dock, near the entrance of the Joliette basin.

Festivals – Theatre and dance in various spots of the city (June-July). Island festival in July.

Pétanque competition – La Marseillaise *pétanque* world championship (in July): selection of games in the Borély park, finals on the Vieux Port. A very popular event frequented by show business celebrities who, after a few throws, let the champions take over.

Folklore – International folklore festival at Château-Gombert which takes place at the beginning of July.

For coin ranges, see Legend at the back of the guide.

EATING OUT

Specialities – As well as the celebrated *bouillabaisse*, the so-called fisherman's dish made with rockfish and found in most restaurants, and the famous *aioli* (garlic sauce), another speciality of Marseilles is a dish made with tripe called *pied-et-paquets*.

☺ **Dégustation Toinou** – *3 cours St-Louis* - ☎ *04 91 33 14 94 – closed Aug*. This is a real institution and inhabitants of Marseille aren't wrong about these things. They flock here to eat oysters and seafood. Platters are paraded on every floor of this contemporary style building with its wood and burnished metal decor. Reasonable prices a stone's throw away from the Vieux Port.

☺ **Salon de thé Couleur des Thés** – *24 rue Paradis* - ☎ *04 91 55 65 57 – closed 15 Aug-1Sept and Sun*. Located on the first floor of a building in the city centre, this tearoom has all the intimacy of a plush, pleasantly decorated apartment. On offer are a salad buffet, charcuterie, savoury tarts and homemade pastries. Fifty varieties of tea which can also be purchased in bulk.

☺ **La Cloche à Fromage** – *27 cours d'Estienne-d'Orves* – ☎ *04 91 54 85 38*. Here you can help yourself to a wide selection of cheeses: from the mildest to the most pungent varieties, there is something for everyone! There is a wonderful terrace in the summer. A few dishes without cheese also available.

Chez Vincent – *25 rue de Glandeves – ☎ 04 91 33 96 78 – closed Aug and Mon –* 🍴. Behind a modest façade lies a simple, bistro-style restaurant, whose owner, Rose, has been cooking here since the 1940s and is much appreciated by the locals. Generous helpings of regional cooking.

Les Arcenaulx – *25 cours d'Estienne-d'Orves – ☎ 04 91 59 80 30 – closed 8-23 Aug and Sun.* Dine surrounded by the books which cover the walls of this restaurant which is combined with a bookshop and publishers, located in the orignal setting of the warehouses of the 17C Arsenal des Galères. Large terrace on cours d'Estienne-d'Orves. Sun-kissed cooking.

Shabu Shabu – *30 rue de la Paix-Marcel-Paul – ☎ 04 91 54 15 00 – closed 28 Jul-1Sept, Mon lunchtime and Sun – booking recommended at weekends.* Every kind of Mediterranean fish prepared as sushi right before your very eyes! The decor here is Japanese but the chef is French, and passionate about Japanese cooking. A most unusual place, not least because it is one of the very few Japanese restaurants in the city.

Chez Fonfon – *140 Vallon-des-Auffes – ☎ 04 91 52 14 38 – closed 2-24 Jan, Sun evening and Mon lunchtime.* The dining room of this renowned restaurant dominates the Vallon des Auffes harbour. Every morning fresh fish and seafood is brought in by "pointus", the local fishing boats.

L'Épuisette – *156 Vallon-des-Auffes – ☎ 04 91 52 17 82 – closed 20 Aug-2 Sept, Sat lunchtime, Sun evening and Mon.* Get a front seat for stormy days! Located above the rocks and facing the Frioul islands, this restaurant almost feels like a ship advancing through the sea. Well-presented food with daily specials.

WHERE TO STAY

Chambre d'hôte Villa Marie-Jeanne – *4 rue Chicot – ☎ 04 91 85 51 31 – 🍴 – 3 rooms.* A very special address in Marseille, this 19C building has been tastefully done up. Situated in a residential neighbourhood, it blends the traditional colours of Provence with antique furniture, wrought iron and contemporary paintings. Garden shaded by plane trees and a nettle tree.

Hôtel Edmond Rostand – *31 rue du Dragon – ☎ 04 91 37 74 95 – closed 21 Dec-6 Jan – 16 rooms – 🛏 5.49€ – restaurant 12.20/12.20€.* In a smart residential area of Marseille, this hotel, whose name bears tribute to the creator of Cyrano de Bergerac, has entirely renovated.

Behind the stone façade and blue shutters are simple, well-kept rooms. Snacks available for residents only.

Hôtel St-Ferréol's – *19 rue Pisançon – ☎ 04 91 33 12 21 – 19 rooms – 🛏 6.86€.* This old house is situated at the heart of the pedestrian quarter, undoubtedly the liveliest in Marseille. Each of the little rooms, decorated with English-style fabrics and with its own marble bathroom, bears the name of an impressionist painter.

New Hôtel Vieux Port – *3 bis rue de la Reine-Élisabeth – ☎ 04 91 90 51 42 – 47 rooms – 🛏 9.15€.* The building is an old one but has been internally renovated, and its setting, right beside the Vieux Port, is ideal. Some rooms have views of the harbour and the old city. Functional and well soundproofed.

S. Sauvignier/MICHELIN

Place du Général-de-Gaulle

ON THE TOWN

Café Parisien – *1 place Sadi-Carnot – ☎ 04 91 90 05 77 – Mon-Wed 4am-9pm, Thurs-Fri until 1am, closed public holidays.* At weekends this baroque style café hosts musical events based on the themes presented in the exhibitions that are organised here every month. The Torcida Brésil has made this place their HQ. "Tango aperitif" evenings are also held, with free entry for guests on the last Fri of the month.

Le Pelle-Mêle – *8 place aux Huiles – ☎ 04 91 54 85 26 – www.pele-mele.com – Tues-Sat from 6pm, closed Aug.* This is a magnificent venue with a vaulted hall at the back, where world-famous jazz groups play.

O'Brady's Irish Pub – *378 avenue de Mazargues – ☎ 04 91 71 53 71 – www.obradys.com – daily 11am-1.30am – closed 25 Dec and 1 Jan.* Situated near the seat of the OM and the Stadium-Velodrome, this award-winning pub is one of the favourite meeting places of OM fans. On match nights the game is broadcast on a giant screen and a lively atmosphere is guaranteed.

O'Malley's – *9 quai Rive-Neuve* – ☎ *04 91 33 65 50* – daily 4pm-2am. Irish pub with a marine decor. There is an authentic and warm atmosphere and an Irish accent is a must-have for staff. Traditional Irish music on Wednesday evenings from 9.30pm.

BOOKS AND FILMS

Books – Nowadays the city is the backdrop to the mystery thrillers (nicknamed bouillabaisse mysteries) by Jean-Claude Izzo (Casino totale and Chourmo) and Philippe Carrese

(Trois jours d'engatse). Fans of French comic books – *bandes dessinées* – will enjoy Les Aventures de Léon Loden, whose hero is a Marseille-based private eye.

Films – As well as Marcel Pagnol's celebrated trilogy, which appeals especially to the nostalgic, the films of Robert Guédiguian, whose work includes the well-known Marius and Jeanette, are redolent with the atmosphere of Marseille. Lesser-known films like Transit by René Allio and Bye-Bye by Karem Dridi also portray the city's unique ambience.

Roman Marseille

At the moment when the rivalry between Caesar and Pompey was at its height, Marseille was forced to decide for one or the other of the two Roman generals. It backed Pompey, making the wrong choice. Besieged for six months, the town at last fell in 49 BC; Caesar stripped it of its fleet, its treasures and its trade. Arles, Narbonne and Fréjus were enriched with its spoils. Nevertheless, Marseille remained a free city and maintained a brilliant university, the last refuge of Greek teaching in the West. After the invasions, Marseille remained an active port which continued to trade with the Far East; it was the object of violent rivalry between the barbarian leaders. In 543 the plague arrived in Gaul for the first time and the town's decline began in the 7C. Pillaging by the Saracens, the Greeks and Charles Martel pushed the town back behind the fortifications of the bishopric on St-Laurent hill.

Maritime development

As early as the 11C the old Phocaean city mobilised all its shipping resources and put its shipyards to work. In 1214 Marseille became an independent republic, but only for a short time, as in 1252 it had to submit to the rule of Charles of Anjou. During this prosperous period (12C-14C), which was marked by the Crusades, Marseille competed with Genoa for the rich supply trade in war material and food to the Crusaders. Not only did the city reap great profit from this, but it was granted ownership of a section of Jerusalem with its own church.

Marseille, now rich again, sought new outlets. Its sailors began to trade along the Catalan coast, competed in their own waters with the men of Pisa and Genoa, and often sailed as far as the Levant, Egypt and North Africa. In the early 15C prosperity was undermined by crises and recession which came to a head in 1423 when the fleet from Aragon pillaged the city. But this was just temporary because under the influence of two clever merchants, the Forbin brothers, trade started up again. Jacques Coeur installed the main office of his bank here.

The Great Plague

In the early 18C Marseille's population was about 90 000. It was a great port which had profited from an edict of franchise since 1669 and from a monopoly of trade with the Levant. It subsequently became a huge warehouse of imported products (textiles, food products, drugs and miscellaneous items); and was preparing to launch into trade with the West Indies and the New World, when in May 1720 it fell victim to a dreadful curse. A ship coming from Syria, the *Grand St-Antoine*, was stricken with several cases of the plague during its journey. When it arrived in Marseille, it was put under quarantine at the Île de Jarre. Despite the precautions taken, the epidemic struck the town in circumstances which are still unclear, exacting a terrible toll. The Parliament at Aix forbade all communication between Marseille and the rest of Provence under penalty of death. But this did not stop the plague from spreading to Aix, Apt, Arles and Toulon. Despite the construction of a "Plague wall" 28km/17.5mi long, ordered by the Papal vice-legate, neither was the Comtat Venaissin spared. In two years 100 000 people died, 50 000 of whom were from Marseille.

Commercial activity

Marseille recovered rapidly: in only a couple of years the city had re-established its incredible demographic and economic energy. By 1765 the city had returned to the demographic level it was at in 1720 with aound 90 000 inhabitants. Trade found new openings with Latin America and the West Indies; Marseille began importing sugar, coffee and cacao. Industrialisation began: soap and glass making, sugar refining, glazed earthenware (*faience*) and textiles. Huge fortunes were made: ship owners and merchants, whose number doubled in the century, displayed their wealth amid the artisans and workers who lived directly from the cargo brought off the docks.

The city welcomed the Revolution with enthusiasm. In 1792, volunteers from Marseille popularized the *Chant de guerre de l'Armée du Rhin*, composed by Rouget de Lisle and soon baptised the *"Marseillaise"* (*see box below*). Marseille was also the first town to demand the abolition of the monarchy. The heavy hand of the Convention, however, soon became unbearable for Marseille, federalist at heart, and it rebelled.

Under the Empire, Marseille became royalist, the city's trade having been hard hit by the British fleet and the continental blockade. Under the Second Empire, Marseille became Republican; extensive urban projects were undertaken (the opening of the present Rue de la République, construction of Palais Longchamp, Notre-Dame-de-la-Garde, the cathedral, Pharo palace and park). The conquest of Algeria put an end to the Barbary pirates and stimulated the economic activity of Marseille, while the opening of the Suez Canal in 1869 was another step forward in its development.

The present and future

The German-Italian bombing of 1940 and that of the Allies in 1943-44 to prepare for their landing in Provence caused widespread damage and resulted in many victims. In January 1943, under the pretext of public health, the Germans evacuated 40 000 inhabitants from the old district in order to raze the streets between rue Caisserie and the Vieux Port.

Like most cities damaged by the war, after the Liberation Marseille threw all its energy into reconstruction programmes. The most striking project of this period was the **Cité Radieuse**, built between 1947 and 1952 on boulevard Michelet. Nicknamed from the outset *Maison de Fada* or crazy house, this first housing complex by **Le Corbusier** is still striking today for its bold and innovative design. The result of research by the architect on housing and its role in society, brings together in one area features of a small town including local services, and leisure and community areas. It is now much studied by architects worldwide and is open to the public.

Today, hit by economic recession, Marseille is seeking a new role, symbolised by the building of the futuristic local government office, designed by Will Alsop. A 25-year "Euro-Mediterranean" development project aims to remodel the city between the Belle de Mai, St-Charles train station and La Joliette, with the creation of cultural, economic, commercial and maritime centres.

OLD MARSEILLE 1

Vieux Port★★

▶ *Begin at the old port, to which all streets lead.*

The Phocaeans landed in this creek in the year 600 BC. It was here that, until the 19C, all Marseille's maritime life was concentrated. The quays were constructed under Louis XII and Louis XIII. In the 19C, the depth of two fathoms was found to be insufficient for steamships of large tonnage; new docks were built at this time.

Église St-Ferréol

Facing the old port stands St-Ferréol or the Church of the Augustinians with its Renaissance façade, rebuilt in 1804. Features of particular interest inside the church include a Gothic nave and an 18C marble altar.

The Corps-de-Ville, a district symbolic of old Marseille, bordering **quai du Port**, was dynamited by the Germans in 1943. Only a few buildings of interest were spared, one of which is the Hôtel de Ville, surrounded nowadays by post-war constructions, built to plans by Fernand Pouillon (1912-1986).

Hôtel de Ville

A town hall has existed on this site since the 13C. The present building and its interesting façade, an example of Provençal Baroque architecture, date from the middle of the 17C. The king's coat of arms above the main entrance is a copy of a work by **Pierre Puget** exhibited in the Musée des Beaux-Arts.

Le Vieux Port and Notre-Dame-de-la-Garde

Passing to the left of the building, notice the 16C **Maison Diamentée**, so called because of the faceted stones of its façade. Today it houses the Musée du Vieux Marseillea *(see MUSEUMS)*.

▶ *Take a few steps into Grand-Rue; no 27 bis is the Hôtel de Cabre (now a branch of the Crédit Agricole bank).*

Hôtel de Cabre

Built in 1535 and spared when much of the district was destroyed in 1943, this is one of the oldest houses in the city. Its composite style bears witness to the long-lasting influence of the Gothic style on civil Marseille architecture.

▶ *Return to place Daviel.*

Pavillon Daviel and Hôtel-Dieu

The former Law Courts building, the Pavillon Daviel (mid-18C), has a beautiful wrought-iron balcony decorated in the style typical of Marseille known as *à la marguerite* or daisy style, and a harmonious façade of pilasters.
The imposing **Hôtel-Dieu** which dominates the port is typical of hospital architecture of the second half of the 18C; note the arrangement of space and the superimposing of its arcaded galleries.

Clocher des Accoules

This 11C bell tower is all that remains of one of Marseille's oldest churches.

▶ *From here go toward the Quartier du Panier.*

Quartier du Panier★

Built on the Moulins hill on the site of ancient Massalia, the Panier district is all that remains of old Marseille since the Liberation. In the past its inhabitants, the majority of whom were of modest means and lived mainly from the sea, made the most of their tiny plots of land by constructing tall buildings. Just at the time when it was gradually becoming something of a ghetto, Le Panier reaped the benefits of a large renovation and development programme to turn the restored Vieille Charité into a museum *(see below)*. The area, with its narrow streets dissected here and there by flights of steps and where the tall façades are gradually regaining their former colours, is best explored on foot, preferably between shopping and lunchtime, at the end of the morning: the **Montée des Accoules**, symbol of the area, but also **rue du Panier**, rue Fontaine-de-Caylus, rue Porte-Baussenque, rue du Petit-Puits, rue Sainte-Françoise, rue du Poirier, and rue des Moulins which leads to place des Moulins. This charming and highly picturesque quarter of Marseille can be seen as a melting pot where Naples, Catalonia and the Mediterranean coast mingle with the French West Indies, Vietnam or the Comoro Islands to produce scenes which delight the senses: washing hangs from windows, the air is full of the scents of basil and *ratatouille*, locals in characteristic blue overalls browse through the papers on the doorsteps and bursts of Marseille French, and its inimitable turns of phrase, can be heard everywhere.

Centre de la Vieille Charité★★

This well-restored former hospice is a fine architectural unit built from 1671 to 1749 based on the plans of Pierre and Jean Puget. The buildings, created originally to shelter the deprived, stand around the central **chapel**★, a fine Baroque building with an ovoid dome by Pierre Puget. The façades looking onto the courtyard present three storeys of arcaded galleries in elegant pink and yellow-tinted Couronne stone.

Nowadays the building houses the **Musée d'archéologie méditerranéenne**, the museum of African, Oceanic and native American art (MAAOA), a poetry centre and a variety of exhibitions *(see MUSEUMS below)*.

▶ *Go round the left side of the Vieille Charité, turn left and left again into rue de l'Evêché, then turn right to reach the Major.*

Cathédrale de la Major

A huge and sumptuous construction started in 1852 in Roman-Byzantine style. It was originally built at the instigation of the future Napoleon III who wished to conciliate both the Church and the people of Marseille.

Ancienne Cathédrale de la Major★

The "Old Major", in stout contrast, is a fine example of mid-11C Romanesque, truncated in the 19C to make space for the building of the new cathedral. Only the chancel, transept and one bay of the nave and side aisles remain.

▶ *Go past the esplanade de la Tourelle and make for the small church of St-Laurent.*

Belvédère St-Laurent

Located on the parvis of St-Laurent church, the old fishermen's parish of the St-Jean district, it offers a fine **view**★ of the Vieux Port, the entrance to the Canebière, the Étoile chain, Notre-Dame-de-la-Garde basilica and the **Forts St-Jean and St-Nicolas**, built by Louis XIV in an attempt to control the town; the Fort St-Nicolas was stormed on 30 April 1790 and members of the Royal Familly were imprisoned in Fort St-Jean. The latter includes earlier constructions such as the Tour du Fanal or Tourette which resembles a minaret.

Place de Lenche

This lively square with façades embellished with wrought-iron balconies is located on the presumed site of the agora of the Greek town; from one of the café terraces there is an interesting view of Notre-Dame-de-la-Garde and the Théâtre de la Criée.

▶ *Go to the landing stage of the legendary ferry-boat which takes you to quai de Rive Neuve.*

B. Kaufmann/MICHELIN

Vielle Charité

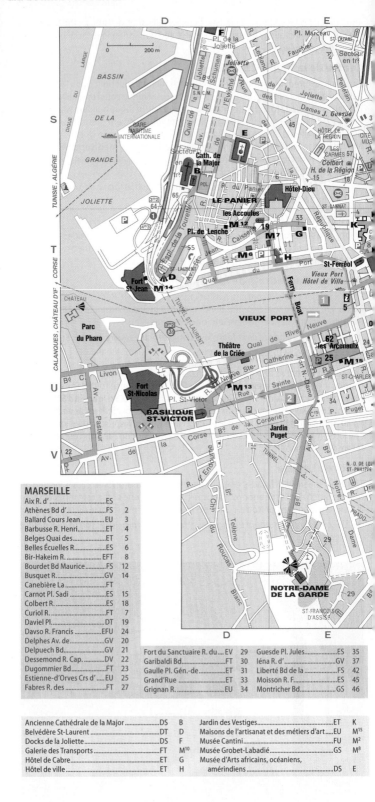

MARSEILLE

Aix R. d'	ES	
Athènes Bd d'	FS	2
Ballard Cours Jean	EU	3
Barbusse R. Henri	ET	4
Belges Quai des	ET	5
Belles Écuelles R.	ES	6
Bir-Hakeim R.	EFT	8
Bourdet Bd Maurice	FS	12
Busquet R.	GV	14
Canebière La	FT	
Carnot Pl. Sadi	ES	15
Colbert R.	ES	18
Curiol R.	FT	7
Daviel Pl.	DT	19
Davso R. Francis	EFU	24
Delphes Av. de	GV	20
Delpuech Bd	GV	21
Dessemond R. Cap.	DV	22
Dugommier Bd	FT	23
Estienne-d'Orves Crs d'	EU	25
Fabres R. des	FT	27

Fort du Sanctuaire R. du	EV	29
Garibaldi Bd	FT	30
Gaulle Pl. Gén.-de	ET	31
Grand'Rue	ET	33
Grignan R.	EU	34

Guesde Pl. Jules	ES	35
Iéna R. d'	GV	37
Liberté Bd de la	FS	42
Moisson R. F.	ES	45
Montricher Bd	GS	46

Ancienne Cathédrale de la Major	DS	B
Belvédère St-Laurent	DT	D
Docks de la Joliette	DS	F
Galerie des Transports	FT	M10
Hôtel de Cabre	ET	G
Hôtel de ville	ET	H

Jardin des Vestiges	ET	K
Maisons de l'artisanat et des métiers d'art	EU	M15
Musée Cantini	FU	M2
Musée Grobet-Labadié	GS	M8
Musée d'Arts africains, océaniens, amérindiens	DS	E

Paradis R.	FUV		St-Louis Cours	FT	56	Thiars Pl.	EU	62
Philipon Bd	GS	50	Ste-Barbe R.	ES	57	Thierry Crs J.	GS	63
Raynouard Traverse	GV	53	Ste-Philomène R.	FV	58	Tourette Quai	DS	64
St-Ferréol R.	FTU		Sembat R. Marcel	FS	60	Trois Mages R. des	FT	66
St-Laurent R.	DT	55	Sibié R.	FT	67	Vaudoyer Av.	DS	65

Musée d'Histoire de Marseille	ET	M³	Musée du Santon Marcel-Carbonel	DU	M¹³
Musée de l'artisanat et des métiers d'art	ET	M¹⁵	Musée du Vieux Marseille	DET	M⁷
Musée de la Marine et de l'Économie			Mémorial des Camps de la mort	DT	M¹⁴
de Marseille	ET	M⁴	Préau des Accoules	DT	M¹²
Musée de la Mode	FT	M⁵	Vieille Charité : Musée d'archéologie		
Musée des Docks romains	DT	M⁶	méditerranéenne	DS	E

RIVE NEUVE 2

Quai de Rive-Neuve

It was only relatively recently that the shallows that inconvenienced this part of the port were dredged and the quayside improved. Surrounded by beautiful buildings in Neo-classical style, the quai de Rive-Neuve is nowadays livelier than its opposite bank. Opposite no 12, the bust of Vincent Scotto stands at the ferry-boat pier.

▶ *Enter the shipyard district via place aux Herbes.*

Quartier des Arsenaux

In the Italian-style **cours Honoré-d'Estienne-d'Orves** are several cafés and restaurants, as well as the last remains of the Arsenal's buildings, at no 23 and no 25.

Place Thiars

This pleasant square, dating from the end of the 18C, is full of restaurants and bars where *bagna freda* (anchovy paste and small raw vegetables) is often served with your aperitif; it is situated on the former naval construction site of the shipyard. In the streets nearby, particularly in rue St-Saens and rue Fortia, a number of restaurants serve *bouillabaisse.*

▶ *To reach the basilica take rue Marcel-Paul (steps) and rue Sainte on the right.*

Basilique St-Victor★

This church is the last relic of the famous abbey known as the "key to Marseille harbour" founded in the early 5C by St John Cassian, a monk from the Far East, in honour of St Victor, patron of sailors and millers, who suffered martyrdom in the 3C by being slowly ground between two millstones. The sanctuary, destroyed in a Saracen raid, was rebuilt in c 1040 and subsequently remodelled and strongly fortified.

From the outside it is truly a fortress. The porch which opens into the Tour d'Isarn is roofed with heavy pointed vaulting (1140) which is among the oldest in Provence.

Crypt★★

The most interesting part is the 5C basilica, erected by St Cassian, which was submerged when the 11C church was built. Near it are the cave of St Victor and the entrance to the catacombs where, since the Middle Ages, St Lazarus and St Mary Magdalene have been venerated. In the neighbouring crypts a remarkable series of ancient, pagan and Christian sarcophagi can be seen. In the central chapel, near the so-called St-Cassian sarcophagus is a shrine (3C) discovered in 1965, which contained the remains of town martyrs on the tomb of which the abbey was built.

Go down rue Neuve-Ste-Catherine and the steps which lead to quai de Rive-Neuve.

Théâtre National de Marseille-La Criée, whose reputation has been made by the Marcel Maréchal company, is located in the former fish auction house (criée), which was moved near to the Estaque in 1975.

▶ *Take the car or the no 60 bus from cours Jean Ballard to go up to the basilica. To reach it on foot take boulevard Aune (at the very end of cours Pierre-Puget) and walk through the pretty park.*

Basilique de Notre-Dame-de-la-Garde

▶ *Leave the car on "Plateau de la Croix" (car parks).*

The basilica was built by Espérandieu in the mid-19C in the then fashionable Romano-Byzantine style. It stands on a limestone outcrop (alt 162m/532ft) on the site of a 13C chapel also dedicated to Our Lady. Surmounting the belfry (60m/197ft high) is a huge gilded statue of the Virgin. The interior is faced with multicoloured marble, mosaics and

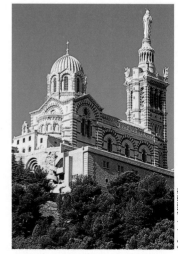

Notre-Dame-de-la-Garde

S. Sauvignier/MICHELIN

mural paintings by the Düsseldorf School. Numerous ex-votos cover the walls, whereas in the crypt is the lovely Mater Dolorosa in marble carved by Carpeaux.

A magnificent **panorama**★★★ can be enjoyed from the parvis of the basilica.

THE CANEBIÈRE 3

Built as Marseille expanded in the 17C, this avenue, the most famous in the city, derives its name from a hemp rope factory (hemp: *canèbe* in Provençal) which once existed here.

▶ *Start on the left-hand pavement of the Vieux Port.*

To the right of rue St-Ferréol a covered passageway and escalator lead to the Centre Bourse shopping centre which houses the **Musée d'Histoire de Marseille**★ (*see MUSEUMS below*). From here make for the Jardin des Vestiges which was brought to light during works for the layout of the quarter.

Jardin des Vestiges (Archeological garden)

The fortifications of the Greek town, the horn shape of the ancient port surrounded by its 1C quays, and an entrance way into the town dating from the 4C make up this archeological garden. During the Phocaean period, this site was located beside a swamp which slowly dried up in the 3C and 2C BC. In the second half of the 2C BC a new wall was built, from which interesting ruins remain: square towers, bastions and stepped curtain walls. Note the construction of the stone blocks hewn out of pink limestone from the cape of Couronne. A road dating from the Roman period enters the town through an older gate (2C BC), one of the flanking towers of which is still identifiable.

Going back along the Canebière, several buildings are remarkable for the quality of their architecture, recalling the past glory of the street, especially on the right-hand side: the mid-18C rocaille facades of buildings between rue St-Ferréol and cours St-Louis; the baroque-style building (1671-72) on the corner of cours St-Louis (nos 1-3), which was to have formed one side of the Place Royale designed by Pierre Pujet, but never finished; and two typical Second Empire buildings, no 53 (now a department store) and no 62 (Hôtel Noailles). In cours Belsunce is the glass canopy of the famous **Alcazar** theatre which, after lying abandoned for decades, will soon see a new lease of life as the city's main library, the **Bibliotèque de Marseille**.

▶ *Go down to the shopping area which extends south of the Canebière. Turn right into boulevard Garibaldi and then immediately left.*

Cours Julien

Until 1972 this was the Marseille wholesale market for market garden produce. It has now been renovated and here you will find specialist restaurants and antique or clothing shops (Madame Zaza of Marseille, Fille de Lune etc); it is a pleasant area for a relaxing stroll. The roads leading off to the east of the cours, such as rue de Bussy-l'Indien, rue Pastoret, rue Crudère, rue Vian, are slightly on the "fringe", their façades covered with occasional artists' graffiti (note the front of La Maison Hantée, rue Vian) and the clubs and cafés which come to life as night falls.

▶ *Take the footbridge spanning cours Lieutard to reach rue Aubagne.*

Splendour and decadence

The fame of this street spread worldwide, thanks to sailors of all nationalities who visited the great Mediterranean port. The famous operettas of Vincent Scotto (Un de la Canebière, 1938) and popular songs from the years between the wars also contributed to making this avenue the symbol of the bustling city. The street's real period of glory lasted for three-quarters of a century, until the Occupation, when it was the junction point for the whole public transport system and where all the city's fashionable cafés, cinemas and department stores were gathered. Today it has lost its prestige; despite a "Plan Canebière" aimed at rehabilitating the area by implanting administrative offices, it is a still far cry from its former glory, especially after nightfall. An indication of its renewal is the recent reopening of the Nouvelles Variétés, one of the great café/concert venues of the 1930s, now transformed into an art house cinema.

MARSEILLE

Aix R. d'	BY	
Briançon Bd de	BX	13
Canebière La	BY	
Catalans R. des	AY	16
Chartreux Av. des	CY	17
Guesde Pl. Jules	BX	35
Guigou Bd	BX	36
Lesseps Bd Ferdinand de	AX	40
Moulin Bd Jean	CY	47
Paradis R.	BYZ	
Pologne Pl. de	CY	51
Pompidou Prom. Georges	BZ	52
Sartre Av. Jean-Paul	CX	59
Strasbourg Bd	BX	61
Verdun R. de	CY	70

Château Borely	BZ	M¹
Docks de la Joliette	AXY	F
Hôtel de ville	BY	H
Monument aux morts de l'armée d'Orient	AY	L
Musée-Boutique de l'O.M.	CZ	M⁹
Réplique du David de Michel-Ange	BZ	V

Rue Aubagne which also has its share of unusual establishments *(for example, the grocery shop at no 34)*, and which leads to the "belly of Marseille", still lively, even if of less economic importance. Rue du Musée and rue Rodolph-Pollack specialize in exotic and African cosmetic hairdressers; **place du Marché des Capucins**, opposite Noailles metro station, is the kingdom of the local stall-holders or partisanes. The air rings with their loud cries, urging passers-by to purchase their lemons and beans. In the narrow **rue Longue-des-Capucins** the atmosphere of which is part souk, part flea market, the air is full of different scents: spices mingled with coffee, pitted or marinated olives, anchovies, herbs and dried fruit.

Rue des Halles-Charles-Delacroix (a former fish market, now demolished), lined with grocery stores and shops selling exotic wares, leads to rue Vacon, where Provençal fabrics are displayed, as well as to "Saint-Fé," the rue St-Ferréol, which is the main pedestrian-only shopping street of the city, and where the fashion boutiques, shoe shops, record stores and fast-food outlets are concentrated, as well as the major stores such as Galleries Lafayette and Virgin Megastore.

The **Musée Cantini** (🕯 *see MUSEUMS below*) is housed in the 17C Hôtel de la Compagnie du Cap Nègre, which was donated to the city. Return to the Canebière and take rue Paradis, a busy shopping street, on the right.

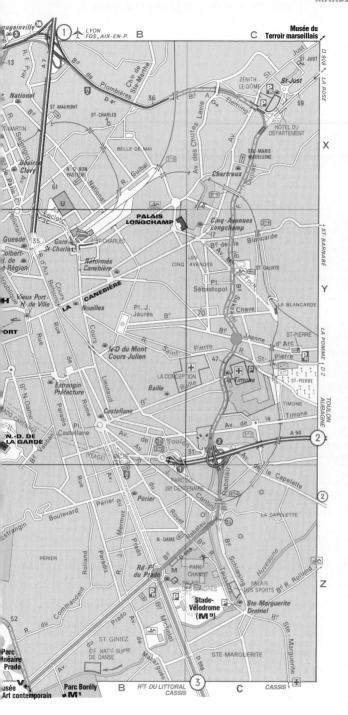

La Corniche

🚗 *You can drive down the corniche but it is almost impossible to find a parking place.*

Parc du Pharo

This park is situated on a promontory above the entrance to the Vieux Port. Enjoy the **view** from the terrace near the Pharo palace, built for Napoleon III. There is an underground auditorium in the park.

INDEX OF STREETS AND SIGHTS IN MARSEILLE

Aix R. d' ... BY, ES
Anthoine R. d' ... AX
Athènes Bd d' ... FS 2
Aubagne R. d' ... FTU
Aune Bd A. ... EV
Baille Bd ... BCY, GV
Ballard Cours Jean ... EU 3
Barbusse R. Henri ... ET 4
Belges Quai des ... ET 5
Belles Écuelles R. ... ES 6
Belsunce Cours ... BY, FST
Bir-Hakeim R. ... EFT 8
Blancarde Bd de la ... CY
Bompard Bd ... AYZ
Bourdet Bd Maurice ... FS 12
Breteuil R. ... EFUV
Briançon Bd de ... BX 13
Brun R. Roger ... GV
Busquet R. ... GV 14
Caisserie R. ... DT
Camas R. du ... GST
Canebière La ... BY, FT
Cantini Av. Jules ... BCZ, GV
Capelette Av. de la ... CYZ
Carnot Pl. Sadi ... ES 15
Castellane Pl. ... BY, FV
Catalans R. des ... AY 16
Chape R. ... GS
Chartreux Av. des ... CY 17
Chave Bd ... BCY, GT
Chutes Lavie Av. ... CX
Colbert R. ... ES 18
Corderie Bd de la ... DEU
Corinthe Av. de ... GV
Corse Av. de la ... DUV
Curiol R. ... FT 7
Dames Bd des ... DES
Daviel Pl. ... DT 19
Davso R. Francis ... EFU 24
Delphes Av. de ... GV 20
Delpuech Bd ... GV 21
Dessemond R. Cap. ... DV 22
Dr-Escat R. ... FV
Dragon R. ... EFV
Dugommier Bd ... FT 23
Dunkerque Bd de ... AX
Duparc Bd Françoise ... CXY
Endoume R. d' ... AY, DV
Estienne-d'Orves Crs d' ... EU 25
Estrangin Bd G. ... ABZ
Évêché R. de l' ... DS
Fabres R. des ... FT 27
Fauchier R. ... ES
Ferrari R. ... GU
Flammarion Bd Camille ... GS
Fleming Bd Alexander ... CX
Foch Av. Mar. ... CY
Fort du Sanctuaire R. du ... EV 29
Fort Notre-Dame R. ... EU
Gambetta Allée ... FS
Garibaldi Bd ... FT 30
Gaulle Pl. Gén.-de ... ET 31
Gènes R. de ... GV
Gouffé Cours ... GV
Grand'Rue ... ET 33
Grignan R. ... EU 34
Guesde Pl. Jules ... BY, ES 35
Guibal R. ... BX
Guigou Bd ... BX 36
Héros R. des ... FGS
Honnorat R. ... FS
Iéna R. d' ... GV 37
Italie R. d' ... FV
Jean-Jaurès Pl. ... BY, GT
Jeanne-d'Arc Bd ... CY
Joliette Pl. de la ... DS
Joliette Quai de la ... DS
Joliette R. de la ... DES
Julien Cours ... FTU
Lazaret Quai du ... AX
Leblanc R. V. ... DS
Leclerc Av. Gén. ... BY, FS
Lenche Pl. de ... DT
Lesseps Bd Ferdinand de ... AX 40
Libération Bd de la ... GS
Liberté Bd de la ... FS 42
Lieutaud Cours ... BY, FTUV
Livon Bd Charles ... AY, DU
Lodi R. de ... GUV
Longchamp Bd ... GS
Loubière R. de la ... GU
Marceau Pl. ... ES
Marché des Capucins
Pl. du ... FT
Mazargues Av. de ... BZ
Menpenti R. ... GV
Mermoz R. Jean ... BZ
Michelet Bd ... BCZ
Moisson R. F. ... ES 45
Montricher Bd ... GS 46
Moulin Bd Jean ... CY 47
National Bd ... BX, FGS
Nationale R. ... FS
Nau R. ... GU
Nedelec Bd Charles ... FS
Neuve Ste-Catherine R. ... DEU
Notre-Dame Bd ... BY, EV
Panier R. du ... DS
Paradis R. ... BYZ, FUV
Paris Bd de ... ABX
Pasteur Av. ... DUV
Pelletan Av. C. ... BXY, ES
Périer Bd ... BZ
Philipon Bd ... GS 50
Pierre Bd Eugène ... GT
Plombières Bd de ... BX
Pologne Pl. de ... CY 51
Pompidou Prom. Georges ... BZ 52
Port Quai du ... DET
Prado Av. du ... BYZ, VF
Président-J.-F.- Kennedy
Corniche ... AYZ
Puget Crs Pierre ... EFU
Pyat R. Félix ... BX
Rabatau Bd ... BCZ
Raynouard Traverse ... GV 53
République R. de la ... ABY, DEST
Rive-Neuve Quai de ... DEU
Roches Av. des ... AZ
Rolland Bd Romain ... CZ
Rolland R. du Cdt ... BZ
Rome R. de ... BY, FUV
Roosevelt Crs Franklin ... GS
Roucas Blanc
Chemin du ... AZ, DV
Rouet R. du ... BYZ, GV
St-Ferréol R. ... FTU
St-Jean Av. ... DT
St-Just Av. de ... CX
St-Laurent R. ... DT 55
St-Louis Cours ... FT 56
St-Pierre R. ... BCY GU
St-Savournin R. ... GST
St-Victor Pl. ... DU
Sainte R. ... DEU
Ste-Barbe R. ... ES 57
Ste-Cécile R. ... GV
Ste-Marguerite Bd ... CZ
Ste-Marthe Ch. de ... BX
Ste-Philomène R. ... FV 58
Sakakini Bd ... CY
Salengro Av. Roger ... BX
Salvator Bd L. ... FU
Sartre Av. Jean-Paul ... CX 59
Schloesing Bd ... CZ
Schuman Av. Robert ... DS
Sébastopol Pl. ... CY
Semard Av. Pierre ... FS
Sembat R. Marcel ... FS 60
Sibié R. ... FT 67
Strasbourg Bd ... BX 61
Tapis Vert R. du ... FST
Teisseire Bd R. ... CZ
Tellène Bd ... AY, DV
Terrusse R. ... GT
Thiars Pl. ... EU 62
Thierry Crs J. ... GS 63
Tilsit R. ... GU
Timone Av. de la ... CY
Toulon Av. de ... BCY GV
Tourette Esplanade de la ... DT
Tourette Quai ... DS 64
Trois Mages R. des ... FT 66
Vallon l'Oriol Chemin ... AZ
Vauban Bd ... BY, EFV
Vaudoyer Av. ... DS 65
Verdun R. de ... CY 70
Vertus R. des ... GUV
Victor-Hugo Pl. ... FS
Voltaire Bd ... FS

Ancienne Cathédrale de
la Major ... DS B
Basilique N. D. de la Garde ... BY, EV
Basilique St-Victor ... DU
Belvédère St-Laurent ... DT D
Cathédrale de la Major ... DS
Château Borely ... BZ M1
Clocher des Accoules ... DT
Docks de la Joliette ... AXY, DS F
Église St-Ferréol ... ET
Église St-Vincent-de-Paul ... GST
Ferry-boat ... ET
Fort St-Jean ... DT
Fort St-Nicolas ... DU
Galerie des Transports ... FT M10
Gare St-Charles ... FS
Hôtel de Cabre ... ET G
Hôtel de ville ... BY, ET H
Hôtel du Département ... CX
Hôtel-Dieu, Pavillon Daviel ... ES
Jardin Puget ... EUV
Jardin Valmer ... AZ
Jardin des Vestiges ... ET K
Le Vieux Port ... ABY, DET
Maisons de l'artisanat et
des métiers d'art ... EU M15
Marégraphe ... AZ
Monument aux morts
de l'armée d'Orient ... AY L
Musée Cantini ... FU M2
Musée Grobet-Labadié ... GS M8
Musée d'Art contemporain ... AZ
Musée d'Arts africains,
océaniens, amérindiens ... DS E
Musée d'Histoire de Marseille ... ET M3
Musée de l'artisanat et
des métiers d'art ... ET M15
Musée de la Marine et de
l'Économie de Marseille ... ET M4
Musée de la Mode ... FT M5
Musée des Docks romains ... DT M6
Musée du Santon
Marcel-Carbonel ... DU M13
Musée du Terroir marseillais ... CX
Musée du Vieux Marseille ... DET M7
Musée-Boutique de l'O.M. ... CZ M9
Mémorial des Camps
de la mort ... DT M14
N.-D.-du-Mont ... GU
Opéra ... EU
Palais Longchamp: Musée
des Beaux-Arts, Muséum
d'Histoire naturelle ... BY, GS
Parc Borély ... BZ
Parc balnéaire du Prado ... BZ
Parc du Pharo ... AY, DU
Plage de la Batterie de
Malmousque ... AY
Plage des Catalans ... AY
Plage du Prophète ... AZ
Port Moderne ... AX
Préau des Accoules ... DT M12
Quartier des Arcenaulx ... EU
Quartier du Panier ... DS
Quartier du Roucas-Blanc ... AZ
Réplique du David de
Michel-Ange ... BZ V
Théâtre de la Criée ... DU
Vallon des Auffes ... AY
Vieille Charité: Musée
d'archéologie
méditerranéenne ... DS E

Vallon des Auffes

Corniche Président-J.-F.-Kennedy★★

This corniche runs for nearly 5km/3mi – almost entirely along the sea-front. It is dominated by elegant villas built at the end of the 19C.

Level with the **Monument aux Morts de l'Armée d'Orient**, attractive views open out towards the coast and the islands. An odd phenonmenon – the islands appear closer to land when the mistral wind is blowing. A viaduct crosses the picturesque Auffes valley.

Vallon des Auffes

Access through boulevard des Dardanelles, just before the viaduct. This tiny fishing port, crowded with traditional boats and ringed with cabanons, inspired Vincent Scotto. For a pleasant and timeless evening, choose an outdoor restaurant along the port, where you can appreciate the changing light of the setting sun, much as the Phocaean inhabitants must have done more than 2 000 years ago.

Promenade de la Plage

This is the extension of the Corniche to the south, running alongside the **plages Gaston-Defferre**, a leisure area bordered by gardens with children's playgrounds which contains a number of pleasure pools and artificial beaches. On the other side of the road there are several restaurants.

The Alcazar Music-Hall of Marseille

Long since closed down, the renowned Alcazar music-hall is still cherished by the people of Marseille and has become something of a legend.

The Alcazar opened its doors in 1857 on the present cours Belsunce and for over a century was the temple of variety shows in Marseille. Here, against a backdrop of Moorish-inspired decor, mime artists, pastoral players, "Marseille review" entertainers, music-hall celebrities, fortune-tellers, bawdy comedians, local eccentrics and, in later years, rock and roll pop stars all performed. The operettas of Vincent Scotto and Sarvil, performed by well-known French singers such as Alibert, Rellys or Chargrin, developed their own style here, while at the same time the spirit of the Alcazar carried more than a hint of Marcel Pagnol.

The music-hall reached its zenith between 1920 and 1950, with such artists as Mayol, Mistinguett, Rina Ketty and Maurice Chevalier, a regular performer here since his very first appearance at the age of 16. Raimu, Fernandel, Tino Rossi and Yves Montand all made their débuts at the Alcazar, the latter in a western-style repertoire which dubbed him the "young swing star of 1941".

Performing at this mythical venue was indeed a test: the audience here, as in the nearby Opéra, were merciless and would not tolerate a single note out of key or any vocal weakness, seizing the first opportunity to heckle, shout jibes or burst into raucous laughter. The performers nonetheless appreciated the skill and generosity of the theatre: stars tried out their shows at the Alcazar before heading up to Paris. The Alcazar closed down in 1964: one of the last personalities to triumph there was the French pop singer Johnny Halliday.

The Pointe Rouge, on the opposite side of the Prado roundabout, with its replica of Michelangelo's *David*, is an important sailing centre.

Château et Parc Borély

Botanical Gardens – ♿ ⏱ *Daily except Sat-Sun. 1-5pm.* ⏱ *Closed 1 and 8 May, Easter Monday, Ascension, Whit Monday, 25 Dec. 1.52€.* ☏ *04 91 55 24 96.*
Built between 1767 and 1778 by the Borély, a family of wealthy merchants, the château will house the town's Museum of Decorative Arts once restoration work is complete. The **park**, which has a network of paths and extends to the east with beautiful **botanical gardens** is the venue every year for the extremely popular Provençal and Marseille boules competition, so typical of Marseille life.
You can continue to the little Montredon beach, where, in "La Campagne Pastré", an attractive 19C bastide, the superb **Musée de la Faïence** *(see MUSEUMS below)* is housed, and as far as the Calanques des Goudes and Callelongue.

The Port

The old port had become inadequate, with ships crowded four or five rows deep, so in 1844 a law authorised the construction of a dock at La Joliette; later the docks of Lazaret and Arenc were built and the port area was enlarged through the addition of further docks to the north.
The city has retained some traditional Marseille activites, based on maritime trade industries: oil pressing, soap making, flour milling, semolina production and metalworking.
The two World Wars, the fact that larger ships could no longer use the Suez canal and decolonization dealt Marseille a heavy blow. Reconversion and modernization, mainly in the oil and chemical sectors, have brought about a shift in the main industrial activities to the area around the Étang de Berre and the Golfe de Fos. The new installations, administered by the Port Autonome de Marseille, have made this one of Europe's leading ports.

The Docks

Guided tours (2hrs) by coach, July and Aug: Wed; low season: by appointment. Contact the Marseille tourist office, 4 La Canebière, 2 weeks in advance. ☏ *04 91 13 89 00, fax 04 91 13 89 20*
The coastal motorway also offers the only good general view of the installations and of port traffic.

La Joliette Docks

Access: Joliette metro station. Entrance at place de la Joliette, through the administrative buildings. Built from 1858 to 1863, based on an English docks design, this huge row of warehouses, almost 400m/1 312ft long, is the embodiment of Marseille's economic peak as the Gateway to the Orient. Situated between the new port of La Joliette and the railway line, the docks receive raw goods, package or sometimes process them, then ship them by sea or rail. The most modern techniques were installed for these activities, such as hydraulic lifts, the first to be used in Marseille.

The Marseillaise

On 20 April 1792, Revolutionary France declared war against Austria. In Strasbourg, General Kellerman asked Claude Joseph Rouget de Lisle, a talented captain and a composer-songwriter in his spare time, to write "a new piece to celebrate the departure of the volunteers"; the Chant de Guerre pour l'Armée du Rhin (War Song for the Rhine Army) was written on the night of 25 to 26 April. Soon adopted by a batallion from Rhône-et-Loire and carried south by commercial travellers, the Chant was heard in Montpellier on 17 June. On 20 June, a young patriot from Montpellier on assignment in Marseille, François Mireur, sang it during a banquet offered by the Marseille Jacobin club, located at rue Thubaneau. Enthusiasm was such that the text of the song was distributed to 500 national guards from Marseille, who had been called to arms for the defence of Paris. Re-named Chant de guerre aux armées des frontières (War Song for the Border Armies), the anthem was sung at each of the 28 stages of the journey towards the capital, with increasing success and virtuosity. On 30 July, the impassioned verses sung by these warm southern voices, ringing out across the St-Antoine district, was referred to by the electrified crowd as the Chant des Marseillais (Song of the Marseillais). A few days later, the new anthem, on the storming of the Tuileries, was given its definitive name. The Marseillaise became the national anthem on 14 July 1795 and once again, after a long period of eclipse, on 14 February 1879.

The exclusive use of stone, brick and cast iron in the construction, which nowadays is a specific feature of this type of architecture, was intended to prevent the risk of fire. Various other installations connected to the activities of the docks, which were renovated in 1991, now hold plays and exhibitions, enabling the visitor to admire the remarkable vaulted cellars.

MUSEUMS

Old Marseille

Musée du Vieux Marseille★

🕐*Closed for renovation.* ☎ *04 91 55 10 19.* The ground floor contains 18C Provençal furniture and domestic objects. The fine staircase with its coffered ceiling goes up to the first floor where a number of 18C cribs in spun glass or resin-and-bread-crumbs and a large collection of santons (1830-early 1900s) are exhibited. Another room is devoted to Marseille's old district, with a relief model of the town in 1848, while another room contains miscellaneous items concerning the great plague of 1720. On the second floor, displays of costumes, engravings and paintings illustrate 19C Marseille life. Also worth noting is the large Camoin (Marseille card-makers since the 18C) donation, which includes the appropriate material needed for the making of playing cards and the different techniques used.

Musée de Marseille

Wooden Tsimshian mask (British Columbia)

Musée des Docks romains★

🕐*Jun to Sept: daily except Mon 11am-6pm; Oct to May: daily except Mon 10am-5pm.* 🕐*Closed public holidays. 1.83€.* ☎ *04 91 91 24 62*
During reconstruction work in 1947 the remains of some commercial Roman warehouses used for storing dolia (large earthenware jars) were uncovered, dating from the 1C to the 3C. The museum contains objects found on the site, which date from the Greek period to the Middle Ages. A model reconstruction illustrates the site and its surroundings. The warehouse complex consisted of a ground floor level opening out onto the quay and a first floor level which was probably connected by a gateway to the main street of the city, the decumanus, which is now rue Caisserie. The ground floor housed the dolia for grain, wine and oil. The history of trade in Marseille is retraced in the museum with the help of ceramic and metal ware and amphorae, retrieved from shipwrecks, and coins and measures. A potter's kiln demonstrates how amphorae were made.

Centre de la Vieille Charité★★

🕐*Jun to Sept: daily except Mon 11am-6pm; Oct to May: daily except Mon 10am-5pm.* 🕐*Closed public holidays. Musée d'Archéologie méditerranéenne: 1.83€; Musée des Arts Africains, Océaniens et Amérindiens: 1.83€; temporary exhibitions: 2.74€; combined ticket (both museums and temporary exhibitions) 4.57€.* ☎ *04 91 14 58 80.*
The rich and varied collection of this museum, bringing together some 900 artefacts from the Near East, Greece, Etruria and Rome, constitutes one of the few provincial museums able to offer an almost complete picture of ancient Mediterranean civilisations.

Musée d'Archéologie méditerranéenne★

First floor, north wing. **Egypt:** Spanning the beginning of the Old Kingdom (2 700 BC) to the Coptic Period (3C and 4C AD), this collection of approximately 1 600 pieces provides a complete overview of art, funerary rites, religion and daily life in Pharaonic Egypt: funerary statuettes, known as *ouchtebis*, two masks of Osiris in beaten gold leaf, a large ibis in silver and gilded wood from the Ptolemaic Period, a black granite staue of the goddess Neith (New Kingdom, 18th dynasty) as well as an offering table bearing 34 royal cartouches (New Kingdom, 19th dynasty).

Near East: Assyrian pieces from the palace of Sargon II at Dur-Sharukin (present-day Khorsabad) and the Assurbanipal Palace at Nineveh. Note two ceramics of exceptional elegance and delicacy (4C BC).

Cyprus – With as many as 185 artefacts, the collection of Cypriot antiquities is the largest to be found in any French provincial museum. It includes pieces of pottery with a shiny red surface bearing incised or light relief decoration dating from the Early Cypriot Bronze Age (2300-2000 BC), Mycenaen-type funerary objects crafted in the Late Cypriot Bronze Age (1600-750 BC) and turned ceramic pieces decorated with concentric circles from the Cypriot Geometric period (1050-750 BC).

Greece, Magna Grecia - Statues of marble Cycladic idols precede an exhibit dating from the Minoan civilisation; ceramics decorated with geometrical motif friezes are characteristic of the 9C and 8C BC. Corinthian works influenced by Eastern art (aruballos and alabaster: perfume vases ornamented with animal or floral motifs), black-figure ceramics, red-figure ceramics and sculptures of a naked young man (couros) or a clothed young woman (koré). **Classical Greece** (5C-4C) produced lekythos with a white background and funerary steles.

Etruria, Rome – Ceramics in bucchero nero, where the carefully-smoothed black paste rivals the shine of the silver pieces; funerary painting from Chiusi and Tarquinia, Vulci in stone sculpture, Cerveteri and Veii (sculpture of koré).

Roquepertuse and the Celtic-Ligurians – Roquepertuse is situated in the commune of Velaux (north of Vitrolles) where various excavation projects have unearthed a remarkable archeological collection. This includes painted, sculpted and engraved fragments, statues of warriors sitting cross-legged, huge birds and the bicephalous **Hermes**★, a magnificent sculpture of two heads attached by a mortice and tenon joint. The "broken heads" portico consists of three monolithic pillars, the upper part of which is hollowed out with cephaliform cavities which were intended to hold skulls.

Musée des Arts Africains, Océaniens et Amérindiens (MAAOA)★★

Second floor, north and east wings. After the Musée de l'Homme in Paris, this museum has the richest collection of artefacts from Africa, Oceania and the Americas of any provincial museum in France. The layout of the museum offers an ideal setting for contemplation: the works are exhibited on one side against a black background, illuminated by indirect lighting, whereas opposite the exhibit is the corresponding explanatory text.

Salle Pierre-Guerre

In this room are reunited objects donated by Pierre Guerre, as well as other recent gifts and acquisitions: masks, sculptures, reliquaries and other daily objects mainly from West Africa.

Salle Antonin-Artaud

The objects in this room recall the civilisations of Oceania and the Americas: ceremonial paddles, a headdress mask from Wayana (Brazil), shrunken human heads (tsantsas of the Jivaros Indians, Ecuador) and other cult objects. The Gastaut collection brings together a unique set of sculpted, engraved and shaped human skulls, illustrating the ancient civilisations of Oceania and Amazonia. Finally, the François Reichenbach Collection consists of popular objets d'arts from Mexico.

Around the Canebière

Musée d'Histoire de Marseille★

&. ⏱*Daily except Sun noon-7pm.* ⏱*Closed public holidays. 1.83€.* ☎ *04 91 90 42 22.*
The museum is located at the end of the Jardin des Vestiges. It traces the history of Marseille in its Provençal context from prehistoric to Gallo-Roman times through archeological finds, documents and models. The model of Greek Marseille in the 3C and 2C BC shows the horn shape of the ancient port, complete with slipways. Celtic-Ligurian customs are evoked through the reconstruction of the Roquepertuse sanctuary portico (2C BC), complete with its "broken heads". The Greek town, funerary customs, metallurgy, etc are all dealt with clearly and accurately. The transport and storage of food is explained by means of the cross-section of a dolium (large urn), and the exhibition of various types of amphorae which once contained wine, oil or different types of fish dressing.

A Roman merchant vessel dating from the 3C, preserved through freeze-drying, shows the wide range of wood used in naval construction of the time: the keel is made of cypress, the stem of umbrella pine, the keys and plugs of olive or ilex, and the planking and interior covering of larch and Aleppo pine.

A new exhibition Le Temps des découvertes de Protis à la reine Jeanne (Discoveries from Protis to Queen Jeanne), is dedicated to the spectacular result of the most recent excavations.

Musée de la Marine et de l'Économie de Marseille

Daily 10am-6.30pm. 1.83€. ☎ 04 91 39 33 33.
This maritime and commercial museum displays several models of sailboats and steamships, paintings, water-colours, engravings and plans illustrate marine history and the history of the port of Marseille, concentrating on the 17C to the present.

Musée de la Mode

Daily except Mon noon-7pm. Closed public holidays. 2.74€. ☎ 04 91 56 59 57.
This museum has temporary exhibitions on costume and fashion themes.

Musée Cantini★

Jun to Sept: daily except Mon 11am-6pm; Oct to May: 10am-5pm. Closed public holidays. 1.83€. ☎ 04 91 54 77 75.
This museum specialises in 20C art after the Second World War until 1960, with particular attention to Fauvist, early Cubist, Expressionist and Abstract art, including works by Matisse, André Derain (*Pine Forest, Cassis*), Raoul Dufy (Factory in the Estaque), Alberto Magnelli (*Stones no 2*, 1932), Dubuffet (*Striking Woman*), Kandinsky, Chagall, Jean Hélion and Picasso. The presence of a number of Surrealist artists in Marseille during the last war, gathered around André Breton at the Villa Air-Bel, explains a selection of paintings from this movement at the Cantini Museum; paintings by André Masson (*Antille*, 1943), Max Ernst (*Monument to the Birds*, 1927), Wilfredo Lam, Victor Brauner, Jacques Hérold, Joan Miró and rare drawings by the Marseille artist Antonin Artaud.

The port of Marseille, a local subject of inspiration along with the Estaque, is represented on canvases by Marquet, Signac and the Marseille specialist in this subject, Louis Mathieu Verdilhan (1875-1928). Finally, the collection features a few works by 20C artists who defy classification: Baltus (*The Bather*), Giacometti (*Portrait of Diego*) and Francis Bacon (*Self-Portrait*).

Longchamp District

Musée Grobet-Labadié★★

Jun to Sept: daily except Mon 11am-6pm; Oct to May: 10am-5pm. Closed public holidays. 1.83€. ☎ 04 91 62 21 82.
The bourgeois interior of this town house has been preserved, with its fine Flemish and French (16C-18C) tapestries, furniture, 18C Marseille and Moustiers faience ware, religious gold and silver plate, wrought-iron work and old musical instruments. Fine paintings hang on the walls: Flemish, German and Italian Primitives, French School covering the 17C-19C. The museum is further enriched by a collection of drawings by European schools from the 15C to the 19C.

Palais Longchamp★

This imposing building was constructed by the Nîmes architect, Henri Espérandieu from 1862 to 1869. In its centre stands a neatly concealed water tower embellished by fountains; it is linked by colonnades to the Musée des Beaux-Arts (*on the left*) and the Muséum d'Histoire Naturelle (*on the right*).

Musée des Beaux-Arts★

Jun to Sept: daily except Mon 11am-6pm; Oct to May: 10am-5pm. Closed public holidays. 1.83€. ☎ 04 91 14 59 30.
On the first floor there is a large gallery devoted to **16C and 17C painting**. There are works from the French School: Vouet (*Madonna with Rose*), Le Sueur, Champaigne, Rigaud, Largillière; the Italian School: Perugino, Cariani, Carracci, Lanfranco, Guercino; the Flemish School: Snijders, Jordaens, several Rubens (*The wild boar hunt*) and Gaspard de Crayer. Provençal artists are represented by Michel Serre, Jean Daret, Finson and Meiffren Comte. On the ground floor, a large room exhibits the works of **Pierre Puget** (1620-94), native of Marseille: (*Infant Jesus Sleeping*), statues (*The Faun*) and low

reliefs (*The Plague at Milan, Louis XIV Riding*). In the stairwell are two murals by Puvis de Chavannes: Marseille as a Greek Colony and as the *Gateway to the Levant*.

On the second floor a sequence of rooms is devoted to **French painting of the 18C and 19C**. The 18C is represented by beautiful canvases by Nattier, Verdussen, Watteau de Lille, Carle Van Loo, Françoise Duparc, Greuze, Joseph Vernet (*Storm*), Mme Vigée-Lebrun (*The Duchess of Orleans*) and sculpture by Chastel. Among the 19C works, those by Courbet (*Deer at Water's Edge*), Millet, Corot, Girodet, Gros, Gérard, Ingres, David, and the Provençal painters Guigou and Casile compete for the viewer's attention. The **Drawings Room** contains Italian and French works, displayed as temporary exhibitions.

Muséum d'Histoire naturelle★

🕐*Daily except Mon 10am-5pm.* 🕐*Closed public holidays. 1.8€.* ☎ 04 91 14 59 50.
Rich zoological, geological and prehistorical collections are exhibited. Four hundred million years of history of the Provence-French Riviera region are retraced, and a safari museum illustrates the diversity of the animal kingdom throughout the world. A gallery is devoted to Provençal flora and fauna.

The various **aquariums** present a standing exhibition on white waters in Provence under the title "Eaux vives, du Verdon aux Calanques".

Southern Districts

Musée d'Art Contemporain *(MAC) (not on town plan)*

🕐 *June to Sept: 11am-6pm; Oct to May: 10am-5pm.* 🕐*Closed Mon and public holidays. 2.74€, no charge Sun mornings when no temporary exhibitions are scheduled.* ☎ 04 91 25 01 07.

From the promenade de la Plage, once level with the Escale Borély, turn into avenue de Bonneveine and continue to the intersection with avenue Haifa, where a large metal thumb sculpted by César can be seen. This single-storey museum, opened in 1994, has been constructed via the juxtaposition of identical modules. The permanent collection, which concentrates on French artists and gives pride of place to artists either born or living in Marseille, brings together the different trends in contemporary art from the 1960s to the present day: structured movements, such as New Realism, the Support-Surface or Arte Povera group, but also eclectic work from the 1980s and maverick art which resists all attempts at classification. This rewarding collection includes: *Compressions and Expansions* by César, work by Richard Baquié (*Amore Mio*, 1985), Jean-Luc Parent (*Viewing Machines*, 1993), Daniel Burren (*Cabane éclatée no 2*), the complex creative approach of Martial Raysse, (Bird of Paradise, 1960), Arman, Jean-Pierre Raynaud, the *Rotazaza* machine by Tinguely, an *Anthropometry* by Yves Klein, contributions by Robert Combas and Jean-Michel Basquiat as well as exhibits of the sometimes underrated art of our culture: cartoons, graffiti.

Musée de la Faïence★ *(not on town plan)*

🕐 🕐*Jun to Sept: daily except Mon 11am-6pm; Oct to May: 10am-5pm.* 🕐*Closed public holidays. 1.83€.* ☎ 04 91 72 43 47.

Walk past the Parc Borély and proceed towards Pointe Rouge. The museum is situated at the far end of the Parc de Montredon. Set up in the Château Pastré, a fine 19C mansion built at the foot of the Marseilleveyre massif, this museum is devoted to the art of ceramics, from the early Neolithic Era up to the present day. A great many of the collections feature exhibits coming from Provence, and particularly Marseille, where the manufacturing of faience pottery was considerable in the late 17C and the 18C. Visitors can enjoy a series of superb exhibits turned out by the Clérissy workshops, which played a key role in reviving the art of faience in the late 17C (sharp firing technique for enamelling blue and manganese pieces), as well as three other manufactures - Madeleine Héraud, Louis Leroy and Fauchier (rocaille ornamentation and yellow enamels). Four well-known factories used the mild firing technique for vitreous glazes during the 18C: La Veuve Perrin (fish motifs, Chinese scenes, large flowers with insect), Gaspard Robert, Honoré Savy (mild firing applied to green pieces) and Antoine Bonnefoy.

The tour then moves on to Provençal collections: Moustiers faience, ceramics from La Tour-d'Aigues and Aubagne (glazed green and yellow pottery), Apt and Le Castellet (glazed pieces featuring different types of clay). The display devoted to the late 19C contains several splendid examples: glazed pottery from Avisseau in the tradition of Bernard Palissy, enamelled stoneware by Ernest Chaplet, Art Nouveau vases by Théodore Deck. Contemporary creations are also represented with the work of Émile Decouer (1930s), Georges Jouve (after 1954) and Claude Varlan (1990).

Château d'If and îles du Frioul

S. Sauvignier/MICHELIN

EXCURSIONS

Îles du Frioul

Summer: departure every hour; winter: departures on the hour and half-hour. 7.62€. Apr to Sept: 9am-5.40pm; Oct to Mar: 9.15am-6.45pm. 3.96€ (tour of the château). Combined ticket If and Frioul islands: 12.20€. Groupement des Armateurs Côtiers Marseillais, 1, quai des Belges, 13001 Marseille. ☎ 04 91 55 50 09. About 1hr 30min including boat trip and a tour of the castle; embarkation quai des Belges.

Château d'If★★

Alexandre Dumas (1802-70), the popular 19C French author of The Three Musketeers, gave this castle literary fame by imprisoning two of his heroes here: the Man in the Iron Mask, the Count of Monte Cristo and Abbé Faria. Built rapidly from 1524 to 1528, Château d'If was an outpost destined to protect the port of Marseille. In the late 16C the castle was encircled by a bastioned curtain wall. The castle, which had fallen into disuse, then became a state prison where Huguenots, the Man in the Iron Mask, and various political prisoners were held; their cells can be visited.

The **panorama**★★★ from the old chapel terrace is remarkable: the harbour, city and the Ratonneau and **Pomègues** islands linked by the new port of Frioul. On the latter, the **hôpital Caroline** is in the process of being restored.

Massif des Calanques★★ – ⓒ See Les CALANQUES.

Musée des Arts et Traditions populaires du Terroir marseillais de Château-Gombert – ⓒ See Chaîne de l'ÉTOILE.

L'Estaque

9km/5.5mi to the north. Leave Marseille by U on the plan, along the coastal motorway. "Just like a playing card – red roofs on a blue sea" is how Paul Cézanne described to Camille Pisarro in July 1876 the charms of this fishing village dotted with factories. The village was made famous by a number of avant-garde painters between 1870 and the First World War. It was partly here that the foundations of modern art were laid by Cézanne, Renoir, Braque, Dufy, Derain, Marquet, Othon Friesz, with, in particular, the birth of Cubism between 1908 and 1910.

The Estaque no longer holds the same attraction for visitors. Inhabitants of Marseille are attracted by the fish shops (the Marseille fish auction house is now located in the nearby Saumaty cove), the restaurants, as well as by the odd stall which continues to make chichi frégi – delicious long fried doughnuts. However, visitors can still enjoy a panoramic view from place de l'Eglise in the old village; the port and islands, with the picturesque rooftops of the old village in the foreground give some idea of what made this village so popular in the past.

L'Estaque was the setting for Marius et Jeannette, a hugely popular French film released in 1996, which focused on the life of this humble yet picturesque neighbour-hood close to Marseille.

Chaîne de l'Estaque★ – ⓒ See Chaîne de l'ESTAQUE.

MARTIGUES

POPULATION 72 375

MICHELIN MAP 340: F-5

LOCAL MAP SEE ÉTANG DE BERRE

Martigues took its name in 1581 after the union of the three villages of Jonquières, Ile and Ferrières established here since the Middle Ages. Set on the banks of the Étang de Berre and linked to the sea by the Canal de Caronte, Martigues, once a small fishing village, has been transformed and enlarged as a result of the expansion of the oil industry and its subsidiaries around Lavéra-Étang de Berre. In the past, painters (Corot, Ziem) and writers (Charles Maurras) alike were captivated by the luminosity and charm of this typical Provençal port; thus Martigues acquired great renown in literary and artistic circles.

The old atmosphere of a little fishing village can be conjured up by a visit to Île Brescon, the island between the Baussengue and Galiffet canals. Stand on the bridge over the Canal St-Sébastien which runs through the middle of the island for the view and whiff of nostalgia. *Av. Louis-Sammut, 13500 Martigues, ☎ 04 42 42 31 10. www.martigues-tourisme.com.*

Local Sport

At the end of June, local teams take part in water-jousting tournaments. The game is played on a raised platform set on boats navigated by oarsmen who row to the sound of pipes and drums. Players are armed with lances and shields and try to knock their opponents over.

Visit

Miroir aux oiseaux★

The pont St-Sébastien on Île Brescon affords a view of the brightly-coloured pleasure craft along the Canal St-Sébastien. Popular with painters, this spot is known as the Birds' Looking Glass.

Église Ste-Madeleine-de-l'Île

The 17C church on Canal St-Sébastien has a Corinthian style front and pilasters, cornices and an imposing organ loft inside.

Martigues, the "Venice of Provence"

G. Magnin/MICHELIN

Address Book

EATING OUT

◎◎ **Le Bouchon à la Mer** – *19 quai L.-Toulmond* – ☎ *04 42 49 41 41 – closed 1-25 Jan, Sun evenings from Sept to June, Sat lunchtime in July-Aug and Mon – 18.29/28.20€.* This small, unpretentious restaurant overlooks the canal and the harbour. Colourful dining room upstairs. Classic cuisine which offers good value for money. To aid digestion take a stroll along the canal side on the island of Brescon.

WHERE TO STAY

◎ **Le Cigalon** – *37 boulevard du 14-Juillet* – ☎ *04 42 80 49 16 – www.lecigalon.fr* – ℗ – *18 rooms: 34/51.22€* – ☼ *6.10€* – *restaurant 30€.* Located a few minutes away from the centre of the "Venice" of Provence, this family-run hotel has a

colourful, eye-catching façade. The rooms are simple but beautifully kept and air-conditioned, the food is Mediterranean and served in a typically Provençal decor.

ON THE TOWN

Le Cours – *8 cours du 4-Septembre* – ☎ *04 42 81 56 14* - Le Cours is an obligatory stopping point for those in search of a drink in Martigues. It consists of a series of bars and terraces which are nonchalantly taken by storm in the summer by those after a bit of sun and relaxation.

Le San Giov' – *14 cours du 4-Septembre* – ☎ *04 42 07 38 37 – Daily 7am-1am.* San Giov' is one of the more fashionable of these bars, instantly recognisable by its red façade. Go upstairs from 9pm onwards: you can't imagine the passion that karaoke unleashes.

Sights

Musée Ziem

◷ *Jul and Aug: daily except Mon 10am-noon, 2.30-6.30pm; Sept to Jun: daily except Mon and Tues. 2.30-6.30pm.* ◷*Closed public holidays. No charge.* ☎ *04 42 80 66 06* Grouped around the works of Félix Ziem (1821-1911), painter of landscapes and oriental scenes, whose granddaughter recently bequeathed his paintings, sketches and travel notebooks to the city, are works by Provençal artists from the 19C and 20C. Also exhibited in the museum are collections of local ethnology and archaeology and an exhibition of contemporary art.

Chapelle de l'Annonciade

◷ *Guided tours (1hr) Wed 10.30am-12.30pm on request. No charge.* ☎ *04 42 42 31 10.* Built at the beginning of the 17C for the Brothers of the White Penitents, this chapel is sumptuously decorated in Baroque style: gilded panelling, frescos representing the life of the Virgin, and a richly painted ceiling, in contrast to the building's sober exterior.

Excursions

Étang de Berre★

Round- trip of 113km/70mi by D 5. ◷ *See Étang de BERRE.*

Chapelle Notre-Dame-des-Marins

3.5km/2.25mi. Leave Martigues by N 568; after 1.5km/0.75mi from the centre bear right at the main crossroads onto D 50 (towards the hospital); 1.2km/0.5mi farther, just before the top of the hill, turn right onto a surfaced path to the chapel (car park).

From the precincts of this chapel, the **panorama**★ sweeps around Port-de-Bouc, Fos, Port-St-Louis, Lavéra complex, the Caronte railway and road bridges, the Chaîne de l'Estaque, Martigues, Étang de Berre with the Arles canal linking it to Fos-sur-Mer, the Étoile and Vitrolles chains, Montagne Ste-Victoire and on clear days Mont Ventoux, Marseille-Provence airport, the towns of Berre and St-Mitre-des-Remparts.

Fos-sur-Mer★

9km/5.5mi by N 568. ◷ *See FOS-SUR-MER.*

MÉNERBES★

POPULATION 1 118

MICHELIN MAP 332: E-11

This old village occupies a picturesque site on a promontory of the Luberon's north face. In 1573 the Calvinists captured the stronghold by a ruse, and it took five years and a large ransom to dislodge them.

Visit

Place de l'Horloge

The square is overlooked by the town hall's bell tower with its simple wrought-iron bell cage. In one corner of the square stands a noble Renaissance mansion with a round-arched doorway.

Church

The church stands at the end of the village and dates back to the 14C when it was a priory dependent on St-Agricol of Avignon. Behind the east end there is a fine **view**★ of Coulon valley, the villages of Gordes and Roussillon (with its ochre cliffs), Mont Ventoux, the Vaucluse plateau and the Luberon.

Citadelle

This 13C fortress (rebuilt in the 16C and 19C) has preserved part of its defence system with its corner towers and machicolations. Owing to its strategic position it played an important part during the Wars of Religion.

Musée du Tire-Bouchon

🕒 *Apr to Oct: 9am-noon, 2-7pm, Sat-Sun and public holidays 10am-noon, 3-7pm (Jul and Aug: 9am-7pm); Nov to Mar: daily 9am-noon, 2-6pm, Sat 10am-noon, 2-6pm, Sun up to 31 Dec 2-6pm. 3.66€. ☎ 04 90 72 41 58.*

Take the western exit from Ménerbes on the road to Cavaillon (D 3). Nestling in the wine-producing estate of La Citadelle, this museum displays a fine collection of corkscrews carved in different materials (horn, ivory, gold and silver) and presenting a variety of shapes (the letter T, animals, an effigy of Senator Volstead, who promoted the laws on Prohibition in the United States in the 1920-1930s) from the 17C up to today. The different methods used to uncork wine are well illustrated through a remarkable

Corkscrew for a weight lifter

Musée du Tire-Bouchon

An Artist's Village

Ever since the English writer **Peter Mayle** published *A Year in Provence*, Ménerbes has become famous throughout the world and it is even said that coachloads of Japanese and American tourists turn up to visit the small Provençal village. However, before Peter Mayle, other artists had already discovered this charming spot in the Luberon: the French author and literary critic François Nourissier has lived here for around 15 years, Picasso stayed here in 1946 and the place has often been frequented by celebrities, including Albert Camus and the painter Nicolas de Staël, who in 1953 bought the small castle west of the town (once a medieval fortress) and had it converted into a private residence.

display of models – wing-nut, narrow-rack, rack-and-pinion, Thomason etc as well as some outstanding collector's pieces: one combining the functions of corkscrew and nutmeg grater, and the very first French corkscrew (17C). Visitors may also be taken on a tour of the wine cellars, complete with a tasting of Côtes-de-Luberon wine.

Abbaye de **MONTMAJOUR**★

MICHELIN MAP 340: C-3

On a hill overlooking the Arles plain lie the ruins of Abbaye de Montmajour, the buildings of which represent two different periods: medieval and 18C.

The struggle against the marshes

The hill was, for a long time, surrounded by marshes. A Christian cemetery was established here and a group of hermits, who looked after the burial ground, were at the origin of the abbey, founded in the 10C under Benedictine rule. The main occupation of these people was the drainage of the marshland: between the Alpilles and the Rhône, firm land was reclaimed little by little.

Decadence

In the 17C the abbey consisted of about 20 monks and "religious" laymen, officers of the crown, to whom the king granted a position in the community and more significantly part of the revenues. Their tendency towards frivolity and love of the good life provoked a reaction: the congregation of reformed monks of St-Maur, in charge of restoring discipline, sent new monks to the abbey in 1639; the monks who had been expelled by force pillaged the abbey. In the 18C part of the buildings collapsed and were replaced by magnificent new constructions. The last abbot, the cardinal of Rohan, was implicated in the affair of the queen's necklace, with the result that in 1786 Louis XVI proclaimed the suppression of the abbey as retribution.

The misfortunes of a national property

In 1791, Montmajour was sold as a national property. It was bought by a second-hand dealer for 62 000 livres, payable over 12 years. To help repay the debt this woman broke up the buildings: furniture, panelling, lead, timberwork and marble were loaded on carts and sold. In spite of that, the woman was late in her payments and in 1793 the sale was annulled. The abbey was sold for 23 000 livres to an estate agent, who broke up the fine stonework and sold the old buildings to people who converted them into lodgings.

During the last century, the people of Arles, friends of old monuments, and the town itself recovered the buildings little by little. In 1872 the restoration of the medieval buildings was started; the 18C buildings remained in ruins. The abbey is now state property.

Tour 45min

Église Notre-Dame★

The 12C building in the main part includes an upper church and a crypt or lower church. The upper church was never completed and consists of a chancel, a transept and a nave with two bays. The crypt a was in part built into the sloping rock and in part raised, due to the incline of the land.

Cloisters★

The cloisters were built at the end of the 12C but only the eastern gallery has preserved its Romanesque characteristics. The capitals bear remarkable historiated decoration which has been associated with that of St-Trophime in Arles.

Monastic buildings

The remaining buildings include the chapter-house with rounded barrel vaulting, the refectory with its interesting pointed barrel vaulting (access from the exterior) and the dormitory, on the first floor above the refectory.

Tour de l'Abbé

This fine keep (1369), the machicolations of which have been rebuilt, was the abbey's main defence. From the platform (124 steps) a fine panorama embraces the Alpilles, Crau plain, Arles, Cévennes, Beaucaire and Tarascon.

Chapelle St-Pierre★

When the abbey was founded, this tiny church was built and half-carved out of the hillside. It includes a church with two naves (capitals carved with geometric designs) and, extending it, a hermitage formed from natural caves.

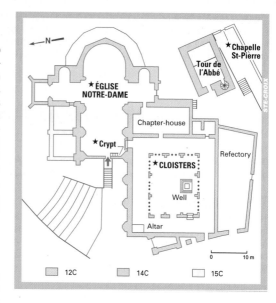

Chapelle Ste-Croix★

Guided tours by appointment. ☎ 04 90 54 64 17.

This charming 12C building is located outside the abbey precincts (200m/218yd to the right towards Fontvieille). It is built in the form of a Greek cross: a square surmounted by a dome with triangular pediments and a bell tower surrounded by four apsidal chapels with oven vaulting. This was the funerary chapel for the Montmajour cemetery. Note the ancient tombs hewn out of the rock which extend over the rocky platform.

DENTELLES DE **MONTMIRAIL**★

MICHELIN MAP 332: D-8 TO D-9

The pine and oak-clad heights, sometimes blanketed with vines, are the final foothills of Mont Ventoux overlooking the Rhône and owe their name (dentelle means lace) to the unique outline of the peaks. The geological cause of these sharp peaks lies in the upper strata of Jurassic limestone having been forced upright by the folding of the earth's crust and then eroded by wind and weather into needle-thin spikes and ridges. Although not very high in altitude (St-Amand: 734m/2 409ft), the Dentelles have a more alpine appearance than their taller neighbour (Mont Ventoux: 1 909m/6 263ft). The hills, broom-covered in May and June, attract painters and naturalists as well as walkers, who come either for a short stroll or for a long hike.

Several wine festivals are organised in the wine-producing villages, from Séguret to Vacqueyras, on the Saturday after Ascension.

Driving Tour

FROM VAISON-LA-ROMAINE

60km/37mi round-trip – about half a day

▶ Leave Vaison-la-Romaine on D 977, the road towards Avignon; turn left after 5.5km/3.75mi onto D 88.

The road climbs into the mountains, disclosing views of the Ouvèze valley to the west.

Séguret★

This picturesque village, built against the side of a steep hill, is worth a visit. At the village entrance walk through the covered passage into the main street and continue past the 15C Mascarons fountain and the 14C belfry to the 12C St-Denis church. From the square *(viewing-table)* the view embraces the Dentelles, the Comtat Venaissin and, to the far north, the line of the Massif Central. A ruined castle and a network of steep streets, lined with old houses, all add character.

▶ *On leaving Séguret turn left onto D 23 for Sablet and then take D 7 and D 79 for Gigondas.*

Gigondas

The village has given its name to the local red Grenache wine, one of the grands crus of the Côtes-du-Rhône appellation. There are many opportunities to sample and buy direct from the producers.

▶ *By way of Les Florets, where there is an alpine club hut, drive to the Col de Cayron.*

Col de Cayron

Alt 396m/1 299ft. This pass is at the centre of the Dentelles' principal peaks which, with faces rearing nearly 100m/300ft high, offer all the complexity of features relished by rock climbers.

▶ Park the car and bear right *(1hr return on foot)* on the unsurfaced road which winds through the Dentelles.

There are splendid **views**★ of the Rhône plain backed by the Cévennes, Vaucluse plateau and Mont Ventoux. The road passes below a ruined Saracen tower (Tour Sarrazine).

▶ *Return to the car and take D 7, then turn left towards Vacqueyras.*

Chapelle Notre-Dame d'Aubune

Near Fontenouilles farm. The Romanesque chapel at the foot of the mountain stands on a small terrace from which there is a good view of the Comtat plain. It is surmounted by an elegant **bell tower**★ ornamented on each of its four sides by tall Antique-style pilasters and rounded bays between larger and smaller pillars – note the decoration on the columns and capitals: straight or twisted fluting, grapes, acanthus leaves and grotesque figures.

▶ *Continue left along D 81 which winds through vineyards and olive groves.*

Address Book

EATING OUT

🍴 **L'Oustalet** – *place du Portail – 84190 Gigondas* – ☎ 04 90 65 85 30 – *closed 15 Nov-28 Dec, Mon from mid-Aug to June and Sun – 21€ lunch - 34.30/57.93€.* Situated in the charming village square, this restaurant is housed in an old building and extends onto a terrace. Whether served on the terrace or in the simple, rustic dining room, the food is made with fresh produce and accompanied by pitchers of local wines.

🍴🍴 **La Bastide Bleue** – *route de Sablet – 84110 Séguret* – ☎ 04 90 46 83 43 – *closed 7 Jan-8 Feb, Wed except evenings in Aug and Tue from Oct-May – 15€ lunch – 21.50€.* Situated in the stables of an old coaching inn, this restaurant serves authentic country cooking. In the summer the shady courtyard serves as a terrace. There is also a swimming pool surrounded by a garden, and a few rooms full of character.

WHERE TO STAY

🛏 **Chambre d'hôte La Farigoule** – *Le Plan-de-Dieu – 84150 Violès – 10km/6.2mi west of Gigondas via D 80 for Orange then D 8 and D 977 for Violès* – ☎ 04 90 70 91 78 – *closed Nov-Mar – 5 rooms: 33.54/50.31€.* This 18C wine-producing estate has maintained all its authenticity. The hosts, formerly booksellers, have given each room the name of a Provençal poet whose books are also provided. Breakfast is served in a vaulted room.

🛏 **Chambre d'hôte Mas de la Lause** – *chemin de Geysset – 84330 Le Barroux* – ☎ 04 90 62 33 33 – www.provence-gites.com – *closed 1 Nov-1 Apr* – 🍴 – *5 rooms: 43/68€ – evening meal 15€.* This mas, dating from 1883, is surrounded by vineyards and apricot trees. Restored in a contemporary style, the rooms have nonetheless retained their Provençal colours. Food is made using local produce and is served under an arbour facing the chateau.

Vineyard at the foot of the Dentelles de Montmirail

Beaumes-de-Venise

A terraced village, on the southernmost foothills of the Dentelles, which produces a delicious fortified sweet white wine from the Muscat grape.

▷ *Leave Beaumes-de-Venise eastwards on D 21, bear left on D 938 and left again on D 78.*

Le Barroux

🕐 *Jun to Sept: 10am-7pm; Apr to Jun and Oct: 2-6pm.* 🕐 *Closed Nov to Mar.* 3€. ☎ 04 90 62 35 21.

Car park at entrance to village. The picturesque village, with sloping streets, is dominated by the lofty silhouette of its **castle**.

This huge quadrilateral construction, flanked by round towers, originally (12C) guarded the Comtat Venaisson plain. Remodelled in the Renaissance, burnt down during the Second World War, then restored once more, the castle was, until the 18C, the seat of several lordships, including that of Rovigliasc (note the coats of arms above the square tower doorway). After visiting the chapel, the lower rooms and the Guard room, walk through the different floors, where contemporary exhibitions are on display in several of the rooms (Salles des Audiences, Salle de la Garenne, Salle du Parlement, among others). There is a fine view from the gardens.

▷ *Leave Le Barroux northwards towards Suzette and meet up with D 90.*

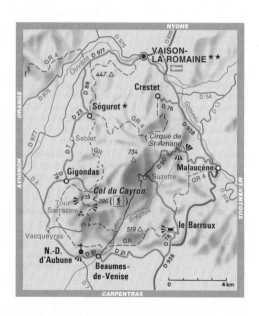

After Suzette the road enters the vertical-walled Cirque de St-Amand.

The road rises to a small pass which affords a good **view**★ on one side of the Dentelles and on the other of Mont Ventoux, Ouvèze valley and the Baronnies.

Malaucène

This typical Provençal town is for the most part surrounded by a large avenue shaded by huge plane trees. The fortified church, rebuilt in the 14C on the site of the former Romanesque church, was once a part of the ramparts: the façade is surmounted by corbelled machicolations. Inside, the Provençal Romanesque nave is covered with splendid pointed-barrel vaulting, the south side chapels with pointed vaulting and the apse with a dome of flat ribs. Note the 18C organ loft with beautifully-carved musical instruments and a pulpit carved out of oak.

Go through Porte Soubeyran, the gate beside the church, into the old village of small streets, old houses, fountains, wash-houses and oratories, with an old belfry crowned by a wrought-iron bell cage at its centre. Take the path to the left of the church to the Calvary for a view of the Drôme mountains and Mont Ventoux.

▶ *D 938 northwest climbs the fertile Groseau valley. Turn left onto D 76.*

Crestet

Leave the car in the castle car park. The village is one of the most typical of Vaucluse, with the 14C church standing in a minute square lined by an arcade and decorated at the centre with a fountain. Narrow streets between Renaissance houses climb the hill crowned by a 12C **castle**, from where there is a good view of the village, the Ouvèze, Mont Ventoux and the Baronnies.

▶ *Return to D 938 and turn left for Vaison-la-Romaine.*

NÎMES★★★

POPULATION 128 471

MICHELIN MAP 339: L-5

Situated on the edge of the garrigue limestone hills and the Petite Camargue plain, Nîmes exudes the air of a great city of the arts, proud of its prestigious Gallo-Roman past, yet nonetheless anxious to open itself up to new ideas. Deeply-marked by its Huguenot past, Nîmes is a city of old traditional industries, particularly textiles and the processing of local agricultural products (canning of fruit, wine production). Among the city's gastronomic specialities note: brandade de morue (see below), marinated olives, caladons (almond biscuits), and crispy little Croquant Villaret, a speciality of Nîmes for more than two hundred years. In the past few years the local Costières de Nîmes wines (red, rosé and white) have gained an excellent reputation.

Nîmes is also the centre for tauromachy (bullfighting). The corridas or bullfights, with their set rules, which take place in the amphitheatre, Camargue races and the running of bulls through the streets have brought immense popularity and fame to the city.

A. Thuillier/MICHELIN

Huguenot cross

A Bit of History

The Chained Crocodile

Capital of Volcae Arecomici, Nemausus (Nîmes' ancient name originated from a sacred spring around which the town settled) was at the head of a vast territory of 24 settlements between the sea the Cévennes and from the River Rhône to the Sète mountains, when it accepted Roman domination. The date of Roman colonisation, its founder and the ethnic origin of its colonists are now matters of controversy. Two theories have been put forward: the founder was either Augustus, who settled here in 31 BC with a Roman colony of veterans of the Egyptian campaign (evidence of this settlement is the famous coin stamped with the chained crocodile), or Caesar with a Latin colony in 44 BC.

Regardless of the issue as to who founded Nîmes, Augustus was the one who heaped privileges on the town and allowed it build fortifications 16km/10mi long. The town, situated on the **Domitian Way**, then proceeded to embellish itself with splendid buildings: a forum with the Maison Carrée to the south, an amphitheatre able to hold 24 000 people, a circus, baths and fountains fed by an imposing aqueduct, the Pont du Gard which yielded 20 000m3/7 063 cubic ft of water a day. In the 2C the city received privileges from the Emperors Hadrian and Antoninus Pius (whose mother came from Nîmes) and continued to flourish and build (Plotinius' basilica, arrangement of the Fountaine district), reaching its zenith with a population of 20 000 to 25 000 inhabitants.

Religious Struggles

The most significant period of Nîmes history, together with that of the Roman occupation, is the period of bitterly-disputed religious differences. In the 5C the Visigoths, who ruled the country (from Toulouse to the River Rhône), clashed with the Catholic population when they tried to impose their beliefs: churches were closed and the Catholics were persecuted well into the 6C.

In the 13C the people of Nîmes sided with the Albigensians. This sect, also know as the Catharist heretics, was in permanent oppostion to the Roman church and protested against the corruption of the clergy at that time. Simon de Montfort headed the terrible crusade against these heretics, and the city surrendered in 1213. The implacable war threw the nobility of northern France against that of the south, and ended in the destruction of the Provençal civilization along with the indepence of the princes who ruled over it. In the 14C a wave of intolerance fell upon the Jews; they were expelled from the city and their possessions confiscated. In the 16C Nîmes became a Huguenot city. It was the Geneva of France: three quarters of its population believed in the Reform.

On 29 September 1567 the Michelade tragedy occurred: 200 Catholics, most of whom were priests, were massacred. There ensued a long dark period of persecution and war in which both sides suffered in turn. The active participation of Nîmes in the War of the Camisards (1700-1704) following the Revocation of the Edict of Nantes was followed later the same century by Protestant revenge at the time of the Revolution. The Restoration of the Bourbon monarchy (1814-1830) was marked by the White Terror perpetrated by the Catholics.

The Conquest of the West

From the Middle Ages local serge was well known throughout Europe for its hard-wearing quality. Legend has it that Christopher Columbus used it to manufacture the sails of his caravels; this same cloth, which was exported via Genoa, was also used to make sailors' trousers. In 1873, a Bavarian emigrant in the United States called Lévy-Strauss had the idea of capitalizing on its robust qualities to make trousers for gold-diggers and migrants setting out to discover the West. The name "bleu de Gênes" or "blue from Genoa" became "blue jeans" and the brand name "denim" (literally "from Nîmes") still bears testimony today to the contribution made by the city in the conquest of the West.

Ferias and bullfighting

The focus of the Whitsun Feria (Feria de Pentecôte), created in 1952 in imitation of Spanish bullfighting festivals, is on the amphitheatre (arènes) and the corridas and novilladas (bullfights with young bulls and novice matadors) held inside it. Although the bull reigns supreme, the whole town becomes involved in its traditions: running the bulls along the boulevards, bullfights for eager amateurs in small bullrings nearby, concerts, exhibitions, folklore parades, dances and impromptu events, all of which

Address Book

Guided tours of the town – Nîmes has been listed as a "Town of Art and History" and the guided tours (2hrs), organised by the tourist office, are conducted by guides approved by the Centre des Monuments Nationaux (National Monuments Centre). They include a visit to the hôtel Fontfroide, which is not open to visitors otherwise. All year round: Sat 2.30pm (July to Sept: 10am); during school term: Tue, Thur, Sat: 2.30pm. 5.34€.

An all-purpose ticket (pass) allows entry to all city monuments and museums and can be purchased at the first sight you visit: 9.15€ (children: 4.57€), valid 3 days.

Hôtel Fontfroide – Guided tours only *(see Practical Information)*.

WHEN (NOT) TO VISIT NÎMES

Those who can't tolerate the heat should avoid the city in August when it becomes a veritable furnace, even at night. Visitors who object to corridas and crowds are advised not to come during the long weekend of Pentecôte (7th Sun-Mon after Easter) when entry to just about anywhere is almost impossible, as is finding accommodation!

ENTERTAINMENT

Programmes – See the daily newspaper *Midi-Libre*, the weekly publication *La Semaine de Nîmes* or its rival the *Gazette de Nîmes*, or *Le César (free)*, provided by the Tourist Information Centre.

Cinema – Art house cinema Le Sémaphore, 25 rue Porte-de-France, ☎ 04 66 67 83 11.

Theatres – L'Armature, 12 rue de l'Ancien-Vélodrome, ☎ 04 66 82 20 52, housed in a hangar which used to be an industrial warehouse, now hosts concerts, plays and exhibitions.

SHOPPING

Maison Villaret – *13 rue de la Madeleine* – ☎ 04 66 67 41 79. Crunchy almond biscuits known as *croquants*.

Brandade Raymond – *34 rue Nationale* – ☎ 04 66 67 20 47. A century dedicating to the producing of this classic Provençal dish!

Wine – *La Vinothèque* – *18 rue Jean-Rebou* – ☎ 04 66 67 20 44. Local wines.

Provençal fabrics – *Olivades* – *4 place de la Maison-Carré* – ☎ 04 66 21 01 31. The textile industry was born during the reign of Louis XI, when the first workshop was founded. In the 18C the textile factories (silk and serge) embraced more than 300 professions and gave work to 10 000 people. The tradition has continued through the centuries with highs and lows and nowadays is represented by prestigious brands such as Cacharel who have made their mark with this shop.

Books – *Librairie Goyard* – *34 bd Victor-Hugo* – ☎ 04 66 67 20 51. For books on the region and on bullfighting.

Markets – Large market on Mon on bd Gambetta. Organic market Fri mornings on av Jean-Jaurès. Flea market Sun mornings in the Costières stadium car park. Evening market, Jul-Aug, Thur 6-10pm ('Les jeudis de Nîmes').

EVENTS

Ferias and bullfighting – There are three ferias in Nîmes: during the so-called "spring" feria which takes place in February, *novilladas* take place throughout the weekend; the Whitsun feria, the most well-known, lasts from the 7th Thursday after Easter to the following Monday and includes a pégoulade along the boulevards, *abrivados, novilladas* and corridas throughout the day and evening as well as other entertainments all over the city; the harvest feria, the most typical of all, takes place in mid-September.

Tickets – As well as single tickets you can also buy a pass which gives access to the shows and the best seats. Don't expect to gain access at the last moment at the Whitsun and Harvest ferias, unless you buy tickets on the black market for astronomical prices.

At the ticket office prices vary from 15.24€ to 76.22€ for a *corrida* and from 4.57€ to 7.62€ for a novillada.

Ticket office: 1 rue Alexandre-Ducros, ☎ 04 66 67 28 02.

Amphitheatre – Since 1988, from October to April, the amphitheatre is covered by a detachable dome consisting of an inflatable, transparent cloth held up by an elliptical beam which in turn leans on pilasters which are fixed to the modern parts of the monument. This structure, which forms a spectacular setting for shows held in the winter, can hold up to 7 000 people. As well as ferias, the amphitheatre also hosts rock and pop concerts, fairs and conventions and Davis Cup tournaments.

Le Printemps du jazz – (3rd week in March) Jazz concerts in a variety of venues around town.

For coin ranges see Legend at the back of the guide.

EATING OUT

☺ **Bistrot des Arènes** – *11 rue Bigot* – ☎ 04 66 21 40 18 – *closed Aug, Sat lunchtime and Sun*. Sample the specialities of Lyons restaurants known as bouchon in a delightfully ornate setting crammed with objects including the French puppet Guignol.

☺ **Le Bistrot au Chapon Fin** – *3 place du Château-Fadaise* – ☎ 04 66 67 34 73 – *closed Aug. Sat lunchtime and Sun*. Located behind the church of St Paul, the old façade of this building is more than a little inviting... Inside, the bistro-style decor, with its feria and movie posters and Nîmes paintings, won't disappoint you. Note the collection of cocks! Daily dishes are listed on a blackboard.

🍽🍽 **Le Bouchon et L'Assiette** – *5 bis rue Sauve –* ☎ *04 66 62 02 93 – closed 2-17 Jan, 29 Apr-2 May, 29 Jul-23 Aug, Tue lunchtime and Wed.* A carefully chosen decor, embellished with paintings and antiques, a warm welcome, and tasty seasonal cooking.

🍽🍽 **Aux Plaisirs des Halles** – *4 rue Littré –* ☎ *04 66 36 01 02 – closed 12-20 Aug, Sun evenings and Mon except evenings in Jul-Aug.* Everyone in town talks about this place. Once you've got past the discreet façade you will find an elegant yellow room with armchairs draped in fabric, a patio which has been turned into a pretty terrace, excellent, well-presented food and a good wine list.

WHERE TO STAY

🛏 **Hôtel Amphithéâtre** – *4 rue des Arènes –* ☎ *04 66 67 28 51 – closed 2-15 Jan – 16 rooms -* 🍴 *5.64€.* Near the amphitheatre in a pedestrian street, this small, family-run hotel with its slightly austere façade, is an excellent address for those travelling on a low budget. It offers quite spacious rooms decorated with rustic furniture.

🛏 **Chambre d'hôte La Mazade** – *In the village – 30730 St-Mamert-du-Gard – 17km/10.5mi west of Nîmes via D 999 and D 1 –* ☎ *04 66 81 17 56 – www.bbfrance. com/couston.html –* 🚫 *– 3 rooms: evening meal 14€.* This is a very original family house: each room has designer decor and is bursting with plants and Mexican objets d'art... This picturesque mix of styles makes for an amusing setting! In the evening, dinner is served under an arbour on the terrace which faces the garden.

🛏🛏 **New Hôtel la Baume** – *21 rue Nationale –* ☎ *04 66 76 28 42 – 34 rooms –* 🍴 *8.38€ – restaurant 12.20/20.58€.* This 17C mansion successfully blends contemporary and antique styles. An interior stone staircase leads to the simple bedrooms, a few of which have pretty, French-style painted ceilings.

ON THE TOWN

Behind the numerous ancient buildings in Nîmes lies the hidden shadow of Bacchus and the tendency to view life as a perpetual party. The whole year is marked out by the ferias and the city in general is characterised by a huge number and variety of cafés including Café-concerts, bodegas, Irish pubs or the great fin-de-siècle cafés: each has its own following.

Haddock Café – *13 rue de l'Agau –* ☎ *04 66 67 86 57 – haddock.cafe@libertysurf.fr – Mon-Fri 11.30am-3pm, 7pm-2am, Sat 7pm-3am.* This wine bar-restaurant cultivates food (wine by the glass, reasonably priced menu) as much as the arts. There is a never-ending series of entertainments including concerts, literary and philosophy evenings and art exhibitions. Behind the wide, metal bar Philippe, the owner, presides over what is definitely one of the most dynamic venues of Nîmes' cultural life.

La Grand Bourse – *2 bd des Arènes –* ☎ *04 66 67 21 91 – daily 7am-1am.* With its Napoleon III style coffered ceiling, a terrace facing the amphitheatre and deep comfortable rattan armchairs, this is the most prestigious café in Nîmes. Excellent, professional service attracts customers of all ages and backgrounds.

Bar Hemingway – *15 rue Gaston-Boissier –* ☎ *02 66 21 90 30 – hotel.imperator@ wanadoo.fr – daily 8am-11pm.* Opening onto a garden with redwood and cedar trees, a fountain and sculptures, the Hemingway bar of the Hotel Imperator Concorde is an oasis of calm and magic. Photographs evoke the presence in this bar of two lovers of tauromachy: Ava Gardner and Ernest Hemingway, who wrote Death in the Afternnon (1962), a magnificent book about bullfighting.

Le Diagonal – *41bis rue Émile-Jamais –* ☎ *04 66 21 70 01 – Tue-Thu 5pm-2am, Fri-Sun and the eve of public holidays 5pm-3am. Closed 3 weeks in Aug.* This 1950s style bar is run by a couple. Rather like the sphinx at the entry of Thebes, the husband poses riddles to customers, if in a rather more convivial atmosphere, judging by the din of the clientele, the board games and the art exhibitions (art previews on the first Thursday of the month). Tapas and house punch, Latino and African music as well as jazz and salsa.

attract large crowds from far and wide. In the narrow streets local associations open up *bodegas* (informal bars or restaurants) in which pride of place is given to Spanish food (*tapas* and *paella*) and sherries (the dry fino, in particular).

Battered by storm

Early in the morning of 8 October 1988, a massive thunderstorm, accompanied by torrential rain, struck Nîmes. Although nothing unusual in the region, the rainfall was such that normally dry streams became engorged with water, and even underground water courses forced their way to the surface. Soon the road from Alès turned into a torrent of mud, which invaded the town, carrying everything in its path, throwing trees and cars against walls, and resulting in eight dead and a devastated city.

Public Buildings 1

This itinerary explores the principal monuments of Roman Nîmes and the "Écusson," the medieval quarter with its winding streets nestling between the tree-lined boulevards. Also worth noting are some of the splendid *hôtels particuliers*, and elegant town houses, many undergoing restoration.

Esplanade

Leave your car in the underground car park.

This ample square, bordered by the columns of the Palais de Justice and numerous outdoor cafés, looks out onto avenue Feuchères. In the middle of the square note the Fontaine Pradier, erected in 1848.
Go down boulevard de la Libération to reach the amphitheatre.

Amphitheatre (Arènes)★★★

Apr to Sept: 9am-6.30pm; Oct to Mar: 9am-5.30pm. Closed 1 Jan, 1 May, 25 Dec and days when performances are held. 4.27€. ☎ 04 66 58 38 00.
Access from the end of rue de l'Aspic.

This beautifully preserved amphitheatre is twin to the one at Arles; most likely from the same period (late 1C-early 2C), with the same layout, similar dimensions and capacity (133m x 101m/436ft x 331ft; seating capacity 24 000). Its differences are slight architectural ones such as the galleries with barrel vaulting of Roman construction which are replaced by the Greek trabeated form. The Nîmes amphitheatre because of its axial dimensions is ranked ninth out of the 20 important amphitheatres discovered in Gaul; however, it is the best preserved of the Roman ones.

From the exterior, the building presents two storeys each of 60 arcades (total height: 21m/65.5ft) crowned with an attic. The building material in hard limestone from Barutel did not require detailed ornamentation: pilasters on the lower register and engaged Doric columns above. Four axial doorways correspond to the four entrances. The main northern gateway has kept its pediment, adorned with bulls. Inside (climb to the topmost tiers to have a view of the whole), an ingenious system of corridors, stairways, galleries and *vomitaria* (sloping corridors) made it possible for the amphitheatre to be evacuated in a few minutes. Under the arena itself a substructure (68 x 37m/223 x 121ft) made of two vast galleries served as backstage.

Having lost its main purpose when gladiator combats were forbidden in 404, the amphitheatre was transformed into a fortress by the Visigoths: arcades were boarded up and towers added, a deep moat was dug around the arena itself and perhaps backed up by a small rampart wall (ruins can be seen in the basement of the Law Courts). In the eastern part of the building, the castle of the Viscounts of Nîmes was later built (two walled arcades lit by small Romanesque windows were preserved). The amphitheatre was, like the one at Arles, overtaken by houses, streets and two chapels; a village was established and numbered 700 inhabitants in the 18C. The demolition of these buildings started in 1809 and restoration began. The first corrida was performed in 1853.

Maison Carrée★★★

Apr to Sept: 9am-7pm; Oct to Mar: 9am-5pm. Closed 1 Jan, 1 May, 25 Dec. No charge. ☎ 04 66 58 38 00.

This magnificent temple, known as the Square House, is the best preserved of the Roman temples still standing. It was built under Augustus' (late 1C BC) reign and was inspired by the Temple of Apollo in Rome. Consecrated to the Imperial cult and dedicated to Augustus' grandsons, the temple faced the forum and was surrounded by a portico of finely carved columns.

The pure lines of the building, its harmonious proportions and the elegance of its fluted columns denote Greek influence, which is also found in the temple's ornamentation. Like all Classical temples, it is composed of a porch defined by a colonnade, and a cella, or inner room, consecrated to a god, which is reached by a stairway of 15 steps. Inside is an exhibition dedicated to the architecture and chequered history of the building, and a superb mosaic was discovered during building work near the Jardin de la Fontaine.

▸ *Take the narrow rue de l'Horloge then turn right into place de l'Horloge and then left into rue de la Madeleine.*

NÎMES

11 Novembre Pl.	DV
11 Novembre Sq. du	DV
Antonin Square	C
Arènes Bd des	CV 2
Arènes Pl. des	CV
Arnavielle R.	AZ
Aspic R. de l'	CUV
Auguste R.	CU 4
Beaucaire R. de	BX
Bernis R. de	CV 6
Bouillargues R. de	BY
Bouquerie Sq de la	CU
Briçonnet R.	BY 8
Carnot Av.	BY, DV
Chapitre Pl. du	DU
Chapitre R. du	CU 12
Cirque Romain R. du	AY 13
Cité Foulc R.	BY
Courbet Bd Amiral	DUV 14
Crémieux R.	DU 16
Curaterie R.	DU 17
Daudet Bd Alphonse	CU 18
Dhuoda R.	AZ
Ducros R. A.	CV 19
Faïta R. V.	BX, DU
Feuchères Av.	DV
Fontaine Quai de la	AX, CU 20
Fresque R.	CV
Gambetta Bd	ABX, CDU
Gamel Av. P.	BZ 22
Gaulle Esplanade de	DV
Générac R. de	AYZ 23
Générac Rte de	AZ
Grand-Temple Pl. du	DU
Grand'Rue	DU 24
Greffes R. des	CDV
Guesde Pl. J.	AY
Guizot R.	CU 26
Halles R. des	CU 27
Henri-IV R.	AYZ
Herbes Pl. aux	CU
Horloge Pl. de l'	CU
Horloge R. de l'	CU 28
Hôtel-Dieu R. de l'	AY
Jamais R. E.	AY, CV
Jean-Jaurès Av.	AYZ
Kennedy Av.	AY
Leclerc Av. du Général	BYZ
Libération Bd de la	DV 30

Arènes	CV	
Carré d'art	CU	
Castellum	AX	
Cathédrale N.-D.-et-St-Castor	CU	
Chapelle des Jésuites	DU	B
Façade romane	CU	D
Fontaine Pradier	DV	
Hôtel Fontfroide	VC	G
Hôtel Meynier de Salinelles	CU	K
Hôtel de Bernis	VC	E
Hôtel de Régis	DU	F
Jardin de la Fontaine	AX	

Rue de la Madeleine

The main shopping street of Nîmes. At no 13, the Boulangerie Villaret is proud of baking the famous "croquants" biscuits in the same oven for two centuries. No 1, the oldest house in "old Nîmes", displays a finely-carved Romanesque façade.

Come out into delightful **place aux Herbes**, a good place for a rest on one of the café terraces, which offer a good view of the west front of the **Cathédrale Notre-Dame-et-St-Castor**, which still has a partly Romanesque frieze depicting scenes of the Old Testament.

▸ *From the narrow street on the left of the cathedral take rue Curaterie and place du Grand-Temple to get to boulevard Amiral-Courbet.*

Porte d'Auguste

This gate, a ruin of the Augustinian fortified wall on the Domitian Way, was flanked originally by two semicircular towers enclosing an interior courtyard, an effective defensive procedure. It still has the two wide passages for chariots and two narrower passages for pedestrians. There is also a bronze copy of the statue of Augustus.

Madeleine R. de la ....CU 32	Perrier R. Gén. .... CU	Saintenac Bd E. ....DU 45
Maison Carrée Pl. de la ......CU 33	Placette Pl. de la ....AY	Sauve R. de .... AX
Mallarmé R. Stéphane ....AX 34	Planas R. du ....BZ	Séguier R. ....BX
Marchands R. des ....CU 35	Pompidou Av. Georges ....AY	Semard R. Pierre......BX, DU
Marché Pl. du CV	Porte de France R. CV	Servie R. de la.........................DV
Marronniers R. des ....BZ	Prague Bd de ....DV 42	Séverine Pl. .... AZ
Martyrs de la s	Président-Allende Bd ....BZ	Seynes R. A.-de......................AZ
Résistance Pl. des ....AZ 36	Puech-du-Teil R. .... AZ	Sully R. ....BX
Mendès-France Av. Pierre ..BZ 39	Régale R. ....CDV	Talabot Bd ....BX
Mistral R. Frédéric ....AYZ	République R. de la ....AYZ, CV 43	Tessier R. G. ....AZ
Montcalm Pl. ....AY	Revoil R. Henri ....AY	Tour l'Évêque R. de la ....BZ
Nationale R. ....CDU	Révolution Pl. de la .... CU	Tour Magne R. de la..............AX
Natoire Bd ....BY	Rouget-de-l'Isle R.................. AX	Triaire Bd Sergent ....ABZ
Notre-Dame R. ....BX, DV	Roussy R. ....DUV	Verdun R. de.....................AY 47
Painlevé R. P. ....BY	St-Gilles R. de ....AYZ	Victor-Hugo Bd................CUV
Pasteur R. ....AX	Ste-Anne R. ....AY 46	Villars R. ....BX
Péri Pl. Gabriel ....DU	Ste-Perpétue R. ....BY	Violettes R. ....CV 49

Maison Carrée.................................CU	Musée du Vieux Nîmes.....................CU M³
Maison natale de Daudet.....................CU L	Porte d'Auguste .... DU
Musée Archéologique, Muséum	Temple de Diane ....AX
d'Histoire naturelle ....DU M¹	Tour Magne ....AX
Musée des Beaux-Arts ....ABX M²	
Musée des Cultures taurines.................CV M⁴	

▶ *Go back to boulevard Amiral-Courbet and just after the Archaeological Museum turn right into rue des Greffes and right again into Grand'Rue.*

Chapelle des Jésuites

The 18C Jesuit college chapel has surprisingly harmonious proportions. The striking two-storey façade is topped by a triangular pediment and has a regular pattern of alternating pilasters, engaged columns and alcoves. The **interior**★ is lit through skylights and consists of a short single-aisle nave with balustraded galleries running along its sides, a transept crowned by a flattened dome above the crossing, and a chancel with a semi-circular vault and prominent ribbing. The richness of the sculpted ornamentation (pilasters, capitals, entablatures) puts the finishing touches to the balance of the building, which houses temporary exhibitions.

▶ *Turn left into rue du Chapitre.*

Rue du Chapitre

No 14. The Hôtel de Regis displays an 18C façade and a lovely 16C paved courtyard.

▷ *Take rue de la Prévôté which leads into place du Chapitre.*

After the old bishopric, which now houses the Muséee du Vieux-Nîmes, return to place aux Herbes before turning left into rue des Marchands.

▷ *Walk under the picturesque covered gallery known as "Passage des marchands". Rue de Bernis will be on your right.*

Rue de Bernis

At the junction with **rue de l'Aspic**, the porch of the **Hôtel Meynier de Salinelles** (No 8) is adorned with three paleochristian sarcophagi imbedded in the wall. At No 14, **Hôtel Fontfroide**, note the superb double spiral grand staircase dating from the 17C. At No 3 rue de Bernis, the **Hôtel de Bernis** has a fine 15C façade with mullioned windows.

▷ *Turn left from rue Fresque, an arched passageway leads into place du Marché, where you will find a palm tree, the symbol of Nîmes, while a bronze crocodile is to be found looking in the water of one of the fountains, a sculpture by Martial Raysse.*

Fountains 2

From place de la Maison Carré go up boulevard Daudet until you reach **place d'Assas** with its numerous outdoor restaurants. Bear right to get to the aristocratic **quai de la Fontaine**, bordered by magnificent private residences.

▷ *Follow the calm, tree-shaded canal with its haughty swans.*

Jardin de la Fontaine★★

Entrance through the monumental gate facing rue Jean-Jaurès. This garden is the unexpected creation of an 18C army engineer, J.-P. Mareschal, and extends from the famous Nemausus spring up the slopes of Mont Cavalier to the white octagonal form of the Tour Magne.

Since the creation of the garden in the 18C, the spring water has been collected in a mirror-like pool surrounded by balustraded walks, before flowing through pools to the canal.

During Antiquity, this sacred district included the spring, a theatre, temple and baths. Recent excavations have uncovered some of the surrounding area: to the east on rue Pasteur an opulent 2C mansion; a district for ordinary local people; and at the crossroads of boulevard Jaurès and rue de Sauve, a sumptuous public building (2C), whose function still arouses speculation. **Temple de Diane** dates from the first half of the 2C and is known as the Temple of Diana but its true function is unknown. It was most likely part of a vast architectural ensemble, still buried, made up of several different levels (traces of stairs). It was occupied by the Benedictine nuns in the Middle Ages, who converted it into a church without too many modifications, and was destroyed during the Wars of Religion in 1577.

Tour Magne★

🕐 *Jun to Sept: 9am-7pm; Oct to May: 9am-5pm.* 🚫*Closed 1 Jan, 1 May, 25 Dec. 2.29€.* ☎ *04 66 67 65 56.*

Located at the top of Mont Cavalier, the city's highest point, the tower is the most remarkable vestige of the massive defences built around the city. It is a three-storey polygonal tower standing 34m/112ft high, but it was weakened by a 16C treasure-seeker who persisted in digging at its base. There is a good **view**★ of Mont Ventoux, the Alpilles, Nîmes, Vistre plain and the garrigues.

▷ *Leave the park and go back down to the canal along rue de la Tour-Magne. Turn left into rue Pasteur.*

Castellum

This was the Roman distribution tank to which water, from Uzès, was brought by the Pont du Gard aqueduct, and then distributed in the town. Above it stands Fort Vauban, the citadel built in 1687 to watch over Protestant Nîmes, which today is a university.

▷ *Return along boulevard Gambetta.*

At No 20, a bourgeois townhouse, is the **Maison Natale d'Alphonse Daudet**, the birthplace of Alphonse Daudet.

Museums

Musée des Beaux-Arts

Apr to Sept: daily except Mon 10am-6pm; Oct to Mar: daily except Mon 11am-6pm. Closed 1 Jan, 1 May, 1 Nov, 25 Dec. 4.27€. 04 66 67 38 21.

The Fine Arts Museum was remodelled in 1986 by the architect J-M. Wilmotte. On the ground floor there is a large Roman mosaic depicting the marriage of Admetus; it was discovered in Nîmes in the 19C. The museum displays works of art from the French, Italian, Flemish and Dutch Schools (15C-19C) including paintings by Bassano (*Susanna and the Elders*), Rubens (*Portrait of a Monk*), Jean-François de Troy (*The Sleeping Reaper*), Delaroche (*Cromwell and Charles I's Coffin*), an astonishing ceramic figure by Andrea della Robia, a *Madonna and Child* and portraits by Nicolas Largillière and Hyacinthe Rigaud. Local works are represented by the delicate portraits of Xavier Sigalon (1787-1837) from Uzès, a seascape by Joseph Vernet, historical paintings by Natoire, a native of Nîmes, and *Landscape Near Nîmes*, dated 1869, by J.-B. Lavastre.

Carré d'Art★

Daily except Mon 10am-6pm. Closed 1 Jan, 1 May, 1 Nov, 25 Dec. 4.27€. 04 66 76 35 70.

This large building, designed by the British architect **Norman Foster** to house both the city's Museum of Contemporary Art and its media library, stands opposite the Maison Carrée, from which it has adopted its sobriety of line and copied several of its architectural features. Its collection includes paintings, sculptures and drawings from 1960 onwards, with three main themes: French art from 1960 to the present day, Anglo-Saxon and Germanic artists and Mediterranean identity(Spain and Italy in particular, with Arte Povera and the Transavangarde movement).

The museum gives precedence to certain key movements in contemporary art such as New Realism, Supports/Surfaces, the BMPT group, Figuration Libre and New Figuration. Some famous names also in the museum's collection include César, Jean Tinguely, Sigmar Polke, Christian Boltanski, Gérard Garouste, Martial Raysse, Julian Schnabel, Miquel Barcélo, Annette Messager, the photographer Thomas Struth and local artist Claude Viallat. The museum's collection of work is displayed on a rotation system on the top two floors which may result in some works being temporarily withdrawn to provide space for exhibitions.

Musée du Vieux Nîmes

Daily except Mon 11am-6pm (Apr to Sept: 10am-6pm). Closed 1 Jan, 1 May, 1 Nov, 25 Dec. 4.27€. 04 66 76 73 70.

This museum is located in what used to be the episcopal palace (17C) at the heart of the old town. It was founded in 1920 by a rival of Frédéric Mistral and contains numerous local exhibits in a remarkably well-restored historical setting. The city of Nîmes actually reflects characteristics of both Languedoc and Provence, and there are some pieces of furniture typical of both these regions on display here; notice in particular a dining hall and a billiard room.

Musée Archéologique★

Daily except Mon 11am-6pm (Apr to Sept: daily except Mon 10am-6pm). Closed 1 Jan, 1 May, 1 and 11 Nov, 25 Dec. 4.27€. 04 66 76 74 80.

The Archaeological Museum is located in the former Jesuit College. In the ground-floor gallery, numerous pre-Roman carvings are displayed, as well as a large collection of Roman inscriptions. Upstairs are Gallo-Roman items used daily (toilet articles, headdresses, kitchen utensils, tools), funerary steles, oil lamps, glassware, pottery (Archaic Greek, Etruscan and Punic), and a coin collection. There is also an extraordinary collection of cork models of the city's main ancient monuments.

Muséum d'Histoire Naturelle

Daily except Mon 11am-6pm (summer: 10am-6pm). Closed 1 Jan, 1 May, 1 Nov, 25 Dec. 4.27€. 04 66 76 73 45.

Located on the first floor of the former Jesuit College. The museum houses a natural history section of stuffed mammals and reptiles from all over the world, and puts on excellent temporary exhibitions.

Excursions

Aire de Caissargues

This motorway rest stop is situated between the Nîmes-Centre and Garon interchanges on motorway A 54.

Here, the fine neo-classical style colonnade of Nîmes' former theatre has been rebuilt at the end of a tree-lined avenue. The exhibition building (🕐*open all year round*) houses remains (moulds) discovered on this motorway site, including the "Dame de Caissargues", the skeleton of a 25–30 year-old-woman, dating from 5 000BC, buried in a contracted foetal position and wearing a shell necklace.

Driving Tour

LA VAUNAGE

Round-trip of 44km/27mi – about 2hr 30min

▷ *Starting from the Esplanade, take rue de la République, then at the end of rue Jean-Jaurès (roundabout) take rue Arnavielle, opposite, which becomes D 940, the road to Sommières.*

Caveirac

An imposing 17C horseshoe-shaped château houses the town hall. Two corner towers roofed with glazed tiles, the mullioned windows, some amusing gargoyles and a fine staircase with a wrought iron balustrade enhance the building. The porch is so big that it straddles the road (D 103).

▷ *Take D 40 and, after St-Dionisy, turn left into D 737 for Nages-et-Solorgues. A rocky signposted pathway leads up the hill to the site of the archaeological remains.*

Oppidum de Nages

Nages was one of the five *oppida* of the Iron Age (800–50 BC) that housed the Vaunage population. The islands of living quarters, arranged on the slope's incline and separated by parallel streets, suggest an early urban plan and give an insight into the characteristics of the Gauls' living arrangements. The rows of small uniform houses with drystone walls, sometimes quite high, are clearly visible. To begin with, these dwellings were on a one-room plan with a hearth at its centre; in the 2C BC they were enlarged and subdivided but the comfort remained rudimentary. The settlement was surrounded by fortifications (there were four successive ones) a part of which has been successfully excavated. No public monument has been uncovered except for a *fanum*, a small native temple (70 BC). Roman infiltration did not hinder the *oppidum's* development which was at its greatest between 70 and 30 BC, the period in which appears the beginning of economic specialisation (presence of a forge).

▷ *On the return trip down, at the village's entrance, take the first street to the left leading to the Roman cistern, which still feeds several of the village's fountains.*

Nages-et-Solourges

Located in the town hall, on the first floor, the **Musée archéologique** (🕐*daily except Sat-Sun.* ☎ *04 66 35 05 26; contact the administration office in the town hall at Nages-et-Solorgues*) displays pottery and various items excavated from the site of Les Castels. Different aspects of the successive inhabitants' daily life are evoked; food-related activities (agriculture, husbandry, hunting), crafts (metalwork, pottery making, weaving), arms, toilet requisites and funerary objects.

▷ *Return to D 40, turning left onto it.*

Calvisson

This peaceful village lies amid vines in the centre of Vaunage plain and is famous for its Easter procession.

▷ *In the centre of town take CD 107 for Fontanès; leave the village and bear left on the sign posted road indicating Roc de Gachonne.*

From the viewing table located at the top of a tower, there is a picturesque view of the red tile-roofed village, Vidourle valley (south-west) and St-Loup peak (east).

▷ *Return to D 40, then turn left onto D 249 and exit at Aubais. D 142 leads to **Aigues-Vives**.*

▶ *After passing under the motorway, it is worth stopping at* **Mus***, the nearby* **Gallargues** *and* **Vergèze***.*

▶ *D 139 leads to Source Perrier.*

Source Perrier

🕐 *Jul and Aug: 9.30-10.30am, 1-6pm, Sat-Sun 9.30-10am, 1-4.30pm; Sept to June: call for information.* 🕐 *Closed in Jan and 1 May. It is advisable to book in advance. 4.12€.* ☎ *04 66 87 61 01.*

The Perrier spring, the Source des Bouillens, forms an underground lake with a temperature of 15°C/50°F; the abundant natural gas which escapes is

Tiled roofs, Calvisson

captured and reinserted in the water under pressure. Its beneficial qualities were discovered by a Dr Perrier, but it was left to an Englishman named Harmosworth to market the product. Annual production now exceeds 800 million bottles thanks to automated bottling procedures. Major markets for Perrier are France, Great Britain and the other members of the European Community, the United States, Canada, Switzerland, Australia and Saudi Arabia. The tour includes a visit to the various plants for bottle making, bottling and labelling.

▶ *Return to Nîmes via D 135 and turn left at Domaine de la Bastide onto D 613.*

NYONS

POPULATION 6 353

MICHELIN MAP 332: D-7

Situated on the River Eygues, where it emerges from a gorge into the Tricastin plain, within a protective ring of mountains, Nyons basks in a pleasant climate in which exotic flora flourishes out of doors; this warm winter climate attracts many visitors. The olive groves surrounding Nyons (olives and oil are marketed by the town) give it a very Provençal look. The town has a truffle market, and on Thursday mornings a colourful weekly market takes place.

Oil Mills
The mills are fully operational between November and February.

Moulin Ramade

Nov to Mar: daily except Sun and public holidays (except for the 1st Sun in Feb) 9am-noon, 2-6.30pm, Sat 10am-noon, 2-6pm; Apr to Oct: 8am-noon, 2-7pm, public holidays 10.30am-noon, 3-6pm. No charge. ☎ *04 75 26 08 18.*
Access to the west via T on the plan and the fourth street on the left. The first gallery houses millstones and presses used in the production of olive oil. The second gallery is specialised in refining and stocking the produce.

Vieux Moulins

Guided tours (30min) daily except Sun and Mon at 10.30am, 11.30am, 3pm, 4pm and 5pm (July and Aug: daily except Sun). Closed in Jan and public holidays. 3.51€. ☎ *04 75 26 11 00*
Access via avenue de la Digue. Old 18C and 19C oil mills can be seen, in which the oil is produced using traditional methods. You may also visit an old soap factory.

Address Book

EATING OUT

La Charrette Bleue – *7km/4.3mi northeast of Nyons via D 94 (Gap road) –* ☎ *04 75 27 72 33 – closed 29 Oct-7 Nov, 17 Dec-31 Jan, Tue evenings Sept-June, Sun evenings mid-Sept to Mar and Wed.* Yes, there is a blue cart perched on the roof of this pretty mas adorned with Roman tiles. If the sun is too bright on the terrace, try the cool dining room with its exposed beams and old flagstones. Country cooking prepared by the book.

WHERE TO STAY

Hôtel Picholine – *promenade Perrière – 1km/0.6mi north of Nyons via promenade des Anglais –* ☎ *04 75 26 06 21 – closed Feb and 15 Oct-6 Nov –* P *– 16 rooms –* ☞ *6.86€ – restaurant 20.58/35.06€.* Situated on a private road, this large building makes for a pleasant stopover in the hills of Nyons. The idle will definitely enjoy the garden, the swimming pool shaded by the light foliage of olive trees and the attractive terrace.

LOCAL PRODUCTS

Moulin Autrand-Dozol – *4 promenade. de la Digue – Le Pont Roman –* ☎ *04 75 26*

02 52 – www.moulin-dozol.com – Sept-Jun: Mon-Sat 9am-noon, 2pm-6.30pm; Jul-Aug: daily except Sun afternoon. Closed in Oct and afternoon of public holidays. This mill, dating from 1750 produces an AOC (with a guarantee of origin) olive oil sold on site, as well as other regional products. The museum has illustrative material on 18C and 19C oil mills, an 18C soap factory and an old Provençal kitchen.

Distillerie Bleu Provence – *58 promenade de la Digue –* ☎ *04 75 26 10 42 – Jul-Aug: Mon-Sat 10.30am and 5pm – 2.74€.* Products on sale and visit of the distillery. From Jun-Sep you can watch the process of plant distillation. Apr-Oct, Tue afternoon: visit of this workshop in floral art or perfume making *(13.72€, by appointment).*

Jardin des Arômes – *Promenade de la Digue,* ☎ *04 75 26 10 35.* A collection of aromatic plants used in the production of medicines and perfumes.

Markets – Traditional market, Thur morning. Provençal market (crafts, regional products) Sun morning, mid-June to mid-Sept.

NYONS			
	Digue Promenade de la 4	Petits Forts R. des 10	
Autiero Pl. 2	Liberté R. de la..............6	Randonne R. 12	
Chapelle R. de la..............3	Maupas R. 8	Résistance R.de la..............14	

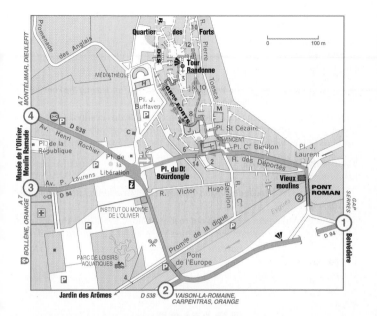

Coopérative Oléicole et Viticol

Place Olivier-de-Serres. Access to the west via ③ on the plan. ⚓ ⏱ *May to Oct: 8.45am-12.30pm, 2-7pm, Sun 9.30am-12.30pm, 2.30-6.30pm; Nov to Apr: 8.45am-12.15pm, 2-6.30pm, Sun 10am-12.30pm, 2.30-6.30pm.* ⏱*Closed 1 Jan, 1 May, 25 Dec. No charge.* ☎ *04 75 26 03 44.*

In this wine and oil cooperative, two adjoining rooms are devoted to the production of virgin olive oil (70% of production), obtained by only one mechanical pressing without further treatment. The remaining olives, the tanche variety, or Nyons black olives, are subsequently processed for canning.

Musée de l'Olivier

Avenue des Tilleuls. Access to the west via ③, *on the plan, then northwest of place Olivier-de-Serres.* ⚓ ⏱*Mar to Oct: daily except Sun 2.45-6pm; Nov to Feb: daily except Sun and Mon 2.45-6pm. 1.83€.* ☎ *04 75 26 12 12.*

This Olive Museum includes a wide variety of utensils, presses, tools and so on used in the production of olives and olive oil; there is also a group of items, such as lamps, showing how oil can be used. Documents enhance the collection. Note as well the giant fossil weighing 148kg/326lb.

Olives, olives everywhere

B. Kaufmann/MICHELIN

Additional Sights

Old Nyons★

This old district is built on a hill overlooking the town. Start from the arcaded place du Dr-Bourdongle. Take rue de la Résistance and rue de la Mairie to rue des Petits-Forts, a narrow alley lined with low-roofed houses (early 14C). In the square at the end of it a 13C tower, Tour Randonne, houses the tiny chapel of Notre-Dame-de-Bon-Secours. Bear left on rue de la Chapelle, to reach rue des **Grands-Forts**★, a long covered gallery where the thick walls have been pierced with windows to allow the light to filter through. Go under the tall vaulted gateway, the ruins of a feudal castle, and bear left into rue Maupas, a stepped street which leads back to rue de la Mairie. Proceed via place St-Cézaire and place Barillon to reach the banks of the River Eygues.

Pont Roman (Vieux Pont)▲

This 13C-14C humpbacked bridge spans the Eygues with a single 40m/131ft arch, one of the boldest in the Midi.

Excursion

Viewpoint (Belvédère)

▶ *Cross the Eygues over the Nouveau Pont, bear left on D 94, leaving the Pont Roman on the left; pass under the tunnel and turn right.*

From the rocky spike (bench) the view embraces old Nyons overlooked by Angèle mountain (alt 1 606m/5 268ft), and the deep, narrow Eygues valley to the right contrasting with the wide basin, to the left, where the new town has spread.

Promenade de Vaulx

Round-trip of 8km/5mi.

▶ *Leave Nyons Promenade des Anglais (northwest of town plan) and after 300m/328yd turn right.*

The narrow, winding but nicely laid out road runs along the hillside through olive groves. It offers good views of Nyons, Eygues Valley and the Baronnies Massif.

▶ *On the descent to D 538, leave the road on the right to Venterol and return to Nyons via D 538.*

ORANGE★★

POPULATION 26 964

MICHELIN MAP 332: B-9

Gateway to the Midi, at the crossroads of two motorways, Orange is famous for its prestigious Roman public buildings which include the triumphal arch and the Roman theatre. These monuments serve as the stage for the international music festival created in 1869 called Chorégies. An important market centre for fruit and early produce, Orange also has industrial (canning, chemicals) and military (air base, Foreign Legion) activities.

Don't Miss: Saturdays from mid-June to mid-September, visitors can enjoy the Marché provençal et des métiers d'art on place de la République, selling a variety of Provençal wares including fabrics, ceramics and santons.

Address Book

EATING OUT

Le Yaca – *24 place Silvain –* ☎ *04 90 34 70 03 – closed 2-28 Nov, Tue evening except Jul-Aug and Wed.* The owner really goes out of her way to please clients. Everything is homemade, fresh and not at all expensive in this small restaurant located a few steps away from Roman theatre. There is a small, vaulted, Provençal style dining room with lamps and flowers on the tables. Terrace in the summer.

Les Acacias – *place de la Mairie – 84100 Uchaux – 9km/5.6mi north of Orange towards Bollène via N 7, D 976 then D 11 –* ☎ *04 90 40 60 59 – closed Tue evening and*

Sat lunchtime. A pizza oven has replaced the old forge and the dining room occupies what used to be the stables... Savour tasty little dishes cooked by the owner's mother. An unpretentious place, with an aroma of the south.

WHERE TO STAY

Hôtel St-Florent – *4 rue du Mazeau –* ☎ *04 90 34 18 53 – www.multimania.com/saintflorent – closed Dec – 18 rooms –* ⬜ *6€.* Situated a stone's throw away from the Roman theatre, this original little hotel is bound to surprise you. All the paintings are by the owner and each room is decorated differently with furniture chosen to fit in with its particular style.

A Bit of History

Roman Orange

Established in 35 BC, the Roman colony of Orange welcome[...]
Second Legion. The town had a well-ordered urban plan, enhanced by p[...]
ings and surrounded by fortifications which protected some 70ha/173 acres. It was a[...]
the head of a vast territory, which the Roman land surveyors laid out with precision.
Lots were attributed with priority to the veterans, the next more mediocre lots were
rented out to the highest bidders and the remaining lots belonged to the collectivity.
In this way the Roman state encouraged colonisation and the development of land
at the natives' expense. Until 412, when the town was ransacked by the Visigoths,
Orange prospered.

Dutch Orange

In the second half of the 12C, the town became the seat of a small principality in Comtat
Venaissin; its prince, Raimbaut d'Orange, was a famous troubadour who sang of his
love for the Comtesse de Die. Through marriage and inheritance Orange ended up
belonging to a branch of the Baux family, heir also to the German principality of Nassau. In the 16C the then prince of Orange and Nassau, William the Silent, transformed
his fief into the United Provinces with himself as first *stadthouder*. At the same time,
the town became Protestant and fell victim to the ravages of the Wars of Religion,
but it succeeded in preserving its autonomy.

Orange is justly proud of the fact that the preferred title of the glorious royal dynasty
of Holland is Prince or Princess of Orange; and its name has been given to a state, cities
and rivers in South Africa and the USA. While governing the Low Countries and even
England, the House of Orange-Nassau did not forget its tiny enclave in France.

In 1622 Maurice of Nassau surrounded the town with strong ramparts and built a
large castle. Unfortunately, for economic reasons as well as through lack of time,
he took the stones necessary for his fortifications from the Roman ruins which had

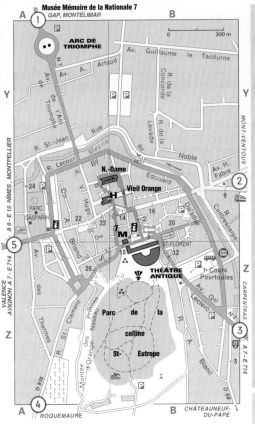

ORANGE

Arc de Triomphe Av. de l'................	AY	
Artaud Av. A.	ABY	
Blanc R. A.	BZ	
Briand Crs A...............	AYZ	
Caristie R.	BY	2
Châteauneuf R. de	BZ	3
Clemenceau Pl. G......	BY	4
Concorde R. de la.......	BY	
Contrescarpe R. de la............	BY	
Daladier Bd E............	ABY	
Fabre Av. H.	BY	
Frères-Mounet Pl. des......................	BY	5
Guillaume-le- Taciturne Av.	BY	
Herbes Pl. aux...........	BY	7
Lacour R.......................	AY	
Leclerc Av. Gén.	BZ	
Levade R. de la...........	BY	
Mistral Av. F................	BY	9
Noble R. du	ABY	
Pourtoules Cours	BZ	
Pourtoules R...............	BZ	12
Princes d'Orange-Nassau Mtée des..................	AZ	
République Pl. de la ..	BY	14
République R. de la ...	BY	16
Roch R. Madeleine.....	BZ	18
St-Clement R...............	AZ	
St-Florent R................	BY	20
St-Jean R.....................	AY	
St-Martin R..................	AY	22
Tanneurs R. des	AY	24
Thermes Av. des.........	AZ	
Tourre R. de	AZ	26
Victor-Hugo R.............	AY	

Hôtel de ville	ABY	H
Musée municipal	BY	M

Arc de Triomphe, Orange

B. Kaufmann/MICHELIN

not been destroyed by the Barbarian invasions. This time nothing was left standing except the theatre, part of the ramparts and the triumphal arch which had been transformed into a fortress.

French Orange

During the war against Holland, Louis XIV coveted the Principality of Orange. It was the count of Grignan, lieutenant-general to the king in Provence and Mme de Sévigné's son-in-law, who captured the town. The ramparts were razed and the castle demolished. In 1713 the Treaty of Utrecht ceded Orange to France.

Roman Monuments *2hr*

Arc de Triomphe★★

At the entry to the city on the N 7. 🅿*Free parking at the crossroads.*

The arch stands on the north side of the city on the old Via Agrippa which linked Lyon to Arles. It ranks third among the Roman constructions of this type owing to its dimensions: 22m/72ft high, 21m/69ft wide and 8m/26ft deep and is one of the best preserved, particularly the north face.

Built c 20 BC and dedicated later to Tiberius, the arch commemorated the campaigns of the II Legion. It has three openings flanked by columns and displays two unusual architectural features: a pediment above the central opening and two attic storeys. It was surmounted at the time of its construction by a bronze quadriga (a chariot drawn by four horses harnessed abreast) flanked by two trophies.

Its exuberant decoration is linked to Roman classicism and the plastic beauty of the Hellenistic style. To be admired are the scenes of battles and arms captured, which recall the conquering of Gaul, and naval symbols evoking Augustus' victory over the fleet of Antony and Cleopatra.

Roman Theatre (Théâtre antique)★★★

🕐*Apr to Sept: 9am-6.30pm; Oct to Mar: 9am-noon, 1.30-5pm.* 🕐*Closed 1 Jan and 25 Dec. 4.57€.* ☎ *04 90 34 70 88.*

Built during Augustus' reign, the theatre is rightly the pride of the city, as it is the only Roman theatre which has managed to conserve its stage wall almost intact. This impressive stage wall (103m/338ft long and 36m/118ft high), which Louis XIV had qualified as the finest wall of the kingdom, is the theatre's external façade. Its upper storey was made up of two rows of corbels pierced with holes to hold up the poles for the *velum*, which shaded the spectators from the sun. Below, 19 blind arcades corresponded with rooms inside, corridors and staircases.

The semicircle, the *cavea*, held up to 8 000 to 9 000 spectators seated according to their social station. It was divided into three sections of 37 tiers of seats and separated by walls. Below, the orchestra was in the shape of a half circle; along it were three low tiers of seats where movable seats were set up for the high-ranking citizens.

On either side of the stage, large rooms, one on top of the other (entrance is now from the lower room, west side), were for receiving the public, and housed the backstage. The stage, fitted with wooden flooring, under which the machinery was kept, measured 61m/200ft long and 9m/30ft wide of performing area; it was raised above the orchestra by about 1.10m/3.5ft. It was held up by a low wall, *pulpitum*. Behind was the curtain slot (the curtain was dropped during the performances).

The stage wall was as high as the topmost tier, and displayed a richly ornate decoration of marble facing, stucco, mosaics, several tiers of columns, and niches for statues, including the imperial one of Augustus (3.55m/11ft) which was brought back to its original location in 1951. The stage wall had three doors, each of which had a particular function. The royal door in the centre was used by the principal actors for their entrances, whereas the two side doors were for secondary actors. From the top row one can hear someone speaking in the semicircle. The actors' masks amplified their voices, and the large sloping roof which protected the stage was also useful acoustically.

From mid-July to the beginning of August the Roman theatre hosts the **Chorégies,** a classical music and opera festival. Visitors can not only enjoy these magnificent and prestigious musical events, but also appreciate the majesty of the theatre. *Ticket office: place Silvain (near the theatre).*

Old Orange

▶ *Starting from the theatre, follow rue Caristie until it joins rue de la République, the city's main street.*

Vieil Orange

The streets of the old town centre are very animated and pleasant to stroll along. Note the statue of the troubadour-prince Raimbaut d'Orange while crossing place de la République and heading towards the cathedral, the **ancienne Cathédrale Notre-Dame**, by turning right into rue Fuseerie then, after place du Cloître, left into rue de Renoyer. This Romanesque building was very badly damaged during the Wars of Religion and the majority of it had to be rebuilt.

There are plenty of lively cafés and restaurants with pavement terraces in place Georges-Clemenceau, where you can admire the **Hôtel de Ville** with its 17C belfry. From place de la République, rue Stassart leads to a little square shaded with plane trees, **place aux Herbes**, which you cross to return to the theatre via rue du Mazeau.

Colline St-eutrope

St Eutrope Hill

▶ *Drive up montée des Princes-d'Orange-Nassau.* P*Leave the car in the car park in front of the public gardens.*

The main avenue crosses the moat of the former castle of the Princes of Orange; the excavations (left of square Reine-Juliana) have uncovered important ruins. At the far north end of the park, near a statue to the Virgin, there is a viewing table offering a beautiful **view**★ of the Roman theatre in the foreground, the city of Orange with its tiled roofs, and the Rhône plain enclosed by mountains.

Additional Sights

Musée municipal

Apr to Sept: 9.30am-7pm; Oct to Mar: 9.30am-noon, 1.30-5.30pm. Closed 1 Jan and 25 Dec. 4.57€ (ticket also gives access to the Roman theatre). 04 90 51 18 24.

This museum which occupies a former palace, built in the 17C by a Dutch nobleman, displays in the courtyard and ground floor lapidary vestiges from the Roman monuments (no longer standing) and the castle of the Princes of Orange. One gallery contains fragments (meticulously reconstructed) of the renowned Roman **land survey** of Orange *(see above)*, unique in France. On these marble tablets, the historians have identified the well-planned grid pattern (with its *cardo* and *decumanus*), the administrative subdivisions and topographical references (roads, mountains, rivers, swamps) and finally written information on the judicial and fiscal status of the land.

The museum's other rooms are devoted to the history of Orange, local traditions, painting, and a collection of printed fabrics from 18C Orange, belonging to the Swiss manufacturing family named Wetter.

Excursions

Caderousse

6km/3.5mi to the west, by D 17.

This village is located on the banks of the Rhône and has often been subject to flooding. On the town hall's façade left of the door, four plaques indicate the level reached by the rise of the floodwaters. Since 1856 a dike has protected the village from the floodwaters; ramparts encircle the whole village and only two doors open at the cardinal points.

Église St-Michel

The church is in the Provençal Romanesque style. Inside, south of the chancel, the Flamboyant-style chapelle St-Claude with its fine vaulting was added in the 16C.

Harmas Jean-Henri-Fabre

8km/5mi by N 7 and D 576. ⏱*Closed for renovation.*

At the entrance of Sérignan-du-Comtat stands the house of Jean-Henri Fabre, the famous entomologist (1823-1915) who lived here for the last 36 years of his life. The visit includes the scientist's office, where display cases contain his collections: insects, shells, fossils, minerals, and a gallery in which his own watercolours (depicting mushrooms from the region) are hung. A tour of the land around his house, which was his main field of observation, now a botanical garden, ends the visit.

Aven d'**ORGNAC**★★

MICHELIN MAP 331: I-8

LOCAL MAP SEE GORGES DE L'ARDÈCHE

The great hole in the ground was known to the local people, who paid little attention to it until 19 August 1935, when the speleologist Robert de Joly (1887-1968) made an initial exploration. The engineer and speleologist, who explored his native Cévennes, also played an important role in improving the equipment and techniques used in underground exploration.

This cave is fascinating because of the natural development of underground streams, fed by infiltration and through fissures in the calcareous rock. The first concretions, which were at times 10m/33ft in diameter, were broken by a major earthquake at the end of the Tertiary Era. These columns, broken or turned upside down, served as a base for more recent stalagmites.

Tour *allow 1hr*

🐌 *The constant temperature in the cave is 13°C/55°F so you are advised to dress warmly, particularly when it is hot outdoors, as the difference in temperature can bring on a chill.*

🐌 *Also bear in mind that during the tour you will have to go up and down 788 steps (they have been counted).*

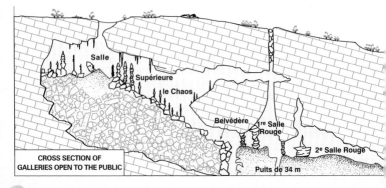

CROSS SECTION OF
GALLERIES OPEN TO THE PUBLIC

Salle
Supérieure

le Chaos

Belvédère
1re Salle Rouge

2e Salle Rouge

Puits de 34 m

The **Salle Supérieure** (Upper Chamber), 17-40m/58-131ft high, 250m/820ft long and 125m/410ft wide, contains magnificent stalagmites. The largest are in the middle; a number of growths give them the shape of pine cones. Unable, due to the height of the vault, to join the stalactites to form pillars, the stalagmites have thickened at the base and become quite large; other more recent and thinner stalagmites have piled on top of them like a stack of plates. Along the walls of the chamber, note the delicate columns which came after the earthquake; some are very tall, either in bayonet-shape or standing very straight. The dim light which comes from the cave's natural opening illuminates the chamber with a strange bluish light.

"Pine cone" stalagmites

In **Le Chaos** (Chaos Chamber), encumbered by concretions which have fallen in from the Salle Supérieure, magnificent curtains of varied colours escape from a fissure in the vault. On a level with the viewpoint of the **Première Salle Rouge** (First Red Chamber), the water filtering in, enriched with carbonate of lime through the calcareous layer, has encouraged the formation of a mass of concretions. Nearby is the well, the deepest in the cave at 34m/112ft which leads into another chamber 180m/591ft deep.

Le Safari Souterraine *Mar to mid-Nov: guided tour (2hr 30min) by request 2 weeks beforehand (Jul-Aug: Tue, Thu and Fri, 2-5pm by advance request). Minimum 7 people.* 18.29€ *(children: 16.46€).* 04 75 38 62 51. Underground expeditions on a more adventurous scale for groups of at least seven people can be organised, but you must book in advance.

Musée de Préhistoire

Apr to Sept: 10am-noon, 2-6pm (July and Aug: 10am-7pm); Oct: 10am-noon, 2-5pm. Closed from 1 Nov to 28 Feb. 4.95€ *(combined ticket for the museum and cave: 8.84€).* 04 75 38 65 10.

Rooms arranged around a patio contain the discoveries of excavations carried out in the Ardèche and the north of the Gard regions. Reconstructions (Acheulean hut from Orgnac III, flint knapping workshop, Lion's Head decorated cave) introduce visitors to the way of life of prehistoric man.

Bois de PAÏOLIVE★

MICHELIN MAP 331: H-7

This limestone area of Bas Vivarais stretches over about 16km2/6sq mi southeast of Les Vans on either side of the River Chassezac. The ground consists of grey Jurassic limestone (Secondary Era), which is both hard and permeable, making it resistant to wind and weather erosion but susceptible to rain water, full of carbonic acid, which has enlarged the fissures into deep defiles and remoulded the rocks into strange forms. Elsewhere residual rock has turned to clay and encouraged the growth of vegetation (especially the common oak).

A Bit of History

Jalès and the Royalists

The basin stretching southeast of Vans, on either side of the village of Jalès, is closely linked to a dramatic period in France's counter-revolutionary history. Between 1790 and 1792, nostalgic followers of the Ancien Régime would congregate at the Château de Jalès. At the time the Civil Constitution of the Clergy was being implemented and this served to accentuate the divide as many bishops ended up supporting the Royalists. On 21 June 1792, the revolutionary cockade was trampled underfoot at Berrias. Hailed as the leader of the Royalist movement in the area, the Comte de Saillans, whose family originally came from the Dauphiné, precipitated the date of the uprising. However, his plot was exposed. A troup of soldiers sent to defeat Saillans' men overcame them not far from Courry, south of Vans, on 11 July. Saillans took refuge at the Château de Banne, then decided to flee the area with a group of his comrades-in-arms. They were arrested on the road to Villefort and taken to Vans. The crowds, who blamed Saillans for the execution of several Republicans, murdered him and his friends in the street. It is said that a few Royalists succeeded in escaping to the Bois de Païolive, where they probably died of hunger.

Visit *allow 2hr*

▷ *D 252 crosses the woods west to east.*

About 300m/328yd from D 901 and some 20m/21yd off to the right coming from Les Vans stand the rocks known locally as L'Ours (The Bear) and Le Lion (The Lion).

Clairière★

A clearing is accessible to cars near D 252 in a right hand bend coming from Les Vans, up an unsurfaced slope. It is established on a doline or sinkhole (a small picnic area has been set up nearby).

Corniche du Chassezac★★

🚶 *30min return on foot. Park in the first car park on the left of the road, going towards Mazet-Plage. A footpath marked "Corniche" follows the tall cliffs which overlook the deep gorge.*
After less than 10 minutes' walk you suddenly come upon the grandiose Chassezac gorge winding past below, at the foot of the cave-pitted cliffs. The footpath, a sheer drop of 80m/262ft above the water, leads to the left, opposite a manor-house, to a viewpoint located upstream.

▷*Return by the way you came.*

Mazet-Plage

▷ *15min return on foot. A surfaced path off D 252 leads 300m/328yd to a campsite along the river bank.*

🚶 This site is at the end of the Chassezac gorge, which is the only means of access. To reach the higher parts of the gorge, to bathing or climbing places, cross the river going in the direction of Casteljau and park in the of the car parks.

▷ *Walk along the Chassezac, going towards the left for about 500m/0.3mi along the shingly beach with its small willows opposite the unusual cave-pitted cliffs.*

Banne

▶ *6km/3.5mi from the crossroads of D 901 and D 252. Leave the car in the square; climb up the slope behind the Calvary.*

The path leads to a platform overlooking the Jalès depression. From the top, where the ruins of Banne's old citadel lie, there is a vast **panorama**★ extending from the River Gard to the lower Ardèche. Half-buried in the platform's southwest side a long vaulted gallery can be seen, which served as stables to the castle of Banne and which was demolished after the defeat of the counter-revolutionaries.

PERNES-LES-FONTAINES★

POPULATION 8 304

MICHELIN MAP 332: D-10

The town located on the border of the Vaucluse plateau was once the capital of Comtat Venaissin (968-1320) before Carpentras. It was the home town of Fléchier (1632-1710), one of the best orators of the late 17C; his funeral orations included those for Turenne and Marie-Thérèse of Austria.

The town gets its name from the 36 or so fountains, in which it takes great pride. These decorate the numerous squares in its urban districts. Most of them were built in the middle of the 18C, following the discovery of a large spring near Chapelle St-Roch. The older fountains have since been restored.

Like most of the towns on the Vaucluse plateau, Pernes-les-Fontaines has canning factories. Fruit – cherries, strawberries, melons, grapes – is especially abundant in the region.

Walking Tour

Allow 1hr for those wishing to explore the winding streets of the old town.
▶ *Start at the church of N.-D.-de-Nazareth.*

Notre-Dame-de-Nazareth

The oldest parts of the church date from the late 11C. The south porch opens through a lovely door (in bad condition) inspired by Antiquity.
Opposite, the willow-shaded River Nesque is spanned by an old bridge, which leads to the porte Notre-Dame.

Porte Notre-Dame★

On one of the bridge's piles is the small 16C chapel of Notre-Dame-des-Grâces with its elegant cast-iron bell tower. On the left is the 17C covered market.

Fontaine du Cormoran

This, the most interesting of the fountains in Pernes, owes its name to the cormorant with outspread wings which is perched on top of it. The base is decorated with low reliefs and masks.

▶ *Turn right onto rue Victor-Hugo which runs parallel to the Nesque river. Take rue de Brancas and immediately turn right.*

Tour de l'Horloge

🕐 *All year round: unaccompanied visits 10am-5pm.* ☎ *04 90 61 31 04*
This keep was once part of the fortified wall which protected the castle of the Counts of Toulouse. From the top of the clock tower there is a sweeping panorama to the west over the Comtat plain and the countryside around Avignon; in the background, to the north and east, the Dentelles de Montmirail and Mont Ventoux.

WHERE TO EAT

🍽️ **Dame l'Oie - Le Troubadour** – 56 rue Troubadour-Durand – ☎ 04 90 61 62 43 – closed 15-28 Feb, Tue in the low season and Mon. Built around a stone fountain surmounted by a fine goose, the yellow and white Provençal decor serves as a showcase for a delightful collection of white ceramic geese. Classic cuisine with a speciality known as caprice de dame l'oie and local wines.

PERNES-LES-FONTAINES

Barreau R.	2
Brancas R. de	3
Briand Pl. Aristide	4
Corti Pl. et Square D.	5
Fléchier Pl.	7
Gambetta R.	9
Giraud Pl. L.	12
Mistral Pl. F.	14
Neuve R.	16
Notre-Dame Pont	18
Porte-Notre-Dame R.	21
Raspail R.	24
République R. de la	27
Zola R. É.	33

Chapelle N.-D.-des-Grâces	B	
Fontaine Reboul	E⁴	
Fontaine de l'Hôpital	E	
Fontaine du Cormoran	E²	
Hôtel de Jocas	F	
Hôtel de Vichet	G	
Hôtel de Villefranche	K	
Hôtel de ville	H	
Magasin Drapier, musée du costume comtandin	M	
Maison Fléchier	N	
Porte Notre-Dame	L	
Tour Ferrande	S	
Tour de l'Horloge	R	

▶ *Continue down rue Victor-Hugo where you will pass in front of the Clos de Verdun, a miniscule park which stands on the site of an old olive-press.*

Tour Ferrande

🔊*Guided tours (15min) by appointment with the tourist office. 2.29€. ☏ 04 90 61 31 04.*

This square crenellated 13C tower, hemmed in between the houses, overlooks a small square which contains the Guilhaumin, or "Gigot", fountain. Go up a narrow staircase to the third floor, which is decorated with beautiful 13C frescoes depicting the Virgin and Child, St Christopher, and retracing the epic adventures of Charles of Anjou in southern Italy.

▶ *Go to the end of rue Gambetta.*

Porte de Villeneuve

This gate is a remnant of the 16C fortifications and is flanked by two round, machi-colated towers.

▶ *Turn back and take rue de la République on the right.*

On the corner of rue Gambetta and rue de la République, the magasin Drapier, which as preserved the appearance of an 18C fashion shop, houses the little musée du costume Comtadin. Opposite, notice the 16C Hôtel de Vichet with its doorway surmounted by an elegant wrought-iron balcony. The nuns of Christian retreat, who occupy the mansion, make the eucharistic host which is then sent all over France and the French-speaking countries of Africa. Pass the 17C hôtel de Villefranche (set back on the right).

▶ *Turn left onto rue Barrau.*

Fontaine de l'Hôpital

This fountain dates from 1760 and draws its name from its position opposite the Hôtel des Ducs de Berton, which was once a hospital.
Come out into place Louis-Giraud. On one side of this square the 19C Augustine church, now a cultural centre, can be seen.

▶ *Take the narrow rue Brancas on your right.*

Hôtel de Ville

This 17C mansion once belonged to the Dukes of Brancas, one of whom was Maréchal de France and the ambassador of Louis XIV in Spain. The courtyard is further enhanced by a striking fountain and its vast portico (1750), set against a wall.

▶ *Turn left into rue du Bariot which leads to Porte St-Gilles.*

Porte de St-Gilles

This square tower was part of the 14C fortifications. It still has its machicolations.

▶ *Cross the tower and continue towards rue Raspail.*

At No 214, set back on the right, there is the Hôtel de Jocas with its beautiful Louis XV doorway. Note the Fontaine Reboul, dating from the end of the 17C and also known as the "Grand' Font" (Big Fount), with its fish-scale ornamentation. Before returning to the porte Notre-Dame, a little turning to the right leads to the Maison Fléchier, birthplace of the famous orator.

▶ *Cross the bridge and continue for 200m/656ft after cours Frizet.*

Croix Couverte

This elegant quadrangular monument, pierced by four ogival openings, is thought to have been built in the 15C by Pierre de Boët of Pernes.

PONT DU GARD★★★

MICHELIN MAP 339: M-5

This aqueduct, one of the wonders of the Ancient world, is certainly worth a journey. It is part of a system which brought spring water from a catchment area near Uzès to Nîmes; it was built in 1C and in spite of its 2 000 years is in very good condition.

Aqueduct

The Romans attached a great deal of importance to the quality of the water which they required for even the smallest town. The water was collected preferably on the north slope so that it did not heat up in the reservoirs. The water channel was made entirely of stone, either vaulted or tiled and pierced with openings only for ventilation and maintenance. Some aqueducts were equipped with settling tanks. The contours of the land were crossed with exceptional engineering skill – the aqueduct followed its course via bridges, ditches, tunnels and siphons. The aqueduct of Nîmes, some 50km/31mi long, had an average incline of 34cm per km or 1:300, falling more steeply just before the valley to reduce the height of the bridge. Its daily flow was about 20 000 m3/44 million gallons.

From the 4C the aqueduct ceased to be maintained, so that lime deposits built up, until finally by the 9C the course had become blocked and it had fallen into disuse. Landowners along the course thereupon began to remove the dressed stones for their own use. In 1743 a road bridge was added downstream of the aqueduct.

Pont du Gard

The GR6, a footpath specifically designed for hikers, follows the traces of the Nîmes aqueduct in a landscape of scrubland.

Canoeing down the Gardon from Collias is also a popular passtime. The river is quite safe and this activity can be enjoyed by all. A good way to cool off on hot days.

Bridge (Pont)★★★

The aqueduct spans the Gardon valley. The golden coloured tone of the old stones harmonises beautifully with the surrounding countryside.

It is composed of colossal dressed blocks of masonry, some weighing as much as six tonnes, which were laid without mortar, the courses being held together with iron clamps. The stone was lifted into position by block and tackle with goats as auxiliaries and a winch worked by a massive human treadmill.

In order to break the sense of monotony the three levels of arches are recessed, the piers in line one above another. Statistical details are: height above the Gardon at low water: 49m/160ft; lowest level: 6 arches, 142m long, piers 6m thick, arches 22m high (465ft, 20ft, 72ft); middle level: 11 arches, 242 m long, piers 4m thick, arches 20m high (792ft, 13ft, 65ft); top level, the one carrying the canal: 35 arches, 275m long, piers 3m thick, arches 7m high (900ft, 10ft, 23ft). The bridge was restored under Napoleon III. The architect varied the span of the arches very slightly within each range; each arch was constructed independently to give flexibility in the event of subsidence. The stones obtruding from the face were scaffolding supports, and were left not only to facilitate maintenance work but to add interest to the surface, as do the ridges on the piers which held the semicircular wooden frames on which the arches were constructed.

Visit

Free access. There is a charge for parking. A variety of cultural events also take place here, at a charge. There are several man-made swimming beaches on the banks of the River Gardon. Beware of the currents.

Left bank

Mid-Apr to mid-Sept: 9am-9pm; mid-Sept to mid-Apr: 9am-6pm. Parking facilities *on both banks 7am-1am. 3.05€ for the first 2 hours; Jul and Aug: 8pm-1am. (4.57€). Free access to the bridge. Activities: 12.20€.* 0825 01 30 30.

▸ *Access from the Vers road (D 981 Uzès to Remoulins).*

After parking your car you will reach a large embankment with a cafeteria, projection room, children's activity centre and a recreational museum with displays on the region's traditional activities.

A walkway leads to the quarry where the stone for the structure was extracted. Note the quarryman's rocky house with niches carved into the walls where beehives were inserted.

Right bank

To the left of the access road, hollowed out of the hill, stands the reception centre which houses a multi-media exhibition/show covering an area of 500m2/598yd2. The show includes films and interactive displays pertaining to the bridge and its construction.

PONT-ST-ESPRIT

POPULATION 9 277

MICHELIN MAP 339: M-3

LOCAL MAP SEE GORGES DE L'ARDÈCHE

The town owes its raison d'être and name to the bridge built in 1265-1309 by the Bridge Brotherhood under the protection of the Holy Spirit (Saint Esprit); it subsequently became an important halting-place on the Rhône.

Walking Tour

▶ Take **rue St-Jacques**, lined with old houses.

The 17C **Hôtel de Roubin** at no 10 and especially the Maison des Chevaliers (Knights' Mansion) at no 2, a former private residence belonging to the Piolenc, a renowned family of merchants from the Rhône valley, who lived on the premises between the 12C and 1988. This townhouse, enhanced by a pretty gemelled bay window in the Romanesque style, is home to the **Musée d'Art Sacré du Gard** (see MUSEUMS).

▶ Go past the old town hall, which now houses the Musée Paul-Raymond (see MUSEUMS), and walk toward place St-Pierre from rue Haut-Mazeau.

Terrasse

This terrace lies on the east side of place St-Pierre and is bounded to the north by the 15C parish church, to the south-west by the Baroque façade of the Chapelle des Pénitents and to the south-east by the former 17C Église St-Pierre (now deconsecrated) topped by a dome. From the terrace there is a good overall view of the bridge.
A monumental double flight of stairs leads to quai de Luynes. Left, almost at the foot of the bridge, the **Maison du Roy** has fine Renaissance windows.

Pont

The bridge, nearly 1 000m/3 281ft long, is slightly curved upstream against the current; 19 of the 25 arches are original. It used to be defended at either end with bastions and two towers in the middle, now destroyed.

To facilitate navigation – the passage through the bridge had, over the centuries, always been feared by sailors – the bridge's first two arches were replaced by one arch (it was subsequently destroyed during the Second World War and rebuilt in reinforced concrete).

> **WHERE TO EAT**
>
> 🍽️🍽️ **Le St-Pancrace** – route de Barjac – 3km/1.8mi northwest of Pont-St-Esprit towards Gorges de l'Ardèche – ☎ 04 66 39 47 81 – closed Wed from Mar-Oct. Well-known by the inhabitants of the region, this restaurant owes its reputation to the quality of the food and the charm of its hosts. Meals are eaten in attractive, airy dining rooms, one of which is on a veranda. Tables are laid out in the garden in summertime.

From the bridge there is a fine view of the Rhône and the town. North of the bridge, where there is now a vast terrace, the citadel once stood; it was built in 1595 and fortified by Vauban in the 17C. From the centre of the terrace the view extends to the 15C Flamboyant doorway of the former Plan collegiate church. Take the stairs for a better look at the doorway's details (partly uncovered).

▶ Cross the intersection and then take rue des Minimes and turn left on rue du Couvent; continue along rue Bas-Mazeau, rue Haut-Mazeau and rue St-Jacques to the car.

PONT-ST-ESPRIT

19 Mars 1962 R. du	28
Allègre Chemin Bd	2
Ancienne Mairie Pl. de l'	3
Bas Mazeau R.	4
Bruguier-Roure R. L.	5
Couvent R. du	6
Doumergue Av. G.	7
Gaulle Av. du Gén.-de	8
Haut Mazeau R.	9
Jean-Jaurès Allées	10
Jemmapes R.	12
Joliot-Curie R.	
Minimes R. des	
Mistral Allées F.	15
Paroisse R. de la	17
Plan Pl. du	18
République Pl. de la	21
St-Jacques R.	25
St-Pierre Pl.	26
Ville Pl. Georges	27

Ancienne collégiale du Plan	N
Hôtel de Roubin	B
Maison des Chevaliers (Musée d'Art sacré du Gard)	M²
Maison du Roy	K
Musée Paul-Raymond	M¹

Museums

Musée d'art sacré du Gard

Daily except Mon 10am-noon, 2-6pm; mid-June to mid-Sept: daily except Mon 10am-noon, 3-7pm). Closed in Feb, 1 Jan, Easter, 1 May, Ascension, Whitsun, 14 July, 1 and 11 Nov, 24 and 31 Dec. 3.05€. ☎ 04 66 39 17 61

The purpose of this **Museum of Sacred Art** is to enlighten the general public on France's religious heritage by presenting and explaining sacred rites and their significance. On the ground floor, a sacristy displaying various sacred articles for celebrating Mass stands alongside a collection of clerical garments (interactive terminal showing a priest donning his robes before celebrating Mass; explanations are then given about the actual proceedings of a religious service). The rooms at garden level encourage visitors to reflect on the meaning of sacred issues, which contribute to reinforcing social cohesion, and on the role of the Bible today in a world characterised by scientific progress. The old tower dominating the garden is devoted to 18C-19C *santons* and cribs, while another room contains a display of household reliquaries, including a few *paperolles* - paintings consisting of rolled sheets of paper that form a decor framing the relics.

The fine collection of religious paintings include The Adoration of the Magi by Nicolas Dipre (c 1495), while the **Royal Court of Justice** ★ on the first floor houses a retable by the Provençal Primitive painter **Raymond Boterie**, illustrating *The Fall of the Angels* (1509-1510). Visitors may also admire a former apothecary's surgery and the pharmacy of the St-Esprit Hospital (early 18C pottery jars and an outstanding collection of medieval ceramic pieces of Hispano-Moorish inspiration).

Musée Paul-Raymond

Daily except Mon and Sat. 10am-noon, 2-6pm (July and Aug: daily except Mon 10am-noon, 3-7pm). Closed Feb and public holidays. 1.83€. ☎ 04 66 39 09 98.

Set up in the former town hall, this museum is laid out over two levels and presents the work of the painter Benn (1905-1989), dedicated to a number of religious themes. It forms a perfect complement to the Museum of Sacred Art mentioned above. In the basement lies the town's former ice-house (1780).

ROCHEFORT-DU-GARD

POPULATION 4 107

MICHELIN MAP 339: N-5

This hanging village with its steep little streets and small shaded squares is a lovely place for a stroll. In 1825 the town hall was installed in St-Joseph's chapel, which was built in 1733. The 19C fountain opposite is surmounted by a triangular pediment and decorated with geometric designs.

All that remains of the "castellas" originally to the east of the village is the looming white silhouette of the Romanesque chapel. The **view**★ from the platform stretches over Notre-Dame-de-Grâce sanctuary, the dried-up lake of Pujaut and the mountains in the background.

Excursion

Sanctuaire Notre-Dame-de-Grâce

🕐*Wed, Sun and public holidays 3-5pm (winter: 4pm).* ☎ *04 90 31 72 01*
2km/just over a mile northeast. Leave Rochefort on D 976 towards Roquemaure. After 700m/765yd take a small road uphill on the left.
On a hillock at the edge of Rochefort forest stands Notre-Dame-de-Grâce sanctuary. Built on the site of a Benedictine priory founded in 798, ravaged in the 18C and restored in the 19C by the Marist Fathers, the sanctuary has housed an almshouse since 1964.
In the sparsely-decorated chapel note the lovely wrought-iron grille closing off the chancel; the altar in polychrome marble is surmounted by a statue of Our Lady of Grace.
By the entrance to the chancel, on the south pillar, hangs an ex-voto (1666), which was offered by Anne of Austria for the birth in 1638 of the future Louis XIV, after 23 years of childless marriage. In a room off the chapel, more than 100 votive offerings from the 17C-20C are exhibited. In the cloisters the echo chamber enabled the priest to hear the confessions of lepers: two people stand in opposite corners facing the wall; when they speak quietly, they can hear each other distinctly.

▶ *Go around the reception office on the south side and take the Way of the Cross.*

⊙ *From the terrace there is a lovely* **view**★ *of the Lance mountains, Mont Ventoux, the Vaucluse plateau, the Montagnette and the Alpilles, and the Rhône valley.*

WHERE TO EAT

🍴**L'Olive Noire** – *2 rue de l'Église* – ☎ *04 90 31 72 11* – *closed 6-20 Jan and Sun* – *10.68€ lunch.* This old oil mill has been converted into a restaurant. From the terrace in the evening, contemplate the superb façade made of local stone and enhanced by clever lighting. Cooking makes use of local produce.

ROUSSILLON★★

POPULATION 1 165

MICHELIN MAP 332: E-10

LOCAL MAP SEE APT: OCHRE TOUR

The village stands on an unusual site on the highest of the hills between Coulon valley and Vaucluse plateau. These striking hills, composed of ochre rock of many different shades featured in the local houses, enhance the village and the surrounding countryside.

Ochre Land

A visit to Roussillon, as well as giving you an opportunity to explore the beautiful village, also gives a good overview of all stages of ochre production, from the quarries where it is extracted, to the processing factory, to colouring the walls of the village.

Range of natural ochre colours

Sentier des ocres★

Departure in front of the cemetery opposite place Pasquier. 1km/0.6mi. Allow 1hr.

This signposted footpath, dotted with information panels, provides an introduction to the ochre hill's flora (holm-oaks, juniper) and its landscape of ancient quarries: note the **aiguilles des fées**, which dominate the famous **chaussée des géants**★★, imposing jagged cliffs.

Conservatoire des ocres et pigments appliqués★

Feb to Oct: guided tours (1hr) 9am-6pm (July and Aug: 7pm); Nov to Jan: daily except Mon 9am-6pm. Price information not provided. ☎ 04 90 05 66 69.
On the road to Apt (D 104), about 1 km/0.6mi from place Pasquier. This workshop, closed in 1963, used to transform ochre extracted from the quarries. Ochre in its natural state is a mixture of argillaceous sand and iron oxide. To obtain a commercially-pure ochre product, the mineral is first washed and the heavier sandy impurities settle to the bottom. The lighter weight mixture of iron oxide and clay is passed through a filter and into settling tanks (one for each colour) where the clay gradually accumulates

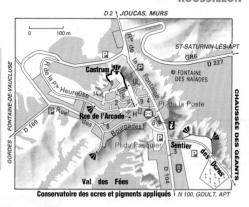

ROUSSILLON

Abbé-Avon Pl. de l'...............................2
Burlière Av. de la.................................3
Casteau R. 4
Église R. de l'......................................5
Eynard Pl. J...6
Forge Pl. de la.....................................7
Lauriers R. des.....................................8
Mairie Pl. de la....................................9
Mathieu Pl. C......................................12
Pignotte Pl...14

in layers. The water is evacuated and the ochre is left to dry all summer; it is then cut into blocks. To finish the drying process and to darken the pigmentation, the ochre is baked in ovens (to obtain a red colour, yellow ochre is baked at 450°C). Finally it is crushed, sifted and put in sacks or barrels.

The Village★

With its narrow little streets, which are sometimes stepped, its splendidly colourful ochre-clad houses, its arcades full of artwork and pottery, Roussillon is a continual enchantment, particularly with the warm light of sunset.

Start from the Tourist Information Office and turn left into rue Bourgades and follow rue de l'Arcade, a partially covered stepped street. Pass under the belfry to get to the castrum.

Castrum

Viewing-table. From this platform the view extends northwards to Vaucluse plateau and the white crest of Mont Ventoux, southwards to the Coulon valley and Grand Luberon.

Go via place Pignotte to reach the far end of the watchpath, from where there is a lovely view of the **Aiguilles du Val des Fées** (Needles of Fairies' Valley), vertical clefts in an ochre cliff-face.

▶ *Rue des Bourgades leads back to the start of the walk.*

ST-BLAISE

MICHELIN MAP 340: E-5

With the sea, the River Rhône, the Étang de Berre as well as other small lagoons and the vast Crau plain not far away, the oppidum of St-Blaise (in the commune of St-Mitre-les-Remparts) is a historic site, the wealth of which depended, during the Hellenic occupation, on the working and trading of salt. After being abandoned for some 400 years, it was reoccupied between the 4C and the 14C.

Visit *Allow 3 to 4hr.*

▶ *Leave the car in the car park and climb a path on the left to the medieval wall surrounding the excavations.*

The settlement of St-Blaise (its ancient name could be Heraclea or Mastramellè) takes the form of a fortified spur, the natural defences of which, huge vertical cliffs, are reinforced by ramparts from the Hellenistic period; these were built on the most accessible side which overlooks Lavalduc valley.

Etruscan St-Blaise

The oldest traces of human existence date back to early 5 000 BC. The group of small lagoons which link the east arm of the River Rhône to Berre lagoon most probably contributed to the discovery of the site by Etruscan sailors in the 7C BC. They established a trading post and began a successful trade: exchanging salt collected here for wine from Etruria. The settling of the Phocaeans at Marseille in c 600 BC brought about serious competition between St-Blaise and Marseille; nevertheless the discovery of Etruscan, Corinthian and Ionian pottery has proved that the settlement progressed.

In the second half of the 7C, the settlement formed a proto-urban town surrounded by a wall. As in Entremont, a lower and an upper town were established. The dwellings were built of stone on a square plan; one in the lower town still has its walls at a height of 0.9m/35in.

A long period of transition (475-200 BC) then took place, after a fire, marked by the departure of the Etruscans from the trading post, and Marseille took over. It has been suggested that there was a possible period of withdrawal judging from the absence of human dwellings.

Hellenistic ramparts★

From the late 3C to the mid 1C BC the settlement reached its apex: commerce picked up under the influence of Marseille which held St-Blaise without, however, making it a colony.

Large projects for levelling of the terrain preceded the establishment of an urban plan and a strong fortified wall. The very high **Hellenistic ramparts**★ were raised under the direction of Greek craftsmen between 175 and 140 BC; they are more than 1km/0.5 mi long and cut by towers and bastions, equipped with three posterns and a gateway and crowned at the top with merlons. The wall was equipped with a system of water evacuation via

Hellenistic ramparts

channels. It had hardly been finished when the settlement underwent a violent siege (dozens of cannonballs have been discovered) which historians are still trying to date. According to a recent theory, having escaped the control of Marseille a short time after the ramparts were completed, St-Blaise may have been taken over by the Romans during their conquest from 125 to 123 BC. After this event, St-Blaise went through a period of total decline; after its brief reoccupation in the mid 1C BC the site was totally abandoned for four centuries.

Paleochristian and Medieval St-Blaise

With the rise of insecurity at the end of the Roman empire, the old settlement was once again inhabited. The Hellenistic fortifications were reused: in the 5C the wall was surmounted by an ornamentation of irregular blocks of stone. Two churches were built: St-Vincent (the apse of which is near the ancient main gate) and St-Pierre (destroyed in the 9C). A necropolis (tombs carved into the rock) extended to the south. The living quarters of this settlement were unfortunately difficult to identify among the other ruins.

In 874, Ugium (the name of the settlement at that time) was destroyed by the Saracens. It recovered slowly, St-Pierre was rebuilt in the 10C, then burned down, then reconstructed again in the 11C (substructures have been found near the chapel of St-Blaise). In 1231, at the plateau's northernmost point a new wall was built to protect the town of Castelveyre (its new name) with its new church Notre-Dame-et-St-Blaise around which the dwellings nestled.

In 1390 Raymond de Turenne's band of brigands pillaged the town. The site was never to be resettled; the last inhabitants settled at St-Mitre. At the end of the spur, a fine view of the Étang de Lavalduc and the Bassins de Fos opens out (& *see Bassins de FOS).*

ST-GILLES★

POPULATION 11 304

MICHELIN MAP 339: L-6

Gateway to the Camargue, and of agricultural importance (fruit, Costières wines), St-Gilles' claim to fame is the old abbey church, the west front of which considerably influenced Romanesque sculpture in Provence and in the Rhône valley.

Feria

St-Gilles has long hosted bullfights and traditional bouvines – Camargue horse races – in the summer months. The third weekend in August the town's "peach and apricot" feria takes place and includes corridas, bull races through the town streets and merrymaking, local style.

A Bit of History

St Giles and the doe

Legend has it that in the 8C St Giles, who lived in Greece, was touched by the grace of God and gave all his money to the poor. He set out from Greece aboard a raft which was borne by the sea to Provence, where he lived alone in a cave for many years. The hermit was befriended by a doe which brought him food, and which he later saved from a huntsman, miraculously snatching the arrow in mid-flight, and so amazing the huntsman that he, being of a rich and noble family, founded an abbey on the site in commemoration of the event. St Giles journeyed to Rome to obtain recognition for the new foundation and was presented by the pope with two doors for the abbey, which he promptly launched on the Tiber and which, after being carried out to sea, landed on the Provençal shore at the same time and place as the saint on his return.

The influence of St Giles (11C-12C)

On the site of St Giles' tomb, a sanctuary was raised which became the object of a fervent cult and a place of pilgrimage, even more frequented because of its location on one of the four major roads to Santiago de Compostela.

In the 12C the monastery reached its peak: the town surrounding it had nine parishes and was extraordinarily prosperous. It owed part of its success to the Crusades: a large amount of Far Eastern goods passed through its port; the crusading pilgrims embarked from here and the people of St-Gilles had trading posts with privileges in the Latin States of Jerusalem. The St-Gilles Fair held in September was in full expansion; it was one of the great trading centres between the Mediterranean and northern countries. This prosperity diminished in the 13C owing to the competition of the royal port of Aigues-Mortes.

Detail of bas relief on doorway of St-Gilles church

B. Kaufmann / MICHELIN

Five artists to create a masterpiece

Art historians identify five stylistic groups with the name of only one master known, that of Brunus.
– Brunus: Matthew, Bartholomew, John the Evangelist, James the Greater, Paul; characteristics: Antique style, heavy, plain.
– Master "of St Thomas": Thomas, James the Less, Peter, low reliefs of the centre door; this sculptor is thought to have worked in the west of France; characteristics: linear quality and typically Romanesque treatment.
– "Soft" Master: apostles, left splay of the centre door, tympanum and lintel of the north door; characteristics: supple drapery modelling the folds around the arms and legs.
– "Hard" Master: apostles, south door; characteristics: long enveloping drapery with voluminous and hard folds sometimes represented in a spiral form, contrasts accentuated by light and shade.
– Master "of St Michael": entablatures on either side of the centre door, St Michael slaying the dragon; characteristic: very expressive style.

The glory and decline of the Counts of Toulouse

Popes and the counts of Toulouse protected and enriched the Benedictine monastery. In the 11C the powerful Count **Raymond IV** became lord of St-Gilles, and built up a vast domain extending from Cahors to the Îles de Lérins, through marriage and inheritance. In 1096 he received Pope Urban II, who consecrated the altar of the new abbey church; the count vowed never to return to his land so as to devote himself entirely to the conquest of the Holy Land; this he did, founding the county of Tripoli, where he died.

His great-grandson, **Raymond VI**, was ordered by Pope Innocent III to fight against the so-called Albigensians, or Catharist heretics, and purge them from his territories. It was at St-Gilles, the extreme limit of the county, that he received the papal legate, Pierre de Castlenau, who was assassinated the next day, 15 January 1208. The pope immediately excommunicated Raymond VI and preached the Crusades. The count submitted and did penance in St-Gilles on 12 June 1209, being led naked into the church and flagellated in front of Castelnau's tomb. However, he soon revolted again, fighting a losing battle against **Simon de Montfort**, and was killed at Muret in 1213.

Abbey Church *45min*

In order to grasp the abbey's importance at the end of the 11C and during the 12C, try to imagine the chancel of the former abbey church extending beyond the present chancel and, on the church's south side, the cloisters with their courtyard surrounded by the chapterhouse, refectory, kitchens and basement storeroom, not to mention the other monastic buildings which stretched as far as the present Rue de la République and rue Victor-Hugo.

Secularised and established as a collegiate church in 1538, it suffered irrevocable destruction in 1562 during the Wars of Religion. The Huguenots threw the monks into the crypt's well and set the monastery on fire: the church's vaulting collapsed; in 1622 the great belfry was destroyed. In the 17C the church was shortened by half and its vaulting lowered so that in the future there would be less upkeep. Thus all that is left of a magnificent medieval building are the fine west face, remains of the chancel and the crypt.

Façade★★

The façade, which dates from the mid 12C, is considered one of the finest examples of Romanesque sculpture in the south of France. The work was carved in a single time span, according to an initial project which was modified during its carving by several different schools of sculpture. The story told is that of Salvation through the different stages in the life of Christ. The sculptors were inspired by the Antique style, notably from the paleo-Christian sarcophagi, as is shown by their use of high relief and the representations of volumes (anatomical proportions) and forms (pleated clothing). The great frieze reads from left to right and recounts all the events of Holy Week from Palm Sunday to the morning of Paschal Resurrection and the discovery of the empty tomb by the Holy Women.

Ancien Chœur de St-Gilles

This is outside the actual church and corresponds to the part which was devastated in the 17C and razed during the Revolution. The bases of the pillars and the walls indicate precisely the former chancel's layout with its ambulatory and radiating chapels. On either side of the ambulatory, two small bell towers were served by spiral staircases; the one on the left remains: the Vis de St-Gilles.

Vis de St-Gilles★

This spiral staircase served the abbey church's north bell tower. Completed in 1142, it has always been admired by the Brotherhood of Stonemasons who during their habitual tour of France stopped to study it (they left graffiti).

Climb to the top (50 steps) to appreciate the rare quality of the cutting and joining of the stone. The steps rest on the central core and the cylindrical walls. The perfection of the interlocking stone composes a spiral vault of nine voussoirs. The art of the stonemason appears in the double concavity and convexity of each voussoir.

Crypt★

This low church (50m/164ft long, 25m/82ft wide) was the scene of one of the West's most important pilgrimages. It lasted three days and some 50 000 people walked past the venerated tomb of St Giles. It was once covered with groined vaulting, which remains in several bays to the right of the entrance. Pointed vaulting from the mid 12C is what remains in the crypt; this vaulting is among the oldest known in France. The decoration of certain arches adorned with a plain band contrasts with that of the others elegantly ornamented with ribbons and ovolo moulding.

Note the staircase and ramp the monks used to reach the upper church. Sarcophagi, ancient altars and Romanesque capitals are also worth admiring.

In Town

Maison des métiers

Grand-Rue, ☎ *04 66 87 09 05.* Craft workshops specialising in ceramics, gold, glass, terrac otta and fabrics for interiors.

Additional Sight

Maison romane

🕐*Daily except Sun 9am-noon, 2-5pm (Jul and Aug: 9am-noon, 3-7pm).* 🕐*Closed in Jan and public holidays. No charge.* ☎ *04 66 87 40 42.*

This Romanesque house is the birthplace of **Guy Foulque**, elected pope in 1265 under the name of Clement IV. It houses an ethnological room presenting tools and objects relating to the old trades: the shepherd, coopery, life in the fields, the vineyards, olive groves and domestic life. In the "medieval" room, with its magnificent chimney, a small lapidary museum containing the ruins of the former abbey church: tympanum, capitals, keystone, 12C low reliefs and sarcophagi.

Camargue Gardoise★

73km/45.6mi – allow half a day

Situated between the Costières and the Petit-Rhône, Saint-Gilles and Aigues-Mortes, the so-called "Camargue gardoise" with its marshes and reeds constitutes what is probably the most austere landscape of the Rhône delta. However its strong links to ancient traditions make it an area that is well worth preserving and exploring.

▷ *Leave St-Gilles via N 572 for Montpellier.*

The road winds its way through the slopes of the hills crossing the territory of the Nîmes Costières with its numerous vineyards where wine can be bought. To the left there is an area of lakes with the large lakes of Scamandre and Charnier visible through the reeds.

▷ *Turn left onto D 179 for Gallician and, from this small wine-producing hamlet, turn right on to the small D 381 road. After the Mas Teissier, turn left and follow D 401 until you reach the canal that links the Rhône to Sète.*

Pont des Tourradons

From this bridge that stands in isolation among the marshes, there are interesting **views**★ of a typical Petite Camargue landscape: a straight canal, ponds and reeds which seem to merge with the sky in a solitary silence. In the summer herds of black bulls peacefully graze in the pastures of the Cailar. This is surely the definitive scenery of the authentic Camargue.

▶ *Take D 104 in the opposite direction and turn right onto D 352 for Vauvert.*

Vauvert

The old centre of this wine-producing village, now a residential suburb of Nîmes, has a covered marketplace which has been converted into an exhibition space.

▶ *Take N 572 towards Aimargues.*

At the level of the roundabout that leads to the village of Cailar (whose signposts were designed and made by the painter François Boirond), stands the tomb of a famous Camargue bull known as *Sanglier (boar)*.

▶ *Before reaching Aimargues, turn left onto D 979 for Aigues-Mortes.*

Château de Teillan

👣 See AIGUES-MORTES.

Saint-Laurent-d'Aigouze

In the middle of the village square, shaded by large plane trees, stands the arena, next to the church whose sacristy seems to function as a *toril*. It is worth a visit particularly at the end of August when the races to celebrate the votive feast take place.

▶ *Continue along D 146 which goes past the Tour Carbonnière (see AIGUES-MORTES). On reaching D 58 turn left towards Arles.*

In this wine-producing area there are a great number of large mas, hidden by the shade of small pine forests.

After 9.5km/5.9mi turn left onto the small D 179 road for Montcalm e St-Gilles.

In the hamlet of **Montcalm** stand the ruins of a large, early 18C house (in very bad repair) where the Marquis de Montcalm stayed before his departure for Canada. On the right, in a large vineyard, stands a chapel dating from the same period.

▶ *The very narrow road runs along the Capettes canal all the way to the Mas des Iscles. At the crossing, park in the Centre du Scamandre car park.*

Centre de découverte du Scamandre

🕐*Nov to Apr: Wed to Fri 9am-5pm; May to Oct: Wed to Sat 9am-5pm.* 🕐*Closed Sun and public holidays. Enquire for information. 1.82€.* ☎ *04 66 73 52 05.*

The main purpose of this centre, situated in the Scamandre nature park, is to preserve and manage the marshes as well as raise public awareness of this fragile ecosystem.

Road D 179 on the right leads to Gallician, frequented by many fishermen and situated on the Capettes canal. The canal runs between the Charnier and Scamandre ponds and is a veritable forest of reeds.

Harvesting reeds

G. Magnin/MICHELIN

▶ *After crossing the canal and Gallician, return to Vauvert via N 572 on the right.*

ST-MAXIMIN-LA-STE-BAUME★★

POPULATION 9 594

MICHELIN MAP 340: K-5

St-Maximin lies at the centre of a small basin, once the bottom of a lake, not far from the source of the Argens in a region of flat depressions; the village is flanked to the north by wooded hills and vineyards and to the south by the mountainous foundations of the Massif de la Ste-Baume. The village takes its name from St Maximus who, according to legend, converted its inhabitants to Christianity and is buried here, on the spot of what subsequently became a Dominican monastery and basilica.

🛈 *Pl. de-l'Hôtel-de-Ville, 83470 St-Maximin-La-Ste-Baume, ☎ 04 94 59 84 59.*

A Bit of History

During the Revolution the Dominicans were expelled but by great good fortune the basilica and monastery housed Lucien Bonaparte, Napoleon's youngest brother, then officer in charge of military stores. He turned the cathedral into a food depot and saved the organ from harm by having the Marseillaise played regularly upon it. The young officer, with an intelligence second only to Napoleon's, became a well-known figure in the town, as he developed into a rousing speaker and was elected president of the local Jacobin club.

Basilica★★ *45min*

The basilica is constructed on the foundations of a 6C Merovingian church, where in 1279 when the tombs of Mary Magdalene and St Maximinus were discovered. The sarcophagus contained the relics of the saints which were hidden in 716 for fear of the Saracens who were devastating the region. The spot was indicated by the saint herself in a dream. In 1295 Pope Bonifacio VIII acknowledged the relics and on the site of the crypt Charles of Anjou had a basilica and monastery built. He installed the Dominican friars who were in charge of guarding the relics and supervised what soon became a major pilgrimage.

EXTERIOR

Devoid of transepts and ambulatory, the basilica has a squat appearance reinforced by the absence of a belfry, its incomplete west front, and the massive buttresses reaching the nave walls high up. It is nonetheless the most important example of the Gothic style in Provence, combining the influences of the north, especially of Bourges, with local architectural traditions.

INTERIOR

The building comprises a nave, chancel and two aisles of remarkable height. The two-storey, 29m/95ft high nave has pointed vaulting; its keystones bear the arms of the counts of Provence and kings of France; the very large chancel is closed off by a pentagonal apse. The aisles, which were only 18m/59ft high to allow for a clerestory, end with quadrangular apsidal chapels. The side chapels were raised less than the aisles so as to allow the light to filter through.

1) The organ, which has a double case and still has the pipes saved by Lucien Bonaparte, was made by the lay Dominican, Isnard of Tarascon and ranks with the one in Poitiers' cathedral, as one of the finest 18C instruments in France.

2) Fine gilded wood statue of John the Baptist.

3) 15C altarpiece of the Four Saints: Lawrence, Anthony, Sebastian and Thomas Aquinas.

4) Rosary altar adorned with 18C gilded wood statue of the Virgin; 16C altar front carved with four low reliefs recounting the life of Mary Magdalene.

5) 17C choir screen carved in wood with wrought iron inlets emblazoned with the arms of France.

6) Choir stall panelling enclosing 94 stalls, decorated with 22 medallions of saints of the Dominican Order, carved in the 17C by the lay brother, Vincent Funel.

7) 17C stucco decoration by J. Lombard before which stand, to the right, a terracotta of Mary Magdalene's communion, to the left, a marble of the saint's ecstasy and, at the centre, the altar surmounted by a glory.

8) Pulpit carved in 1756 by the Dominican, Louis Gaudet, with representations on the sounding board, of immense size, of the ecstasy of Mary Magdalene, and on the staircase, panels of her life. The rail is cut from a single piece of wood and is a masterpiece in itself.

9) 15C Provençal School predella (lower part of the altarpiece) illustrating the beheading of John the Baptist, St Martha taming the Tarasque on Tarascon Bridge and Christ appearing to Mary Magdalene.

10) 16C painted wood retablea by Ronzen of the Crucifixion, surrounded by 18 medallions.

Crypt

The crypt was the funeral vault of a late 4C-early 5C Roman villa. It contains 4 sarcophagi of the 4C: Saint Mary Magdalene, Saints Marcella and Susan, Saints Maximinus and Cedonius. At the back there is a 19C reliquary containing a cranium long venerated as that of Mary Magdalene. Four marble and stone tablets depict carved figures of the Virgin, Abraham and Daniel (c 500).

Sarcophagus of St Cedonius (detail), Basilica of St-Maximin

D. Pazery/MICHELIN

Royal Monastery★

9am-6pm. No charge. ☎ *04 94 86 55 66.*

Started in the 13C at the same time as the basilica against which it has been built to the north, the former royal monastery was completed in the 15C. The elegant **cloisters**★ include 32 bays. Its garden contains an abundance of foliage: boxwood, yew, lime and cedars. It serves as the stage set for the St-Maximinus Musical Evenings *(Soirées Musicales de St-Maximin)* in the summer.

The convent buildings include a chapel with fine vaulting in the form of a depressed arch, the refectory of five bays and the **chapterhouse**, with its lovely pointed vault above slender columns ending in foliated capitals and held by very low corbels; it is entered through a door flanked by two windows. The large 17C guest-house now houses the town hall.

Abbaye de ST-MICHEL-DE-FRIGOLET

MICHELIN MAP 340: D-2

Located some 18km/11mi south of Avignon, this abbey nestles in a hollow, fragrant with rosemary, lavender and thyme, sheltered by cypresses, pines and olives.

A Bit of History

The abbey was founded in the 10C by monks from Montmajour (*see MONTMAJOUR*), who came to this idyllic spot to recover from the fevers they contracted while draining the marshes around their mother house. They dedicated the chapel to Our Lady of Goodly Remedy (Notre-Dame-du-Bon-Remède), which became the object of a pilgrimage which continues even to this day.

Monks from different orders inhabited the conventual buildings before everything was confiscated and sold during the Revolution. The abbey was converted into a boarding school which Frédéric Mistral attended from 1839 to 1841. The school shut down in 1841 and the abbey was abandoned. In 1858 the abbey was bought by the Reverend Padre Edmond and the Premonstratensians were installed. In 1880 religious persecution drove the monks out and the abbey underwent a real siege at that time. The religious community was once again dispersed in 1903, as a result of the Law of Congregations: the Premonstratensians fled to Belgium. During the First World War the abbey was converted into a military round-up camp; later the Premonstratensians returned to their abbey.

Abbey *45min*

Église Abbatiale and Notre-Dame-du-Bon-Remède

Built in the 19C by R.P. Edmond, the abbey church is lavishly decorated. It was built around the 11C Chapelle de Notre-Dame-du-Bon-Remède, which was the abbey's precursor, and which serves as the apse of the church's north aisle; it contains lovely **gilt panelling**★, a gift from Anne of Austria. The panelling includes 14 framed canvases attributed to the School of Nicolas Mignard. In the hall, added in the 19C, onto which opens the refectory, note the handsome modern santon figures in olive-wood.

Cloisters (Cloître)

🐾*Guided tours (1hr) daily at 3pm, Sun at 4pm.* ○*Closed public holidays. 3.81€.* ☎ *04 90 95 70 07.*

Early 12C. In the north gallery a number of Roman ruins have been collected: friezes, capitals, masks.

Museum (Musée)

The museum contains Provençal furniture, a fine collection of 18C-19C pharmacy jars and the chapel's Renaissance doorway.

Église St-Michel

This very plain 12C church was once the monastery's church. It has a fine stone roof topped by an openwork crest. The façade was redone in the 19C. The interior was heightened by 1.5m/4ft, thus modifying the building's equilibrium.

ST-RÉMY-DE-PROVENCE★

POPULATION 9 340

MICHELIN MAP 340: D-3

LOCAL MAP SEE ALPILLES

Gateway to the Alpilles, St-Rémy symbolises the essence of Provence: boulevards shaded by plane trees, fountains gracing the squares, charming alleyways, and a festive atmosphere, especially on market day and during traditional fairs. Sitting within a region that is a great fruit and market gardening centre, it is a town of gardeners, and has long specialised in the production and trade of flower and vegetable seeds. St-Rémy's main source of income, however, is tourism, encouraged by its thyme and rosemary-scented streets and the presence of impressive Roman ruins.

🛈 *Pl. Jean-Jaurès, 13210 St-Rémy-De-Provence, ☎ 04 90 92 05 22. www.saintremy-de-provence.com.*

A Bit of History

The village, founded after the destruction of Glanum *(see below)*, developed under the protection of the Abbaye de St-Rémi of Reims, from which its name is derived. Birthplace of the famous astrologist Michel Nostradamus, St-Rémy has been dazzled by the genius of Van Gogh and the inspiration of the Provençal poets from Roumanille to Marie Mauron (1898-1986).

Plateau des Antiques★★ *2hr*

1km/0.5mi south of St-Rémy.

▷　Leave St-Rémy by D5 (◷*see circled 3 on the town plan).*

🅿 *Leave your car in the parking area on the right, in front of the triumphal arch.*

The Roman monuments lie on a plateau below the Alpilles' last foothills, In this pleasant spot, from where the view extends over the Comtat plain, Durance valley and Mont Ventoux, stood the prosperous city of Glanum. It was abandoned after Barbarian invasions at the end of the 3C; two magnificent monuments – the mausoleum and commemorative arch – remain.

Mausoleum★★

This monument is 18m/60ft high and is one of the most outstanding in the Roman world and the best preserved; it lacks but the pinecone finial crowning its dome. For a long time it was believed to have been built as a sepulchre for a noble from Glanum and his spouse. However, the excavations conducted by Henri Rolland have established that it was not a tomb but a cenotaph; that is to say, a monument built in memory of the deceased, around 30 BC.

Mausoleum (detail)

Low reliefs representing battle and hunting scenes adorn the four walls of the square podium. The first storey, pierced by four arches, bears on the frieze (depicting naval scenes) of the northern architrave an inscription which says "Sextius, Lucius, Marcus, sons of Caius of the Julii family, to their parents". This suggests a posthumous dedication from the three brothers in honour of their father and grandfather. The second storey is made up of a rotunda with a Corinthian colonnade which encloses the statues of the two figures.

Arc Municipal★

Perhaps contemporary with the mausoleum, that is to say the first years of Augustus' reign, this arch is the oldest Roman arch of the Narbonensis region. It indicated, on the main route to the Alps, the entrance to Glanum. Its perfect proportions (12.50m/40ft long, 5.50m/17ft wide and 8.60m/27ft high) and the exceptional quality of its carved decoration show Greek influence, quite evident at Glanum.

The sole arcade is carved with a lovely festoon of fruit and leaves; inside, it is adorned with a finely-carved hexagonal coffered ceiling. On either side of the opening are allegorical symbols of victory and on the sides groups of two prisoners, men and women, down by the victors' booty. The despondency of these figures is well rendered.

Art historians feel that the unique form of this arch, mutilated very soon after construction, has inspired some of the 12C Romanesque doorways such as St-Trophime at Arles.

Glanum★

🕐 *Apr to Sept: 9am-7pm; Oct to Mar: 9am-noon, 2-5pm (last admission 30min before closing).* 🚫*Closed 1 Jan, 1 May, 1 and 11 Nov, 25 Dec. 5.49€.* ☎ *04 90 92 23 79 or* ☎ *04 90 92 35 07.*

The excavations, unearthed since 1921, are located at the main gap of the Alpilles, which dominate them. The site consists of a group of complex structures reflecting several different periods of occupation, grouped by archaeologists into three phases.

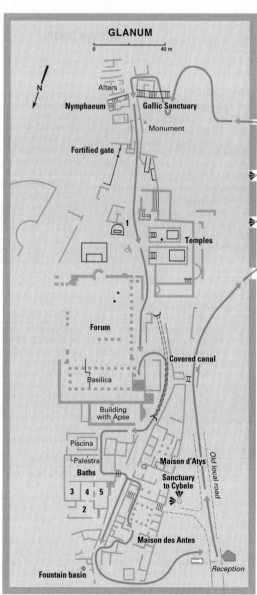

GLANUM

0   40 m

Altars

Nymphaeum   Gallic Sanctuary

Monument

Fortified gate

Temples

1

Forum

Covered canal

Basilica

Building with Apse

Piscina

Palestra   Maison d'Atys

Baths   Sanctuary to Cybele

3   4   5

2

Old local road

Maison des Antes

Fountain basin   Reception

A Bit of History

The Three Glanum– The origin of the site is a sanctuary venerated by Celtic-Ligurian people known as the Glanics. This native settlement rapidly came into contact with the merchants of Massalia owing to its location close to two important roads. Glanon (or Glanum I) developed under Hellenistic influence as can be seen in the construction, particularly in the technique of bonding (large carved blocks of stone perfectly set without mortar) in the 3C and 2C BC. This Hellenistic community included public buildings (temple, agora, assembly hall, a rampart, which was probably ceremonial and controlled the procession to the sanctuary), houses with peristyles, and a fortified district to the south (sanctuary).

The second phase (Glanum II) began with the Roman conquest during the late 2C and with the occupation of the country by Marius' army which stopped the Teutonic army. The town most probably suffered when the Teutons passed through; the new buildings were then made by the bonding of irregular stones and the majority of the public buildings disappeared.

The last phase (Glanum III) follows the conquest of Marseille by Caesar in 49 BC. Romanisation intensified, and under Augustus the town was rebuilt. In the centre,

Address Book

For coin ranges, see Legend at the back of the guide.

EATING OUT

Le Monocle – *48 rue Carnot – closed 20 Dec-31 Jan, Sat and Sun –*. Immerse yourself in the world of science fiction in this resolutely original restaurant with its supernatural murals. Both refined and served in generous portions, the southern food is anything but fictitious. Try and get here early, as there are not many tables.

La Cassolette – *53 rue Carnot – 04 90 92 40 50 – closed 7 Nov-1 Feb, Mon evening in low season and Tue except on public holidays –*. You really have to get into the thick of the old quarter of St-Rémy to find this little house where the young owners concoct bona fide regional dishes. Dine in one of the two dining rooms, with glossy walls.

La Maison Jaune – *15 rue Carnot – 04 90 92 56 14 – closed 8 Jan-8 Mar, Sun evenings in the winter, Tue lunchtime Jun-Sep and Mon – booking essential.* This restaurant has a yellow façade and sits in the heart of the city. Also yellow are the patterned floor tiles of the pretty terrace on two levels which is shaded by an awning and faces the church. Furniture is made of teak and wrought iron. The Provençal cuisine is light and makes use of fresh market produce.

WHERE TO STAY

Cheval Blanc – *6 avenue Fauconnet – 04 90 92 09 28 – closed Nov-Feb – 22 rooms – 5.34€.* A family-run establishment set in the heart of the city. First-floor reception area, rustic-style rooms which are gradually being done up, and sitting room with local furniture. Breakfast is served on the veranda.

L'Amandière – *avenue Plaisance du Touch – 1km/0.6mi northeast of St-Rémy via the Avignon road then take the Noves road – 04 90 92 41 00 – closed end Oct to mid-Dec and beginning Jan to mid-Mar – 26 rooms – 6.40€.* A peaceful area, a modern building, a pleasant pool and garden as well as the added bonus of a warm welcome... What more could one ask for? The medium-sized rooms are simply decorated and some of them have small terraces or balconies. Well-presented breakfast served on the veranda or on the terrace.

Chambre d'hôte La Chardonneraie – *60 rue Notre-Dame – 13910 Maillane – 7km/4.3mi northwest of St-Rémy via D 5 – 04 90 95 80 12 - closed Dec and Jan – 4 rooms.* Forming part of an old Provençal mas, this charming house is full of allure with its shimmering colours, antique furniture, small garden and swimming pool. At breakfast time the owner will point out the most picturesque footpaths from which to explore the area.

ON THE TOWN

Café des Arts – *30 bd Victor-Hugo – 04 90 92 13 41 – summer: daily except Tue, 7.30am-2am; rest of year 7.30am-12.30am – closed Feb and first half of Nov.* An artistic meeting point in the town, this café is frequented by celebrities in search of a bit of peace within these modest walls which for decades have also served as a showcase for the paintings of local artists. Don't forget to check out the decoration in the dining room.

SHOPPING

Le Petit Duc – *7 bd Victor-Hugo – 04 90 92 08 31 – www.petit-duc.com – daily 10am-1pm, 3pm-7pm except Wed.* Using recipes drawn from books of magic spells, the delicacies of Le Petit Duc will surprise you not only for their flavours but also for their names: *oreilles de la bonne déesse* (ears of the good goddess), *pastilles d'amour* (love lozenges) and in particular the town speciality, *pignolat de Nostradamus*.

Santonnier Laurent-Bourges – *Maillane road – D5 –* ☎ *04 90 92 20 45 – daily 9am-7pm.* From his home in the heart of the countryside, Laurent Bourges has dedicated himself to the profession of santon craftsmanship for 44 years. Pay him a visit and he will show you his atelier and, who knows, perhaps divulge some secrets of his ancestral know-how. You might even encounter some celebrities searching for figures to complete their collection of santons.

EVENTS

Festival Organa – Organ festival in July in the Collégiale St-Martin.

Glanum en fête – Theatre on the Glanum archaeological site (June).

Jazz dans les Alpilles – Espace Dourguin.

Fête de la transhumance – Whit Monday (7th Mon after Easter): goats, ewes and rams cross the town in celebration of the end of winter as animals move to open pastures. The festivities include a cheese fair, an antique fair and a display of Provençal donkeys.

Feria provençale – Typical Camargue races in mid-August, which includes abrivados, and the so-called *carreto ramado*, a ritual procession of a cart drawn by 40 horses.

Noël – At Christmas a gros souper (Christmas dinner) market is set up, offering basic ingredients to make a Christmas meal; a pastoral played by the town's inhabitants.

Fêtes de la route des peintres – Painting festivals take place between May and October for four weekends. During the festival the streets are filled with paintings and sculptures by over 200 artists, with a huge variety of styles and talent.

the old buildings were razed, their debris levelled and filled to make room for a vast horizontal esplanade on which were erected the great public buildings: forum, basilica, temples and baths.

Visit

In the Visitors' Centre (ticket office), two models of the site, reconstructed frescoes and various fragments of architecture and domestic objects all help to shed further light on the different phases of the site's history.

Gallic Sanctuary

Set up in terraces facing the rising sun, this sanctuary dates from the 6C BC. In this area kneeling warriors were uncovered, as well as stelae with carved skulls identical to those found in the great Salian towns.

Nymphaeum

The source round which Glanum possibly developed is marked by a pool with masonry walls of large, Greek-style stones. In 20 BC Agrippa built a temple next to it, dedicated to Valetudo, goddess of health (ruins of three fluted columns). A staircase leads to the bottom still fed with water from the spring.

Fortified Gate

This remarkable Hellenistic vestige used, like at St-Blaise, the Massaliote technique of large well-matched rectangular blocks of stone with merlons and gargoyles. The ramparts, which succeeded at least two protohistoric ramparts, defended the sanctuary and included a postern with a zigzag passageway and a carriage gate.

Temples

Southwest of the forum (on the left as you go north) stood twin temples surrounded by a *peribolus*, the southern section of which partially covered an assembly hall with its tiered seats. These Roman public buildings, the oldest of their kind in Gaul, date back to 30 BC. Important vestiges of their lavish decoration (blocks of cornice, roof decorations etc) as well as exquisite sculpture (particularly the portraits of Octavian and Julia which can be found in the Hôtel de Sade) have been excavated. These vestiges have made it possible, partially, to reconstruct the smaller of the two temples. A monumental fountain (1) stood opposite the temples in front of the forum and here a trapezoidal square belonging to a Hellenistic building was laid out, surrounded by magnificent head capital colonnades (exhibited at the Hôtel de Sade).

Forum

The forum was built on the ruins of pre-Roman buildings which archaeologists are seeking to identify. It was closed to the north by the basilica (a multi-purpose building mostly for commercial and administrative activities) of which 24 foundation pillars remain and under which Sulla's House was discovered. In the house were uncovered mosaics (2), most likely the oldest ones found in Gaul. South of the basilica lay the forum square lined on each side by a covered gallery and closed to the south by a great decorated apsidal-ended wall. Discovered underneath the square were a house and a large Hellenistic building.

Covered Canal

This remarkable work, probably a channel which drained the water from the valley and the town, was so constructed that the stone covering also served as Glanum's main street pavement.

Baths

These baths date back to the time of Julius Caesar. Their clear plan followed the classical route: *a gymnasium* (3), *frigidarium* (4), *tepidarium* (5), *caldarium* (6), *palestra*, set up for physical exercise and athletic games, once lined with porticoes, and finally a cold swimming pool, possibly supplied with running water.

Maison d'Atys

This house was originally divided into two parts (peristyled court to the north and pool to the south) joined by a large door. Later a sanctuary to Cybele was set up in the area where the peristyle stood; note the votive altar dedicated to the goddess' ears.

Maison des Antes

Beside Maison d'Atys, this lovely Greek-style house, built according to the 2C BC taste, was laid out around a peristyled central courtyard and cistern. The entrance bay of one of the rooms has preserved its two pilasters (*antes*).

The City

Place de la République

Beside the ring road, this square is on the site of the medieval ramparts and is the heart of the town, animated by its café terraces and the bustle on its market days.

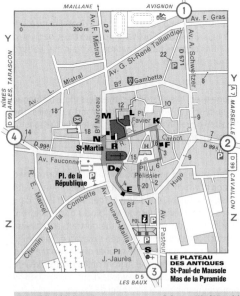

ST-REMY-DE-PROVENCE

8 Mai 1945 R. du	Z	20
Commune R.	Z	2
Estrine R.	YZ	3
La-Fayette R.	Z	6
Hoche R.	Z	4
Libération Av. de la	Y	7
Mauron Av. Ch.	Y	8
Mirabeau Bd	YZ	9
Nostradamus R.	Y	10
Parage R.	Y	12
Pelleten R. C.	YZ	14
Résistance Av.	Z	15
Roux R.	Z	16
Salengro R. R.	Y	18

Ancien hôpital St-Jacques	Z	E
Chapelle Notre-Dame-de-		
Pitié (Donation Mario Prassinos)	Y	S
Fontaine Nostradamus	Y	K
Hôtel Estrine (Centre d'Art-		
Présence-Van-Gogh)	Z	F
Hôtel Mistral de Mondragon	Y	M
Hôtel d'Almeran-Maillane	Y	R
Hôtel de Lubières " maison de l'Amandier "	Y	N
Hôtel de Sade	Y	L
Maison Natale de Nostradamus	Z	D
Musée des Alpilles Pierre-de-Brun	Y	M

St-Paul-de-Mausole cloister

Collégiale St-Martin

This collegiate church with its striking façade was rebuilt around 1820 after it had partially caved in. The only remaining 14C feature is the bell tower crowned with a crocketed spire. The lovely organ case in the gallery inside was reconstructed in 1983. The organ is used every year during the festival of organ music.

The vestiges of the old 14C fortifications line Rue Hoche; here can also be seen the **Maison natale de Nostradamus** (Nostradamus' Birthplace) and the 17C **Ancien Hôpital St-Jacques**.

▶ *Take boulevard Victor-Hugo and turn right into rue de 8 mai 1945. In place Jules-Pélissier stands the town hall, which was formerly a 17C monastery. Turn right into rue Lafayette, then left into rue Estrine.*

Hôtel Estrine

No 8. This handsome private mansion was built in the 18C for Marquis Joseph de Pistoye and was subsequently purchased by Louis Estrine, a master rope-maker from Marseille, from whom the house gets its name. Recent renovation work has restored the residence to its former glory. Built on three storeys from ashlar masonry, it features a central concave section on its façade into which opens the doorway, surmounted by an elegant wrought iron balcony. Inside, the grand stone staircase leads up to the rooms on the first floor, which are paved with floor tiles and decorated with plaster-work. The mansion now houses the **Centre d'Art–Présence Van Gogh**, devoted to Vincent Van Gogh: an audiovisual display and thematic exhibitions illustrate his work and the time he spent at St-Rémy. The upper floors are given over to interesting temporary exhibitions of contemporary art (Ⓞ*mid-Mar to end of Oct and Dec: daily except Mon 10.30am-12.30pm, 2.30-6.30pm. 3.5€. ☎ 04 90 92 34 72).*

On the corner of rue Carnot and rue Nostradamus is the 19C **Fontaine Nostradamus**, decorated with a portrait of the famous medic and astrologer.

A couple of yards further on, place Favier (Le Planet or the former herbal market place) is lined with fine 15C and 16C hôtels, converted into museums: the **hôtel de Sade** (15C-16C) and the 16C *hôtel* **Mistral de Mondragon**. A little further on is the Hôtel d'Almeran-Maillane, where Charles Gounod gave his first hearing of "Mireille" in 1863.

▶ *Return to boulevard Marceau, where a detour to the right reveals (at no 11) the former* **hotel de Lubières**, *also known as the "house of the almond tree."*

Additional Sights

Archeological stone collection★

Ⓞ*Apr to Sept: 10am-noon, 2-6pm (Jul and Aug: 7pm); Oct to Mar: 10am-noon, 2-5pm.*
Ⓞ*Closed 1 Jan, 1 May, 1 and 11 Nov, 25 Dec. 2.44€. ☎ 04 90 92 64 04.*

The **hôtel de Sade** contains an important collection (part of which is open to the public), where remarkable finds from the Glanum excavations can be seen. Of particular note are a very fine acroterion from the temple dedicated to the goddess Valetudo, and the remains of 4C baths and a 5C baptistery (in the courtyard). The second floor displays objects evoking daily life at Glanum from the Greeks to the Gallo-Roman occupation: tools, bronze and bone objects, funerary urns, pottery, oil lamps (among them note the rare candelabrum with two rows of lamps, one above the other), jewellery (note the magnificent ring made of rock crystal adorned with the finely carved head of a woman).

Musée des Alpilles Pierre-de-Brun

🕐*Mar to Oct: 10am-noon, 2-6pm (Jul and Aug: 7pm); Nov to Dec: 10am-noon, 2-5pm.* 🕐*Closed Jan and Feb, 1 May, 25 Dec. 2.74€.* ☎ *04 90 92 68 24.*
This museum is located in the vast 16C Mistral de Mondragon mansion built round a fine courtyard with a round turreted staircase and overlooked by loggias. The exhibits relate to popular arts and traditions. Documents concerning Nostradamus as well as minerals from the Alpilles are also displayed.

Donation Mario Prassinos★

🕐*Chapelle N.-D.-de-Pitié – Mar to Dec: daily except Mon 2-6pm (Jul and Aug: daily except Mon 11am-1pm, 3-7pm).* 🕐*Closed Jan and Feb, 1 May, 1 and 11 Nov, 25 Dec. No charge.* ☎ *04 90 92 35 13*
Mario Prassinos (1916-1985), a Greek artist who settled at Eygalières, carried out a series of mural paintings on the theme of Agony in the Chapelle Notre-Dame-de-Pitié, a former place of pilgrimage at times of pest or famine. It is a bleak work of branches and trunks of trees juxtaposed in black and white, evoking the Crucifixion of Christ. An alternating display of copper engravings, prints, Indian ink drawings on paper completes this bequest.

Ancien Monastère de St-Paul-de-Mausole

♿ 🕐*Apr to Oct: daily 9.30am-6pm, Sat-Sun and public holidays 10.30am-7pm; Nov to end of Mar: daily 10.30am-1pm, 1.30-5pm. 2.59€.* ☎ *04 90 92 77 00*
Located near the Roman monuments, to which its name is linked, this monastery of Augustinian and later Franciscan canons was transformed into a convalescent home in the mid 18C. It preserves the memory of Vincent Van Gogh who asked to be interned here from 3 May 1889 to 16 May 1890. He had a workroom on the ground floor and a bedroom on the first floor. While here he painted: his life at the hospital, nature (Cypress Trees, The Sower), self-portraits, and the extraordinary work Starry Night. The small church dates from the end of the 12C (18C façade) and has a fine square bell tower with Lombard arcades. Beside it the **cloisters**★ present a fine Romanesque decor: the capitals of the small columns are carved with varied motifs (foliage, animals, masks).

Mas de la Pyramide

200m/219yd from the Monastery of St-Paul-de-Mausole. ♿ 🕐*9am-noon, 2-5pm (Apr to Sept: 9am-7pm). 3€.* ☎ *04 90 92 00 81*
This mas hewn out of the rock has an unusual interior layout. It was built for the most part in the old Roman quarries from materials that were also used for the neighbouring town of Glanum. The rooms house a museum of rural life, which displays tools and agricultural equipment once used by local peasants. At the centre of the estate, the vertical "pyramid" rock is a lone reminder of the old ground level of the site before mining work in the quarries began.

La STE-VICTOIRE★★★

MICHELIN MAP 340: I-4

East of Aix-en-Provence lies Montagne Ste-Victoire, a limestone range which reaches an altitude of 1 011m/3 297ft at its peak, the Pic des Mouches. Oriented west to east, this range forms on its south side a sheer drop down to the Arc basin, whereas on its north side it slopes gently in a series of limestone plateaux towards the Durance plain. A striking contrast exists between the bright red clay of the foot of the mountains and the white limestone of the high mountain ridges, especially between Le Tholonet and Puyloubier. The mountain, immortalised by Paul Cézanne (1839-1906) in his paintings, was depicted about 60 times by the artist.

Maison de la Ste-Victoire, 13100 Antonin-sur-Bayon, ☎ 04 42 66 84 40.

Driving Tour

Round-trip of 74km/46mi, allow 1 day (not including tour of Aix).

▷ *Leave Aix-en-Provence on D 10 going east; turn right towards the Barrage de Bimont.*

Barrage de Bimont

This vaulted dam across the River Infernet is the principal architectural undertaking on the Canal de Verdon extension. It stands in a beautiful, wooded site at the foot of montagne Ste-Victoire.

Downstream, superb gorges descend (*1hr there and back on foot*) to the Barrage Zola (a dam built by engineer François Zola, father of the famous author, Émile Zola), the second undertaking in the scheme which supplies water to local towns and villages and irrigation to some 60 local *communes*.

> **WHERE TO EAT**
>
> ⊜⊜ **Au Moulin de Provence** – *33 avenue des Maquisards – 13120 Vauvenargues –* ☎ *04 42 66 02 22 – moulin.de.provencewanadoo.fr.* After Exploring the village, linger for a moment in this pleasant family-run establishment, offering regional cooking and modest rooms. From the terrace and the pastel-coloured sitting room there are views of the Ste Victoire mountain.

▷ *Return to D 10 and turn right. Park the car in the small car park to the right of the road at Les Cabassols farm.*

Croix de Provence★★★

3hr 30min round-trip on foot.

▷ *Walk along the Venturiers path, a mule track which rises rapidly through a pinewood before easing off into a winding path (easier walking).*

The first staging post is at 900m/2 950ft, the Notre-Dame de Ste-Victoire priory, built in 1656 and occupied until 1879. It comprises a chapel, a conventual building and parts of cloisters; a terrace laid in a breach in the wall gives a **view** of the Arc basin and

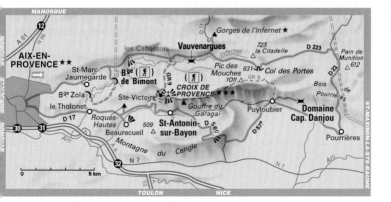

Étoile chain. Bear left of the cloisters to make the short climb to reach the 945m/3 100ft high summit, Croix de Provence, marked by a 17m/56ft cross upon an 11m/36ft base. The **panorama**★★★ of Provençal mountains includes: Massif de la Ste-Baume and Chaîne de l'Étoile to the south, then towards the right the Vitrolles, Crau

Massif Ste-Victoire

J. Malburet/MICHELIN

plain, Durance valley, Luberon, Provençal Alps and more to the east the Pic des Mouches. To the east on the crest is **Gouffre du Garagaï**, a chasm 150m/492ft deep, a source of legends and superstitions.

Vauvenargues

Nestling in the Infernet valley, this village has retained its 17C château, which stands on a rock spur. It belonged to **Picasso**, who lived here at the end of his life (1881-1973); he is buried in the park in front of the château.

Beyond Vauvenargues, the road follows lovely steep wooded **gorges**★ of the Infernet, overlooked on the left by the 723m/2 370ft high Citadelle, and reaches the Col des Portes pass. During the descent, the Alpine foothills can be distinguished on the horizon.

At Puits de Rians, take D 23 to the right which skirts Montagne Ste-Victoire on its eastern side and crosses the Bois de Pourrières (woods); to your left is the Pain de Munition (alt 612m/2 005ft).

▶ *In Pourrières turn right towards Puyloubier.*

Domaine Capitaine Danjou

   ⏱ *Daily 10am-noon, 2-5pm. No charge.* ☎ *04 42 66 38 20.*

In Puyloubier, a path to the right leads to the château, now the Foreign Legion's Pensioners' Hospital. The tour includes the workshops (pottery, book-binding, iron-works) and a small museum.

▶*Return to Puyloubier and take D 57B; then turn right onto D 56c.*

More good views of Montagne Ste-Victoire, also of Trets basin and Massif de la Ste-Baume can be enjoyed before the road climbs the slopes of Montagne du Cengle. The D 17, on the left, winds between the imposing mass of Montagne Ste-Victoire and the Cengle plateau.

Saint-Antonin-sur-Bayon

⏱*10am-6pm, Sat-Sun and public holidays 10am-7pm.* ⏱*Closed 1 Jan, 25 Dec. Price information not provided.* ☎ *04 42 66 84 40*

The **Maison de la Sainte Victoire** has a permanent exhibition on the mountain and explains its ecosystem, history (dinosaur eggs) and the reforestation attempts made after the devastating fire in 1989.

Before returning to Aix, it is worth making a detour to **Beaurecueil** which affords the best views of Sainte-Victoire, particularly at sunset when the mountain and surrounding countryside are tinted by the sun's rays.

▶ *Return to Aix via the "route Paul Cézanne" which goes through Le Tholonet.*

Les STES-MARIES-DE-LA-MER★

POPULATION 2 232

MICHELIN MAP 340: B-5 7

LOCAL MAP SEE CAMARGUE

Between the Mediterranean and the Launes and Impérial lagoons, at the heart of the Camargue, Les Stes-Maries-de-la-Mer can be distinguished by its fortified church. A new marina extends to the west.

🛈 *5 av. Van-Gogh, 13460 Stes-Maries-De-La-Mer, ☎ 04 90 97 82 55. www.lessaintes-maries.com*

A Bit of History

According to Provençal legend, the boat abandoned to the waves in c 40 by the Jews of Jerusalem, which, without the aid of sail or oar, landed safely on the shore of Les Saintes-Maries, carried Mary, the mother of James, Mary Magdalene, Martha and her brother Lazarus, St Maximinus, Mary Salome, the mother of James Major and John, and Cedonius, the man born blind. Sarah, the two Marys' black servant left behind on the shore, wept aloud until Mary Salome threw her mantle on the water so that Sarah could walk over it to join the others. The legend continues that after erecting a simple oratory to the Virgin on the shore, the disciples separated; Martha went to Tarascon, Mary Magdalene to Ste-Baume. The two Marys and Sarah remained in Camargue and were buried in the oratory.

Sights

Church★

From the exterior, the massive crenellated walls of this fortified church are decorated with Lombard arcades at the east end. The keep-like structure of the upper chapel, surrounded at the base by a watchpath and crowned by a crenellated terrace, is dominated by a bell gable (restored in the early 20C). On the south side note the two fine lions devouring their prey which are believed to have supported a porch.

Interior

Enter through the small door on place de l'Église. The Romanesque nave is very dark. The chancel, raised when the crypt was constructed, has blind arcading held up by eight marble columns with splendid carved capitals, two of which are historiated – one illustrating the Incarnation, the other Abraham's Sacrifice of Isaac. South of the nave, protected by a wrought-iron railing, is a well of fresh water for use in time of siege. In the third bay on the north side, above the altar is the Saints Marys' boat which is carried in procession by the gypsies in May and the parishioners in October.

Nineteen centuries of pilgrimage

The saints' tomb rapidly became the object of a cult attracting pilgrims from afar, whereas gypsies and other nomads developed a particular veneration for Sarah.

By the mid 9C the oratory (believed to date from the 6C) had been replaced by a fortified church which, in 869, was being incorporated into the town ramparts under the personal supervision of the archbishop of Arles, when suddenly the Saracens made a lightning raid and carried off the archbishop. In the short time it took to collect the ransom of 150 *livres* of silver, 150 mantles, 150 swords and 150 slaves, the prelate died; unperturbed, the Saracens returned with the corpse, set it apart on a throne with a great show of respect as if nothing were wrong, and departed with the ransom before the Arlesians discovered their loss.

In the 11C the monks of Montmajour established a priory and in the 12C rebuilt the church which was at the same time incorporated into the fortifications. At the end of the 14C the church's fortress-like appearance was reinforced by the addition of machicolations.

During the Barbarian invasions the saints' remains were buried under the chancel. In 1448, King René ordered the exhumation of the saints, whose relics were then enshrined with great ceremony and have remained the object of a deep and widespread veneration ever since.

Address Book

EATING OUT

◎◎ **L'Hippocampe** – *rue Camille-Pelletan* – ☎ *04 90 97 80 91* – ⏱ *closed 2 Nov-17 Mar and Tue except 12 Jul-17 Sept.* Situated in a little village house away from the crowds, this restaurant serves well-presented food in two dining rooms which open onto a patio. In the summer you can enjoy the pleasant Mediterranean evenings on the terrace under the arcades. Four well-kept rooms.

WHERE TO STAY

◎ **Méditerranée** – *4 rue Frédéric-Mistral* – ☎ *04 90 97 82 09* – ⏱ *closed 3 weeks in Jan* – ⊬ – *14 rooms* – ⊡ *4.57€*. A simple family hotel with plenty of good points: a flower-decked façade, a shady terrace where breakfast is served on fine days, recently decorated rooms, reasonable prices and a good choice of restaurants nearby.

◎◎ **Chambre d'hôte Mazet du Maréchal Ferrand** – *route du Bac – 5km/3.1mi from Stes-Maries via the D 570 for Arles and route du Bac via D 85* – ☎ *04 90 97 84 60* – ⊬ – *3 rooms*. With no trace of formality the owner makes you feel right at home. Rooms are all on the ground floor and are simple and colourful. Breakfast is served under the mulberry tree or in a small room with typically Provençal colours.

SHOPPING

Les bijoux de Sarah – *12 place de l'Église*, ☎ *04 90 97 73 73*. Handmade jewellery. Their speciality is a "gypsy" pendant which is supposed to bring good luck and protect against the evil eye.

Market – Traditional market Monday and Friday in place des Gitans.

EVENTS

Pilgrimages des saintes – Each saint merits her own pilgrimage: the celebrations for Mary, mother of James, are held on 24 and 25 May while the feast day of Mary Salome falls on the Sunday closest to 22 October. On the afternoon of the first day, the shrines are brought down from the upper chapel to the chancel. The next day the saints' statues, preceded by the women of Arles in costume, surrounded by Camargue gardians on horseback, are marched in procession through the streets, to the beach and into the sea. Finally, after vespers, the shrines are returned to their chapel on high.

Gypsy Celebration – In May gypsies from all over the world flock to the crypt of their patron saint Sarah, canonised without any formal ceremony. They also carry the richly dressed statue of Sarah through the streets to the sea.

Camargue traditions – The 26 May is Baroncelli-Javon Memorial Day (*see Musée Baroncelli*); it is one of much celebration and local colour. Camargue gardians with the women of Arles in traditional costume take part in such events as the local dance, the farandole, the roundup (ferrade), horse racing and bull running.

Christmas – A picturesque Midnight Mass is held with local additions such as the Camargue guardians and the women of Arles performing the local dance.

South of this altar note the Saints' Pillow, a worn block of marble incorporated in a column and discovered during the excavations of 1448 when the saints' relics were discovered. In the fourth north bay is a pagan altar.

Crypt

Built under the sanctuary. The altar has been built with part of a sarcophagus; it holds the reliquary containing the presumed relics of St Sarah. Right of the altar stands the statue of Sarah and ex-votos offered by the gypsies.

Upper Chapel

The chapel is richly panelled in bright green and gold in the Louis XV style. It houses the reliquary shrine of the two Marys. Frédéric Mistral set the final scene of his romance Mirèio in the chapel where his heroine, Mireille, came to pray for help. There is a statue of Mireille by A. Mercié standing in the main square.

Watchpath (Chemin de ronde)

⏱ *Sept to end of June: 10am-noon, 2-6pm (Jul and Aug: 10am-8pm). 1.52€.* ☎ *04 90 97 82 55.*
53 steps. Climb to the paved watchpath which encircles the church roof, commanding an unforgettable **view**★ of the sea, the town, and the vast Camargue plain.

Musée Baroncelli

⏱ *Mar to mid-Nov: 10am-noon, 2-6pm. 1.52€.* ☎ *04 90 97 82 55.*
Located in the former town hall, this museum displays the literature collected by **Marquis Folco de Baroncelli-Javon** (1869-1943), who revived Camargue traditions,

on the subject of the agro-pastoral way of life in the Camargue and on the history of the town of Les Saintes-Maries. The exhibition comprises also: dioramas illustrating Camargue fauna, including a herons' nesting site; 18C Provençal furniture; display cases devoted to Van Gogh and the marquis de Baroncelli and his friends, such as the Russian painter Ivan Prashninikoff.

SALON-DE-PROVENCE★

POPULATION 34 054

MICHELIN MAP 340: F-4

The town lies at the heart of France's olive growing country. The olive oil industry was established here in the 15C and developed by Colbert. Today mineral oils hold an important position in the town's commerce. A large agricultural market centre, Salon is also the seat of the officers' training school for the French Air Force, which was established in 1936.

🛈 *56 cours Gimon, 13300 Salon-De-Provence, ☎ 04 90 56 27 60. www.salon-de-provence.org.*

▶ **Orient Yourself:** The town is in two parts: the old city climbing up the hill to the castle, and the new district which lies at its feet. They are divided by a broad belt of tree-shaded avenues. Market day in Salon is Wednesday, on place Morgan. There is also an antique market held there the the first Sunday of each month.

A Bit of History

Michel Nostradamus chose Salon as his home. Born in St-Rémy-de-Provence in 1503, he studied medicine in Montpellier and travelled for twelve years in Europe and the Far East to try to improve the remedies which he kept secret; he also studied esotericism.The success he achieved with his remedy for the plague epidemics of Aix and Lyon aroused the jealousy of his colleagues. When the epidemics ceased, he retired to Salon (1547) and took up astrology. His book of predictions entitled *Centuries*, written in the form of verse quatrains, was fantastically successful and attracted the attention of Catherine de' Medici. She came to him and had him read Charles IX's horoscope, showering him profusely with gifts. Nostradamus then studied meteorology and his *Almanach* was also successful. He died in Salon in 1566. His son César wrote a remarkable work entitled Stories and Chronicles of Provence.

Nostradamus

On 11 June 1909, the area from Salon to Aix was badly shaken by a severe earth tremor destroying the villages of Vernègues and Rognes and damaging parts in Salon, Lambesc and St-Cannat; some 60 people died.

Town Centre *2hr*

▶ *On foot, follow the itinerary indicated on the town plan.*

Château de l'Empéri

Built on top of Puech rock, this massive castle dominates the old town. Once the residence of the archbishops of Arles, lords of Salon, the castle was begun in the 10C, rebuilt in the 12C and 13C and remodelled in the 16C; it was transformed into barracks in the 19C but damaged during the 1909 earthquake. A vaulted passage leads to the courtyard decorated with a Renaissance gallery.

The 12C Chapelle Ste-Catherine, the main reception room with its finely carved chimney and some 30 rooms, houses the Empéri Museum.

Hôtel de Ville

This elegant 17C mansion with two corner turrets and a carved balcony nowadays houses the town hall. On place de l'Hôtel-de-Ville stands the statue of Adam de Craponne (1527-76), a native son of Salon and civil engineer, who made the region fertile through the construction of the irrigation canal bearing his name which carries water from the Durance along the original river course through the Lamanon gap.

Porte Bourg-Neuf

This gate opposite the town hall is all that is left of the old 13C ramparts.

Musée de l'Empéri

Église St-Michel

⊘*Closed for restoration work.* This 13C church possesses a five-bay arcaded tower and another tower added in the 15C. Note the portal's Romanesque carved tympanum. In the centre of the old town the house of Nostradamus is to be seen, before passing through the **porte de l'Horloge** to reach place Crousillat with its charming 18C fountain, the **Fontaine moussue**.

▶*Continue along rue des Frères-Kennedy, then turn right into rue Pontis.*

Collégiale St-Laurent

This 14C and 15C church is a good example of southern French Gothic. Inside, admire a monolithic 15C polychrome Descent from the Cross, carved from a single block of stone; the third north chapel contains Nostradamus' tomb.

▶ *Turn back to rue Frères-Kennedy and make for place des Centuries, in front of the castle.*

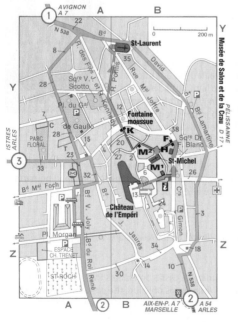

SALON-DE-PROVENCE

Ancienne Halle Pl.	BY	2
Capucins Bd des	BZ	3
Carnot Cours	AY	4
Centuries Pl. des	BY	6
Clemenceau Bd Georges	AY	7
Coren Bd Léopold	AY	8
Craponne Allées de	BZ	10
Crousillat Pl.	BY	12
Farreyroux Pl.	BZ	13
Ferrage Pl.	BZ	14
Fileuses de Soie R. des	AY	15
Frères J. et R.-Kennedy R. des	AY	
Gambetta Pl.	BZ	18
Gimon Cours	BZ	
Horloge R. de l'	BY	20
Ledru-Rollin Bd	AY	22
Massenet R.	AY	23
Médicis Pl. C. de	BZ	24
Mistral Bd Frédéric	BY	26
Moulin d'Isnard R.	BY	27
Nostradamus Bd	AY	28
Pasquet Bd	BZ	30
Pelletan Cours Camille	AY	32
Raynaud-d'Ursule R.	BZ	34
République Bd de la	AY	33
St-Laurent Square	BY	35
Victor-Hugo Cours	BY	38

Hôtel de ville	BY	H
Maison de Nostradamus	BY	M²
Musée Grévin de Provence	BY	M¹
Porte Bourg-Neuf	BY	F
Porte de l'Horloge	BY	K

Address Book

For coin ranges, see Legend at the back of the guide.

EATING OUT

La Fabrique – *75/77 rue de l'Horloge – ☎ 04 90 56 07 39 – la.fabrique@wanadoo.fr – closed Sun lunchtime – booking recommended in the evening.* Situated near the Porte de l'Horloge, this Provençal-coloured restaurant has an infinite variety of homemade pasta which is cooked with every kind of sauce, using old recipes and always served with a smile. All this in the droll setting of an old garage.

Le Clos des Arômes – *20 montée du Château – ☎ 04 90 56 91 06 – closed Sun evenings and Wed.* You'll find this restaurant in the attractive pedestrian quarter at the foot of the castle, just outside the city centre. There is a charming terrace shaded by an acacia tree; the food is of good quality and prepared by a female chef.

L'Eau à la Bouche – *place Morgan – ☎ 04 90 56 41 93 – closed 23-31 Dec, Sun evenings and Mon.* Joined to a fishmongers, this restaurant brings over fish and seafood from the shop before cooking it so freshness and quality are guaranteed! You will eat either in the simple dining room or on the veranda which is very pleasant in the summer.

WHERE TO STAY

Angleterre – *98 cours Carnot – ☎ 04 90 56 01 10 – closed 22 Dec-5 Jan – 25 rooms – ⊃ 5.64€.* This early 20C building near the museums has various sized rooms with double glazing. The breakfast room has a glazed cupola.

Chambre d'hôte Domaine du Bois Vert – *quartier Montauban – 13450 Grans – 7km/4.4mi south of Salon via D 16 and D 19 for Lançon – ☎ 04 90 55 82 98 – www.multimania.com/leboisvert – closed 5 Jan-15 Mar – 3 rooms.* A park of oak and pine trees surrounds this traditional old house and the old-fashioned, rustic rooms have hexagonal floor tiles. Breakfast is served in the large living room or on the terrace facing the garden. Attractive swimming pool.

ON THE TOWN

Le St-Michel – *place des Centuries – ☎ 04 90 56 27 45 – June-Aug: daily 8am-2am; rest of year: Mon-Sat 8am-8.30pm. Closed during Feb school holidays, Christmas and New Year.* As well as serving a variety of beers, this brasserie also has incomparable views of the Château-musée de l'Empéri, which dominates the old town from the imposing rock.

Le Longchamps – *8 place Eugène-Pelletan – ☎ 04 90 56 21 29 – daily 7am-1am – closed Christmas and New Year.* Longchamps is currently the fashionable bar to go and have a drink or simply to go and lend support to the OM whose matches are shown here!

Additional Sights

Musée de l'Empéri★★

Jul and Aug: daily except Tues 10am-6pm; Sept to Jun: daily except Tues 10am-noon, 2-6pm. Closed 1 Jan, 1 and 8 May, 1 Nov, 24, 25 and 31 Dec. 3.06€. ☎ 04 90 56 22 36.
This museum covers the history of the French army from the time of Louis XIV to 1918. The fine rooms enhance the pleasant display of 10 000 items (uniforms, flags, decorations, cutting and thrusting weapons and firearms, cannons, paintings, drawings, engravings, figures on foot or on horseback) which illustrate the military past with special reference to the Napoleonic years.

Musée Grévin de Provence

9am-noon, 2-6pm, Sat-Sun 2-6pm (Jul and Aug: 6.30pm). Closed Easter, 1 and 8 May, Ascension, 14 July, 24, 25 and 31 Dec, 1 Jan. 3.05€. ☎ 04 90 56 36 30.
Some 2 600 years of the history of Provence are retraced here, in the form of 15 waxwork scenes, from the legendary marriage of Gyptis and Protis to the modern day.

Maison de Nostradamus

9am-noon, 2-6pm, Sat-Sun 2-6pm (Jul and Aug: 6.30pm). Closed 1 Jan, Easter, 1 and 8 May, Ascension, 14 Jul, 24, 25 and 31 Dec. 3.05€. ☎ 04 90 56 64 31.
This is the house in which *Nostradamus* spent the last 19 years of his life. Ten animated tableaux with audiovisual back-up illustrate his life and work.
Leave the city centre heading east via D 17, turn left onto the Val de Cuech road and then immediately left onto rue du Pavillon (the museum is signposted).

Château de La Barben

Musée de Salon et de la Crau

🕙*Daily except Tues 10am-noon, 2-6pm, Sat-Sun 2-6pm (Jul and Aug: 6.30pm).* 🚫*Closed public holidays. 3.04€.* ☎ *04 90 56 28 37.*

This museum is in a huge 19C mansion, known as the "Pavillon", and is concerned with local history and the popular arts and traditions of Salon and the surrounding area at the end of the 19C. Traditional activities and everyday customs are evoked thematically: sheep-raising, the manufacture of local household soap known as savon de Marseille, popular worship etc. The natural history section has diorama displays of a variety of naturalised birds.

Driving Tour

Round-trip of 57km/35.6mi – allow half a day.

▸ Leave Salon-de-Provence on D 572 heading east. After Pélissanne a small road on the left leads to la Barben, which occupies a precipitous site in the small Touloubre valley.

Château de La Barben★

🕙*Jun to Aug: guided tours (45min) 10am-noon, 2-6pm; Mar to May and Sept: daily except Tues 10am-noon, 2.30-5.30pm; Oct to Feb: daily except Tues 10.30am-noon, 2.30-5pm.* 🚫*Closed in Jan and 25 Dec. 6.86€.* ☎ *04 90 55 25 41*

The access ramp to the castle offers a plunging view onto the formal French gardens. The present castle was originally a medieval fortress, built before AD 1 000, belonging to the Abbaye St-Victor from Marseille and then to King René, who sold it to the powerful Forbin family. This family owned it for some 500 years and remodelled and enlarged it several times, especially in the 14C and 17C, when it was transformed into a stately home. Its round tower was recently rebuilt after the earthquake of 1909. In front of a noble 17C façade is the terrace (Henri IV staircase with double flight of stairs), from where there is a good view of the gardens designed by Le Nôtre and of the Provençal countryside.

Inside, note the painted ceilings, 16C-17C Aubusson, Flemish and Brussels tapestries, and a fine painting by Largillière. The great drawing room is covered by a Second Empire Aubusson carpet. The reception hall is decorated with Cordoban leathera made near Avignon in 1680. On the second floor the Empire-style bedroom of Pauline Borghese, Napoleon's sister, and her boudoir ornamented with paper painted by Granet and representing the Four Seasons, are also worth noticing.

Vivarium

In the castle's former vaulted sheep's pen is a display of reptiles and tropical and European freshwater fish. The aviary contains birds from the five continents.

Parc Zoologique

Kids ♿ 🕙*10am-6pm. 9.15€ (children: 4.57€).* ☎ *04 90 55 19 12.*

This 30ha/12 acre zoo features a number of enclosures in which over 600 animals roam in relative freedom: big cats, monkeys, elephants, giraffes, bison, zebras and birds of prey.

▶ *Continue left along D 572.*

The road follows the fertile Touloubre valley; after the viaduct carrying the TGV south-east, there is a lovely view of the Trévaresse range before you.

St-Cannat

The town was the birthplace of **Admiral Suffren** (1729-88); the house in which he was born is now the town hall containing a small **museum** *(Musée Suffren et du Vieux St-Cannat* ○*May to Sept: Tues to Fri and the 1st Sun in the month 3-6.30pm.* ○*Closed public holidays. No charge.* ☎ *04 42 50 82 00).*

▶ *Leave St-Cannat by the N 7, in the Avignon direction, then turn left onto D 917.*

Lambesc

This small town possesses a number of fine mansions and fountains from the 17C and 18C. The large 18C church has a remarkable dome. On a 16C gate is a belfry with a clock and Jack.

▶ *Continue along N 7, in Cazan turn left onto D 22. 1km/0.5mi southwest of Cazan is a road marked Château-Bas, with a car park at the end.*

Château-Bas

The fascinating ruins of a Roman temple and chapel stand in a charming site at the far end of the castle (16C-18C) estate. *Go to the vault and request access to the temple.* The **Temple Romain** (○*Daily 9.30am-12.30pm, 1.30-6.30pm, Sun and public holidays 10am-12.30pm, 2.30-6.30pm.* ○*Closed 1 Jan, 25 Dec. No charge.* ☎ *04 90 59 13 16)* probably dates from the late 1C BC, a period characterised by many impressive buildings such as the Commemorative Arch at St-Rémy-de-Provence or the Maison Carrée in Nîmes. The remains include part of the foundations, the left side wall, a wall ending in a square pilaster, surmounted by a beautiful Corinthian capital, and a 7m/23ft fluted column still standing intact. Among the surrounding ruins are a second temple and a semicircular precinct (Roman), probably the ruins of a sanctuary.

Abutting the left wall of the temple is the 12C **Chapelle St-Césaire**.

▶ *Continue along D 22 and turn right onto D 22C.*

Vieux-Vernègues

After passing through Vernègues, the post-1909 village built on the plateau after the earthquake had destroyed the original hill-top settlement, which was then abandoned, the uphill road circles the old village (the ruins are not open to the public) and goes on to the small tower from where there is a vast **panorama**★ *(viewing able)* of a large area of Provence.

Follow the winding road to **Alliens** which has preserved some remains of the city ramparts.

▶ *Turn left onto D 71D and, just after crossing the EDF canal, turn left again onto D 17D for Lamanon.*

Site de Calès

Leave the car in the car park of the fire brigade station and walk to the cobbled path behind the church.

🚶 There are two paths; one leads to the caves and castle ruins *(blue signposts - 1hr 30min there and back)*, the other to the chapels *(green signposts - 2hr 30min there and back)*. The site is closed in July and August.

Nestling on the slopes of the Défens mountain, the Calès site features an impressive cluster of cliff dwellings overlooked by a medieval castle and chapels dating from the same period.

Caves (Grottes)

Carved out of the rock right at the foot of the cliffs to form a natural amphitheatre, the caves were used as quarries during the construction of the castle in the Middle Ages, and subsequently converted into outbuildings and habitations. Visitors may observe the various architectural features of these strange dwellings: holes made for beams, gutters, stairs as well as silos dug out of the rock and used to store food. The caves were inhabited until the castle was destroyed in the late 16C.

Of the 12C fortress there remain only a few vestiges. From the edge of the terrace, on which a statue of Notre-Dame-de-la-Garde has been erected, there are **views** through the pine forest: northwards, of the Durance valley and the Luberon; eastwards, of the cliff dwellings; and southwards, of the Lamanon gap, where the Durance used to flow, the Salon plain, Estaque chain, Crau plain and Berre lagoon.

Go back down towards the cirque and follow the green signposts on the left, leading to the **Chapelle St-Denis**, a typical example of rural church architecture in Provence, which was built around the same time as the castle. Turning right into a path leading to the St-Jean plateau, you will reach the ruins of a double chapel, once an important place of pilgrimage.

▶ *Return to Salon via D 12F and N 538.*

SAULT

POPULATION 1 206

MICHELIN MAP 332: F-9

The town is built in a semicircle, 765m/2 510ft up on a rock promontory at the west end of the Vaucluse plateau above the Gorges de la Nesque. Its position makes it an ideal centre for excursions to Mont Ventoux and the Baronnies and Lure mountains. It is at the centre of an important lavender-growing region and is known for its nougat and honey.

Av. de-la-Promenade, 84390 Sault, ☎ 04 90 64 01 21. www.Saultenprovence.com.

Sights

Church (Église)

The 12C-14C building has a fine Romanesque nave.

Terrace

At the north end of the town, offering a lovely view of the Vaucluse plateau, the entrance to the Nesque gorges and Mont Ventoux.

Museum

🕐*Jul and Aug: daily except Sun 3-6pm. No charge. ☎ 04 90 64 02 30.*
Located on the first floor of the library, the museum contains prehistoric and Gallo-Roman remains, coins, arms, geological finds and a collection of old documents, as well as a mummy and other Egyptian artefacts.

Excursions

MONT VENTOUX★★★

Allow 2hr – ascent via the eastern face.

▶ *Leave Sault on D 164. For description and local map, ⓘsee Mont VENTOUX.*

Address Book

EATING OUT

Restaurant Le Provençal – *rue Porte-des-Aires* – ☎ *04 90 64 09 09 – closed 12 Nov-1 Jan and Tue except May-June –* 🍴 *– 14/20€.* Don't be fooled by the simple façade: this restaurant is well known by inhabitants of the region for its unpretentious, friendly atmosphere. Dishes prepared by a young chef and imbued with all the colour of the region, to be enjoyed in the dining room or on the shaded terrace.

Ferme-auberge Les Bayles – *84390 St-Trinit – 9km/5.6mi east of Sault via D 950 and a secondary road –* ☎ *04 90 75 00 91 – closed Jan – booking essential – 15/22€.* This old sheepfold makes an ideal setting for a return to nature. Chicken, guinea-fowl, duck and rabbit are all on the menu at this farm-inn. Five simple rooms and a cottage are available for hikers, cyclists and riders. Riding centre and swimming pool.

PLATEAU D'ALBION

Round-trip of 30km/19mi – 1hr 30min.

▶ *Leave Sault on D 30 towards St-Christol.*

The Albion plateau, with its fissured calcareous landscape, has all the physical characteristics of a limestone *causse*. Over 200 underground caves or *avens* have been discovered here, many with narrow openings which are difficult to spot. The most beautiful viewed from above is the "Crirvi" cave near St-Christol; the deepest in the region include the Aven Jean-Nouveau with its 168m/550ft vertical shaft at its entrance, and the 600m/1 970ft deep Aven Autran, also near St-Christol, with abundant flowing water at its base. The distinctive feature of these caves is their ability to absorb rainwater down into the branches of an underground system buried deep in the calcareous rock: the main branch of this vast system emerges in the famous Fontaine de Vaucluse.

St-Christol

Lovely Romanesque church built in the 12C and enlarged by the addition of an aisle in the 17C. The most interesting features are the columns, decorated with fantastic animals, and the Carolingian altar, which is carved on three sides.

▶ *Turn back on D 30 towards Sault then, after 4km/2.5mi, turn right onto D 95.*

St-Trinit

A 12C church is all that remains of an old medieval priory which was accountable to the Abbaye St-André at Villeneuve-lès-Avignon.

▶ *Continue to Aurel on D 950 towards Sault, then take D 1 which branches off to the right, and finally D 95.*

Aurel

From D 950 the village, overlooking the Sault plain and its fields of lavender, appears suddenly below, along with its old fortifications and robust church with its light-coloured stone.

GORGES DE LA NESQUE★★

75km/46.9mi – allow approximately 3hr.

▶ *Leave Sault to the south-east along D 942, a scenic road that runs along the Nesque river.*

The River Nesque rises on the east face of Mont Ventoux and after some 70km/45mi flows into a tributary of the Sorgue, west of Pernes-les-Fontaines. In its upper reaches, the most attractive part of its course, the river has cut a spectacular gorge through the calcareous rock of the Vaucluse plateau.

Monieux

This picturesque old village perched above the Nesque is overlooked by a high 12C tower connected to the village by what remains of a defensive wall. Some of the village's medieval houses have retained their old doors.

Viewpoint (Belvédère)★★

Alt 734m/2 408ft. The viewpoint (*left of the road*), signalled by a stele bearing verses from Mistral's Calendau, overlooks the gorges and the jagged **Cire rock** (872m/2 860ft high). The descent begins with a passage through three tunnels, between which the road affords beautiful views of the site. At this point the Nesque runs in a cleft buried so deep in lush vegetation that only the murmuring of the fast flowing crystal-clear waters over its pebble-strewn bed can be heard.

D 942 moves slightly away from the gorge to cross the Coste Chaude coomb. At the exit to the fourth tunnel there is a good **view** back along the gorge to the Rocher du Cire. The road runs below the ruined hamlet of Fayol, buried beneath luxuriant Provençal vegetation. The landscape then changes suddenly as the river emerges into the Comtat Venaissin plain, and the horizon expands to include Mont Ventoux to the east and Carpentras and its countryside straight ahead. The beautiful Hermitage coomb leads to the village of **Villes-sur-Auzon**, an important agricultural centre which lies on the wooded slopes of Mont Ventoux. It is centred on a large square overlooked by old houses and is ringed by a street of plane trees and splashing fountains.

▶ *Take D 1 towards la Gabelle.*

As the road crosses the plateau, Mont Ventoux, the Dentelles de Montmirail and the Carpentras basin fill the horizon. At the entrance to La Gabelle the view extends to the opposite slope, with the Nesque gorges in the foreground and the Luberon mountains in the background.

▸ *From La Gabelle continue north, cross D 1 and head towards Flassan.*

The road descends into a cool valley studded with pines and spruce.

Flassan

The minute village has ochre walled houses and a typically picturesque Provençal square.

▸ *D 217 and D 1 on the left lead back to Sault.*

Abbaye de SÉNANQUE★★

MICHELIN MAP 332: E-10

Nestling in the hollow of a small canyon of the Senancole, which opens onto the Vaucluse plateau, the harmonious ensemble of buildings of the Abbaye de Sénanque (lovely view coming from Gordes on D 177) stands in a desolate site. On arrival, as one takes in the abbey church's east end, set in a sea of lavender, in the summer months and bathed in sunlight, one feels perfectly in tune with the tranquil atmosphere which this seat of Cistercian monasticism exudes.

A Bit of History

Foundation and development

The foundation, in 1148, of Sénanque by a group of monks who had come from Abbaye de Mazan (Haut-Vivarais) fits into the great Cistercian expansion of the 12C. This monastic movement, directed and inspired by St Bernard of Clairvaux, preached an ascetic ideal and prescribed the strict application of the early Benedictine rule in its monasteries: isolation, poverty and simplicity must lead the monk to purity and beatitude.

The way of life of the Cistercians was thus very demanding, very difficult even: divine service, prayer and pious reading alternated with manual labour to fill very long days where time of rest did not exceed seven hours; meals taken in silence were frugal and the monks slept in a common dormitory without any comfort. Cistercian austerity influenced the architectural and artistic conceptions of the Order. St Bernard decreed that buildings be exceedingly plain and stripped of all ornamentation that could divert the attention of those who prayed: no coloured stained glass windows, statues, paintings, or carved tympana and proud bell towers. This lack of ornamentation can be found in the other two Provençal abbeys, daughter-houses of Sénanque: Abbaye du Thoronet *(see The Green Guide French Riviera)* and Abbaye de Silvacane. They have come down to us almost as they were at the height of the Cistercian movement.

Sénanque prospered very rapidly to the point that, as early as 1152, the community had enough members to found another abbey in Vivarais. It profited from numerous gifts starting with the land of the Simiane family and later the land of the lords of Venasque. The monastery rapidly set up, sometimes quite far away, outlying farms (*granges*) worked by lay brothers recruited from the peasant population, who performed the duties essential to the running of a farm.

Sénanque's peak occurred in the early 13C, but as elsewhere, success and prosperity caused corruption. As with the Cluny Order in the past, the Cistercian Order accumulated wealth incompatible with its vow of poverty: disorder ensued.

Decadence and renaissance

In the 14C Sénanque entered a decadent period. Recruitment and f
while lack of discipline increased. And yet, thanks to the energetic rule
the end of the 15C, the situation improved and until the mid 16C the mo
strove to respect the ideals of its founders. Unfortunately, in 1544, Séna
the Vaudois revolt: monks were hanged by the heretics and several buildings were razed.
This was the final blow; the abbey was never able to recover. At the end of the 17C, in spite
of the efforts of the abbots, the community numbered only two monks. Nevertheless
the south wing of the monastery was rebuilt at the beginning of the 18C.

Sold as state property in 1791, Sénanque miraculously fell into the hands of an intel-
ligent owner who not only preserved it from destruction but also consolidated it.
Bought by an ecclesiastic in 1854, it was returned, soon after, to its monastic vocation;
new buildings were added flanking the older ones and 72 monks were installed. The
anticlerical beliefs of the Third Republic brought about their eviction twice. In 1927
a dozen monks returned and remained for some 40-odd years, then moved for a
period to the Lérins Islands (St-Honorat) and finally returned to resume monastic
life in the abbey in October 1989.

Tour *about 1hr*

This is a fine example of Cistercian architecture. The early monastery is almost complete with the exception of the lay-brothers' wing, which was rebuilt in the 18C. The
medieval parts are built in local ashlar stone. The abbey church has kept its original
roof of limestone slabs (lauzes) surmounted by a small square bell tower; contrary to
custom it was built facing north rather than east, as the builders had to compensate
for the rigours of the local terrain.

▶The tour starts on the first floor of the dormitory, north-west of the cloisters.

Dormitory (Dortoir)

This vast pointed barrel vaulted room with transverse arches, lit by a 12-lobed oculus
and narrow windows, is paved in brick. This is where the monks slept fully dressed
on a simple straw pallet. They were roused in the middle of the night for the first
service (nocturns) which took place at 2 am, soon followed by matins at dawn. The
dormitory now houses an exhibition on the abbey's construction.

Abbey Church (Église)⋆

Begun in 1160 with the sanctuary and transept, the church was completed in the early
13C with the nave. The purity of line and great and austere beauty, emphasised by
the absence of all decoration, create a place of worship and meditation.

Stand at the back of the nave to admire the harmony of the proportions and masses.
The transept crossing is crowned by a large dome on elaborate squinches (small
arches, curved stone slab, fluted pilasters which recall the style of churches from
Velay and Vivarais). The sanctuary ends with a semicircular apse pierced by three
windows, symbolising the Trinity, and flanked by four apsidal chapels. Nave, transept
and aisles are covered with flat stones resting on the vault itself.

Abbaye de Sénanque

B. Kaufmann/MICHELIN

Cloisters (Cloître)★

Late 12C. The cloisters' galleries are covered with rounded barrel vaulting with transverse arches held up by carved brackets. Decoration appears on the capitals (leaf-work, flowers, rope and palm-leaf moulding and interlacing) and yet it remains discreet.

The cloisters open onto the different rooms of the conventual buildings, each of which has its specific function.

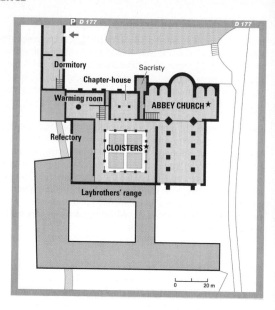

Conventual Buildings (Bâtiments conventuels)★

Chapter-house (salle capitulaire)

The room is roofed with six-pointed vaults held up at the centre on two pillars. Under the abbot's leadership the monastic community met here to read and comment on the Scriptures, receive the novices' vows, to keep vigil over the dead and to make important decisions.

Warming room (chauffoir)

Access via a narrow passage. One of the two original chimneys remains in a corner. The heat was essential to the transcribers who were bent over their manuscripts all day.

Refectory (réfectoire)

Parallel to the west gallery of the cloisters. It was extensively damaged in the 16C and has recently been restored to its original appearance.

Lay-brothers' wing (bâtiment des convers)

South of the cloisters, this building which was remodelled in the 18C housed the lay-brothers, who lived separately from the monks, meeting them only during certain services or when working in the fields.

Abbaye de SILVACANE★★

MICHELIN MAP 340: G-3

Set in a pastoral landscape on the Durance's south bank, the Abbaye de Silvacane, with its pink-tiled roofs and small mutilated square bell tower, offers a beautiful example of plain Cistercian beauty. It is a perfect setting for musical events.

A Bit of History

From its founding to the present

In the 11C the monks from St-Victor of Marseille established themselves on this insalubrious land surrounded by "a forest of reeds" (Sylva cana), from which the monastery derives its name.

The monastery became affiliated with Cîteaux and in 1144 received a donation from two benefactors: Guillaume de la Roque and Raymond de Baux, allowing a group of Cistercians from the Abbaye de Morimond to settle here.

Protected by Provence's great lords, the abbey prospered; it accomplished large land improvement projects in the region and in turn founded Abbaye de Valsainte near Apt. In 1289 a violent confrontation occurred between it and the powerful Abbaye de Montmajour of the Benedictine Order; monks pursued each other and some were even taken as hostages. The conflict ended in a trial and Silvacane was returned to its rightful owners, the Cistercians.

But even more serious were the pillaging of the abbey in 1358 by the lord of Aubignan and the severe frosts of 1364 which destroyed the olive and wine crops. This set off a period of decline which ended in 1443 with the annexation of the abbey to the chapter of St-Sauveur Cathedral in Aix.

It became the village of Roque-d'Anthéron's parish church in the early 16C, and suffered during the Wars of Religion. When the Revolution broke out the buildings were already abandoned; the abbey was sold as state property and converted into a farm.

In 1949 the buildings were bought by the state and are gradually being restored: on the foundations discovered in 1989, to the west, the monastic buildings, the fortified wall in coated quarry-stone, and the monks' guest-house have all now been restored.

Tour *about 1hr*

Church (Église)

The church, which was built on a slope between 1175 and 1230, features different levels which are noticeable when one is viewing the west façade, which has several openings: a central door, two side doors topped with small off-centred windows, three windows and an oculus adorned with mouldings on the upper floor. The three-bayed nave ends in a flat east end. Each arm of the transept has two chapels.

Note how the architect had to take into account the very steep slope of the land by placing the south aisle, nave, the north aisle and the cloisters at different levels.

In the north chapel of the north arm of the transept (1) are the fragments of the tomb of Bertrand de Baux, grandson of the founder, who began the church's construction.

Cloisters

Located at a lower level (1.6m/4.5ft) than the church, the cloisters date from the second half of the 13C, although the gallery vaulting is still Romanesque. Powerful rounded arches open on to the yard; they were originally adorned with paired bays.

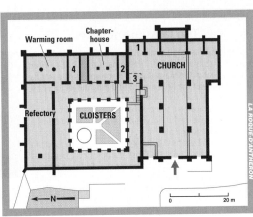

Conventual buildings

Except for the refectory these were all built from 1210 to 1230.
The **sacristy** (2) is a long narrow room next to the **library** (3) located under the north arm of the transept. The **chapter-house** recalls the one at Sénanque: six-pointed vaults falling on two central pillars. After the **parlour** (4), which was used as a passage to the exterior, comes the **warming house**; also with pointed vaulting, it has kept its chimney. Above is the **dormitory**. The large and magnificent **refectory** was rebuilt from 1420 to 1425. The capitals are more decorated than in the other rooms; the room is well lit by high windows and a large rose window; the pulpit remains.
The lay-brothers' wing has completely disappeared. Excavations have uncovered, outside, the ruins of the gatehouse and the abbey's precinct wall.

TARASCON ★

POPULATION 10 826

MICHELIN MAP 340: C-3

A tradition dating back some 2 000 years has created Tarascon, the city of the Tarasque. In the 19C century Alphonse Daudet brought fame to the town through his character Tartarin. And yet the city has its own claim to fame in the shape of its magnificent castle, with walls which drop straight down to the swift-flowing River Rhône. The city is on the boundary of a rich market gardening region and has thus become an important fruit and vegetable dispatching centre. Market day is Tuesday, in the town centre.

🛈 *59 r. des Halles, 13150 Tarascon, ☎ 04 90 91 03 52. www.tarascon.org.*

Château du Roi René ★★1hr

🕐*Apr to Sept: 9am-7pm; Oct to Mar: 9am-noon, 2-5pm.* 🕐*Closed 1 Jan, 1 May, 1 and 11 Nov, 25 Dec. 5.49€.* ☎ *04 90 91 01 93.*
Its location on the banks of the Rhône, its massive appearance which contrasts with its elegant inner architecture, and its exceptional state of preservation, make this building one of the finest medieval castles in France. In the 13C, the castle, opposite the royal city of Beaucaire, defended Provence's western boundary. Captured by Raymond de Turenne in 1399, it was restored soon after to its owners, the Anjou family; Louis II, father of René, decided to have it entirely rebuilt. From 1447 to 1449, **King René** completed the building, which was his favourite residence, contributing all his taste and refinement to the interior decoration.
It is made up of two independent parts: the seigneurial living quarters on the south side flanked by round towers on the town's side and square towers on the Rhône side, offering a compact mass of walls rising up 48m/157ft; and the inner courtyard on the north side, defended by shorter rectangular towers.

The Tarasque monster

Tarascon was established on an island in the Rhône as Massalia's trading post. The Romans took it over after the defeat of the Massaliotes. The present castle stands on the site of the Roman camp built by the legionaries. According to a Provençal legend, an amphibious creature periodically climbed out of the Rhône into the town, where it devoured children and cattle and killed anyone attempting to cross the river. To save the town, St Martha came from Les Stes-Maries-de-la-Mer and subdued the beast with the sign of the Cross; the now docile beast was thereupon captured by the townspeople. In celebration of the miracle, Good King René, who often resided in the castle, organised stupendous festivities in 1474. The legend is still recalled in an annual fête.

La Tarasque

G. Magnin/MICHELIN

Le Château du Roi René

Outer Courtyard (basse cour)

A wide moat spanned by a bridge (once a drawbridge) isolates the group of buildings from the rest of the city. This section includes the recently restored service buildings, including the Hospital of St-Nicolas' **dispensary**: in a finely-panelled 18C room there are 200 apothecary jars.

Cour d'honneur (main courtyard)

Enter the seigneurial living quarters through the keep's zigzag passageway to the main courtyard, around which are the apartments with their lovely, finely-carved façades adorned with mullioned windows. A graceful polygonal staircase turret (1) serves the different floors; near it a niche shelters the busts of King René and Jeanne of Laval, his second wife. Still on the south side of the main courtyard, climb up some steps to the Flamboyant screen of the chantry (2); opening onto the corner tower is the lower chapel (3), and above it the upper chapel.

To the east and north lie the L-shaped main living quarters which partly overlook the town and include the private apartments, which rise above a lovely gallery (4) with pointed barrel vaulting, and communicate with the clock tower.

Seigneurial Living Quarters

The tour of the west wing, which rises above the river, is a visit through the state rooms: the ground floor – banqueting hall (two chimneys); first floor – reception hall

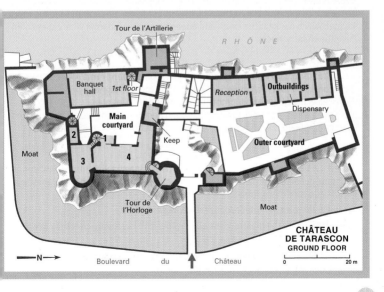

Address Book

For coin ranges, see Legend at the back of the guide.

EATING OUT

🍽 **Bistrot des Anges** – *place du Marché* – ☎ 04 90 91 05 11 – 🕐 *closed Sun* – 🍴. A pretty restaurant, decorated with bright Provençal colours and furnished with wrought-iron tables and chairs. A single menu, which changes every day, guarantees fresh produce. Terrace in the square in summer.

WHERE TO STAY

🛏🛏 **Chambre d'hôte du Château** – *24 rue du Château* – ☎ 04 90 91 09 99 – *ylaraisonwanadoo.fr* – 🕐 *closed Nov-20 Dec* – 🍴 – *5 rooms*. Staying in this carefully restored 18C house, situated in a quiet road leading to the château, is like going back in time. Breakfast is served on the flower-decked patio, beneath the dovecot with its red-ochre walls. A dream of a place at a reasonable price.

🛏🛏 **Cadran Solaire** – *rue du Cabaret Neuf* – *13690 Graveson* – *10km/6.25mi north of Tarascon on N 570* – ☎ 04 90 95 71 79 – 🕐 *closed 1-15 Nov* – 🅿 – *12 rooms* – 🍴 *5.95€*. A sundial adorns the pretty façade of this former coaching inn. Natural beige colours, rush matting on the floor and country furniture in the recently renovated rooms.

SHOPPING

Souleïdo – *39 rue Proudhon* – ☎ 04 90 91 08 80. 🕐 *Shop open Mon-Fri 8.30am-noon, 1.30-6pm (Fri 5pm)*. The main shop of these famous Provençal fabrics.

Choix du Roy – *26 rue des Halles (in the former hôtel de la Monnaie)* – ☎/fax 04 90 43 50 07. A wide choice of Provençal fabrics, by the metre or made up. By appointment: 9am-12.30pm, 2-7.30pm.

Régis Morin – *56 rue des Halles* – ☎ 04 90 91 01 17 – 🕐 *Tue-Sun 6.30am-1pm, 3-8pm – closed second half of Aug*. This chocolate and cake maker is the creator of delicious chocolate sweets filled with hazelnut praline, and of chocolates known as "Besuquettes de Tartarin".

EVENTS

Fêtes de la Tarasque – *Last weekend of June, Fri-Mon*. A huge model of the Tarasque with champing jaws and swinging tail is paraded through the streets; with a swing of its tail, the monster knocks down those it can reach. The stout, bearded character of Tartarin, whom Alphonse Daudet invented in 1872, also takes part in the procession. Various events associated with bulls (Camargue-style races, novilladas) and a musical fireworks display complete the celebrations.

Christmas – Santon fair last weekend of Nov; Christmas Eve, pastoral procession at the church of Ste-Marthe (also at St-Michel-de-Frigolet).

(two vast rooms with painted wood ceilings). Then continue to the king's bedroom (in the southwest tower) with a chimney and heating platter; on the second floor are the audience chamber and council room, which were vaulted to support the terraces. In these rooms there are several fine 17C Flemish tapestries. Return to the south wing to see the chaplain's room (sacristy, host oven, corner for the treasury) and the royal chapel, which has kept the king's and queen's oratories and from where they could hear the chantry voices.

Terrace

Access via the artillery tower. The terrace offers a wide **panorama**★★ of Beaucaire, Tarascon, the Rhône, Vallabrègues undertaking, the Montagnette hills, the Alpilles, Fontvieille, the Abbaye de Montmajour, Arles and St-Gilles plain.
Go back down by the clock tower; the ground floor houses the galley room, named to commemorate the graffiti and boat drawings made by past prisoners.

The Town

Even if it is best known for its castle, the town is also worth a visit, for its warm-toned old stone buildings and narrow streets, lined with fine mansions, whose façades have often been carefully restored.

▶ *Enter the town by Porte St-Jean and follow rue Pelletan.*

On the right note the theatre's Baroque façade, with its chubby-cheeked cherubs.

▶ *Continue along rue Proudhon.*

A fine mansion (*no 39*) houses the family business, **Souleïado**, whose shop sells Provençal fabrics printed in warm, bright colours.

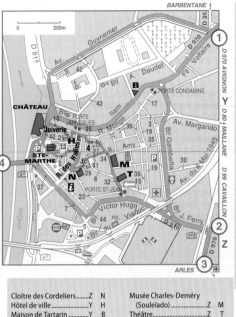

TARASCON

Ancien Collège R. de l'	Z	2
Aqueduc R. de l'	Y	3
Arc de Boqui R.	Y	4
Berrurier Pl. Colonel	Z	5
Blanqui R.	Z	6
Briand Crs Aristide	Z	7
Château R. du	Y	10
Clerc de Molières R.	Y	13
Halles R. des	YZ	
Hôpital R. de l'	Y	15
Jean-Jaurès R.	Y	17
Jeu de Paume R. du	YZ	19
Juifs R. des	Y	21
Ledru-Rollin R.	Z	23
Marché Pl. du	Z	25
Millaud R. Ed.	YZ	27
Mistral R. Frédéric	Z	29
Monge R.	Y	
Moulin R. J.	Z	30
Pelletan R. E.	Z	32
Proudhon R.	YZ	34
Raffin R.	Y	35
République Av. de la	Z	37
Révolution R. de la	YZ	39
Roi René Bd du	Y	40
Salaire R.	Z	41
Salengro Av. R.	Y	42
Semard Av. P.	Z	44
Victor-Hugo Bd	Z	

Cloître des Cordeliers	Z	N	
Hôtel de ville	Y	H	
Maison de Tartarin	Y	B	
Musée Charles-Deméry (Souleïado)	Z	M	
Théâtre	Z	T	

▶ *Continue along this street then, just after the 17C Chapelle de la Persévérance, turn left into rue **Arc de Boqui**, which is completely covered.*

▶ *At the end of this street, turn right towards place du Marché.*

Hôtel de Ville

This 17C building features an elegantly carved façade enhanced by a stone balcony. The first-floor Salle des Consuls, with its panelling and portraits, may be visited. Rue du Château leads to the picturesque **Juiverie**, the town's former Jewish ghetto. At the far side of this district are the castle and the collégiale Ste-Marthe.

▶ *Return to place de la Mairie by rue Robert.*

Turn right into rue des Halles, the main street of old Tarascon, where the market was once held. It is lined with picturesque arcaded houses (15C). In rue Ledru-Rollin, on the left, are the 17C galleries of the old cloister, the Cloître des Cordeliers, where exhibitions are held.

▶ *Return to boulevard Victor-Hugo by rue Ledru-Rollin.*

Additional Sights

Église Ste-Marthe★

Guided tours available, ask at the tourist office or at the Amis de la Collégiale association. ☎ 04 90 91 09 50.

Founded in 12C, this church was rebuilt in the 14C and modified over the following centuries, and finally restored in 1944 after being partly destroyed. The south door is a fine example of the Romanesque style; alas, its lovely carved decoration has partially disappeared.

The interior is unfortunately not well enough lit to appreciate fully the paintings by Pierre Parrocel Nicolas Mignard.

In the staircase to the crypt is the Renaissance-style tomb of Jean de Cossa (former Seneschal of Provence), attributed to the school of Francesco Laurana. The crypt itself contains the sarcophagus (3C-4C) of St Martha, ornamented with carvings.

Musée Charles-Deméry (Souleïado)★

May to Sept: 10am-6pm (last admission 1hr before closing); Oct to Apr: daily except Mon, Sun and Public holidays 10am-5pm. Closed 1 Jan, 1 and 11 Nov, 25 Dec. 6.10€. ☎ 04 90 91 50 11.

Frédéric Mistral

Born on 8 September 1830 into a farming family, Mistral spent his childhood at the Mas du Juge, on the road to Graveson. From schooling in Maillane, he went to boarding school at St-Michel-de-Frigolet, then studied at the Collège Royale in Avignon where he met Roumanille. After studying law at Aix he returned to the family home, more attracted to the charm of the Provençal language than the complexities of the *Code Napoléon*. At the death of his father he had to leave the Mas du Juge for the Maison du Lézard (house facing the museum), a small family home at the village's entrance, where he lived with his mother and finished writing *Mirèio* (1859). He married in 1876 and moved to a new house which has religiously safeguarded his memory (🔥 *see below*). In 1904 he was awarded the Nobel Prize for Literature, and he was buried in the village cemetery on his death in 1914.

This interesting museum, established in a typical Provençal interior on the same site as the family business, contains several rare pieces of printed cloth, popular 18C-19C Provençal costumes and a large collection of earthenware, pottery and paintings.

Maison de Tartarin

🕐 *Jul-Aug : daily except Sun and Wed, 9.30am-12pm, 2-7pm ; Apr-Jun and Sept: daily except Sat-Sun and Wed, 9.30am-12pm, 2-7pm ; Oct. : daily except Sat-Sun and Wed, 9am-12pm, 1.30-7pm; guided tours upon request(45mn) . 🕐Closed 1 Jan, 1 and 8 May, 1 and 11 Nov, 25 Dec. 2€ ☎04 90 91 05 08.*

Arranged in homage to the most famous of Tarascon citizens, the fictitious Tartarin, this house consists of three rooms decorated in the 1870s style. On the ground floor are the office and living room, above is the bedroom. Costumed models, furniture and documents help relive the atmosphere of Daudet's novel: The New Don Quixote or the Wonderful Adventures of Tarascon. Behind the house is a tropical garden, where a conservatory contains an effigy of the Tarasque with a "tarascaire" (knight of the Tarasque).

EATING OUT

🍽🍴**Auberge de la Tour** ★ *– rue A.-de-Tres – ☎ 04 90 07 34 64 – closed Nov, Sun evening and Mon*. The relaxed atmosphere gives this village-centre restaurant the feel of a bistro. The cuisine is local, carefully prepared dishes with a Provençal flavour.

La Montagnette

Round-trip of 45km/28mi – allow 4hr.

▸ *Leave Tarascon by D 80 to the east (in direction of Maillane) and continue along N 570 via D 80A, then, on the left D 32.*

Maillane

In the fertile countryside known as the Petite Crau de St-Rémy, Maillane offers the charm typical of a Provençal town with its small squares shaded with plane trees and white tile-roofed houses. Its renown is largely due to the fame of **Frédéric Mistral**, the Provençal poet and one of the founders of the Félibrige movement. **Museon Mistral** – 🕐*Apr to Sept: guided tours (30min) daily except Mon 9.30-11.30am, 2.30-6.30pm; Oct to Mar: daily except Mon 10-11.30am, 2-4.30pm. 🕐Closed public holidays. 3.05€. ☎ 04 90 95 74 06.*

Museon Mistral

This museum is located in the house which Mistral had built and then lived in from 1876 to 1914. Mistral's memory is evoked throughout the various rooms – office, living room, dining room, bedroom – which have been kept as they were at this death.

▸ *Continue to Graveson via D 5, then left onto D 28.*

Graveson

The village church has a Romanesque apse and a carved bell tower. At the end of cours Nationale is the **Musée Auguste-Chabeaud** ★ *(Jun to Oct: 10am-noon, 1.30-6.30pm; Nov to May: 1.30-6.30pm. 🕐Closed 1 Jan and 25 Dec. 3.05€. ☎ 04 90 90 53 02)*, which houses a collection of paintings by this painter, sculptor and poet, who was born in

Nîmes and died in Graveson in 1955. Following periods of residence in Paris, the artist moved to the Mas de Martin at the foot of the Montagnette hills, where he found inspiration in the countryside, rural scenes and festivals of Provence in the Rhône valley. His technique of using smooth lines of pure colour outlined with black has obviously drawn comparisons with the Fauvist School, yet the keen expression and fervour shown in his work classifies him more as an Expressionist painter. Note: *Old Provençal Women, Shepherd Leaning on a Stick, Girls in the Wind, The Olive Harvest.*

Musée des Arômes et du Parfum

🕐*10am-noon, 2-6pm.* 🕐*Closed 1 Jan and 25 Dec. 3.05€.* ☎ *04 90 95 81 55.*

A few miles to the south on D 80, the Fragrance and Perfume Museum occupies an old mas that once belonged to the monks of St-Michel-de-Frigolet. Traditional techniques related to the making of aromatic scent are presented and explained by a fascinating exhibition: copper stills, collection of old flasks, semicircular racks displaying all types of essences (*orgues de parfumier*) and receptacles for catching the essential oils and floral water after distillation (*essenciers*).

Continue to D 570 and turn right towards Graveson, then left towards Tarascon. Turn left immediately onto D 81.

After crossing over D 970, the road climbs and winds among pines, olive trees and cypresses, in a pleasant setting for a picnic. A cross marks the road to the abbey.

Abbaye de St-Michel-de-Frigolet

👢 *See ST MICHEL-DE-FRIGOLET.*

▶ *Continue along D 80, then D 35E.*

Barbentane

👢 *See BARBENTANE.*

▶ *Leave Barbentane to the south, on D 35.*

Boulbon

An impressive fort dominates the town, which is laid out against the Montagnette hillside. The Romanesque St-Marcellin chapel contains a number of statues, particularly the 14C recessed tomb with recumbent figures and mourners.

▶ *Return to Tarascon on D 35.*

La TOUR-D'AIGUES

POPULATION 3 328

MICHELIN MAP 332: G-11

Nestling at the foot of the Luberon mountains, the region around Aigues is a delightful countryside made up of fertile, sun-drenched vineyards, orchards (cherries) and market gardens, in stark contrast with the wild barrenness of the neighbouring hills. Founded in the 10C or 11C, the town owes its name to a tower which was a precursor of the keep of the present castle. In high season the Festival du Sud Luberon is held here.

🏛 *Le Château, 84240 La Tour-D'aigues,* ☎ *04 90 07 50 29.*

Sights

Château

🕐*Jul and Aug: 10am-1pm, 2.30-6.30pm; Apr to Jun and mid-Aug to end of Oct: Sun-Mon 10am-1pm, 2.30-6pm; Tues 2.30-6pm; Sat-Sun and public holidays 2-6pm; Nov to Mar: 10am-noon, 2-5pm, Sun-Mon 2-5pm, Tue 10am-noon.* 🕐*Closed 1 Jan, 24, 25 and 31 Dec. 4.50€ (children under 8 years, free)* ☎ *04 90 07 50 33. www.chateau-latourdaigues. com.*

The château was rebuilt from 1555 to 1575 in the Renaissance style by an Italian architect (Ercole Nigra) on a vast terrace overlooking the Lèze; Catherine de' Medici stayed here in 1579. Burned in 1782 and again in 1792 when it was ruined, it is now being progressively restored by the Vaucluse département.

Château de la Tour-d'Aigues — entrance gate

The monumental entrance gate takes the form of a richly-decorated triumphal arch: Corinthian columns and pilasters, a frieze of the attributes of war and an entablature surmounted by a triangular pediment. In the centre of the bailey is the keep restored to its 16C Italian plan; in a corner the chapel.

Inside, the network of underground cellars now house exhibition, projection and conference rooms as well as collections from the two museums below.

Musée des Faïences

During the course of the restoration work carried out on the château's cellars a large quantity of glazed earthenware was discovered. The finest pieces from these finds have been brought together in this museum which offers the visitor a comprehensive illustration of the work produced in Jérôme Bruny's Tour-d'Aigues factory between 1750 and 1785. The collection contains some fine examples of faience ware; white stanniferous-enamelled faience, tableware emblazoned with the coat of arms of the Bruny family, and polychrome and *en camaïeu faience*, including an oval dish representing a fox-hunting scene in orange-tinted monochrome from an engraving by Jean Bernard Oudry. Examples of 18C European (Delft, Moustiers, Marseille) and Asian (China, Japan) porcelain are also displayed, as well as 16C marble medallions of laurel-crowned heads, and 17C-18C enamelled terracotta ornamental tiles.

Musée de l'Habitat rural du Pays d'Aigues

This museum contains a modern display drawing heavily on audiovisual methods: a history of Provençal man's evolution from his origins to the present. Slides, illuminated maps, miscellaneous objects (early casts, tools, reconstruction of a silkworm farm) and models depict the development of local rural life.

Driving Tours

112km/70mi – allow 1 day.

At the foot of the Luberon mountains flows the Durance, the great fluctuating river which follows a course parallel to the Mediterranean before joining the Rhône at Avignon. This was not always the case, however; at the end of the last Ice Age, the swollen waters burst through the Lamanon gap on a more direct route to the sea, depositing a huge mass of rock and stone over the wide expanse of what is now the Plaine de la Crau.

The Durance's flow is irregular, with violent rain storms provoking devastating flood-waters, though the river is gradually being harnessed to serve the local economy. The Serre-Ponçon reservoir helps to control its course as well as maintaining irrigation of the plains of the Basse-Durance during dry periods.

It is rare for any one region to be as well served by canals as Provence is between the Durance and the sea. Each was constructed for one of three purposes: irrigation (such as the 16C Canal de Craponne one of the oldest in Provence), the provision of town and factory water and the production of electricity.

The river's waters have regained their purity, as show by the numerous fish, cormorants, herons and beavers which make it their home.

▷ *Leave Tour-d'Aigues by D 135 eastwards and proceed towards Mirabeau.*

On the left after the village, N 96 goes through the **Défilé de Mirabeau** where the river bends sharply to the west and emerges from Haute-Provence int the Vaucluse through this dramatic narrow channel cut out by the action of the water.

▷ *After crossing the Durance by the **Pont Mirabeau**, and the motorway, turn right onto N 96 near the Centrale de Jouques power station and follow the green waters of the EDF canal, which begins at the Cadarache dam and runs parallel to the Durance until Mallemort.*

Peyrolles-en-Provence

Little remains of the town's medieval fortifications except for a belfry crowned by a wrought-iron bell cage and a round tower (in ruins) near the church.

Château

Once a residence of King René, this castle was converted into a mansion in the late 17C. The interior features a grand sweeping staircase and 18C gypsum furnishings. From the east terrace, decorated with a fountain portraying a gladiator, there is a pretty view of the Durance valley.

Église St-Pierre

🔊*Guided tours 9-11.30am by appointment with Mme Chaïb. Town hall ☎ 04 42 57 89 82* This church has retained its Romanesque nave, despite being remodelled many times.

Chapelle de St-Sépulcre

Built on a rocky spur in the 12C in the form of a Greek cross. Its walls bear frescoes: the creation of Adam and Eve (above the doorway) and a procession of saints with halos.

Peyrolles-en-Provence – Chapelle du St-Sépulcre

Meyrargues

The town is dominated by its château (now a hotel) rebuilt in the 17C. A pleasant walk leads to the remains of a Roman aqueduct (below the castle) which brought water to Aix-en-Provence and continues to the wild Étroit gorges.

▷ *On leaving the town, turn right onto D 561 in direction of Roque-d'Anthéron, then left onto D 15 towards Puy-Ste-Réparade.*

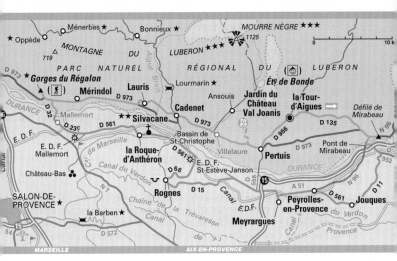

Le Tambour d'Arcole

In the main square there is a statue of André Estienne, the famous drummer boy, born in Cadenet in 1777. He served in Napoleon's northern Italy campaign of 1796 and, in the midst of the battle against the Austrians and Italians for the Arcole Bridge, he swam the river and beat such a tattoo that the Austrians mistook it for artillery fire; as they retreated the French advanced to capture the bridge and win the battle.

The town is also the birthplace of Félicien David (1810-76), whose travels to the Far East brought an Oriental touch to his music (*Le Désert*, 1844).

Rognes

Rognes is located on the north face of the Chaîne de la Trévaresse. It is famous on two accounts: for the well-known Rognes stone (quarries on D 15 going to Lambesc) much used for construction locally, and for its truffles (market in December). The **church** (*information available at the tourist office.* ☎ *04 42 50 13 36*) built in the early 17C is decorated with a remarkable group of **ten altarpieces**★ (17C-18C).

▷ *Take the picturesque D 66 to return to D 561, and turn left.*

Centrale de St-Estève-Janson (power station)

This is where the Canal de Marseille begins. Dug in the 19C, it supplied the city with drinking water for many years.

Bassin de St-Christophe

A vast reservoir in a setting of rocks and pine trees, at the foot of the chaîne des Côtes.

▷ *The road crosses and then follows the EDF canal.*

Abbaye de Silvacane★★

ⓖ See Abbaye de SILVACANE.

La Roque-d'Anthéron

At the centre of the town stands the 17C **Château de Florans** flanked by round towers. This acts as a backdrop to the prestigious International Piano Festival. The **Musée de Géologie Provençale** (🕐 *Jul to mid-Sept: daily except Sat-Sun 10am-noon, 3pm-7pm; mid-Sept to end of June: Tues, Wed, Thu, Sun (except last Sun in the month) 10am-noon, 2-6pm. 1.52€.* ☎ *04 42 50 47 87*), which houses paleontology and mineral collections, is situated on place Paul-Cézanne.

▷ *Continue along D 561 to D 23c on the right. Beyond the town of Mallemort turn onto D 32 to cross the river; turn left onto D 973. Continue for 2km/1mi and just before a bridge, bear right onto a small road which skirts a quarry.*

Gorges du Régalon★

1hr 15min there and back on foot. Some yards further on bear right, ignoring the uphill road on the left. Leave the car in the parking area; take the path opposite which skirts the stream; cross the olive grove on your left and go through a narrow gap to enter the gorges. Note: 🙂 (a) it will be colder (an advantage on hot days), 🙂 (b) the rocks are often wet and slippery – therefore go suitably clad and shod; 🙂 (c) on showery, rainy days the stream becomes a rushing torrent and the expedition should not be ventured.

🚹 The route follows the bed of the stream, runs beneath a huge rock caught fast between the sides of the gorges, and over a rocky and sometimes slippery section before coming to a cave. The tunnel bends sharply into a passage 100m/328ft long and 30m/98ft high but only 80cm/30in wide in places. The cave and passage are the most remarkable parts of the gorges.

▷ *At the end retrace your steps.*

▷ *After returning to the car, take D 973 on the left.*

Lauris

A picturesque village whose small streets, lined with houses from the 16C, 17C and 18C, are perfect for a stroll. The 18C church is topped with an attractive rounded bell tower in wrought iron. From the Promenade de la Roque, the visitor is able to explore the terraced gardens of the castle, built at the steepest part of the village and dominating the wide valley of the Durance.

Cadenet

11 place du Tambour-d'Arcole – 84160 – ☎ 04 90 68 38 21.

This small town was an important centre for basket making, thanks to the proximity of the Durance; from the beginning of the 19C until the mid 20C, its willow beds were harvested for the production of wicker. The industry reached its zenith between the 1920s and 1930s after which, as a result of competition from rattan imported from the Far East, production diversified into providing containers, household items and various decorative objects. The last business closed down in 1978.

Musée de la Vannerie

Apr to end of Oct: daily except Tues 10am-noon, 2.30-6.30pm, Wed and Sun 2.30-6.30pm. Closed 1 May. Price information not provided. ☎ 04 90 68 24 44.

avenue Philippe-de-Giraud. Situated on the site of the former La Glaneuse workshop, the museum contains, in addition to basket-making tools, small articles for daily use, colonial chaises-longues, prams and cradles, demijohns (containers encased in wickerwork), trunks and cases. On the mezzanine, an audio-visual montage evokes life in Cadernet in the olden days.

Church

Jul to end of Aug: Mon to Wed and Sat 10.30am-noon, 5.30-7pm. ☎ 04 90 68 06 79

The 14C structure, remodelled in the 16C and 17C, has a fine square bell tower. Inside the church the north aisle contains beautiful **baptismal fonts**★ made from a 3C Roman sarcophagus decorated with low reliefs.

Pertuis

Capital of Aigues country and birthplace of Mirabeau's father, the town retains, as reminders of its past, a 14C battlemented tower (St-Jacques), 13C clock tower, a castle ruin and the Église St-Nicolas. This church, rebuilt in the 16C, contains a 16C triptych and two 17C marble statues given to the monks of the town by Cardinal Barberini.

▷ *Return to La Tour d'Aigues by D 956.*

UZÈS★★

POPULATION 7 649

MICHELIN MAP 339: L-4

Set in the severe yet charming garrigues countryside, Uzès is established at the tip of a limestone plateau, overlooking the Alzon valley. A ducal seat, bishopric and consular seat, Uzès has preserved its lay-out as a medieval stronghold, embellished in the 17C and 18C as a result of economic prosperity (acquired through the manufacture of linen, serge and silk). The town has overflowed its former fortifications, now replaced by boulevards, and has developed on the plateau. It has been restored to its earlier appearance as a result of the renovation work undertaken in the protected district.

Pl. Albert-ler, 30700 Uzès, ☎ 04 66 22 68 88. www.uzes-tourisme.com.

A Bit of History

The duchy of Uzès

The old House of Uzès goes back to Charlemagne through its women. After the execution, in 1632, of the Duke of Montmorency in Toulouse, the Duke of Uzès became the most powerful duke and peer of the kingdom.

Poet in exile

Uzès has its place in the history of French literature, because it was here that **Jean Racine** (1639-99) stayed in 1661 when he was 22 years old. Having been educated under the severe discipline of Port-Royal and the Jansenist College of Harcourt in Paris, Racine sought a change. His family, who watched with horror as their son considered a career in the theatre, sent him to his uncle, vicar general of Uzès. To entice him away from his worldly associations, his uncle promised him an allowance once he had taken

Address Book

EATING OUT

🍴 **Le San Diego** – *10 bd Charles-Gide –* ☎ *04 66 22 20 78 –* 🕐 *closed Mon and Sun evening .* An unassuming place on the circular boulevard which encircles the old town. Both the owner and the cooking have an accent of the south; Provençal flavours are much in evidence in the two vaulted dining rooms whose exposed stone walls are decorated with brightly coloured paintings.

🍴 **Les Fontaines** – *6 rue Entre-les-Tours –* ☎ *04 66 22 41 20 –* 🕐 *closed 20 Jan-6 Mar, 15 Nov-8 Dec, Wed and Thu except evenings in Jul-Aug.* This 16C restaurant has a Provençal-style vaulted dining room, or you can eat on the terrace in the charming interior paved courtyard, bordered with arcades. Simple cooking.

🍴 **Zaïka** – *passage Marchand –* ☎ *04 66 03 27 37 –* 🕐 *closed 15 Dec-31 Jan, Sun evening, Mon and Tue – booking essential.* In India, Zaïka means "taste," and there is certainly plenty to appreciate in that area in this restaurant, with its lovely smell of spices. Its cuisine is a great success, served in an exotic setting decorated with colourful Indian chairs.

WHERE TO STAY

🛏 **Le Mas de Caroubier** – *684 rte de Vallabrix – 30700 St-Quentin-la-Poterie – 5km/3.1mi northeast of Uzès via D 982 and D 5 –* ☎ *04 66 22 12 72 – contactmas-caroubier.com –* 🕐 *closed Jan –* 🚫 *– 4 rooms – evening meal 19/22.87€.* This mas set at the end of a lane is a haven of tranquillity. Everything here is conducive to a peaceful stay: the warm welcome, the quiet garden, the charming rooms decorated with patterned fabrics, the blue water in the swimming pool. Additional attractions include pottery, painting or Provençal cookery courses.

🛏🛏 **Hôtel d'Entraigues** – *8 rue de la Calade –* ☎ *04 66 22 32 68 –* 📶 *– 19 rooms: – * 📶 *9.15€ – restaurant 20.58/42.69€.* A 15C building situated in the old town, opposite the Tour Fenestrelle. The lovely terrace and the mosaic-lined swimming pool will appeal to the aesthetic senses. The standard of comfort varies between the old rooms, but they have a certain charm, nonetheless.

🛏🛏🛏 **Chambre d'hôte Le Mas Parasol** – *rue Damon – 30190 Garrigues-Ste-Eulalie – 10km/6.25mi southwest of Uzès via D 982 –* ☎ *04 66 81 90 47 – www.masparasol.fr –* 🕐 *closed 15 Nov-Feb – 7 rooms - evening meal 25€.* This mas is bound to appeal, with its brightly coloured, refined rooms, its collection of old advertising watercolours, and its restored gypsy caravan. The young owner organises special breaks.

ON THE TOWN

La Sorbetière – *place Albert-1er –* ☎ *04 66 22 34 32 –* 🕐 *Oct-May: Mon-Fri, Sun 8am-8pm, Sat 8am-11pm; June-Sept: daily 8am-11pm.* It's easy to overindulge here on the terrace, beside the fountain! There is a choice of over 60 teas, as well as ice creams and pastries, which can also be enjoyed inside in the vaulted room, furnished with low table and cosy armchairs. Salads and crepes are also available. Regular exhibitions and concerts.

SHOPPING

Fairs and markets – Annual truffle day (*journée de la truffe*), place aux Herbes, 3rd Sun in Jan. Garlic Fair (and St-Jean bonfire celebrations) in the same square, 24 June. Traditional market, Sat morning. Wine fair, around 15 Aug, on the Esplanade.

Olive oil – Two mills are open to the public, at Collorgues and Martignargues.

Les Truffières du Soleil (Michel Tournayre) – *Mas du Moulin de la Flesque –* ☎ *04 66 22 08 41.* Find out everything you always wanted to know about truffles. Visit to plantations and tasting.

Atelier Pichon – *6 rue St-Étienne and 7 rue Jacques-d'Uzès.* Manufacture of traditional ceramics, founded in 1802.

holy orders. Racine spent rather more than a year at his uncle's. In his letters, full of humour, he spoke little of theology but much of the countryside, the food, the local dialect (which he could not understand) and his first poems.

The young poet did not pursue the religious vocation so desired by his family, but returned to Paris to become France's greatest classical dramatist.

Old Town ★★*2hr 30min*

▶ *Start at avenue de la Libération and turn right onto boulevard des Alliés.*

Église St-Étienne

📷*Guided tours only.*

This church was built in the 18C in the Jesuit style, based on the design of the architect Pierre Bondon. It occupies the site of an earlier church which was destroyed during

the Wars of Religion. It features a curvilinear façade dec[...]
Ionic capitals and with flame ornamentation. The rectan[...]
remnant of the 13C building.

On place de l'Église stands the house where **Charles G**[...]
was born, uncle of the author **André Gide** (1869-1951) [...]
Prize for Literature in 1947. Gide spent his holidays with [...]
his sojourns in If It Die (Si le Grain ne Meurt).

▸ *Take rue St-Étienne towards place aux Herbes.*

Rue St-Étienne

No 1. An imposing Louis XIII-style faceted door. Farther on to the left in a blind alley
is a fine Renaissance façade.

Place aux Herbes★

This picturesque, asymmetrical square is surrounded by covered walkways and
has plane trees growing in it. Among the medieval houses, which were converted
in the 17C and 18C, notice the **Hôtel de la Rochette**, dating from the 17C and
slightly set back and, to the north, a corner house decorated on the side with
a turret.

▸ *Near this house turn right into an alleyway, which leads to the unusual and narrow
rue Pélisserie. Turn right into rue Entre-les-Tours.*

Tour de l'Horloge

This clock tower dates from the 12C and is crowned with a wrought-iron bell cage.
It was the bishop's tower; it confronted the duke's tower and king's tower at a time
when these three powers shared Uzès.

Hôtel Dampmartin

On the corner of rue Jacques-d'Uzès and place Dampmartin. This mansion displays a
Renaissance façade flanked by a round tower; a carved frieze surrounds the first-floor
window. Enter into the Renaissance courtyard (staircase).

▸ *Cross place Dampmartin, also surrounded by covered walkways, and take rue de la
République.*

Hôtel de Joubert et d'Avéjan

No 12. Fine Henri II-style façade (restored).

▸ *Continue along the street, then turn right into boulevard Gambetta and continue to
the Hôtel de Ville.*

Hôtel de Ville

This dates from the 18C and has a finely laid-out courtyard. From the façade on the
side of the château there is a view of the enormous outline of the Ducal Palace and
the chapel roof of varnished tiles.

▸ *Turn left along rue Boucairie, formerly a leather workers' street.*

At the corner of rue Rafin stands the Hôtel des Monnaies (Old Mint); a sign reminds us
that the bishops of Uzès were permitted to strike their own coins during the Middle
Ages.

Hôtel du Baron de Castille

The late-18C front of this mansion is preceded by a colonnade.

Ancien Palais épiscopal

This sumptuous episcopal palace was built at the end of the 17C; its right wing houses
the public library and a museum, the Musée Municipal Georges-Borias (see
MUSEUMS).

Cathédrale St-Théodorit

The 17C cathedral behind a 19C remodelled west front contains a fine Louis XIV-style
organa. Note the painted shutters which were closed over the instrument in the
past, during Lent.

...estrelle★★

...er which abuts the cathedral's ...wall is 12C and is the only relic of ...ormer Romanesque cathedral. This ...nd of round bell tower is unique in France: it rises 42m/138ft above a square base with six storeys which recede one above the other.

Promenade Jean-Racine

This avenue, which runs into Promenade des Marronniers, overlooks the ducal park, the garrigues, and the Alzon valley where the River Eure was tapped at its source by the Romans and diverted along the Pont du Gard aqueduct to provide water for Nîmes.

To the left stands the Pavillon Racine, an old tower, once part of the fortifications, restored in the late 18C.

▶ *Return and follow Le Portalet.*

Maison du Portalet

No 19 Le Portalet. This is a pretty Renaissance house.

▶ *Return to avenue de la Libération via boulevard Victor-Hugo.*

Tour Fenestrelle

Museums

Duché★

🕐*Mid-Sept to end of June: unaccompanied visits of the tower, guided tours of the apartments (45min) 10am-noon, 2-6pm (Jul to mid-Sept: 10am-1pm, 2-6.30pm).* 🕐*Closed 25 Dec. 9.50€.* ☎ *04 66 22 18 96.*

From the outside, the ducal palace appears as a feudal mass with buildings of various periods exemplifying the rise of the Uzès family.

Courtyard

From left to right are: Tour de la Vicomté (14C tower) with its octagonal turret, commemorating the lords of Uzès' elevation to a viscounty in 1328; Tour Bermonde, a square 11C keep. To the right, at a right angle, lies the Renaissance **façade**★ erected by the first duke in c 1550 based on plans by Philibert Delorme. At the façade's far end stands a Gothic chapel (restored in the 19C).

Tour Bermonde

This tower is entered up a spiral staircase (*135 steps*).

From the terrace the **panorama**★★ which unfolds over the old roofs of Uzès and the *garrigues* landscape is really beautiful; the bell cage of the clock tower can be seen nearby.

Cellars (Caves)

The enormous 11C vaulted cellars house a waxwork reconstruction of the marriage of Jacques de Crussol and Simone d'Uzès in 1486.

Apartments

To get into these, go through the doorway in the façade, which opens onto the beautiful Renaissance main staircase, which has coffered, diamond-pointed vaulting. Particularly worth noting in the visit are: the Louis XV great hall, decorated with plasterwork and a Trianon console; the library; the dining room decorated with Renaissance and Louis XIII furniture; and the 15C chapel, which was renovated in 19C. On the left as you leave notice the 12C **Tour de la Vigie**.

Musée Municipal Georges-Borias

🕐*Feb to Oct: daily except Mon 3-6pm; Nov to Dec: daily except Mon 2-5pm.* 🕐*Closed in Jan, 1 Nov, 25 Dec. 1.52€.* ☎ *04 66 22 40 23.*

F. Gégot/MICHELIN

The museum's collections include archaeological finds, popular arts and traditions, old documents; pottery from St-Quentin-la-Poterie; paintings by Sigalon, Chabaud and Borias; engravings by Subleyas; and souvenirs of André Gide (manuscripts, rare editions).

Additional Sights

Uzès National Stud (Haras national d'Uzès)

Jul to Feb: guided tours (1hr) 2-5pm; Mar to Jun: daily except Sun and public holidays 2-5pm. 2.29€. ☎ 04 66 22 68 88

3.5km/2.2mi west.

▸ Leave Uzès by the Alès road. After 2km/1mi turn left onto the chemin du Mas-des-Tailles (signposted).

This horse farm was established in 1974 on a property which included, among other things, a large house dating from the end of the 19C, outbuildings and stables. Modern installations were added to enhance the premises, namely a riding school, race courses and an obstacle course for the dressage and training of their horses, stallions and Provençal donkeys.

Musée du bonbon Haribo

& Jul to Sept: 10am-7pm; Oct to Jun: daily except Mon 10am-1pm, 2-6pm. Closed first 3 weeks in Jan. 3.81€ (under 15 years: 2.29€). ☎ 04 66 22 74 39.

Kids Pont-des-Charettes, at the entrance to Uzès on D 981 (Remoulins road).

Everything you always wanted to know about sweet manufacturing, in particular the various different shaped 'jelly' sweets, so beloved of children. Flavour space for smelling and tasting.

Parc Aquatique de la Bouscarasse

Route d'Alès End of May to mid-Sept: Mon-Fri 10am-7pm, weekend 10am-8pm – Closed mid-Apr to end May. ☎ 04 66 22 50 25.

UZÈS

4-Septembre R.	A 35	Évêché R. de l'	B 12	Port Royal R.	B 20
Alliés Bd des	A 2	Foch Av. Mar.	A 13	Raffin R.	B 21
Boucairie R.	B 4	Foussat R. Paul	A 14	République R.	A 23
Collège R. du	B 6	Gambetta Bd	A	St-Étienne R.	A 25
Dampmartin Pl.	A 7	Gide Bd Ch.	AB	St-Théodorit R.	B 27
Dr-Blanchard R.	B 8	Marronniers Prom. des	B 16	Uzès R. J.-d'	A 29
Duché Pl. du	A 9	Pascal Av. M.	B 17	Victor-Hugo Boulevard	A 32
Entre les Tours R.	A 10	Pelisserie R.	A 18	Vincent Av. Gén.	A
		Plan de l'Oume R.	B 19		

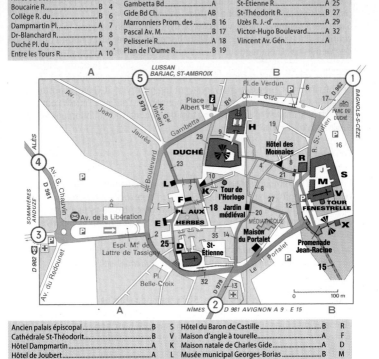

Ancien palais épiscopal	B	S	Hôtel du Baron de Castille	B	R
Cathédrale St-Théodorit	B	V	Maison d'angle à tourelle	A	F
Hôtel Dampmartin	A	K	Maison natale de Charles Gide	A	D
Hôtel de Joubert	A	L	Musée municipal Georges-Borias	B	M
Hôtel de la Rochette	A	E	Pavillon Racine	B	X
Hôtel de ville	A	H			

🧒 With 2 500m²/2990sq yd of swimming and paddling pools, this place is ideal for families with young children. The large shady park is full of luxuriant plants, with wooden tables for picnics, as well as an open-air theatre and a small snack bar. An exhibition on a theme connected with plants is held in the last weekend of May.

Moulin de Chalier

♿🕐 *Mar to Oct: 10am-noon, 2-7pm (Jul and Aug: 9am-7pm); Nov to Feb: school holidays, Wed, Sat-Sun 10am-noon, 2-6pm.* 🕐*Closed 2nd week in Jan. 5.34€ (children: 3.81€), 8.99P for both museums (children: 5.95€).* ☎ *04 66 22 58 64.*

4km/2.5mi. Leave Uzès on D 982, the Anduze road. Turn right just before Arpaillargues onto a road running downhill. This 18C stone mill houses the **Musée 1900** with its collection of vehicles, posters and other objects evoking daily life during the Belle Époque. Exhibits include a wide range of vehicles dating from 1870 onwards: a 1907 Renault, luxury limousines from the 1930s, 1950s motorbikes; fire-fighting equipment (including an 1850 Parisian fire engine). The early days of cinema, photography and radio are also represented by magic lanterns (1870), a photo enlarger (1880) and crystal receivers, as well as an entire section devoted to traditional agricultural activities in the region (18C oil mill).

The nearby **Musée du Train et du Jouet** (Toy and Train Museum), entertainingly-set out in the decor of a recreated railway station, houses a 400m/1 300ft long miniature railway as well as models of the region's most impressive sites; the amphitheatre at Nîmes, the Pont du Gard aqueduct and the fortifications at Aigues-Mortes.

St-Quentin-la-Poterie

Galerie Terra-Viva – ♿ *End of Mar to end of Dec: daily except Mon 10am-1pm, 2.30-6pm (May to end of Sept: daily 10am-1pm, 2.30-7pm). Closed from beginning of Jan to mid-Mar and 25 Dec. No charge.* ☎ *04 66 22 48 78.*

5km/3mi. Leave Uzès by R on the map, the Bagnols-sur-Cèze road. After 2km/1mi turn left onto D 5 and then left again onto D 23. The excellent quality of its clay sub-soil gave rise to the rapid development of the pottery industry in the village, particularly during the 14C when over 110 000 glazed earthenware tiles were made for the decoration of the Palais des Papes at Avignon. Large-scale production continued up to the beginning of this century; the last brick factory closed its doors in 1954 and the last pipe factory stopped operating in 1974.

Since 1983, ceramists, along with glass artists, have been attracted to the village to continue the tradition. An old oil mill in the centre of the village houses the Maison des Métiers de la Céramique (Ceramic Workers Centre) which displays a collection of 250 ceramic pieces of Mediterranean origin. On the ground floor, the Galerie Terra Viva presents displays of contemporary ceramic art. The small Musée des Terrailles, on the first floor, provides an overview of the history of St-Quentin pottery since Neolithic times. Every two years, the town organizes the large Terralha pottery fair, which is held around 14 July, bringing together around 100 exhibitors and attracting thousands of visitors.

Excursion

51km/31mi – about 6hr

From Uzès to Remoulins, this tour of la Gardonnenque follows the Gardon valley, passing through a typical landscape of the garrigue: rocks uncovered by the action of rain, frost, drought and wind, interspersed with scrub oak, cistus, gorse, asphodel and wild aromatic plants. Through these parched, arid limestone hills, rivers carve picturesque gorges.

▶ *Leave Uzès by the road to the south and turn right onto D 979, the road to Nîmes, which winds through the countryside offering splendid views of Uzès.*

Pont St-Nicholas

The nine-arched bridge, built in the 13C by the Bridge Brotherhood, spans the River Gardon in a particularly beautiful spot. D 979 cuts into the overhanging rock as it climbs, affording good views of the Gardon; the right-hand bend at the top (car park) presents a spectacular **view**★ along the course of the Gardon gorges.

▶ *Turn left onto D 135 and, just before Poulx, left again onto D 127. This is a poorly surfaced road, and passing is sometimes difficult, if not impossible, except in lay-bys hewn out of the rock.*

Site de la Baume★

🚶 *Park the car after the final bend and take the path (1hr return) which leads to the foot of the gorges.*

After passing some ruined buildings, the path reaches a picturesque spot on the banks of the Gardon, which is very popular in summer with bathers. On the opposite bank, the entrance to the cave, the Grotte de la Baume can be seen in the cliff face.

Poulx

Now a residential suburb of Nîmes, this village still has a pretty little Romanesque church.

▶ *Continue along D 427, which crosses the garrigue, interspersed with vineyards and orchards. In Carbrières turn left onto D 3, towards the Gardon valley.*

Collias

A centre for water sports and horseriding, the GR 63 footpath also passes by here, allowing access to the Gardon gorges. The village is also popular among rock climbers, on account of its towering cliffs.

▶ *Follow D 3 which climbs the Alzon valley, then turn right onto D 981.*

Château de Castille

🔑 *Not open to the public.* A small Romanesque chapel and a funerary chapel surrounded by columns stand to the right of the avenue of yew trees leading to the château. Built in the 16C and remodelled in the 18C by the Baron de Castille, it possesses a colonnade and various balustrades.

▶ *Continue along D 981.*

Pont du Gard★★★

🕐 *See PONT DU GARD.*

▶ *Turn left onto D 228.*

Castillon-du-Gard★

A hilltop village with superbly restored houses built of reddish stone. It can claim the exclusivity of being the only village with a view of the famous bridge.
Return to D 981 and continue to Remoulins, which has preserved the remains of its fortifications and a Romanesque church with a bell gable.
At Remoulins take N 100 towards Avignon, then turn right onto D 108 to reach Domazan.

Musée du Vélo et de la Moto★

🔑 *Closed temporarily.*

🧒 *At Domazan.* This bicycle and motorbike museum has an exceptional, humorously presented collection of two-wheeled vehicles through the ages. Prize exhibits include an engraved velocipede (1869) which belonged to Yves Montand, a bicycle with articulated handlebars, an early ancestor of the scooter, the "auto-armchair", a moped specially designed for clergymen, a helix cycle (ridden lying down), and a solar tricycle dating from 1980 which only ever worked in theory.

VAISON-LA-ROMAINE★★

POPULATION 5 663

MICHELIN MAP 332: D-8

LOCAL MAPS SEE DENTELLES DE MONTMIRAIL AND MONT VENTOUX

Built along the banks of the River Ouvèze, in the middle of a corrie of wooded hills, Vaison-la-Romaine, a small Provençal town full of charm, will enchant those who love old historical places. Rarely does a town offer such a complete and picturesque ensemble: vast fields of ancient ruins, Romanesque cathedral and cloisters, and old district dominated by its castle. As well as becoming a busy tourist centre during the music festivals, Vaison thrives as an agricultural centre where wine, fruit and mountain produce (honey, lavender, truffles) are the source of prosperous trading.

🛈 *Av. du-Chanoine-Sautel, 84110 Vaison-La-Romaine, ☎ 04 90 36 02 11. www.vaison-la-romaine.com.*

A Bit of History

The City of the Vocontii

Southern capital of the Vocontii, a Celtic tribe, Vaison (Vasio Vocontiorum) became part of Roman Provence which was conquered at the end of the 2C BC and covered all south-eastern Gaul. Very early on it received the status of federated city (and not colony) which allowed it a great deal of autonomy. Allied with Caesar during the Gallic Wars (58-1 BC), the Vocontii lived side by side with the Romans; and among them illustrious men appeared: the historian Trogus-Pompeius and Nero's tutor Burrhus. Cited as one of the Narbonensis' most prosperous cities under Roman rule, Vaison covered some 70ha/173 acres and had a population of approximately 10 000. Unlike the colonial examples of Arles, Nîmes and Orange, the city did not expand with a Romanised urban plan, as was customary, because a pre-existing rural plan prevented the surveyors from tracing a regular grid plan and placing living quarters and public buildings in their rightful place. The result was a very loose urban lay-out. Immense dwellings were built right in the centre of the city, replacing the earlier buildings. It was not until the last third of 1C AD, under the Flavians, that it was decided to create straight streets: properties had to be remodelled accordingly, the façades of houses were realigned and their axes modified, while porticoes and colonnades were erected.

VAISON-LA-ROMAINE

11 Novembre Pl. du	Y	40
Aubanel Pl.	Z	2
Bon Ange Chemin du	Y	3
Brusquet Chemin du	Y	4
Burrus R.	Y	5
Cathédrale Pl. de la	Y	6
Chanoine-Sautel Pl.	Y	7
Coudray Av.	Y	8
Daudet R. A.	Y	9
Église R. de l'	Z	10
Évêché R. de l'	Z	12
Fabre Cours H.	Y	13
Foch Quai Maréchal	Z	14
Géoffray Av. C.	Z	15
Gontard Quai P.	Z	17
Grande-Rue	Y	18
Jean-Jaurès R.	Y	22
Mazen Av. J.	Y	23
Mistral R. Frédéric.	Y	24
Montée du Château	Y	25
Montfort Pl.	Y	26
Noël R. B.	Y	27
Poids Pl. du	Y	29
République R.	Y	32
St-Quenin Av.	Y	33
Sus Auze Pl.	Y	34
Taulignan Crs	Y	35
Victor-Hugo Av.	Z	36
Vieux Marché Pl. du	Y	38
Cloître	Y	B
Musée archéologique Théo-Desplans	Y	M

Address Book

EATING OUT

☞ **Auberge d'Anaïs** – 84340 Entrechaux – 5km/3.1mi southeast of Vaison via D 938 then D 54 – ☎ 04 90 36 20 06 – auberge. anais.free.fr – closed 15 Nov-1 Mar, Mon from Apr-Sept and Sat in Mar and from Oct-15 Nov. Surrounded by vines and olive trees, this inn is a popular meeting place among locals who enjoy its relaxed, colourful dining room, its tasty cooking and the lively atmosphere, thanks to the son of the house. But keep it to yourself – it's a well-kept secret! A few rooms and a swimming pool.

☞☞ **Brin d'Olivier** – 4 rue Ventoux – ☎ 04 90 28 74 79 – closed 21-31 Jan, 25 Mar-4 Apr, 20 Jun-4 Jul, 23 Sept-4 Oct, 25 Nov-6 Dec, Wed, Thu lunchtime and Sat lunchtime . A nice place near the Roman bridge, with two dining rooms decorated in rustic Provençal style. Patio with a lovely olive tree. Local cooking.

☞☞ **Le Girocèdre** – in the village – 84110 Puyméras – 6km/3.75mi northeast of Vaison, in the direction of Nyons then St-Romain via D 71 – ☎ 04 90 46 50 67 – closed 3-31 Mar, 15 Nov-15 Dec, Tue in low season and Mon. At the top of the village is this building perched on an outcrop of rock, whose caves, originally carved out to raise silkworms, today serve as wine cellars. Under the cedars, olive, fig and tamarisk trees, the terrace is delightful in summer. Two small cottages.

WHERE TO STAY

☞ **Chambre d'hôte L'Oliveraie** – route de St-Roman – 84280 Cairanne – 17km/10.6mi west of Vaison via D 975, D 69 then D 51 – ☎ 04 90 30 72 85 – ⚠ – 5 rooms. Set on a hillside surrounded with olive trees, this recently built house offers modern rooms and a terrace overlooking Cairanne and the Rhône valley. To enjoy the view at its best, add a lovely sunset with glass of Côtes-du-Rhône. Swimming pool.

☞ **Chambre d'hôte Domaine le Puy de Maupas** – route de Nyons – 84110 Puyméras – 7km/4.4mi northeast of Vaison via D 938 then D 46 – ☎ 04 90 46 47 43 – closed 1 Nov-15 Mar – ⚠ – 5 rooms – evening meal 20€. A house set among vines, next to the cellar of this wine-producing property. In the evening you will enjoy the nightly concert of the frogs in the pond. Breakfast is served facing Mont Ventoux. Evening meals offer the opportunity to taste the house wines. Swimming pool.

☞☞ **Chambre d'hôte L'Évêché** – rue de l'Évêché – ☎ 04 90 36 13 46 – evecheaol. com – closed 15 Nov-15 Dec – ⚠ – 4 rooms. This pleasant 16C house in the upper part of the town was once part of the bishop's palace. Carefully decorated rooms, prettily furnished, arranged on several levels. Attractive collection of etchings from a book about lock making. Lovely view over the lower town from the terrace.

☞☞ **Chambre d'hôte La Calade** – rue Calade – 84110 St-Romain-en-Viennois – 4km/2.5mi northeast of Vaison via D 938 then D 71, Nyons direction – ☎ 04 90 46 51 79 – closed end Oct-end Mar – ⚠ – 4 rooms. A former barn built against the village walls welcomes its guests in a lovely courtyard, where breakfast is served on fine days. Its slightly monastic rooms will appeal to those who like the ascetic style. The terrace, at the top of the tower, offers a splendid view.

☞☞ **Chambre d'hôte Les Auzières** – 84110 Roaix – 6km/3.75mi west of Vaison via D 975 in the direction of Orange – ☎ 04 90 46 15 54 – closed Nov-Mar – ⚠ – 5 rooms – evening meal 22.87€. It's hard to find anywhere more isolated than this! This huge house, surrounded by vines and olive trees, offers spacious, cool rooms. Around the big wooden table in the dining room your hosts will make sure you appreciate the local cooking. Swimming pool.

The archeologists have established that the luxurious domi were much larger than those in Pompeii. They were built over a period of 250 years, and yet Vaison was not restricted to just this kind of dwelling; excavations have unearthed small palaces, modest dwellings, huts and tiny shops. The large public buildings, except for the theatre and baths, have not been traced.

Over the centuries

Partially destroyed in the late 3C, Vaison rose again during the 4C with a reduced urban plan. The seat of a bishopric, it ranked highly in the 5C and 6C in spite of Barbarian occupation, and two synods took place here in 442 and 529.

The following centuries were marked by a sharp decline and by the desertion of the lower town, to the profit of the old town on the river's south bank where the count of Toulouse built a castle. The medieval upper town was abandoned in the 18C and 19C and the modern town fortified the Gallo-Roman city.

ROMAN RUINS★★ *about 2hr*

Jul and Aug: Puymin 9.30am-6.45pm, Villasse 9.30am-12.30pm, 2-6.45pm; June and Sept: Puymin 9.30am-6pm, Villasse 9.30am-12.30pm, 2-6pm; Mar to May and Oct: 10am-12.30pm, 2-6pm; Nov to Feb: 10am-noon, 2-4.30pm (Closed Tues from Nov to end of Jan other than School holidays). Closed 1 Jan and 25 Dec. 6.25€ (children: 2.13€), ticket gives access to all the monuments. ☎ 04 90 36 02 11.

The ancient ruins are spread over 15ha/37 acres. The centre of the Gallo-Roman city (forum and precincts) is covered by the modern town, and therefore only the peripheral quarters, rich with information on life at Vaison and its inhabitants in the 1C AD, have been uncovered.

At present the excavations are progressing towards the cathedral in the La Villasse quarter and around Puymin hill, where a shopping district and a sumptuous domus, the **Peacock villa** with its mosaics, were recently unearthed. On the northern boundary of the ancient town, the excavated baths (some 20 rooms) have revealed that they were used until the late 3C and then destroyed.

Quartier de Puymin

Maison des Messii

This *domus*, a large urban dwelling belonging to a wealthy Vaison family (partly buried under the modern road network), features a very elaborate interior which favoured a sumptuous and comfortable lifestyle. As one enters, via the Roman street, a vestibule then a corridor lead to the *atrium* (1) around which the various rooms have been laid out, including the *tablinum* (study and library reserved for the head of the family). The atrium had in its centre, under the open section, a square basin (*impluvium*) which caught the rainwater.

Note the room (2) where Apollo's head (in the museum) was found, the main reception hall or *oecus* (3), the peristyle and its basin. The annexes include the kitchen (4) with its twin hearths, and the private bath (5) with its three rooms: *caldarium, tepidarium, frigidarium*.

Portique de Pompée

This elegant public promenade, a sort of public garden, 64m x 52m/210ft x 171ft, consisted of four galleries with niches (*exedra*), covered originally with a lean-to-roof, surrounding a garden and pool, in the centre of which stood a square aedicule. The well-excavated north gallery presents three exedra into which were placed the casts of the statues of Sabina, Diadumenos (Roman copy of the statue by Polyclitus which is exhibited at the British Museum) and Hadrian. The west gallery is also almost entirely excavated, while the other two galleries are buried under the modern buildings.

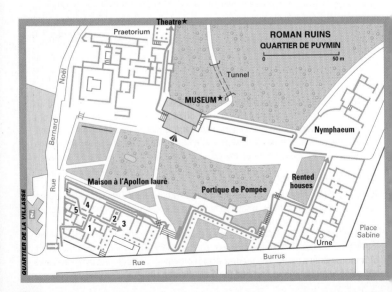

A destructive torrent

At 11 o'clock on the morning of 22 September 1992, huge gushes of water swept through the town, transforming the River Ouvèze into a destructive torrent. The consequences were devastating; 37 people lost their lives, 150 houses were destroyed and the town's industrial estate was completely washed away. With the exception of its parapet which has since been rebuilt, the Roman bridge alone was able to withstand the river's onslaught. The town has bravely risen out of its ruins and has now recovered its pleasing air.

Rented Houses

This residential complex consists of a block of dwellings (to rent) several storeys high, for citizens of modest means. Note the large urn (*dolium*) for provisions.

Nymphaeum

This features various buildings of a cistern set around a spring, which was collected into an elongated basin, called a nymphaeum.
Further on to the east the shopping district and Peacock villa were excavated (*not open to the public*).

Musée archéologique Théo-Desplans★

  Jul and Aug: 9.30am-6.45pm; Jun and Sept: 9.30am-6.30pm; Mar to May and Oct: 10am-1pm, 2.30-6pm; Nov to Feb: 10am-noon, 2-4.30pm (Feb: 5pm); Closed Tues from Nov to end of Jan other than School holidays). Closed 1 Jan and 25 Dec. 6.25€ ticket gives access to all the monuments (children: 2.13€). ☎ 04 90 36 51 38 or b 04 90 36 02 11.

This fascinating and pleasant archaeological museum displays the finds excavated at Vaison. Different aspects of Gallo-Roman civilization are presented thematically: religion, living quarters, pottery, glassware, arms, tools, ornaments, toiletries and Imperial coins. The statues are remarkable. They are all in white marble; in chronological order: Claudius (dating from 43) wearing a heavy oak crown; Domitian in armour; naked Hadrian (dating from 121) in a majestic pose in the Hellenistic manner; Sabina, his wife, represented more conventionally as a great lady in state dress. Two other pieces are worthy of interest: the 2C marble head of Apollo crowned with laurel leaves, and a 3C silver bust of a patrician and mosaics from the Peacock Villa.

▶ *Go to the theatre by following the west slope of the Puymin.*

Théâtre Romain★

The theatre was built in the 1C, repaired in the 3C and dismantled in the 5C. Its dimensions (95m/312ft diameter, 29m/95ft high) reveal that it was slightly smaller than the one in Orange (103m/338ft, 36m/118ft); it had a seating capacity of 6 000 people (Orange held 9 000 to 10 000 spectators). Also like the theatre in Orange, it was built against the hillside; its tiers were rebuilt by Jules Formigé (1879-1960; Inspector-General of Historical Monuments). The entire stage was hewn out of the rock and the pits containing the machinery and curtain have been well preserved. Discovered amid the ruins were the fine statues exhibited in the museum. Another feature, unique among the Roman theatres in Provence, is the existence of part of a top gallery portico.

Quartier de La Villasse

Main street and baths

On entering the site of the excavations, walk on the paved main street, under which runs a drain going down towards the Ouvèze and the modern buildings. On the west side of the street is a parallel passageway lined with colonnades reserved for pedestrians only; shops, located in the main houses' outbuildings, lined it. On the east side of the street lie the baths, which are surrounded by deep drains. The great room has a pilastered arcade.

Maison au buste d'argent
(House of the Patrician of the Silver Bust)

Across from the baths in the shop street is the entrance (1) to the vast domus, in which was discovered the silver bust (*see museum above*) of its opulent owner.

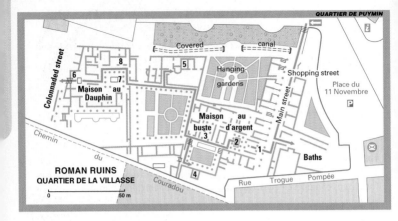

Sprawled over about about 5 000m2/53 820sq ft, the *domus* is complete: paved vestibule, atrium (2), tablinum (3), a first peristyle with garden and pool and then a second larger peristyle also enhanced with garden and pool.

On the south side of the house stands another where mosaics (4) were found as well as frescoes around an atrium. North of the second (larger) peristyle is the private bath (5) which is preceded by a courtyard. Nearby, to the east, lies a large hanging garden which enhanced the wealthy property.

Maison au Dauphin (Dolphin House)

In its early stages c 40 BC, this house occupied the north-eastern section of a large enclosure in a non-urban setting. The central part of this vast house, which covers 2 700m2/29 060sq ft, is laid out around a peristyle (7) decorated by a pool in dressed stone. To the north, covering 50m2/538sq ft, there are the private baths (8) with the *triclinium*, a large dining room used for banquets, along the west edge. The atrium (6) led into the colonnaded street; this was one of the entrances to the house.

To the south stands another peristyle, a pleasant garden complemented by a large pool, with three exedra and faced with white marble, as well as fountains and formal gardens.

Colonnaded Street

Not completely excavated, this street borders the Maison au Dauphin along 43m/141ft. It was not a paved street; its surface, like many other street surfaces, was made of gravel.

Additional Sights

The exceptional archaeological site for which Vaison is justly famous should not cause the visitor to neglect the medieval town, starting with the cathedral, which is reached from Quartier de la Villasse by following avenue Jules-Ferry.

Ancienne Cathédrale Notre-Dame-de-Nazareth

This beautiful Provençal Romanesque style building still has its 11C chevet, made from a solid rectangular block of masonry, its apsidal chapels and its walls, reinforced in the 12C at the same time that the nave was covered in by a barrel-vault. The discovery of Gallo-Roman architectural fragments leads experts to believe that the cathedral was built on the ruins of a civic building with a basilical ground plan.

Outside, the chevet is decorated with cornices and foliated friezes imitating Antique decoration. Inside, the nave includes two bays with pointed barrel vaulting and one bay topped by an octagonal dome on squinches decorated with the symbols of the Evangelists. It is lit through windows cut at the base of the vaulting.

Cloître★

🕒 *Jul and Aug: 10am-12.30pm, 2-6.45pm; Jun and Sept: 10am-12.30pm, 2-6pm; Mar to May and Oct: 10am-12.30pm, 2-6pm; Nov to Feb: 10am-noon, 2-4.30pm.* 🕒*Closed 1 Jan and 25 Dec. 1.22€.* ☎ *04 90 36 02 11*

The cloisters are adjacent to the cathedral and were originally built in the 12C and 13C; the southeast gallery is a 19C reconstruction. The capitals in the east arcade are the most elaborately decorated: acanthus leaves, interlaced designs or figures.

▶ *Return to the avenue and turn right along quai Pasteur, which runs along the right bank of the Ouvèze.*

Pont Romain

The Roman bridge has only one arch, 17.20m/56.5ft wide. Apart from the parapet, rebuilt after the dramatic flood on 22 September 1992, the bridge is as it was 2 000 years ago.

Haute Ville★ (Upper Town)

▶ *Start from place du Poids and go through the 14C fortified gateway, dominated by the belfry tower and its 18C wrought-iron bell cage.*

Roman bridge over the Ouvèze

The 14C fortifications which surround the city's steeply sloping streets were built in part using stones from the ruins of the Roman town. Take the time to amble through the picturesque maze of alleyways (rue de l'Église, rue de l'Évêché, rue des Fours) and squares (place du Vieux-Marché) decorated with lovely fountains. The successful restoration of the warm-coloured stone houses roofed with old Roman tiles, evokes a typical Provençal village of yesteryear.

The church dates from the 15C and there is a fine view of Mont Ventoux from the parvis. A steep path leads to the castle, built by the counts of Toulouse at the end of the 12C on a rock overlooking the upper town.

Chapelle de St-Quenin★

ⓒ*Contact the tourist office for information on opening times, ☎ 04 90 36 02 11.*

The unusual triangular chevet and its remarkable decoration have given rise to a number of theories among archaeologists. Some see it as a temple of Diana, others as a Merovingian chapel. It is now believed to be a Romanesque building constructed in the 12C with older elements.

EXCURSIONS

There are two signposted footpaths with loop around the surrounding countryside, one of 18km/11mi and one of 37km/23mi. Maps are available at the Tourist office.

Rasteau

ⓒ*Jul and Aug: daily except Tues 10am-6pm; from Easter to Jun and Sept: daily except Tues 2-6pm.* ⓒ*Closed Oct to Easter. 0.56€. ☎ 04 90 46 11 75.*
10km/6.2mi west by D 975.

The vineyards of Rasteau produce wines under the two official appellations of Côtes-du-Rhône and Rasteau (dessert wines known as vins doux naturels). The Musée du Vigneron with a display of winegrowing equipment used long ago and a large collection of vintage Châteauneuf-du-Pape will certainly be of interest to amateur oenologists.

Brantes

▶ *28km/17.5mi east by D 938, then left onto D 54 until Entrechaux. There take D 13 towards Mollans and finally turn right onto D 40.*

This fortified village presents an impressive **site**★ at the foot of Mont Ventoux, on the northern face of the Toulourenc valley. It contains a Chapelle des Pénitents Blanc, now used for exhibitions, the remains of a Renaissance manor house (lovely sculpted doorway) and a richly decorated church.

VALLON-PONT-D'ARC

POPULATION 1 914

MICHELIN MAP 331: I-7

LOCAL MAP SEE GORGES DE L'ARDÈCHE

An outdoor pursuits resort, Vallon is the recommended starting point for travel-ling down the Gorges de l'Ardèche by boat. To the south-east, on the hillside, stand the ruins of old Vallon, a feudal village.'

🚇 1 pl. de l'Ancienne-Gare, 07150 Vallon-Pont-D'arc, ☎ 04 75 88 04 01. www.vallon-pont-darc.com.

Sights

Town Hall Tapestries

   🕐 *Daily except Sat-Sun 10-11am, 3.30-4.30pm, Sat-Sun and public holidays by appointment. 2.29€ ☎ 04 75 88 02 06.*
The town hall (mairie) is located in an old Louis XIII-style mansion, formerly the residence of the counts of Vallon. In the ground floor marriage room hang seven Aubusson tapestries remarkable for their bright colours.

"Grotte Chauvet-Pont d'Arc" Exhibition

No 1, rue de Mariou.   🕐*Mid-Mar to mid-Nov: daily except Mon 10am-noon, 2-5.30pm (Jun to Aug: daily except Mon 10am-1pm, 3-8pm). 3.81€ (children: 2.29€). ☎ 04 75 37 17 68, www.culture.fr/culture/arcnat/chauvet/fr.*

With a view to preserving the invaluable heritage discovered in the Grotte Chauvet in 1994, a huge exhibition has been organised to enlighten visitors on this major breakthrough dating back to the Upper Palaeolithic Era. A display of photographs, explanatory documents and films explore the various representations of art in the decorated caves of the Ardèche, as well as the daily life of nomadic hunters back in those Prehistoric days (reconstituted scenes).

Excursions

Silkworm Farm (Magnanerie)

3km/2mi towards Ruoms on D 579. Access along a road branching off to the left coming from Vallon.

📷 🕐*Mid-Apr to end of Sept: guided tours (45min) 10am-noon, 2-6pm.* 🕐*Closed Sun. 4.50€ (children: 2.30€). ☎ 04 75 88 01 27.*
In the village of Les Mazes one of the last Vivarois silkworm farms still in operation can be seen. From the covered terrace (couradou) visit the cocoonery, a vast room containing silkworms on trays made of reeds. The tour shows the development of the silkworm from a tiny larva, the size of a pinhead, to a cocoon enveloped in silken threads.

Pont-d'Arc★★

5km/3mi to the south-east via D 290. *See Gorges de l'ARDÈCHE.*

WHERE TO STAY

🍽️🛏️ **Mondial-Camping** – *1.5km/1mi southeast of Vallon-Pont-d'Arc* – ☎ *04 75 88 00 44 – open 25 Mar-10 Oct – booking advised – 244 places.* A pleasant site with spacious places, well marked out and surrounded with greenery. Restaurant, games room and bar/disco. When it comes to swimming, there is a choice between the swimming pool bordered with palm trees and, of course, the Ardèche.

VALRÉAS

POPULATION 9 069

MICHELIN MAP 332: C-7

Lying in the fertile Coronne valley, Valréas is an important centre for agriculture and light industry (printers, factories making metal furniture, cardboard or plastic articles).

Av. du Mar.-Leclerc, 84600 Valréas, ☎ 04 90 35 04 71.

A Bit of History

The papacy located in Avignon wanted to possess Valréas, a neighbour to the Comtat Venaissin. In 1317, John XXII bought the town from the Dauphin Jean II, but a strip of land still separated the two pontifical states. Worried about the expansion of the papal lands in this region, King Charles VII forbade further sales of land to the popes, thus creating this papal enclave. In 1791, after a referendum, France annexed the territory. Valréas is a now a canton of Vaucluse département entirely surrounded by the Drôme département.

Le Petit St-Jean

This is a charming tradition which has survived 500 years. Every year, on the night of 23 June, a small boy (3-5 years old) is crowned Le Petit St-Jean (Little St John). Symbolising St Martin, the city's patron saint, Le Petit St-Jean parades through torch-lit streets on a litter, blessing people along the way. A procession of 300 costumed figures follows him in a colourful and animated atmosphere. For one year Valréas is placed under his protection.

The Town

The town lies within plane tree-shaded boulevards planted on the site of former ramparts of which only the **Tour du Tivoli** remains. In the old town are several fine houses: at no 36 Grande-Rue is the **Hôtel d'Aultane**, its door topped by a coat of arms; on the corner of rue de l'Échelle is **Hôtel d'Inguimbert** adorned with modillions and mullioned windows; on place Gutenberg stands **Château Delphinal** with machicolations.

Hôtel de Ville

Jul and Aug: unaccompanied tours at the same time as a visit to the Exhibition of Visual Arts daily except Tues 10.30am-12.30pm, 4-8pm; Sept to Jun: guided tours (30min) daily except Sun 3-5pm. Closed public holidays. No charge. ☎ 04 90 35 00 45.

This former 18C mansion belonged to the Marquis de Simiane, who married Pauline de Grignan, granddaughter of Mme de Sévigné. The oldest part of the mansion dates back to the 15C; a majestic façade overlooks place Aristide-Briand. The library, on the first floor, with its 17C wood panelling from the former hospital, contains papal bulls and manuscripts. Note the second floor room with its fine timber ceiling.

Address Book

EATING OUT

Délice de Provence – *6 La Placette (town centre) – ☎ 04 90 28 16 91 – closed 27 Oct-9 Nov, Tue evening and Wed.* A pleasant little place to stop and cheer yourself up with classic cooking, in the town centre. A good choice of menus at very reasonable prices.

WHERE TO STAY

Le Grand Hôtel – *28 avenue du Gén.-De-Gaulle – ☎ 04 90 35 00 26 – closed 21 Dec-28 Jan, Mon lunchtime in high season, Sat evening from Nov-Mar and Sun – P – 15 rooms – 7.62€ – restaurant 15.09/45.73€.* A large building on the boulevard which encircles the town centre. The décor may not be very up to date, but this is a useful address for travellers passing through. Regional cooking and simple rooms.

VALRÉAS

Ancien Collège R. de l'........................	2
Borello R. Charles...............................	3
Château Robert R.	5
Daurand R. J.-F.	6
Échelle R. de l'	7
Fabre Pl. Henri	9
Faye R. Jules	10
Ferry Pl. Jules	12
Foch Av. Maréchal	13
Grande-Rue	14
Gutenberg Pl.	15
Maury Pl. Cardinal	16
Meynard Av.	17
Niel R. Jules	18
Pasteur R. Louis	19
Recluse Pl. de la	21
Recluse R. de la	22
République Pl. de la	23
St-Antoine R.	24
St-Jean R.	25

Chapelle des Pénitents Blancs.............	E
Hôtel d'Aultane	K
Hôtel d'Inguimbert	N
Hôtel de ville	H
Musée du Cartonnage et de l'Imprimerie	M
Tour de Tivoli	B
Tour de l'Horloge.................................	F

Église Notre-Dame-de-Nazareth

The most interesting part of this Provençal Romanesque church is its south door of four recessed orders resting on small columns.

Chapelle des Pénitents Blancs

To visit, ask at the tourist office. ☎ 04 90 35 04 71

On place Pie a lovely wrought-iron gate announces the way to the 17C chapel. The chancel is adorned with carved stalls and a lovely flowered coffered ceiling. The garden is overlooked by Château Ripert or clock tower; from the terrace there is a lovely view of old Valréas and the hills of the Tricastin.

Musée du Cartonnage et de l'Imprimerie

Valréas, an important centre of cardboard production, offers tourists interested in the manufacturing industries an opportunity to follow the different processes involved in the manufacture of cardboard since the 19C in this instructive museum.

Excursion

Round-trip of 40km/25mi – allow 2hr.

▶ *Leave Valréas west on D 941.*

Grignan★

See GRIGNAN.

▶ *Take D 541 and turn left onto D 71.*

Chamaret

A clock tower, converted from a fine belfry, relic of the massive castle perched high on a rock, dominates the landscape with an all-encompassing view of Tricastin.

▶ *Continue along D 71.*

The road is bordered by fields of lavender separated by truffle oaks and cypresses.

Montségur-sur-Lauzon

▶ *In front of the town hall, take the street on the left, turn right and then take the uphill path to the hillock on which lies the old village.*

A network of streets allows the visitor to discover the old town and leads to the castle's old Romanesque chapel. From the watchpath, a fine panoramic view of the Tricastin countryside, Baronnies and Mont Ventoux unfolds.

▶ *Take D 71B going east.*

There are good views of Montagne de la Lance and the Nyons countryside.

Truffle markets

Richerenches is known as the truffle capital. It has received the title of *site remarqable du goût*, an award given to places that promote the culinary excellence of their local specialities. Every year in January, a special Mass is held for members of the Confrèrie du diamant noir ("Brotherhood of the black diamond"), and the congregation is invited to put truffles in the collection box. You will have to buy yours at the market, however: in Richerenches on Saturday and Valréas on Wednesday *(Nov-Mar)*.

Richerenches

Founded as a command post by the Knights Templars in the 12C, *the town* is now an important truffle market. Built on a rectangular plan, it still retains its fortified wall flanked by four round corner towers; go through the belfry, a rectangular machicolated tower with a heavy nailed door. Left of the church lie important temple ruins.

▶ *D 20, southeast, crosses Visan and continues on to Notre-Dame-des-Vignes.*

Chapelle Notre-Dame-des-Vignes

🕐*Summer: 10-11.30am, 3-6pm.*
The nave of this 13C chapel is decorated with 15C panelling; in the chancel is a 13C polychrome wood statue of the Virgin, the object of a popular pilgrimage on 8 September.

▶ *Go past Visan and take D 976 to return to Valréas.*

VENASQUE★

POPULATION 785

MICHELIN MAP 332: D-10

Built on a foothill of the Vaucluse plateau, Venasque dominates the Carpentras plain. The rich calcareous soil, benefiting from irrigation, nourishes vegetables and fruit that are distributed nationwide. The Ouvèze, Sorgue and Durance rivers have created vast, fertile alluvial plains that have brought prosperity to market towns such as Orange, Avignon, Cavaillon and Carpentras; some of these same towns have become very large dispatching centres.

🛈 *Grand'rue, 84210 Venasque, ☎ 04 90 66 11 66.*

A Bit of History

The village was, before Carpentras, the Comtat's bishopric and gave its name to the Comtat Venaissin. Located between the Rhône and Durance rivers and Mont Ventoux, the territory was under the counts of Toulouse's rule; and like all the county's other possessions it was affected by the Albigensian heresy and united under the crown in 1271. It was ceded three years later to Pope Gregory X by Philip III, the Bold, and remained under papal authority until 1791 when it once again became part of France. This enclave had its own administration; its law courts were located at Carpentras, capital of the Comtat, having superseded Pernes-les-Fontaines in 1320. Made up of the rich Vaucluse Plain, Comtat Venaissin occupies the largest and most southerly basin of the Rhône Valley.

The Village

Stroll through the peaceful streets of the village, among the artists' workshops (painters, potters and ceramicists) and the tastefully restored houses, often decorated with pergolas.

During the walk, admire **place des Comtes-de-Toulouse**, a reminder of the village's history. From **esplanade de la Planette** and **Tours Sarrasines**, remains of medieval fortifications, there are fine views to be had of Mont Ventoux and the Dentelles de Montmiral.

EATING OUT

😕😕 **Restaurant Les Remparts –** *rue Haute – ☎ 04 90 66 02 79 – 🕐 closed 15 Nov-15 Mar.* Restaurant built on the old fortifications of this hilltop village, whose streets are pleasant to explore. Eat in one of the smart, colourful dining rooms, decorated with old cinema posters. A few simple rooms.

B. Kaufmann/MICHELIN

Merovingian Baptistery

Baptistery★

🕐*Mid-Mar to mid-Nov: daily except Wed. 10am-noon, 2-6pm, Sun 2-6pm (Jun to Sept: 10am-noon, 3-7pm); mid-Nov to mid-Mar: daily except Wed. 10am-noon, 2-5pm, Sun 2-5pm.* 🕐*Closed between Christmas and New Year's Day 2.29€.* ☎ *04 90 66 62 01.*

Entrance right of the presbytery. The baptistery, most likely from the 6C or the Merovingian period and remodelled in the 11C, is one of France's oldest religious buildings. The Greek cross plan, with groined vaulting over the centre square, has unequal arms ending in apsidal chapels, each oven-vaulted with blind arcading on slender marble columns with Antique or, in the case of the east apsidal chapel, Merovingian capitals. The hollow in the floor was for the font.

Église Notre-Dame

The church, which is connected to the Baptistery by a long corridor, has been subject to considerable alterations and contains, in the chancel, a 17C carved altarpiece. In the second north chapel is a 15C Avignon School **Crucifixion**★.

Excursion

10km/6mi east on D 4 towards Apt. The **Route des Gorge**s is a winding yet picturesque road that goes up the gorges through the **Forêt de Venasque** on the Vauclause plain. After climbing some 400m/1 312ft the road reaches Col de Murs pass (alt 627m/2 057ft). Beyond the pass the first bends on the way down to Murs reveal extended views of Apt basin and Roussillon.

Mont VENTOUX★★★

MICHELIN MAP 332: E-8

Mont Ventoux is the most dominant feature of Provence's Rhône valley. It proudly commands the Rhône valley to the west, Vaucluse plateau to the south and the small Baronnies range to the north. The climb to Mont Ventoux is one of the loveliest excursions of Provence; the panorama from the peak is immense. With a height of only 1 909m/6 263ft, Mont Ventoux cannot rival the Alps or Pyrenees for altitude; and yet its location in front of the Alps, far from any rival peak, its bold outline above Carpentras plain and the Vaucluse plateau, all combine to give it an astonishing majesty.

Vegetation

The lower slopes are covered with the trees and plants typical of Provence, while at the summit polar species such as Spitzbergen saxifrage and Icelandic poppy flourish. The flowers are at their best in early July. The forests which once covered the mountainside were felled from the 16C on, to supply the naval shipyards in Toulon; replanting has been going on since 1860. Aleppo pine, holm and downy oaks, cedar, beech, pitch pine, fir and larch form a forest cover which at about 1 600m/5 249ft is replaced by a vast field of white shingle. During the autumn a climb to the top through the multicoloured landscape is enchanting.

Weather

There is nearly always a wind on Mont Ventoux, as its name suggests (*vent* means wind), particularly when the mistral is blowing. The temperature at the top is on average 11°C/20°F lower than at the foot; rainfall is twice as heavy and filters through the fissured limestone of Vaucluse Plateau. In winter the temperature may drop at the observatory to − 27°C /-17°F), the mountain is usually snow-capped above 1 300m/4 265ft to 1 400m/4 593ft from December to April, and the slopes at Mont Serein on the north side and Chalet-Reynard on the south provide good skiing.

Address Book

For coin ranges, see Legend at the back of the guide.

EATING OUT

◎◎ **Le Vieux Four** – *in the village* – 84410 Crillon-le-Brave – ☎ 04 90 12 81 39 – closed 15 Nov-1 Mar, Mon and lunchtime during the week – ⌂. This young female chef has set up her restaurant in the old village bakery. You can eat in the bakehouse, with its old oven still in place, or on the terrace, on the ramparts, with a view of Mont Ventoux

◎◎ **La Maison** – *84340 Beaumont-du-Ventoux* – ☎ 04 90 65 15 50 – closed Nov-5 Apr, Mon and Tue from Sept-June and lunchtime in Jul-aug except Sun. A prettily restored former farm, in a little village surrounded by vines and orchards. Its charm is evident as soon as you step onto the terrace under the lime trees. Provençal cooking is served in the yellow dining room. Three simple, smart rooms.

◎◎ **Le Mas des Vignes** – *route du mont Ventoux* – 84410 Bédoin – 6km/3.75mi east of Bédoin – ☎ 04 90 65 63 91 – closed 2 Nov-30 Mar, lunchtime Jul-Aug except Sun and public holidays, Tue lunchtime and Mon – ⌂. From this pretty mas overlooking the valley and the course of the famous race up Mont Ventoux, the view extends as far as the Dentelles de Montmirail and the Comtat plain. Enjoy the simply served cooking, based on fresh produce, in the dining room or on the terrace.

WHERE TO STAY

◎ **Hôtel Garance** – *84410 Ste-Colombe* – 4 km/2.5mi east of Bédoin via the road to Mont-Ventoux – ☎ 04 90 12 81 00 – Ⓟ – 13 rooms – ⌂ 5.95€. A restored old farm in a hamlet surrounded by vines and orchards and overlooked by Mont Ventoux. The rooms have contemporary furniture, Provençal colours and old floors. Those at the back are preferable, with a view of the "giant of Provence". Swimming pool.

◎◎◎ **Hostellerie de Crillon le Brave** – *place de l'Église* – 84410 Crillon-le-Brave – ☎ 04 90 65 61 61 – closed 2 Jan-8 Mar – Ⓟ – 18 rooms – ⌂ 14.48€ – restaurant 38.11/70.13€. This 17C building situated opposite Mont Ventoux is reminiscent of Cézanne's paintings. Provençal rooms, lovely vaulted dining room in the former stables, gorgeous shaded terrace and elegant Italian garden. Local food and wines.

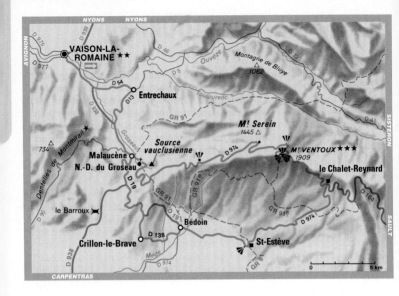

Ascent★★

Ascent of the North face. ☺*Roads may be blocked Nov to May; call in advance* ☎ *08 36 68 02 84 (Météo France).*
Round-trip of 63km/39mi starting from Vaison-la-Romaine – allow 1 day – ⌚see map.

The itinerary uses D 974, a road made in 1933 for tourists ascending Mont Ventoux by the north side. Although the incline is similar to the one on the south side, it is less trying during the hot summer months because of the breeze. During a storm, the road can be obstructed by fallen earth for the last 3km/2mi but does not stop traffic. These conditions simply require more attention on the part of the driver.

▷ *Leave Vaison-la-Romaine by D 938, to the south-east. After 3.5km/2mi turn left onto D 54.*

Entrechaux

The village, overlooked by the ruins of a castle with its 220m/700ft defensive keep, was formerly a possession of the bishops of Vaison.

▷ *Return to the Malaucène road via D 13.*

Malaucène

⌚ *See DENTELLES-DE-MONTMIRAIL.*

▷ *Leave Malaucène east on D 974.*

Chapelle Notre-Dame-du-Groseau

⊶*Not open to the public.* This chapel is all that is left of a Benedictine abbey, a dependant of St-Victor's of Marseille. The square building is the 12C abbey church's former chancel; the nave has been destroyed.

Source vauclusienne du Groseau

This spring forms a pool of clear water as it emerges from several fissures at the foot of a steep slope (over 100m/328ft), beneath trees to the left of the road. The Romans built an aqueduct to carry the water to Vaison-la-Romaine.

The road continues up the northern slope revealing a good view of the Vaucluse plateau, climbing up the steepest and most ravined face of the mountain; it crosses pastures and pinewoods near the Mont Serein refuge.

The viewpoint beyond the Ramayettes hut offers a fine **view**★ of the Ouvèze and Groseau valleys, the Massif des Baronnies and Plate summit.

Mont Serein

Winter sports resort: chalets are charmingly set in the snow fields; and it is well equipped with ski-lifts.

Fr. Isler/MICHELIN

Mount Ventoux

The panorama becomes wider and includes the Dentelles de Montmirail and the heights along the Rhône's west bank. Two more long hairpin bends lead to the top.

Mont Ventoux Summit★★★

The summit, which rises to an altitude of 1 909m/6 263ft, is spiked with scientific equipment: an air force radar station and a television mast. In summer the summit may be shrouded in cloud or midday mist; it is advisable to set out early or remain at the top until sunset. In winter the atmosphere tends to be clearer but the last stage of the ascent should be made on skis.

The view from the car park extends over the Alps, particularly the Vercors range *(viewing table)*. The platform on the south side offers a **panorama**★★★ *(viewing table)*: it swings from the Pelvoux massif to the Cévennes by way of the Luberon, Ste-Victoire, Estaque hills, Marseille, the Étang de Berre, the Alpilles and the Rhône valley.

On very clear days the Canigou is visible way over to the southwest in the Pyrenees. At night the Provençal plain is a wonderful sight as it is transformed into a dark carpet studded with clusters of glittering lights. The sight extends to the Étang de Berre and coast where the lighthouses regularly probe the darkness.

The corniche road, which winds down the south face through a vast tract of shining white shingle to woods, is the oldest road built (c 1885) to serve the observatory. In 22km/13.5mi of hairpin bends to Bédoin (alt 310m/1 017ft), it descends 1 600m/5 249ft.

Le Chalet-Reynard

Excellent local slopes have made Le Chalet-Reynard a popular resort for skiers from Avignon, Carpentras and other nearby towns.

The road goes through the forest; pine trees, beeches, oaks and cedars give way to vines, peach and cherry orchards and a few small olive groves. The view extends across the Comtadin plain; beyond Vaucluse plateau appears the Luberon.

▶ *Leave D 164 on the left to return to Sault (see SAULT) by the Nesque valley.*

St-Estève

From the famous sharp bend, now straightened, which featured in the Ventoux car racing competition to the summit, there is a good **view**★ on the right of the Dentelles de Montmirail, the Comtat plain, and left onto Vaucluse plateau.

Bédoin – This village, which is perched on a hill, has picturesque small streets, leading to the classical Jesuit-style church, which contains several elegant altars.

▶ *Take D 138.*

Crillon-le-Brave

&. ⚡*Easter to Sept: guided tours (1hr, last admission 1hr before closing time) 3-7pm. 4.57€. ☎ 04 90 65 93 53.*

Nestling on a overhang facing the Mont Ventoux, Crillon-le-Brave is a quaint perched village with vestiges of its former fortifications. Beside the Town Hall stands the fascinating **Maison de la Musique Mécanique**, where you can see and hear a bird flageolet (1740), a 1900 orchestrion featuring nine instruments, several barrel organs, and an organ used for merry-go-rounds at funfairs.

▶ *North of the village, take the untarred road leading up to the Belvédère du Paty.*

Belvédère du Paty★

From this viewpoint, there is a panoramic viewa down onto the picturesque terraced village of Crillon-le-Brave and the ochre clay quarries; to the right emerge the Alpilles, and opposite them the Comtat Venaissin, bounded by the Vaucluse plateau, and to the left is Mont Ventoux.

▶ *Take D 19 and D 938 to return to Vaison-la-Romaine.*

VILLENEUVE-LÈS-AVIGNON★

POPULATION 10 730

MICHELIN MAP 339: N-5

A tour of Villeneuve-lès-Avignon is the natural complement to a visit to Avignon. This town, the "City of the Cardinals," offers a view—one of the most famous in the Rhône valley—over the "City of the Popes." The best time to contemplate it is at the end of the afternoon, beneath a setting sun, when Avignon appears in all its splendour.

▤ *1 pl. Charles-David, 30400 Villeneuve-Lès-Avignon, ☎ 04 90 25 61 55. www.villeneu-velesavignon.com.*

A Bit of History

In 1271 after the Albigensian Crusade, the King of France, Philip III the Bold, acquired the county of Toulouse which extended to the banks of the Rhône. On the opposite shore was Provence and the Holy Roman Empire. The river belonged to the crown, which raised the thorny question of rights: whenever the river flooded parts of Avignon, the French king claimed them as his territory and demanded taxes from the unfortunate citizens.

At the end of the 13C, Philip the Fair founded a new town (in French: *ville neuve*) on the plain, and its population grew rapidly. Grasping the great military importance of the spot, he built a powerful fortification at the entrance to Pont St-Bénézet. The cardinals, arriving at the papal court in the 14C and finding no suitable accommodation in Avignon, began to build magnificent residences (*livrées*) across the river in Villeneuve, until eventually there were 15 of these. The prosperity, which the cardinals' patronage of churches and monastic houses brought to the town, remained long after the papal court had returned to Rome. The kings John the Good and Charles V had built Fort St-André in order to watch over the neighbouring papal kingdom. In the 17C and 18C fine *hôtels* lined Grande-Rue. In the monasteries, which developed into real museums, an active and brilliant life style flourished until the Revolution swept away the aristocratic and ecclesiastic regimes.

Address Book

EATING OUT

◱◱ **Le St-André** – *4 bis montée du Fort* – ☎ *04 90 25 63 23* – ◷ *closed Nov, Tue lunchtime and Mon*. If you need to gather strength for the climb to the St-André fort, stop in this pleasant, cool restaurant with its Provençal decor, which borders the narrow road which leads there.

WHERE TO STAY

◱◱ **Hôtel de l'Atelier** – *5 rue de la Foire* – ☎ *04 90 25 01 84* – ◷ *closed beginning Nov to mid-Dec* – *19 rooms.* A 16C building which has retained its charm: old furniture, beams and exposed stone walls, spacious and personalised rooms. In winter the large fireplace heats the sitting room, while in summer breakfast is served on the shady terrace.

VILLENEUVE-LÈS-AVIGNON

Abbé-Vallat Bd 2
Amelier R. de l' 3
Bugade Impasse de la 4
Carpanedo Bd des
    Frères 6
Chartreuse Pl. de la 8
Croix Pl. de la 9
Fabrigoule R. Marcel 10
Hôpital R. de l' 12
Jean-Jaurès Pl. 13
Laune R. de la 14
Meissonnier Pl. J. 16
Mûriers Allée des 17
St-Marc Pl. 18

Chapelle N.-D.-de-Belvézet .... D
Musée municipal
    Pierre-de-Luxembourg .... M
Porte fortifiée .... B

The Town

▶ *Coming from Nîmes or Avignon on D 980, turn left up montée de la Tour.*

Tour Philippe-le-Bel

Same hours as for Notre-Dame church. 1.52€.

Built on a rock, near the Rhône, this tower was the key structure in the defence work at the west end of Pont St-Bénézet, on royal land. When it was first built (1293-1307) it was the present one storey-high building. The second floor and watch turret were added in the 14C. The upper terrace (176 steps) gives a lovely viewaa of Villeneuve and Avignon, Mont Ventoux, the Montagnette hills and the Alpilles.

▶ *Continue to place de l'Oratoire and take rue de l'Hôpital.*

Église Notre-Dame

🕐*Apr to Sept: daily except Mon 10am-12.30pm, 3-7pm (mid-Jun to mid-Sept: daily); Oct to Mar: daily except Mon 10am-noon, 2-5.30pm.* 🕐*Closed in Feb, 1 Jan, 1 May, 1 and 11 Nov, 25 Dec.* ☎ *04 90 27 49 66*

This collegiate church dedicated to Our Lady was founded in 1333. The tower which ends the building on the east side was built as a separate belfry, the ground floor of which straddled the public footpath. The monks obtained permission to redirect the path. They blocked off the belfry arcade, converted it into a chancel and linked it to the existing church by adding an extra bay to the nave. Inside, a number of works of art can be found: starting from the back of the church note the tomb of Cardinal Arnaud de Via, rebuilt with its original 14C recumbent figure (second north chapel), a copy of the famous Pietà kept in the Louvre since 1904 (third south chapel), *St Bruno* by Nicolas Mignard and a *Calvary* by Reynaud Levieux.

Rue de la République

The street is lined with a number of livrées (nos 1, 3, 45 and 53). One of these palaces (recently restored), which belonged to Cardinal Pierre de Luxembourg, a cardinal who died having already won saintly repute at the early age of 19 (in 1387), houses the local museum (see below). At no 60 a gateway gives access to the Chartreuse du Val de Bénédiction.

Additional Sights

Musée municipal Pierre-de-Luxembourg

Apr to Aug: daily except Mon 10am-12.30pm, 3-7pm (mid-June to beginning of Sept: daily); Oct to Mar: daily except Mon 10am-noon, 2-5.30pm. Closed in Feb, 1 Jan, 1 May, 14 July, 1 and 11 Nov, 25 Dec. 3.05€. ☎ 04 90 27 49 66.

This museum, in the hotel Pierre-de-Luxembourg, displays magnificent works of art on four floors.

On the ground floor you will find the 14C polychrome ivory **Virgin**★★, carved from an elephant's tusk; it is one of the finest works of its kind. Also worth admiring are: the marble **Virgin**★★ with two faces from the School of Nuremberg (14C); the death mask of Jeanne of Laval, second wife of King René, by Laurana; the chasuble said to have belonged to Innocent VI; and the 17C veil of the Holy Sacrament, adorned with small pearls.

The first floor houses the museum's most beautiful work of art: **Coronation of the Virgin**★★, painted in 1453 by Enguerrand Quarton, from Laon; this artist painted in Aix, then Avignon (from 1447). Fascinated by landscapes and Provençal light, he used bright colours which emphasised the scene's majesty. The Virgin with her large cloak dominates this composition which encompasses heaven and earth in the subjects painted. Note interesting paintings by Nicolas Mignard (*Jesus in the Temple,* 1649) and Philippe de Champaigne (Visitation c 1644), Reynaud Levieux (*Crucifixion*), Simon de Châlons and Parrocel (*St Anthony and the Infant Jesus*).

Coronaton of the Virgin by Enguerrand Quarton

Coronation of the Virgin by Enguerrand Quarton

Chartreuse du Val de Bénédiction★ *1hr.*

60 rue de la République. 9.30am-5.30pm (Apr to Sept: 9am-6.30pm). Closed 1 Jan, 1 May, 1 and 11 Nov, 25 Dec. 5.49€. ☎ 04 90 15 24 24

In 1352 the papal conclave met in Avignon and elected the General of the Carthusian Order as Pope, but he refused the throne out of humility. To commemorate this gesture Innocent VI, who became Pope instead, founded a charter house on his livrée in Val de Bénédiction. The house, enlarged by the Pope's nephews after his death, became the most important one in France.

The Carthusian Order was founded in 1084 by St Bruno. It consisted of Fathers, who used the title Dom, and Brothers, who lived a communal life like monks in other orders. The Fathers, however, lived singly in cells spending their time in prayer, study and manual work. Three times a day the monks met in chapel to sing the offices; they took their meals alone except on Sundays when brief periods of conversation were allowed.

The charter house now houses colloquia and seminars and also the Centre National des Écritures du Spectacle (CNES), established to promote the act of writing for public performance (plays, opera and songs). The Rencontres de la Chartreuse, held annualy, is linked with the famous Avignon theatre festival.

Porte du cloître

The cloister door separates place des Chartreux from allée des Mûriers. The proportions and ornamentation of the 17C door can be admired from inside.

▷ *Pass through the reception area at the end of allée des Mûriers.*

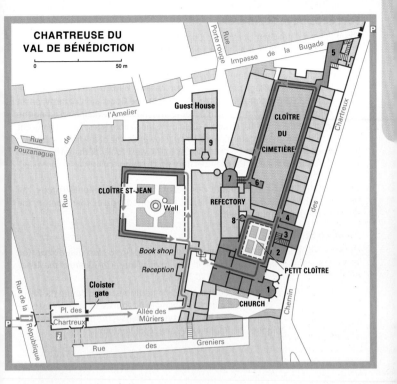

CHARTREUSE DU VAL DE BÉNÉDICTION

Church

Go through the nave; the apse opens out with a **view**★ on to Fort St-André. On the north side, the apse of the other nave and a bay contain the tomb of Innocent VI (**1**): the white marble recumbent figure lies on a high plinth of Pernes stone.

Petit Cloître

The east gallery opens into the chapter-house (**2**) and the Sacristans' yard (**3**) with its well and picturesque staircase. The lavabo (**8**) is a small circular building with a beautiful 18C dome.

Cloître du Cimetière

The great cloisters, 80m/262ft x 20m/66ft, with their warm Provençal colouring, are lined with cells for the Fathers, each cell consisting of a small open court and two rooms, one of which communicates with the cloisters by a hatch. The first cell (**4**) can be visited. The others have been restored and are used as lodgings for writers-in-residence. At the northeast end of the cloisters a passage leads to the bugade (**5**), the depressed groin-vaulted wash-room, which has preserved its well and chimney for drying clothes. Opening off the west gallery is a small chapel of the dead (**6**) off which is another chapel (**7**) which was part of Innocent VI's livrée; it is decorated with lovely frescoes attributed to Matteo Giovanetti (14C), one of the decorators of the Palais des Papes. They illustrate scenes from the life of John the Baptist and the life of Christ.

Refectory

(⌐ *Not open to the public*) The Tinel (18C) is used for con certs. On leaving the cloisters, skirt the crenellated east end of the Tinel; note the bakery (**9**) with its hexagonal tower. On the northeast side, the guest house, remodelled in the 18C, features a lovely façade on its north side.

Cloître St-Jean

The cloisters' galleries have disappeared; however, several of the Fathers' cells remain. In the centre stands the monumental Fontaine St-Jean (18C) which has kept its well and lovely old basin.

Fort et abbaye St-André★

⊙Apr to Sept: 10am-6pm; Oct to Mar: 10am-1pm, 2-5pm. ⊙Closed 1 Jan, 1 May, 1 and 11 Nov, 25 Dec. 4€, no charge 1st Sun in the month from Oct to end of May. ☎ 04 90 25 45 35.

This fort includes a Benedictine abbey, the 12C Romanesque Chapelle Notre-Dame-de-Belvézet, and the village of St-André, of which there remain but a few walls. The fort was built in the second half of the 14C by John the Good and Charles V, on an island called Mount Andaon, which became attached to the mainland when the tributary of the Rhône which circled it dried up in the Middle Ages. The magnificent Porte Fortifiéea (fortified gate), flanked by twin towers is one of the finest examples of medieval fortifications to be seen. Access to the west tower of the fortified gate allows the visitor to discover the chamber from which the portcullises were controlled, and a 18C bakery.

The terrace (85 steps) commands a very beautiful **view**★★ of Mont Ventoux, the Rhône, Avignon and the Palais des Papes, the Comtadin plain, the Luberon, the Alpilles and Tour Philippe-le-Bel.

Abbaye St-André

⊙Apr to Sept: daily except Mon 10am-12.30pm, 2-6pm; Oct to Mar: daily except Mon 10am-12.30pm, 2-5pm. Jul to end of Sept: ⟋⟍ guided tours (1hr30min) of the Abbey Palace Wed and Sat at 4pm. 4€. ☎ 04 90 25 55 95.

Of the Benedictine abbey founded in the 10C and partly destroyed during the Revolution, there remain the entrance gate, left wing and terraces, held up by massive vaulting. Walk through the pleasant **Italian-style gardens**★; the upper terrace gives a lovely **view**★ of Avignon, the Rhône valley and Mont Ventoux.

Little Red Riding Hood

But Little Red Riding Hood had her local map with her, and so she did not fall into the trap. She did not take the path through the wood and she did not meet the big bad wolf. Instead, she chose the picturesque touring route straight to Grandmother's house, and arrived safely with her cake and her little pot of butter.

The End

With Michelin maps, go your own way.

A

Abbaye de Senánque............. 228
Abbaye de St-Roman 183
Aigues-Mortes 106
Aïoli 99
Aire de Caissargues............... 282
Aix-en-Provence 110
  Albertas, Place d'................. 117
  Cathédrale St-Sauveur........... 118
  Cloître St-Sauveur.............. 117
  Cours Mirabeau 115
  Events......................... 112
  Fondation Vasarely.............. 120
  Hôtel de Ville 117
  Hotels 111
  Musée des Tapisseries........... 119
  Musée Granet................... 119
  Nightlife....................... 111
  Old Aix 115
  Quartier Mazarin............... 118
  Restaurants.................... 111
  Shopping...................... 112
Almonds.........................93
Les Alpilles......................122
Ancient myths 90
Ansouis..........................126
Apt 128
Archeological excavations 42
Architecture.....................68
L'Ardèche, Gorges de 14, 132
Arles.............................139
  Abbaye de Montmajour 149
  Allée des Sarcophages 147
  Les Alyscamps 147
  Amphitheatre.................. 144
  Cloître St-Trophime 146
  Crau Plain.................... 150
  Cryptoporticus................. 145
  Église St-Honorat 147
  Église St-Trophime 145
  Entertainment 140
  Espace Van-Gogh 146
  Events........................ 140
  Fondation Vincent Van Gogh-Arles 149
  Hôtel de Ville 145
  Hotels 141
  Marais du Vigueirat 150
  Musée de l'Arles
    et de la Provence antique 147
  Musée Réattu.................. 148
  Museon Arlaten................ 148
  Nightlife...................... 141
  Palais Constantin.............. 145
  Plaine de la Crau 149
  Restaurants................... 141
  Roman Theatre 144
  Sarcophagi 148
  Shopping 140
  Tours 140
Artichauts à la barigoule............101
Aubagne.........................151
Aven d'Orgnac 138
Avignon 153
  Cathédrale Notre-Dame-des-Doms 163
  Collection Lambert 169
  Events 154
  Hotels 155
  Musée Angladon................... 168
  Musée Calvet 168
  Musée Lapidaire 169
  Musée Louis-Vouland 169
  Muséum Requien 169
  Nightlife.......................... 155
  Old Avignon 165
  Palais des Papes................... 156
  Petit Palais....................... 168
  Place Du Palais................... 163
  Pont St-Bénézet.................. 164
  Promenade des Papes............. 163
  Quartier De La Balance 163
  Remparts......................... 164
  Restaurants....................... 154
  Rocher des Doms 163
  Shopping.......................... 154
  Tours 154

B

Bagnols-sur-Cèze...................171
Barbentane 174
Beaucaire 181
Belvédère......................... 327
Belvédère du Serre de Tourre 134
Belvédères de Gaud 134
Berre, Étang de.................... 184
Boat Trips.........................33
Bollène 188
Bonaparte, Napoleon...............211
Bonnieux 190, 241
Books.............................43
Bories 228
Bouillabaisse......................99
Boules 95
Brantes 353
Bullfighting.......................36

C

Calanques, Massif des 192
Calendar of Events 37
Calvisson 282
Camargue 15, 196
Camargue Gardoise 305
camping...........................30
Cap Canaille 210
Card games........................96
Carpentras........................ 203
Car rental 27
Cassis............................ 208
Cavaillon.........................210
Cell Phones 52
Cézanne..........................85
Cézanne, Paul......................113
Château d'If...................... 265
Château du Roi René 332
Châteauneuf-du-Pape..............214
Cheeses........................... 100
Children 37
La Ciotat.........................215

INDEX

Grotte de La Cocalière 218
Colorado de Rustrel 131
Consulates 21
Corniche des Crêtes 209
Corniche du Chassezac 292
Costumes 98
Côtes du Rhône 92
Crestet 273
Croix de Provence 317
Currency 50
Cycling 35

D

Daube provençale 101
Défilé de Ruoms 235
Driving 26

E

Economy 92
Electricity 49
Embassies 21
En-Vau 195
L'Estaque 265
L'Estaque, Chaîne de 218, 265
L'Étoile, Chaîne de 221
Euro 50
Eygalières Alpilles 125

F

Fairs 42
Farandole 97
Fauchier 86
Félibrige 89
Festivals 97
Films 43, 46
Fine Arts 83
Fishing 94
Flora 59
Fontaine-de-Vaucluse 223
Food 99
Fos-sur-Mer 226

G

Gauguin, Paul .85
Glanum 311
Gogh, Vincent Van 85
Gordes 226
Gorges de la Nesque 327
Grand Luberon 238
Le Grau-du-Roi 229
Grignan 230

H

La Haute Corniche 136
Hellenistic ramparts 302
Herbs 100
Holidays 49
Horseback Riding 34
Hostels 30
Hotels 28

I

Îles du Frioul 265
International Visitors 21
L'Isle-sur-la-Sorgue 232

L

Labeaume 234
Lançon Viewing Table 187
Language 88
Lavender 17, 92
Legends 90
Le Luberon 127
Leroy 86
Les Baux-de-Provence 175
Literature 88
Lourmarin 239
Luberon 14
Le Luberon 235

M

Malaucène 273
Marinas 32
Marine parks 16
Markets 40
Marseille 15, 243
  Ancienne Cathédrale de la Major 251
  Basilique de Notre-Dame-de-la-Garde . . 254
  Basilique St-Victor 254
  Belvédère St-Laurent 251
  Books 248
  Canebière 255
  Cathédrale de la Major 251
  Centre de la Vieille Charité 251, 261
  Corniche Président-J.-F.-Kennedy 259
  Cours Julien 255
  Crypt 254
  Église St-Ferréol 249
  Entertainment 245
  Events 246
  Ferry 245
  Films 248
  Hôtel-Dieu 250
  Hôtel de Cabre 250
  Hôtel de Ville 249
  Hotels 247
  Jardin des Vestiges 255
  La Corniche 257
  Longchamp District 263
  Metro 245
  Musée Cantini 263
  Musée d'Archéologie
    méditerranéenne 261
  Musée d'Histoire de Marseille 262
  Musée de la Faïence 264
  Musée des Arts Africains,
    Océaniens et Amérindiens 262
  Musée des Beaux-Arts 263
  Musée des Docks romains 261
  Musée du Vieux Marseille 261
  Musée Grobet-Labadié 263
  Muséum d'Histoire naturelle 264
  Old Marseille 249, 261
  Palais Longchamp 263

Pavillon Daviel 250
Place de Lenche. 251
Port 260
Quartier du Paniera 250
Restaurants. 246
Rive Neuve 254
Shopping. 245
Southern Districts. 264
Tours 245
Vieux Port 249
Martigues. 266
Massif des Calanques. 265
Ménerbes. 241, 268
Minitel. 52
Mistral, Frédéric. 336
Money. 49
Monieux. 327
La Montagnette. 336
Montmajour, Abbaye de 269
Montmirail, Dentelles de 270
Mont Ventoux. 326
Morgiou 195
Motorhomes 27
Mourre Nègre 238

N

Nature. 56
Nature parks 16
Nîmes 273
Amphitheatre. 277
Carré d'Art. 281
Castellum. 280
Entertainment 275
Esplanade 277
Events 275
Hotels 276
Jardin de la Fontaine 280
Maison Carrée 277
Musée Archéologique. 281
Musée des Beaux-Arts. 281
Musée du Vieux Nîmes 281
Muséum d'Histoire Naturelle 281
Restaurants. 275
Rue de la Madeleine. 278
Shopping. 275
Tour Magne. 280
Tours 275
Nostradamus, Michel. 321
Noves. 170
Nyons 284

O

Ochre. 95, 129
Ochre Land 300
Olive oil. 95
Olives. 17, 93, 100
Olive trees 59
Oppède-le-Vieux. .241
Orange 286
D'Orgnac, Aven 290
Outdoor Fun 32

P

Païolive, Bois de 292
Pastis. 92
Pernes-les-Fontaines 293
Petit Luberon 241
Petrol. 27
Plateau d'Albion. 327
Pont-d'Arc 354
Pont-St-Esprit 297
Pont du Gard. 295
Port-Pin. 195
Post 49
Provençal furniture. 86
Puget, Pierre 84

R

Rasteau. 353
Restaurants 30
Roquemaure. 215
Roussillon. 130, 300

S

Salon-de-Provence. 321
Salt marshes 95
Sanctuaire de Répit 228
Santon. 88
Sault. 326
Saumane-de-Vaucluse. 225
Scuba diving. 32
Seasons. 19
Séguret. 271
Sénanque, Abbaye de 328
Shopping 39
Sightseeing. 42
Silvacane, Abbaye de. 331, 340
Source Perrier. 283
St-Blaise 301
St-Gilles. 303
St-Maximin 307
St-Michel-de-Frigolet, Abbaye de . . . 309
St-Rémy-de-Provence 125, 310
La Ste-Baume 307
La Ste-Victoire 317
Ste-Victoire, Montagne 120
Les Stes-Maries-de-la-Mer 319
Sugiton. 195

T

Tapenade 100
Tarascon 332
Telephones 52
Thalassotherapy .30
Themed Tours. 16
Tipping. 51
Tolls 27
La Tour-d'Aigues 337
Tour Fenestrelle. 344
Tourist Offices
French. 20
Local 21
Regional. 21

Troubadours 88
Truffles 93
Truffles 18

U
Uzès 341

V
Vaison-la-Romaine 348
Vallon-Pont-d'Arc 132, 354
Vallon-Pont-d'Arc 132

Value Added Tax .39
Vaucluse. 14
La Vaunage 282
Vauvenargues. .318
Venasque 357
Ventoux, Mont 359
Villeneuve-lès-Avignon. 170, 362

W
Web Sites 20
Wine 18, 99, 101

MAPS AND PLANS

THEMATIC MAPS

Principal sights 8-9
Driving tours 10-11
Places to stay 28-29
Relief map 57
Greco-Roman Marseille 243

TOWN PLANS

Aigues-Mortes 109
Aix-en-Provence 114, 115
Apt 129
Arles 143
Avignon 160-161
Les Baux-de-Provence 177
Beaucaire 181
Bollène 188
Bonnieux 190
Carpentras 205
Cavaillon 211
Marseille 252-253, 256-257
Nîmes 278, 279
Nyons 285
Orange 287
Pernes-les-Fontaines 294
Pont-St-Esprit 298
Roussillon 301
St-Rémy-de-Provence 314
Salon-de-Provence 322
Tarascon 335
Uzès 345
Vaison-la-Romaine 348
Valréas 356

MONUMENTS AND SITES

Avignon, Palais des Papes . . . 157, 158
Montmajour Abbey 270
Aven d'Orgnac 290
St-Maximin Basilica 308
St-Rémy, excavations 311
Sénanque Abbey 330
Silvacane Abbey 331
Tarascon Castle 333
Vaison-la-Romaine,
    Roman ruins 350, 352
Chartreuse du Val
    de Bénédiction 365

LOCAL MAPS FOR TOURING

Les Alpilles 125
Apt: Ochre tour 131

Gorges de l'Ardèche 134-135
Étang de Berre 185
Les Calanques 192-193
La Camargue 199
Luberon 236-237
Dentelles de Montmirail 272
Ste-Victoire mountains 317
Mont Ventoux 360

MICHELIN MAPS

Motorists who plan ahead will always have the appropriate maps at hand. Michelin products are complementary: for each of the sites listed in The Green Guide, map references are indicated which help you find your location on our range of maps. The image below shows the Local maps to use for each geographic area covered in this guide.

To travel the roads in this region, you may use any of the following:

• the regional maps at a scale of 1:250 000 - 300 000 no 528 and 524, which cover the main roads and secondary roads, and include useful indications for finding tourist attractions. These are good maps to choose for travelling in a wide area. In a quick glance, you can locate and identify the main sights to see. In addition to identifying the nature of the road ways, the maps show castles, churches and other religious edifices, scenic view points, megalithic monuments, swimming beaches on lakes and rivers, swimming pools, golf courses, race tracks, air fields, and more.

And remember to travel with the latest edition of the map of France no 721, which gives an overall view of the region of Provence, and the main access roads which connect it to the rest of France. The entire country is mapped at a 1:1 000 000 scale and clearly shows the main road network.

Michelin is pleased to offer a route-planning service on the Internet: www.ViaMichelin.com. Choose the shortest route, a route without tolls, or the Michelin recommended route to your destination; you can also access information about hotels and restaurants from The Red Guide, and tourists sites from The Green Guide.

There are a number of useful maps and plans in the guide, listed on the following page.

Bon voyage!

Key

Selected monuments and sights

Tour - Departure point

Catholic church

Protestant church, other temple

Synagogue - Mosque

Building

Statue, small building

Calvary, wayside cross

Fountain

Rampart - Tower - Gate

Château, castle, historic house

Ruins

Dam

Factory, power plant

Fort

Cave

Troglodyte dwelling

Prehistoric site

Viewing table

Viewpoint

Other place of interest

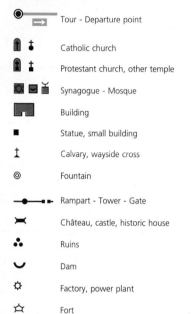

Sports and recreation

Racecourse

Skating rink

Outdoor, indoor swimming pool

Multiplex Cinema

Marina, sailing centre

Trail refuge hut

Cable cars, gondolas

Funicular, rack railway

Tourist train

Recreation area, park

Theme, amusement park

Wildlife park, zoo

Gardens, park, arboretum

Bird sanctuary, aviary

Walking tour, footpath

Of special interest to children

Abbreviations

A   Agricultural office (Chambre d'agriculture)

C   Chamber of Commerce (Chambre de commerce)

H   Town hall (Hôtel de ville)

J   Law courts (Palais de justice)

M   Museum (Musée)

P   Local authority offices (Préfecture, sous-préfecture)

POL.   Police station (Police)

🛡   Police station (Gendarmerie)

T   Theatre (Théâtre)

U   University (Université)

	Sight	Seaside resort	Winter sports resort	Spa
Highly recommended ★★★	☆☆☆	🏖🏖🏖	❄❄❄	⚕⚕⚕
Recommended ★★	☆☆	🏖🏖	❄❄	⚕⚕
Interesting ★	☆	🏖	❄	⚕

Additional symbols

🛈	Tourist information
▬▬ ▬	Motorway or other primary route
❶ ❶	Junction: complete, limited
⊢⊨⊣ ▬	Pedestrian street
ɪ = = = = ɪ	Unsuitable for traffic, street subject to restrictions
▭▭▭ - - - -	Steps – Footpath
🚆 🚆	Train station – Auto-train station
🚌 🚌 S.N.C.F.	Coach (bus) station
─┼─	Tram
Ⓜ	Metro, underground
P R	Park-and-Ride
♿	Access for the disabled
✉	Post office
☎	Telephone
▱	Covered market
⁕⤬⁕	Barracks
△	Drawbridge
ʊ	Quarry
✗	Mine
B F	Car ferry (river or lake)
🛥	Ferry service: cars and passengers
⛴	Foot passengers only
③	Access route number common to Michelin maps and town plans
Bert (R.)...	Main shopping street
AZ B	Map co-ordinates

Hotels and restaurants

Hotels- price categories:

	Provinces	Large cities
🛏	<40 €	<60 €
🛏🛏	40 to 65 €	60 to 90 €
🛏🛏🛏	65 to 100 €	90 to 130 €
🛏🛏🛏🛏	>100 €	>130 €

Restaurants- price categories:

	Provinces	Large cities
🛏	<14 €	<16 €
🛏🛏	14 to 25 €	16 to 30 €
🛏🛏🛏	25 to 40 €	30 to 50 €
🛏🛏🛏🛏	>40 €	>50 €

20 rooms: Number of rooms:
38.57/57.17 € price for one person/ double room

🛏 *6.85 €* Price of breakfast; when not given, it is included in the price of the room (i.e., for bed-and-breakfast)

120 sites: Number of camp sites and cost
12.18 € for 2 people with a car

12.18 € lunch- Restaurant: fixed-price menus
16.74/38.05 € served at lunch only – mini/maxi price fixed menu (lunch and dinner) or à la carte

rest. Lodging where meals are served
16.74/38.05 € mini/maxi price fixed menu or à la carte

meal 15.22 € "Family style" meal

reserv Reservation recommended

🚫 No credit cards accepted

P Reserved parking for hotel patrons

🏊 Swimming Pool

▤ Air conditioning

🚭 Hotel: non-smoking rooms Restaurant: non-smoking section

♿ Rooms accessible to persons of reduced mobility

The prices correspond to the higher rates of the tourist season

NOTES

NOTES

NOTES

NOTES

Manufacture française des pneumatiques Michelin

Société en commandite par actions au capital de 304 000 000 EUR
Place des Carmes-Déchaux – 63000 Clermont-Ferrand (France)
R.C.S. Clermont-Fd B 855 200 507

No part of this publication may be reproduced in any form
without the prior permission of the publisher.

© Michelin, Propriétaires-éditeurs
Dépot légal mars 2006 – ISSN 0763-1183

Pre-Press : Nord Compo à Villeneuve d'Ascq
Printing and Binding : IME à Baume-les-Dames
Made in France, mai 2007